XML Data Management

XML Data Management

Native XML and XML-Enabled Database Systems

Akmal B. Chaudhri
Awais Rashid
Roberto Zicari
Editors

Addison-Wesley

Boston • San Francisco • New York • Toronto • Montreal
London • Munich • Paris • Madrid
Capetown • Sydney • Tokyo • Singapore • Mexico City

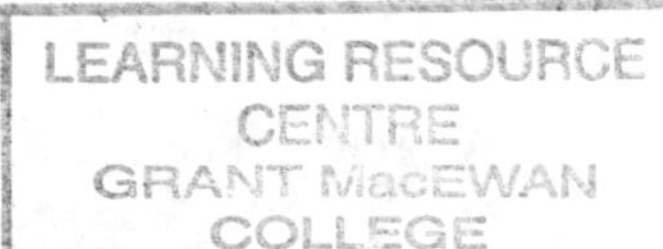

The publisher offers discounts on this book when ordered in quantity for bulk purchases and special sales. For more information, please contact:

U.S. Corporate and Government Sales
(800) 382-3419
corpsales@pearsontechgroup.com

For sales outside of the U.S., please contact:

International Sales
(317) 581-3793
international@pearsontechgroup.com

Visit Addison-Wesley on the Web: www.awprofessional.com

Library of Congress Cataloguing-in-Publication Data

XML data management : native XML and XML-enabled database systems / Akmal B. Chaudhri, Awais Rashid, Roberto Zicari [eds.].
p. cm.
Includes bibliographical references and index.
ISBN 0-201-84452-4 (alk. paper)
1. Database management. 2. XML (Document markup language) I. Chaudhri, Akmal B. II. Rashid, Awais. III. Zicari, Roberto.

QA76.9.D3 X555 2003
005.7'2—dc21 2002038298

ISBN: 0-201-84452-4
Text printed on recycled paper
1 2 3 4 5 6 7 8 9 10—CRS—0706050403
First printing, March 2003

For my mother, Nusrat, and in memory of my father, Bashir.
—Akmal B. Chaudhri

To my wife, Rouza.
—Awais Rashid

For Greta, Sophia, Carla.
—Roberto Zicari

Contents

Preface

The past few years have seen a dramatic increase in the popularity and adoption of XML, the eXtensible Markup Language. This explosive growth is driven by its ability to provide a standardized, extensible means of including semantic information within documents describing semi-structured data. This makes it possible to address the shortcomings of existing markup languages such as HTML and support data exchange in e-business environments.

Consider, for instance, the simple HTML document in Listing P.1. The data contained in the document is intertwined with information about its presentation. In fact, the tags describe only how the data is to be formatted. There is no semantic information that the data represents a person's name and address. Consequently, an interpreter cannot make any sound judgments about the semantics as the tags could as well have enclosed information about a car and its parts. Systems such as WIRE (Aggarwal et al. 1998) can interpret the information by using search templates based on the structure of HTML files and the importance of information enclosed in tags defining headings and so forth. However, such interpretation lacks soundness, and its accuracy is context dependent.

Listing P.1 An HTML Document with Data about a Person

```
<html>
<head>
   <title>Person Information</title>
</head>
```

```
<body>
<p> <b>Name: </b>John Doe</p>
<p> <b>Address: </b>10 Church Street, Lancaster LAX 2YZ, UK</p>
</body>
</html>
```

Dynamic Web pages, where the data resides in a backend database and is served using predefined templates, reduce the coupling between the data and its representation. However, the semantics of the data can still be confusing when exchanging information in an e-business environment. A particular item could be represented using different names (in the simplest case) in two systems in a business-to-business transaction. This enforces adherence to complex, often proprietary, document standards.

XML provides inherent support for addressing the above problems, as the data in an XML document is self-describing. However, the increasing adoption of XML has also raised new challenges. One of the key issues is the management of large collections of XML documents. There is a need for tools and techniques for effective storage, retrieval, and manipulation of XML data. The aim of this book is to discuss the state-of-the-art in such tools and techniques.

This preface introduces the basics of XML and some related technologies before moving on to providing an overview of issues relating to XML data management and approaches addressing these issues. Only an overview of XML and related technologies is provided because several other sources cover these concepts in depth.

P.1 What Is XML?

XML is a W3C standard for document markup. It makes it possible to define custom tags describing the data enclosed by them. An example XML document containing data about a person is shown in Listing P.2. Note that tags in XML can have attributes. However, for simplicity, they have not been used in this example.

Listing P.2 An XML Document with Data about a Person

```
<?xml version="1.0" standalone="yes"?>
<person>
  <name>
     <surname>Doe</surname>
     <firstname>John</firstname>
  </name>
  <address>
```

```
        <housenumber>10</housenumber>
        <street>Church Street</street>
        <town>Lancaster</town>
        <postcode>LAX 2YZ</postcode>
        <country>UK</country>
    </address>
</person>
```

Unlike the HTML document in Listing P.1, the document in Listing P.2 contains only the data about the person and no representational information. The data and its meaning can be read from the document and the document formatted in a range of fashions as desired. One standard approach is to use XSL, the eXtensible Stylesheet Language.

The flexible nature of XML makes it an ideal basis for defining arbitrary languages. One such example is WML, the Wireless Markup Language. Similarly, the XML schema language used to describe the structure of XML documents is based on XML itself.

P.1.1 Well-Formed and Valid XML

Although XML syntax is flexible, it is constrained by a grammar that governs the permitted tag names, attachment of attributes to tags, and so on. All XML documents must conform to these basic grammar rules. Such conformant documents are said to be *well formed* and can be interpreted by an XML interpreter, which means it's not necessary to write an interpreter for each XML document instance.

In addition to being well formed, the structure of a particular XML document can be validated against a Document Type Definition (DTD) or an XML schema. An XML document conforming to a given DTD or schema is said to be *valid*.

P.1.2 Data-Centric and Document-Centric XML

XML documents can be classified on the basis of data they contain. *Data-centric* documents capture structured data such as that pertaining to a product catalog, an order, or an invoice. *Document-centric* documents, on the other hand, capture unstructured data as in articles, books, or e-mails. Of course, the two types can be combined to form *hybrid* documents that are both data-centric and document-centric. Listings P.3 and P.4 provide examples of data-centric and document-centric XML, respectively.

Listing P.3 Data-Centric XML

```
<order>
  <customer>Doe</customer>
  <position>
    <isbn>1-234-56789-0</isbn>
    <number>2</number>
    <price currency="UKP">30.00</price>
  </position>
</order>
```

Listing P.4 Document-Centric XML

```
<content>
  XML builds on the principles of two
  existing languages, <em>HTML</em>
  and <em>SGML</em> to create a simple
  mechanism  . . .
  The generalized markup concept . . .
</content>
```

P.2 XML Concepts

This section provides an overview of basic XML concepts: DTDs, XML schemas, DOM, and SAX.

P.2.1 DTDs and XML Schemas

Both DTDs and XML schemas are mechanisms used to define the structure of XML documents. They determine what elements can be contained within the XML document, how they are to be used, what default values their attributes can have, and so on. Given a DTD or XML schema and its corresponding XML document, a parser can validate whether the document conforms to the desired structure and constraints. This is particularly useful in data exchange scenarios as DTDs and XML schemas provide and enforce a common vocabulary for the data to be exchanged.

XML DTDs are subsets of SGML (Standard Generalized Markup Language) DTDs. An XML DTD lists the various elements and attributes in a document and the context in which they are to be used. It can also list any elements a document cannot contain. However, it does not define constraints such as the number of instances of a particular element within a document, the type of data within each element, and so on. Consequently, DTDs are inherently suitable for document-centric XML as compared to data-centric XML because data-typing and instantiation constraints are less critical in the former case. However, they can be and are being used for both types of documents.

Listing P.5 shows a DTD for the simple XML document in Listing P.2. It describes which primitive elements form valid components for the three composite ones: *person*, *name*, and *address*. The keyword *#PCDATA* signifies that the element does not contain any tags or child elements and only *parsed character* data.

Listing P.5 A DTD for the Simple XML Document in Listing P.2

```
<!ELEMENT person (name, address)>
<!ELEMENT name (surname, firstname)>
<!ELEMENT surname (#PCDATA)>
<!ELEMENT firstname (#PCDATA)>
<!ELEMENT address (housenumber, street, town, postcode, country)>
<!ELEMENT housenumber (#PCDATA)>
<!ELEMENT street (#PCDATA)>
<!ELEMENT town (#PCDATA)>
<!ELEMENT postcode (#PCDATA)>
<!ELEMENT country (#PCDATA)>
```

XML schemas differ from DTDs in that the XML schema definition language is based on XML itself. As a result, unlike DTDs, the set of constructs available for defining an XML document is extensible. XML schemas also support namespaces and richer and more complex structures than DTDs. In addition, stronger typing constraints on the data enclosed by a tag can be described because a range of primitive data types such as string, decimal, and integer are supported. This makes XML schemas highly suitable for defining data-centric documents. Another significant advantage is that XML schema definitions can exploit the same data management mechanisms as designed for XML; an XML schema is an XML document itself. This is in direct contrast with DTDs, which require specific support to be built into an XML data management system.

Listing P.6 shows an XML schema for the simple XML document in Listing P.2. The *sequence* tag is a *compositor* indicating an ordered sequence of subelements. There are other compositors for *choice* and *all*. Also, note that, as shown for the *address* element, it is possible to constrain the minimum and maximum instances of an element within a document. Although not shown in the example, it is possible to define custom complex and simple types. For instance, a complex type *Address* could have been defined for the *address* element.

Listing P.6 An XML Schema for the Simple XML Document in Listing P.2

```
<?xml version="1.0"?>
<xs:schema xmlns:xs="http://www.w3.org/2001/XMLSchema">
  <xs:element name="person">
    <xs:complexType>
      <xs:sequence>
     <xs:element name="name">
       <xs:complexType>
         <xs:sequence>
        <xs:element name="surname" type="xs:string"/>
        <xs:element name="firstname" type="xs:string"/>
      </xs:sequence>
        </xs:complexType>
     </xs:element>
     <xs:element name="address" minOccurs="0" maxOccurs="1">
       <xs:complexType>
         <xs:sequence>
        <xs:element name="housenumber" type="xs:integer"/>
        <xs:element name="street" type="xs:string"/>
        <xs:element name="town" type="xs:string"/>
        <xs:element name="postcode" type="xs:string"/>
        <xs:element name="country" type="xs:string"/>
      </xs:sequence>
        </xs:complexType>
     </xs:element>
   </xs:sequence>
      </xs:complexType>
  </xs:element>
</xs:schema>
```

P.2.2 DOM and SAX

DOM and SAX are the two main APIs for manipulating XML documents in an application. They are now part of the Java API for XML Processing (JAXP version 1.1). DOM is the W3C standard Document Object Model, an operating system– and programming language–independent model for storing and manipulating hierarchical documents in memory. A DOM parser parses an XML document and builds a DOM tree, which can then be used to traverse the various nodes. However, the tree has to be constructed before traversal can commence. As a result, memory management is an issue when manipulating large XML documents. This is highly resource intensive especially in cases where only a small section of the document is to be manipulated.

SAX, the Simple API for XML, is a *de facto* standard. It differs from DOM in that it uses an event-driven model. Each time a starting or closing tag, or processing instruction is encountered, the program is notified. As a result, the whole document does not need to be parsed before it is manipulated. In fact, sections of the document can be manipulated as they are parsed. Therefore, SAX is better suited to manipulating large documents as compared to DOM.

P.3 XML-Related Technologies

This section describes some of the technologies related to XML—namely, XPath, XSL, and SOAP.

P.3.1 XPath

XPath, the XML Path Language, provides common syntax and semantics for locating and linking to information contained within an XML document. Using XPath the information can be addressed in two ways:

- A hierarchical fashion based on the ordering of elements in a document tree
- An arbitrary manner relying on elements in a document tree having unique identifiers

A few example XPath expressions, based on the sample XML document in Listing P.2, are shown in Listing P.7. Example 1 expresses all children named *firstname* in the current focus element. Example 2 selects the child node *surname* whose parent node is *name* within the current focus element, while example 3 tests whether an element is present in the union of the elements *name* and *address*. Note that, although not shown in the examples, it is also possible to specify constraints such as *first address of the third person in the document*.

Listing P.7 Example XPath Expressions

```
1. select="firstname"
2. select="name/surname"
3. match="name | address"
```

P.3.2 XSL

Since an XML document does not contain any representational information, it can be formatted in a flexible manner. A standard approach to formatting XML documents is using XSL, the eXtensible Stylesheet Language. The W3C XSL specification is composed of two parts: XSL Formatting Objects (XSL FO) and XSL Transformations (XSLT).

XSL FO provides formatting and flow semantics for rendering an XML document. A rendering agent is responsible for interpreting the abstract constructs provided by XSL FO in order to instantiate the representation for a particular medium.

XSLT offers constructs to transform information from one organization to another. Although designed to transform an XML vocabulary to an XSL FO vocabulary, XSLT can be used for a range of transformations including those to HTML as shown in Listing P.8. The example style sheet uses a set of simple XSLT templates and XPath expressions to transform a part of the XML document in Listing P.2 to HTML (see Listing P.9).

Listing P.8 An XSL Style Sheet for the XML Document in Listing P.2

```
<?xml version="1.0"?>
<xsl:stylesheet xmlns:xsl=
    "http://www.w3.org/1999/XSL/Transform" version="1.0">
   <xsl:template match="/">
      <html>
         <head><title>Person Information</title></head>
         <body>
            <xsl:apply-templates select="person/name"/>
         </body>
      </html>
   </xsl:template>
   <xsl:template match="name">
      <xsl:apply-templates/>
   </xsl:template>
   <xsl:template match="surname">
      <p><b><xsl:text>Surname: </xsl:text></b>
       <xsl:value-of select="."/></p><br/>
   </xsl:template>
   <xsl:template match="firstname">
      <p><b><xsl:text>First name: </xsl:text></b>
      <xsl:value-of select="."/></p>
   </xsl:template>
</xsl:stylesheet>
```

Listing P.9 HTML Resulting from the Transformation in Listing P.8

```
<html>
   <head>
      <title>Person Information </title>
   </head>
   <body>
      <p>
         <b>Surname: </b>Doe
      </p>
      <br>
      <p>
      <b>First name: </b>John
      </p>
   </body>
</html>
```

P.3.3 SOAP

SOAP is the Simple Object Access Protocol used to invoke code over the Internet using XML and HTTP. The mechanism is similar to Java Remote Method Invocation (RMI). In SOAP, method calls are converted to XML and transmitted over HTTP. SOAP was designed for compatibility with XML schemas though their use is not mandatory. Being based on XML, XML schemas offer a seamless means to describe and transmit SOAP types.

P.4 XML Data Management

So far, we have discussed the basics of XML and some of its related technologies. The discussion emphasizes the fundamental advantages of XML, hence providing an insight into the reasons behind its growing popularity and adoption. As more and more organizations and systems employ XML within their information management and exchange strategies, classical data management issues pertaining to XML's efficient and effective storage, retrieval, querying, indexing, and manipulation arise. At the same time, previously uncharted information-modeling challenges appear.

Database vendors have responded to these new data and information management needs. Most commercial relational, object-relational, and object-oriented database systems offer extensions and plug-ins and other mechanisms to support the management of XML data. In addition to supporting XML within existing database management systems, native XML databases have been born. These are designed for seamless storage, retrieval, and manipulation of XML data and integration with related technologies.

With the numerous approaches and solutions available in the market, organizations and system developers with XML data management needs face a variety of challenges:

- What are the various XML data management solutions available?
- What are the features, services, and tools offered by these different XML data management systems?
- How can an in-house, custom solution be developed instead of using a commercially available system?
- Which XML data management system or approach is the best in terms of performance and efficiency for a particular application?
- Are there any good practice and domain or application-specific guidelines for information modeling with XML?
- Are there other examples and applications of XML data management within a particular domain?

This book is intended to be a support mechanism to address the above challenges. It provides a discussion of the various XML data management approaches employed in a range of products and applications. It also offers performance and benchmarking results and guidelines relating to information modeling with XML.

P.5 How This Book Is Organized

This book is divided into five parts, each containing a coherent and closely related set of chapters. It should be noted that these parts are self-contained and can be read in any order. The five parts are as follows:

Part I: Introduction
Part II: Native XML Databases
Part III: XML and Relational Databases
Part IV: Applications of XML
Part V: Performance and Benchmarks

The parts are summarized in the sections that follow.

P.5.1 Part I: Introduction

This part contains a chapter that focuses on guidelines for achieving good grammar and style when modeling information using XML. Brandin, the author, argues that good grammar alleviates the need for redundant domain knowledge required for interpretation of XML by application programs. Good style, on the other hand, ensures improved application performance, especially when it comes to storing, retrieving, and managing information. The discussion offers insight into information-modeling patterns inherent in XML and common XML information-modeling pitfalls.

P.5.2 Part II: Native XML Databases

Two native XML database systems, Tamino and eXist, are covered in this part. In Chapter 2, Schöning provides an overview of Tamino's architecture and APIs before moving on to discussing its XML storage and indexing features. Querying, tool support, and access to data in other types of repositories are also described. The chapter offers a comprehensive discussion of the features that are of key importance during the development of an XML data management application.

In a similar fashion, Chapter 3 by Meier introduces the various features and APIs of the Open Source system eXist. However, in contrast with Chapter 2, the main focus is on how query processing works within the system. As a result, the author provides deeper insight into its indexing and storage architectures. Together both chapters offer a balanced discussion, both on high-level application-programming features of the two systems and underlying indexing and storage mechanisms pertaining to efficient query processing.

Finally in Chapter 4, we have included an example of an embedded XML database system. This is based upon the general-purpose embedded database engine, Berkeley DB. Berkeley DB XML is able to store XML documents natively, and it provides indexing and an XPath query interface. Some of the capabilities of the product are demonstrated through code examples.

P.5.3 Part III: XML and Relational Databases

This part provides an interesting mix of products and approaches to XML data management in relational and object-relational database systems. Chapters 5, 6, and 7 discuss three commercial products: IBM DB2, Oracle9i, and MS SQL Server 2000, respectively, while Chapters 8 and 9 describe more general, roll-your-own strategies for relational and object-relational systems.

Chapter 5 by Benham highlights the technology and architecture of XML data management and information integration products from IBM. The focus is on the DB2 Universal Database and Xperanto. The former is the family of products providing relational and object-relational data management support for XML applications through the DB2 XML Extender, extended SQL, and support for Web services. The latter is the planned set of products and functions for addressing information integration requirements, which are aimed at complementing DB2 capabilities with additional support for XML and both structured and unstructured applications.

In Chapter 6, Hohenstein discusses similar features in Oracle9i: the use of Oracle's CLOB functionality and OracleText cartridge, for handling data-centric XML documents, and XMLType, a new object type based on the object-relational functionality in Oracle9i, for managing document-centric ones. He presents the Oracle SQL extensions for XML and provides examples on how to use them in order to build XML documents from relational data. Special features and tools for XML such as URI (Uniform Resource Identifier) support, parsers, class generator and Java Beans encapsulating these features are also described.

In Chapter 7, Rys covers a feature set, similar to the ones in Chapters 5 and 6, for MS SQL Server 2000. He focuses on scenarios involving exporting and importing structured XML data. As a result, the focus is on the different building blocks such as HTTP and SOAP access, queryable and updateable XML views, rowset views over XML, and XML serialization of relational results. Rowset views and XML serialization are aimed at providing XML support for users more familiar with the relational world. XML views, on the other hand, offer XML-based access to the database for users more comfortable with XML.

Collectively, Chapters 5, 6, and 7 furnish an interesting comparison of the functionality offered by the three commercial systems and the various similarities and differences in their XML data management approaches. In contrast, Chapters 8 and 9, by Edwards and Brown, respectively, focus on generic, vendor-independent solutions.

Edwards describes a generic architecture for storing XML documents in a relational database. The approach is aimed at avoiding vendor-specific database extensions and providing the database application programmer an opportunity to experiment with XML data storage without recourse to implementing much new technology. The database model is based on merging DOM with the Nested Sets Model, hence offering ease of navigation and the ability to store any well-formed XML document. This results in fast serialization and querying but at the expense of update performance.

While Edwards' architecture is aimed at supporting the traditional relational database programmer, Brown's approach seeks to exploit the advanced features offered by the object-relational model and respective extensions of most relational database systems. He discusses object-relational schema design based on introducing into the DBMS core types and operators equivalent to the ones standardized in XML. The key functionality required of the DBMS core is an extensible indexing system allowing the comparison operator for built-in SQL types to be overloaded. The new SQL 3 types thus defined act as a basis during the mapping of XPath expressions to SQL 3 queries over the schema.

P.5.4 Part IV: Applications of XML

This part presents several applications and case studies in XML data management ranging from bioinformatics, geographical and engineering data management, to customer services and cash flow improvement, through to large-scale distributed systems, data warehouses, and inductive database systems.

In Chapter 10, Direen and Jones discuss various challenges in bioinformatics data management and the role of XML as a means to capture and express complex biological information. They argue that the flexible and extensible information model employed by XML is well suited for the purpose and that database technology must exhibit the same characteristics if it is to keep in step with biological data management requirements. They discuss the role of the NeoCore XML management system in this context and the integration of a BLAST (Basic Local Alignment Search Tool) sequence search engine to enhance its ability to capture, manipulate, analyze, and grow the information pertaining to complex systems that make up living organisms.

Kowalski presents two case studies involving XML and IBM's DB2 Universal Database in Chapter 11. Her first case study is that of a customer services unit that needs to react to problems from the most important customers first. The second case study focuses on improving cash flow in a school by reducing the time for reimbursement from the Department of Education. The author presents the scenario and the particular problem to be solved for each case study, which is followed by an analysis identifying existing conditions preventing the solution of the problem. A description of how XML and DB2 have been used to devise an appropriate solution concludes each case study.

Chapter 12, by Eglin, Hendra, and Pentakalos, describes the design and implementation of the JEDMICS Open Access Interface, an EJB-based API that provides access to image data stored on a variety of storage media and metadata stored in a relational database. The JEDMICS system uses XML as a portable data exchange solution, and the authors discuss issues relating to its integration with the object-oriented core of the system and the relational database providing the persistent storage. A very interesting feature of the chapter is the authors' reflection on their experiences with a range of XML technologies such as DOM, JDOM, JAXB, XSLT, and Oracle XSU in the context of JEDMICS.

In Chapter 13, Wilson and her coauthors offer insight into the use of XML to enhance the GIDB (Geospatial Information Database) system to exchange geographical data over the Internet. They describe the integration of meteorological and oceanographic data, received remotely via the METCAST system, into GIDB. XML plays a key role here as it is utilized to express the data model catalog for METCAST. The authors also describe their implementation of the OpenGIS Web Map Server (WMS) specification to facilitate displaying georeferenced map layers from multiple WMS-compliant servers. Another interesting feature of this chapter is the implementation of the ability to read and write vector data using the OpenGIS Geographic Markup Language (GML), an XML-based language standard for data interchange in Geographic Information Systems (GISs).

Rine sketches his vision of an Interstellar Space Wide Web in Chapter 14. He contrasts the issues relating to the development and deployment of such a facility with the problems encountered in today's World Wide Web. He mainly focuses on adapters as configuration mechanisms for large-scale, next-generation distributed systems and as the means to increase the reusability of software components and architectures in this context. His approach to solving the problem is a configuration model and network-aware runtime environment called Space Wide Web Adapter Configuration eXtensible Markup Language (SWWACXML). The language associated with the environment captures component interaction properties and network-level QoS constraints. Adapters are automatically generated from the SWWACXML specifications. This facilitates reuse because components are not tied to interactions or environments. Rine also discusses the role of the SWWACXML runtime system from this perspective as it supports automatic configuration and dynamic reconfiguration.

In Chapter 15, Meo and Psaila present an XML-based data model used to bridge the gap between various analysis models and the constraints they place on data representation, retrieval, and manipulation in inductive databases. XDM (XML for Data Mining) allows simultaneous representation of source raw data and patterns. It also represents the pattern definition resulting from the pattern derivation process, hence supporting pattern reuse by the inductive database system. One of the significant advantages of XML in this context is the ability to describe complex heterogeneous topologies such as trees and association rules. In addition, the inherent flexibility of XML makes it possible to extend the inductive database framework with new pattern models and data-mining operators resulting in an open system customizable to the needs of the analyst.

Chapter 16, the last chapter in this part, describes Baril's and Bellahsene's experiences in designing and managing an XML data warehouse. They propose the use of a view model and a graphical tool for the warehouse specification. Views defined in the warehouse allow filtering and restructuring of XML sources. The warehouse is defined as a set of materialized views, and it provides a mediated schema that constitutes a uniform query interface. They also discuss mapping techniques to store XML data using a relational database system without redundancies and with optimized storage space. Finally, the DAWAX system implementing these concepts is presented.

P.5.5 Part V: Performance and Benchmarks

XML database management systems face the same stringent efficiency and performance requirements as any other database technology. Therefore, the final part of this book is devoted to a discussion of benchmarks and performance analyses of such systems.

Chapter 17 focuses on the need to design and adopt benchmarks to allow comparative performance analyses of the fast-growing number of XML database management systems. Here Bressan and his colleagues describe three existing benchmarks for this purpose, namely XOO7, XMach-1, and XMark. They present the database and queries for each of the three benchmarks and compare them against four quality attributes: simplicity, relevance, portability, and scalability. The discussion is aimed at identifying challenges facing the definition of a complete benchmark for XML database management systems.

In Chapter 18, Patel and Jagadish describe a benchmark that is aimed at measuring lower-level operations than those described in Chapter 17. The inspiration for their work is the Wisconsin Benchmark that was used to measure the performance of relational database systems in the early 1980s.

Schmauch and Fellhauer describe a detailed performance analysis in Chapter 19. They compare the time and space consumed by a range of XML data management approaches: relational databases, object-oriented databases, directory servers, and native XML databases. XML documents are converted to DOM trees, hence reducing the problem to storing and extracting trees. Instead of using a particular benchmark, they derive their test suite from general requirements that the storage of XML documents has to meet. Different-sized XML documents are stored using the four types of systems, selected fragments and complete documents are extracted, and the disk space is used and performance is measured. Similar to the next chapter, Chapter 20, the authors offer a thorough set of empirical results. They also provide detailed insight into existing XML data management approaches using the four systems analyzed. Finally, the experiences presented in the chapter are used as a basis to derive guidelines for benchmarking XML data management systems.

In Chapter 20, Fong, Wong, and Fong present a comparative performance analysis of a native XML database and a relational database extended with XML data management features. They do not use any existing benchmarks but instead devise their own methodology and database. The key contribution of this chapter is a detailed set of empirical results presented as bar graphs.

P.6 Who Should Read This Book

This book is primarily aimed at professionals who are experienced in database technology and possibly XML and who wish to learn how these two technologies can be used together. We hope they can learn through the discussions about alternative architectural approaches, case studies, and performance benchmarks. Since the book is divided into a number of self-contained parts, it can also be used as a reference, and only the relevant sections that the reader is interested in can be read. The book may also be useful to students studying advanced database courses.

P.7 Resources

Web sites that provide useful material that supports or complements this book include

- Ron Bourret's excellent Web site: http://www.rpbourret.com/xml
- Cover pages at Oasis: http://www.oasis-open.org/cover/xmlAndDatabases.html

Acknowledgments

Our sincere thanks to all the contributors who worked very hard to complete their chapters on time. We would also like to thank Alicia Carey, Brenda Mulligan, and Mary T. O'Brien at Addison-Wesley for all their help and support in getting this book to publication. Our grateful thanks to the external reviewers for their constructive comments, which helped improve the overall quality of this book.

—Akmal B. Chaudhri,
Awais Rashid,
Roberto Zicari

Chapter 8

For helpful discussions on this topic, I am indebted to Ignacio Vera, Sian Hope, Thomas Varsamidis, and Michael Baxter of the School of Informatics at the University of Wales, Bangor; Ronald Bourret and Akmal Chaudhri, gurus of XML databases; Tony Eastwood of ETL Solutions; Raimundo Lozano of Hospital Clinic (Barcelona); Mike Malloch of theKnowNet; Oggy East of Semantise; and Ian Williams of Arval PHH. I would also like to thank Loulou Smith, my parents Ann and Graham Edwards, my grandmother Margaret King, and my late grandfather Edmund King for all their support and encouragement in this and many other endeavors.

Chapter 12

Thanks to all the great people in the OAI team for making this project a success.

Chapter 13

The authors would like to thank the ONR, PE 63782N, and Dr. Dick Root, program manager, for funding this effort under the Generation and Exploitation of the Common Environment Program.

Chapter 14

I am very grateful to Professor Robert Simon and Professor Elizabeth White in offering many suggestions and conceptual ideas for this research topic.

Chapter 19

This research was funded by the German Ministry of Education and Research (BMBF).

Part I

What Is XML?

This part contains a chapter that focuses on guidelines for achieving good grammar and style when modeling information using XML.

Chapter 1

Information Modeling with XML

Chris Brandin

1.1 Introduction

When XML first came into use, it was seen primarily as a data interchange standard. Since then it has come to be used for more and more things—even serving as the core for development and deployment platforms such as Microsoft's .NET. Increasingly, XML has become the means to model components of information systems, and those components automatically construct themselves around what has been expressed in XML. This represents the real potential of XML—the ability to model the behavior of an entire application in XML once, instead of repeatedly in different ways for each component of an application program.

As long as XML was used as a container for data managed by legacy systems, it was sufficient to consider only syntax when building documents. Now that XML is being used to do more than simply express data, it is important to consider grammar and style as well. Obviously, proper syntax is necessary for parsers to be able to accept XML documents at all. Good grammar insures that once XML information has been assimilated, it can be effectively interpreted without an inordinate need for specific (and redundant) domain knowledge on the part of application programs. Good style insures good application performance, especially when it comes to storing, retrieving, and managing information.

Proper XML syntax is well understood and documented, so that topic will not be discussed here. This chapter does not discuss how to build XML schemas or DTDs, as they are also well documented elsewhere. This chapter is intended as a practical guide to achieving good grammar and style when modeling information in

XML—which translates to building flexible applications that perform well with minimal programming effort. Grammar is often regarded as being either right or wrong. True, there are "wrong" grammatical practices; but past that, there is good grammar and bad grammar—and everything in between. Arguably, there is no such thing as wrong style, only a continuum between the good and the bad.

1.2 XML as an Information Domain

XML allows us to model information systems in a natural and intuitive way. This is because XML allows us to express information in ways that better match the way we do business. We now have an information-modeling mechanism that allows us to characterize what we want to do, rather than how we have to do it. XML simply does a much better job of reflecting the way the real world operates than the data-modeling mechanisms that preceded it. XML brings a number of powerful capabilities to information modeling:

- **Heterogeneity:** Where each "record" can contain different data fields. The real world is not neatly organized into tables, rows, and columns. There is great advantage in being able to express information, as it exists, without restrictions.
- **Extensibility:** Where new types of data can be added at will and don't need to be determined in advance. This allows us to embrace, rather than avoid, change.
- **Flexibility:** Where data fields can vary in size and configuration from instance to instance. XML imposes no restrictions on data; each data element can be as long or as short as necessary.

XML is also self-describing and informationally complete; applications can use this feature to automatically build themselves with little or no programming required. Companies such as BEA, TIBCO, and Microsoft offer frameworks for building applications, with a minimum of effort, that use XML as the basis for expressing information. In environments like these, XML becomes a universal information-structuring tool where system components no longer need to be programmed separately as discreet silos of functionality. NeoCore offers an XML Management System (XMS) that brings an entirely transparent persistence mechanism to the fold, requiring no separate database design process, indexing instructions, or use-case predefinition. Moreover, NeoCore's XMS carries forward the characteristics of XML that make it powerful as an information domain—heterogeneity, extensibility, and flexibility. All that is required to store, retrieve, and manage information is that it be expressed in XML, and that queries be expressed as XPath or

XQuery patterns. This can have a profound effect on rapid application development efficiency, especially when changes have to be made. When we build XML-centric systems, we can often accommodate changes by modifying the underlying XML, and information system components will adjust themselves accordingly without the need for reprogramming.

1.3 How XML Expresses Information

XML expresses information using four basic components—tags, attributes, data elements, and hierarchy. Each of these components serves a unique purpose; each represents a different "dimension" of information. In order to illustrate these basic components, we will use a simple XML fragment from an application dealing with readings from colorimeters (devices that measure colors using tri-stimulus readings).

Data elements are represented in **bold** type in Listing 1.1. In XML, a data element equates to "data" as we have traditionally thought of it. If we simply extract the data elements, we get "**0, 255, 255**", which is meaningless unless you know what the data definitions are. XML adds context to data, thereby giving it meaning, by adding tags (represented in regular type in the listing). Tags describe what data elements are. Attributes (represented in ***Italics*** in the listing) tell us something about or how to interpret data elements. Colorimeters can represent RGB tri-stimulus values in a variety of resolutions. If the reading had been taken with a resolution of 16 bits, for example, values of "**0, 255, 255**" would represent a very dark cyan, instead of pure cyan. So, we need the "*resolution=8*" attribute to correctly interpret the RGB reading values in Listing 1.1.

Listing 1.1 Simple XML Fragment

```
<colorimeter_reading>
      <RGB resolution=8>
            <red> 0 </red>
            <green> 255 </green>
            <blue> 255 </blue>
      </RGB>
</colorimeter_reading>
```

Now we have data (data elements), we know what they are (tags), and we know how to interpret them (attributes). The final step is to determine how to string it all together, and that is where hierarchy comes in. So far, we have represented three dimensions of information explicitly. The last dimension, how everything relates, is implied spatially. This means that much of what we need to know is contained in how we order the components of XML information. In order to give data meaning, a complete context must be provided, not just the most immediate tag or attribute. For example, if we simply say "*red=0*", it will not mean much because we have not provided an adequate context. If we include all tags in the hierarchy leading up to the reading of "0", we achieve a more complete context: "`<colorimeter_reading><RGB><red>` 0". Although we have a complete understanding of what the data element represents and its value, some ambiguity as to how to interpret the value still remains. The attribute "*resolution58*" belongs to the tag "`<RGB>`". Because "`<RGB>`" is a part of our context, any attribute belonging to it (or any attribute belonging to any tag in our context for that matter) applies. Now we know how to interpret the value of the data element as well. Related information is represented in the hierarchy as siblings at various levels; as a result, hierarchy tells us how data elements are related to each other.

1.4 Patterns in XML

In order to effectively model information using XML, we must learn how to identify the natural patterns inherent to it. First, we must determine whether we have used XML elements properly. To do this we will analyze the XML fragment shown in Listing 1.2.

Listing 1.2 Example XML Fragment

```
<colorimeter_reading>
        <device> X-Rite Digital Swatchbook </device>
        <patch> cyan </patch>
        <RGB resolution=8>
                <red> 0 </red>
                <green> 255 </green>
                <blue> 255 </blue>
        </RGB>
</colorimeter_reading>
```

We examine each data element and ask the following question:

- Is this data, or is it actually metadata (information about another data element)?

We examine every attribute and ask the following questions:

- Does the attribute tell us something about or describe how to interpret, use, or present data elements?

- Is the attribute truly metadata, and not actually a data element?
- Does it apply to all data elements in its scope?

We examine every tag and ask the following question:

- Does this tag help describe what all data elements in its scope are?

We examine the groupings we have created (the sibling relationships) and ask:

- Are all members of the group related in a way the parent nodes describe?
- Is the relationship between siblings unambiguous?

If the answer to any of the preceding questions is "no," then we need to cast the offending components differently.

After insuring that information has been expressed using the components of XML appropriately, we examine how everything has been stitched together. To do this we create an information context list from the XML fragment. This is done by simply taking each data element and writing down every tag and attribute leading up to it. The resulting lines will give us a flattened view of the information items contained in the XML fragment. A context list for the example XML fragment in Listing 1.2 would look like the one shown in Listing 1.3.

Listing 1.3 Context List for Example XML Fragment

```
<colorimeter_reading><device> X-Rite Digital Swatchbook
<colorimeter_reading><patch> cyan
<colorimeter_reading><RGB resolution=8><red> 0
<colorimeter_reading><RGB resolution=8><green> 255
<colorimeter_reading><RGB resolution=8><blue> 255
```

If we convert these lines to what they mean in English, we can see that each information item, and its context, makes sense and is contextually complete:

1. This colorimeter reading is from an X-Rite Digital Swatchbook.
2. This colorimeter reading is for a patch called cyan.
3. This colorimeter reading is RGB-red and has an *8-bit* value of 0.
4. This colorimeter reading is RGB-green and has an *8-bit* value of 255.
5. This colorimeter reading is RGB-blue and has an *8-bit* value of 255.

Next we examine the groupings implied by the tag hierarchy:

- `"<colorimeter_reading>" contains "<device>", "<patch>", and "<RGB>" (plus its children).`
- `"<RGB>" contains "<red>", "<green>", and "<blue>".`

"`<colorimeter_reading>`" represents the root tag, so everything else is obviously related to it. The only other implied grouping falls under "<RGB>". These are the actual readings, and the only entries that are, so they are logically related in an unambiguous way.

Finally, we examine the scope for each attribute:

- `"resolution=8" has the items "<red>", "<green>", and "<blue>" in its scope.`

"*resolution=8*" logically applies to every item in its scope and none of the items not in its scope, so it has been appropriately applied.

A self-constructing XML information system (like NeoCore XMS) will use the structure of and the natural patterns contained in XML to automatically determine what to index. Simple queries are serviced by direct lookups. Complex queries are serviced by a combination of direct lookups, convergences against selected parent nodes, and targeted substring searches. With NeoCore XMS no database design or indexing instructions are necessary—the behavior of XMS is driven entirely by the structure of the XML documents posted to it. Index entries are determined by inference and are built based on the natural patterns contained in XML documents. NeoCore XMS creates index entries according to the following rules:

- An index entry is created for each data element.
- An index entry is created for each complete tag context for each data element —that is, the concatenation of every tag leading up to the data element.
- An index entry is created for the concatenation of the two preceding items (tag context plus data element).

For the XML fragment in Listing 1.2, the following items would be added to the pattern indices (actually, this list is not complete because partial tag context index entries are also created, but a discussion of those is beyond the scope of this chapter):

1. **X-Rite Digital Swatchbook**
2. **cyan**
3. **0**

4. **255**
5. **255**
6. <colorimeter_reading><device>
7. <colorimeter_reading><patch>
8. <colorimeter_reading><RGB><red>
9. <colorimeter_reading><RGB><green>
10. <colorimeter_reading><RGB><blue>
11. <colorimeter_reading><RGB ***resolution=8***>
12. <colorimeter_reading><device> **X-Rite Digital Swatchbook**
13. <colorimeter_reading><patch> **cyan**
14. <colorimeter_reading><RGB ***resolution=8***><red> **0**
15. <colorimeter_reading><RGB ***resolution=8***><green> **255**
16. <colorimeter_reading><RGB ***resolution=8***><blue> **255**

Entries 1–5 are data only, entries 6–11 are tag context only, and entries 12–16 are both.

At this point it is important to consider how performance will be affected by the structure of the XML document. Because the inherent patterns inferred from the XML itself can be used to automatically build a database, the degree to which those patterns match likely queries will have a big effect on performance, especially in data-centric applications where single data elements or subdocuments need to be accessed without having to process an entire XML document.

1.5 Common XML Information-Modeling Pitfalls

We could easily arrange the XML fragments from the previous section in other, perfectly acceptable ways. There are many more, albeit syntactically correct, unfortunate ways to arrange the information. Common mistakes made when creating XML documents include:

- Inadequate context describing what a data element is (incomplete use of tags)
- Inadequate instructions on how to interpret data elements (incomplete use of attributes)
- Use of attributes as data elements (improper use of attributes)
- Use of data elements as metadata instead of using tags (indirection through use of name/value pairings)

- Unnecessary, unrelated, or redundant tags (poor hierarchy construction)
- Attributes that have nothing to do with data element interpretation (poor hierarchy construction or misuse of attributes)

These mistakes sap XML of its power and usefulness. Time devoted to good information modeling will be paid back many times over as other components of applications are developed. We can put a great deal of intelligence into XML documents, which means we do not have to put that intelligence, over and over again, into every system component.

Because XML is very flexible, it is easy to abuse. Sometimes the best way to illustrate how to do something is by counterexample. Much, if not most, of the XML we have seen is not well designed. It is not difficult to design XML with good grammar and good style, and doing so will save a lot of time and effort in the long run—to say nothing of how it will affect performance. The following sections contain a few examples of poorly constructed XML fragments.

1.5.1 Attributes Used as Data Elements

This may be the most common misuse of XML. Attributes should be used to describe how to interpret data elements, or describe something about them—in other words, attributes are a form of metadata. They are often used to contain data elements, and that runs counter to the purpose of attributes.

Listing 1.4 contains no data elements from readings at all; the attributes apply to nothing. Attributes that apply to nothing, obviously, describe how to interpret nothing.

Listing 1.4 XML with No Data Elements

```
<colorimeter_reading>
      <device> X-Rite Digital Swatchbook </device>
      <patch> cyan </patch>
      <RGB resolution=8 red=0 green=255 blue=255 />
</colorimeter_reading>
```

If we examine each attribute, especially the data portion (the part to the right of the equal sign), we can determine whether they actually represent data, or metadata:

- ***resolution=8***: This is a true attribute because the value "8" does not mean anything by itself; rather it is an instruction for interpreting data elements, and therefore it is metadata.

- ***red=0***: This is clearly actually data because it is a reading from the colorimeter; moreover, in order to be correctly interpreted, it requires the ***"resolution=8"*** attribute. This attribute does not tell us how to interpret data—it is data. Consequently it should be recast as a tag/data element pair.
- ***green=255, blue=255***: The previous analysis of ***"red=0"*** applies.

1.5.2 Data Elements Used as Metadata

This is often a result of emulating extensibility in a relational database. Instead of creating columns accounting for different fields, a database designer will create two columns: one for field type and one for field contents. This basically amounts to representing metadata in data element fields and is shown in Listing 1.5.

Listing 1.5 XML Data Elements Used as Metadata

```
<colorimeter_reading>
      <device> X-Rite Digital Swatchbook </device>
      <patch> cyan </patch>
      <RGB>
            <item>
                  <band> red </band>
                  <value> 0 </value>
            </item>
            <item>
                  <band> green </band>
                  <value> 255 </value>
            </item>
            <item>
                  <band> blue </band>
                  <value> 255 </value>
            </item>
      </RGB>
</colorimeter_reading>
```

If we decompose this document into an information context, we get Listing 1.6.

Listing 1.6 Information Context for Listing 1.5

```
<colorimeter_reading><device> X-Rite Digital Swatchbook
<colorimeter_reading><patch> cyan
<colorimeter_reading><RGB ><item><band> red
<colorimeter_reading><RGB ><item><value> 0
<colorimeter_reading><RGB ><item><band> green
<colorimeter_reading><RGB ><item><value> 255
<colorimeter_reading><RGB ><item><band> blue
<colorimeter_reading><RGB ><item><value> 255
```

Listing 1.6 translates to approximately the following in English:

1. This colorimeter reading is from an X-Rite Digital Swatchbook.
2. This colorimeter reading is for a patch called cyan.
3. This colorimeter reading item is RGB band red.
4. This colorimeter reading item is RGB and has a value of 0.
5. This colorimeter reading item is RGB band green.
6. This colorimeter reading item is RGB and has a value of 255.
7. This colorimeter reading item is RGB band red.
8. This colorimeter reading item is RGB and has a value of 255.

The last six lines are contextually weak. Lines 3, 5, and 7 don't contain any readings; they contain metadata about the lines following them. Lines 4, 6, and 8 don't adequately describe the readings they contain; they are informationally incomplete and ambiguous. In fact, lines 6 and 8 are exactly the same, even though the readings they represent have different meanings.

1.5.3 Inadequate Use of Tags

This is often a result of emulating extensibility in a relational database. Instead of building separate tables for different data structures, a database designer will create one table for many different data structures by using name/value pairs. This represents unnecessary indirection of metadata and an inappropriate grouping of data elements, to the detriment of performance (because what should be direct queries become joins) and reliability (because grouping is ambiguous). This is shown in Listing 1.7.

Listing 1.7 Use of Name/Value Pairs

```
<colorimeter_reading>
      <device> X-Rite Digital Swatchbook </device>
      <patch> cyan </patch>
      <mode> RGB </mode>
      <band> red </band>
      <value> 0 </value>
      <band> green </band>
      <value> 255 </value>
      <band> blue </band>
      <value> 255 </value>
</colorimeter_reading>
```

If we decompose this document into an information context, we get Listing 1.8.

Listing 1.8 Information Context for Listing 1.7

```
<colorimeter_reading><device> X-Rite Digital Swatchbook
<colorimeter_reading><patch> cyan
<colorimeter_reading><mode> RGB
<colorimeter_reading><band> red
<colorimeter_reading><value> 0
<colorimeter_reading><band> green
<colorimeter_reading><value> 255
<colorimeter_reading><band> blue
<colorimeter_reading><value> 255
```

Translated to English, Listing 1.8 becomes:

1. This colorimeter reading is from an X-Rite Digital Swatchbook.
2. This colorimeter reading is for a patch called cyan.
3. This colorimeter reading is in RGB mode.
4. This colorimeter reading is red.
5. This colorimeter reading has a value of 0.
6. This colorimeter reading is green.
7. This colorimeter reading has a value of 255.
8. This colorimeter reading is blue.
9. This colorimeter reading is has a value of 255.

The last six lines are contextually weak, and line 3 represents nothing but context. Lines 3, 4, 6, and 8 do not contain any readings; they contain metadata about the lines following them. Lines 5, 7, and 9 don't describe the readings they contain at all; they are informationally incomplete and ambiguous. In fact, lines 7 and 9 are exactly the same and contained within the same group, even though the readings they represent have different meanings and should belong to different groups. We could add tags to encapsulate reading elements into groups so that the bands and reading values are unambiguously related to each other. But first, we should determine whether each data element truly represents data. If we examine the data elements, we can determine whether they really represent data or metadata, and whether they have an adequate context:

- **X-Rite Digital Swatchbook**: This is clearly data.
- **cyan**: This is also clearly data.
- **RGB**: Although this could be considered data in the academic sense, it is not of much value by itself. Furthermore, it is needed to understand the meaning of data elements following it.
- **red**, **green**, and **blue**: These are also data in the academic sense only. They lack adequate context as well. For example, a colorimeter reading in the red band could mean a number of different things.
- **0**, **255**, and **255**: These are the actual colorimeter readings; they are clearly data. They are, however, nearly devoid of critical context—namely the color mode and the color band they represent.

1.6 A Very Simple Way to Design XML

One great advantage of XML information modeling over traditional data modeling is that it serves as a much more intuitive analog of reality. Because of this, a very simple method for designing XML documents produces surprisingly good results. In fact, it will produce better results than many, if not most, "industry standard" XML schemas. Forget that you will be using a computer to manage information—in fact, forget almost everything you know about computers. Instead, imagine that you will be managing your information manually, and design simple forms accordingly. First, make the preprinted parts of the forms into tags; second, make the parts you fill in into data elements; and third, change things like units into attributes. Obviously, doing so will not produce totally optimum results, but it will serve quite well—and it's a good way to start.

Let's look at a simple example—a telephone number directory. We will start with a manual entry form.

Telephone Directory Listing	
Name:	John A. Doe
Address:	123 Main Street
City:	Pleasantville
State:	Maryland
Zip Code:	12345
Telephone:	(999) 555-1234

If we convert this directly into an XML document (spaces become underscores), we get Listing 1.9.

Listing 1.9 Telephone Directory Listing as XML

```
<Telephone_Directory_Listing>
        <Name> John A. Doe </Name>
        <Address> 123 Main Street </Address>
        <City> Pleasantville </City>
        <State> MD </State>
        <Zip_Code> 12345 </Zip_Code>
        <Telephone> (999) 555-1234 </Telephone>
</Telephone_Directory_Listing>
```

Now we will make some small changes. First, we will separate the name into first, middle initial, and last name, and group them together. We will also group the address and separate the telephone number and area code into its own group. Separating fields, such as the name, makes it possible to use the components as individual query terms that will be serviced with direct lookups instead of requiring partial content scans within fields. This significantly improves performance in cases where a query, for example, might be for "John Doe" instead of "John A. Doe". The resulting XML is shown in Listing 1.10.

Listing 1.10 Telephone Directory Listing in XML after Changes

```
<Telephone_Directory_Listing>
      <Name>
            <First> John </First>
            <MI> A. </MI>
            <Last> Doe </Last>
      </Name>
      <Address>
            <Street> 123 Main Street </Street>
            <City> Pleasantville </City>
            <State> MD </State>
            <Zip_Code> 12345 </Zip_Code>
      </Address>
      <Telephone>
            <Area_Code> 999 </Area_Code>
            <Number> 555-1234 <Number>
      </Telephone>
</Telephone_Directory_Listing>
```

The XML document in Listing 1.10 would serve as a good basis for a telephone directory. When thinking about additional information that may have to be added to some listings (additional address lines, additional telephone numbers, etc.), it is important to remember that XML is extensible; a field has to be added only when it is necessary—not globally to all listings.

Many businesses are basically forms driven. For example, clinical trials in the pharmaceutical industry start with forms that have to be approved before the computer systems managing the information can be designed. Because forms can be converted into XML so easily, it is now possible to build systems that are driven primarily by business objectives in intuitive ways, rather than by abstract computing paradigms.

1.7 Conclusion

One of the most promising things about XML, and the new breed of tools built on it, is that we can build applications that are driven by a single information model rather than multiple data models accommodating each application function. We can change the behavior and functionality of application programs by changing the underlying XML rather than by changing code. Additionally, we can optimize performance by changing the way information is expressed. Even in environments not fully leveraging XML as a central information model, it is important to design good XML for the sake of readability and maintainability. Building good applications efficiently requires that we learn not only to use XML correctly, but that we learn also to use it well.

Part II

Native XML Databases

Two native XML databases are covered in this part.

Chapter 2

Tamino—Software AG's Native XML Server

Harald Schöning

2.1 Introduction

In 1999, Software AG released the first version of its native XML server Tamino, which included a native XML database. The term *native* has become popular since then, being used with differing meanings. While some sources (e.g., Bourret 2002) define a native XML database system only by its appearance to the user ("Defines a [logical] model for an XML document . . . and stores and retrieves documents according to that model. . . . For example, it can be built on a relational, hierarchical, or object-oriented database. . . ."), Software AG takes the definition further by requiring that a native XML database system be built and designed for the handling of XML, and not be just a database system for an arbitrary data model with an XML layer on top. At first glance, this might not make a difference at the user level, but a fundamental difference is inside the system. XML is different from other well-known data models (e.g., relational, object-oriented) in a number of aspects. As a consequence, mapping XML to another data model always causes an "impedance mismatch," leading to limitations in functionality and/or performance.

XML by itself leaves many choices for the modeling of data. Two modeling approaches are contrasted by R. Bourret: Data-centric documents have a regular structure, order typically does not matter, and mixed content does not occur. This is the type of information usually stored in a relational or object-oriented database. Document-centric documents are characterized by a less regular structure, the occurrence of mixed content, and the significance of the order of the elements in the document. Of course, all choices in between these two extremes are possible.

Tamino XML Server handles these kinds of XML documents uniformly and is designed to process XML documents efficiently regardless of their structure. In addition, Tamino can store other types of data (e.g., images, HTML files, etc.) that are relevant in a Web context.

Tamino XML Server has a complete database system built in, providing transactions, security, multiuser access, scalability, and so on. In addition, Tamino is tailored to fit the needs of XML: It supports relevant XML standards and is optimized for XML processing. Tamino is available on Windows, several flavors of UNIX (including Solaris, AIX, HP-UX, Linux), and OS/390.

2.2 Tamino Architecture and APIs

Figure 2.1 provides an overview of Tamino's architecture. The primary access to Tamino XML Server is via HTTP—that is, via one or more Web servers, which may be local or remote to the Tamino server. This makes the Internet and an intranet first-class clients of Tamino. Tamino provides the so-called X-Port component (i.e., an extension for the most popular Web servers, which guarantees efficient communication between a Web server and the Tamino XML Server using Software AG's TCP/IP-based transport software XTS—extended transport system—which supports SSL-protected communication). If the client application uses SSL communication with the Web server, the whole path from client application to Tamino database server is secure.

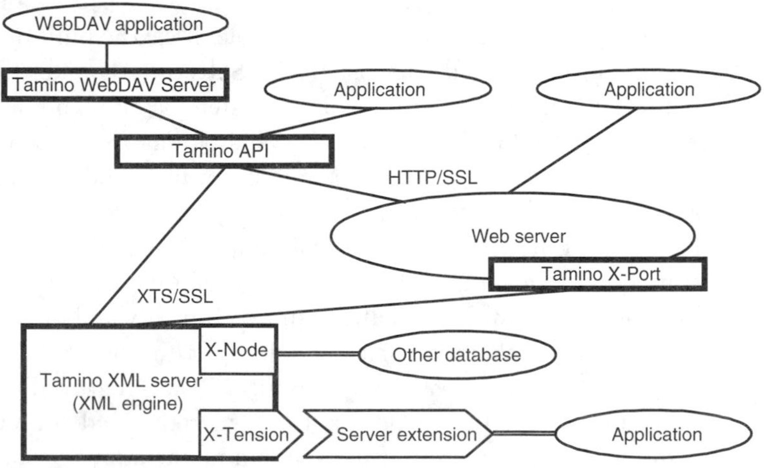

Figure 2.1 Tamino Architecture

Tamino XML Server directly supports the HTTP methods GET, PUT, DELETE, HEAD to read documents, store or replace documents, delete documents, and get information about documents stored in Tamino. More elaborate functionality is transported via the GET or the POST method (using multipart form data)—for example, queries or schema definitions. Clients can be browsers or applications using Tamino's APIs, which map a convenient programming interface to HTTP calls. Such APIs are available for Java, ActiveX, JavaScript, and .NET. The Java API offers the Java programmer comfortable access to data stored in Tamino by using different object models (DOM, SAX, JDOM) or stream-based access. Included with the Tamino API for Java is the Tamino EJB API that allows enterprise application developers to write business applications using Tamino XML Server as a resource manager in an Enterprise Java Beans environment.

Starting with Tamino version 4, an option accesses Tamino without having to pass through a Web server, which saves some overhead for applications in the intranet. Again, this access is based on XTS and therefore can also be SSL secured.

The Tamino administration tool, Tamino Manager, is embedded in Software AG's administration framework, System Management Hub. It provides a browser-based fully functional graphical administration interface to Tamino, as well as a command-line facility for administration. The concept of a single point of control is illustrated in Figure 2.2: From one instance of Tamino Manager, you can manage all Tamino servers in your local network.

By default, documents are completely stored inside Tamino. It is possible, however, to integrate other data sources into the Tamino XML view.

Tamino X-Node provides access to external relational databases as well as to Software AG's Adabas. Data residing in these systems can be included in the XML documents delivered by Tamino XML Server. Also, information included in XML documents stored in Tamino can be propagated to the external systems.

The second option providing openness in Tamino XML Server is a feature called Tamino X-Tension: An element, attribute, or subtree of an XML document, rather than being stored, can be passed to a user-provided mapping function. This function takes over responsibility for the storage of data. It can access an external system or can decide to store information at some other place in Tamino's data store. For retrieval, the corresponding mapping function is used to retrieve the same part of the XML document.

2.3 XML Storage

XML documents can have some schematic information (e.g., in the form of a DTD or W3C XML Schema), but they are not required to. Even if a schema exists,

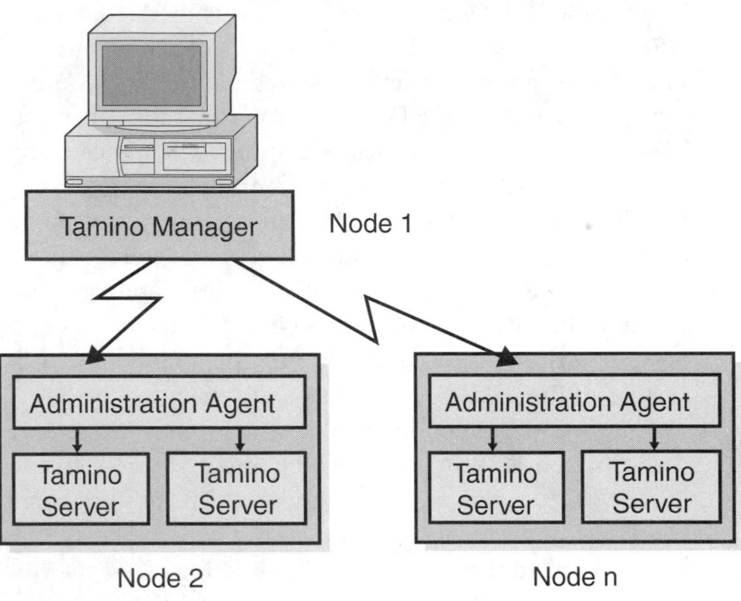

Figure 2.2 Tamino Administration Provides a Single Point of Control

comments and processing instructions may occur at any place without previous declaration in the schema. Thus, the classical database approach of handling objects of a predefined type cannot be applied to the storage of XML. It is mandatory that schemas remain optional. Schemas may also be partial (i.e., describe only parts of the data, as discussed later in this chapter), and they can be easily modified even for existing data.

The descriptive power of DTDs is not sufficient for database purposes. For example, DTDs lack information such as data type, which is needed for the proper indexing of information. As a consequence, DTDs are not a sufficient basis for an XML database schema. In 2001, W3C published the recommendation for W3C XML Schema, a schema definition language that covers most of the expressive power of DTDs but also extends this power with a number of new concepts. In particular, an elaborated type system has been added, which makes XML Schema a suitable basis for a database schema description. In addition, XML Schema offers extensibility features that can be used to enhance standard schematic descriptions by database-specific information without compromising the interpretability of the schema by nonproprietary standard tools. Tamino XML Server uses this concept and supports the schematic description of documents via W3C XML Schema.

2.3.1 Collections and Doctypes

A Tamino database consists of multiple so-called *collections* (see Figure 2.3). These collections are just containers to group documents together. Each document stored in Tamino's data store resides in exactly one collection. A collection has an associated set of W3C XML Schema descriptions. In each schema description, doctypes can be defined using a Tamino-specific notation in the extensibility area of W3C XML Schema (*appinfo* element). A doctype identifies one of the global elements declared in a W3C XML Schema as the root element. Within a collection, each document is stored as a member of exactly one doctype.

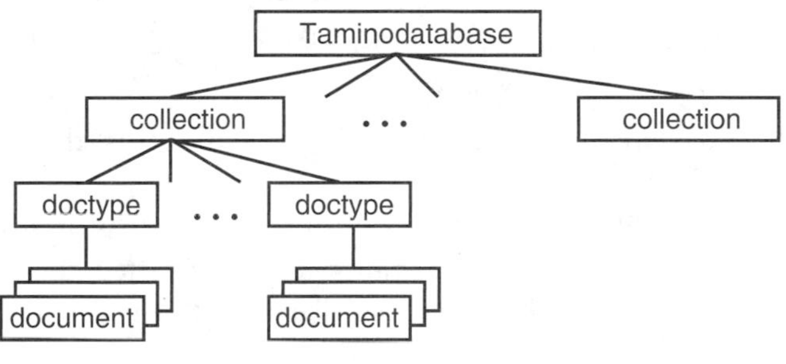

Figure 2.3 Organization of Data in a Tamino Database

The root element of the document identifies the doctype. As a consequence, within a collection, there is a 1:1 relationship between the doctype and root element type. If a document is to be stored in a collection, and no doctype corresponds to the document's root element, such a doctype is created dynamically. In this case, there is no associated user-defined schema. In cases where an associated user-defined schema exists, Tamino validates incoming documents against this schema.

Tamino's configuration data (e.g., character-handling information about available server extensions, etc.) are also stored in XML documents in (system) doctypes in (system) collections. Consequently, configuration can be done by storing or modifying XML documents via the normal Tamino interface.

Tamino XML Server can also store arbitrary objects (non-XML objects)—for example, images, sound files, MS Word documents, HTML pages, and so on. These are organized in a dedicated doctype called nonXML. When these objects are read from Tamino XML Server, Tamino sets the appropriate MIME type.

Tamino assigns an identifier (called ino:id) to each document or non-XML object. In addition, the user can specify a name. This name must be unique within a doctype and can be used for directly addressing the document or object via a URL.

2.3.2 Schemas

As already mentioned, schemas for XML documents play a different role than in relational databases—they are much more loosely coupled to documents and might well describe only parts of a document. With the wildcard mechanism in XML Schema, it is possible to allow subtrees (using the *any* element) or attributes (using the *anyAttribute* element) to occur in specified places of a document, without a detailed description of these subtrees or attributes. Three *processContents* options control the behavior of the validation:

- *strict:* Requires that all elements or attributes that occur at the corresponding location are declared as global items and match the declaration.
- *lax:* Requires that those elements and/or attributes declared as global items match the declaration.
- *skip:* Does not require any checks against declarations.

In addition, the namespace of such elements or attributes can be restricted. For example, a declaration that allows for completely unrestricted subtrees of XML elements below an element *myelement* looks like that shown in Listing 2.1:

Listing 2.1 Subtree of XML Elements

```
<element name="myelement">
 <complexType>
   <sequence>
     any maxOccurs="unbounded" processContents="skip"/>
   </sequence>
 </complexType>
</element>
```

These capabilities of W3C XML Schema already provide some flexibility for the documents associated with this schema and are fully supported by Tamino. However, some scenarios require even higher flexibility. Consider the case of electronic data interchange, where a standard schema that all participants can understand is required. There might be some need for unilateral extension of the standard schema, be it due to a new version of the standard schema, or due to the need for certain participants to enhance the commonly understood information by proprietary bits. Such extensions are not preplanned; hence they cannot be represented in the schema, and W3C XML Schema has no means to support such extensions. For such cases, Tamino XML Server has introduced the *open content* option. If this option is specified, the document is validated against the schema. If information items are found that are not described in the schema, they are accepted nevertheless.

Consider the very simple XML schema for Tamino shown in Listing 2.2.

Listing 2.2 Simple XML Schema

```
<?xml version = "1.0" encoding = "UTF-8"?>
<xs:schema xmlns:xs = "HTTP://www.w3.org/2001/XMLSchema"
xmlns:tsd = "HTTP://namespaces.softwareag.com/tamino/
TaminoSchemaDefinition">
  <xs:annotation>
    <xs:appinfo>
      <tsd:schemaInfo name = "City">
        <tsd:collection name = "mycollection"></tsd:collection>
        <tsd:doctype name = "City">
          <tsd:logical>
            <tsd:content>open</tsd:content>
          </tsd:logical>
        </tsd:doctype>
      </tsd:schemaInfo>
    </xs:appinfo>
  </xs:annotation>
  <xs:element name = "City">
    <xs:complexType>
      <xs:sequence>
        <xs:element name = "Monument" minOccurs = "0"
maxOccurs = "unbounded">
          <xs:complexType>
            <xs:sequence>
              <xs:element name = "Name" type = "xs:string"/>
              <xs:element name = "Description" type = "xs:string"/>
            </xs:sequence>
          </xs:complexType>
        </xs:element>
      </xs:sequence>
      <xs:attribute name = "Name" type = "xs:string"/>
    </xs:complexType>
  </xs:element>
</xs:schema>
```

The schema describes documents that contain information about monuments in a city. A city has a name and may have zero or more monuments. You will notice the xs:annotation element as a child of the xs:schema element. This element type has been introduced in the W3C XML Schema recommendation to allow applications to add their annotations to an XML schema without compromising the interpretability of the schema by other applications. Tamino XML Server uses this feature, adding its information below the xs:appinfo child. This information is Tamino specific. For this reason, the names used are from a Tamino namespace rather than from the XML Schema namespace. The Tamino information comprises the name of the schema when it is stored in Tamino, the name of the collection it applies to, and the name of the doctype(s) defined in this schema. For each doctype, open or closed content can be specified. In this example, open content has been specified. Hence, Tamino accepts the document shown in Listing 2.3 without complaining about validation errors.

Listing 2.3 Undeclared Attribute and Element

```
<?xml version = "1.0" encoding = "UTF-8"?>
<City Name="Darmstadt">
 <Monument built="1897-1899">
    <Name>Russian Chapel</Name>
    <Location>Mathildenhöhe</Location>
    <Description>Built for Nikolai II, czar of Russia.</Description>
 </Monument>
</City>
```

An undeclared attribute is *built* in the Monument element, and an undeclared *Location* element child is below Monument. If `<tsd:content>closed </tsd:content>` had been specified, it would have caused a validation error.

XML schemas can evolve in many aspects: Attributes and elements can be added or removed, and types can change (e.g., by modifying or adding restricting facets, etc.). If a schema is modified for a doctype for which documents are stored in Tamino XML Server, Tamino guarantees the validity of these documents with respect to the new schema. For some modifications, validation can be guaranteed without accessing the documents (e.g., when adding an optional attribute in the case of closed content). For other modifications, Tamino revalidates existing documents in the course of the schema modification.

2.3.3 Access to Other Databases—Tamino X-Node

As already mentioned, data stored in relational databases or in Adabas can be integrated into documents stored in Tamino via the X-Node component. For the user, the fact that parts of the data reside in another data source is transparent. These data behave just like regular parts of a document. They are also declared as part of a document in a Tamino schema. As an example, suppose a relational database contains statistical data about cities. We want to enhance the city information stored in Tamino by the number of inhabitants. Any update of the statistics should be immediately reflected in the documents delivered by Tamino. Thus, we do not replicate the information into Tamino, but we access the information every time it is needed. When accessing a document of the doctype *City*, Tamino looks up the external database for the inhabitants' information and integrates it into the resulting document as if the information were stored in Tamino. Modification of data stored in another database would be possible in the same way: When you store a City document that contains information about the number of inhabitants, the external database is updated. In many scenarios, an update of the external database is not desired. In this case, you can tell Tamino XML Server not to propagate changes.

Listing 2.4 is a Tamino schema snippet that includes a corresponding X-Node definition.

The correspondence between data stored in Tamino and data stored in the other database system must be explicitly described. In addition, user and password to access the other database can be specified, and some other database information as well (e.g., the encoding used in the external database).

Listing 2.4 Tamino Schema Example

```
<xs:element name = "City">
  <xs:annotation>
    <xs:appinfo>
      <tsd:elementInfo>
        <tsd:physical>
          <tsd:map>
            <tsd:subTreeSQL table = "Cities" datasource = "mydb">
              <tsd:primarykeyColumn>name</tsd:primarykeyColumn>
              <tsd:accessPredicate>
              name=<tsd:nodeParameter>/City/@Name
</tsd:nodeParameter>
              </tsd:accessPredicate>
            </tsd:subTreeSQL>
            <tsd:ignoreUpdate></tsd:ignoreUpdate>
          </tsd:map>
        </tsd:physical>
      </tsd:elementInfo>
    </xs:appinfo>
  </xs:annotation>
  <xs:complexType>
    <xs:sequence>
```

```
          <xs:element name = "Monument" minOccurs = "0" maxOccurs =
"unbounded">
            <xs:complexType>
              <xs:sequence>
                <xs:element name = "Name" type = "xs:string">
</xs:element>
                <xs:element name = "Description" type = "xs:string">
                   </xs:element>
              </xs:sequence>
            </xs:complexType>
          </xs:element>
        </xs:sequence>
        <xs:attribute name = "Name" type = "xs:string"
use = "required">
          <xs:annotation>
            <xs:appinfo>
              <tsd:attributeInfo>
                <tsd:physical>
                  <tsd:map>
                    <tsd:nodeSQL column = "name"></tsd:nodeSQL>
                  </tsd:map>
                </tsd:physical>
              </tsd:attributeInfo>
            </xs:appinfo>
          </xs:annotation>
        </xs:attribute>
        <xs:attribute name = "Inhabitants" type = "xs:string">
          <xs:annotation>
            <xs:appinfo>
              <tsd:attributeInfo>
                <tsd:physical>
                  <tsd:map>
                    <tsd:nodeSQL column = "POPULATION"></tsd:nodeSQL>
                  </tsd:map>
                </tsd:physical>
              </tsd:attributeInfo>
            </xs:appinfo>
          </xs:annotation>
        </xs:attribute>
```

```
    </xs:complexType>
  </xs:element>
```

Attached to the *City* element, a connection between this element and the table *Cities* in database *mydb* is defined. The *accessPredicate* defines how rows of this table and elements in corresponding documents relate: Here, equality of the *Name* attribute of the XML element *City* to the *name* column of *Cities* is required. Consequently, a mapping of this attribute to the column is specified. From rows matching this criterion, the *POPULATION* column is included as XML attribute *Inhabitants* into the *City* element. The mapping on table level defines ignoreUpdate. As a consequence, should an XML document of this type be stored in Tamino with the *Inhabitants* attribute contained, the new value would not be propagated to the database *mydb*.

2.3.4 Mapping Data to Functions—Tamino X-Tension

For access to data stored in other databases, the correspondence between parts of an XML document and data in the database can easily be described in a declarative manner. For other data sources (e.g., ERP systems), a more procedural mapping is needed. For this purpose, Tamino's X-Tension component supports mapping functions. A Tamino X-Tension package can be made up of map-in and map-out functions, event-handling functions, and query functions (discussed shortly). These functions can be written in Java or as COM objects (on Windows platforms). The administrator can specify whether they run in the same address space as the Tamino Server (which is faster) or in a separate address space (which is safer). X-Tension functions are loaded dynamically when they are referenced. They can be added to an online Tamino Server without interruption to normal operations.

Map-in functions accept whole documents or parts of documents as parameters. The functions are responsible for storing the XML passed to them. This includes the option to pass documents to middleware systems such as Software AG's EntireX Communicator for further processing. Analogously, map-out functions output XML documents or parts thereof. With this mechanism, the logic to store parts of a document somewhere can be described programmatically. The X-Tension mechanism has full access to Tamino functionality via callbacks. As a consequence, it is also possible to store the XML passed to an X-Tension function in Tamino. While this may seem strange at first glance, it can make sense in scenarios where the same information is received in multiple different formats. In this case, the map-in function can transform the data into a standard format (e.g., using XSLT style sheets) and then store it in Tamino. Then, data can be retrieved in the standard format or—via the map-out function—in the format sent to Tamino. X-Tension mapping is specified in the Tamino schema as shown in Listing 2.5.

Listing 2.5 X-Tension Mapping Example

```
<?xml version = "1.0" encoding = "UTF-8"?>
<xs:schema xmlns:xs = "HTTP://www.w3.org/2001/XMLSchema" xmlns:tsd
= "HTTP://namespaces.softwareag.com/tamino/TaminoSchemaDefinition">
  <xs:annotation>
    <xs:appinfo>
      <tsd:schemaInfo name = "City">
        <tsd:collection name = "mycollection1"></tsd:collection>
        <tsd:doctype name = "City">
          <tsd:logical>
            <tsd:content>open</tsd:content>
          </tsd:logical>
        </tsd:doctype>
      </tsd:schemaInfo>
    </xs:appinfo>
  </xs:annotation>
  <xs:element name = "City">
    <xs:annotation>
      <xs:appinfo>
        <tsd:elementInfo>
          <tsd:physical>
            <tsd:map>
              <tsd:xTension>
               <tsd:onProcess>transform.transformIn</tsd:onProcess>
               <tsd:onCompose>transform.transformOut</tsd:onCompose>
              </tsd:xTension>
            </tsd:map>
          </tsd:physical>
        </tsd:elementInfo>
      </xs:appinfo>
    </xs:annotation>
    <xs:complexType>
      <xs:sequence>
        <xs:element name = "Monument" minOccurs = "0" maxOccurs =
"unbounded">
          <xs:complexType>
            <xs:sequence>
```

```
                    <xs:element name = "Description" type = "xs:string">
                        </xs:element>
                  </xs:sequence>
                  <xs:attribute name = "Name" type = "xs:string">
</xs:attribute>
                </xs:complexType>
              </xs:element>
            </xs:sequence>
            <xs:attribute name = "Cityname" type = "xs:string">
</xs:attribute>
          </xs:complexType>
        </xs:element>
</xs:schema>
```

When a document is stored in the *City* doctype in *mycollection1*, the function *transform.transformIn* is called. This user-provided function applies some transformation to the document in order to match the schema for *City* in collection *mycollection* (rename attribute *Cityname* to *Name*, transform *Monument* attribute *Name* to child element *Name*) and then store the result in doctype *City* in collection *mycollection*. Analogously, the function *transform.transformOut* retrieves the document from *mycollection* and applies reverse transformations.

Again, the fact that mapping is used is transparent to the user. In particular, it does not affect the available functionality on the data. For example, there are no restrictions on the queries allowed on such data.

For an X-Tension function, the information about transactional events (commit, rollback) is usually important. If the X-Tension function is used to store data in a transactional external system, the corresponding transaction on the foreign system has to be rolled back if the Tamino transaction is rolled back. If the external system does not support transactions, data stored by the X-Tension function in the course of a Tamino transaction has to be explicitly removed on rollback. To enable such actions, X-Tension packages can register callback functions that are invoked on events such as commit or rollback of a transaction, end of session, and so on.

As a special case, mapping does not need to be symmetric. For example, one can include random values into documents delivered by Tamino, if the map-out function is a random number generator and no map-in function is specified. Analogously, one may specify a map-in function that sends its input via e-mail to a certain recipient or passes it to a workflow system. The map-out function might then deliver status information (e.g., where the data currently are in the work flow) rather than the information passed in.

2.3.5 Internationalization Issues

XML is based on Unicode (Unicode Consortium 2000). Consequently, Tamino internally works with Unicode only. However, not all systems interacting with Tamino are based on Unicode. Hence, Tamino has to care for encoding differences and encoding conversions. The first obvious place where Tamino can encounter non-Unicode encoding is in the XML declaration in a document:

```
<?xml version="1.0" encoding="iso-8859-1"?>
```

The XML 1.0 specification requires XML processors to understand the Unicode encodings UTF-8 and UTF-16, and it leaves open whether an XML processor accepts other encodings. Tamino XML Server supports a plethora of non-Unicode encodings, including the ISO-Latin family, and many others. When such documents are sent to Tamino XML Server, Tamino converts them into Unicode before processing them and also resolves character references by replacing them with the corresponding Unicode character. Analogously, users can specify an encoding when retrieving data. In this case, Tamino converts the query results to the desired encoding before sending them to the user.

This is, however, not the only place where encoding issues occur. On the HTTP level, messages can also carry encoding information. This encoding information can even differ from the information included in the XML documents. Here, Tamino XML Server has to do conversions as well.

Among the facets for string types defined by W3C XML Schema, there is no collation facet. In the context of a database, where sorting is an important operation, it is highly desirable to be able to influence the order of strings according to language-specific rules. For example, according to Spanish language rules, the word llamar is sorted after the word luz (i.e., "luz" > "llamar"). Because W3C XML Schema does not support the concept of user-defined facets, Tamino adds collation information in the appinfo element as shown in Listing 2.6:

Listing 2.6 Collation Information

```
<xs:attribute name = "Name" type = "xs:string" use = "required">
  <xs:annotation>
    <xs:appinfo>
      <tsd:attributeInfo>
        <tsd:logical>
          <tsd:collation>
            <tsd:language value = "es"></tsd:language>
          </tsd:collation>
        </tsd:logical>
```

```
        </tsd:attributeInfo>
      </xs:appinfo>
    </xs:annotation>
  </xs:attribute>
```

2.3.6 Indexing

Indexes are indispensable in database systems because otherwise large quantities of data could not be queried in a satisfactory way. Tamino XML Server supports three types of indexes that are maintained whenever documents are stored, modified, or deleted.

The *standard index* is a value-based index, as it is well known from relational databases. It serves for a fast lookup when searching for elements or attributes having certain values, or for relational expressions on such values (*find all books with a price less than 50*). In the *City* example presented earlier, a standard index on the *Name* attribute of *City* would accelerate searches for a dedicated city. Indexes are also defined in the Tamino schema, again using the appinfo mechanism of W3C XML Schema.

Standard-indexes are type-aware: Indexes on numerical values support numerical order (i.e., 5 < 10); indexes on values of a textual data type are ordered lexicographically ("5" > "10").

Global elements may be referenced in multiple contexts. If an index is to be established only for a subset of these contexts, a *which* element can be used to specify the paths for which an index is to be created.

Text indexes are the prerequisite for efficient text retrieval functionality. In text indexing, the words contained in an element or attribute are indexed, such that the search for words within the content of an element or attribute is accelerated. Note that text indexes can not only be defined on leaf elements, but also on elements that contain other elements. Thus, it is possible to text-index whole subtrees or even a whole document. In any case, the index is based on the result of applying the text() function known from XPath (Clark and DeRose 1999) to the element or attribute. This result is tokenized, and each token is included in the index. Note that this tokenization is a nontrivial task. Even in English text, where words are separated by whitespace and therefore are easily recognizable, the role of punctuation characters such as colon and dash has to be defined. Do they separate tokens, or are they part of a token? For other languages, the same characters may have to be treated separately. Based on decades of experience with text retrieval at Software AG, Tamino defines default handling of such characters that fits the needs of most character-based languages. However, Tamino XML Server offers a configuration mechanism to override its default handling for dedicated characters.

The words in some languages are not separated by whitespace, and tokenization has to work differently (e.g., it must be dictionary-based). This holds for Japanese, Chinese, Korean, and so on. Tamino XML Server supports tokenization for these languages.

Non-XML objects representing text are automatically text-indexed to provide basic search facilities on them.

A special index for text search is the so-called word fragment index. It is used to speed up wildcard search in cases where the search term uses a wildcard for both the prefix and the postfix of the words to be searched.

There is also an XML-specific type of index, called *structure index*. It comes in two flavors. The condensed structure index keeps the information about all paths that occur in any instance of a specific doctype. This can accelerate query execution in many cases (e.g., for documents without associated schema, doctypes with open content, or when the xs:anyAttribute is used). If such an index does not exist, misspelled names might lead to a sequential scan of all documents of a doctype. This index also helps when a schema is modified: The validity of some changes can be assessed without looking at the instances of a doctype. The full structure index records not only the existence of paths in a doctype, but also the documents in which the path occurs. This can be used for optimization whenever a query asks for optional parts of a doctype (e.g., elements or attributes with *minOccurs=0* or children of them).

2.3.7 Organization on Disk

Tamino databases are made up of two persistent parts (called *spaces*):

- The data space contains all the documents and objects stored in Tamino. Doctypes are organized in clusters in order to accelerate sequential access. Based on the document size, Tamino XML Server chooses appropriate compression techniques. Tamino's choice can, however, be overruled by the specification of a dedicated compression method in the Tamino schema of the corresponding doctype.
- The index space contains the index data for the documents stored in Tamino.

Both spaces can be distributed over many different volumes of external storage, thus allowing Tamino to store terabytes of data. Tamino can be configured to automatically extend spaces when they run full.

For transactional logging, Tamino has a *journal space*, which is a fixed-size container. It is used as a circular buffer containing all logs necessary to roll back transactions, or to redo transactions after a system crash. Long-time logging, which can be used to bring the database to a current state after the restoration of a previously done backup, is stored in sequential files.

2.4 Querying XML

As already mentioned, Tamino XML Server supports methods to directly retrieve documents that were previously stored using Tamino (e.g., direct addressing of documents via URL). This includes documents with mapping to external data sources or to functions. However, just retrieving documents by their name or by their identifier is only part of the functionality needed in an XML database system. Powerful query facilities must complement the direct access methods.

2.4.1 Query Language—Tamino X-Query

Currently, there is no standardized XML query language. However, there is W3C activity to define an XML query language, called XQuery (Boag et al. 2002), but it is still in draft status. As a consequence, database systems that store XML have to use another language for querying. A common choice is XPath (Clark and DeRose 1999), which is also the basis for Tamino's query language. However, Tamino has extended XPath in two aspects:

- While the navigation-based approach of XPath fits the needs of retrieval in data-centric environments, document-centric environments need a more content-based retrieval facility. Therefore, Tamino XML Server also supports full-text search over the contents of attributes and elements (including their children, ignoring markup). For this purpose, Tamino defines a new relational operator ~= (the *contains* operator). With the Tamino text search capabilities, the occurrence of a word or a phrase in the content of an element can be tested. Case is ignored in text search. An asterisk represents a wildcard for the search: //*[.~="XML" ADJ "database*"] finds all elements that contain strings such as "XML databases", "xml databases", "xml database systems". Text search functionality is independent of the existence of text indexes—they just accelerate the search.
- To enable the user to integrate dedicated functionality into queries, Tamino allows user-defined functions to be added to the query language. This is another functionality of the X-Tension component.

With the progress of the W3C standardization efforts for XQuery, Tamino XML Server will also support this query language.

2.4.2 Sessions and Transactions

Tamino operations (including queries) can be executed inside or outside a session context. In the latter case, such an operation is a transaction on its own—that is, after its execution, all resources used by this operation are released. In case of an error, all effects of the operation have been wiped out; otherwise all effects of the operation are made persistent.

A session groups multiple operations together. The session is the unit of user authentication. In a *connect* request, the user presents his credentials and sets the default operation modes for all operations executed in the session. Among them is the isolation level for the session, which is analogous to the isolation levels in SQL: The higher the isolation level, the fewer anomalies can occur. On the other hand, the higher the isolation level, the higher the impact on parallel operations. The isolation level defined for a session can be overridden on the statement level. Within a session, multiple consecutive transactions can occur.

2.4.3 Handling of Results

The result of a Tamino query is well-formed XML. If a query returns more than one document (or document fragment), the pure concatenation of them would not yield well-formed XML because an XML document must have exactly one root. Therefore, Tamino wraps the result set in an artificial root element. This also contains context information such as error messages. To facilitate handling of large response sets, Tamino offers a cursor mechanism on query results. Cursor information is also included in the result wrapper. The result of fetching just one result element at a time for the query /City/Monument/Name looks like that shown in Listing 2.7.

Listing 2.7 Result of /City/Monument/Name Query

```
<?xml version="1.0" encoding="iso-8859-1" ?>
<ino:response xmlns:ino="HTTP://namespaces.softwareag.com/tamino/
response2"
       xmlns:xql="HTTP://metalab.unc.edu/xql/" ino:sessionid="15"
       ino:sessionkey="18362">
  <xql:query>/City/Monument/Name</xql:query>
  <ino:message ino:returnvalue="0">
    <ino:messageline>fetching cursor</ino:messageline>
  </ino:message>
  <xql:result>
    <Name ino:id="3">Russian Chapel</Name>
  </xql:result>
  <ino:cursor ino:handle="1">
```

```
    <ino:current ino:position="3" ino:quantity="1" />
    <ino:next ino:position="4" />
    <ino:prev ino:position="2" />
  </ino:cursor>
  <ino:message ino:returnvalue="0">
    <ino:messageline>cursor fetched</ino:messageline>
  </ino:message>
</ino:response>
```

2.4.4 Query Execution

When a query is sent to Tamino XML Server, the first step is to transform it into Unicode. After this, the query is parsed and checked for syntactical correctness. In the following optimization step, the query is matched against the schema definitions. Depending on the existence of a schema, open or closed content definition, and existence of full or condensed structure index, some queries will return to the user with an empty result even before accessing data. The next step is the selection of appropriate indexes to use for the evaluation of the query. Index-based selection of documents is then performed, and the remaining parts of the query are evaluated on the result.

2.5 Tools

Several tools complement Tamino's functionality. Some of the most remarkable tools are sketched in the sections that follow.

2.5.1 Database Browsing

During application development, but also in later phases of database operation, a simple-to-use but powerful tool to view the database contents is very useful. The Tamino X-Plorer (see Figure 2.4) organizes the schemas defined in Tamino and all the instances in a tree view. Queries can be used to tailor the set of documents shown. A paging mechanism enables browsing, even if a very large number of instances are stored for a doctype. Applications can be launched directly from the X-Plorer window.

2.5.2 Schema Editing

As mentioned previously, Tamino's schema description is based on the W3C XML Schema. Unfortunately, schema documents based on the W3C XML Schema can become quite lengthy and complex in structure. For the users' convenience,

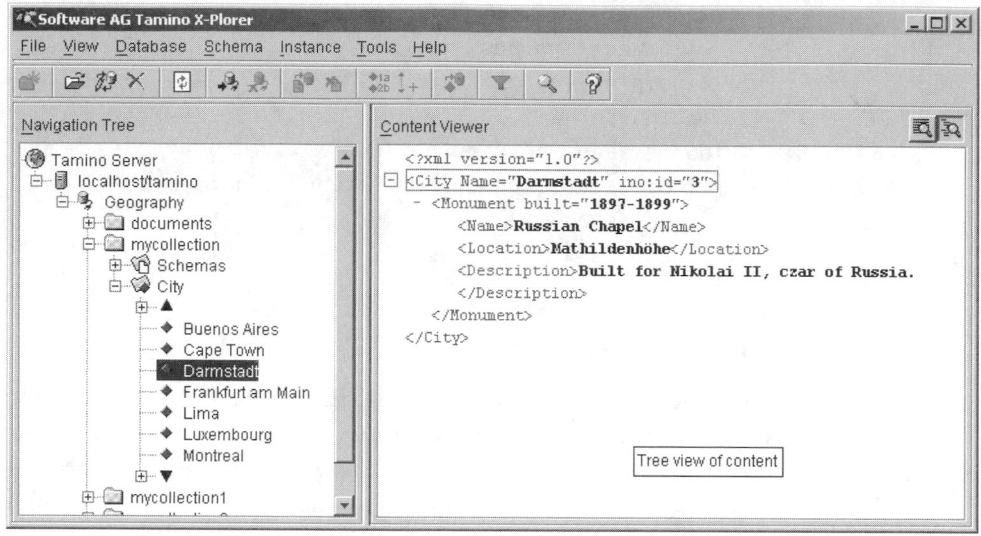

Figure 2.4 Tamino X-Plorer

Tamino's Schema Editor (see Figure 2.5) provides its own graphic interface for defining schemas and enhancing them with Tamino-specific information.

2.5.3 WebDAV Access

With WebDAV (Web-based Distributed Authoring and Versioning), a standard way of reading and writing documents over the Web has been defined (Goland et al. 1999). The WebDAV protocol enhances the HTTP protocol. It provides methods for organizing documents in hierarchies (folders), locking documents over the Web (check-in and check-out), instance-based authorization, versioning, assignment of properties to documents, and querying documents. With this functionality, a WebDAV-enabled data management system can serve as a very convenient file system. This is the reason why many tools (including Windows Explorer and Microsoft Office products) support WebDAV-based resource management. In Windows Explorer, for example, you can browse through a WebDAV server as if it were a file system.

The Tamino WebDAV Server implements the WebDAV standard on Tamino XML Server, thereby converting a Tamino XML Server to a WebDAV data source. As a consequence, you can use Windows Explorer to browse a Tamino database and use Microsoft Word to open a document stored in Tamino and then save it back to Tamino, and so on.

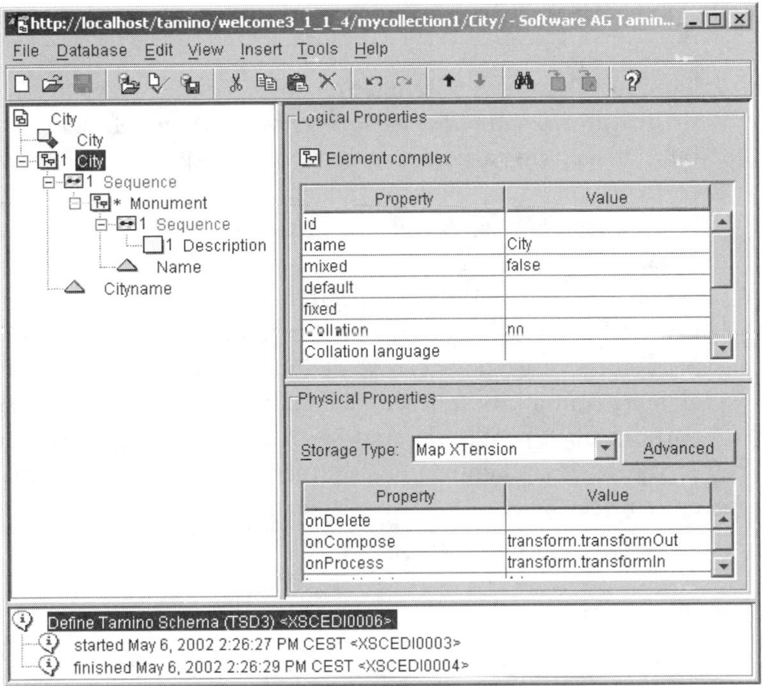

Figure 2.5 Tamino Schema Editor

2.5.4 X-Application

Tamino X-Application is Software AG's suite for rapid application development. It is focused on HTML-based Web applications. Tamino X-Application is based on Java Server Pages (JSP). By embedding JSP tags into HTML pages, it becomes possible to browse, display, insert, update, and delete Tamino data within an HTML Web page. A rich tag library provides the necessary functionality. Because JSP is server based, X-Application's functionality does not depend on a particular client platform. Additional modules allow the quick creation of Tamino-enabled HTML pages:

- A plug-in module for Macromedia's Dreamweaver HTML editor allows WYSIWYG design of X-Application Web pages in an environment Web designers are familiar with.
- The X-Application generator can automatically generate an HTML access layer for existing XML document types. This access layer can be used to browse, display, insert, update, and delete document instances.

2.6 Full Database Functionality

Tamino XML Server is made up of a complete database system. It supports all the features required for a database system, including multiuser operation, support for transactions, a powerful backup concept, mass load facilities, scalability, and performance.

Security is essential for a database system. The Tamino security concept consists of several components. For a secure transport of data to and from Tamino XML Server, SSL-secured communication can be used. In addition, Tamino can restrict the Web servers that are allowed to communicate to a dedicated database.

Access restrictions can be defined on collection level, on doctype level, and on element and attribute level. Hence, it is possible to allow access to only a specific part of a document for a certain user. For user authentication, Tamino can make use of the basic authentication facilities of Web servers or (starting after version 3) authenticate against its own user database or an external user database.

2.7 Conclusion

Tamino XML Server provides the full functionality required in a modern database system that has been thoroughly designed for handling XML. XML documents are stored natively in Tamino's data store, not mapped to any other data model. Tamino XML Server supports an XML-specific query language, which includes text retrieval facilities. Dedicated indexing techniques accelerate the execution of queries. However, Tamino remains storage structure independent: The operations and queries accepted by Tamino do not depend on the existence of any indexing structure. Storage in Tamino XML Server provides high flexibility: Schemas are optional, may be declared as only partially describing the documents, or can fully describe document structures. Data can be completely or partially stored in Tamino, or data can be stored partially in another database system (Tamino X-Node), or in any other way using the Tamino X-Tension feature. A set of graphical tools facilitates Tamino application development.

Chapter 3

eXist Native XML Database

Wolfgang M. Meier

3.1 Introduction

eXist is an Open Source effort to develop a native XML database system, tightly integrated with existing XML development tools like Apache's Cocoon. eXist covers most of the basic native XML database features as well as a number of advanced techniques like keyword searches on text, queries on the proximity of terms, and regular expression-based search patterns. The database is lightweight, completely written in Java, and may be easily deployed, running either standalone, inside a servlet engine, or directly embedded in an application.

While on first sight, eXist has many similarities to Apache's Xindice, each project addresses different types of applications, and each is based on different architectures. eXist especially puts strong emphasis on efficient, index-based query processing. eXist's search engine has been designed to provide fast XPath queries, using indexes for all element, text, and attribute nodes. Based on path join algorithms, a wide range of query expressions are processed using only index information. eXist will not load the actual nodes unless it is really required to do so, for example, to display query results.

eXist started as an Open Source project in January 2001 and has already gone a long way since the first versions were released to the public. A growing number of developers and projects are actively using the software in a variety of application scenarios. Applications show that eXist—despite its relatively short project history—is already able to address true industrial system cases, for example, as a core retrieval component in a multilingual documentation publishing system, containing technical maintenance documentation for several car models produced by an Italian car manufacturer.

The following sections introduce eXist's features and provide a quick overview of how to develop standalone and Web-based applications using the different interfaces provided with eXist. Finally, we will take a closer look at eXist's indexing and storage architecture to see how query processing works.

3.2 Features

In this section we discuss some of the key features of eXist—namely, schema-less data storage, collections, index-based query processing, and XPath extensions for performing full-text searches.

3.2.1 Schema-less XML Data Storage

eXist provides schema-less storage of XML documents. Documents are not required to have an associated schema or document type definition. In other words, they are allowed to be well formed only. This has some major benefits: Besides the fact that one usually finds a lot of documents without a valid document type definition, many XML authors typically tend to create the DTD or schema after writing the document to which it applies. In practice, DTDs may also evolve over a longer period of time, so documents follow slightly different versions of the same DTD or schema. Therefore, an XML database should support queries on similar documents, which may not have the same structure.

3.2.2 Collections

Inside the database, documents are managed in hierarchical collections. From a user's point of view, this is comparable to storing files in a file system. Collections may be arbitrarily nested. They are not bound to a predefined schema, so the number of document types used by documents in one collection is not constrained. Arbitrary documents may be mixed inside the same collection.

Users may query a distinct part of the collection hierarchy or even all the documents contained in the database using XPath syntax with extensions.

3.2.3 Index-Based Query Processing

Evaluating structured queries against possibly large collections of unconstrained documents poses a major challenge to storage organization and query processing. To speed up query processing, some kind of index structure is needed. eXist uses a numerical indexing scheme to identify XML nodes in the index. The indexing scheme not only links index entries to the actual DOM nodes in the XML store, but also provides quick identification of possible relationships between nodes in the document node tree, such as parent-child or ancestor-descendant relationships. Based on these features, eXist's query engine uses fast path join algorithms to evaluate XPath expressions, while conventional approaches are typically based on top-down or bottom-up traversals of the document tree. It has been shown that path join algorithms outperform tree-traversal based implementations by an order of magnitude (Li and Moon 2001; Srivastava et al. 2002). We will provide details on the technical background at the end of this chapter.

Indexing is applied to all nodes in the document, including elements, attributes, text, and comments. Contrary to other approaches, it is not necessary to explicitly create indexes. All indexes are managed by the database engine. However, it is possible to restrict the automatic full-text indexing to defined parts of a document.

3.2.4 Extensions for Full-Text Searching

During development, the main focus has been to support document-centric as opposed to data-centric documents. Document-centric documents usually address human users. They typically contain a lot of mixed content, longer sections of text, and less machine-readable data. However, querying these types of documents is not very well supported by standard XPath. eXist thus provides a number of extensions to efficiently process full-text queries. An additional index structure keeps track of word occurrences and assists the user in querying textual content. Special full-text operators and functions are available to query text nodes as well as attribute values.

3.3 System Architecture Overview

This section provides an overview of the eXist architecture.

3.3.1 Pluggable Storage Backends

Though eXist provides pluggable storage backends (see Figure 3.1), storing documents either in the internal XML store or an external relational database system (e.g., MySQL or PostgreSQL), it has been designed to be a pure native XML database. As a proof of concept for the indexing and storage architecture, the first releases of eXist implemented only the relational backend. These versions served as a testing platform to explore whether the basic design would meet XML database management needs. Beginning with version 0.6, the relational backend has been supplemented by a new native database backend, which has been written from scratch in Java. The pure native backend (which is covered in the following sections) will yield much better performance for many types of applications.

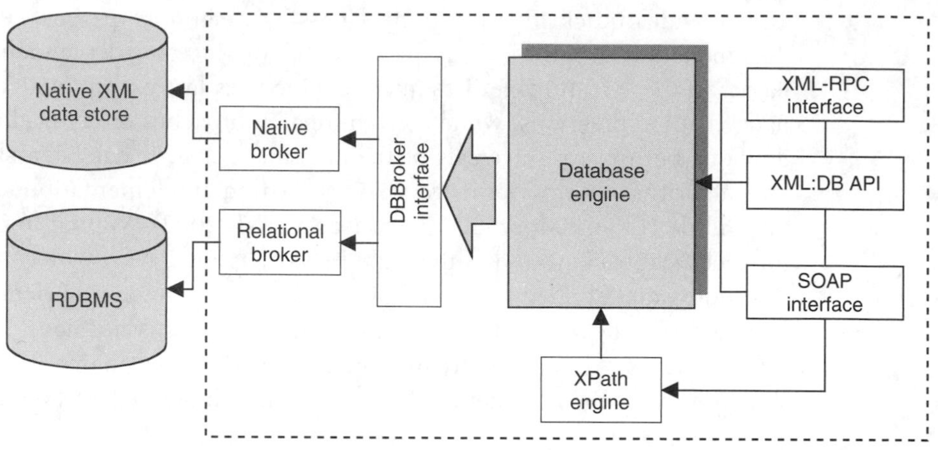

Figure 3.1 The eXist Architecture

However, the relational backend code has been kept as well. Relational DBMSs provide high reliability and have been investigated for years, which is important for applications that require reliability more than speed.

Backend implementation details are hidden from eXist's core. All calls to the storage backend are handled by broker classes, implementing the DBBroker interface. To use the relational backend instead of the internal native XML store, JDBC connection parameters have to be specified in the configuration file. New storage backends may be added at any time.

3.3.2 Deployment

The database engine may either run as a standalone server, embedded into an application, or in connection with a servlet container. All three alternatives are thread safe and support concurrent operations by multiple users. Embedding the database into an application without running an external server process is supported by the XML:DB API driver. It is also possible to use eXist from a read-only file system—for example, to deploy an application on a CD-ROM.

3.3.3 Application Development

Applications may access a remote eXist server via HTTP, XML-RPC (XML Remote Procedure Call), SOAP, and WebDAV (Web-based Distributed Authoring and Versioning) interfaces. Developers programming in Java should have a look at the XML:DB API supported by eXist: It is an API proposed by the XML:DB initiative that tries to standardize common development interfaces for access to XML database services. Using the XML:DB API, you may keep your code unchanged while switching between alternative database systems like Xindice and eXist.

eXist's integration with Cocoon also relies completely on the XML:DB API. Cocoon may use eXist as its data store, reading all XML files from the database instead of the file system. Access to the retrieval and document management facilities of eXist is provided via XSP logic sheets. XSP—eXtensible Server Pages—is Java code inside XML, comparable to JSP—Java Server Pages, which typically embeds Java in HTML.

3.4 Getting Started

Current versions of eXist are available at the project's Web page (http://exist-db.org). The software is distributed either as a zip or tar file and runs with Java Development Kit version 1.3 or 1.4. All required Java libraries, Apache's Jakarta Web server, and Cocoon are included in the distribution. Hardware requirements are low: Any machine with at least 64MB of main memory is sufficient.

Details on the installation of eXist are provided in the documentation. For the native storage backend, the installation process is fairly simple and limited to unpacking the distribution and starting either the standalone server or the included Web server. To access the features discussed below, it is recommended that you use eXist with the Web server. Once the server has been started, it will provide XML-RPC, SOAP, and WebDAV interfaces to communicate with the database engine. You may also browse through the Cocoon-based project pages, which are available at http://localhost:8080/exist/index.xml. There you will find a query interface to send queries to the server and a simple administration tool used to add or view XML documents, create or remove collections, and so on.

The database engine will create all required files the first time it is accessed. The documentation also describes how to put XML files into the database. To try out the XPath expressions given as examples later in this chapter, you may use the simple Web-based query-interface. An online version is also available at eXist's home page.

However, there is no preferred way to work with eXist. Several command-line clients are included in the distribution. They serve as examples for client-side programming and use different APIs and programming languages to access eXist.

3.5 Query Language Extensions

Let's take a quick look at some useful extensions eXist adds to standard XPath to enable you to efficiently use the database.

3.5.1 Specifying the Input Document Set

Since a database may contain an unlimited set of documents, two additional functions are required by eXist's query engine to determine the set of documents against which an expression will be evaluated: `document()` and `collection()`. `document()` accepts a single document name, a list of document names, or a wildcard as parameters. The wildcard (*) selects all documents in the database. The `collection()` function specifies the collection whose documents are to be included into query evaluation. For example:

```
collection('/db/shakespeare')//SCENE[ SPEECH[ SPEAKER='JULIET']]/
TITLE
```

The root collection of the database is always called `/db`. By default, documents found in subcollections below the specified collection are included. So you don't have to specify the full path to `/db/shakespeare/plays` in the preceding expression.

3.5.2 Querying Text

The XPath standard defines only a few limited functions to search for a given string inside the character content of a node, which is a weak point if you have to search through documents containing larger sections of text. For many types of documents, the provided standard functions will not yield satisfying results. For example, you might remember to have read something about "XML" and "databases" in some chapter of a book, but you may not be sure exactly where it was. Using standard XPath, you could try a query like:

```
//chapter[ contains(., 'XML') and contains(., 'databases')]
```

Still you can't be sure to find all matches—for example, "databases" might have been written with a capital letter at the start of a sentence. Also, query execution will probably be quite slow for large sets of documents, because the XPath engine has to scan over the entire character content of all chapters and their descendant nodes in all books to find matches.

The solution: eXist offers two additional operators and several extension functions to provide efficient, index-based access to the full-text content of nodes. For example, you might remember that the words "XML" and "database" were mentioned near to each other but not in the same paragraph. So with eXist, you could query:

```
//section[ near(., 'XML database', 50)]
```

This query will return all sections containing both keywords in the correct order and with less than 50 words between them. Besides making query formulation easier and in many cases more exact, using eXist's full-text search extensions instead of standard XPath expressions yields a much better query performance. The query engine will process the previous query based entirely on indexing information. We will have a closer look at how this works later.

In cases where the order and distance of search terms are not important, eXist offers two other operators for simple keyword queries. The following XPath expression will select the scene in the cavern from Shakespeare's *The Tragedy of Macbeth*:

```
//SCENE[ SPEECH[ SPEAKER &= 'witch' and LINE &= 'fenny snake']]
```

&= is a special text search operator. It selects context nodes containing all of the space-separated terms in the argument on the right. To find nodes containing any of the terms, the `|=` operator is provided. For example, we may use the subexpression `LINE |= 'fenny snake'` in the preceding query to get all lines containing either `"fenny"` or `"snake"`.

Note that eXist's default keyword tokenizer will treat dates, floating point numbers, and any character sequence containing at least one digit as a single keyword. The operators accept simple wildcards, for example, `'witch*'` will select `'witch'` as well as `'witches'`. To match more complex string patterns, regular expression syntax is supported through the match, match-all, and match-any functions. For example, to find all lines containing "live", "lives", as well as "life", you may use the following expression:

```
//SPEECH[ match-all(LINE, 'li[ fv] e[ s] ')]
```

Match-all and match-any perform a search on keywords in a similar fashion as the &= and `|=` operators, while match corresponds to the `contains` function. More information on this topic is available in the eXist documentation.

3.5.3 Outstanding Features

eXist's XPath query engine currently implements major parts of the standard requirements, though at the time of writing it is not yet complete. Only abbreviated XPath syntax is supported so, for example, node-axis specifiers like previous-sibling/next-sibling still wait to be implemented. However, the existing functionality covers most commonly needed XPath expressions. Some work is under way in the project to rewrite the query processor. In the long run, we would like to replace XPath with an XQuery-based implementation.

3.6 Application Development

This section presents a quick introduction into programming applications with eXist. We first look at the XML:DB API, which is mainly of interest to Java developers. To those who prefer other programming languages, eXist offers SOAP and XML-RPC interfaces. A small SOAP example using .NET and C# is provided later in this section. Finally, we will see how eXist integrates with Apache's Cocoon.

Due to space restrictions, the examples are simple. The distribution contains more complex examples for each of the APIs discussed here.

3.6.1 Programming Java Applications with the XML:DB API

The preferred way to access eXist from Java applications is to use the XML:DB API. The XML:DB API provides a common interface to native or XML-enabled databases and supports the development of portable, reusable applications.

The vendor-independent XML:DB initiative tries to standardize a common API for access to XML database services, comparable to JDBC or ODBC (Open Database Connectivity) for relational database systems. The API is built around four core concepts: drivers, collections, resources, and services. Drivers encapsulate the whole database access logic. They are provided by the database vendor and have to be registered with the database manager. As in eXist, collections are hierarchical containers, containing other collections or resources. A resource might be either an XML resource or a binary large object. Other types of resources might be added in future versions of the standard. Currently, eXist supports only XML resources. Finally, *services* may be requested to perform special tasks like querying a collection with XPath or managing collections.

Every application using the XML:DB API has to first obtain a collection object from the database. This is done by calling the static method `getCollection` of class DatabaseManager. To locate the specified collection, the method expects a fully qualified URI (Uniform Resource Identifier) as parameter, which identifies the database implementation, the collection name, and optionally the location of the database server on the network.

For example, the URI "xmldb:exist:///db/shakespeare" references the Shakespeare collection of an eXist database running in embedded mode. Internally, eXist has two different driver implementations: The first talks to a remote database engine using XML-RPC calls; the second has direct access to a local instance of eXist. Which implementation will be selected depends on the URI passed to the `getCollection` method. To reference the Shakespeare collection on a remote server, you use "xmldb:exist://localhost:8080/exist/xmlrpc/db/shakespeare".

The DriverManager keeps a list of available database drivers and uses the database ID specified in the URI ("exist") to select the correct driver class. Drivers may be registered for different databases by calling `DatabaseManager.registerDatabase` at the start of a program. For example, the code fragment shown in Listing 3.1 registers a driver for eXist.

Listing 3.1 Registering a Driver for eXist

```
Class cl = Class.forName("org.exist.xmldb.DatabaseImpl");
Database driver = (Database)cl.newInstance();
DatabaseManager.registerDatabase(driver);
```

Once you have obtained a valid collection object, you may browse through its child collections and resources, retrieve a resource, or request a service. Listing 3.2 presents a complete example, which sends an XPath query passed on the command line to the server.

Listing 3.2 Querying the Database

```
import org.xmldb.api.base.*;
import org.xmldb.api.modules.*;
import org.xmldb.api.*;

public class QueryExample {
  public static void main(String args[]) throws Exception {
     String driver = "exist.xmldb.DatabaseImpl";
     Class cl = Class.forName(driver);
     Database database = (Database)cl.newInstance();
     database.setProperty("create-database", "true");
     DatabaseManager.registerDatabase(database);

     Collection col =
        DatabaseManager.getCollection("xmldb:exist:///db");
          (XPathQueryService) col.getService("XPathQuery-Service",
"1.0");
     service.setProperty("pretty", "true");
     service.setProperty("encoding", "ISO-8859-1");
     ResourceSet result = service.query(args[0]);

     ResourceIterator i = result.getIterator();
     while(i.hasMoreResources()) {
        Resource r = i.nextResource();
        System.out.println((String)r.getContent());
     }
}
```

The sample code registers the driver for a locally attached eXist database and retrieves the root collection. By setting the "create-database" property to "true", the database driver is told to create a local database instance if none has been started before. A service of type "XPathQueryService" is then requested from the collection. To execute the query, method `service.query(String xpath)` is called. This method returns a `ResourceSet`, containing the query results. Every resource in the `ResourceSet` corresponds to a single result fragment or value. To iterate through the resource set we call `result.getIterator()`.

To have the client query a remote database, the URI passed to `DatabaseManager.getCollection()` has to be changed as explained previously: For example, to access a database engine running via the Tomcat Web server, use `DatabaseManager.getCollection("xmldb:exist://localhost:8080/exist/xmlrpc/db")`.

3.6.2 Accessing eXist with SOAP

In addition to the XML:DB API for Java development, eXist provides XML-RPC and SOAP interfaces for communication with the database engine. This section presents a brief example of using SOAP to query the database. A description of the XML-RPC interface is available in the "Developer's Guide" that can be found on the home page of eXist.

XML-RPC as well as SOAP client libraries are available for a large number of programming languages. Each protocol has benefits and drawbacks. While a developer has to code XML-RPC method calls by hand, programming with SOAP is usually more convenient, because most SOAP tools will automatically create the low-level code from a given WSDL (Web Services Description Language) service description. Additionally, SOAP transparently supports user-defined types. Thus the SOAP interface to eXist has a slightly cleaner design, because fewer methods are needed to expose the same functionality. On the other hand, SOAP toolkits tend to be more complex.

eXist uses the Axis SOAP toolkit from Apache, which runs as a servlet. Once the Tomcat Web server contained in the eXist distribution has been started, the developer is ready to access eXist's SOAP interface. Two Web services are provided: The first allows querying of the server; the second is used to add, view, and remove documents or collections.

Listing 3.3 presents an example of a simple client written in C# with Microsoft's .NET framework. For this example, the wsdl.exe tool provided with .NET to automatically generate a client stub class from the WSDL Web service definition (query.wsdl) was used, which describes eXist's query service. The tool produces a single file (QueryService.cs), which has to be linked with the developer's own code. Using the automatically generated classes, all the SOAP-related code is hidden from the developer. The developer does not even have to know that a remote Web service is being accessed.

Listing 3.3 Simple .NET Client in C#

```
using System;

public class SoapQuery {
    static void Main(string[] args) {
        string query;
        if(args.Length < 1) {
            Console.Write("Enter a query: ");
            query = Console.ReadLine();
        } else
            query = args[0];
        QueryService qs = new QueryService();

        // execute the query
        QueryResponse resp = qs.query(query);
        Console.WriteLine("found: {0} hits in {1} ms.", resp.hits,
        resp.queryTime);

        // print a table of hits by document for every collection
        foreach (QueryResponseCollection collection in
resp.collections) {
            Console.WriteLine(collection.collectionName);
            QueryResponseDocument[] docs = collection.documents;
            foreach (QueryResponseDocument doc in docs)
                Console.WriteLine('\t' + doc.documentName.
PadRight(40, '.') +
                    doc.hitCount.ToString().PadLeft(10, '.'));
        }

        // print some results
        Console.WriteLine("\n\nRetrieving results 1..5");
        for(int i = 1; i <= 5 && i <= resp.hits; i++) {
            byte[] record = qs.retrieve(resp.resultSetId, i,
"UTF-8", true);
            string str = System.Text.Encoding.UTF8.GetString
(record);
            Console.WriteLine(str);
        }
    }
}
```

The client simply instantiates an object of class QueryService, which had been automatically created from the WSDL description. The XPath query is passed to method `query`, which returns an object of type `QueryResponse`. `QueryResponse` contains some summary information about the executed query. The most important field is the `result-set id`, which is used by the server to identify the generated result-set in subsequent calls. To actually get the query results, the `retrieve` method is called with the `result-set id`. The XML is returned as a byte array to avoid possible character-encoding conflicts with the SOAP transport layer.

3.6.3 Integration with Cocoon

The combination of eXist and Cocoon opens a wide range of opportunities, starting from simple Web-based query interfaces to—from a future perspective—a complete content management system. Cocoon provides a powerful application server environment for the development of XML-driven Web applications, including configurable transformation pipelines, XML server pages for dynamic content generation, and output to HTML, PDF, SVG (Scalable Vector Graphics), WAP (Wireless Access Protocol), and many other formats (for a complete description, see http://xml.apache.org/cocoon). Cocoon enables developers to create complex Web applications entirely based on XML and related technologies. Web site creators and developers are allowed to think in XML from A to Z.

Cocoon sites are configured in an XML file called `sitemap.xmap`. Most important, this file defines the processing pipelines Cocoon uses to process HTTP requests. Pipelines may be arbitrarily complex, using any mixture of static and dynamic resources. Basically every processing step in the pipeline is supposed to produce an SAX stream, which is consumed by the next step.

To use eXist, no changes to Cocoon itself are required. Beginning with version 2.0, Cocoon supports pseudo protocols, which allow the registration of handlers for special URLs via source factories. Current Cocoon distributions include a source factory to access XML:DB-enabled databases. Once the handler has been registered, it is possible to use any valid XML:DB URI wherever Cocoon expects a URL in its site configuration file.

As a practical example, suppose that you have written a small bibliography for an article. The bibliography has been coded in RDF (Resource Description Framework), using Dublin Core for common fields like title, creator, and so on. Additionally, you have written an XSLT style sheet to transform the data into HTML for display. The source file (xml_books.xml) as well as the XSLT stylesheet (bib2html.xsl) have been stored in eXist in a collection called "/db/bibliography".

You would like to get the file formatted in HTML if you access it in a browser. Adding the snippet shown in Listing 3.4 to the <map:pipelines> section of Cocoon's sitemap.xmap will do the job:

Listing 3.4 Additions to Cocoon's sitemap.xmap to Obtain HTML Output

```
<map:pipeline>
 <!" . . . more definitions here . . . ">
 <map:match pattern=/xmldb/db/bibliography/*.html">
```

```
        <map:generate src="xmldb:exist:///db/bibliography/{1}.xml"/>
        <map:transform src="xmldb:exist:///db/bibliography/
bib2html.xsl"/>
        <map:serialize type="html"/>
    </map:match>
    <!" . . . ">
</map:pipeline>
```

If you browse to any location matching the pattern "xmldb/db/bibliography/*.html" relative to Cocoon's root path (e.g., `http://localhost:8080/exist/xmldb/db/bibliography/xml_books.html`), you will get a properly formatted HTML display. Instead of loading the files from the file system, Cocoon will retrieve the XML source and the style sheet from eXist.

You may also like to add a little search interface to be able to find entries by author, title, or date. Cocoon offers XSP to write XML-based dynamic Web pages. Similar to JSP, XSP embeds Java code in XML pages. To better support the separation of content and programming logic, XSP also enables you to put reusable code into logic sheets, which correspond to tag libraries in JSP. A logic sheet should help limit to a minimum the amount of Java code used inside an XSP page.

eXist includes a logic sheet based on the XML:DB API, which defines tags for all important tasks. You could also write all the XML:DB-related code by hand, but using the predefined tags usually makes the XML file more readable and helps users without Java knowledge understand what's going on. To give the reader an idea of how the XSP code might look, Listing 3.5 shows a simple example.

Listing 3.5 Using the XML:DB XSP Logic Sheet

```
<xsp:page
      xmlns:xsp=http://apache.org/xsp
      xmlns:xmldb="http://exist-db.org/xmldb/1.0"
>
      <html>
         <body>
            <h1>Process query</h1>
               <xmldb:collection uri="xmldb:exist:///db/bibliography">
                  <xmldb:execute>
                     <xmldb:xpath>"document(*)//rdf:
Description[dc:title"
                     + "&amp;="" + request.getParameter("title") + ""]"
                     </xmldb:xpath>
                     <p>Found <xmldb:get-hit-count/> hits.</p>

                     <xmldb:results>
                        <pre>
```

```
                        <xmldb:get-xml as="string"/>
                    </pre>
                </xmldb:results>
            </xmldb:execute>
        </xmldb:collection>
    </body>
</html>
</xsp:page>
```

The Cocoon version included with eXist has been configured (in cocoon.xconf) to recognize the xmldb namespace and associate it with the XML:DB logic sheet. All you have to do is to include the correct namespace declaration in your page (xmlns:xmldb="http://exist-db.org/xmldb/1.0").

The page executes a query on the dc:title element using the HTTP request parameter "title" to get the keywords entered by the user. As required by the XML:DB API, any action has to be enclosed in an xmldb:collection element. The query is specified in the xmldb:xpath tag using a Java expression, which inserts the request parameter into an XPath query. The xmldb:results element will iterate through the generated result set, inserting each resource into the page by calling xmldb:get-xml.

Note that in this simple example, all resources are converted to string to display the results in a browser. If you wanted to post-process results—for example, by applying a style sheet to the generated output—you would use `<xmldb:get-xml as="xml"/>`.

To tell Cocoon how to process this page, you finally have to insert a new pattern into the sitemap, as shown in Listing 3.6.

Listing 3.6 Processing Pattern to Be Inserted into Cocoon Sitemap

```
<map:match pattern="bibquery.xsp">
  <map:generate type="serverpages" src="bibquery.xsp"/>
  <map:serialize type="html"/>
</map:match>
```

To see if the page works, you may now enter into your Web browser the URL http://localhost:8080/exist/bibquery.xsp?title=computer.

3.7 Technical Background

The following sections take a closer look at the design of eXist's indexing and storage architecture. We start with a brief discussion of conventional approaches to query execution and the problems they face when processing queries on large collections of XML documents. Second, we examine the numbering scheme used by eXist to identify nodes in index files. We then provide details on the concrete implementation of the storage and indexing components. Finally, we explain how the query engine uses the information collected in index files to process XPath expressions.

3.7.1 Approaches to Query Execution

XML query languages like XPath or XQuery use regular path expressions to navigate the logical structure of XML documents. Following a conventional approach, an XPath processor typically uses some kind of top-down or bottom-up tree traversal to evaluate regular path expressions. For example, the Open Source XPath engine Jaxen is based on a generalized tree-walking model, providing an abstraction for different APIs like DOM, DOM4J, or JDOM.

Despite the clean design supported by these tree-traversal based approaches, they become very inefficient for large document collections. For example, consider an XPath expression selecting all sections in a large collection of books whose title contains the string "XML":

```
/book//section[ contains(title, 'XML' )]
```

In a conventional top-down approach, the XPath processor has to follow every child path beginning at `book` to check for potential `section` descendants. This implies walking every element in the document tree below the document's root node `book`, because there is no way to determine the possible location of `section` descendants in advance.

While computing costs for traversing the document tree are acceptable as long as the document is completely contained in the machine's main memory, performance will suffer if the document's node tree has been stored in some persistent storage. A great number of nodes not being `section` elements have to be loaded just to test for their names and types. As a result, a lot of disk I/O is generated. Additionally, the whole procedure has to be repeated for every single document in the collection, which is unacceptable for very large collections.

Thus some kind of index structure is needed to efficiently process regular path expressions on large, unconstrained document collections. To speed up query execution, the query engine should be able to evaluate certain types of expressions just using the information provided in the index. Other types of expressions will still require a tree traversal, which is comparable to a full-table scan in a relational database system.

Consider a simple path expression like "//ACT/TITLE" to retrieve the titles for all acts in the play. To evaluate this expression, an indexing scheme should provide two major features: First, instead of traversing all elements in the document to find ACT elements, the query processor should be able to retrieve the location of all ACT and TITLE nodes in the document tree by a fast index lookup. This can be done, for example, by mapping element names to a list of references that point to the corresponding DOM nodes in the storage file.

However, knowing the position of potential ancestor and descendant nodes alone is not sufficient to determine the ancestor-descendant relationship between a pair of nodes. Thus, as a second requirement, the information contained in the index should support quick identification of relationships between nodes to resolve ancestor-descendant path steps.

3.7.2 Indexing Scheme

Several indexing schemes for XML documents have been proposed by recent research (Lee et al. 1996; Shin et al. 1998; Li and Moon 2001; Zhang et al. 2001). The approach taken by the eXist project has been inspired by these contributions. eXist's indexing system uses a numbering scheme to identify XML nodes and determine relationships between nodes in the document tree. A numbering scheme assigns numeric identifiers to each node in the document—for example, by traversing the document tree in level-order or pre-order. The generated identifiers are then used in indexes as references to the actual nodes. In eXist, all XML nodes are internally represented by a pair of document and node identifiers. Much of the query processing can be done by just using these two identifiers, which will be shown in the next section. Thus eXist will not load the actual DOM node unless it is really required to do so.

How does the numbering scheme work? For example, a numbering scheme might use the start and end position of a node in the document to identify nodes. Start and end positions might be defined by counting word numbers from the beginning of the document. A scheme based on this idea has been described in Zhang et al. (Zhang et al. 2001; see also Srivastava et al. 2002). According to this proposal, an element is identified by the 3-tuple (document ID, start position:end position, nesting level). Using these 3-tuples, ancestor-descendant relationships can be determined by the proposition: A node x with 3-tuple $(D_1, S_1{:}E_1, L_1)$ is a descendant of a node y with 3-tuple $(D_2, S_2{:}\ E_2, L_2)$ if and only if $D_1 = D_2$; $S_1 < S_2$ and $E_2 < E_1$. However, the 3-tuple identifiers generated by this numbering scheme consume a lot of space in the index.

eXist's indexing scheme has been inspired by another proposal, contributed by Lee et al. (Lee et al. 1996; see also Shin et al. 1998). It models the document tree as a complete k-ary tree, where k is equal to the maximum number of child nodes of an element in the tree structure. This implies that every nonleaf node in the tree is supposed to have exactly the same number of children. An identifier is assigned to each node by traversing the tree in level-order. For any node having less than k children, virtual child nodes are inserted to fill the gap. This means that some identifiers are wasted to balance the tree into a complete k-ary tree. Figure 3.2 shows the identifiers assigned to the nodes of a very simple XML document.

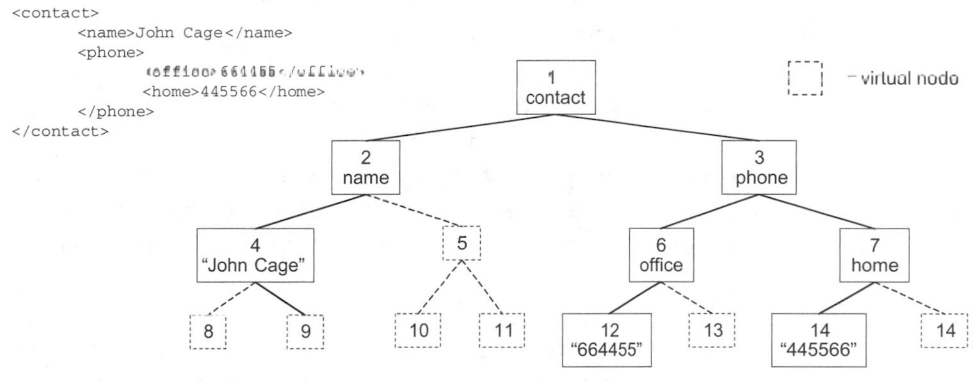

Figure 3.2 Level-Order Numbering Scheme

The generated identifier has a number of important properties: From a given identifier, we are always able to calculate the ID of its parent, sibling, and (possibly virtual) child nodes.

Implementing the corresponding W3C DOM methods for each node type is straightforward. For example, to get the parent of a given node, we simply calculate the parent identifier, which is then used to retrieve the actual parent node by an index lookup. All axes of navigation are supported as required by W3C DOM methods. This significantly reduces the storage size of a single node in the XML store: We don't need to store soft or hard links to parent, sibling, or child nodes with the DOM node object, because this information is implicitly contained in the generated identifier. Thus an element node will occupy between 4 and 8 bytes in eXist's XML node store—depending on the number of attributes.

Yet the completeness constraint imposes a major restriction on the maximum size of a document to be indexed. In practice, many documents contain more nodes in some distinct subtree of the document than in others. For example, a typical article will have a limited number of top-level elements like chapters and sections, while the majority of nodes consists of paragraphs and text nodes located below the top-level elements. In a worst case scenario, where a single node at some deeply structured level of the document node hierarchy has a maximum of child nodes, a large number of virtual nodes has to be inserted at all tree levels to satisfy the completeness constraint, so the assigned identifiers grow very fast even for small documents. For example, the identifiers generated by a complete 10-ary tree with height 10 will not fit into a 4-byte integer.

To overcome the limitations imposed by level-order numbering, we decided to partially drop the completeness constraint in favor of an alternating numbering scheme. The document is no longer viewed as a complete k-ary tree. Instead we recompute the number of children each node may have for every level of the tree and store this information in a simple array in the document object. Thus the completeness constraint is replaced by the following proposition:

```
For two nodes x and y of a tree, size(x) = size(y) if level(x) =
level(y), where size(n) is the number of children of a node n and
level(m) is the length of the path from the root node of the tree
to m.
```

In other words, two nodes will have the same number of (possibly virtual) children if they are located on the same level of the tree. This approach accounts for the fact that typical documents will have a larger number of nodes at some lower level of the document tree while there are fewer elements at the top level of the hierarchy. Changing k at a deeper level of the node tree—for example, by inserting a new node—has no effect on nodes at higher levels. The document size limit is raised considerably to enable indexing of much larger documents. Figure 3.3 shows the numeric identifiers generated by eXist for the document used in Figure 3.2.

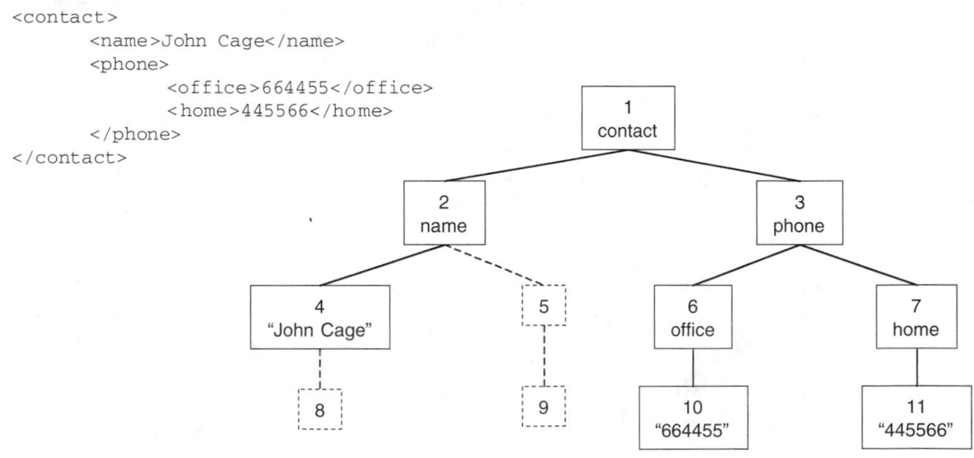

Figure 3.3 Alternating Level-Order Numbering Scheme

Using an alternating numbering scheme does not affect the general properties of identifiers as described previously: From a given identifier, we are still able to compute parent, sibling, or child node identifiers using the additional information on tree-level-arity stored in the document object.

To have enough spare IDs for worst case scenarios and later document updates, eXist uses 8-byte Java long integers for identifiers.

3.7.3 Index and Storage Implementation

Index organization might be compared to the traditional inverted index that represents a common data structure in many information retrieval systems. An inverted index is typically used to associate a word or phrase with the set of documents in which it has been found and the exact position where it occurred (Salton and McGill 1983).

Contrary to traditional information retrieval systems, an XML database needs to know the position and structure of nodes. Thus, instead of simply storing word positions, eXist uses the generated node identifiers to keep track of node occurrences. Additionally, to support the structured query facilities provided by XML query languages, different index structures are needed. Currently, eXist uses four index files at the core of the native XML storage backend:

1. dom.dbx collects DOM nodes in a paged file and associates node identifiers to the actual nodes.
2. collections.dbx manages the collection hierarchy.
3. elements.dbx indexes elements and attributes.
4. words.dbx keeps track of word occurrences and is used by the full-text search extensions.

Index implementation is quite straightforward. Basically, all indexes are based on B+-tree classes originally written by the former dbXML (now Xindice) project. To achieve better performance, many changes have been made to the original code—for example, to provide efficient page-buffering and locking mechanisms.

Node identifiers are mapped to the corresponding DOM nodes in the XML data store (dom.dbx). The XML data store represents the central component of eXist's native storage architecture. It consists of a single paged file in which all document nodes are stored according to the DOM. The data store is backed by a multiroot B+-tree in the same file to associate a node identifier to the node's storage address in the data section (see Figure 3.4). The storage address consists of the page number and the offset of the node inside the page. To save storage space, only top-level elements are added to the B+-tree. Other nodes are found by traversing the nearest available ancestor node.

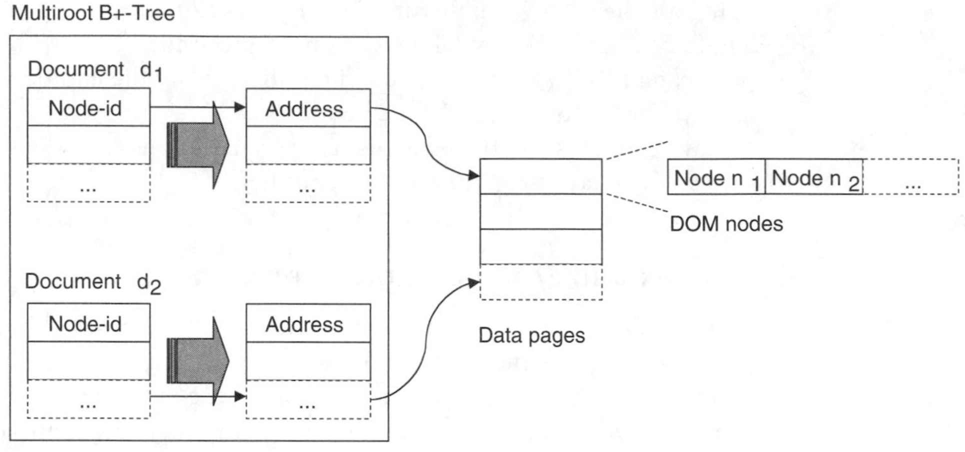

Figure 3.4 XML Data Store Organization

Ordered sequential access to the nodes in a document will speed up a number of tasks, such as serializing a document or fragment from the internal data model into its XML representation. Thus nodes are stored in document order. Additionally, the indexer tries to use subsequent physical data pages for all nodes belonging to the same document.

Only a single initial index lookup is required to serialize a document or document fragment. eXist's serializer will generate a stream of SAX events by sequentially walking nodes in document order, beginning at the fragment's root node. Thus any XML tool implementing SAX may be used to post-process the generated SAX stream—for example, to pretty-print the XML code or apply XSLT transformations on the server side.

The index file elements.dbx maps element and attribute names to node identifiers (see Figure 3.5). Each entry in the index consists of a key—being a pair of <collection id, name id>—and an array value containing an ordered list of document IDs and node IDs, which correspond to elements and attributes matching the qualified name in the key. To find, for example, all chapters in a collection of books, the query engine will need a single index lookup to retrieve the complete set of node IDs pointing to chapter elements.

Organizing index entries by entire collections might seem inefficient at first sight. However, we have learned from earlier versions of eXist that using <document id, name id> pairs for keys leads to decreasing performance for collections containing a larger number (>5,000) of rather small (<50KB) documents. Filtering out those nodes that do not match the input document set for a query yields a much

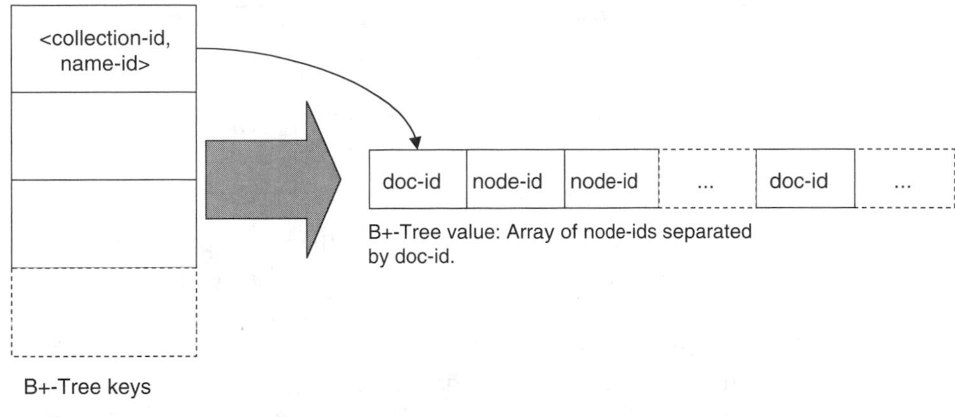

Figure 3.5 Index Organization for Elements and Attributes

better overall performance. As a result, splitting large collections containing more than a few thousand documents into smaller subcollections is recommended.

Finally, the file words.dbx corresponds to a traditional inverted index as found in many IR (Information Retrieval) systems. By default, it indexes all text nodes and attribute values by tokenizing text into keywords. In words.dbx, the extracted keywords are mapped to an ordered list of document and node IDs. The file follows the same structure as elements.dbx, using <collection id, keyword> pairs for keys. Each entry in the ordered list points to the text or attribute node where the keyword occurred.

It is possible to exclude distinct parts of a given document type from full-text indexing or switch it off completely.

3.7.4 Query Language Processing

Given the index structures presented previously, we are able to access distinct nodes by their node IDs and retrieve a list of node identifiers for a given qualified node name or the set of text or attribute nodes containing a specified keyword. The DBBroker interface has method definitions for each of these tasks.

However, we have not yet explained how the query engine could use the provided methods to efficiently evaluate path expressions. eXist's query processor will first decompose a given regular path expression into a chain of basic steps. For example, the XPath expression `/PLAY//SPEECH[ SPEAKER=' HAMLET' ]` is logically split into subexpressions as shown in Figure 3.6.

Figure 3.6 Decomposition of Path Expression

To process the first subexpression, the query processor will load the root elements (PLAY) for all documents in the input document set. Second, the set of SPEECH elements is retrieved for the input documents via an index lookup from file elements.dbx. Now we have two node sets containing potential ancestors and descendants for each of the documents in question.

To find all nodes from the SPEECH node set being descendants of nodes in the PLAY node set, an ancestor-descendant path join algorithm is applied to the two sets. Several path join algorithms have been proposed by recent research (Li and Moon 2001; Srivastava et al. 2002; Zhang et al. 2001). eXist's algorithm differs from the proposed algorithms due to differences in the numbering schemes.

We will not discuss the algorithm in depth here. Basically, a node set in eXist is a list of <document id, node id> pairs, ordered by document ID and node ID. The algorithm takes the set of potential ancestor nodes and the set of descendant nodes as input. It recursively replaces all node identifiers in the descendant set with their parent's node ID and loops through the two sets to find equal pairs of nodes. If a matching pair is found, it is added to the resulting node set.

The result returned by the algorithm will become the context node set for the next subexpression in the chain. So the resulting node set for the expression PLAY//SPEECH becomes the ancestor node set for the expression SPEECH[SPEAKER], while the results generated by evaluating the predicate expression SPEAKER="HAMLET" represent the descendant node set.

To evaluate the subexpressions PLAY//SPEECH and SPEECH[SPEAKER], eXist does not need access to the actual DOM nodes in the XML store. Both expressions are entirely processed on the basis of the numeric identifiers provided in the index file. The path join algorithm determines ancestor-descendant relationships for all candidate nodes in all documents in one single step. Since node sets are implemented using simple Java arrays, execution times for the path join algorithm are very short. More than 90 percent of the overall query execution time is spent for index lookups.

Yet to process the equality operator in the predicate subexpression SPEAKER="HAMLET", the query engine will have to load the real DOM nodes from storage to determine their value and compare it to the literal string argument. Since a node's value may be distributed over many descendant nodes, the engine has to do a conventional tree traversal, beginning at the subexpression's context node (SPEAKER).

If we replace the equality operator with one of eXist's full-text operators or functions, the preceding query will perform a magnitude faster. For example, we may reformulate the query as follows:

```
/PLAY//SPEECH[ SPEAKER |= ' hamlet ghost' ]
```

Since the exact match query expression has been replaced by an expression based on keywords, the query engine is now able to use the inverted index to look up the keywords "hamlet" and "ghost" and obtains node identifiers for all text nodes containing the search term. Second, if there are multiple search terms, the retrieved node sets are merged by generating the union (for the &= operator and near function) or intersection set (for the |= operator). Finally, the resulting set of text nodes is joined with the context node set (SPEAKER) by applying an ancestor-descendant path join as explained previously. While the equality operator, as well as standard XPath functions like contains, requires eXist to perform a complete scan over the contents of every node in the context node set, the full-text search extensions rely entirely on information stored in the index.

Replacing exact match query expressions by equivalent expressions using full-text operators and functions will be easily possible for many queries addressing human users. For example, to find all items in a bibliographic database written by a certain author, we would typically use an XPath query like

```
//rdf:Description[ dc:creator="Heidegger, Martin"]
```

Query execution time will be relatively slow. However, it is very likely that a keyword-based query would find the same or even more true matches while being much faster. For the preceding query, we could replace the equality comparison by a call to the near function:

```
//rdf:Description[ near(dc:creator, "heidegger martin")]
```

3.7.5 Query Performance

Table 3.1 shows experimental results for a data set containing movie reviews. We compared overall query execution times for a query set using standard XPath expressions with corresponding queries using eXist's full-text query extensions. Both sets of queries were equivalent in that they will generate the same number of hits. Table 3.1 shows the standard XPath queries.

Additionally, we compared these results with those of another Open Source query engine (Jaxen, see http://www.jaxen.org), which is based on conventional tree traversals. For this experiment, Jaxen has been running on top of eXist's persistent DOM, using standard DOM methods for traversing the document tree.

Table 3.1 Average Query Execution Times (in secs.) for eXist and External XPath Engine

XPath Query	Exist	eXist + Extensions	Jaxen
`/movie[ .//genre='Drama']//credit[ @role='directors']`	3.44	1.14	21.86
`/movie[ genres/genre='Western']/title`	0.79	0.23	7.58
`/movie[ languages/language='English']/title`	1.45	0.97	8.50
`/movie[ .//credit/@charactername='Receptionist']`	3.12	0.21	51.48
`/movie[ contains(.//comment, 'predictable')]`	2.79	0.20	31.49
`/movie[ .//credit='Gable, Clark']`	4.47	0.35	33.72
`/movie[ .//languages/language='English']/title[starts-with(.,'42nd Street')]`	1.63	0.32	32.64
`/movie[ languages/language='English' and credits/credit='Sinatra, Frank']`	5.16	0.58	13.26

The data set contained 39.15MB of raw XML data, distributed over 5,000 documents taken from a movie database. Document size varied from 500 bytes to 50KB. We formulated queries for randomly selected documents that might typically be of interest to potential users. The experiment was conducted on a PC with an AMD Athlon 4 processor with 1,400MHz and 256MB memory. Execution times for retrieving the actual results have not been included. They merely depend on the performance of eXist's serializer and are approximately the same for all tested approaches.

The results show that eXist's query engine outperforms the tree-traversal based approach by an order of magnitude. As expected, search expressions using the full-text index perform much better than corresponding queries based on standard XPath.

In a second experiment, the complete set of 5,000 documents was split into 10 subcollections, each containing 500 documents. To test the scalability of eXist, we added one more subcollection to the database for each test sequence and computed performance metrics for both sets of queries. Figure 3.7 shows average query execution times for eXist.

We observe that query execution times increase linearly with increasing source data size. This indicates the linear scalability of eXist's indexing, storage, and querying architecture.

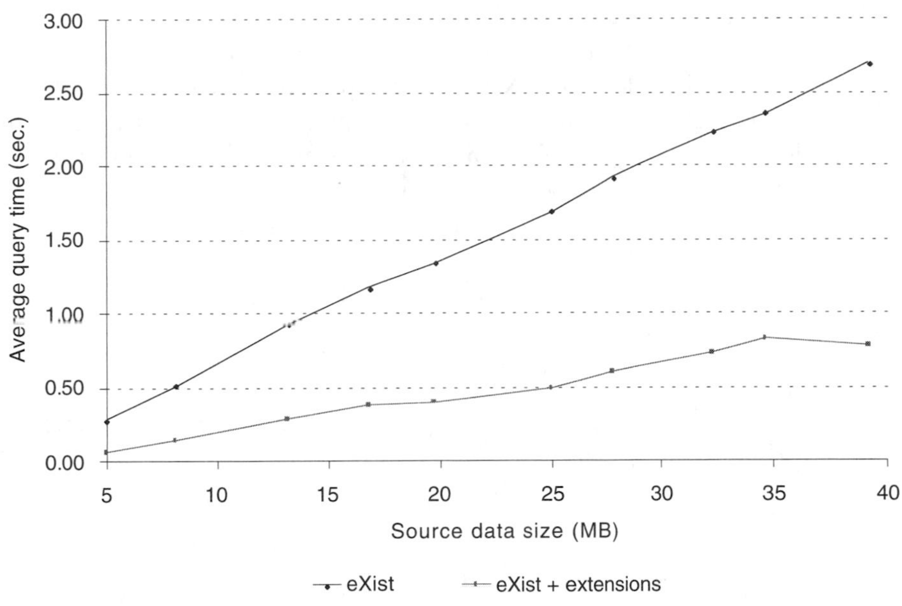

Figure 3.7 Average Query Execution Times by Source Data Size

3.8 Conclusion

eXist's user community has been continuously growing since eXist was released to the public. Applications prove that eXist may be effectively used to implement XML-based services in a wide range of scenarios, dealing with different types of XML documents and data volumes.

Yet much work remains to be done to implement outstanding features. Being an Open Source project, eXist strongly depends on user feedback and participation. Interested developers are encouraged to join the mailing list and share their views and suggestions.

Some of eXist's weak points, namely indexing speed and storage requirements, have already been subject to a considerable redesign. The project is currently concentrating on complete XPath support, possibly using existing implementations developed in other projects. However, XPath has some restrictions. For example, in the current eXist implementation, complex queries involving multiple source documents have to be split manually into several XPath expressions. Additionally, for some types of applications, a more sophisticated transformation of query results is required. XQuery may provide a good alternative to overcome these limitations. It would be worthwhile to invest some work into implementing XQuery for eXist.

Another issue is XUpdate—a standard proposed by the XML:DB initiative for updates of distinct parts of a document. XUpdate is defined as a service in the XML:DB API. However, eXist currently does not implement updates off single nodes in the DOM tree, which is clearly a major restriction for applications using large documents. It is possible to implement the missing functions by extending the basic indexing concepts described earlier.

At the time of writing, we have already started to simplify the created index structures, making them easier to maintain on node insertions or removals. However, some work remains to be done on these issues.

Chapter 4

Embedded XML Databases

John Merrells and Michael Olson

4.1 Introduction

Much discussion of database systems concentrates on the services that such systems provide. For example, most database systems support transactions and multiple concurrent users. All database systems have some mechanism for storing and retrieving data. All database systems have an underlying data model, which defines the data types that they can store and the operations that are supported on those types. Examples include relational databases, object-oriented databases, and XML databases. All of these details are important, of course. You must understand the services your database provides if you are to choose the right one.

The huge success of relational database systems like Oracle and IBM's DB2 has created a general perception that a database system is a heavyweight, standalone engine with complicated user interface tools of its own. These database systems are installed and maintained by professional database administrators. Programmers and end users interact with them by typing SQL queries.

In fact, there is a fast-growing market for embedded database engines that are different from the relational products that dominate public perception. Embedded databases are intended for use by professional software developers, rather than by end users or database administrators. They provide the same data management services, including transactions, recovery, and concurrency, but in a very different package. Embedded databases have carved out a comfortable niche among certain users, and their success in managing general-purpose data suggests that they will also be important in the XML database market. For example, content management systems, reliable message queues, Web services registries, and user preference and authentication repositories are all services that should naturally be delivered using XML, and that need to store and maintain XML data internally. No direct end-user access to the backing store is required. An embedded XML database is a natural way to store the XML data for systems like these.

4.2 A Primer on Embedded Databases

Embedded databases run directly in the application or system that uses them. They do not require a separate database server, since all the data management logic is linked into the application's address space. They generally offer a carefully tuned function call or class method API that developers can use to store, fetch, and update records. Embedded databases do not, as a rule, include end-user query tools.

Fundamentally, an embedded database system is intended for use by a software developer building an application or server that needs fast, reliable data management. The only way to store and fetch records in an embedded database is to write code that calls the database APIs. Unlike client/server database systems, most embedded databases include no end-user query tools, graphical user interfaces, or report generators. The programmer must design and build into the application any query interfaces that the end user needs. In fact, most end users who run those applications have no idea that they are using a database at all. The end user focuses on the task at hand—sending e-mail, looking up information in a directory, or shopping on an e-commerce site—and the programmer decides what to store and how to find it again later.

The most significant advantage that an embedded database has over a client/server system is speed. Because all database operations happen inside the application process, an embedded database incurs none of the overhead that inter-process communication imposes. Since most computers can do many thousands of local function calls in the time that it takes to do a network operation, embedded databases exhibit far less latency. In addition, because no extra copying of the data occurs when it moves from one address space to another, throughput is much higher.

Also, because there is no separate server, embedded databases are typically easier for end users to install and administer. Embedded database systems require the programmer who develops the application to handle administrative tasks like backup and failure recovery, so the end user can ignore them, or can at least use tools and interfaces that are consistent with the application to handle them. Because no separate server process is required at runtime, there are fewer moving parts, reducing the likelihood of runtime problems because some component has failed separately from the others.

Of course, there are trade-offs. Embedded database systems are not generally suitable for applications that have to support *ad hoc* queries by end users. Embedded databases require developers to write more code, on average, than client/server databases. And embedded databases require developers to consider carefully, when they design their applications, the kind of data they need to manage and how they will store it and search for it. Embedded databases, as a rule, are harder for developers to use than client/server databases, but easier for end users. Since there are many more end users than developers in the world, favoring the end user makes sense.

Developers need not make trade-offs regarding scalability, reliability, or performance when they choose an embedded database. The techniques for handling large amounts of data and many concurrent users, for surviving system failures without losing data, and for providing fast data access work just as well in embedded products as they do in standalone database engines. Of course, the individual product offered by any particular vendor will behave differently, but scalability, reliability, and performance are features of a particular implementation and do not depend on where the actual machine code executes.

There are many applications in which embedded databases have been more successful than client/server relational databases over the past several years. Many of the services that underlie the Internet, including e-mail, naming and directory services, Web search, and shopping cart applications, need fast, reliable data storage but cannot afford the overhead of an SQL query to a remote database server for every operation. Those applications use embedded database systems for speed and reliability. Increasingly, devices like network routers and gateways, storage systems, and entertainment systems including personal video recorders and set-top boxes need to store and manage critical data, and rely on embedded database systems. At the low end, devices like cell phones and PDAs often need data storage and synchronization in a small-footprint package and take advantage of embedded database systems for that.

4.3 Embedded XML Databases

Whether a database is embedded or client/server is an architectural matter. The query language that it supports, and the data types that it can store, are features of a particular database system. Embedded databases can specialize in storing XML data in the same way that client/server databases do.

In fact, there are reasons to prefer an embedded database system for many XML applications.

The early success of XML has been in connecting legacy applications to one another over the Web. In these cases, a software developer generally needed to write code to import and export data, to convert native-format data in the application to

XML format for transmission over the network, and to do the corresponding conversion to native format at the other end. XML provides the common language that enables interoperability between heterogeneous systems.

Services are required within the network and at the edges of the network to facilitate this interoperability. The applications that map legacy data formats to XML, and the servers that transmit it reliably and securely over the network, need database services. Translations of XML documents to a relational or object form can be mitigated by using an XML database, and the cost of interaction with a client/server database can be avoided by using an embedded XML database.

Since the developer is writing new code, and since there is no need for direct access to the XML repository by end users, it makes sense to embed the XML database directly in the application. This simplifies installation and management of the new software, and improves performance.

Even though the main job of the data import and export services is to transform data, developers may also want to store the XML data in its native format. This can be important in applications like financial services or accounting software, where the exact format of a trade order, an invoice, or a purchase order must be preserved. Such systems often need to provide nonrepudiation services, so that a trading partner cannot later claim that he never issued a particular request. Storing the request in the exact format in which it arrived, along with any authenticating information, can prevent fraud.

Converting documents from a legacy format to XML can be very expensive, owing either to the volume of data to be converted or to the cost of fetching it from the legacy system. Because of this, the data conversion software may want to cache the XML version of the data for later reuse. An embedded XML database maintains the cache locally to the process that does the conversion, which dramatically speeds up cache fetches.

XML databases, whether client/server or embedded, offer several advantages over relational or object-oriented systems. These advantages include the ability to operate on XML data natively, a closer match between the application's data model and the database engine, and the optional enforcement of XML schema. An embedded XML database offers several advantages over a client/server product, including improved performance, ease of administration by end users, an installation and management regimen that matches the application's, greater reliability due to fewer components in the deployed system, and a smaller footprint than standalone systems.

As XML becomes a more important piece of the computing infrastructure, new applications that operate on XML data natively will appear. This fact has created enormous interest among database vendors in adding native support for XML to their products. Many XML applications will need the performance and ease of deployment and administration that embedded databases provide.

4.4 Building Applications for Embedded XML Databases

An embedded XML database is a library that links directly into the address space of the application that uses it. This has significant implications for the design of both the embedded database and the application.

Because an embedded XML database needs to run inside the application, the database code itself cannot make many assumptions about how the application operates or what platform-specific services the application uses. What threading model should the database use? In practice, it must be able to use whatever threading model the application designer has selected. Similarly, the embedded database system must give the application developer control over resource consumption, whether concurrent access to the data is supported (and, if so, what degree of concurrency is required), and so on.

The good news for application developers is that the embedded database system leaves so many policy decisions in the developer's hands. This means that an embedded database system can support small, single-user applications efficiently, or can handle thousands of concurrent users on a large multiprocessor box with huge amounts of memory and disk.

The bad news, of course, is that the developer has so many policy decisions to make. Building an application with an embedded XML database forces the developer to think not just about the data that the application will manage, but also about how the database code will operate inside the application.

The rest of this chapter covers some of the issues that arise in the design and implementation of applications using embedded XML databases. The examples refer to the interfaces provided by Berkeley DB XML, an Open Source-embedded XML database available from Sleepycat Software (http://www.sleepycat.com).

4.4.1 Overview of Berkeley DB XML

Berkeley DB XML is an embedded XML database. It is built on top of Berkeley DB, the general-purpose embedded database engine. The Berkeley DB XML product stores XML documents, indexes them, and provides an XPath query interface. XML documents are organized into containers, which may share a common schema or may be schema-less. Each container is configured by the client application with an indexing strategy. Listing 4.1 shows an example of using a container.

Listing 4.1 Opening and Using a Berkeley DB XML Container

```
#include "dbxml/DbXml.hpp"

using namespace DbXml;
```

```
int main()
{
  try
  {
     XmlContainer container (0, "test")
     container.open(0,DB_CREATE);
     XmlDocument document;
     string content(
     "<book><title>The Cement Garden</title></book>");
     document.setContent(content);
     u_int32_t id= container.putDocument(0, document);
     document = container.getDocument(0,id);
     string s(document.getContentAsString());
     cout << id << " = " << s << "\n";
     container.close();
  }
  catch(XmlException &e)
  {
     cerr << e.what() << "\n";
  }
}
```

Physically, a Berkeley DB XML container consists of several Berkeley DB tables, including a table that stores configuration information for the container, a data dictionary for the container schema, a table to store the XML document text, and tables for each index that the programmer creates. Berkeley DB XML stores statistical information about each index. This information allows the XPath query optimizer to choose an access path that minimizes the cost of executing queries at runtime.

The underlying Berkeley DB library, which handles low-level storage and transaction and recovery services, is written in C. The XML parser, XPath query processor, and other code specific to Berkeley DB XML is written in C++ and makes calls to the Berkeley DB library. Berkeley DB XML includes Java language bindings.

The rest of this chapter discusses the issues that confront programmers when they design and implement applications that use an embedded XML database. The text includes examples based on Berkeley DB XML to illustrate key points.

4.4.2 Configuration

Embedded XML databases must leave important policy decisions in the hands of the developer building the final application. Examples include:

- Memory available to the embedded database system for managing its cache of recently used documents, information on locking, and other shared state
- Whether the application requires transaction and recovery services
- The degree of concurrency that the application requires
- Whether the application will use multiple concurrent processes for different users, multiple threads inside a single process, or some combination of the two

Embedded databases generally provide sensible default settings for all of these policy decisions but permit the programmer to override any of them as the application requires.

Berkeley DB XML uses an abstraction called an environment (see Listing 4.2) to manage the shared state of a set of document collections. Generally, calling methods on the environment or on a particular container change any configuration setting. Many of the settings cannot be changed after the initial configuration step by the application. For example, the size of the shared memory region is fixed once the environment is opened. As a result, most applications create the environment, change any of the default configuration parameters as required by the application, and then open it and begin normal processing.

Listing 4.2 Using a Berkeley DB XML Container within an Environment

```
DbEnv environment(0);
// Configure the environment here.
environment.open(0, DB_CREATE | DB_INIT_MPOOL, 0);
XmlContainer container(&environment, "test");
container.open(0, DB_CREATE);
// Use the container here.
container.close();
environment.close(0);
```

4.4.3 Indexing and Index Types

Any document collection in a Berkeley DB XML container can be indexed in several different ways. When a container is created, the programmer must consider the common queries that are likely to be evaluated over the container. The common queries will run faster if the container is indexed so that the attributes or elements used in the search can be looked up efficiently. Indexes are kept up to date automatically when new documents are added to the container, and the XPath query processor uses these indexes to search collections expeditiously.

It is not enough merely to decide what the most common attributes or elements for searches will be. XPath permits a variety of queries over a container, and different index types support different queries efficiently.

Indexing and optimizing queries are important topics not just in embedded XML databases, but also in client/server systems. However, the configurability of embedded systems often requires the programmer to make explicit decisions about indexing. Fundamentally, creating an index trades off query time against disk space, since the index entries must be stored, and against update speed, since every index must be updated when a new or changed record is written to the database.

Berkeley DB XML indexing strategies are best illustrated by example. Consider the XML document in Listing 4.3:

Listing 4.3 XML Document

```
<book bookID="books/mit/AbelsonS85">
<author>Abelson, H</author>
<title>Structure and Interpretation of Computer Programs</title>
<isbn>0-262-51036-7</isbn>
</book>
```

Depicted as a graph, the document consists of a series of nodes (book, bookID, author, title, ISBN), edges that connect the nodes (book.bookID, book.author, book.title, book.ISBN), and values (1234, Abelson, H, Structure and Interpretation of Computer Programs, 0-262-51036-7). This document is illustrated in Figure 4.1.

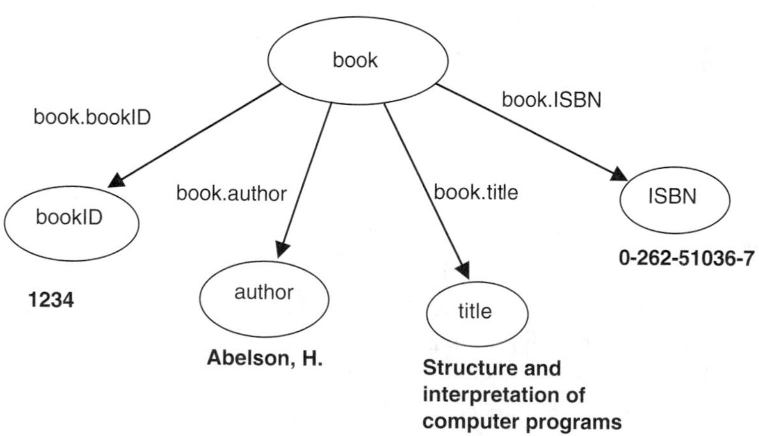

Figure 4.1 Graphical Version of an XML Document

Many indexing strategies could be used to index this XML document. When creating a container, the application developer must specify the indexes that are to be maintained for that container. Each index specification is represented by a string. For example, the index "node-element-equality-string" specifies an index of elements with string values. The index specification string consists of four components: path type, node type, key type, and syntax type. There are multiple possible values for each of these types, offering a total of 16 possible combinations.

- **Path type:** Either *node* or *edge*. Using the book example, an index with path type of *node* would contain five entries, one for each node in the graph (book, bookID, author, title, ISBN). An index with path type of *edge* would have four entries, one for each edge in the graph (book.bookID, book.author, book.title, and book.ISBN).
- **Node type:** Specifies which document nodes should be included in the index. Supported node types are *element* and *attribute*. In the book example, an index with node type *element* would have four entries (for book, author, ISBN, and title). An index with node type *attribute* would have a single entry, for the `bookID` node, as it is the only attribute in the original XML document.
- **Key type:** Determines the kind of index key that is created. The legal values are *equality*, *presence*, and *substring*. An index of key type *equality* will provide fast searches for specific nodes that match a given value. An index of key type *substring* enables fast substring searches. An index of key type *presence* will quickly find any node that matches the search key.
- **Syntax type:** Dictates how a value will be interpreted for comparison. The choices are *string*, *number*, and *none*. String and number are interpreted as you would expect. None means that the index is for presence only.

The code example in Listing 4.4 demonstrates the creation of a container with the declaration of an index for the nodes named `title` of type `node-element-equality-string`. In other words, all document element nodes named `title` will have an index key created for them containing the value of the node as a string.

Listing 4.4 Creating an Index on a Collection in Berkeley DB XML

```
XmlContainer container(0, "test");
container.open(0, DB_CREATE);
container.declareIndex(0, "", "title",
"node-element-equality-string");
container.close();
```

4.4.4 XPath Query Processing

Berkeley DB XML uses XPath for queries. Query processing consists of four steps:

1. The XPath parser translates the text query into an internal representation.
2. The query plan generator creates an initial query plan.
3. The query optimizer considers various execution strategies and chooses one likely to minimize the execution cost.
4. The query execution engine runs the optimized plan against a document container and delivers results to the application. The results may be computed eagerly or lazily.

The efficiency of the query evaluation is dependent upon the class of query and the suitability of the indexes configured for the collection. Each indexing strategy is suitable for a different class of XPath query.

Presence Keys

An index of type *node-element-presence-none* has keys that record the presence of an element type within a document. They are suitable for path navigation expressions such as */book/author/name/first* as the index will find all documents that contain the element types that appear in the path. They are also suitable for expressions containing element type value predicates such as */book[author='john']* as the index will find all documents that have elements of type *book* and *author*.

An index of type *node-attribute-presence-none* has keys that record the presence of an attribute name within a document. They are suitable for expressions that include path navigation expressions to attributes such as */book/@bookID* as the index will find all documents that contain bookID attributes. They are also suitable for expressions that include attribute value predicates such as */book[@bookID='a1b2c3']* for the same reason.

Equality Keys

An index of type *node-element-equality-string* has keys that record the value of an element type. They are suitable for expressions that include element type value predicates such as */book[author='john']* as the index will find all documents that have elements of type *author* with the value *john*. An equality index is always more specific than a presence index, so query processing favors an equality lookup over a presence lookup.

An index of type *node-attribute-equality-string* has keys that record the value of an attribute. They are suitable for expressions that include attribute value predicates such as */book[@bookID='a1b2c3']* as the index will find all documents that have *bookID* attributes with the value *a1b2c3*. An equality index is always more specific than a presence index, so query processing favors an equality lookup over a presence lookup.

An index with key type *equality* and syntax type *number* has equality keys that are compared numerically, rather than lexically. The numeric syntax is provided to support queries such as */book[(year=>1980 and year<1990) or year=2000]* or */book[@bookID>1000]*.

The query processor also makes use of equality indexes for satisfying queries that use the XPath function *starts-with*. For example, */book[starts-with(title, 'Structure')*.

Substring Keys

An index with key type *substring*—for example, *node-element-substring-string*—has keys that support substring queries. In XPath, substring searches are expressed using the XPath function *contains*—for example, */book[contains (title,'Computer')]*. The XML indexer creates one key for every three-character substring of the node value. So, for example, the node value "abcde" creates the keys *{abc, bcd, cde}*.

Edge Keys

An index of type *edge-element-presence-none* is a more specific form of the *node-element-presence-none* index and is suitable for expressions containing long path navigations. If an XML document is viewed as a graph, with the elements being nodes, then the index keys are formed from the edges between the nodes. For example, the contrived XML fragment *<a><b><c>d</c></b></a>* has element nodes *{a,b,c}* and edges *{a-b,b-c}*. A query with an expression such as */book/author/name* can be efficiently satisfied with lookups into the index for the edges *{book-author,author-name}*. An edge index is always more specific than a node index, so query processing favors an edge lookup over a node lookup.

The other indexes of node type *edge* are also supported. Each works in the same way as its *node* counterpart. For example, indexing the above XML fragment with *edge-element-equality-string* would give one key, *b.c=d*.

Listing 4.5 shows an example query.

Listing 4.5 Running a Query against a Berkeley DB XML Collection

```
XmlContainer container(0, "test");
container.open(0, DB_CREATE);
XmlDocument document;
```

```
string content("<book><title>The Rachel Papers</title></book>");
document.setContent(content);
container.putDocument(0, document);
XmlResults results(container.queryWithXPath(0, "/book"));
XmlValue value;
for(results.next(0, value);
     !value.isNull();
     results.next(0, value))
{
   XmlDocument document(value.asDocument(0));
   cout << document.getID() << " = " << value.asString(0) << "\n";
}
container.close();
```

4.4.5 Programming for Transactions

Most databases support transactions. An embedded database allows the programmer to determine where the transaction boundaries appear in an application. The developer can choose to make a group of related changes in a single transaction, so that all of them succeed or they are all rolled back together. This affects the way that developers write embedded XML database applications, as the next few sections will describe.

Choosing where to begin and end a transaction requires the developer to think about the application and the work that it is doing. Generally, a single transaction should include a set of related changes to the database. In the case of an XML database, two different containers may include documents that refer to one another, and the programmer may want to ensure that neither container is ever changed without a corresponding change to the other. If the two changes are made in a single transaction, then the database will always be consistent. Listing 4.6 shows an example transaction.

Listing 4.6 Transactional Updates in Berkeley DB XML

```
int main()
{
  try
  {
    DbEnv environment(0);
    environment.open(0, DB_CREATE | DB_INIT_LOCK | DB_INIT_LOG |
              DB_INIT_MPOOL | DB_INIT_TXN, 0);
```

```
    XmlContainer container1(&environment, "test1");
    XmlContainer container2(&environment, "test2");
    container1.open(0, DB_CREATE | DB_AUTO_COMMIT);
    container2.open(0, DB_CREATE | DB_AUTO_COMMIT);
    DbTxn *txr;
    environment.txn_begin(0, &txn, 0);
    try
    {
     XmlDocument document;
     string content("<book><title>Fever Pitch</title></book>");
     document.setContent(content);
     container1.putDocument(txn, document);
     container2.putDocument(txn, document);
     txn->commit(0);
    }
    catch(XmlException &e)
    {
     txn->abort();
     cerr << e.what() << "\n";
    }
    container1.close();
    container2.close();
    environment.close(0);
  }
  catch(XmlException &e)
  {
    cerr << e.what() << "\n";
  }
}
```

4.4.6 Two-Phase Locking and Deadlocks

Most database systems support transactions using two low-level services, called *two-phase locking* and *write-ahead logging*. The locking service guarantees that concurrent transactions cannot interfere with one another, since each locks the values that it touches for the duration of the transaction. The logging service lets transactions commit or roll back, by keeping track of changes that must be backed out if the transaction fails.

Locking guarantees that transactions cannot modify the same XML documents at the same time. To enforce the locking protocol, a database system makes one of the transactions wait to acquire a lock until the transaction that holds the lock has run to completion. If the two transactions want to update the same documents at the same time, they may deadlock against one another. A deadlock can arise, for example, when two transactions are waiting for one another to complete. This is shown in Figure 4.2.

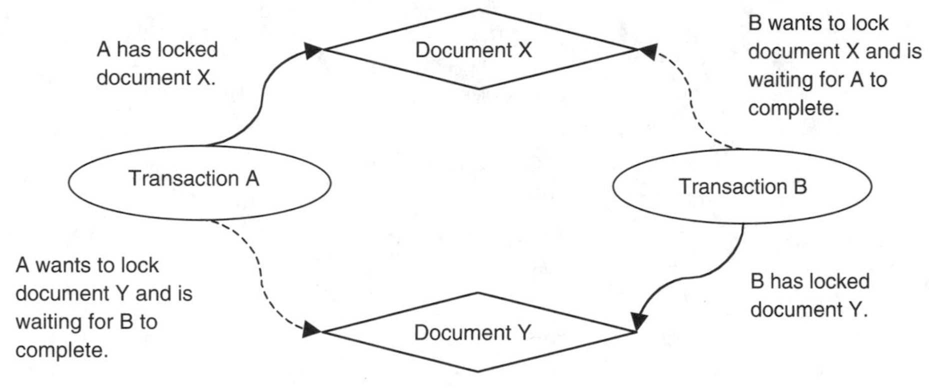

Figure 4.2 Deadlock

In Figure 4.2, the database system must terminate either transaction A or transaction B and roll back all its changes. The remaining transaction can then proceed to completion.

A client/server database can do this on behalf of the application. An embedded database requires the programmer to watch for deadlock errors and to roll back a transaction in the case of a deadlock (see Listing 4.7).

Fortunately, the code to identify and deal with deadlocks in an embedded XML database application is straightforward. Inside a transaction, any database operation may result in a deadlock. The embedded database can report the situation to the application, which must then abort the deadlocked transaction.

Listing 4.7 Deadlock Detection and Rollback

```
int main()
{
   try
   {
```

```
        DbEnv environment(0);
        environment.set_lk_detect(DB_LOCK_DEFAULT)
        environment.open(0, DB_CREATE | DB_INIT_LOCK | DB_INIT_LOG |
                DB_INIT_MPOOL | DB_INIT_TXN, 0);
        XmlContainer container1(&environment, "test1");
        XmlContainer container2(&environment, "test2");
        container1.open(0, DB_CREATE | DB_AUTO_COMMIT);
        container2.open(0, DB_CREATE | DB_AUTO_COMMIT);
        bool retry = true;
        while(retry)
        {
         DbTxn *txn;
         environment.txn_begin(0, &txn, 0);
         try
         {
          XmlDocument document;
          string content("<book><title>Fight Club</title> </book>");
          document.setContent(XmlDocument::XML,
                              content, strlen(content));
          container1.putDocument(txn, document);
          container2.putDocument(txn, document);
          txn->commit(0);
          retry = false;
         }
         catch(DbDeadlockException &e)
         {
          txn->abort();
          retry = true;
         }
        }
        container1.close();
        container2.close();
        environment.close(0);
       }
       catch(XmlException &e)
       {
       cerr << e.what() << "\n";
      }
    }
```

Rolling back a deadlocked transaction is easy to do programmatically. The embedded database system uses the log to undo all the changes that the transaction made and then releases all its locks. This can be a very expensive operation for two reasons, however. First, if the number of changes is high, then the work to undo all of them can be substantial. Second, all the work that the transaction did before it rolled back was done for a reason. It is likely that the end user will want that work to be retried. Rolling back a transaction usually means that the same sequence of updates needs to happen again in a new transaction, duplicating the work that failed in the first case.

It is much better to design database applications, including embedded XML database applications, to minimize or eliminate deadlocks. One way to do that is to keep transactions short. If a transaction touches only one or two items, it is less likely to encounter a conflict with another transaction. Another technique is to always touch items in the same order in all transactions. In Figure 4.2, the problem is that B locked Y before locking X, and A locked X before locking Y. If both transactions locked the documents in the same order, then one would still have to wait on the other, but there would be no deadlock, and no work would have to be rolled back and redone.

4.4.7 Reducing Contention

Contention can lead to deadlocks in database applications, but it can also cause more general performance problems. Embedded XML databases in particular must offer the programmer ways to measure and reduce contention. Since the database code executes using the threading model and degree of concurrency that the programmer selects, an embedded XML database's performance is much more profoundly affected by application design choices than a client/server system is.

Contention can arise from multiple transactions that need to operate on the same data at the same time. The locking subsystem will permit multiple transactions to read the same XML document in a container, but if any of them wants to modify the document, that transaction must have exclusive access to the document. As a result, it is important to lay out data in the database, and to consider query patterns, to minimize the number of concurrent transactions that want write access to the same document.

Another common source of contention is for the disk arm, in moving documents between memory and disk. Most XML database systems, whether client/server or embedded, maintain an in-memory cache of recently used documents. If that cache is smaller than the working set of the application, then the I/O subsystem will be forced to fetch documents from disk frequently. Under a heavy update load, contention is worse, since removing a document from the cache may first require writing the changed version back to stable storage before reusing the space it occupied for a new document. Thus, what might have been a single read operation turns into a write, followed by a read. Cache sizing is important in database applications generally, but because an embedded XML database gives the programmer much finer control over cache size than is common for client/server products, the matter demands more attention with an embedded database.

Finally, a third common source of contention in database applications is the transaction log. When a transaction makes changes to the database, the log records information that allows the database system to reapply or roll back the changes as necessary. Every update operation that an application makes turns into a log write. An embedded XML database allows the programmer to determine the number of threads and processes that can write to the database at the same time. As a result, an embedded XML database may exhibit log contention because of the application design. If the embedded XML database supports a service like group commit, it will monitor and adjust for that contention. Otherwise, the programmer must consider the commit throughput that the log supports and design the application accordingly.

4.4.8 Checkpoints

Both embedded and client/server XML databases use a technique called *checkpointing* to limit the time that an application will have to spend recovering the database after a system failure. Performing a checkpoint guarantees that the actual database contents on disk are consistent with the change log up to a particular point. As a result, after a system failure, the change log prior to that point can be ignored.

An XML database server can take periodic checkpoints on the application's behalf. An embedded XML database, by contrast, requires the programmer to decide when, and how frequently, to take a checkpoint. The code to take a checkpoint is straightforward, but the programmer must do the work periodically to ensure that the system can start up quickly after a failure. The example in Listing 4.8 makes use of Win32 threads, but any threading package can be used with Berkeley DB XML.

Listing 4.8 Checkpoints

```
void checkpoint(DbEnv *environment)
{
  while(true)
  {
   ::Sleep(60 * 1000); // 60 seconds
   int r = environment->txn_checkpoint(0, 0, 0);
   if(r != 0)
   {
    exit(1);
```

```
      }
    }
  }

  int main()
  {
    try
    {
      DbEnv environment(0);
      environment.open(0, DB_CREATE | DB_INIT_LOCK | DB_INIT_LOG |
                DB_INIT_MPOOL | DB_INIT_TXN, 0);
      HANDLE checkpointThread =
        ::CreateThread(0, 0, (LPTHREAD_START_ROUTINE)&checkpoint,
                       &environment, 0, 0);
      // Create containers, add documents, perform queries, etc.
      ::CloseHandle(checkpointThread);
      environment.close(0);
    }
    catch(XmlException &e)
    {
     cerr << e.what() << "\n";
    }
  }
```

After a checkpoint, the application can also reclaim the space occupied by log records that are no longer needed. This allows the programmer to bound the space that is consumed by the log during normal processing.

4.4.9 Recovery Processing after Failures

A client/server XML database system automatically runs recovery when the database server restarts after an abnormal shutdown. Since an embedded XML database has no server process of its own, the application programmer is responsible for running recovery prior to beginning normal processing.

Berkeley DB XML makes this operation fairly simple, but every Berkeley DB XML application must begin by recovering the database. Listing 4.9 shows an example of recovery at start-up.

Listing 4.9 Recovery at Start-up

```
DbEnv environment(0);
environment.open(0, DB_CREATE | DB_INIT_LOCK | DB_INIT_LOG |
```

```
            DB_INIT_MPOOL | DB_INIT_TXN | DB_RECOVERY, 0);
// Create containers, add documents, perform queries, etc.
environment.close(0);
```

4.5 Conclusion

Embedded XML databases offer the same data management services as their client/server counterparts. Applications can get transactions, scalability, and reliability by storing data in an embedded XML database. Because the database code runs directly in the address space of the application, performance can be orders of magnitude better in an embedded XML database. However, embedded products require more sophistication on the part of the software developer and suit a narrower range of uses. End users generally cannot use embedded XML databases directly. An application programmer must write code to store and retrieve XML documents in the database.

Part III

XML and Relational Databases

This part provides a mix of products and approaches to XML data management in relational and object-relational database systems.

Chapter 5

IBM XML-Enabled Data Management Product Architecture and Technology

Shawn E. Benham

5.1 Introduction

This chapter contains current and "under consideration" aspects of XML architecture and technology in IBM DB2 data management products. Focus areas are DB2 Universal Database (DB2) product offerings and information integration-related product and technology offerings. The chapter is structured as follows:

- Product and technology offering summaries (names and brief summaries)
- Current architecture and technology (overall design, how they work, examples of what you can do)
- The future (a look ahead)

5.2 Product and Technology Offering Summaries

This section provides brief summaries of current product and technology focus areas.

5.2.1 DB2 Universal Database

The DB2 Universal Database (DB2) family of products provides relational and object-relational data management support for XML applications. There are three specific areas of XML support. The first one is the DB2 XML Extender, an IBM object-relational "datablade" that provides access to, storage options, and transformation support for XML data through user-defined functions and stored procedures. DB2 Universal Database for Linux, UNIX, and Windows also provides extended SQL support that includes the creation of XML fragments from relational data through the use of a subset of SQL/XML valve functions. Additionally, Web service capabilities and support for extracting and using XML data in other products (such as WebSphere MQ) are provided.

5.2.2 Information Integration Technology

Information integration refers to the IBM technology infrastructure for integrating structured, semi-structured, and unstructured data. Xperanto is the code name for a project to address customer requirements for integrating diverse and distributed information. An online Xperanto project demo (http://xperanto.dfw.ibm.com/demo/) previews a number of the technology underpinnings.

Solving information integration challenges will require a combination of existing data management products/function and additional DB2 technology that supports operations on structured, unstructured, and semi-structured information. The Xperanto project will evolve these technologies to deliver a unified view across enterprise information and allow it to be searched, cached, replicated, transformed, and analyzed to meet the needs of the business. The intent is shown in Figure 5.1.

A focus for information integration is XML support, but it is more than that. It is a "home" for federation and distributed query application technology built for business integration and information integration requirements. From a product perspective, information integration offerings will have DB2 capabilities, additional federated source support, strong XML function, and support for structured and unstructured data.

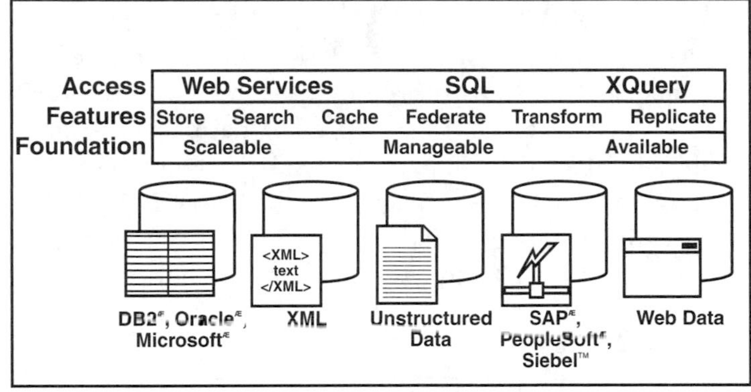

Figure 5.1 Xperanto Project

5.3 Current Architecture and Technology

This section contains general XML support architecture and technology/function in current and near term DB2 XML-enabled data management products. The section is organized so that common/shared function is covered first. Additional information integration function is covered later.

5.3.1 Shared Architecture and Technology

This section contains the shared architecture and technology of XML-related function provided in DB2 Universal Database and information integration offerings. The three key shared areas of function are the DB2 XML Extender, SQL/XML support, and Web service support.

XML data typically originates outside the DBMS (it can also be generated from within the database through composition functions) from a variety of locations including the file system, from a message system such as MQSeries or Web services, or from any other mechanism that will put XML data into memory. From there it is ingested into the database and stored in one of several ways, the principal ones are XML Column and XML Collection (described later in this chapter). Once stored in the database, applications can interact with the data using any combination of XML Extender-specific extensions to the DBMS or SQL/XML-standard extensions to the SQL language.

5.3.2 XML Extender Architecture

The focal point for much of IBM relational database XML function is the XML Extender. It provides the ability to store and access XML documents, to generate XML documents from existing relational data, and to insert rows into relational tables from XML documents. The XML Extender provides data types, functions, and stored procedures to manage XML data in DB2. The XML Extender is available for use with DB2 for z/OS and OS/390, DB2 for iSeries, and DB2 Universal Database for Linux, Unix, and Windows. The overall architecture of the XML Extender is shown in Figure 5.2.

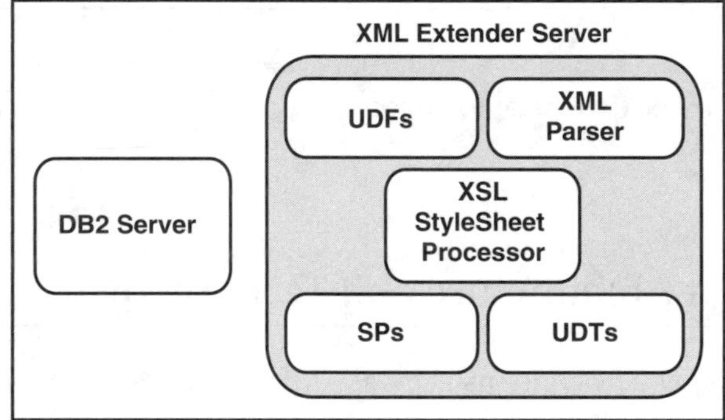

Figure 5.2 XML Extender

The XML Extender architecture provides

- XML object storage and processing support for DB2 and information integration technology offerings.
- XML application request support. XML Extender user-defined functions (UDFs) and user-defined types (UDTs) provide function for document access, indexing, shredding, searching, and processing.

XML documents can be stored in several ways. The storage options are shown in Figure 5.3.

XML documents stored with the XML Extender can be stored intact in a relational column (XML Column support), stored as fragments (i.e., shredded) in a collection of tables (XML Collection), or stored as files linked from the DBMS (in that case, the database simply serves as an XML index and points to the external documents). You can also store XML documents as Character Large Objects (CLOBs).

Storing documents intact in XML Columns makes sense when the entire document must be maintained and be retrievable. It is also useful when update operations are minimal. Storing documents in a collection of tables (shredding) makes sense

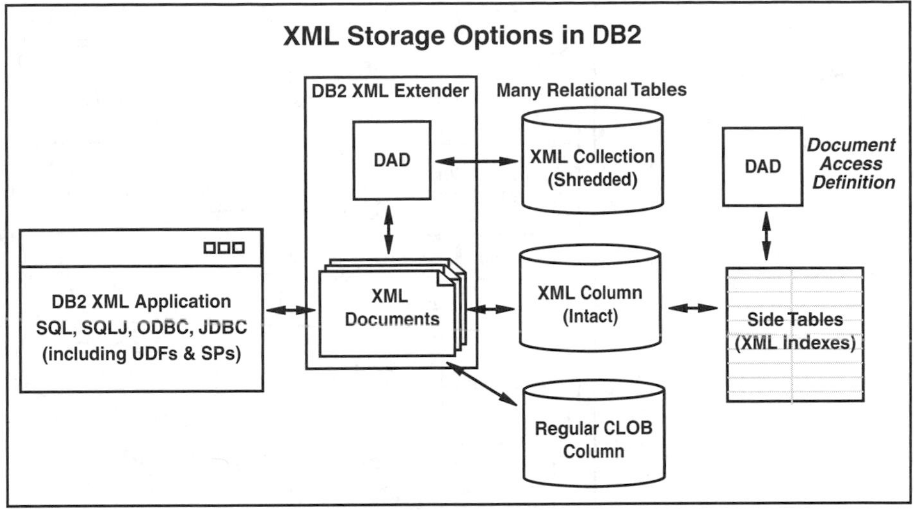

Figure 5.3 XML Storage Options in DB2

when fragments are subject to frequent update. Side tables are used for two reasons: as a method to improve performance for operations on XML column data and as a system for maintaining pointers to XML documents not stored in the data management system. Combinations of these approaches can also be used.

5.3.3 XML Extender Technology

The XML Extender architecture provides functional support for typical application requirements, such as storing, accessing, and retrieving XML data. Figure 5.4 provides an overview of data movement operations.

As stated earlier, the XML Extender offers two key storage models: XML Columns and XML Collections. Additional detail on related functions is provided below.

XML Columns

Storing XML data in relational columns is made possible through specific types and functions. The types are

- **XMLVarchar:** Allows small XML documents to be stored as column data
- **XMLCLOB:** Similar, but for large XML documents
- **XMLFile:** A special type used to associate or link data in a relational column within the database to an XML document stored outside the database

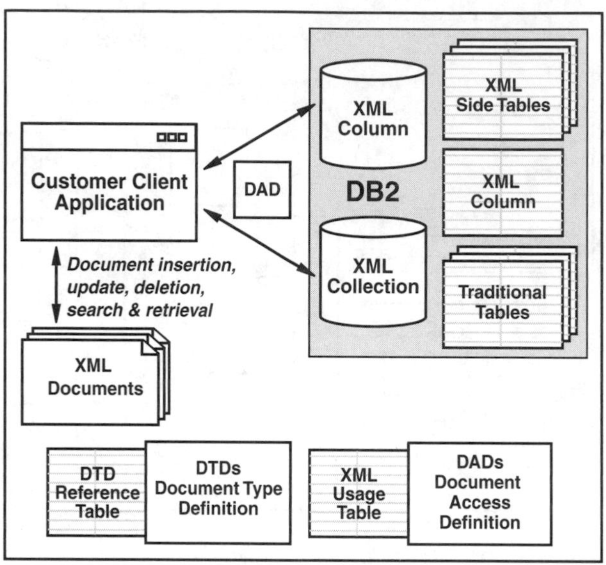

Figure 5.4 XML Column and XML Collection

From an application perspective, use of XML Columns is recommended when XML documents already exist and/or when there is a need to store XML documents in their entirety. XML data stored in XML Columns can be easily searched and updated. UDFs are supplied for operations on the element nodes in the XML documents. The XML Extender uses the XPath W3C recommendation for locating elements and attributes. The XML Columns approach is useful for documents frequently read but infrequently updated. This approach is also optimal when it is known which elements will be of interest because it is possible to replicate key elements to side tables to dramatically speed access to specific elements. An example is shown in Figure 5.5.

Data Access Definition (DAD) Files

A data access definition (DAD) file is used for both XML Column and XML Collection approaches to define the "mapping" between XML document elements/attributes and relational column data. A DAD file is used for column data when mapping from side tables to XML documents. It is also used for Collection data when composing or decomposing XML documents. Here is a quick example of an XML column DAD for storing an XML document:

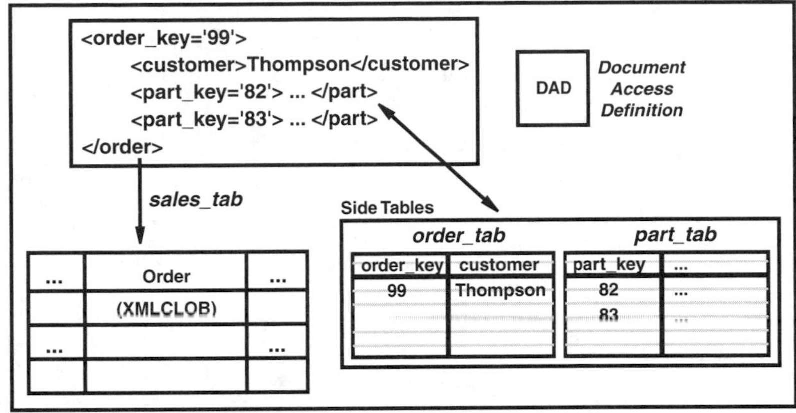

Figure 5.5 Side Table Example

```
<?xml version="1.0"?><!DOCTYPE DAD SYSTEM
"c:\dxx\dtd\dad.dtd"><DAD>    <dtdid>Order.dtd</dtdid>
      <validation>YES</validation> <Xcolumn>
         <table name="order"><column name="customer_num"
type="Integer" path="/Order/Customer" multi_occurrence="NO">

      </column></table></Xcolumn></DAD>
```

DAD files are also used for composing documents. One way to compose a document is to use an XML Collection SQL Node Mapping DAD. Listing 5.1 provides an example.

Listing 5.1 SQL Node Mapping

```
<?xml version="1.0"?>
<!DOCTYPE DAD SYSTEM "c:\dxx\dtd\dad.dtd">
<DAD>
<validation>NO</validation>
<Xcollection>
<SQL_stmt>select book_id, price_date, price_text from book_table
ORDER BY book_id</SQL_stmt>
<prolog>?xml version="1.0"?</prolog>
<doctype>!DOCTYPE book SYSTEM "c:\dtd\book.dtd"</doctype>
<root_node>
<element_node name="book">
  <attribute_node name="id">
    <column name="book_id"/>
```

```
      </attribute_node>
      <element_node name="price">
        <attribute_node name="date">
          <column name="price_date"/>
        </attribute_node>
        <text_node><column name="price_text"/></text_node>
      </element_node>
    </element_node>
    </root_node>
    </Xcollection>
    </DAD>
```

The mapping information in the DAD file is used to define a map between an XML document and the data in Table 5.1. The hierarchical view of the map is shown in Figure 5.6.

Table 5.1 Relational View of Book_Table

Column1	Column 2	Column 3
book_id	price_date	Price_text

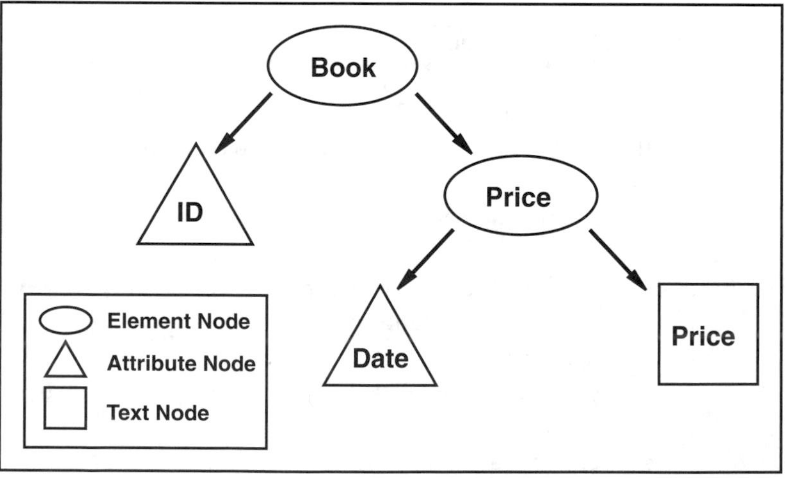

Figure 5.6 Hierarchical View of Map

XML Collections

An XML collection approach is used when the goal is to break down documents into small relational table sets of untagged data or when it is necessary to generate XML documents from a particular set of relational column data. It is also useful when updates to small sections of documents (or small documents in their entirety) are required and when update performance is important. XML documents are composed from relational columns by using a DAD file to define the publishing map (relational to XML). You can use an SQL node DAD or an RDB node DAD to compose documents. Listing 5.2 provides an example of an RDB node DAD mapping document. It shows how to compose an XML document from a simple relational table (personal_table) that contains six columns.

Listing 5.2 RDB Node DAD

```
<?xml version="1.0"?>
<!DOCTYPE DAD SYSTEM "c:\dxx\dtd\dad.dtd">
<DAD>
   <dtdid>personal_dtd</dtdid>
   <validation>NO</validation>
   <Xcollection>
   <prolog>?xml version="1.0"?</prolog>
   <doctype>!DOCTYPE personal SYSTEM "personal.dtd"</doctype>
   <root_node>
      <element_node name="personnel" multi_occurrence="NO" >
      <RDB_node>
         <table name="personal_table" />
      </RDB_node>
        <element_node name="person">
           <attribute_node name ="id">
             <RDB_node>
                <table name="personal_table"/>
                <column name="person_id" type="varchar(32)" />
             </RDB_node>
           </attribute_node>
           <attribute_node name="contr">
             <RDB_node>
                <table name="personal_table"/>
                <column name="person_contractor"
type="varchar(32)" />
             </RDB_node>
           </attribute_node>
           <attribute_node name="salary">
```

```
                    <RDB_node>
                        <table name="personal_table"/>
                        <column name="person_salary" type="varchar(32)" />
                    </RDB_node>
                  </attribute_node>
                  <element_node name="name">
                      <element_node name="family">
                        <text_node>
                          <RDB_node>
                             <table name="personal_table"/>
                             <column name="person_family"
type="varchar(32)"/>
                          </RDB_node>
                        </text_node>
                      </element_node>
                      <element_node name="given">
                        <text_node>
                          <RDB_node>
                              <table name="personal_table"/>
                              <column name="person_given"
type="varchar(32)"/>
                          </RDB_node>
                        </text_node>
                      </element_node>
                  </element_node>
                  <element_node name="email">
                    <text_node>
                 <RDB_node>
                    <table name="personal_table"/>
                    <column name="person_email" type="varchar(32)" />
                       </RDB_node>
                     </text_node>
                   </element_node>
                </element_node>
             </element_node>
          </root_node>
          </Xcollection>
       </DAD>
```

5.3.4 Using Both XML Collections and XML Columns

Sometimes using both storage approaches makes sense. For example, consider an insurance claim. From a legal perspective, the entire document and each version of the document must be stored for recall upon demand. Additionally, a given document could have key fields and metadata that would be useful to query and in some cases update. For example, the current state of a claim (e.g., open, working, closed) will require updates. Additionally, an application developer might need to index the document using side tables so that document searches are completed quickly. Shredding the original claim document into smaller fragments could have value when you need to send a specific and consistent piece of the original document to drive follow-on business processes, such as claims follow-up, billing, analysis for fraud, and so on.

5.3.5 Transforming XML Data

The transformation is provided through XSL and XML Style Sheet Transformation (XSLT) support. The most common functional requirement is to publish SQL or shredded XML as displayed HTML or transformed XML suitable for Web services. The steps to do this are

1. Transform relational data to XML through use of a DAD file.
2. Transform XML to HTML or another XML dialect with an XSL style sheet.

A simple example is shown in Figure 5.7.

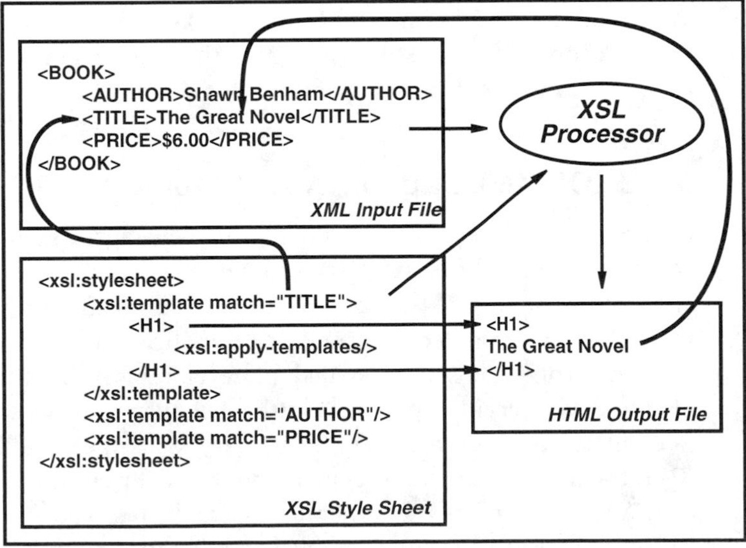

Figure 5.7 Transformation Example

Regarding step 2, a common need is to take XML and transform it to an intercompany standard format (which is common when one company purchases another) to support enterprise application integration (EAI) requirements or external standard formats (for business-to-business applications). XSL is extremely powerful and allows for element restructure, element change, and the ability to generate new results from an existing XML data set. XSL transforms are supported with UDFs delivered with the XML Extender.

5.3.6 Searching, Parsing, and Validating XML Data

XPath statements are used to locate portions within an XML document. The XML Extender supports a subset of the XPath standard (for finding elements and attributes). You do not need another parser to go through a document to find specific information. There is a restriction: You must parse entire XML documents, not shredded documents.

The XML Extender also provides support for XML Schema and provides a UDF for validating XML documents with named schemas. This support can be used to verify documents built from previously shredded XML source or new XML documents built directly from relational data.

5.3.7 XML Extender Federated Support

The XML Extender supports federated environments. XML documents can be transparently composed from one or many data sources with a single SQL statement. With DB2, the DB2 family and Informix IDS data sources can be used for composing or decomposing XML documents. With additional information integration function, you can extend these capabilities to include non-DB2 data sources.

5.3.8 SQL/XML Support Architecture

DB2 SQL/XML support is of interest to developers familiar with SQL who are attempting to build new XML data applications or who want to extend existing SQL applications so that XML fragments can be requested from relational data. The data model purposely reflects current SQL application development models because many enterprise tools are designed for developing SQL applications and a great deal of SQL development expertise is in the data management community.

Initial work on the SQL/XML standard focused on publishing relational data in XML fragments suitable for standalone results or embedding in application generated XML documents. To generate the fragments, you use constructor functions. The functions provide considerable flexibility to the application developer, allowing a variety of ways to build the XML fragment. For example, you could use the XMLATTRIBUTES function to map columns to XML attributes. You would use the XMLAGG function to generate a sequence of XML values.

The implementation in DB2 is at a system function level—it is not a set of UDFs like the XML Extender. SQL/XML data generation and function are undertaken within the engine. Data source access and processing are pushed down when possible to the local database manager and can be pushed down to other DB2 database managers (e.g., distributed, z/OS, iSeries) when a federated query is executed. The overall architecture is shown in Figure 5.8.

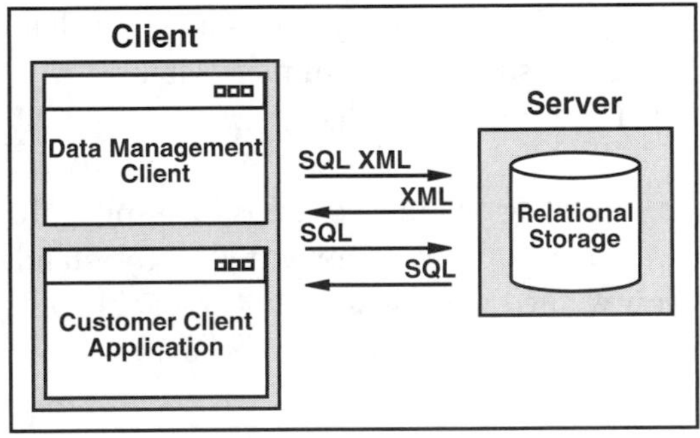

Figure 5.8 SQL/XML Architecture

The output from SQL/XML queries is XML fragments. No schema is generated with the result set so validation of results must be done by the calling application (the results might be embedded into a larger document, and an existing schema could be used for validation). The current implementation relies on a new internal data type (XML).

SQL/XML functions are available for use over DB2 federated systems and can transparently generate XML from data stored in DB2, non-DB2 data sources (more on that later), and nonrelational data. Developers can expect

- Compensation for data sources that don't provide capability to publish their data as XML documents
- Pushdown support, whenever possible, for better performance, to data sources (such as DB2 for z/OS) that provide similar functionality

5.3.9 SQL/XML Support Technology

IBM SQL/XML support is provided just like any other SQL support as callable SQL/XML publishing functions. The statements are documented in the *DB2 SQL Reference*, but here are a few usage notes and examples:

- XMLATTRIBUTES: Provides mapping from columns to attributes of an XML element.
- XMLELEMENT: Provides mapping from columns to XML content. It can be used to generate nested elements.
- XMLAGG: Used to generate a sequence of values. It is used most often in the context of a JOIN statement.
- XML2CLOB: A mandatory statement that converts XML results into CLOB data. This is how the implementation ensures that the calling application can process the results.

The following section contains examples of SQL/XML statements. The examples are similar to those documented in the standards document (Melton 2002).

If you wanted to view a table (i.e., Table 5.2) as an XML fragment, you could use the SQL statement shown in Listing 5.3.

Table 5.2 Employees Table

Name	Dept	Hire_Date
John	Shipping	2001-10-10
Mark	Accounting	1999-04-01

Listing 5.3 SQL/XML Statement 1

```
SELECT XML2CLOB(XMLELEMENT(NAME "Employees",
       XMLAGG(XMLELEMENT(NAME "Emp", XMLATTRIBUTES(name),
       XMLELEMENT(NAME "Dept", Dept),
       XMLELEMENT(NAME "Hire_date", Hire_date)))))
FROM employees
```

Listing 5.4 Result from SQL/XML Statement 1

```
<EMPLOYEES>
<EMP NAME="John">
   <DEPT>Shipping</DEPT>
   <HIRE_DATE>2001-10-10</HIRE_DATE>
</EMP>
<EMP NAME="MARK">
   <DEPT>Accounting</DEPT>
   <HIRE_DATE>1999-04-01</HIRE_DATE>
</EMP>
</EMPLOYEES>
```

SQL/XML works well with information integration federated functionality. For example, customers can generate an XML fragment describing a customer where the information is stored in Oracle and DB2 tables. A sample set of statements and results could look like those shown in Listing 5.5.

Listing 5.5 SQL/XML Statement 2

```
SELECT XML2CLOB(XMLELEMENT(NAME "customer",
       XMLATTRIBUTES(c.id),
       XMLELEMENT(NAME "name", c.name),
       XMLELEMENT(NAME "porders",
             SELECT XMLAGG(XMLELEMENT(NAME "porder",
                  XMLATTRIBUTES(p.id, p.acctID as "acct"),
                   XMLELEMENT(NAME "date", p.date))
       ORDER BY p.id)
       FROM ora_purchaseOrder p WHERE p.custid = c.id))))
FROM db2_customer c
```

The output for Listing 5.5 could look like Listing 5.6.

Listing 5.6 Result from SQL/XML Statement 2

```
<CUSTOMER ID="C1"><NAME>John Doe </NAME>
            <PORDERS>
                  <PORDER ID="P01" ACCT="A1">
                        <DATE>2001-10-10</DATE>
                  </PORDER>
                  <PORDER ID="P02" ACCT="A2">
                        <DATE>1991-11-17</DATE>
```

```
            </PORDER>
        </PORDERS>
</CUSTOMER>
```

Another way to use XMLELEMENT is shown in Listing 5.7, which contains nested results and an example of concatenated data. To produce an XML element named Emp for each employee, with nested elements for the employee's full name and the date the employee was hired, issue:

Listing 5.7 SQL/XML Statement 3

```
SELECT e.empno, varchar (XML2CLOB(XMLELEMENT(NAME "EMP",
    XMLELEMENT(NAME "name", e.firstname CONCAT' 'CONCAT e.lastname),
    XMLELEMENT(NAME "hiredate", e.hiredate))),82)
AS "result" FROM employee e
```

Listing 5.7 could produce the result shown in Listing 5.8.

Listing 5.8 SQL/XML Statement 3

```
000010 <EMP><NAME>CHRISTINE
HAAS</NAME><HIREDATE>1965-01-01</HIREDATE></EMP>
000020 <EMP><NAME>MICHAEL
THOMPSON</NAME><HIREDATE>1973-10-10</HIREDATE></EMP>
000030 <EMP><NAME>SALLY KWAN</NAME><HIREDATE>1975-04-
05</HIREDATE></EMP>
000050 <EMP><NAME>JOHN GEYER</NAME><HIREDATE>1949-08-
17</HIREDATE></EMP>
000060 <EMP><NAME>IRVING STERN</NAME><HIREDATE>1973-09-
14</HIREDATE></EMP>
000070 <EMP><NAME>EVA PULASKI</NAME><HIREDATE>1980-09-
30</HIREDATE></EMP>
...
```

In all cases, note the use of the XML2CLOB statement to convert generated or existing XML to a CLOB data type so that SQL applications can process it. Over time, expect the depreciation of the DB2 XML2CLOB statement as the SQL/XML standard progresses. Some final notes:

- The implementation handles the mapping of SQL names to XML names.
- Invalid characters (in the context of XML) are processed, ensuring that SQL identifiers are mapped cleanly to XML names.

5.3.10 Data Management Web Services Architecture

IBM provides an extremely flexible architecture and a large selection of products and downloadable tools for creating data management Web services. From a DB2 perspective, three general levels of complexity should be considered when defining how database Web services will be created and the tools and approaches that you will need:

- Simple SQL statements executed on relational data in an existing DB2 database. If all you need is the ability to run a SELECT statement that returns a predictable result to successfully host a new or existing application as a Web service, the requirements are an existing relational database client/server infrastructure, network support, and a Web application server. You should also consider using the WORF (Web Services Object Runtime Framework) unless you want to hand-code the Web Services Description Language (WSDL) document, database access code, and so on.
- Moderately complex operations. In this case, you should also make use of the WORF tools provided with DB2 and the WebSphere Studio Application Developer product. The WORF provides the ability to:
  - Consume DADX files. These files define a Web service using a set of operations that are defined by SQL statements and, optionally, DB2 XML Extender DAD files.
  - Generate WSDL documents.
  - Automatically generate test pages.
- XML document or data-centric operations requiring access to XML Collections and/or SQL update operations on XML Columns. In this case, you should also use the DB2 XML Extender.

All three approaches can be used to support internal EAI and external (business-to-business—B2B, business-to-customer—B2C) Web service requests. If you were considering the XML document approach to Web services, the overall implementation architecture could look like Figure 5.9.

5.3.11 Data Management Web Services Technology

DADX file consumption and the generation of WSDL documents are the key technologies provided with the WORF and the focus area for defining a Web service that makes use of existing database application function. The starting point in the cycle is creating a DADX file that defines what a Web service can do and contains the statements that perform database operations. A simple DADX file is shown in Listing 5.9.

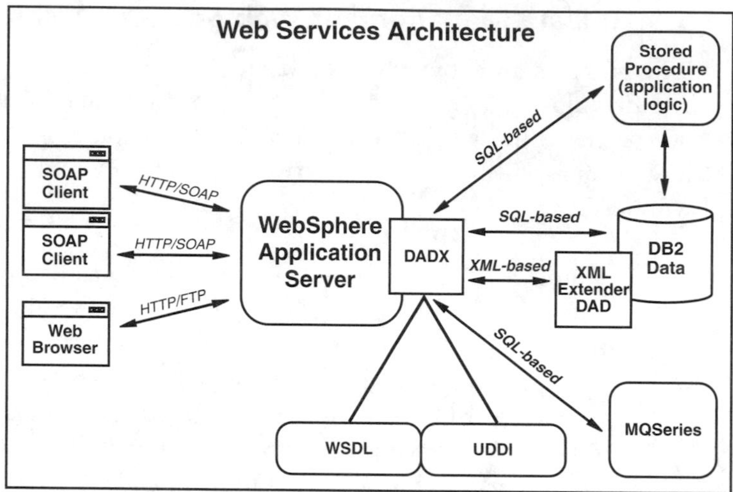

Figure 5.9 Web Services Architecture

Listing 5.9 A Simple DADX File

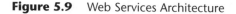

```
<?xml version="1.0" encoding="UTF-8"?>
<DADX xmlns="http://schemas.ibm.com/db2/dxx/dadx">
<operation name="somerandomSELECT">
<query>
<SQL_query>
SELECT * FROM newzoobabies
</SQL_query>
</query>
</operation>
</DADX>
```

In Listing 5.9, the file defines a Web service that on demand executes a query returning data from the relational table "newzoobabies" (perhaps indicating any new arrivals at the local zoo). In this case the returned data is tagged XML.

Web services, and DADX files, can be much more complex and be a part of large-scale B2C and B2B solutions involving complex operations that make use of more than one Web service. DADX files support runtime variable input as needed to better define a service or to make better reuse of services.

For example, consider a situation where a customer needs 100,000 widgets. The customer sends out a SOAP-based message with the above constraints to a public directory and finds an entry for the company JIMCO that is a provider of widgets. Next, the customer sends a request to JIMCO. This B2C situation is quite straightforward on the surface: JIMCO either has what is specified or not. But consider an extension of this scenario from the JIMCO perspective. Even if one company cannot meet the entire contract by itself, there are ways to get the work done—for example, if JIMCO has a defined set of relationships with subcontractors that can be dynamically called on demand as work peaks are experienced by JIMCO. The true goal, then, is to make sure JIMCO can not only query its own capacity to meet the customer needs, it can use a federated query to consider its own and subcontractor capacity at the same time and provide a unified statement of "can or cannot do" to the original customer. To accomplish the above, the application must support a combination of in-bound Web services *and* a federated query across local capacity information and defined subcontractor capacity information accessed with UDFs that call a defined set of B2B out-bound Web services. The overall view of this approach is shown in Figure 5.10.

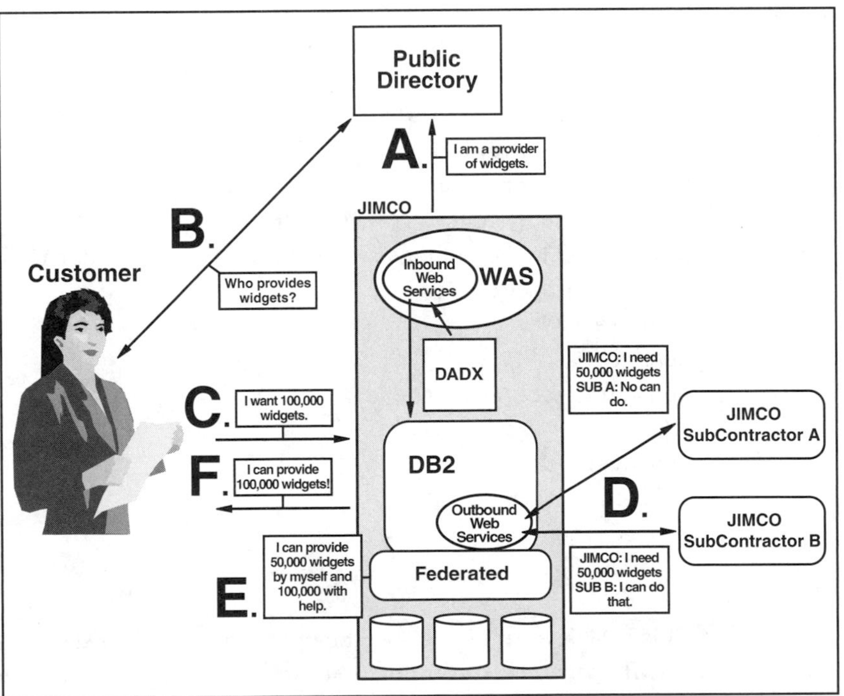

Figure 5.10 JIMCO Example

Previously, you saw a DADX file containing a simple SQL query. The scenario after that DADX file described a more complex situation that would require even more SQL operations. DADX files, however, can also be used with the XML Extender—they are not limited to pure SQL and relational operations. DADX files can be used with XML Extender DAD files to generate or store XML documents. The following DADX file example shows one potential approach for generating an XML document.

Listing 5.10 DADX File for Use with XML Extender DAD File

```
<?xml version="1.0"?>
<DADX  xmlns="http://schemas.ibm.com/db2/dxx/dadx"
                 xmlns="http://www.w3.org/2001/XMLSchema">
<wsdl:documentation
xmlns:wsdl="http://schemas.xmlsoap.org/wsdl/"
xmlns="http://www.w3.org/1999/xhtml">
Provides queries for part order information at myco.com.
See
<a href="../documentation/PartOrders.html"
target="_top">PartOrders.html</a>
for more information.
</wsdl:documentation>
<operation name="findAll">
<wsdl:documentation
xmlns="http://schemas.xmlsoap.org/wsdl/">
Returns all the orders with their complete details.
</wsdl:documentation>
<retrieveXML>
<DAD_ref>
getstart_xcollection.dad
</DAD_ref>
<no_override/>
</retrieveXML>
</operation>
</DADX>
```

This DADX references a specific operation, <retrieveXML> which is used to generate XML documents. Within that element, the <DAD_ref> element specifies the name of the DAD file that contains the mapping information required to generate the XML document.

5.3.12 Information Integration-Specific Architecture and Technology

This section covers the architecture and technology of XML-related database function specific to DB2 information integration technology. Information integration refers to the IBM technology infrastructure for integrating structured, semi-structured, and unstructured data. The primary topics for this section are heterogeneous federated data operations (mentioned previously in the SQL/XML section) and access and support for unstructured data sources.

Heterogeneous Federated Data Access and Application Support

IBM federated functionality provides access to and powerful application support for XML, relational, and industry-specific (such as life sciences) data types. DB2 Universal Database for Linux, Unix, and Windows provides the overall federated base function set and access to DB2 family and Informix Dynamic Server data. IBM's information integration portfolio includes the base federation layer from DB2 and extends the data types you can access to include XML, other relational types (such as Oracle, Microsoft, and Sybase), and additional formats. Figure 5.11 shows the overall architecture from an XML perspective.

The use of this technology in the context of XML ranges from:

- Simple data access (use an XML wrapper, a defined data source connector and mapping structure, to enable relational engine access to XML data sources)
- Complex distributed requests ranging across multiple data sources (one or more being XML, one or more being relational, one or more being something else, or a mix)

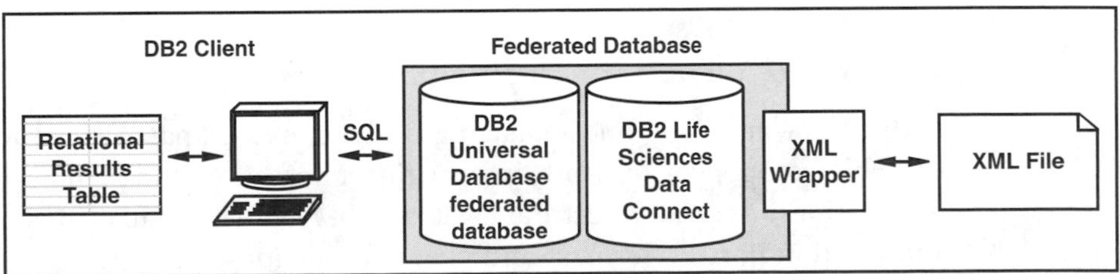

Figure 5.11 Overall Architecture for a Single Additional XML Data Source

XML application support includes

- Local joins of table data in multiple relational databases for use as real-time input to Web service definitions or data input.
- Greatly enhanced SQL/XML query results gathered from local and remote (DB2 and other relational) data stores that result in a single XML fragment reflecting a single view of all accessible sources in a single unit of work. An example was included earlier in the SQL/XML section.
- Business process integration support. For example, using XML, relational, and life sciences data source wrappers (BLAST, as an example) to support requests for the aggregation of results across data types (relational, multi-vendor) and special-purpose vertical industry data.

In addition to planned information integration product functionality, there are related program downloads of interest to XML application developers. For example, out on alphaworks (http://www.alphaworks.ibm.com/) there is a package called the XML Wrapper Generator. It helps integrate XML data sources. Specifically, the tool can load XML schema files and then graphically map the XML schema to a relational schema. Using the tool GUI, a developer can customize the map. Once the map is complete, the tool can automatically generate DDL statements (mentioned below) required to make the XML data source visible to a federated server. SQL queries can then be executed against the XML data source.

Setting up a database for federated operations involves the creation and definition of wrappers for each accessed type (CREATE WRAPPER), registering data servers (CREATE SERVER), and identifying data server tables (a combination of CREATE NICKNAME statements and potentially several CREATE FEDERATED VIEW statements where the view is a compilation of several nicknames that describe an XML document). For life sciences data, some additional steps are related to setting up access (BLAST data, for example, requires an active daemon executable to be available to handle requests for BLAST data).

Access and Support for Unstructured Data

Support for accessing and managing unstructured or partially structured data is a valuable component for both information integration and standard XML database applications. At an architectural level, the IBM Content Management and Enterprise Information Portal offerings (and planned functions) provide

- Scalability to handle the massive amounts of data often required for collections of unstructured text, structured text, binary format, and semi-structured documents
- Federated access to unstructured content

- An integration services layer. From a technology perspective, the Enterprise Information Portal extends available text services to include:
  - Standard text operation (search, aggregate, workflow) support useful for extracting information from XML and unstructured text documents
  - Workflow support
- Text mining support

The text mining services, for example, can crawl and organize large volumes of unstructured information. Mined text can be indexed, categorized, and summarized as needed for additional search and/or analysis. Results can be fed to structured data stores for additional analysis as part of generalized federated query analysis or directly staged feeds for use by EAI applications. In conjunction with the XML Extender, final results can be transformed to XML for use as externalized application feeds to drive B2B or B2C activity based on staged XML data flows between partners (WSDL, creation, for example) or to customers.

5.4 Future Architecture and Technology

This section provides a glance at the challenges and potential directions for IBM XML data management development.

5.4.1 The Vision

The vision is to deliver a data store and application processing interface that helps developers create and run XML as well as current relational data applications without worrying about how the data are stored or in what form they are stored. The data management system provides a consistent way to store and access all digital media. Relational users will see a world-class RDBMS that also handles XML extremely well. XML users will see a strong XML database with native type, function, and indexing that also supports current relational applications.

5.4.2 Application Interface, Data Type, and API Goals

The vision (see Figure 5.12) has two major components: the application view of the data and the storage of the data. From an application perspective, there will be support for XML data as a native type and general functional support, making it easier to access, query, and make good use of XML information. Currently, with the XML Extender, data are stored as a CLOB or shredded into relational tables using existing SQL and specialized UDTs. Similarly, SQL/XML support currently makes use of

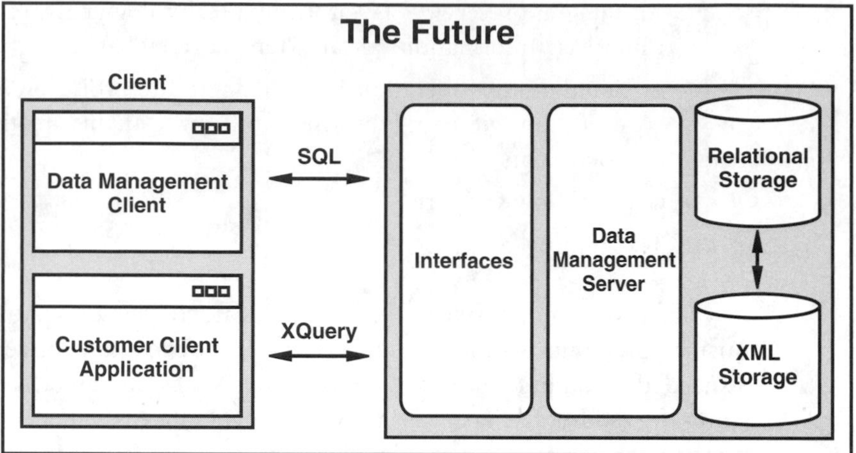

Figure 5.12 The Future

the CLOB type to contain composed XML data. This use of object-relational technology to represent XML will be replaced with a native XML data type within the database and function supporting use of that type. This native XML type will allow for more straightforward application development because developers can

- Count on improved scalability for large XML documents
- Nest XML manipulation operations
- Access, view, store, and manipulate XML data using operators specifically optimized for XML

The focus on application interface and data type enhancements also correlates to likely directions for SQL/XML development (e.g., constructor functions, shredding functions) and improvements to overall navigation function within XML documents (through use of path expressions).

New API development objectives are to expose true XML and relational data types, including support for materializing XML data to the application either in DOM form or through a series of SAX events. At the high end, application-serving function will become much more tightly integrated with the database engine. At a lower level, additional support will be provided for developers to create table or scalar functions from WSDL descriptions.

Specific to support for storing and manipulating XML is development on a new API, based on XQuery, to interact with the XML and relational data. This API will provide callable support for XML, structured (relational data, through XML views), semi-structured (XML fragments), and unstructured (text) applications. This level of XQuery support will provide developers the ability to:

- Automatically create low-level XML views of existing relational data without the need for a DAD file
- Use not only the full set of XQuery, but also the union of XQuery capabilities with relational capabilities
- Create application-specific views using XQuery
- Store XML data automatically without a DAD file
- Query XML and relational data with one statement
- Query data and metadata
- Perform queries on data efficiently, passing function down to the engine and materializing only the minimum set of required data for queries
- Use high-performance text search functions including advanced capabilities such as linguistic search, stemming, proximity search, thesaurus similarity search, classification and categorization, and automated summarization

The net result is that developers will have the ability to quickly load, query, and manipulate both XML and relational data with a standard API while leveraging existing strengths of relational function augmented with XQuery capability.

Listing 5.13 shows an example of XQuery statements. The result set is a new document that contains a set of all hippos that live in fresh water that weigh less than one ton. This statement shows not only XQuery itself, but XQuery with full text (the contains clause) and user-defined function support originally developed for object relational support (a function called legs2weight that is not an XQuery-bodied function but rather a function written in a third-generation language such as C and accessible to XQuery as though it were a built-in function).

Listing 5.13 XQuery Statements

```
<zoo_hippos habitat_type='fresh water'
body_configuration='slender'>
{
for $a in document("/attractions/zoos/animals.xml")
where $a/type="Hippo" and
      contains($a/habitat, "fresh water") and
      legs2weight($a/legs/text()) < 2000
return
      <hippo legs={$a/legs} food={$a/food}>
```

```
            {$a/name}
        </hippo>
}
</>
```

5.4.3 Storage, Engine, and Data Manager Goals

An application view of XML is not sufficient if the data engine does not have robust support for storing and manipulating that type. Relational engines must undergo significant XML-related modifications to:

- Not only support structured data, but also support semi-structured data extremely well.
- Support sequential operations and data, not just set-based.
- Handle sparse attribute processing.
- Provide flexible schema support. This includes support for features such as transformations, schema migration, and constraint enforcement.
- Have a full suite of integrated tools for management of relational as well as XML data.
- Support search, composition, and interrogation (which includes taking full advantage of metadata for improved performance).
- Provide high performance, exploiting the last quarter century of optimizer technology. XQuery support will be deeply integrated into the query compiler—enjoying the same world-class optimization provided to relational users.

Most importantly, the data store must help developers create XML applications with at least the same level of ease and power available to SQL developers now. In terms of overall XML and SQL support, the architecture would look like Figure 5.13.

Object-relational extensions will no longer be required to support XML; the functionality will be part of the core engine. Transformations, intermediary stored procedures, and data-mapping files will not be required.

Developers can submit XQuery or SQL requests and receive relational or XML data in response as application needs dictate. They can even mix and match XQuery and SQL in the same unit of work. They can choose the right language and interface to use based on characteristics of the application, while choosing the right storage model based on characteristics of the data. XQuery support will take advantage of XML storage to provide improved performance for operations involving multiple documents. For example, it is currently feasible to search through one XML docu-

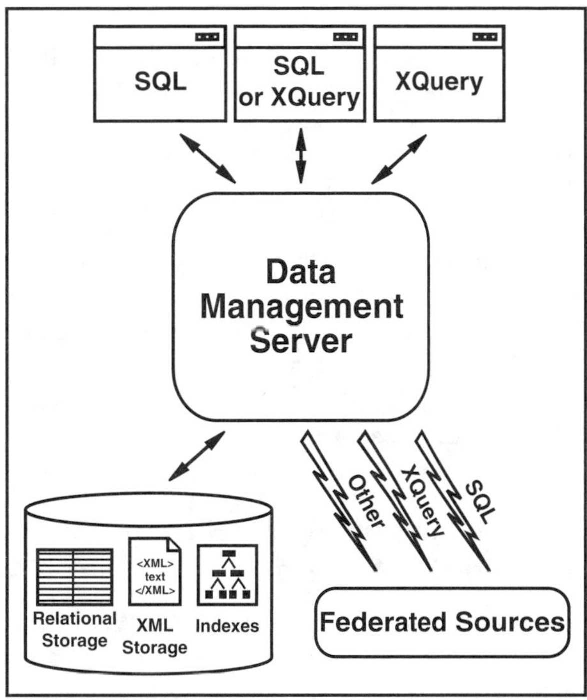

Figure 5.13 Future Architecture

ment for a particular string or attribute using XSL or an XPath processor. However, if you need to search an entire collection of whole XML documents for an attribute, without preindexing elements/attributes of interest, executing XQuery statements on natively stored XML documents using local engine function will provide superior performance.

Overall function support will show similar levels of improvement. For example, today, XML Extender applications must call UDFs to invoke XML processing capabilities; in the future, those capabilities will be part of the built-in function set of the database engine. This set of capabilities will be available through most existing APIs such as ODBC, JDBC, and even as an embedded language (the XQuery equivalent of embedded SQL).

Indexing methods will be available specifically for XML data that are developed and tuned specifically for XML data. The methods will take into account, not only the hierarchical nature of XML data, but also all of the information set. These indexes will vary considerably from existing relational indexes because they will be able to efficiently index the entire document and not just select portions.

A key part of the vision is supporting a flexible approach to data schemas. Typically, for relational data, arbitrary schema support is very difficult. You can create views on data, but you really don't have a lot of flexibility in terms of changing the underlying structure. With XML data, XML Repository (XR), and XSLT support, changing the data schema becomes possible without copying the data into a new database. For example, an application could make use of several schemas (some of which are versioned) and then have a set of documents that work well with each schema. Later, a requirement is received requiring a restructure of the data (adding a new field). This is not a problem because you can create a -01 version of the schema that allows for the new usage without requiring changes to the stored document. This is quite different from the relational model; with the relational model, if you change or add a data type, you need to unload everything, create a new table, and then put the data back.

5.4.4 Why Support Both XML and Relational Storage in One System?

From a user and developer perspective, the simple answer is that there *are not* two systems. There is just one data management system used to store data, and the system will worry about the format and location as needed. From an architectural perspective, the simple answer is that there are advantages to providing underlying function that allows for the storage of data in its native type. And there are advantages to starting with current relational technology and adding in XML support in a manner that takes advantage of what relational engines already have. Here are some specific points:

- XML has a linear/hierarchical structure; SQL data are structured as relations. Data access methods must exist that are optimized for both structures so as to provide reasonable performance for query and insert, update, and delete operations.
- Relational metadata is captured in a distinct catalog and tends to be static; XML metadata is distributed within the document, and the validity of the data can vary as required (different/versioned schemas). Simply verifying that an existing XML document or data set is correct, and reverifying that as needed, is a new step from a relational perspective.
- Relational data are usually much more dense in the sense that typically all/most columns have values. XML documents can be sparse, and missing information is indicated simply through the lack of an element or attribute.
- An XML document has an implicit order—document order, child order under parents, and so on. Relational data has no order beyond that derived from data values.

Regarding the advantages of starting with an existing base of relational technology, here are some reasons:

- Leverage existing transaction management, data storage, and security function.
- Reuse existing data flow capacity.
- Take full advantage of scalability and parallelization technology.
- Exploit local engine level access to existing relational data sets. This approach allows developers to extend to and support new data without losing current structured data and federated data framework.

5.4.5 Why Not Object-Relational Long Term?

The primary reason is that an OR approach does not provide the level of performance and function required for the efficient handling of a data type of this importance (XML). Specifically, an OR future:

- Does not fully address XML document linear structures.
- Requires users to pre-specify storage models for data.
- Relies on a UDT, UDF approach instead of native support.
- Relies on existing LOB technology.
- Cannot easily address XQuery semantics and behavior. XQuery requires two-value logic in some cases and three-value logic in others. Also, it has an approach for empty sequences that is quite different from standard relational null handling.

The overall issue with an OR approach is that the engine never really understands that it is processing XML data.

5.4.6 Impacted Technology Areas

Achieving this vision will require many changes and additions. Key areas are

- New storage and runtime support (XML type, native storage, XPath retrieval, search, and full expression support, security enhancements, access control list support, versioning)
- Indexing (automatic function, statistics)
- Compiler updates to support XML (SQL/XML and XQuery handling, XQuery parser, optimization support, new runtime operators)

- Logging and locking mechanisms
- Transaction management
- Utilities

In summary, because XML is being fully integrated into all facets of the database management system, any area that provides specific relational function will require change or new function to support XML.

5.5 Conclusion

IBM offers a variety of current XML data products and approaches as well as an encompassing vision of the future for XML data management. Users familiar with SQL and standard relational database application development who need to quickly generate XML fragments can make use of engine-level support that resembles their current tool set and leverages current knowledge. Developers who require the creation of complete XML documents from existing relational data, or who wish to directly load entire XML documents or shred them into relational tables, will find the function they require along with support for common APIs, validation calls, and transformation support. Functional support for XML operations in a database is just one part of the story: Web service application development tools as well as scalable document content management are all available now.

As for the future, the vision is to deliver overall XML data store and data management capabilities at a level equivalent to existing relational data product offerings. The new XML function will be accompanied by additional work in federated information access, increasing support for unstructured data, and a continuing higher-level focus on solving information integration issues.

Notices

IBM may have patents or pending patent applications covering subject matter described in this document. The furnishing of this document does not give you any license to these patents. You can send license inquiries, in writing, to:

IBM Director of Licensing
IBM Corporation
North Castle Drive
Armonk, NY 10504-1785
U.S.A.

The following paragraph does not apply to the United Kingdom or any other country where such provisions are inconsistent with local law:

INTERNATIONAL BUSINESS MACHINES CORPORATION PROVIDES THIS PUBLICATION "AS IS" WITHOUT WARRANTY OF ANY KIND, EITHER EXPRESS OR IMPLIED, INCLUDING, BUT NOT LIMITED TO, THE IMPLIED WARRANTIES OF NON-INFRINGEMENT, MERCHANTABILITY OR FITNESS FOR A PARTICULAR PURPOSE. Some states do not allow disclaimer of express or implied warranties in certain transactions, therefore, this statement may not apply to you. This information could include technical inaccuracies or typographical errors.

All statements regarding IBM's future direction or intent are subject to change or withdrawal without notice, and represent goals and objectives only.

This information contains examples of data and reports used in daily business operations. To illustrate them as completely as possible, the examples include the names of individuals, companies, brands, and products. All of these names are fictitious and any similarity to the names and addresses used by an actual business enterprise is entirely coincidental.

COPYRIGHT LICENSE

This information contains sample code. You may copy, modify, and distribute the sample code in any form without payment to IBM, for any purpose, but you do so at your own risk. The sample code is provided "AS IS" without warranty of any kind.

The following terms are trademarks or registered trademarks of IBM Corporation in the United States, other countries, or both: DB2, DB2 Universal Database, IBM, iSeries, OS 390, WebSpheres, and z/OS.

Microsoft and Windows are registered trademarks of Microsoft Corporation.

UNIX is a registered trademark of the Open Group in the United States and other countries.

Other company, product, and service names may be trademarks or service marks of others.

Chapter 6

Supporting XML in Oracle9i

Uwe Hohenstein

6.1 Introduction

Recently there is huge interest in XML. XML has been recognized as an adequate format for data exchange for Internet applications, because XML is portable across computers and applications and independent of existing databases and programming languages. First-class support for XML is a requirement for modern information platforms for the Web. Since XML documents must be held persistently, the relevance of XML has passed over to the area of databases that have to care for the adequate storage and handling of documents.

Much research and development effort has been focused recently on so-called "native" XML databases like Tamino (Schöning and Wäsch 2000), which promise optimized storage and retrieval of XML documents. Although native XML databases and query technology are important capabilities, a common opinion is that they will be successful in the mainstream market only if they are efficiently and effectively combined with SQL and relational database technology in an overall system architecture.

Indeed, relational database technology is well established and widespread, supporting efficient data management for even huge databases and providing scalability even for thousands of parallel users. Relational database systems offer powerful SQL query mechanisms, conforming to standards and providing effective query optimization. Taking up emerging requirements, vendors of relational database systems are extending their products to support storage and retrieval of XML data. In this way, they benefit from important existing features such as concurrency control, security, backup/recovery, and query optimization. Handling documents is done either by storing native XML in one relational column, or by supporting the definition of mappings between a relational schema to an XML schema, or a DTD. The mapping can be used to automatically compose/decompose XML during retrieval/insertion (Cheng and Xu 2000a).

We focus in this chapter on Oracle as a representative for relational database technology and discuss how to use Oracle9i as an XML database—that is, how to store and retrieve XML documents in an Oracle database.

To achieve full integration of XML and relational data, two aspects of functionality need to be addressed. From a data storage perspective, both XML data and relational data should be supported in the same database. From a query language point of view, both SQL-based and XML-based query features should be available to access data, regardless of how the data are stored. This implies that SQL should also be supported over a relational view of XML data, and XML query capabilities should be available over native XML data as well as an XML view of relational data.

Oracle attempts to satisfy these needs. Oracle's solution makes sure that XML queries can be evaluated efficiently on "real" XML documents and on XML "views" of relational data. This goal was first postulated by the Xperanto project (Carey et al. 2000; Shanmugasundaram et al. 2001).

There are two principal approaches to relational databases so far:

1. Document-centric documents are better stored in a coarse-grained manner in unstructured LOBs (Large Objects).
2. A fine-grained storage in attributes of one or more tables is suited for data-centric documents.

Approach 1 provides a simple solution for a relational DBMS, as no new features are required, at least at first glance. Moreover, the first approach places no restrictions on the kinds of document since documents are just taken as they are. Unfortunately, there is currently no SQL for querying, but this may not be a drawback in view of XQuery for searching documents by contents. At least we can state that there is no query performance comparable to SQL. XML-specific query features are then demanded for LOB columns. Another disadvantage to the first approach is that XML, more precisely the underlying LOB, is the unit of work: No modification of document parts is possible—only a complete replacement of the document.

In the diverging principle of approach 2, the powerful query mechanisms of SQL can still be used (even if SQL violates the spirit of XML), thereby offering outstanding query performance. Furthermore, document parts can be easily modified as their values are stored in table columns. This approach also makes it possible to "reuse" relational data: We get an opportunity to compose XML documents of table data. These capabilities for viewing XML data as relational data are useful to maximize the applicability of relational technology and tools for data mining, analysis, report generation, and so on. As a general hindrance, XML documents must possess a certain structure, at least given by a DTD. Thus, this approach is less flexible concerning the kinds documents to handle.

Oracle supports both approaches and a combination of them as well. Oracle's CLOB (Character Large Object) functionality can be used to handle XML documents in the sense of approach 1. When storing XML documents as a whole, the retrieval by means of associative search criteria is an essential problem. Much attention has been recently focused on query languages for XML (Robie et al. 1998), and the need for standardization of XML queries has been recognized (Chamberlin et al. 2001). Despite achieving progress, an integration of full-text search in XML queries has not yet been addressed. Some proposals are discussed in Shinagawa et al. 2000; Fiebig and Moerkotte 2000; Shanmugasundaram et al. 1999; McHugh and Widom 1999; Cheng and Xu 2000b; Florescu and Kossmann 1999a; Deutsch et al. 1999. Oracle solves the problem with the OracleText cartridge, which allows for text retrieval including adequate XML support. Furthermore, Oracle9i introduces a new object type `XMLType` to encapsulate XML documents in a coarse-grained manner. The methods of `XMLType` support easy handling of documents. Later, we will discuss how to store XML documents simply as a CLOB, and how the new Oracle9*i* object type `XMLType` eases the handling in addition. The power of OracleText is examined from the perspective of associative search capabilities.

The general principles of storing XML documents in relational database columns are discussed in Shanmugasundaram et al. 1999, Kanne and Moerkotte 2000, and Florescu and Kossmann 1999a. Oracle's XML SQL Utility (XSU) pursues a model-based approach. A schematic mapping defines how to map tables and views, including object-relational features, to XML documents. XSU also helps to store documents in a fine-grained manner, mapping XML structures into tables. This is done by automatically extracting relational information from stored XML using an inverse XML-to-relational mapping information. Flexibility is obtained by means of user-defined object views, the structure of which directly determines the nesting of the resulting XML. XSU is available for Java and the proprietary PL/SQL database programming language of Oracle. We will discuss the XML SQL utility later in this chapter.

We will also discuss how to build XML documents—for example, for placing relational contents on the Web. We focus on SQL enhancements to work with XML. Oracle extends classical SQL with new SQL functions for publishing relational data as XML (Shanmugasundaram et al. 2000). A JSP-like complementary approach helps to produce XML documents via Web access.

Also, we briefly tackle further concepts, such as uniform resource identifiers (URIs) that point into the database referring to tables, tuples, and rows. An XML parser, according to SAX and DOM interfaces, includes a validation with respect to a DTD or XML Schema. The parsers are particularly executable and callable in the database server. The parser as well as the other tools support XSLT for post-processing documents, especially query results. A class generator takes DTDs and XML Schemas as input and produces Java or C++ classes that allow the construction of valid XML documents. Oracle also offers Java Beans for viewing and interactively designing documents.

6.2 Storing XML as CLOB

In this section we discuss how to store XML as a CLOB.

6.2.1 Using CLOB and the OracleText Cartridge

The simplest approach for handling XML documents is to use relational tables with one or more CLOB columns, supplemented by structured information that classifies and characterizes the documents. Using relational concepts, the XML documents can thus be organized in the sense of containers as provided by native XML databases. However, storing and retrieving documents is only possible as a whole. In fact, updates of XML repositories are still a fundamental research issue for which Oracle has no solution as yet.

In Oracle there is principally no difference between CLOBs and strings except that a CLOB can hold up to 4GB. Both CLOBs and strings offer the same functionality, such as comparisons and substring search. This allows for only few search capabilities unless you're using additional structured information. Such querying is in general too simple for advanced XML applications.

The OracleText cartridge helps to remedy this deficit: OracleText is a server-based implementation for free-text search in any kind of document. Due to the relevance of XML, the cartridge offers special support for XML documents: New query forms `WITHIN`, `INPATH`, and `HASPATH` with XPath expressions can be used for retrieving documents. However, to benefit from these features, creating text indexes and defining section groups must be performed up-front, as we will explain later.

Let us assume that Listing 6.1 is an XML document that describes a customer placing orders.

Listing 6.1 Customer Example

```
<?xml version="1.0" encoding="UTF-8" standalone="yes" ?>
<!DOCTYPE Kunde SYSTEM "kunde.dtd">
<Customer>
  <CNo> 10 </CNo>
  <Name>
    <Firstname> Lucky </Firstname>
```

```
    <Lastname> Luke </Lastname>
  </Name>
  <Address>
    <Zip> 12345 </Zip>
    <City> Bull </City>
    <Street> Cows Xing </Street>
    <Houseno> 8 </Houseno>
  </Address>
  <Phone> 012/3456 </Phone>
  <Phone> 023/4567 </Phone>
  <Order ONo="4711">
    <Entry> 01.01.99 </Entry>
    <Positions>
      <Position PNo="1">
        <Price Currency="US$"> 1.11 </Price>
        <Amount> 111 </Amount>
        <Part> Screw </Part>
      </Position>
      <Position PNo="2">
        <Price Currency="Euro"> 2.22 </Price>
        <Amount> 22 </Amount>
        <Part> Nut </Part>
      </Position>
    </Positions>
  </Order>
</Customer>
```

6.2.2 Search Predicates in OracleText

The essential concept of OracleText is a `CONTAINS` function, which can be used in SQL directly to specify search patterns. Let us assume that customer documents are stored in a CLOB column `txt` in a table `DocTab` (`id INTEGER, txt CLOB`). For example, *Retrieve those tuples in* `DocTab` *that contain "Lucky" in the column* `txt`.The SQL code for this is shown in Listing 6.2.

Listing 6.2 Simple contains Query

```
SELECT id, txt, SCORE(1)
FROM DocTab
WHERE CONTAINS (txt, 'Lucky', 1) > 0
```

Rather than yielding a not/found result, the function CONTAINS assesses the occurrences of a term. It returns a score value in the range of 0...100 determining the relevance of the search pattern: 0 means "not found in the document," while 100 represents a perfect match. The value is computed by a complex formula based on the number of occurrences. Usually, CONTAINS is used in a comparison CONTAINS (. . .)>0 to ask for any occurrences. The third parameter of CONTAINS is an integer such as 1, which is a placeholder for the relevance. Its value can be obtained by applying the SCORE function to the placeholder: SCORE(1) yields the relevance of the term "Lucky" as part of the result.

OracleText provides several operators to affect the search string, for instance:

- Logical operators such as & (AND), | (OR), and ~ (NOT) are possible: Taking "Lucky & Luke' as a search term, both terms "Lucky' and "Luke' must occur in the document. The overall relevance is the minimum of both individual relevances.
- NEAR($term_1$, . . . ,$term_n$,m) requires the list of terms to occur in a sentence of a given length m.
- Special functions vary the search strings and expand queries: stem ($) to search for terms with the same linguistic root, soundex (!) to include words that have similar sounds, fuzzy search (?) for words that are spelled similarly to the specified term (e.g., because of misspellings), as well as the well-known SQL wildcards (_) and (%).
- Thresholds like "term.n" can be defined to eliminate texts that score below a threshold number n.
- A thesaurus is available with corresponding operators such as Preferred Term, Related Term, Broader Term, Narrower Term, and Synonym.

Listing 6.3 demonstrates the power:

Listing 6.3 More Complex contains Query

```
SELECT id, SCORE(1)
FROM DocTab
WHERE CONTAINS (txt, '!Smith | $sing', 1) > 0
```

This query takes also into account documents that contain "Smythe" (due to "!") just as "sang" and "sung" (due to "$").

Further important concepts are

- **Stoplists:** Identify the words in a language that are not to be indexed. For instance, it is not sensible to index articles and pronouns like "the" and "my".

- **Filtering:** Allows indexing documents in binary formats such as Word documents or PDF. Oracle stores them in their native format and uses filters to build temporary plain text versions for indexing.
- **Lexers:** Can be installed to define case sensitivity and the handling of special characters. For example, the lexer can be told to remove characters like ".", "!", and "?" from a token before indexing, because their purpose is only to indicate the end of a sentence.
- **Datastore:** A datastore preference specifies how the text is stored. Besides keeping documents in a text column, it is possible to store documents in several columns, in a nested table, in several rows, or in a file. Files can be handled directly or via a URL. The `txt` column then contains a URL pointing to the document instead of keeping the text itself.

This so far is the general functionality of OracleText, which can certainly be used for XML documents, too, but does not exhaust the full potential of XML.

6.2.3 XML-Specific Functionality

In order to satisfy the need for queries that are more related to XML, `CONTAINS` can be combined with advanced text operators:

- A `WITHIN` operator restricts the occurrence of a term to a text section instead of searching in the whole document: `CONTAINS(txt, 'term WITHIN SENTENCE',1) > 0`. Predefined sections are `SENTENCE` and `PARAGRAPH` to look for terms in a sentence or paragraph, respectively. Further sections are XML elements and their attribute zones. Corresponding queries are `'term WITHIN tag'` and `'term WITHIN attr@tag'`. The first one demands the term to occur between a pair `<tag> . . . </tag>`, while the second one searches for the term in the attribute value `<tag attr=" . . . ">`.
- Two additional operators `HASPATH` and `INPATH` allow for XPath queries. `HASPATH` exists in two different forms, the first one `'HASPATH(xpath)'` asking for the existence of a certain xpath without any search term. A second conditional form `'HASPATH(xpath="value")'` checks the value of an element specified by an `xpath`. Only equality and inequality are allowed in those conditions.
- The `INPATH` operator has the form `term INPATH(xpath)` and restricts the search to an arbitrary XPath fragment: The document must possess a fragment qualified by `xpath`, and the term must occur within.

All the other operators such as "&" and "|" can still be used and combined with these XML operators. The form `WITHIN` allows for terms like `'Screw WITHIN Part'` and is quite general as any occurrence of the <Part> tag is taken into account: The form is equivalent to `'Screw INPATH(//Part)'`, asking for the tag at any level. Nesting `WITHIN` operators, e.g. `'Screw WITHIN Part WITHIN Order'`, is also possible, but offers not the flexibility of XPath expressions. In contrast, `INPATH` uses an XPath expression to determine the element more precisely, for instance, beginning from the root and using conditions: `'Screw INPATH(/Customer [ CNo="10"] /Order/Part)'`.

To demonstrate the differences between `INPATH` and `HASPATH`, let us consider another example:

- `'Luke INPATH(/Name/Lastname)'` finds <Name> . . . <Lastname> xyzLukeXyz </Lastname> . . . </Name>. The term `'Luke'` must be embedded in <Name> and <Lastname> elements.
- `'HASPATH(/Name/Lastname="Luke")'` is only satisfied if the inner element matches the given value exactly, i.e., without any leading or following characters: <Name> . . . <Lastname>Luke</Lastname> . . . </Name>. A value `xyzLuckyXyz` is not accepted any longer.
- `'Luke INPATH(/Name/Lastname[ Lastname="Luke"])'` has the same effect.

Oracle supports the full XPath syntax. Hence, more complex queries than those presented so far are possible. The following example shows an attribute-sensitive search:

```
'Screw INPATH(//Order[ @ONo="4711"])'
```

The term "`Screw`" must occur at any level in a customer's `Order` element having an `ONo` attribute with value 4711.

Note OracleText supports an XML-like retrieval of text documents, but the result is always a CLOB. Hence to extract information from a resulting document, an XML parser must be used. The object type `XMLType`, which will be discussed shortly, offers additional functionality to extract parts from a document. Furthermore, in spite of querying with Xpath, SQL is still used to formulate the body of the query.

6.2.4 Prerequisites

In order to use the `CONTAINS` function, some prerequisites are necessary, making the handling complicated. Generally, `CONTAINS` requires a text index for the column that contains text documents. It is just then that indexing takes place—that is, that terms are correctly found in documents. Furthermore, the `WITHIN` operator needs a text section, called *section group*, which can be defined and added to an index. The most comfortable way for XML is to use a `PATH_SECTION_GROUP`, because it takes into account all the tags and attributes by default and supports all the operators WITHIN, HASPATH, and INPATH. The definition of a PATH_SECTION_GROUP section group myGroup is as follows:

```
CTX_DDL.create_section_group('myGroup', 'PATH_SECTION_GROUP')
```

Afterwards, the text index on the txt column can be created by using a special index type CTXSYS.context and by setting the section group myGroup, as shown in Listing 6.4.

Listing 6.4 CTXSYS.context Index

```
CREATE INDEX myIdx ON DocTab(txt) INDEXTYPE IS CTXSYS.context
PARAMETERS ('SECTION GROUP myGroup')
```

Without a section group, no CONTAINS queries are possible.

The PARAMETERS clause is also important for setting other preferences like datastore, filter, wordlist, and lexers. For example, the type of source of the text can be specified in PARAMETERS analogously by creating a datastore preference: PARAMETERS ('section group myGroup datastore myStorage . . . '). Again, the preference myStorage and others have to be defined beforehand, as shown in Listing 6.5.

Listing 6.5 myStorage Preferences

```
CTX_DDL.create_preference('myStorage', 'FILE_DATASTORE')
CTX_DDL.set_attribute('myStorage',
'/home/text:/local1/home/myTexts')
```

Using the property FILE_DATASTORE, the values of the text attributes are interpreted as filenames. Searching the files is done according to the paths /home/text and /local1/home/myTexts that are defined by means of set_attribute.

As mentioned previously, a PATH_SECTION_GROUP is the most comfortable section group as it supports all the CONTAINS queries without any further action. All the tags and all their attributes are automatically indexed.

Another section group is AUTO_SECTION_GROUP. It behaves similar to PATH_SECTION_GROUP and places indexes on all tags and attributes. But tags and attributes can be used only in WITHIN queries; INPATH and HASPATH are not allowed.

On the other extreme, XML_SECTION_GROUP requires a definition of all the tags to be indexed. Every tag or attribute to be used must be specified explicitly by calling add_. . ._section procedures in the manner shown in Listing 6.6.

Listing 6.6 add_ . . . _section Procedures

```
CTX_DDL.create_section_group('myXmlGroup', 'XML_SECTION_GROUP')
CTX_DDL.add_attribute_section('myXmlGroup', 'mySection1',
'attr@tag')
CTX_DDL.add_zone_section('myXmlGroup', 'mySection2', 'docType(tag)')
```

`mySection1` is the name of an attribute section that indexes the attribute `attr` within `tag`. `mySection2` represents a zone section—that is, the search area has elements `<tag>` . . . `</tag>` for a certain document type `docType`. The `docType` is optional. Afterwards, `WITHIN mySection1/2` can be used.

Further groups that can be used for plain or HTML text are:

- `BASIC_SECTION_GROUP`
- `HTML_SECTION_GROUP` for HTML documents
- `NEWS_SECTION_GROUP` for newsgroups (formatted according to RFC1036)

6.3 XMLType

Since XML documents can be considered a new structured data type in object-relational databases, new advantages arise, which are discussed in Klettke and Meyer (2000), Banerjee et al. (2000), and Cheng and Xu (2000a) in general.

6.3.1 Object Type XMLType

Oracle9i follows this approach and introduces a new object type `XMLType`. The main purpose of `XMLType` is to encapsulate the CLOB storage and to provide XPath-based methods to ease the handling of XML documents. `XMLType` can be used like any other Oracle type in tables. `XMLType` provides several methods for processing XML documents:

- `STATIC createXML(xml VARCHAR | CLOB)`
- `MEMBER getClobVal() RETURN CLOB`
- `MEMBER getStringVal() RETURN VARCHAR`
- `MEMBER getNumberVal() RETURN NUMBER`
- `MEMBER isFragment() RETURN NUMBER`

The static method `createXML` takes an XML string or a CLOB and creates an `XMLType` object, thereby checking well-formedness but not the validity with respect to a DTD or an XML schema. The methods `getClobVal` and `getStringVal` return the `XMLType` content in a serialized format. `getNumberVal` yields a `NUMBER` value and requires the text to be numeric. Hence, `getNumberVal` cannot be applied to elements of the form <CNo> "10" </CNo>; the XPath function `text()` must be used beforehand to extract the numeric value "10". Two further methods of `XMLType` benefit from an XPath subset for querying:

- `MEMBER existsNode(VARCHAR xpath) RETURN NUMBER` applied over the `XMLType` document checks if an XPath determines any valid nodes.
- `MEMBER extract(VARCHAR xpath) RETURN XMLType` extracts fragments out of `XMLType` documents and returns them as an `XMLType` object.

The function `existsNode` is useful to ask for the existence of elements, while `extract` returns a fragment qualified by XPath. Hence, `existsNode` covers the XML-specific parts of OracleText. The function `extract` provides parser functionality, which is not available in OracleText. Moreover, it is important to note that both functions do not demand OracleText or explicit indexing.

Let us now assume a table `XMLTypeTab (id:INTEGER, txt: XMLType)` using an `XMLType` column instead of a CLOB. Listing 6.7 presents an example of how to handle `XMLType` objects.

Listing 6.7 XMLType Example

```
INSERT INTO XMLTypeTab
VALUES(1, SYS.XMLType.createXML
     ('<?xml version="1.0"?> <Customer> <CNo> 10 </CNo> <Name>
     . . .
     </Customer>')
```

An XML document, given as a string, is created with `createXML`, thereby checking the well-formedness—this is the easiest way to create `XMLType` objects. Later we describe another way, namely SQL functions that return `XMLType` objects by extracting information from a given `XMLType` or by using relational data.

Listing 6.8 shows an example how to extract information.

Listing 6.8 Qualify XML Documents

```
SELECT x.txt.extract('Customer//Phone')
FROM XMLTypeTab x
WHERE x.txt.existsNode('Customer//Order') = 1
AND x.txt.extract('/Customer/CNo/text()').getNumberVal() = 10
```

This example shows how to qualify XML documents and how to extract parts. A SELECT-FROM-WHERE is used to formulate the overall query. The query computes a list of phone numbers for customer 10. The extract function in SELECT uses an XPath to extract any occurrence of the Phone-tag beneath a Customer-tag. existsNode requires the existence of an Order-tag for the customer. Owing to the XPath function text() and the XMLType method getNumberVal(), XPath and SQL can be combined in conditions. Extracting the CNo-element, text() computes the text of that element, whereupon getNumberVal() yields an integer that can be used in SQL conditions.

The same type of extract-condition is possible in UPDATE and DELETE statements—for example, to delete the documents that contain a customer with CNo=10 having placed an order.

There are some restrictions on XPath expressions. The following features are currently not available:

- conditions in [ ]
- functions count(), sibling:: etc.

That is, only path expressions with / and //, possibly ending with text(), wildcards, attribute access, and indexing [i] are currently allowed. However, text indexes can be defined for XMLType objects, too, so that the full OracleText functionality becomes available.

The method extract is a simple and easy-to-use substitute for an XML parser. Combined with getNumberVal and getStringVal, it can especially be employed to extract data from XML and to store in structured tables. Listing 6.9 shows an example.

Listing 6.9 Extract Method Example

```
INSERT INTO Customer (No, Name, Address)
(SELECT x.extract('/Customer/CNo/text()').getNumberVal(),
        x.extract('/Customer/Name/Firstname/text()').getStringVal()
        || ' ' ||
        x.extract('/Customer/Name/Lastname/text()').getStringVal(),
        x.extract('/Customer/Address/Zip/text()').getStringVal()
        || ' ' ||
        x.extract('/Customer/Address/City/text()').getStringVal()
        || ' ' ||
        x.extract('/Customer/Address/Street/text()').getStringVal()
        || ' ' ||
        x.extract('/Customer/Address/Houseno/text()').getStringVal()
FROM XMLTypeTab x
```

Here, parts of the XML document are extracted and stored in a table `Customer (No INT, Name VARCHAR, Address VARCHAR)`. The `firstname` and `lastname` values are concatenated ('||') to a single name, just as the parts (`Zip`, `City`, etc.) of an address are.

6.3.2 Processing of XMLType in Java

The JAR archive `xdb_g.jar` contains a Java class `oracle.xdb.XMLType` that directly corresponds to the object type `XMLType`. This Java class possesses the same functionality as the SQL object type. All the `XMLType` methods are also available for the Java class—for example, `java.lang.String getStringVal()`, `oracle.sql.CLOB getClob()` in the same manner. However, both methods `createXML(Connection, oracle.sql.clob)` and `createXML(Connection, String)` require a JDBC database `Connection` as a first parameter.

For example, the processing of `XMLType` objects in Java is shown in Listing 6.10.

Listing 6.10 XMLType Objects and Java

```
OracleResultSet ors = (OracleResultSet)stmt.executeQuery
                      ("SELECT x.txt.extract( . . . ) FROM
                      XMLTypeTab x"); . . .
while (ors.next()) {
   oracle.xdb.XMLType t = (oracle.xdb.XMLType) ors.getOPAQUE(1);
   . . .  handling of XMLType t in Java with getStringVal, extract
                      etc.  . . .
}
```

`OracleResultSet` is a subclass of JDBC's `ResultSet`, enhancing the original JDBC methods. `OracleResultSet` has a method `OPAQUE getOPAQUE(int)` that can be used to read `XMLType` objects from the database. Similarly, the JDBC `Statement` classes possess a `setObject` method to pass XMLType Java objects to statements as parameters. In order to handle null values and to register output parameters, there is also a type constant `OracleTypes.OPAQUE`.

6.4 Using XSU for Fine-Grained Storage

Handling XML documents in a fine-grained manner is supported by Oracle's XSU (XML SQL Utility). XSU is a programmatic interface for Java and PL/SQL programs. XSU supports two directions:

1. XSU transforms data from object-relational tables or views into XML; XML documents are generated out of relational data.
2. Splitting XML documents into pieces and storing them in tables the other way around.

6.4.1 Canonical Mapping

The basis for both directions is a schematic mapping from relational structures to XML. Given an SQL query related to any tables or views, an XML document is produced:

- The whole query result is enclosed by `<ROWSET>` . . . `< /ROWSET>`
- Each tuple of the result is put in `<ROW>` . . . `</ROW>`
- Attribute values turn into tags `<Name>` . . . `</Name>` taking the column name

If aliases are used in SQL queries, the aliases are taken as tags instead of column names. Thus, an alias is useful to give expressions such as `COUNT(*)` a readable name.

These basic mechanisms produce XML documents. This allows for only simple XML documents having a limited nesting level—that is, `<ROWSET>`, `<ROW>`, `<Attributename>`. But the mapping is also able to handle object-oriented concepts in the following way:

- **Object types:** If an attribute is object-valued, then the object type's attributes become inner tags according to the internal structure.
- **Collections:** The name of a V Array or a nested table type becomes a tag to enclose the collection.

  The elements of the inner collection use the collection tag and append `_ITEM`.
- **References:** A type tag with an object identifier uses the syntax `<Tag REFTYPE="REF T"> 0ABD1F6. . . </Tag>`.

Furthermore, it is worth mentioning that attributes or aliases starting with an at sign (@) have a special meaning: The values are taken for tag attributes instead of tag values.

The example in Listing 6.11 assumes two tables and three user-defined types for keeping customer information and their phone numbers.

Listing 6.11 Customers and Phone Numbers

```
CREATE TABLE Customer (CNo INT, FirstName VARCHAR, LastName
                  VARCHAR, Zip VARCHAR, City VARCHAR, Street
                  VARCHAR, Houseno VARCHAR);
CREATE TABLE Phonelist (CNo INT, Phone VARCHAR);
CREATE TYPE Name_Type AS OBJECT (First VARCHAR, Last VARCHAR);
CREATE TYPE Address_Type AS OBJECT (Zip VARCHAR, City VARCHAR,
                                    Street VARCHAR, Houseno VARCHAR);
CREATE TYPE Phone_Tab AS TABLE OF VARCHAR;
```

The next query (see Listing 6.12) produces a nested structure, constructing objects of type Name_Type with first name and last name, building an Address_Type object, and putting the customer's phones in a Phone_tab.

Listing 6.12 Nested Structure Query

```
SELECT c.CNo AS @CNo,
       Name_Type(c.FirstName,c.LastName) AS Name,
       Address_Type(c.Zip,c.City,c.Street,c.Houseno) AS Address,
       CAST (MULTISET (SELECT Phone FROM Phonelist WHERE CNo=c.CNo)
                     AS Phone_Tab) AS Phones
FROM Customer c
```

The query result possesses the following structure:

```
(Cno int, Name Name_Type, Address Address_Type, Phones Phone_Tab)
```

whereby Phone_Tab represents an inner table—that is, each value is a list of phone numbers. Each user-defined object type possesses a constructor like Address_Type to create objects; the parameters correspond to the internal type structure. CAST/MULTISET converts a SELECT-FROM-WHERE query into a collection, here of type Phone_Tab. That is, we obtain a "nested result table" having an inner table of phone numbers for each customer.

Processing the query in interactive SQL produces an XML document with a complex nested structure, as shown in Listing 6.13.

Listing 6.13 Query Output

```
<?xml version="1.0"?>
<ROWSET>
   <ROW NUM="1" CNO="10">
      <NAME>
         <FIRSTNAME> Lucky </FIRSTNAME>
         <LASTNAME> Luke </LASTNAME>
      </NAME>
      <ADDRESS>
         <ZIP> 12345 </ZIP>
         <CITY> Bull </CITY>
         <STREET> Cows Xing </STREET>
         <HOUSENO> 8 </HOUSENO>
      </ADDRESS>
      <PHONES>
         <PHONES_ITEM> 012/3456 </PHONES_ITEM>
         <PHONES_ITEM> 023/4567 </PHONES_ITEM>
      </PHONES>
   </ROW>
   <ROW NUM="2" CNO="20">
   . . .
</ROWSET>
```

Each tuple is put into <ROW> . . . </ROW> and automatically numbered by an attribute NUM. The attributes of an object type are taken as tags—for example, FIRSTNAME and LASTNAME according to the inner structure of the Name attribute. The XML representation of a nested table uses a PHONES tag for the whole collection, and PHONES_ITEM for each entry.

Since the column CNo is renamed to @CNo, the value is taken as an attribute value CNO="10" in the XML document.

Similarly, an object view can be defined as shown in Listing 6.14.

Listing 6.14 Create a View

```
CREATE TYPE Customer_Type AS OBJECT
( CNo     INTEGER,
  Name    Name_Type,
  Addr    Address_Type,
  Phones  Phone_List
);
CREATE VIEW MyCustomer OF Customer_Type AS
SELECT . . . query from above . . . ;
```

The object type Customer_Type describes the structure of the query that is used to define the object view. Then, SELECT * FROM MyCustomer would return the same XML document. The mapping is then based upon the structure of the object type Customer_Type.

Hence, the approach gains power pretty much from object-relational features and object view mechanisms: Applying object-relational concepts allows for nesting of tags to any depth according to the complex structure. Particularly, the object-relational concepts provide a powerful means to obtain nested XML structures even in case of 1NF tables.

Oracle's XSU defines a Java interface and two packages in the proprietary PL/SQL language to use XSU in programs:

1. OracleXMLQuery and DBMS_XMLQuery, respectively
2. OracleXMLSave and DBMS_XMLSave, respectively

In the following sections, only the handling in Java is presented. The principles of the PL/SQL packages are similar.

6.4.2 Retrieval

Listing 6.15 shows how to use XSU for executing a query in a Java environment and producing XML.

Listing 6.15 XSU Example

```
Connection conn = //JDBC database connection
   Drivermanager.getConnection("jdbc:oracle:thin:@myhost:1521:mydb",
"scott", "tiger");
OracleXMLQuery q = new OracleXMLQuery(conn,
"SELECT . . . FROM  . . .  WHERE  . . . ");
org.w3c.dom.Document domDoc =q.getXMLDOM();  // DOM representation
XMLDocument xmlDoc = (XMLDocument)domDoc;
StringWriter s = new StringWriter(10000);
xmlDoc.print(new PrintWriter(s));
System.out.println(s.toString());
q.close();
```

The JDBC database connection specifies the URL of the database and the schema "scott" to be queried. The Java class OracleXMLQuery possesses two constructors that take an SQL query either as a string value or as a JDBC ResultSet:

- `OracleXMLQuery(Connection conn, String query)`
- `OracleXMLQuery(Connection conn, ResultSet rset)`

The resulting document can be obtained in different forms by various `get` methods:

- `java.lang.String getXMLString([int metaType])`
- `java.lang.String getXMLString(org.w3c.dom.Node root [ ,int metaType])`
- `org.w3c.dom.Document getXMLDOC([ int metaType ])`
- `org.w3c.dom.Document getXMLDOC(org.w3c.dom.Node root [ ,int metaType])`
- `void getXMLSAX(org.xml.sax.ContentHandler sax)`

`getXMLString` creates a string representation as output. A variant of `getXMLString` uses a `node-parameter` that becomes the root of the resulting document. An optional `int`-parameter `metaType` specifies whether a DTD or a XML Schema is to be created for the document. The constants for `metaType` are `DTD`, `SCHEMA`, and `NONE` (the default).

The `getXMLDOC` method possesses the same parameters but returns the resulting document in a DOM representation. The code in Listing 6.15 passes the `Document` object to a `PrintWriter` for output. Using the DOM representation, the complete functionality of the Oracle XML Development Kit (XDK) can be used then, for example, to parse the document, to perform XSLT transformations, to extract parts of the document, to create a DTD, and so on.

A further method `getXMLSAX` assigns a SAX-`ContentHandler` to the document. Hence, the document can be handled in a SAX-conforming manner. The parameter `sax` must be previously registered.

`OracleXMLQuery` has various methods for processing results incrementally:

- `void setMaxRows(int max)`: Processes a certain amount of tuples
- `void setSkipRows(int n)`: Skips n tuples (being already read)
- `restart()`: Executes the query again (for the next increment)
- `long getNumRowsProcessed()`: Returns the total number of processed tuples
- `void keepObjectOpen(boolean)`: Lets the query (i.e., the underlying ResultSet) remain open for the database session

These methods are useful to convert a query result piecewise into several XML documents: Setting the bulk to n by means of `setMaxRows`, a loop skips i*n tuples in the i-th run before restarting the query.

Further methods of `OracleXMLQuery` enable one to rename the predefined tags:

- `void setRowTag(java.lang.String tagname)`: Renames the `ROW` tag.
- `void setRowsetTag(java.lang.String tagname)`: Renames the `ROWSET` tag.
- `void setRowldAttrName(java.lang.String tagname)`: Renames the `NUM` attribute of the `ROW` tag.
- `void setRowIdAttrValue(java.lang.String tagname)`: Determines an attribute the values of which are taken for the `NUM` attribute; passing the null object, the rows are sequentially numbered starting with 1.
- `void useTypeForCollElemTag(boolean)`: Tags the entries of the inner collection with the type name of the collection; by default `_ITEM` is attached to the collection tag.
- `void useUpperCaseTagNames()`: Puts tag names in uppercase.
- `void useLowerCaseTagNames()`: Puts tag names in lowercase.

However, the best flexibility is obtained by transforming documents with the help of style sheets. XSL (eXtensible Stylesheet Language) is a powerful language to describe transformations. Particularly, the sublanguage XSLT (XSL Transformations) allows one to transform XML into another text-based format. XSLT is thus ideal to perform additional transformations on the resulting XML document. In XSU, a style sheet is registered as follows by passing a Java String or Reader object:

- `void setXSLT(java.lang.String stylesheet)`
- `void setXSLT(Reader stylesheet)`

Additional methods are not explained here in detail. For instance:

- `void setStylesheetHeader(java.lang.String uri [, java.lang. String type ])` : Sets the style sheet header in the document
- `org.w3c.dom.Document getXMLSchema()`: Creates an XML schema for the result
- `String getXMLMetaData(int metaType, boolean mitVersion)`: Generates a DTD or an XML schema as a string

6.4.3 Modifications

The other way around, XML documents that conform to the canonical mapping can be stored in a relational table or in a view in a fine-grained manner. Using views, several tables beneath the view definition can be filled. Otherwise, only the storage in one table is possible.

The piece of code in Listing 6.16 shows the principle. Assume the URL of an XML file is given.

Listing 6.16 Using Views

```
OracleXMLSave sav = new OracleXMLSave(conn, "MyCustomer");
sav.insertXML(sav.getUrl("http://www.myServer.com/myFile.xml"));
sav.close();
```

The method `getURL(String)` of class `OracleXMLSave` is useful for processing files by means of a URL: Given a string that contains a filename or a URL, `getURL` creates a `java.net.URL` object, which can be used for `insertXML`. The content of the file is stored in the view `MyCustomer`.

The referenced XML document must certainly have a structure that fits to the tables in order to store the derived tuples. One exception to the rule is that tags in the document may be omitted; tags that do not occur are stored as `NULL` values.

The constructor of `OracleXMLSave` takes a table or view that is to be filled. Views are useful if XML documents are to be spread across several tables; the view abstracts from the underlying tables, thus defining a mapping that breaks down documents into pieces. The mechanism of view update is used thereby. In general, updating views requires an `INSTEAD OF` trigger that defines the effect of `INSERT`, `UPDATE`, and `DELETE` on the underlying base tables.

`OracleXMLSave` possesses three main methods for manipulation:

- `int insertXML(org.w3c.dom.Document)`
- `int updateXML(org.w3c.dom.Document)`
- `int deleteXML(org.w3c.dom.Document)`

The methods are also available with alternative parameters of type `java.lang.String`, `Reader`, `InputStream`, and `java.net.URL`, each representing the XML document. All the methods return the number of modified tuples.

In case of `updateXML` and `deleteXML`, the given document is taken as a pattern for qualifying documents—that is, the document determines the query values of the resulting `WHERE` condition. Which attributes are really participating in the condition are specified separately by means of the method `void setKeyColumnList(String[] )`. Several attribute names can be passed as a String array. The corresponding tag values are extracted and used in the condition.

The document also defines the values to be changed or stored in case of `updateXML` and `insertXML`. That is, the document contains the new values being used for `UPDATE . . . SET (updateXML)` and `INSERT INTO . . . VALUES (insertXML)`. The attributes to be modified are specified in a method `void setUpdateColumnList(String[] )`. See Listing 6.17 for an example.

Listing 6.17 insertXML Example

```
OracleXMLSave sav = new OracleXMLSave(conn, "MyCustomer");
String[] list = new String[2];
list[0] = "CNo";          // insert only CNo and
list[1] = "Name";         // Name in view MyCustomer
sav.setUpdateColumnList(list);
Document doc = sav.getUrl("myUrl");
sav.insertXML(doc);       // extract CNo and Name and insert them
```

This program performs the following SQL statement:

```
INSERT INTO MyCustomer (CNo, Name)
VALUES (:cno, :n)
```

The host variables `:cno` and `:n` are the `CNo`- and `Name` values extracted from the XML document. An update is shown in Listing 6.18.

Listing 6.18 updateXML Example

```
list[0] = "Name";             // modify Name and Address
list[1] = "Address";          // in view MyCustomer
sav.setUpdateColumnList(list);
sav.setKeyColumnList("CNo");
sav.updateXML(doc);          // all entries having the
                             //CNo-value are changed
```

Hence, the effect of `updateXML` is shown in Listing 6.19.

Listing 6.19 Effect of updateXML

```
UPDATE MyCustomer
SET Name    = :name,     /* from the document */
    Address = :address   /* from the document */
WHERE CNo = :cno         /* from the document */
```

Further methods allow for bulk operations and determine the Commit behavior:

- `void setBatchSize(int n)`: Helps reduce client/server communication—n operations are collected and transmitted as a bulk operation to the database server.
- `void setCommitBatch(int n)`: Defines simple transactional behavior—a commit is performed after every n operations.

Again, tags can be renamed by using the set methods such as setRowTag. Furthermore, a style sheet can be registered with setXSLT; it is executed before the document is written to the database. This is another effective manner to affect the storage—that is, use XSLT to transfer an XML document into a suitable form that can then be handled by the canonical mapping.

6.5 Building XML Documents from Relational Data

Oracle's version 9i provides several new SQL functions and PL/SQL packages that can be used to handle XML documents. The SQL functions process XMLType objects—for example, to ask for the existence of certain nodes, to extract fragments, or to create XMLType objects by using SQL queries and table data.

6.5.1 SQL Functions existsNode and extract

Two built-in SQL functions extract and existsNode handle XMLType objects in SQL statements. They behave similar to the methods of XMLType of the same name even if the signature is slightly different; the result is again an XMLType object. Both methods are directly usable in SQL statements, as shown in Listing 6.20.

Listing 6.20 extract and existsNode Example

```
SELECT extract(x.txt, '/Customer//Phone')
FROM XMLTypeTab x
WHERE existsNode(x.txt, 'Customer//Order') = 1
AND extract(x.txt, '/Customer/CNo/text()').getNumberVal() = 10
```

The principle is exactly the same as described earlier except that the XMLType object is passed as a parameter. Hence, there is nothing really new. The main benefit of these functions is that both can be used in function indexes, thus speeding up performance for queries like the one shown in Listing 6.20.

6.5.2 The SQL Function SYS_XMLGen

SYS_XMLGen is a standalone function that assumes one SELECT expression, the result of which is then converted into XML. The function converts a value into an XMLType object similar to XSU—that is, the structure is defined by a canonical mapping. Again, object views can be used to affect the structure of the XML document. But in contrast to XSU, only one expression is allowed in the query.

```
SELECT SYS_XMLGen(Lastname) FROM Customer WHERE CNo > 1
```

The result of this query consists of one XMLType object for each tuple. Each object represents a document like <LASTNAME> Luke </LASTNAME> putting a database value Luke into tags. Similar to XSU, the attribute names are directly taken as tags. In case of function calls or complex SELECT expressions, the tag <ROW> will be used by default. However, <ROW> can be renamed by calling SYS_XMLGenFormatType.createFormat within SYS_XMLGen, as shown in Listing 6.21.

Listing 6.21 SYS_XMLGen Example

```
SELECT SYS_XMLGen(c.Address.Zip || ' ' || c.Address.City,
                  SYS_XMLGenFormatType.createFormat('TOWN')
).getClobVal()
FROM MyCustomer c
WHERE CNo = 1
```

Listing 6.21 creates the XML document shown in Listing 6.22.

Listing 6.22 Example Output Using SYS_XMLGenFormatType

```
<?xml version="1.0"?>
<TOWN> 12345 Bull </TOWN>
```

The getStringValue/getClobValue methods produce a string for an XMLType object. Without calling SYS_XMLGenFormatType, the result would be the XML document shown in Listing 6.23.

Listing 6.23 Example Output without SYS_XMLGenFormatType

```
<?xml version="1.0"?>
<ROW> 12345 Bull </ROW>
```

Because the SELECT expression uses a concatenation as a function call, there is no direct column name that could be taken. Using SYS_XMLGenFormatType, a style sheet can be registered, too, to transform the resulting document afterwards.

The single argument used in SYS_XMLGen can be any expression—for example, an XMLType object, a function call, or an object-valued attribute. Despite the limitation to one expression, the function possesses the same power as XSU, if complex objects or object views are used. For example:

```
SELECT SYS_XMLGen(VALUE(x))
FROM MyCustomer x
```

The expression VALUE(x) selects an object of the complex object view MyCustomer: The object is now processed. This view determines the inner structure of the query result and thus the structure of the XML document.

If you pass an XMLType object into SYS_XMLGen, the function encloses the fragment with an element whose tag name is the default "ROW". Hence, the SYS_XMLGen function is useful for converting XMLType fragments (e.g., resulting from extraction) into a well-formed document. Thanks to SYS_XMLGen, the result receives an outer tagging:

```
SELECT SYS_XMLGen(x.doc.extract('/Customer/Phone'))
FROM XMLTypeTab x
```

The extract method returns for each tuple a fragment:

```
<PHONE> 012/3456 </PHONE> <PHONE> 023/4567 </PHONE>
```

consisting of several PHONE elements: There are several occurrences of <PHONE> in the document. SYS_XMLGen then puts <ROW> around the fragment (ROW because extract() is an invocation of a method):

```
<ROW> <PHONE> 012/3456 </PHONE> <PHONE> 023/4567 </PHONE> </ROW>.
```

Owing to the surrounding ROW tag, each tuple is now well formed with regard to XML.

6.5.3 The SQL Function SYS_XMLAgg

While SYS_XMLGen processes each tuple individually—each tuple becomes an XMLType object—SYS_XMLAgg is an aggregate function that takes the whole result and aggregates all the tuples to a single XMLType, enclosing it with a tag ROWSET. The tag ROWSET can again be renamed with SYS_XMLGenFormatType. As an example, in Listing 6.24 we combine SYS_XMLAgg with extract.

Listing 6.24 SYS_XMLAgg Example

```
SELECT SYS_XMLAgg(x.doc.extract('//Customer/Phone'),
       SYS_XMLGenFormatType.createFormat('LIST')) .getClobVal()
FROM XMLTypeTab x
```

The extract method returns an XMLType fragment for each tuple i first of all:

```
<PHONE> phone 1 of tuple i </PHONE> <PHONE> phone 2 of tuple i
</PHONE>  . . .
```

that is, a list of PHONE elements. These fragments are aggregated by SYS_XMLAgg. The result is one XMLType object, as shown in Listing 6.25.

Listing 6.25 Example Aggregated Output

```
<LIST>
   <PHONE> phone 1 of tuple 1 </PHONE>
   <PHONE> phone 2 of tuple 1 </PHONE>
   . . .
   <PHONE> phone 1 of tuple 2 </PHONE>
   . . .
</LIST>
```

The result concatenates all the phone numbers of all the tuples. The association between a phone number and its customer tuple is, however, now lost.

The functions SYS_XMLGen and SYS_XMLAgg can be combined, too: SYS_XMLGen yields an XMLType object for each tuple so that all those objects can be aggregated by SYS_XMLAgg, as shown in Listing 6.26.

Listing 6.26 Using SYS_XMLGen and SYS_XMLAgg Together

```
SELECT SYS_XMLAgg(SYS_XMLGen(CNo)).getClobVal()
FROM Customer
GROUP BY Cname
```

The GROUP BY query itself computes the set of customer numbers having the same name. Using SYS_XMLAgg the numbers of each group are concatenated to one single tuple, as shown in Listing 6.27.

Listing 6.27 Example Concatenated Output

```
<ROWSET>
  <CNO> 10 </CNO>
  <CNO> 20 </CNO>
</ROWSET>
<ROWSET>
  <CNO> 15 </CNO>
  <CNO> 25 </CNO>
  <CNO> 35 </CNO>
</ROWSET>
```

6.5.4 PL/SQL Package DBMS_XMLGen

The PL/SQL package DBMS_XMLGen makes it possible to generate XML documents from query results in PL/SQL. PL/SQL is Oracle's main proprietary language for writing stored procedures. The result is a CLOB or an XMLType object. The queries can be quite complex and may use object-relational features such as objects, references, nested tables, and so on. Thus, the functionality is comparable to XSU, but there are some essential differences: It is not possible to store, modify, and delete XML documents into the database on the one hand. On the other hand, the performance of XSU is worse than DBMS_XMLGen, the functionality of which is integrated in the database kernel.

Listing 6.28 shows the principle of DBMS_XMLGen.

Listing 6.28 DBMS_XMLGen Example

```
DECLARE
  qCtx DBMS_XMLGen.ctxHandle;
  result CLOB;
BEGIN
  qCtx := DBMS_XMLGen.newContext('SELECT  . . . ');
  result := DBMS_XMLGen.getXML(qCtx);
  DBMS_XMLGen.closeContext(qCtx);
END;
```

DBMS_XMLGen.ctxHandle is a context class representing a query and controlling all the functions. A context is created with newContext by passing an SQL query. Using getXML, an XML document can be generated as a CLOB. Analogously, getXMLType returns an XMLType object.

The package DBMS_XMLGen has again several procedures and functions to affect the naming of tags:

- setRowTag(ctx ctxHandle, name VARCHAR): Renames <ROW>
- setRowSetTag(ctx ctxHandle, name VARCHAR): Renames <ROWSET>

and so on. Furthermore, the query result can be processed incrementally:

- setMaxRows(ctx ctxHandle, n NUMBER): Restricts the tuples to be handled to n
- setSkipRows(ctx ctxHandle, n NUMBER): Leaves out the first n tuples
- getNumRowsProcessed(ctx ctxHandle) RETURN NUMBER: returns the number of tuples that have been processed so far
- restartQuery(ctx ctxHandle): Executes the query again

Additional procedures are available to reflect the functionality known from XSU.

6.6 Web Access to the Database

XSQL is a Java servlet for visualizing SQL query results. XSQL combines the power of SQL, XML, and XSLT to publish dynamic Web content based on database information. The servlet is similar to JSP (Java Server Pages) and follows the same mechanisms. Moreover, XSQL is interoperable with JSP. XSQL can be integrated in many popular Web servers like Apache 1.3.9 and higher, Oracle9iAS, or WebLogic 5.1. Thanks to Java, the servlet is easily extensible to one's needs.

6.6.1 The Principle of XSQL

The overall principle of XSQL is similar to JSP: A GET request with a URL of the form http://mycompany.com/myQuery.xsql references a file myQuery.xsql with a specific extension .xsql, denoting an XSQL servlet. The .xsql file mixes XML and SQL. The Web server recognizes the suffix .xsql, which has to be registered at the Web server before, and passes the file content to the XSQL servlet. The servlet processes the file and executes all the embedded SQL statements in the sense of server-side templates. The result, an XML document, is passed back to the caller.

In the easiest case, the XSQL file myQuery.xsql could have the content shown in Listing 6.29.

Listing 6.29 XSQL Example

```
<?xml version="1.0"?>
<xsql:query connection="demo" xmlns:xsql="urn:oracle-xsql">
  SELECT . . . FROM . . . WHERE . . .
</xsql:query>
```

Principally, the file is an ordinary XML document. Queries are embedded by the special tag `<xsql:query . . . >`, the result of which is inserted at this place instead. `xsql` is the nickname for the namespace `"urn:oracle-xsql"` that defines all the XSQL tags.

The attribute `connection="demo"` fixes a database connection to be used for the query. The name "demo" refers to an entry in an XML configuration file named `XSQLConfig.xml`, which contains the details about the JDBC connection, as shown in Listing 6.30.

Listing 6.30 JDBC Connection

```
<connectiondefs>
   <connection name="demo">
      <username>scott</username>
      <password>tiger</password>
      <dburl> jdbc:oracle:thin:@myhost:1521:mydb </dburl>
      <driver> oracle.jdbc.driver.OracleDriver </driver>
      <autocommit> true </autocommit>
   </connection>
   <connection name="lite">
      <username>system</username>
      <password>manager</password>
      <dburl> jdbc:Polite:POlite </dburl>
      <driver> oracle.lite.poljdbc.POLJDBCDriver </driver>
      <autocommit> true </autocommit>
   </connection>
</connectiondefs>
```

The entry "demo" for <connection name> specifies a JDBC connection to the schema scott/tiger, using the database URL (<dburl>) (i.e., the database mydb on myhost using Oracle's "thin" JDBC driver); the database server is listening on port 1521 for incoming JDBC requests. Several connections can be specified that way. Here, a second connection "lite" is defined.

The result of <xsql:query> is processed in the manner of XSU. That is, the result is embedded in <ROWSET>, whereby each tuple becomes a <ROW> element. Again, object-relational concepts such as object-, reference-, and collection-valued attributes can be used in order to give the document a nested structure, according to the canonical XSU mapping. Using aliases helps to rename attributes to tags and to avoid invalid XML names.

The file content is an arbitrary XML document following the XML rules. It can embed xsql queries in any number, combine different query results, nest them, and so on (see Listing 6.31).

Listing 6.31 XSQL Query Examples

```
<Tag1>
   <xsql:query  . . . > Query1 </xsql:query>
   <Tag2>
      <xsql:query  . . . > Query2 </xsql:query>
   </Tag2>
   <xsql:query  . . . > Query3 </xsql:query>
</Tag1>
```

Several queries can be executed and aggregated to a valid XML document that way.

Being a valid XML document, an XSLT style sheet can be registered for the .xsql file, thus further processing the resulting document:

```
<?xml-stylesheet type="text/xsl" href="myXsl.xsl?>
```

myXsl.xsl is the style sheet that is applied to the resulting document. Integrating XSLT has several well-known advantages:

- Style sheets are useful if the browser is unable to display XML. Then XSLT can convert XML into HTML, for instance.
- Moreover, it is possible to present the same information in different ways, tailored to the capabilities of a specific client (PDA, browser, etc.). Common formats are HTML, Tiny HTML, HDML (Handheld Device Markup Language) for hand-held devices, WML (Wireless Markup Language) for wireless devices, and SVG (Scalable Vector Graphics).

The <xsql:query> element possesses various attributes such as fetch-size, skip-rows, max-rows, id-attribute (renaming the NUM-attribute), row-element (<ROW> tag), rowset-element (<ROWSET> tag), id-attribute-column (determining the column for setting the NUM attribute), and tag-case, which all can be used to control the naming of tags.

By default, an empty query result returns an XML document <ROWSET/>. However, putting <xsql:no-rows-query> SELECT . . . </xsql:no-rows-query> within an <xsql:query . . . > element, a query is registered as a substitute: If the original query yields an empty result, then <xsql:no-rows-query> is executed instead.

6.6.2 Posting XML Data into the Database

The XSQL approach also allows for storing XML documents in a fine-grained manner according to inverse canonical mapping. That is, the documents are "posted" into the database. The target is a table or a view. The principle is analogous to XSU; however, the table/view, the key, and the columns to be modified are specified by xsql attributes. The same holds for the batch size (commit-batch-size) and the registration of XSLT style sheets (transform). The XSQL tags are <xsql:insert-request>, <xsql:update-request>, and <xsql:delete-request> to insert, update, and delete documents, respectively (see Listing 6.32).

Listing 6.32 XSQL Update Example

```
<xsql:update-request table="MyCustomer" columns="Name"
key-columns="CNo">
   . . .  XML document  . . .
</xsql:update-request>
```

As an alternative, XSQL also can directly execute DML (Data Manipulation Language) statements using `<xsql:dml> . . . </xsql:dml>`. Consequently, data can be inserted, modified, and deleted in the database in an SQL-like manner via the Web by means of XSQL. The attribute `commit="yes"` sets an autocommit mode:

```
<xsql:dml commit="yes"> DELETE FROM MyCustomer WHERE . . .
<xsql:dml>
```

Analogously, an anonymous PL/SQL block can be executed in the database server.

6.6.3 Parameterization

Queries can be parameterized in a simple way. First of all, parameter names must be declared by using the `bind-params` attribute of `<xsql:query>` (see Listing 6.33).

Listing 6.33 XSQL bind-params Example

```
<?xml version="1.0"?>
<xsql:query connection="demo" bind-params="x y"
xmlns:xsql="urn:oracle-xsql">
  SQL-query
</xsql:query>
```

The value of the `bind-params` attribute is a space-separated list of parameter names whose left-to-right order indicates the positional bind variable to which its value will be bound in the statement. Here, two parameters x and y are declared. Hence, the SQL query possesses two parameters, which are denoted as "?". The first occurrence of "?" corresponds to the first parameter (i.e., x), and the second one to y. A GET request specifies values for the parameters, thus replacing "?" in the query:

```
http://mycompany.com/myQuery.xsql?x=1&y=2
```

Furthermore, parameters can be initialized with default values. In Listing 6.34, the parameter values are x=10 and y=20, unless the GET request provides different values.

Listing 6.34 XSQL Default Values for bind-params Example

```
<?xml version="1.0"?>
<example x="10" y="20">
 <xsql:query connection="demo" bind-params="x y"
 xmlns:xsql="urn:oracle-xsql">
    SELECT . . .
 </xsql:query>
</example>
```

The full power of XML is available in XSQL. For example, for any XSQL action element we can substitute the value of any attribute or the text of any contained SQL statement, by using a lexical substitution parameter. This allows one to dynamically set style sheets as href={ @name} .xsl, to parameterize configuration files as connection="{ @name}", or to control the result size or commit behavior by max-rows="{ @name} ". Listing 6.35 shows the principle.

Listing 6.35 XSQL max-rows Example

```
<example max="10" connection="demo" xlmns:xsql="urn:oracle-xsql">
   <xsql:query max-rows="{@max}"> SELECT . . . </xsql:query>
</example>
```

max="10" defines a default value for the whole <example> element. The attribute can be referenced by { @max}. The value of max is here used to restrict the query result to a certain number of tuples by means of max-rows. If the xsql-file is invoked without any further parameters, then max=10 is taken; otherwise, the default value is overridden by the actual parameter. Those substitutions { @var} can also be used to replace text in SQL queries: ORDER BY { @var}.

<xsql:include-request-params/> and <xsql:include-request-param name="P"/> are special forms to create an XML representation for all parameters or a certain parameter P, respectively. <xsql:include-request-params/> generates something like that shown in Listing 6.36.

Listing 6.36 XSQL include-request-params Example

```
<request>
   <parameters>
```

```
        <Param1> value </Param1>
        <Param2> value </Param2>
         . . .
    </parameters>
    <session>
        <SessionVariable1> value <SessionVariable1>
         . . .
    </session>
    <cookies>
        <CookieName1> value <CookieName1>
         . . .
    </cookies>
</request>
```

Param1 and Param2 are parameter names. <xsql:include-request-param name="P"/> returns the value of only one parameter P as value </P>. This is useful to give XSLT style sheets an opportunity to access the parameters—for example, to control XSL processing in a more powerful way. Even session variables and cookies are displayed by tags <session> and <cookies>, respectively. Additional advanced features assign constants or results of queries to session variable and cookies. Other concepts are known from JSP. <xsql:include-xml href="url"/> includes the XML contents of a local or remote resource referenced by the URL: The URL can be absolute, HTTP-based to retrieve XML from another Web site, or relative to include XML from a file on the file system, thus interpreting the URL relative to the XSQL page being processed. <xsql:include-xsql href="url"/> includes the results of one XSQL page into another page. This allows one to easily aggregate content from a page that has already been built.

6.5.9 Servlet Invocations

Besides a GET request via HTTP, .xsql files can be executed in the following ways:

- Invoking a Java program from the command line:

  ```
  java oracle.xml.xsql.XSQLCommandLine myQuery.xsql output-file
  parameter5value . . .
  ```

  The Java program helps in learning the XSQL servlet by experience. Furthermore, the program is useful in generating XML for static data in order to store it in the file system. Successive accesses refer to the pregenerated data to avoid unnecessary generations. An output file is passed to the command, just as additional parameter values are. Using the special parameter xml-stylesheet, a URL to a style sheet can be registered. The parameter posted-xml provides a URL of an XML resource to be treated as if it were posted as part of the request. `user-agent` can be used to simulate a particular HTTP User-Agent string so that an appropriate style sheet for that User-Agent type will be selected when processing the page.

- A shell command behaves similarly:

  `xsql myQuery.xsql output-file parameter=value . . .`

- Java programs can use an `oracle.xml.xsql.XSQLRequest` object in the manner demonstrated in Listing 6.37.
- Using the JSP mechanisms `<jsp:include>` and `<jsp:forward>`, XSQL files become part of a JSP application. This lets XSQL and JSP cooperate.

Listing 6.37 XSQLRequest Example

```
URL url = new URL ("myQuery.xsql");
XSQLRequest req = new XSQLRequest(url);
Hashtable params = new Hashtable(2);
params.put("x", "value1");
params.put("y", "value2");
req.process(params,new PrintWriter(System.out),
                   new PrintWriter(System.err));
```

The first three types of invocations do not require a servlet installation in the Web server.

6.7 Special Oracle Features

In this section we will discuss some of the special features provided by Oracle.

6.7.1 URI Support

Oracle9i introduces new `URIType` object types that represent URIs (Uniform Resource Identifiers). A URI generalizes the concept of URL. A URI references not only HTML and XML documents, it also possesses "pointer" semantics to point into a document. Hence, a URI consists of two parts:

- A URL referencing a document
- A fragment that identifies a fragment within that document

A typical example for a URI is http://www.xml.com/xml_doc#//Customer/Address/Zip'. The part in front of the number sign (#) identifies the place of the document, while the final part references a fragment in the document. This mechanism follows the W3C XPointer specification. Oracle provides four object types to support the URI concept:

- `UriType` is an abstract object type that supplies the basic mechanisms.
- The subtype `HttpUriType` implements the HTTP protocol for accessing (external) Web pages.
- `DBUriType` is another subtype that allows referencing data in the database, so to speak, by means of intra-database references.
- The purpose of class `UriFactoryType` is to create those `UriType` objects.

The `UriType` object types are ordinary Oracle attribute domains. An object of that type holds a URI to an external document or to database data. Moreover, further subtypes of `UriType` can be added to support and implement other protocols such as gopher.

The subtype `DBUriType`, in particular, can be understood as a pointer to one entry in the database, which might be a table, a single row, a value, maybe complexly structured. The basis for referencing data via `DBUriType` is the implicit XML representation of a database shown in Listing 6.38.

Listing 6.38 XML Representation for DBUriType

```
<?xml version="1.0"?>
<oradb SID="mydb">
  <PUBLIC>
    <ALL_TABLES>
     . . .
    </ALL_TABLES>
    <EMP>
      <ROW>
        <EMPNO>1001</EMPNO>
        <ENAME>John</ENAME>
         . . .
      </ROW>
      <ROW>
        <EMPNO>1002</EMPNO>
        <ENAME>Mary</ENAME>
         . . .
      </ROW>
    </EMP>
  </PUBLIC>
  <SCOTT>
```

```
    <CUSTOMER>
      <ROW>
        <CNO>10</CNO>
        <NAME>Lucky Luke</NAME>
        <ADDRESS>
           <ZIP>12345</ZIP>
           <CITY>Bull</CITY>
           <STREET>Cows Xing</STREET>
           <HOUSENO>8</HOUSENO>
        </ADDRESS>
         . . .
      </ROW>
  </SCOTT>
</oradb>
```

The organization of this virtual XML database document reflects the hierarchy of database concepts:

- <oradb> with the Oracle system identifier (SID) as attribute
- Database schema (e.g., <PUBLIC> and <SCOTT>)
- Table in the schema (e.g., <EMP>, <CUSTOMER>)
- Tuple in the table (<ROW>)
- Attribute value (<CNO>)

Complex attribute values are handled as in XSU. For instance, the "virtual" XML document presents an object-valued attribute `Address` being structured as `<ADDRESS> <ZIP> 12345 </ZIP> <CITY> . . . </HOUSENO> </ZIP>`.

The virtual XML document takes into account the access privileges that are valid at the time of access. Hence, only those tables that are accessible by the user become part of the document. `NULL` values are not displayed, and the whole element for the attribute value is absent. In the future, the special null attribute `<xsi null="true">` will be used to this end.

A DBUri path refers to exactly one element in the "database document"—that is, an attribute value, a single tuple, or the whole table. The path is specified in a simplified XPath format.

- `/SCOTT/CUSTOMER` denotes the whole table.
- `/SCOTT/CUSTOMER/ROW[ CNO="10"]` determines a tuple by means of a predicate.

- /SCOTT/CUSTOMER/ROW[CNO="10"] /NAME refers to an attribute value of a tuple.
- /SCOTT/CUSTOMER/ROW[CNO="10"] /ADDRESS/ZIP points to a value of an object.

In any case, the predicate has to determine exactly one tuple. It does not need to include the key of the table. Logical operators and, or, and not(), the usual comparisons, and some arithmetic operators are allowed. Not all features of XPath and XPointer are supported. For example, the wildcard "*" and the operator "//" are missing. The only XPath-function being allowed is text(). This function eliminates embedding tags and references just the text itself. Hence, the DBUri /SCOTT/CUSTOMER/ROW[CNO="10"] /NAME/text() qualifies the text "Lucky Luke" instead of the element <NAME> Lucky Luke </NAME>.

DBUriType objects are accessible from a browser or a Web server. Certainly, a servlet must be called being able to transform a DBUri. A Java servlet oracle.xml.uri.OraDbUriServlet can execute the DBUri reference and return the value. However, the servlet can run only on the Oracle Servlet Engine (OSE). Anyway, anybody can implement such a servlet and plug it into a Web server. Using the Oracle servlet, the following URL returns the name of customer 10:

```
http://machine.oracle.com:8080/oradb/SCOTT/CUSTOMER/ROW[ CNo=10] /
Name/text()
```

The servlet engine runs on the machine machine.oracle.com with a Web service at port 8080 listening to requests. The appended DBUri is then executed by the servlet. The result of this "query," the name of customer 10, is visualized in the browser. Note that a non-SQL programmer can now easily access data and documents stored in the database.

The MIME type of the generated document is chosen automatically. In the case the DBUri ends in a text() function, then "text/plain" is used, else an XML document is produced with the mime type "text/xml".

DBUriType objects are useful in several scenarios:

- Links to other related documents can be held in the database, as some kind of intra-database link.
- A "lazy fetching" of documents can be implemented: Only the first few characters of a document are stored in a table, the complete document is referenced by a URI in the database.
- XSL style sheets can be stored in the database and referenced during parsing with import/include.

The URIType object types encapsulate in principle a VARCHAR value that holds the URI string. URIType possesses the following methods:

- CLOB getClob(): Returns the value pointed to by the URI as a CLOB.
- VARCHAR getUrl(): Returns the URL that is stored in the URIType object.
- VARCHAR getExternalUrl(): Is similar to getUrl; however, it calls the escape mechanism (e.g., to convert white spaces into "%20").

The type UriFactory should be used to create UriType objects. Let us assume a table UrlTab(id INTEGER, uri URIType). A URI can be stored as shown in Listing 6.39.

Listing 6.39 URI Example

```
INSERT INTO UrlTab
VALUES
(1,SYS.UriFactory.getUri('http://www.oracle.com/CUSTOMER/ROW
[ CNo=10] /Name'))
```

The method getUri(VARCHAR) takes a string and creates a URIType object in the following manner:

- If the prefix is "http://", then the object will be of type HttpUriType.
- If the prefix is "/oradb/" or unknown, then an object of type DBUriType is created.

In principle, new protocols can be added as further subtypes of UriType. Any subtype must be registered in UriFactory by means of a method registerHandler. Afterwards the protocol is recognized by getUri in the same way.

Oracle's SQL possesses a standalone function SYS_DBURIGen that simplifies creating a DBUriType object. URIs are defined in a descriptive manner in Listing 6.40 instead of specifying an XPath, which is useful to generate a DBUri dynamically for given target columns.

Listing 6.40 SYS_DBURIGen Example

```
SELECT SYS_DBURIGen(CNo, Name)
FROM Customer
WHERE CNo=10
```

This query produces a URI "/SCOTT/CUSTOMER/ROW[CNO="10"] /NAME", which references the name of the customer with CNo=10. The first parameter CNo characterizes the key of the object to be referenced, while the second parameter determines the target—that is, the Name value. The key may consist of several attributes, which are all listed in the parameter list. All the parameters except the last one are considered the key. The last parameter always specifies the database object to be referenced.

The generated URI points to an element—that is, including tags like <ROW> . . . </ROW>. If the URI refers to the text, then 'text()' can be applied as the last parameter.

The following generates a URI /SCOTT/CUSTOMER/ROW[CNO='10'] /NAME/text():

```
SELECT SYS_DBURIGen(CNo, Name, 'text()') FROM Customer WHERE CNo=10
```

The scenario in Listing 6.41 presents an application for URIs. Given a table ClobTab(id INTEGER, doc CLOB), we are able to define a view Shorttext(id, header, link), which presents the first 20 characters of doc in a column named header and maintains a link to the real CLOB document.

Listing 6.41 CLOB view Example

```
CREATE VIEW Shorttext
AS SELECT id, shorten(doc) AS header,
          SYS_DBURIGen(id,doc,'text()') AS link
FROM ClobTab
```

The view uses a user-defined function shorten that extracts the first 20 characters.

6.7.2 Parsers

Oracle9i provides several components, utilities, and interfaces to provide the advantages of XML technology in building Web-based database applications. Most of them are summarized in the XDK (XML Development Kit). XDKs are available for Java, C/C++, and PL/SQL, containing building blocks for reading, manipulating, transforming, and viewing XML documents. The XDK for Java is composed of the following components:

- An XML parser parses and creates XML documents using industry standard DOM and SAX interfaces. The SAX and DOM interfaces conform to the W3C recommendations version 2.0.

- The parser includes an integrated XSL Transformation (XSLT) processor for transforming XML data using style sheets. Using the XSLT processor, XML documents can be transformed from XML to any text-based format, such as XML, WML, or HTML.
- Moreover, the parser is able to validate a document against a DTD or an XML schema.

XDK supports XML1.0, DOM1.0, 2.0, SAX1.0, 2.0, and XSLT1.0. As Java is one possible language for implementing stored procedures in Oracle, the XDK allows plugging applications with XML processing into the database server.

6.7.3 Class Generator

An XML Class Generator creates source files from an XML DTD or XML Schema definition. Given a DTD or XML Schema, a class generator produces a set of Java or C++ classes. These classes enable one to construct XML documents in a program incrementally by calling constructors and methods. This is useful, for instance, when a Java program has to create an XML document that confirms a customer's order.

Here we want to explain only the general principle for the Java class generation in case of DTDs. For each element of a DTD, a corresponding Java class is generated. The class possesses constructors to initialize the XML element. Methods represent the DTD rules; for each element E on the right side is a corresponding `addNode` method to add parts. In addition to these basic mechanisms for constructing documents, further methods such as `print(OutputStream)` and `validateContent()` validate the constructed document. Listing 6.42 shows how to build an XML document.

Listing 6.42 Building an XML Document Example

```
CNo id = new CNo("1");
Firstname f = new Firstname ("Lucky");
Lastname l = new Lastname ("Luke");
Name name = new Name;
name.addNode(f);
name.addNode(l); // Name element is ready now
Zip z = new Zip("12345");
City c = new City("Bull");
Street str = new Street ("Cows Xing");
```

```
Houseno hno = new Houseno("8");
Address addr = new Address();
addr.addNode(z);
addr.addNode(c);
addr.addNode(str);
addr.addNode(hno);  // Address element is ready now
Phone ph1 = new Phone ("012/3456");
Phone ph2 = new Phone ("023/4567");
Price pr = new Price("1.11");
pr.setCURRENCY(CURRENCY_Dollar);  // attribute of Price
Position p = new Position ("1");
p.addNode(pr);
 . . .
Order ord = new Order("4711");
 . . .
Customer c = new Customer();
c.addNode(id);
c.addNode(name);
c.addNode(addr);
c.addNode(ph1);
c.addNode(ph2);
c.addNode(ord);

c.validateContent();   // validate the document
c.print(System.out);   // print the document
```

Using the generated Java classes, XML documents can be constructed gradually in a Java program. At first, the leaves of the document tree are created by using constructors of `CNo`, `Firstname`, `Lastname`, and so on. Higher elements like `Name` or `Address` are then built. The `addNode` method adds either a component to an element or a repetitive element such as `Phone`. The `validateContent` method finally checks the validity of the constructed document, which is useful as the methods themselves do not guarantee valid documents. For instance, exchanging `addNode(f)` with `addNode(1)`, an invalid document would emerge.

A command-line utility for the class generator offers the same functionality.

6.7.4 Special Java Beans

Most of Oracle's XML functionality is accompanied with Java Beans that encapsulate the concepts presented earlier in this chapter. These Oracle XML TransViewer beans are provided as part of XDK for Java Beans. They facilitate the addition of graphical or visual interfaces to an XML application. The first three beans are nonvisual:

- The DOM Builder bean builds a DOM tree from an XML document. It encapsulates the XML parser for Java's `DOMParser` class with a bean interface and extends the functionality with asynchronous parsing.
- The XSL Transformer bean accepts an XML file, applies the transformation specified by an input XSL style sheet, and creates the resulting output file. When integrated with other beans, XSL Transformer enables an application to view the results of transformations immediately.
- The DBAccess bean is dedicated to the storage of XML documents. This bean maintains CLOB tables that hold several XML documents. The tables manage filenames and related XML contents. DBAccess can be used by other TransViewer beans as a kind of intermediate XML storage (e.g., keeping XSL style sheets under development and transformation results).

The following beans are visual:

- The Treeviewer bean displays XML documents graphically as a tree. The branches and leaves of this tree can be manipulated with a mouse.
- The XML SourceView bean allows visualization of XML documents, and the editing. of XML and XSL files is displayed such that syntax is highlighted with color. Thanks to the Java Bean approach, the XML SourceView bean can easily be integrated with DOM Builder bean. Hence, it allows for pre- and post-parsing visualization.
- DBViewer is a Java Bean that can be used to display the results of database queries as XML documents in a scrollable swing panel. XSL style sheets can easily be applied to modify the shape of result.
- XML Transform Panel is a bean that applies XSL transformations on XML documents and shows the result. It allows the editing of XML and XSL files.

6.8 Conclusion

Oracle is a relational database system that takes into account new requirements that emerged in the area of managing XML documents. We described in this chapter the comprehensive support for XML that Oracle provides in Version 9i, Release 1.

The chapter's main focus is put on the storage and retrieval of XML documents in a database: The essential building blocks are the XML SQL Utility (XSU), the new

XMLType object type, and the OracleText cartridge. XSU is useful when XML documents are distributed among several tables and columns in a fine-grained manner. The other way around, table data can be used to construct XML documents in a powerful and flexible manner. The XMLType object type pursues a different approach and encapsulates XML documents in Large Objects (LOBs); hence, the documents are stored as a whole unit. Methods provide typical XML functionality such as qualifying documents by XPath queries and extracting document parts. In addition, OracleText supports full text retrieval capabilities including support for XPath.

Furthermore, Oracle contains other useful tools such as XML parsers for the DOM and SAX interfaces and class generators for building XML documents programmatically.

Nevertheless, some important concepts that have been discussed in the database/XML community quite recently are still missing in Oracle. For example, Xperanto (Carey et al. 2000; Shanmugasundaram et al. 2001) publishes relational data as XML views that can be queried and translates arbitrarily complex XQuery statements into executable SQL. XQuery is an emerging standard for a pure XML world defined by the W3C XML Query Language Working Group. It offers XML-only querying wherever a document may be, in databases, files, or messages. Pushing most of the query evaluation down into the SQL engine, XML-based queries can be optimized and efficiently executed. XSU principally behaves in a similar way but does not support yet the XQuery language, neither for XMLType objects, nor for XML views. Also the ability to query XMLType with SQL is still limited.

Oracle's XML DB, which is now available in Oracle9i Release 2, provides solutions to some of these points. The object type XMLType can be used transparently, no matter whether data is stored in CLOBs or in table columns. Hence even relational tables can be queried with XPath. Furthermore, XML DB promises to support an early prototype of XQuery, although the complete W3C recommendation is expected in late 2002. XDB will introduce enhanced native XML storage. The development on the product and research is shaped by ongoing standardization activities, in which a new part of the SQL standard, called SQL/XML (Eisenberg and Melton 2001), was created by the SQLX group as an emerging part of the ANSI and ISO SQL standards. Currently a working draft, the SQL/XML specification has as its major goal to create a "well-defined relationship between XML and SQL." SQL/XML is an extension to SQL to include processing of XML data. Oracle XDB aspires to be the first implementation of SQL/XML. These extensions enable Oracle to develop in the direction of an XML repository.

Chapter 7

XML Support in Microsoft SQL Server 2000

Michael Rys

7.1 Introduction

A large amount of the data that is interchanged between applications originates from relational databases and is finally stored again in relational databases. Since much of the interchange is expected to use XML as the transport format, relational database systems have been extended with XML capabilities. This chapter presents the XML support in Microsoft's SQL Server 2000 database system including the functionality provided by the SQLXML Web releases (see http://msdn.microsoft.com/sqlxml). This chapter is based on earlier publications, such as (Rys 2001).

7.2 XML and Relational Data

Over the past few years, XML and the languages/vocabularies defined with XML have established themselves as the most prevalent and promising lingua franca of business-to-business, business-to-consumer, or generally, any-to-any data interchange and integration. One of the major reasons for the emergence of XML in this space is that XML is a simple, platform-independent, Unicode-based syntax for which simple and efficient parsers are widely available. Another important factor in favor of XML is its ability to not only represent structured data, but to provide a uniform syntax for structured data, semi-structured data (data that is sparse or is of heterogeneous types), and marked-up content.

A large amount of the data that is interchanged originates from relational databases and is finally stored again in relational databases, since they have a proven track record in providing the required efficient and flexible management of data in such usage contexts.

Since relational systems today are predominantly used to manage structured data (an educated guess would be 80 percent or more), most of the XML generated and being consumed at this time in the context of data interchange is also fitting the relational model of structured data. Therefore, relational systems have first focused on providing XML capabilities that fit the most common usage scenario while still providing some support for dealing with data that does not fit into the structured mold. For example, Microsoft SQL Server 2000 provides the mechanisms to easily and efficiently transform relational schemata into a specific XML language (i.e., schema) used for the data transport and back into relations.

This chapter focuses on how Microsoft SQL Server 2000 provides the basic technology to enable a relational database to become a component in an application scenario that uses an XML-based data interchange. It will provide an overview of the features that are needed to provide database access, that transform relational query results into XML, and how to elegantly provide rowset abstractions over XML to shred XML into relations. Next it will present the mechanism that provides queryable and updateable XML views that also can be used to efficiently bulk load XML data into the relational database. The chapter will discuss how these features can be used in the context of any-to-any data interchange and emphasize the ease-of-use of building the XML views. The discussion of generating XML for SQL queries will describe canonical, heuristic-based, and user-defined strategies and point out their use scenarios and also some of their potential shortcomings.

7.3 XML Access to SQL Server

Figure 7.1 shows a high-level architectural block diagram of SQL Server 2000's XML support. It is interesting to note that depending on the overall system or service architecture, different access components and/or protocols are preferable. If there is a limited amount of business logic, or when most of the business logic can be completely pushed either to the client (for example, via ECMAScript embedded in the HTML page) or to the database server (into the database's stored procedures), a simple HTTP or SOAP access mechanism suffices. For two-tier architectures or where the business logic needs to be performed on the Web server (the middle tier), a closer coupling of the business logic to database access is often used due to performance and programmability reasons. Thus, the XML database access story should also be accessible through the standard access components such as OLEDB, ADO, and the .NET APIs.

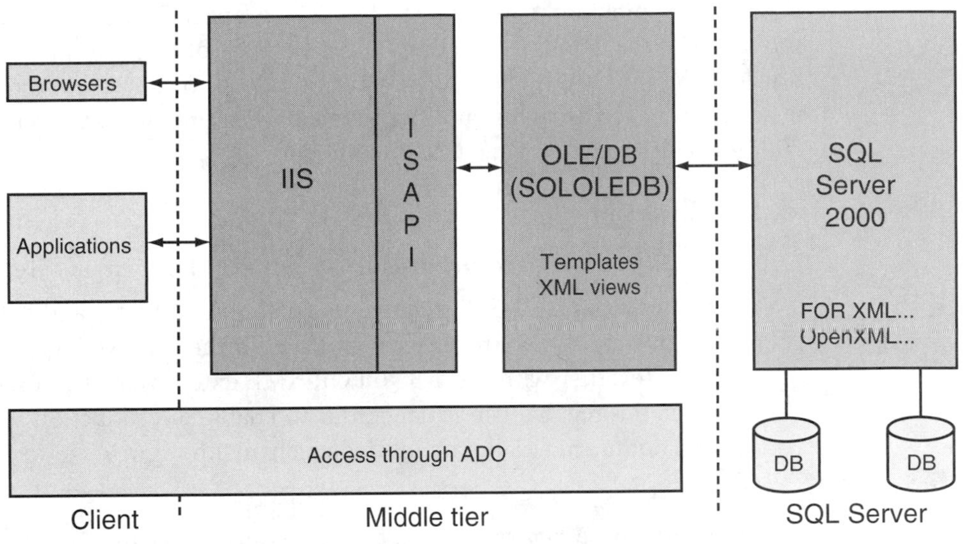

Figure 7.1 Architectural Overview of the XML Access to SQL Server

For these reasons, SQL Server 2000 provides all access to its XML features (except Bulkload) via the SQLOLEDB provider, ADO, and a .NET interface as well as via an IIS ISAPI extension that provides access to the functionality via HTTP and SOAP. In the following sections, we will discuss each XML feature in detail and show where it fits into the architecture and how it can be accessed both via HTTP/SOAP and ADO.NET.

7.3.1 Access via HTTP

Several ways exist to access SQL Server via HTTP. The most common one is to write an active server page that accesses the database via ADO. SQL Server 2000 introduces an HTTP access mechanism via an ISAPI extension that avoids ASP if no mid-tier business logic is needed and—with the latest Web release—can also expose templates, user-defined functions, and stored procedures as SOAP methods.

The URL formats of the new HTTP access methods start with:

```
http://domainname/vroot
```

The SQL Server ISAPI is registered with IIS to handle messages to a particular *virtual root* (vroot). The ISAPI will receive the requests for that particular vroot, and after performing authorization, will then pass the appropriate commands via the

SQLOLEDB provider (in Web releases via a special-purpose SQLXML OLEDB provider) to the database. The virtual root as part of the URL provides an abstraction mechanism that encapsulates the accessed database server and database instances, the access rights, and the enabled access methods. Currently, SQL Server 2000 provides the following access methods:

- *Ad hoc* URL query mechanism:

  `http://domainname/vroot?sql=select+xmldoc+from+table`

  Allows arbitrary T-SQL statements (including updates and data definition statements). Query results are returned in their native binary representation. Together with the T-SQL FOR XML extensions, it can return XML. Since this mechanism is dangerous to enable in production systems, we will not further elaborate on this mechanism.

- Direct query access:

  `http://domainname/vroot/dbobject/Table[ @column1=value] /@column2`

  Provides native access to the binary representation of the data while only allowing a safer set of queries via an XPath-like simple query syntax. An example will be shortly presented where it is used.

- Template access:

  `http://domainname/vroot/template/templatefile?param`

  Templates are XML documents that provide a parameterized query and update mechanism to the database. Since they hide the actual query (or update) from the user, they provide the level of decoupling that makes building loosely coupled systems possible.

  Elements in the `urn:schemas-microsoft-com:xml-sql` namespace are processed by the template processor and used to return database data as part of the resulting XML document. Elements in other namespaces are returned to the client unmodified. The templates support named parameters to parameterize the queries. For security purposes, only values can be parameterized and not query components.

- XPath XML view access:

  `http://domainname/vroot/schema/schemafile/XPATH?param`

  This URL provides a way to query an XML view that is specified by the annotated schema referenced by the schema file in an *ad hoc* way using XPath queries. The URL can be parameterized in the same way templates are. More details on XPaths against annotated schemata are presented shortly.

- SOAP access:

  `http://domainname/vroot/soaptypename?wsdl`

  This URL provides the WSDL (Web Services Description Language) file for the exposed Web service. Each user-configured SOAP type name provides the WSDL file and a configuration file. The services exposed via SOAP can then be accessed using any Web service access mechanism (see http://msdn.microsoft.com/sqlxml for details).

`dbobject`, `template`, and `schema` designate three types of *virtual names* for use with the ISAPI extension. They provide an abstraction for the access methods, and in the case of the last two types of virtual names, they also provide the location of the files that are associated with the access. In addition, all access mechanisms can be parameterized with predefined parameters that among others allow specifying the output encoding, the character set used in the URL, and a server-side XSLT transform.

One of the most important aspects of providing access to a database via HTTP is security. The URL access mechanism has to guarantee that only authorized people can access those parts of the database to which they are allowed access. The ISAPI extension provides three authentication modes on a per-vroot basis. This allows the database administrator to set the database internal access rights for the authenticated users inside the database since only those users who are authenticated will be allowed access. The first mode is the standard HTTP/HTTPS-based basic authentication that prompts for a database user/password combination via HTTP (only secure with a secure HTTP connection). The second mode allows every user who connects to the server to impersonate the vroot-specific Windows or SQL Server user. The user/password combination is associated with the vroot and cannot be changed or retrieved by the user. The final authentication mode takes advantage of Windows ACL such that the authentication is done by a previous authentication event (e.g., the login to the client account), and the credentials are then passed on to the database. This allows the use of a single vroot with multiple access rights without prompting for the user/password combination.

7.3.2 Using the XML Features through SQLOLEDB, ADO, and .NET

All the XML features are also accessible through SQLOLEDB and in later Web releases via a special SQLXML OLEDB provider that provides better performance. Both of the OLEDB providers have been extended with a stream interface that is accessible via ADO's stream interface. XML and XPath were added as new dialects to SQLOLEDB. XML indicates that the input is a template file; XPath indicates that the input is an XPath query with its associated annotated schema. Using a FOR XML query as described shortly does not necessitate a new dialect, but as for any XML-specific result, the result needs to be returned via the stream interface and not the rowset interface of SQLOLEDB or ADO. Some of the predefined URL parameters such as the output encoding or the XSLT transform are also exposed as SQLOLEDB and ADO properties.

Finally the latest Web release also includes a new .NET class named Microsoft.Data.SqlXml that provides access to SQL Server and its XML features. It provides the following three primary classes:

- **SqlXmlCommand**: Used to send a Transact-SQL statement to the database, execute a stored procedure, or query the database using other technologies (such as annotated schemas and XML templates) and get the results back as XML. This object supports a wide range of options, which are discussed in detail in http://msdn.microsoft.com/sqlxml.
- **SqlXmlParameter**: Used to specify the value for a parameter in the command. This can be a parameter to an *ad hoc* query, stored procedure, XPath query, or XML template.
- **SqlXmlAdapter**: Used to populate a *DataSet* object with an XML result set, or update the database with an XML DiffGram.

For more information about the definition and use of these APIs, the reader is referred to http://msdn.microsoft.com/sqlxml.

7.4 Serializing SQL Query Results into XML

SQL Server provides both a SQL-centric and an XML-centric way to generate XML from relational data. This section describes the SQL-centric approach.

Programmers that are familiar with writing SQL select queries want to easily generate XML from their query result. Unfortunately, such a serialization into XML can be done many different ways. SQL Server therefore provides different modes for the serialization with different levels of complexity and XML-authoring capability. All three modes are provided via a new select clause called FOR XML. The modes are raw, auto, nested, and explicit. The syntax of the FOR XML clause is ([ ] indicates optional, | indicates alternative):

```
FOR XML (raw | (auto | nested) [, elements] | explicit) [, binary
base64] [, xmldata]
```

All modes basically map rows to elements and column values to attributes. The optional directive *elements* changes the mapping of all column values to subelements in the auto and nested modes (the explicit mode has column-specific control over the mapping). The optional directive binary base64 is required in the raw and explicit modes if a binary column is returned, such as binary, varbinary, or image. It indicates for all modes that the binary data should be returned inline in the XML document in base64 encoding. In the auto and nested modes, a direct query will be generated if no mode is specified. The optional directive xmldata will generate an inline schema using the XML-Data Reduced schema language as part of the result that describes the structure and data types of the XML query result.

Before we describe the modes in detail, we need to understand some of the general architectural design decisions that are common for all the current FOR XML modes.

The first requirement for the current implementation was to not impact the database system's relational engine. Therefore the serialization process has to happen as a post-processing step on the resulting rowset after the query execution is done. Thus the serialization process is not part of the general query processing (see Figure 7.2). As a consequence to the current implementation, FOR XML query results cannot be assigned to columns but need to be returned directly to the OLEDB provider. It also means that information about the lineage of the data in case of nonprimary key-foreign key joins is lost, since we cannot tell if the master data in the join comes from one or multiple rows.

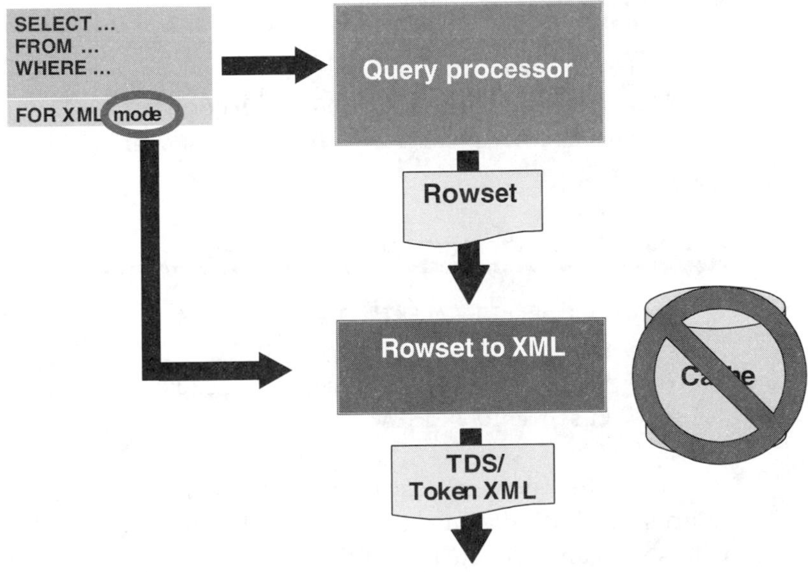

Figure 7.2 FOR XML Processing Model

The second requirement wants to avoid the caching of large XML fragments on the server. In order to avoid such caching, the serialization rules for hierarchical results in the auto, nested, and explicit modes therefore require that rows containing parent data need to be directly followed by their children and children's children data.

Furthermore, due to the open-world assumption of XML (in contrast to the closed-world assumption of relational systems), relational NULL values are serialized by the absence of the instance value. Finally, when a row is mapped to an element, a query returning multiple top rows will generate an XML fragment. To make it into a well-formed XML document, a root element needs to be added via the template mechanism or via the root property of SQLOLEDB.

Later Web releases provide both client-side (in the SQLXML provider) and server-side processing of FOR XML. Since not all information of the auto mode is available on the client side, a new mode called *nested* replaces the auto mode.

7.4.1 The Raw Mode

The raw mode is the simplest mode. It performs a so-called canonical mapping where any row of the query result is mapped into an element with the name row and any column value that is not null into an attribute value of the attribute with the column name. For example, the query in Listing 7.1 may return the results in Listing 7.2.

Listing 7.1 Example Query Using Raw Mode

```
SELECT CustomerID, OrderID
FROM Customers LEFT OUTER JOIN Orders
ON Customers.CustomerID = Orders.CustomerID
FOR XML raw
```

Listing 7.2 Result of Query Using Raw Mode

```
<row CustomerID="ALFKI" OrderID="10643" />
<row CustomerID="ALFKI" OrderID="10692" />
<row CustomerID="ANATR" OrderID="10308" />
<row CustomerID="FISSA" />
```

Since the query results do not contain nested rowsets, the raw mode only returns flat XML documents where the hierarchy of the data is lost. However, it works with any SQL query, and the serialization process is very efficient.

7.4.2 The Auto and Nested Modes

The auto and nested modes apply heuristics on the returned rowset to determine nesting of the data. They basically map each row to an element while using the table alias as the element name. Nesting is determined by taking schema-level lineage information provided by the SQL Server query processor into account.

Basically, the left-to-right appearance of a table alias in the SELECT clause determines the nesting. Columns of aliases that are already placed in the hierarchy are grouped together even if they appear interspersed with columns of other aliases. Computed and constant columns are associated with the deepest hierarchy so far encountered (or with the top level of the first alias). These heuristics together with the loss of the instance level lineage make it impossible to provide differently typed sibling elements: The generated hierarchy will be a simple hierarchy that will introduce a new level for every new table alias.

Due to the streaming requirement, the serialization process then looks at each row that arrives from the query processor, opens a new hierarchy level for the level where all the ancestor data is unchanged, previously closing any lower hierarchies of the sibling. The hierarchy serialization of the auto mode together with the lineage issue of the first requirement means that multiple, indistinguishable parents will be merged to one parent and that parents without children and parents with children without properties will be represented as parents with children without properties. The serialization process also means that if children are not directly following their parent, a duplicate parent will be generated where it reappears in the rowset stream.

For example, the auto mode query in Listing 7.3 may return the results in Listing 7.4.

Listing 7.3 Example Query Using Auto Mode

```
SELECT Customers.CustomerID, OrderID
FROM Customers LEFT OUTER JOIN Orders
ON Customers.CustomerID = Orders.CustomerID
ORDER BY Customers.CustomerID
FOR XML auto
```

Listing 7.4 Result of Query Using Auto Mode

```
<Customers CustomerID="ALFKI">
  <Orders OrderID="10643" />
  <Orders OrderID="10692" />
</Customers>
<Customers CustomerID="ANATR">
```

```
  <Orders OrderID="10308" />
</Customers>
<Customers CustomerID="FISSA">
  <Orders />
</Customers>
```

Note the order by clause to group all children with their parent and the empty Orders element.

7.4.3 The Explicit Mode

The explicit mode allows generating arbitrary XML without any of the auto mode limitations. However, the explicit mode expects that the query be explicitly authored to return the rowset in a specific format. This format, commonly known as a universal table format, provides enough information to generate arbitrary XML. In particular, the explicit mode can generate arbitrary tree structured hierarchies, collapse or hoist hierarchical levels independently of the involved tables, and can generate IDREFS type collection attributes.

The general format and approach is best explained with an example. Explaining every detail of the explicit mode is beyond the scope of this chapter. Therefore, the reader is referred to the documentation for the details. The goal is to generate an XML document of the form shown in Listing 7.5.

Listing 7.5 Desired Form of XML Document

```
<Customer cid="ALFKI">
  <name>Alfreds Futterkiste</name>
  <Order oid="O-10643" />
  <Order oid="O-10692" />
</Customer>
<Customer cid="BOLID">
  <name>Bolido Comidas preparadas</name>
  <Order oid="O-10326" />
</Customer>
```

Note that while this example still consists only of a simple hierarchy, one Customer column has to be mapped to an attribute and the other one to a subelement, a task that cannot be accomplished by the auto mode. In order to generate XML of this format, the explicit mode expects a universal table of the format shown in Table 7.1.

Table 7.1 Universal Table Format

Tag	Parent	Customer!1!cid	Customer!1!name!element	Order!2!oid
1	0	ALFKI	Alfreds Futterkiste	NULL
2	1	ALFKI	NULL	O-10643
2	1	ALFKI	NULL	O-10692
1	0	BOLID	Bolido Comidas preparadas	NULL
2	1	BOLID	NULL	O-10326

Each row corresponds to an element (with the exception of IDREFS where each row is an element of the list). The columns Tag and Parent are used to encode the hierarchy levels for each row (if the parent tag is 0 or NULL, the tag is the top level). The column names encode the mapping of the hierarchy levels to the element name; in the given example in Table 7.1, level 1 corresponds to an element of name Customer. The column names also encode the name of the attribute (or subelement) of the values in that column as well as additional information such as whether the value is a subelement or some other information (such as IDREFS, CDATA section, etc.).

The serialization process takes each row, and based on the tag level and the parent tag, determines what level the element is. It uses the information encoded in the column name to only generate the column attributes and subelements for the current level. Thus all other columns can contain NULL. Due to the streaming requirement, children have to immediately follow their parent; thus the key field columns of the parent often contain the key values like in the example in Table 7.1 because they were used to group the children with their parent element. However, the explicit mode cares only about the order and does not care about the parent's key value.

In principle, the explicit mode does not care about the query that generates the universal table format. One could create a temporary table of this format, insert the data, and then perform an explicit mode query over the temporary table that guarantees the right grouping of children and parents to generate the XML. This however, would most likely not perform. Thus, the best way today to generate this format by means of a single query is to issue a selection for each level, union all them together, and use an order by statement to group children under their parents. This basically generates a left outer join where each join partner is placed into its own vertical and horizontal partition of the rowset. Thus the query for generating the universal table and therefore the XML in our example would look like Listing 7.6.

Listing 7.6 Query for Generating the Universal Table

```
SELECT 1 as Tag,
       NULL as Parent,
  CustomerID AS "Customer!1!cid",
  CompanyName AS "Customer!1!name!element",
    NULL AS "Order!2!oid"
FROM Customers
WHERE CustomerID = 'ALFKI' OR CustomerID='BOLID'

UNION ALL
SELECT 2,
       1,
       Customers.CustomerID,
       NULL,
       'O-'+CAST(Orders.OrderID AS varchar(32))
FROM Customers INNER JOIN Orders
ON   Customers.CustomerID=Orders.CustomerID
WHERE Customers.CustomerID = 'ALFKI'
OR Customers.CustomerID='BOLID'

ORDER BY "Customer!1!cid"
FOR XML explicit
```

Users who prefer a simpler way to formulate these queries can use the XML view and XPath mechanism (explained shortly) to generate such explicit mode queries under the covers.

■ 7.5 Providing Relational Views over XML

In many cases, data will be sent to the database server in the form of an XML message that needs to be integrated with the relational data after optionally performing some business logic over the data inside a stored procedure on the server. This requires programmatic access to the XML data from within a stored procedure. Unfortunately, neither the DOM nor SAX provides a well-suited surface API for dealing with XML data in a relational context. Instead the new API needs to provide a *relational view over the XML data*—that is, it needs to allow the SQL programmer to shred an XML message into different relational views.

SQL Server 2000 provides such a rowset mechanism over XML by means of the OpenXML rowset provider (see Figure 7.3). OpenXML provides two kinds of rowset views over the XML data: the *edge table* view and the *shredded rowset* view. The edge table view provides the parent-child hierarchy and all the other relevant information of each node in the XML document in form of a self-referential rowset. The shredded rowset view utilizes an XPath expression (the row pattern) to identify the nodes in the XML document tree that will map to rows and uses a relative XPath expression (the column pattern) for identifying the nodes that provide the values for each column. The OpenXML rowset provider can appear anywhere in an SQL expression where a rowset can appear as a data source. In particular, it can appear in the FROM clause of any selection.

In order to have access to some of the implicit meta information in the tree such as hierarchy and sibling information, a column pattern can also be a so-called meta property of the node selected by the row pattern. Examples of such meta properties

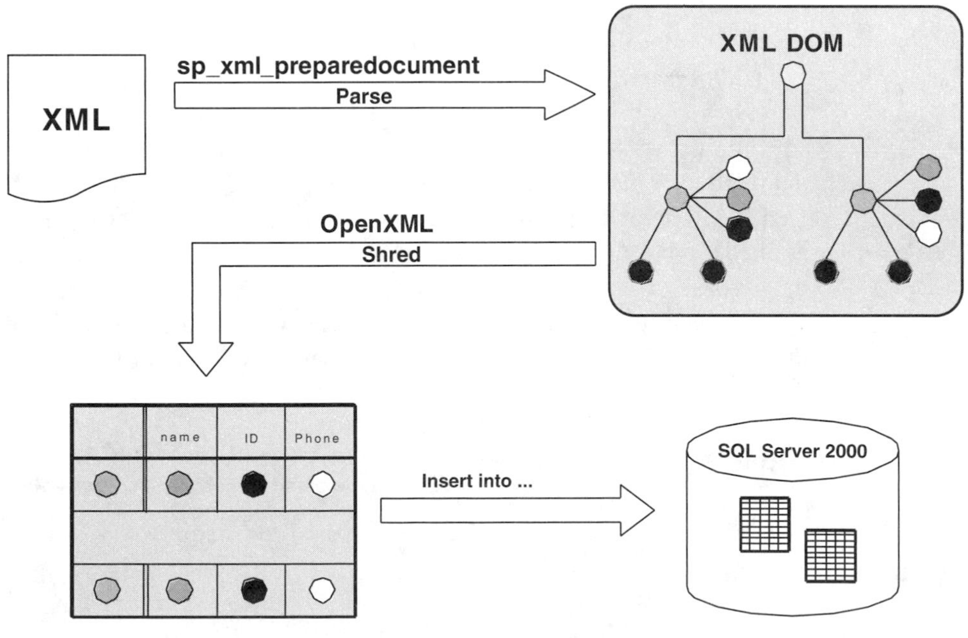

Figure 7.3 Open XML Processing Model

are @mp:id that provides the node ID (the namespace prefix mp binds to a namespace that is recognized by OpenXML as providing the meta properties), @mp:parentid that provides the node ID of the parent node, @mp:prev that provides the node ID of the previous sibling, and the special metaproperty @mp:xmltext that deals with unknown open content (the so-called overflow).

The following presents the syntax of the OpenXML rowset provider ([ ] denote optional parts, | denotes alternatives):

```
OpenXML(hdoc, RowPattern [, Flag] ) [ WITH SchemaDeclaration |
TableName]
```

The hdoc parameter is a handle to the XML document that has been previously parsed with the built-in stored procedure sp_xml_preparedocument. RowPattern is any valid XPath expression that identifies the rows or, in case of the edge table view, the roots of the trees to be returned. The optional Flag parameter can be used to designate default attribute- or element-centric column patterns in the shredded rowset view. If the WITH clause is omitted, an edge table view is generated; otherwise, the explicitly specified schema declaration or the implicitly through TableName-given rowset schema is used to define the exposed structure of the shredded rowset view. A schema declaration has the following form:

```
(ColumnName1 ColumnType1 [ ColPattern1], ColumnName2 ColumnType2 [
ColPattern2], . . .)
```

The ColumnName provides the name of the column, ColumnType the relational datatype exposed by the rowset view, and ColumnPattern the optional column pattern (if no value is given, the default mapping indicated with the flag parameter is applied). Note that XML data types are automatically coerced to the indicated SQL data types.

For example, the T-SQL fragment in Listing 7.7 parses a hierarchical Customer-Order XML document and uses the rowset views to load the customer and order data into their corresponding relational tables.

Listing 7.7 T-SQL Fragment

```
create procedure Load_CustOrd (@xmldoc ntext)
as
declare @h int

-- Parse document
```

```
exec sp_xml_preparedocument @h output, @xmldoc

-- Load the Customer data, note the use of the attribute-centric
-- default mapping and the name of the table in the WITH clause

insert into Customers
  select * from OpenXML(@h, '/loaddoc/Customer') with Customers

-- Load the Order data. Since we need to get the customer id from
the
-- parent element, we need to give the explicit schema declaration
and
-- use the element-centric default for the rest.

insert into Orders(OrderID, CustomerID, OrderDate)
  select *
  from OpenXML(@h, '/loaddoc/Customer/Order', 2)
       with (
         oid int,
         customerid nvarchar(10) '../@CustomerID',
         OrderDate datetime)

-- Remove the parsed document from the temp space

exec sp_xml_removedocument @h
go

-- Now load some data

exec Load_CustOrd N'<loaddoc>
  <Customer CustomerID="NEWC1" ContactName="Joe Doe"
            CompanyName="Foo Inc.">
    <Order>
      <oid>1</oid>
      <OrderDate>2000-01-01T11:59:59</OrderDate>
    </Order>
  </Customer>
  <Customer CustomerID="NEWC2" ContactName="Jane Doe"
            CompanyName="Bar Inc.">
    <Order>
      <oid>2</oid>
      <OrderDate>2000-12-31T11:59:59</OrderDate>
```

```
    </Order>
    <Order>
      <oid>3</oid>
      <OrderDate>2001-01-01T08:00:00</OrderDate>
    </Order>
  </Customer>
</loaddoc>'
```

One of the advantages of this rowset-oriented API for XML data is that it leverages the existing relational model for use with XML and provides a mechanism for updating a database with data in XML format. Utilizing XML in conjunction with OpenXML enables multirow updates with a single stored procedure call and multi-table updates by exploiting the XML hierarchy. In addition, it allows the formulation of queries that join existing tables with the provided XML data.

One disadvantage is that it internally uses a materialized DOM representation and thus does not scale to large (more than 100KB) XML documents due to the memory requirements. Thus, for loading large XML documents, the bulk load facility described shortly should be used.

7.6 SQLXML Templates

Templates are XML documents that provide a parameterized query and update mechanism to the database. Templates can contain either T-SQL statements, Updategrams, XPath queries, or a combination thereof. Examples for Updategrams and XPath queries are given in section 7.7. Listing 7.8 shows the basic structure of a parameterized template that retrieves a Customer-Order hierarchy for a specific region and applies an XSLT post-processing step that transforms the template result into another XML document or some other format (such as HTML).

Listing 7.8 Example of a Parameterized Template

```
<root xmlns:sql ="urn:schemas-microsoft-com:xml-sql"
      sql:xsl="CustOrd.xsl" >
  <sql:header nullvalue="NULL" >
    <sql:param name="City">%</sql:param>
    <sql:param name="state">WA</sql:param>
  </sql:header>
```

```
    <sql:query>
      SELECT Customers.CustomerID, OrderID
      FROM Customers LEFT OUTER JOIN Orders
      ON Customers.CustomerID = Orders.CustomerID
      WHERE City LIKE @City
      AND Region LIKE @state
      ORDER BY Customers.CustomerID
      FOR XML auto
    </sql:query>
  </root>
```

The optional `sql:xsl` attribute on the template root element points to the file that the server-side XSLT transformation will apply to the template results. The transformation will take place inside the OLEDB provider. The `sql:header` contains the parameter declarations. Each parameter declaration provides the name of the parameter and a default value. The optional attribute `nullvalue` declares that the specified string (`"NULL"` in Listing 7.8) will be interpreted as the `NULL` value if passed as the parameter value. The parameters will be referenced by name inside the queries using their native variable reference mechanism. `sql:query` can contain arbitrary T-SQL statements (best placed into a CDATA section to avoid problems with < or other special characters). In Listing 7.8, it is a FOR XML query. The result of the template before the application of the XSLT transform with the default parameter values may look like Listing 7.9.

Listing 7.9 Result of Template before XSLT Transform

```
<root xmlns:sql ="urn:schemas-microsoft-com:xml-sql" >
  <Customers CustomerID="LAZYK">
    <Orders OrderID="10482" />
    <Orders OrderID="10545" />
  </Customers>
  <Customers CustomerID="TRAIH">
    <Orders OrderID="10574" />
    <Orders OrderID="10577" />
    <Orders OrderID="10822" />
  </Customers>
</root>
```

7.7 Providing XML Views over Relational Data

The previous sections presented an SQL-centric approach to generating and consuming XML. This section introduces an XML-centric mechanism that allows the definition of virtual XML views over the relational database that can then can be queried and updated with XML-based tools.

7.7.1 Annotated Schemata

The core mechanism of providing XML views over the relational data is the concept of an *annotated schema*. Annotated schemata consist of a schema description of the exposed XML view and annotations that describe the mapping of the XML schema constructs onto the relational schema constructs. SQL Server 2000 supports both the older XML Data Reduced (XDR) schema language as well as the W3C XML Schema format. Since the schema documents are XML documents and their content model is open, the annotations can be placed inline.

In order to simplify the definition of the annotations, each schema provides a default mapping if no annotation is present. The default mapping maps an attribute or a noncomplex subelement (i.e., content type is text only) to a relational column with the same name. All other elements map into rows of a table or view with the same name. Since SQL Server 2000 does not support nested relations, hierarchy is not mappable without an annotation.

Listing 7.10 shows a simple XML view that defines a Customer-Order hierarchy over the Customers and Orders table of the relational database. Everything that is in the default namespace belongs to the XDR schema definition; the annotations are associated with the familiar namespace `urn:schemas-microsoft-com:xml-sql`.

Listing 7.10 Simple XML View

```
<Schema xmlns="urn:schemas-microsoft-com:xml-data"
        xmlns:sql="urn:schemas-microsoft-com:xml-sql">
<ElementType name="Customer" sql:relation="Customers">
    <AttributeType name="ID" />
    <attribute type="ID" sql:field="CustomerID" />
    <element type="Order">
      <sql:relationship key-relation="Customers"
                        key="CustomerID"
                        foreign-relation="Orders"
                        foreign-key="CustomerID"/>
    </element>
</ElementType>
```

```
<ElementType name="Order" sql:relation="Orders">
    <AttributeType name="OrderID" />
    <attribute type="OrderID" />
  </ElementType>
</Schema>
```

The Customer element is mapped to the Customers table using the `sql:relation` annotation; its attribute ID is mapped to the table's CustomerID column with the `sql:field` annotation. Finally, the similarly mapped Order element is parented under the Customer element. The sql:relationship annotation provides the hierarchy information as a conceptual left-outer join that describes how the child data relates to the parent data. Additional annotations exist to define XML-specific information such as defining ID-prefixes and CDATA sections, and annotations to define limit values to deal with value-driven horizontal partitions.

In order to define the annotations in a graphical way, a utility called the SQL XML View Mapper is available for download from the Microsoft Web site.

The annotated schema does not retrieve any data per se but only defines a virtual view by projecting an XML view on the relational tables. It actually defines two potential views, customers containing orders and just orders, since neither XML Schema language defines an explicit root node. Thus, we need additional information to actually determine which of the two views will be used. This information will be provided implicitly by the query, the Updategram, and Bulkload as explained in the following sections.

7.7.2 Querying Using XPath

XPath is a tree navigation language and is defined in a W3C recommendation. XPath is not a full-fledged query language (it does not provide constructive elements such as projection or subtree pruning) but serves as a basis for navigating the XML tree structure. Each XPath basically consists of a sequence of location steps that navigate the tree with optional predicates to constrain the navigation paths.

SQL Server 2000 uses a subset of XPath 1.0 to select data from the virtual XML views provided by annotated schemata. The first location step of the XPath determines the exact view used of the many potential views defined by the annotated schema by determining the first hierarchy. Instead of returning only a collection of nodes, the selected nodes and their complete subtree is serialized in the resulting XML fragment.

In principle, XPath constructs that are easily mapped to the relational constructs of SQL Server are supported. The currently supported constructs include the non-order, non-recursive navigation axes, all data types, all relational and Boolean operators, all but one arithmetic operation, and variables. Notably not supported in the current release are the `id()` function and the order and recursive axes such as the descendent axis.

Since the views are virtual views, the XPath query together with the annotated schema is translated into a FOR XML explicit query that returns only the XML data that is required by the query. The implementation goes to great length to provide the expected XPath semantics such as preserving the node list order imposed by the parent orders when navigating down the tree and the XPath data type coercion rules. The only two places where the implementation differs from the W3C XPath semantics is with respect to the coercion rules of strings with the < and > comparison operations and with respect to node-to-string conversions in predicates. In the first case, the implementation does not try to coerce to a number but does a string-based comparison on the default collation, which provides support for date-time comparisons. In the second case, XPath mandates a "first-match" evaluation semantics that cannot be mapped to the relational system. Instead, the implementation performs the more intuitive "any-match" evaluation.

For example, the XPath:

```
/Customer[ @ID='ALFKI']
```

against the preceding annotated schema may result in the XML in Listing 7.11.

Listing 7.11 XPath Query Result

```
<Customer ID="ALFKI">
  <Order OrderID="10643" />
  <Order OrderID="10692" />
</Customer>
```

The XPath query can be passed via a URL or a template, or via the XPath dialect of the client provider. The following shows each access method for the query example (`/Customer[ @ID='ALFKI']`), assuming that the schema file is called CustOrd.xdr. First the URL:

```
http://domainserver/dbvroot/schema/CustOrd.xdr/Customer[ @ID=
'ALFKI']
```

The template wraps the result with a root element and parameterizes the ID. The mapping-schema attribute on the `sql:xpath-query` element indicates the location of the annotated schema relative to the template file.

Listing 7.12 XPath Query Template

```
<root>
  <sql:header xmlns:sql="urn:schemas-microsoft-com:xml-sql" >
    <sql:param name="cid">ALFKI</sql:param>
  </sql:header>

  <sql:xpath-query mapping-schema="CustOrd.xdr"
                   xmlns:sql="urn:schemas-microsoft-com:xml-sql" >
    /Customer[ @ID=$cid]
  </sql:xpath-query>
</root>
```

Finally, the Visual Basic fragment in Listing 7.13 shows how to use ADO to post an XPath query.

Listing 7.13 XPath Query Using ADO

```
conn.Open strConn
Set cmd.ActiveConnection = conn
cmd.Dialect = "{ec2a4293-e898-11d2-b1b7-00c04f680c56}"
cmd.CommandText = "/Customer[ @ID='ALFKI']"
cmd.Properties("Output Stream").Value = Response
cmd.Properties("Base Path") = "c:\schemas"
cmd.Properties("Mapping schema") = "CustOrd.xdr"

cmd.Execute , , adExecuteStream
```

7.7.3 Updating Using Updategrams

Updategrams provide an intuitive way to perform an instance-based transformation from a before state to an after state. Updategrams operate over either a default XML view implied by its instance data (if no annotated schema is referenced) or over the view defined by the annotated schema and the top-level element of the Updategram. Listing 7.14 is a simple example.

Listing 7.14 Updategram Example

```
<root xmlns:updg="urn:schemas-microsoft-com:xml-updategram">
  <updg:sync mapping-schema="nwind.xml" nullvalue="ISNULL">
    <updg:before>
      <Customer CustomerID="LAZYK" CompanyName="ISNULL"
```

```
                Address="12 Orchestra Terrace">
        <Order oid="10482"/>
      </Customer>
    </updg:before>
    <updg:after>
      <Customer CustomerID="LAZYK"
                CompanyName="Lazy K Country Store"
                Address="12 Opera Court">
        <Order oid="10354"/>
      </Customer>
    </updg:after>
  </updg:sync>
</root>
```

Updategrams use their own namespace `urn:schemas-microsoft-com:xml-updategram`. Each `updg:sync block` defines the boundaries of an update batch that uses optimistic concurrency control to perform the updates transactionally. The before image in `updg:before` is used both for determining the data to be updated as well as to perform the conflict test. The after image in `updg:after` gives what has to be changed. If the before state is empty or missing, the after state defines an insert. If the after state is empty or missing, the before state defines what has to be deleted. Otherwise the necessary insertions, updates, and deletions are inferred from the difference between the before and after image. Several optional features allow the user to deal with identity and aligning elements between the before and after state. The `nullvalue` attribute indicates that the fields with the specified value need to be compared or set to NULL, respectively.

In Listing 7.14, the customer with the given data (including a company name set to NULL) gets a new company name and address. In addition, the relation to the order 10482 is removed and replaced by a new relation to order 10354.

7.7.4 Bulkloading

Neither Updategrams nor the OpenXML mechanism previously described is well suited to load large amounts of XML data into the database since they both require the whole XML document to be loaded into memory before they perform the insertion of the data. Bulkload is provided as a COM object that allows loading large amounts of XML data via an annotated schema into either an existing database or after creating the relational schema implied by the annotated schema. Transacted and nontransacted load mechanisms are available, and Bulkload can be integrated into a data transformation system (DTS) workflow.

For efficiency, the XML data are streamed in only once via the SAX parser to perform the load. Therefore, the loaded XML data needs to satisfy certain conditions in order to provide the correct loading of the data. For example, all the data that generates a new row needs to appear in the same element context. In order to avoid buffering a potentially large amount of XML data, the information that contains the key of the parent has to appear before any of its children.

Listing 7.15 is a sample Visual Basic script that uses the Bulkload object to load a file into the database.

Listing 7.15 Visual Basic Script for Bulkload

```
set objBL = CreateObject("SQLXMLBulkLoad.SQLXMLBulkLoad")

'open SQL Server connection
objBL.ConnectionString = "provider=SQLOLEDB.1;data
source=mydatabase;database=Northwind;uid=user;pwd=password"

'set Bulkload properties
objBL.ErrorLogFile = "c:\blklderror.xml"
objBL.CheckConstraints = True
objBL.Transaction = True
objBL.KeepIdentity = True
objBL.SchemaGen = False

objBL.Execute "c:\annotatedschema.xdr", "c:\data.xml"

Set objBL = Nothing
```

7.8 Conclusion

This chapter presented the basic technologies required to enable a relational database with XML to cover the current main scenarios of exporting and importing structured XML data. Based on SQL Server 2000's XML support, it gave an overview of the different building blocks such as HTTP and SOAP access, queryable and updateable XML views, rowset views over XML, and XML serialization of relational results. Rowset views over XML and the XML serialization of relational results can be characterized as providing XML support for users feeling comfortable in the context of the relational world, whereas the XML views provide XML-based access to the database for people more familiar with XML.

The next generation of relational systems will not stop at this level though. Besides working on standardizing the server-side aspects of XML generation

(Eisenberg and Melton 2001), they will also add support to deal with native XML documents in the form of an XML data type. Besides the logical next step to provide better support for the semi-structured and marked-up uses of XML, they will be providing support for the increased expectation that more and more of the XML messages and documents will have to be stored and queried in their native form. Thus, XQuery support both over the XML views described in this chapter and the XML data type will be another important capability of the second phase of XML support in relational database systems.

Chapter 8

A Generic Architecture for Storing XML Documents in a Relational Database

Richard Edwards

8.1 Introduction

The relational database is by far the most pervasive data storage paradigm encountered across all application domains in industry and academia. The majority of organizations with a substantial IT infrastructure will have successfully implemented some sort of relational database technology, and many of these will have teams of programmers, database administrators, and other technical staff to design, deploy, support, maintain, and evolve their relational database solutions. Even many non-technical staff involved in the provision or use of database systems will have a reasonable appreciation of the capabilities and approximate structure of the underlying relational database platform. The relational data model is, in short, one of computer science's most prominent success stories, and one of the IT industry's biggest revenue earners.

In a typical application, a database server acts as an information repository for a user interface—the "client"—that runs on the user's desktop machine. In this "client/server" architecture, the client sends requests to create, retrieve, modify, or delete data stored on the server. More sophisticated applications may involve multiple client applications interacting with information partitioned across heterogeneous data servers. Furthermore, in a multitiered architecture, additional application layers (often acting as database proxy servers, information brokers, or business rule enforcers) may lie between the user interface and the database(s).

The advent of object-oriented approaches to programming may have encouraged innovative thinking in terms of data representation and manipulation, but—while many client applications are written using object-oriented programming languages—the underlying data storage technologies that serve these applications are still predominantly relational. The attractiveness (to the application designer at least) of object databases has to some extent been thwarted by the maturity, robustness, speed, security, and scalability of the many available commercial and Open Source relational database products, coupled with their increasing support for hybrid object-relational functionality (such as object persistence and native Java support).

The increasing use of the Internet as a platform for applications has added to the popularity of the relational database management system (RDBMS) as an information store, with many RDBMS vendors incorporating Web support into the feature sets of their product ranges. Likewise, the providers of content-serving Web application platforms (including Web-savvy scripting languages and other server-side technologies) have all addressed the issue of connection to relational data sources.

XML is well established as a platform-independent information exchange format. Thus far, it has predominantly been used for the encapsulation of data and metadata that will often (in part, at least) have originated from, or be destined for, a relational database. In the expanding information economy, many business-to-business (B2B) applications are exchanging data across the Internet in this way, often with no direct human intervention. The wide availability of standard techniques and tools for creating, parsing, validating, and transforming XML has greatly assisted the goal of systems interoperability, through the automated exchange and verification of XML-encoded data and the validation of its structure and content against agreed schemata.

The rapid take-up of XML is catalyzing a reappraisal of data storage approaches, and in particular the future role of RDBMS products in XML-compliant architectures. The move by many organizations to mobilize information in and out of their secure, proprietary, relational data stores through the medium of XML-compliant markup languages (often incorporating descriptive annotations and metadata) is highlighting the many benefits of standards-based interoperable solutions and—in certain situations—the advantages of the semi-structured paradigm over more rigid and inflexible data models.

RDBMS vendors have not been slow in incorporating XML-related functionality into their products, and most now offer some degree of XML support. There are (for example) SQL extensions in many products that allow data to be extracted from relational tables and recast in XML format. Those that permit the storage of XML data may offer one or more options as to the level of granularity of storage.

XML documents may be stored as single entities, rather like flat files stored on a file server. At first sight, this may seem a relatively pointless exercise (after all, we could just store flat files on a file server!), but it does have the benefit that user access permissions can be more closely integrated with other database object permissions.

XML documents may be stored as linked "chunks"—a useful approach if the XML data is "document centric"; that is, it has recognizable paragraphs of plain text or "mixed content" (where text is interspersed with markup).

XML documents may be broken down into small components that are stored in regular relational tables. This approach often requires an explicit mapping between the XML schema and the database tables—that is, between elements and tables, and between attributes and columns.

The latter strategy may prove the most satisfactory if the aim is to support schema-aware searches and low-level editing, but it is likely to prove expensive as regards the marshalling of data back into XML format (since this may involve a large number of table joins). In practice, our choice will be determined by our application's requirements with regard to querying, cross-linking, and document component reuse, among other factors.

Despite these innovations, there is little industry consensus as to the most appropriate way to support XML within the relational data model. Applications that bind too closely to product-specific database extensions run the risk of vendor tie-in and incompatibility with other products, and systems that involve more than one RDBMS platform may require substantially different interfaces to each. Some organizations are evaluating the native XML database technologies that are emerging, but many are reluctant to make a decision until these products have matured and reached the levels of scalability, performance, and cost-effectiveness of RDBMSs.

In this chapter, a simple generic architecture for the storage, manipulation, and retrieval of well-formed XML documents in relational databases is presented (it will be assumed that the reader has a working knowledge of XML, Java, JDBC, relational database concepts, SQL, and common database extensions such as stored procedures). The generic architecture of the repository has the benefit that it allows for rapid prototyping and experimentation, particularly for the reader who is uncertain of which XML schema(s) they will ultimately be using in their real world applications. While it may be less scalable than a schema-specific model (where there is an explicit mapping between XML fragments and database objects) and will doubtless be less functional than a native XML database, it does at least allow the RDBMS-savvy application developer to dip a toe in the waters of XML and gain hands-on experience of working with data in this format, and it should serve as a useful pointer towards the requirements for a fully functional enterprise-scalable system.

Since we can store any well-formed XML, we can, by definition, also store XML Schema Definitions (XSD) and Extensible Stylesheet Language Transformations (XSLT) alongside the documents to which they refer. Furthermore, since we are dealing with XML, should it become necessary to migrate all of the content at some later stage, we can simply export our data (as XML) and upload it to the desired platform.

8.2 System Architecture

The repository we will build consists of a relational database, containing tables and the stored procedures needed to access them, and Java classes that provide an interface layer upon which applications can be built. The stored procedures form a rudimentary API for the Java classes; the classes do not need to know about the underlying table design—all they require knowledge of are the stored procedures that insert, select, update, and delete information for them. This (logical) three-tier architecture—consisting of database objects (the tables), a data-access level (the stored procedures), and repository-aware Java classes—provides a basic platform upon which we can build applications that persist and manipulate XML documents in a relational database. The files in the code download for this chapter are summarized in Table 8.1.

Table 8.1 Code Download Files

Type	Name	Description
Java classes	xmlrepDB.java	Various database access utilities
	xmlrepSAX.java	Various SAX-related utilities
	scanXML.java	Performs a well-formedness check
	uploadXML.java	Uploads an XML file into the database
	extractXML.java	Retrieves an XML file from the database
SQL scripts	create_xmlrep_db.sql	Creates all the database objects
	hello-world-xml.sql	Manually creates some XML in the database

There are also some example XML files for you, the reader, to test the system with. The code samples have been tested on various Windows PCs running Java 2, Microsoft SQL Server, and the Apache Xerces class library, but they should work on other platforms; the majority of the SQL is generic, and I have tried to keep the stored procedures as simple as possible.

8.2.1 Installing Xerces

Go to http://xml.apache.org/dist/xerxes-j/ and download the most recent binaries. For my Windows PC, I downloaded Xerces-J-bin.2.0.1.zip and unzipped the contents to C:\Program Files\Javasoft\xerxes-2_0_1. Add the jar files to your `classpath` environment variable. Xerces comes with some excellent examples that can be tested from the command line to ensure that the Java environment and XML libraries are working properly before we start.

8.3 The Data Model

The data model we will use for the database tables is based loosely on the W3C's Document Object Model (DOM). Briefly put, the DOM represents an XML document as a node tree, with a top-level document node supporting a tree of nodes (representing elements) and leaves (representing text, CDATA, entity references, processing instructions, and comments). Like the DOM, our data model will need to support namespaces, must maintain the distinction between elements and attributes, and should be able to accommodate text and CDATA content of any length.

Listing 8.1 shows an example XML document (in this case a WML file designed to be displayed on a WAP-enabled mobile device), and Figure 8.1 shows the corresponding DOM; note that a document node is above the root element `<wml>`. For simplicity, attributes have not been shown in the diagram, text leaves are represented by a graphic, and whitespace (consisting of carriage returns and spaces for indentation) has been ignored.

Listing 8.1 Example XML Document

```
<?xml version="1.0"?>
<wml>
 <card id="cFirst" title="First card" newcontext="true">
  <p align="center">
   <img src="/images/logo.wbmp" alt="Logo" align="middle"/>
   <br/>
   Content of the first card.
  </p>
  <p>
   <a href="#cSecond">Next card</a>
  </p>
 </card>
 <card id="cSecond" title="Second card">
  <p align="center">
   Content of the second card.
  </p>
 </card>
</wml>
```

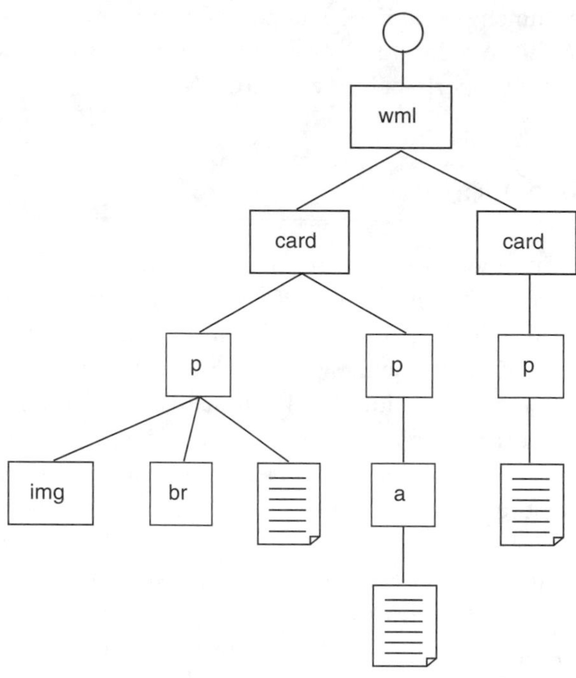

Figure 8.1 Example XML Document Represented as a Node Tree

The W3C's DOM specifications (Levels 1, 2, and 3) detail the methods and interfaces that are required of a "DOM-compliant" application. These methods are largely concerned with the creation, querying, and manipulation of nodes, and the DOM provides a rich interface for interacting with XML document content.

Most DOM applications create DOM representations of XML documents in memory, which allows for rapid access but creates a limitation on the size of documents that may be considered; this problem becomes even more significant in a Web services environment in which multiple users or agents may be carrying out DOM manipulations simultaneously. Clearly, if an XML database can provide a DOM-compliant API, then the problem of memory limitations can be avoided almost entirely; despite the increased latency (since calls to DOM methods will require round trips to the database, rather than in-memory computations), this situation will be substantially more scalable as we consider large documents in multiuser environments. The system described in this chapter could easily be extended to provide full DOM compliance and hence provide a migration path for applications that are starting to feel the pinch of memory limitations.

8.3.1 DOM Storage in Relational Databases

So how can we create a DOM representation of an XML document in a relational database, and is it possible to do so in a way that will be able to offer reasonable performance? Since the DOM is a node tree, we can learn much from the SQL experts who have tackled the issue of storing trees in relational databases. The two most common approaches are known (in Joe Celko's terminology [Celko 2000]) as the Adjacency List Model and the Nested Sets Model. The former does not store child order—not a problem for some trees (such as a hierarchical view of the components of an electric toaster), but this model is clearly incompatible with XML, in which elements are ordered—we cannot arbitrarily change the order of paragraphs in an XHTML document, for example. Another problem of the Adjacency List Model is that it is costly to recreate the original tree, as it typically involves a recursive "walk" over the entire node set, since (typically) each node only knows about its parent.

8.3.2 The Nested Sets Model

Fortunately, the second approach, the Nested Sets Model, turns out to be an almost perfect match for XML; in fact, we might say that XML is an ideal serialization syntax for Nested Sets data. In the Nested Sets Model, each node is stored with two integer coordinates (we will call them x and y, representing left and right), which allow us to preserve order and a sense of location in the hierarchy. These coordinates are assigned at the time of storage (or creation) by walking the node tree from top-down and from left to right, numbering as we go. Figure 8.2 shows the previous node tree with the nodes numbered in accordance with the Nested Sets Model.

This two-coordinate system provides simple methods for navigation and structure elucidation, for example:

- The next sibling (x', y') of any given node (x, y) has $x' = y + 1$.
- The first child (x', y') of any given node (x, y) has $x' = x + 1$.
- The descendant nodes (x', y') of a given node (x, y) have x , x' , y and x , y' , y.
- The ancestor nodes (x', y') of a given node (x, y) have $x' < x > y'$ and $x' , y . y'$.
- The parent node of (x, y) has the largest x' in the set defined by $x' , x . y'$.

This labeling scheme clearly facilitates the rapid serialization of documents (or fragments thereof), at the expense of relabeling parts of the document when new nodes are added or shuffled around.

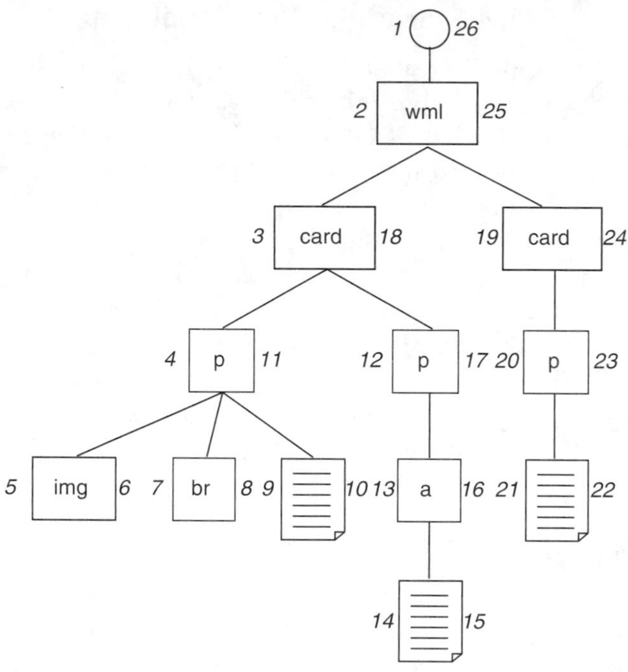

Figure 8.2 Sample Node Tree, with Nested Sets Coordinates

■ 8.4 Creating the Database

In order to store XML data in this fashion, we need tables that reflect the abstract structure of the DOM, with the added information required by the Nested Sets Model. We need one or more tables in which to store information about the node, such as its type, its *x* and *y* coordinates, any attributes, and its name (which may include a namespace) or its content (in the case of a text or CDATA node). We need to be mindful of the possible contents of each type of node; an element node will have a name and may have a namespace and/or a list of attributes (treated as name/value pairs), whereas a text leaf just has text content. Furthermore, since we want to build a repository for more than one document, we need a table to store some information about the documents (at the very least, a unique document ID), and rows in the node table will need to hold a reference to the document to which they belong (we could construct a multidocument repository as if it were one large XML document, comprising many smaller documents, but for many applications the overhead of maintaining the *x*, *y* coordinates would probably prove too costly).

8.4.1 The Physical Data Model

In this section we will walk through the database creation script create_xml-rep_db.sql. But before we begin, let's take a look at the physical data model shown in Figure 8.3. There are 12 tables in all; one (`node_type`) is a lookup table that defines the different types of nodes we will be storing. The remaining 11 tables will store information regarding the nodes, attributes, and leaves for each XML document we import. The *x* and *y* values (respectively, the left and right Nested Sets coordinates) for each node will be stored in the *node* table.

The first step in building the database tables is to create a new database called "xmlrep". Next, we need to create a login called "xmlrep_user" (we will use this later to connect to the repository). This is shown in Listing 8.2.

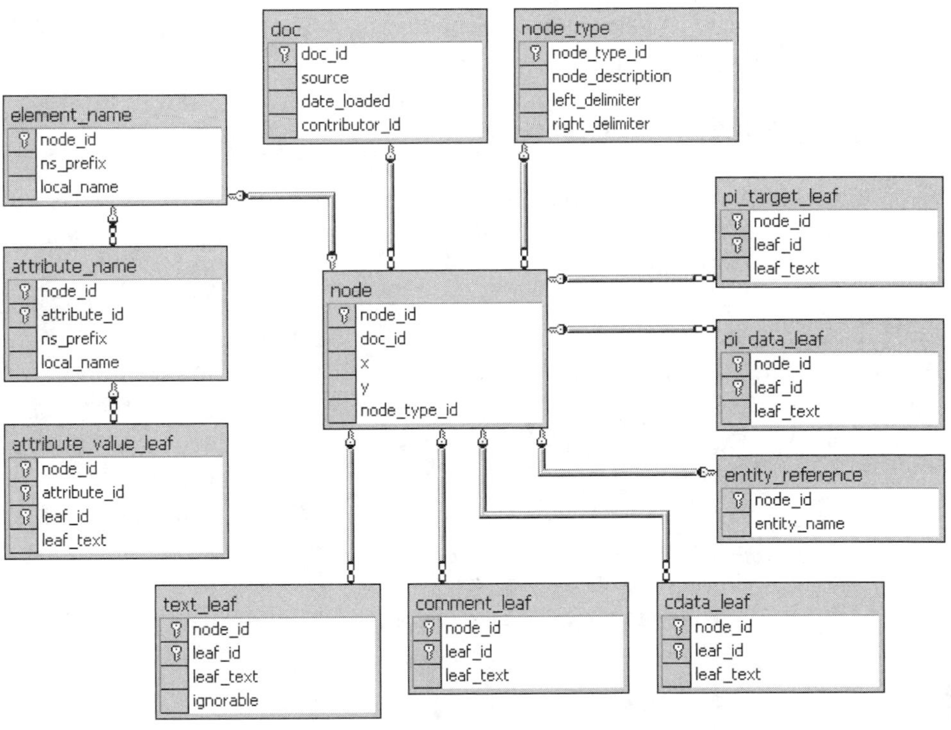

Figure 8.3 The Physical Data Model for the XML Repository

Listing 8.2 Create xmlrep_user

```
-- Create a login (arguments: user-id, password, default-db,
language)
IF NOT EXISTS (SELECT * FROM master.dbo.syslogins
WHERE loginname = 'xmlrep_user')
EXEC sp_addlogin 'xmlrep_user', 'fishcakes', 'xmlrep', 'British'
GO
-- Grant access for the user to this database
EXEC sp_grantdbaccess 'xmlrep_user', 'xmlrep_user'
GO
```

8.4.2 Creating User-Defined Data Types

Some user-defined data types will be useful, both for the tables and for the stored procedures we will create later to access them. (If we want to change the lengths of the various varchar fields, then this is our opportunity to do it.) This is shown in Listing 8.3.

Listing 8.3 Create User-Defined Types

```
EXEC sp_addtype 't_attribute_name', 'VARCHAR(50)', 'NOT NULL'
EXEC sp_addtype 't_doc_id', 'NUMERIC(6,0)', 'NOT NULL'
EXEC sp_addtype 't_element_name', 'VARCHAR(50)', 'NOT NULL'
EXEC sp_addtype 't_entity_ref', 'VARCHAR(50)', 'NOT NULL'
EXEC sp_addtype 't_leaf_id', 'TINYINT', 'NULL'
EXEC sp_addtype 't_leaf_text', 'VARCHAR(255)', 'NULL'
EXEC sp_addtype 't_node_type_id', 'TINYINT', 'NOT NULL'
EXEC sp_addtype 't_node_id', 'NUMERIC(10,0)', 'NOT NULL'
EXEC sp_addtype 't_ns_prefix', 'VARCHAR(25)', 'NOT NULL'
EXEC sp_addtype 't_seq_no', 'TINYINT', 'NOT NULL'
EXEC sp_addtype 't_source', 'VARCHAR(255)', 'NULL'
EXEC sp_addtype 't_user_id', 'VARCHAR(50)', 'NULL'
EXEC sp_addtype 't_xpath_maxlen', 'VARCHAR (1000)', 'NOT NULL'
EXEC sp_addtype 't_xy_index', 'INT', 'NOT NULL'
GO
```

8.4.3 Creating the Tables

As for the tables, let's start by creating the node_type lookup table and populate it with some data. The node_type table needs to contain the types of nodes that can appear, each of which has a numerical ID (node_type_id) and a human-readable description (`node_description`); the two remaining columns (`left_delimiter` and `right_delimiter`) store the characters that come before and after a node of the specified type (respectively); for example, a CDATA section starts with "<![CDATA[" and finishes with "]]>". The code is shown in Listing 8.4.

Listing 8.4 Create node_type Lookup Table

```
-- Create lookup table
CREATE TABLE dbo.node_type (
  node_type_id     t_node_type_id NOT NULL,
  node_description VARCHAR(50)    NOT NULL,
  left_delimiter   VARCHAR(9)     NOT NULL,
  right_delimiter  VARCHAR(9)     NOT NULL,
  CONSTRAINT PK_nt PRIMARY KEY CLUSTERED (node_type_id),
  CONSTRAINT IX_nt UNIQUE NONCLUSTERED (node_description))
GO
-- Insert data
INSERT INTO node_type VALUES (1, 'ELEMENT', '<', '>');
INSERT INTO node_type VALUES (3, 'TEXT_NODE', '', '');
INSERT INTO node_type VALUES (4, 'CDATA_SECTION_NODE', '<![CDATA[',
']]>');
INSERT INTO node_type VALUES (5, 'ENTITY_REFERENCE_NODE', '&',
';');
INSERT INTO node_type VALUES (7, 'PROCESSING_INSTRUCTION_NODE',
'<?', '?>');
INSERT INTO node_type VALUES (8, 'COMMENT_NODE', '<!--', '-->');
INSERT INTO node_type VALUES (9, 'DOCUMENT_NODE', '', '');
GO
```

The `doc` table stores the unique `doc_id` and some metadata, the name of the source document (`source`), the date it was loaded (`date_loaded`), and a reference to the user who loaded it (`contributor_id`). This is shown in Listing 8.5.

Listing 8.5 Create doc Table

```
CREATE TABLE dbo.doc (
  doc_id          t_doc_id  IDENTITY (1, 1) NOT NULL,
  source          t_source  NOT NULL,
  date_loaded     DATETIME  NOT NULL,
  contributor_id  t_user_id NOT NULL,
  CONSTRAINT PK_d PRIMARY KEY CLUSTERED (doc_id))
GO
```

The `node` table (see Listing 8.6) will be the hub of most database activity—every node of every document stored in the repository will have an entry here. Each node will be assigned an arbitrary `node_id` (for performance reasons, this unique identity will be designated as the primary key for the table) and `x` and `y` coordinates. Each node will have a reference (`doc_id`) to the containing document and a type (`node_type_id`).

Why not make `doc_id` and `x` a combination primary key (since these two columns uniquely identify a node in a document)? Well, since many database management systems sort (or "cluster") data according to the primary key, we will be introducing a large overhead in managing this table (with resulting performance and data contention side effects) in the event that nodes are created, moved, or destroyed, since each of these activities could involve changes to the *x* coordinates of many nodes. The use of an arbitrary unique identifier (`node_id`, in this case) will allow nodes to be added and manipulated rapidly, without incurring the expense of resorting any entries (although there will be a performance hit from maintenance to the index `IX_n`).

Listing 8.6 Create node Table

```
CREATE TABLE dbo.node (
  node_id      t_node_id      IDENTITY (1, 1) NOT NULL,
  doc_id       t_doc_id       NOT NULL,
  x            t_xy_index     NOT NULL,
  y            t_xy_index     NULL,
  node_type_id t_node_type_id NOT NULL,
  CONSTRAINT PK_n PRIMARY KEY CLUSTERED (node_id),
  CONSTRAINT IX_n UNIQUE NONCLUSTERED (doc_id, x),
  CONSTRAINT FK_n_d FOREIGN KEY (doc_id)
    REFERENCES dbo.doc (doc_id),
  CONSTRAINT FK_n_nt FOREIGN KEY (node_type_id)
    REFERENCES dbo.node_type (node_type_id))
GO
```

If a given node is an element, there will be an entry in the `element_name` table (see Listing 8.7), which again has `node_id` as its primary key. Each element may have a namespace prefix (`ns_prefix`) and will certainly have a name (`local_name`). In common with many of the other tables, the `node_id` column is a foreign key reference back to the `node_id` in the `node` table.

Listing 8.7 Create element_name Table

```
CREATE TABLE dbo.element_name (
  node_id    t_node_id      NOT NULL,
  ns_prefix  t_ns_prefix    NULL,
  local_name t_element_name NOT NULL,
  CONSTRAINT PK_en PRIMARY KEY CLUSTERED (node_id),
  CONSTRAINT FK_en_n FOREIGN KEY (node_id)
    REFERENCES dbo.node (node_id))
GO
```

The XML specification permits very long element names and namespace prefixes, which creates a problem for storage in some RDBMSs (in some systems, character fields are restricted to 255 characters). We could store these items as linked lists of text fields (indeed, we will use this technique later for handling text and CDATA), but for the purposes of this demonstration (and to make querying simpler), we will make a restriction on the lengths of these fields (their lengths are determined by the user types `t_element_name` and `t_ns_prefix`, respectively).

An element may have one or more attributes (e.g., `<p align="center">`, where `p` is the element name, `align` is an attribute name, and `center` is the value). In the DOM, an attribute is treated as a special type of node. However, since attributes are anchored to the containing element and have different properties to other nodes (e.g., we cannot have an element with two attributes of the same qualified name), we will not store attribute information in the `node` table. Attribute names are stored in the `attribute_name` table (see Listing 8.8); each entry is uniquely identified by the `node_id` of the containing element and an arbitrary `attribute_id`. The namespace prefix (if any) is stored in `ns_prefix`, and the name is stored in `local_name`.

Listing 8.8 Create attribute_name Table

```
CREATE TABLE dbo.attribute_name (
  node_id      t_node_id        NOT NULL,
  attribute_id t_seq_no         NOT NULL,
  ns_prefix    t_ns_prefix      NULL,
  local_name   t_attribute_name NOT NULL,
  CONSTRAINT PK_an PRIMARY KEY CLUSTERED (node_id, attribute_id),
  CONSTRAINT FK_ann_en FOREIGN KEY (node_id)
    REFERENCES dbo.element_name (node_id))
GO
```

The attribute_value_leaf table (see Listing 8.9) follows the same pattern, but since attribute values are often long, we need to allow for any length. This can be achieved in some RDBMSs with a very long (or unbounded) varchar column, but since we want to make our solution as portable as possible, we can achieve the same effect by creating a list of finite length varchar fields.

Listing 8.9 Create attribute_value_leaf Table

```
CREATE TABLE dbo.attribute_value_leaf (
  node_id      t_node_id   NOT NULL,
  attribute_id t_seq_no    NOT NULL,
  leaf_id      t_leaf_id   NOT NULL,
  leaf_text    t_leaf_text NOT NULL,
  CONSTRAINT PK_avl PRIMARY KEY CLUSTERED (node_id, attribute_id,
leaf_id),
  CONSTRAINT FK_avl_an FOREIGN KEY (node_id, attribute_id)
    REFERENCES dbo.attribute_name (node_id, attribute_id))
GO
```

If the length of the attribute value exceeds the length of the leaf_text column, a new row is added for the overspill and given a sequential leaf_id, and so on, until the whole of the value has been accommodated. To rebuild the value, a query will have to select all rows from attribute_value_leaf for a given node_id and attribute_id, order them by leaf_id, and pass the result set back to a function that knits the leaves back together.

The contents of text nodes are stored in text_leaf (see Listing 8.10), again with a leaf_id to determine the sequence order of the chunks into which the content was split in the event that it was too large for the leaf_text column. Since some XML applications make the distinction between textual content that is ignorable (such as whitespace and carriage returns, that may have been included for readability) and that is not ignorable (anything else), we will have an ignorable column to store a flag to indicate this situation.

Listing 8.10 Create text_leaf Table

```
CREATE TABLE dbo.text_leaf (
  node_id    t_node_id   NOT NULL,
  leaf_id    t_leaf_id   NOT NULL,
  leaf_text t_leaf_text NOT NULL,
  ignorable BIT          NOT NULL,
  CONSTRAINT PK_tl PRIMARY KEY CLUSTERED (node_id, leaf_id),
  CONSTRAINT FK_tl_n FOREIGN KEY (node_id)
```

```
    REFERENCES dbo.node (node_id))
GO
```

Processing instructions consist of a reference to the target application followed by data, separated by whitespace. Since the target and the data may be long, we will store them with the same leafing mechanism, in `pi_target_leaf` and `pi_data_leaf`, respectively. These tables are shown in Listing 8.11.

Listing 8.11 Create pi_target_leaf and pi_data_leaf Tables

```
CREATE TABLE dbo.pi_target_leaf (
  node_id   t_node_id   NOT NULL,
  leaf_id   t_leaf_id   NOT NULL,
  leaf_text t_leaf_text NOT NULL,
  CONSTRAINT PK_pitl PRIMARY KEY CLUSTERED (node_id, leaf_id),
  CONSTRAINT FK_pitl_n FOREIGN KEY (node_id)
    REFERENCES dbo.node (node_id))
GO
CREATE TABLE dbo.pi_data_leaf (
  node_id   t_node_id   NOT NULL,
  leaf_id   t_leaf_id   NOT NULL,
  leaf_text t_leaf_text NOT NULL,
  CONSTRAINT PK_pidl PRIMARY KEY CLUSTERED (node_id, leaf_id),
  CONSTRAINT FK_pidl_n FOREIGN KEY (node_id)
    REFERENCES dbo.node (node_id))
GO
```

Entity references (unparsed) are generally short, so a simple `entity_reference` table—with just a `node_id` and `leaf_text` column—will suffice. This is shown in Listing 8.12.

Listing 8.12 Create entity_reference Table

```
CREATE TABLE dbo.entity_reference (
  node_id     t_node_id    NOT NULL,
  entity_name t_entity_ref NOT NULL,
  CONSTRAINT PK_er PRIMARY KEY CLUSTERED (node_id),
  CONSTRAINT FK_er_n FOREIGN KEY (node_id)
    REFERENCES dbo.node (node_id))
GO
```

The remaining tables, comment_leaf (for XML comments) and cdata_leaf (for CDATA sections), will doubtless need to store large amounts of information, and hence we will revert to a leafing mechanism for these. These tables are shown in Listing 8.13.

Listing 8.13 Create comment_leaf and cdata_leaf Tables

```
CREATE TABLE dbo.comment_leaf (
  node_id   t_node_id   NOT NULL,
  leaf_id   t_leaf_id   NOT NULL,
  leaf_text t_leaf_text NOT NULL,
  CONSTRAINT PK_col PRIMARY KEY CLUSTERED (node_id, leaf_id),
  CONSTRAINT FK_col_n FOREIGN KEY (node_id)
    REFERENCES dbo.node (node_id))
GO
CREATE TABLE dbo.cdata_leaf (
  node_id   t_node_id   NOT NULL,
  leaf_id   t_leaf_id   NOT NULL,
  leaf_text t_leaf_text NOT NULL,
  CONSTRAINT PK_cdl PRIMARY KEY CLUSTERED (node_id, leaf_id),
  CONSTRAINT FK_cdl_n FOREIGN KEY (node_id)
    REFERENCES dbo.node (node_id))
GO
```

It will have become obvious that a number of assumptions and restrictions have been introduced (the reader is invited to make such changes as are necessary to meet their particular requirements). For documents with a large amount of mixed content, or with substantial CDATA sections, these last two tables shown in Listing 8.13 could have a text column instead of numerous varchar leaves. An RDBMS will store text as a linked list of (for example) 2K data pages, so some sort of optimization analysis is recommended.

Finally, we will need to set the permissions for the user, as shown in Listing 8.14.

Listing 8.14 Grant Permissions

```
-- Grant permissions to the repository user(s)
GRANT SELECT ON node_type TO xmlrep_user
GRANT SELECT, INSERT, UPDATE, DELETE ON attribute_name TO
xmlrep_user
GRANT SELECT, INSERT, UPDATE, DELETE ON attribute_value_leaf TO
xmlrep_user
```

```
GRANT SELECT, INSERT, UPDATE, DELETE ON cdata_leaf TO xmlrep_user
GRANT SELECT, INSERT, UPDATE, DELETE ON comment_leaf TO xmlrep_user
GRANT SELECT, INSERT, UPDATE, DELETE ON doc TO xmlrep_user
GRANT SELECT, INSERT, UPDATE, DELETE ON element_name TO xmlrep_user
GRANT SELECT, INSERT, UPDATE, DELETE ON entity_reference TO
xmlrep_user
GRANT SELECT, INSERT, UPDATE, DELETE ON node TO xmlrep_user
GRANT SELECT, INSERT, UPDATE, DELETE ON pi_data_leaf TO xmlrep_user
GRANT SELECT, INSERT, UPDATE, DELETE ON pi_target_leaf TO
xmlrep_user
GRANT SELECT, INSERT, UPDATE, DELETE ON text_leaf TO xmlrep_user
GO
```

The stored procedures in Listing 8.15 will be useful for error checking later; they return the leaf size (the length of `t_leaf_text`), the maximum element name length (`t_element_name`), the maximum namespace prefix length (`t_ns_prefix`) and the maximum entity name length (`t_entity_ref`).

Listing 8.15 Stored Procedures for Error Checking

```
CREATE PROCEDURE dbo.leafSize AS
SELECT length AS value FROM systypes WHERE name = 't_leaf_text'
GO
CREATE PROCEDURE dbo.elementNameLength AS
SELECT length AS value FROM systypes WHERE name = 't_element_name'
GO
CREATE PROCEDURE dbo.nsPrefixLength AS
SELECT length AS value FROM systypes WHERE name = 't_ns_prefix'
GO
CREATE PROCEDURE dbo.entityRefLength AS
SELECT length AS value FROM systypes WHERE name = 't_entity_ref'
GO
GRANT EXECUTE ON dbo.leafSize TO xmlrep_user
GRANT EXECUTE ON dbo.elementNameLength TO xmlrep_user
GRANT EXECUTE ON dbo.nsPrefixLength TO xmlrep_user
GRANT EXECUTE ON dbo.entityRefLength TO xmlrep_user
GO
```

Time for a quick recap: Thus far, we have decided on a suitable database model, consisting of a DOM-style node tree in which the nodes are labeled according to the Nested Sets Model (to allow for easy navigation and retrieval). We have built the database, populated the lookup table, built some useful stored procedures, created a user, and set the permissions.

8.4.4 Serializing a Document out of the Repository

In order to reconstruct an XML file from this repository, we will need a stored procedure to pull all the data together from the tables. Essentially, this will involve a large union query over all the tables. This procedure also needs to include the bits of character data that delimit the various components of XML (for example, angle brackets around element names). We also need to ensure that everything is returned in the correct order (this involves a bit more effort than just sorting by values of *x*, as we will see). The procedure can take up to three arguments: the ID of the document, the x value of the node at which to start (allowing us to retrieve a fragment of the document rather than the whole; if this argument is not supplied, the procedure serializes the whole document), and an optional flag that will cause some additional attributes to be included for each element (the *x* and *y* coordinates, and the `node_id`). This is shown in Listing 8.16.

Listing 8.16 Create rep_serialise_nodes Procedure

```
CREATE PROCEDURE dbo.rep_serialise_nodes
                 @doc_id  t_doc_id,
                 @start_x t_xy_index = 1,
                 @incl_xy BIT = 0
AS
BEGIN
-- Get the y coordinate of the start node
 DECLARE @start_y t_xy_index
 SELECT @start_y = y
   FROM node
  WHERE doc_id = @doc_id
    AND x = @start_x
 -- Get the x coordinate of the first element
 -- (we may be starting with the document node)
 DECLARE @first_el t_xy_index
 SELECT @first_el = MIN(x)
   FROM node
  WHERE doc_id = @doc_id
    AND node_type_id = 1
    AND x >= @start_x
 -- Rebuild the document:
```

```
-- Start with the left delimiter for the type of node
SELECT n.x AS seq_no_1,
       1   AS seq_no_2,
       0   AS seq_no_3,
       0   AS seq_no_4,
       0   AS seq_no_5,
       t.left_delimiter AS parsed_text
  FROM node n,
       node_type t
 WHERE n.doc_id = @doc_id
   AND n.node_type_id = t.node_type_id
   AND t.left_delimiter > ''
   AND n.x >= @start_x
   AND n.x < @start_y
UNION
-- Element names (each prefixed with namespace reference, if any)
SELECT n.x, 2, 0, 0, 0, ISNULL(e.ns_prefix + ':', '') +
e.local_name
  FROM element_name e,
       node n
 WHERE n.doc_id = @doc_id
   AND n.x >= @start_x AND n.x < @start_y
   AND n.node_id = e.node_id
UNION
-- If user requested optional attributes, need to declare the
'xmlrep' namespace at the root element
SELECT n.x, 3, 0, 0, 1, '
xmlns:repository="http://www.rgedwards.com/" '
  FROM node n
 WHERE n.doc_id = @doc_id
   AND n.x = @first_el
   AND @incl_xy = 1
UNION
-- Optional attributes describing node coordinates (elements only)
SELECT n.x, 3, 0, 1, 1,
  ' ' + 'repository:x="' + CONVERT(VARCHAR(11), x)
  + '" repository:y="' + CONVERT(VARCHAR(11), n.y)
  + '" repository:nodeID="' + CONVERT(VARCHAR(11), n.node_id) +
'"'
  FROM node n
 WHERE n.doc_id = @doc_id
   AND n.x >= @start_x AND n.x < @start_y
```

```
   AND n.node_type_id = 1  -- ELEMENT
   AND @incl_xy = 1
UNION
-- Attribute name (each prefixed with namespace reference, if any)
-- followed by equal sign and opening quote
SELECT n.x, 3, a.attribute_id, 1, 0,
       ' ' + ISNULL(a.ns_prefix + ':', '') + a.local_name + '="'
  FROM attribute_name a,
       node n
 WHERE n.doc_id = @doc_id
   AND n.x >= @start_x AND n.x < @start_y
   AND n.node_id = a.node_id
UNION
-- Attribute value
SELECT n.x, 3, a.attribute_id, 2, a.leaf_id, a.leaf_text
  FROM attribute_value_leaf a,
       node n
 WHERE n.doc_id = @doc_id
   AND n.x >= @start_x AND n.x < @start_y
   AND n.node_id = a.node_id
UNION
-- Closing quote after attribute value
SELECT n.x, 3, a.attribute_id, 3, 0, '"'
  FROM attribute_name a,
       node n
 WHERE n.doc_id = @doc_id
   AND n.x >= @start_x AND n.x < @start_y
   AND n.node_id = a.node_id
UNION
-- Text leaves
SELECT n.x, 4, 0, 0, x.leaf_id, x.leaf_text
  FROM text_leaf x,
       node n
 WHERE n.doc_id = @doc_id
   AND n.x >= @start_x AND n.x < @start_y
   AND n.node_id = x.node_id
UNION
-- Comment leaves
SELECT n.x, 5, 0, 0, c.leaf_id, c.leaf_text
  FROM comment_leaf c,
       node n
 WHERE n.doc_id = @doc_id
```

```
    AND n.x >= @start_x AND n.x < @start_y
    AND n.node_id = c.node_id
UNION
-- Processing instruction target leaves
SELECT n.x, 6, 0, 1, p.leaf_id, p.leaf_text
  FROM pi_target_leaf p,
       node n
 WHERE n.doc_id = @doc_id
   AND n.x >= @start_x AND n.x < @start_y
   AND n.node_id = p.node_id
UNION
-- Space after PI target leaves (if there are data leaves)
SELECT n.x, 6, 0, 2, p.leaf_id, ' '
  FROM pi_data_leaf p,
       node n
 WHERE n.doc_id = @doc_id
   AND n.x >= @start_x AND n.x < @start_y
   AND p.leaf_id = 1
   AND n.node_id = p.node_id
UNION
-- Processing instruction data leaves
SELECT n.x, 6, 0, 3, p.leaf_id, p.leaf_text
  FROM pi_data_leaf p,
       node n
 WHERE n.doc_id = @doc_id
   AND n.x >= @start_x AND n.x < @start_y
   AND n.node_id = p.node_id
UNION
-- CDATA leaves
SELECT n.x, 7, 0, 0, c.leaf_id, c.leaf_text
  FROM cdata_leaf c,
       node n
 WHERE n.doc_id = @doc_id
   AND n.x >= @start_x AND n.x < @start_y
   AND n.node_id = c.node_id
UNION
-- Entity references
SELECT n.x, 8, 0, 0, 0, e.entity_name
  FROM entity_reference e,
       node n
 WHERE n.doc_id = @doc_id
   AND n.x >= @start_x AND n.x < @start_y
```

```
    AND n.node_id = e.node_id
UNION
-- Right delimiter
SELECT n.x, 9, 0, 0, 0, t.right_delimiter
  FROM node n,
       node_type t
 WHERE n.doc_id = @doc_id
    AND n.node_type_id = t.node_type_id
    AND t.right_delimiter > ''
    AND n.x >= @start_x AND n.x < @start_y
UNION
-- Left braces for closing tags (elements only)
SELECT n.y, 10, 0, 0, 0, t.left_delimiter + '/'
  FROM node n,
       node_type t
 WHERE n.doc_id = @doc_id
    AND n.node_type_id = t.node_type_id
    AND n.node_type_id = 1  -- ELEMENT
    AND t.left_delimiter > ''
    AND n.x >= @start_x AND n.x < @start_y
UNION
-- Element name leaves
SELECT n.y, 10, 0, 3, 0,
       ISNULL(e.ns_prefix + ':', '') + e.local_name
  FROM node n,
       element_name e
 WHERE n.doc_id = @doc_id
    AND n.x >= @start_x AND n.x < @start_y
    AND n.node_id = e.node_id
UNION
-- Right braces for closing tags (elements only)
SELECT n.y, 10, 0, 4, 0, t.right_delimiter
  FROM node n,
       node_type t
 WHERE n.doc_id = @doc_id
    AND n.node_type_id = t.node_type_id
    AND n.node_type_id = 1  -- ELEMENT
    AND t.right_delimiter > ''
    AND n.x >= @start_x AND n.x < @start_y
-- Correct order for concatenation
 ORDER BY seq_no_1, seq_no_2, seq_no_3, seq_no_4, seq_no_5
END
```

```
GO
GRANT EXECUTE ON dbo.rep_serialise_nodes TO xmlrep_user
GO
```

8.4.5 Building an XML Document Manually

As a test, consider the following XML document (hello-world.xml):

```
<message author="me">Hello world!</message>
```

A node tree representation for this document is shown in Figure 8.4; the unlabeled node at the top is the document node.

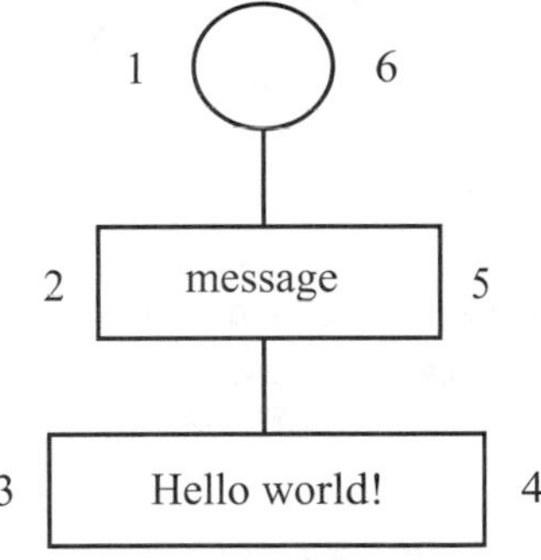

Figure 8.4 The "Hello world!" Example as a Node Tree

We can create this XML document manually in the repository as shown in Listing 8.17 (the script is in hello-world-xml.sql); later on we will create a Java class that will upload XML files automatically, but for now this will serve to illustrate the processes involved.

Listing 8.17 "Hello world!" Example

```
-- Declare some variables
DECLARE @doc_id t_doc_id
DECLARE @node_id t_node_id
-- Insert a row into the doc table and get the unique doc_id
INSERT INTO doc (contributor_id) VALUES ('your-name');
SELECT @doc_id = @@IDENTITY;
-- Create the document node (node type = 9)
```

```
INSERT INTO node (doc_id, x, y, node_type_id) VALUES (@doc_id, 1,
6, 9);
-- Create the node for the root element and get the unique node_id
INSERT INTO node (doc_id, x, y, node_type_id) VALUES (@doc_id, 2,
5, 1);
SELECT @node_id = @@IDENTITY;
-- Set the element name for the root element
INSERT INTO element_name (node_id, local_name) VALUES (@node_id,
'message');
-- Set the name and value for the attribute ('author') of the root
element
INSERT INTO attribute_name (node_id, attribute_id, local_name)
VALUES (@node_id, 1, 'author');
INSERT INTO attribute_value_leaf (node_id, attribute_id, leaf_id,
leaf_text) VALUES (@node_id, 1, 1, 'me');
-- Create the text node (node type = 3) and get the unique node_id
INSERT INTO node (doc_id, x, y, node_type_id) VALUES (@doc_id, 3,
4, 3);
SELECT @node_id = @@IDENTITY;
-- Create the text content
INSERT INTO text_leaf (node_id, leaf_id, leaf_text, ignorable)
VALUES (@node_id, 1, 'Hello world!', 0);
```

If we execute the `rep_serialise_nodes` stored procedure for this laboriously hand-crafted document, we get the results shown in Listing 8.18.

Listing 8.18 Results from rep_serialise_nodes Procedure

```
seq_no_1 seq_no_2 seq_no_3 seq_no_4 seq_no_5 parsed_text
-------- -------- -------- -------- -------- ------------
2        1        0        0        0        <
2        2        0        0        0        message
2        3        1        1        0         author="
2        3        1        2        1        me
2        3        1        3        0        "
2        9        0        0        0        >
3        4        0        0        1        Hello world!
5        10       0        0        0        </
5        10       0        3        0        message
5        10       0        4        0        >
(10 row(s) affected)
```

The sequence numbers can be discarded—they were there only to allow the procedure to sort the text items into the correct order—and the `parsed_text` column needs to be stitched back together (we will create a Java class to do this for us later), but this simple demonstration indicates the capabilities of the database we have created.

8.5 Connecting to the Repository

In this section, we will describe how to connect to the XML repository.

8.5.1 The xmlrepDB Class

First we will create a class (xmlrepDB.java) that will handle the connection to the database and provide methods to execute SQL commands, handle long strings that need splitting into leaves, and handle any exceptions that may arise (see Listing 8.19).

Listing 8.19 xmlrepDB Class

```
// Import core Java classes
import java.lang.*;
import java.sql.*;
// The xmlrepDB class
public class xmlrepDB {
   // Login ID and password
   private String username = "xmlrep_user";
   private String password = "fishcakes";
   // Other variables
   private Connection con;
   public Statement stmt;
   public int leafSize;
   public int elementNameLength;
   public int nsPrefixLength;
   public int entityRefLength;
```

In Listing 8.20, we include a `main()` method for command-line testing.

Listing 8.20 Main Method for Command-Line Testing

```
public static void main(String args[]) {
  // Instantiate the class
  xmlrepDB dbTest = new xmlrepDB();
  // Connect to the repository and attempt a query
  System.out.println("Connecting to the repository...");
  dbTest.connect();
  System.out.println("Attempting some queries...");
  System.out.println("Leaf size = " + dbTest.leafSize);
  System.out.println("Element name length = " +
     dbTest.elementNameLength);
  System.out.println("Namespace prefix length = " +
     dbTest.nsPrefixLength);
  System.out.println("Entity reference length = " +
     dbTest.entityRefLength);
  System.out.println("Disconnecting from the repository...");
  dbTest.disconnect();
  System.out.println("Done");
}
```

The connect() method (see Listing 8.21) initializes the connection to the repository using an ODBC data source called XMLREP, creates a SQL statement object, and retrieves the leaf size and the maximum element name, namespace prefix, and entity name lengths (which we will use for error trapping later).

Listing 8.21 Connect Method

```
public void connect() {
  try {
     // Load the jdbc-odbc bridge
     Class.forName ("sun.jdbc.odbc.JdbcOdbcDriver");
     // Connect to the database (and disable AutoCommit mode)
     String url = "jdbc:odbc:XMLREP";
     con = DriverManager.getConnection(url, username, password);
     con.setAutoCommit(false);
     // Create a SQL query object
     stmt = con.createStatement();
     // Determine the maximum text leaf size etc.
     leafSize = intExecSQL("rep_leafSize;");
     elementNameLength = intExecSQL("rep_elementNameLength;");
```

```
        nsPrefixLength = intExecSQL("rep_nsPrefixLength;");
        entityRefLength = intExecSQL("rep_entityRefLength;");
      } catch (java.sql.SQLException ex)
        {sqlEx (ex, "[End of SQLException]");
      } catch (java.lang.Exception ex) {javaEx(ex);}
  }
```

The disconnect() method closes the statement, commits the current transaction, and closes the connection to the repository. This is shown in Listing 8.22.

Listing 8.22 Disconnect Method

```
  public void disconnect() {
    try {
        // Close the statement
        stmt.close();
        // Commit the transaction
        commitTran();
        // Close the connection
        con.close();
      } catch (java.sql.SQLException ex)
        {sqlEx (ex, "[End of SQLException]");
      } catch (java.lang.Exception ex) {javaEx(ex);}
  }
```

The voidExecSQL() method will execute any SQL statement that does not return a result set (such as an insert, an update, or a delete statement), as shown in Listing 8.23.

Listing 8.23 voidExecSQL Method

```
  public int voidExecSQL(String sqlCmd) {
      try {stmt.executeUpdate(sqlCmd);
      } catch (java.sql.SQLException ex) {sqlEx (ex, sqlCmd);
      } catch (java.lang.Exception   ex) {javaEx(ex);}
  }
```

The intExecSQL() method will execute any SQL statement that returns a result set with an integer value column, as shown in Listing 8.24.

Listing 8.24 intExecSQL Method

```
public int intExecSQL(String sqlCmd) {
   // Return variable
   int resInt = -1;
   try {
      // Execute the query
      ResultSet rs = stmt.executeQuery(sqlCmd);
      // Loop through the records
      while (rs.next()) {
         // Read the value field
         resInt = rs.getInt("value");
      }
      // Close the result set
      rs.close();
   } catch (java.sql.SQLException ex) {sqlEx (ex, sqlCmd);
   } catch (java.lang.Exception   ex) {javaEx(ex);}
   // Return the result
   return resInt;
}
```

The replace() method (see Listing 8.25) comes in handy for replacing occurrences of a given string within another longer string; for example, we need to watch out for characters in text content that will confuse the SQL expressions we will be building (specifically, we will need to escape quotes, as quotes are delimiters for string content in SQL statements).

Listing 8.25 replace Method

```
   public String replace(String theStr, String findStr, String
replaceStr) {
      // Variables
      boolean anotherHit;
      int lastIndex = 0;
      int thisIndex;
      // Check there is a string to search for
      if (findStr == "") {return theStr;}
      // First occurrence
      thisIndex = theStr.indexOf(findStr, lastIndex);
      anotherHit = (thisIndex > 0);
      // Loop over occurrences
      while (anotherHit == true) {
```

```
            // Replace this occurrence
            theStr = theStr.substring(0, thisIndex) + replaceStr +
                  theStr.substring(thisIndex + 1, theStr.length());
            lastIndex = thisIndex + replaceStr.length();
            // Next occurrence
            thisIndex = theStr.indexOf(findStr, lastIndex);
            anotherHit = (thisIndex > 0);
        }
        // Done
        return theStr;
    }
```

The insertValue() method (see Listing 8.26) will cut a string into leaves, if it exceeds the maximum length parameter.

Listing 8.26 insertValue Method

```
    public void insertValue(boolean leavesAllowed, String
beforeCountSQL, String longString, int offset) {
        // Variables
        int startPage;
        int endPage;
        int offsetI;
        // Replace each single quote with 2 * single quotes
        // N.B. check requirements for other RDBMS
        longString = replace(longString, "'", "''");
        // How many leaves?
        int numPages = (longString.length() / leafSize) + 1;
        // Are leaves allowed?
        if (leavesAllowed == false && numPages > 1) {
            trapError("[Error] : '" + longString
                    + "' exceeds the maximum length.");
        }
        // Loop over pages
        for (int i = 1; i <= numPages; i++) {
            startPage = (i - 1) * leafSize;
            endPage = (i * leafSize) - 1;
            if (endPage > longString.length()) {endPage =
longString.length();}
            offsetI = i + offset;
            if (leavesAllowed) {
```

```
                voidExecSQL(beforeCountSQL + ", " + offsetI + ", '"
                    + longString.substring(startPage, endPage) + "'");
            } else {
                voidExecSQL(beforeCountSQL + ", '"
                    + longString.substring(startPage, endPage) + "'");
            }
        }
    }
    // * Handle long strings (start with leaf_id = 1)
    public void insertValue(boolean leavesAllowed, String
beforeCountSQL,
                            String longString) {
        insertValue(leavesAllowed, beforeCountSQL, longString, 0);
    }
```

Methods for handling exceptions are shown in Listing 8.27.

Listing 8.27 Exception-Handling Methods

```
    // * SQL exception handler
    public void sqlEx(java.sql.SQLException ex, String sqlString) {
       // Print SQLException details
       System.out.println("SQL exception(s)");
       while (ex != null) {
          System.out.println("SQLCommand: " + sqlString);
          System.out.println("SQLState: " + ex.getSQLState());
          System.out.println("Message: " + ex.getMessage());
          System.out.println("Vendor: " + ex.getErrorCode());
          ex = ex.getNextException ();
       }
       gracefulExit();
    }
    // * Java exception handler
    public void javaEx(java.lang.Exception ex) {
       // Print the exception
       System.out.println("[Java error]");
       ex.printStackTrace();
       gracefulExit();
    }
    // * Errors we detect in the code
    public void trapError(String msg) {
      System.out.println("[Error] " + msg);
```

```
        gracefulExit();
      }
      // * Graceful exit
      public void gracefulExit() {
         System.out.println("[Attempting a graceful exit...]");
         // Rollback the transaction
         rollbackTran();
         // Close the connection
         try {
            con.close();
         } catch (java.sql.SQLException ex) {
            System.out.println("Error occurred whilst terminating
   connection.");}
         // Stop further processing
         System.exit(1);
      }
```

Finally, methods that will roll back or commit the current transaction are shown in Listing 8.28.

Listing 8.28 Transaction-Handling Methods

```
      // -- SQL transaction methods
      // * Rollback transaction
      private void rollbackTran() {
         try {con.rollback();}
         catch (java.sql.SQLException ex)
           {sqlEx (ex, "ROLLBACK TRANSACTION");}
      }
      // * Commit transaction
      private void commitTran() {
         try {con.commit();}
         catch (java.sql.SQLException ex)
           {sqlEx (ex, "COMMIT TRANSACTION");}
      }
   }
```

The class connects to the database through the JDBC-ODBC Bridge, so we need to create an ODBC data source called `XMLREP`. With this in place, and with `xmlrepDB` compiled (`"javac xmlrepDB.java"`), we can now test the connection, as shown in Listing 8.29.

Listing 8.29 Test Database Connection

```
C:\xmlrep>java xmlrepDB
Connecting to the repository...
Attempting a query...
Leaf size                = 255
Element name length      = 50
Namespace prefix length = 25
Entity reference length = 50
Disconnecting from the repository...
Done
```

8.6 Uploading XML Documents

In order to upload XML files, we need a program that can read them, understand the content model, discern content from syntax, and set the *x* and *y* coordinates of each node. Fortunately, the XML community has done almost all of the hard work for us already. The Simple API for XML (SAX) provides methods for sequential parsing of XML files, so all we will need to do is write methods to handle the various events that the SAX parser will invoke as it steps through the file. Some features of SAX are worth noting here. A SAX parser understands the XML content model and acts as an XML processor (i.e., it has some intelligence built into it)—by default, the SAX `ContentHandler` will parse entity references, ignore comments, and treat CDATA sections in the same way as text. Since we want entity references to remain unparsed, and we need to maintain the distinction between CDATA and text, we need to implement the SAX `LexicalHandler` as well; the SAX `LexicalHandler` interface provides a method for handling comments, and methods that denote the beginning and end of CDATA sections. Finally, if we want to handle DTD (Document Type Definition) content, we need to implement the `DTDHandler` interface, which provides methods regarding entity definitions and notation declarations.

8.6.1 The xmlrepSAX Class

First, let's create a class (xmlrepSAX.java) that will initialize a SAX2 parser and handle any exceptions that may arise (in this case, we are using the `Xerces` parser from http://xml.apache.org/, but the reader can change this by altering the value of `DEFAULT_PARSER_NAME`). Note that SAX2 parsers are namespace-aware; whereas a SAX1 parser (or a SAX2 parser with this feature disabled) would treat an element such as `<my-ns:my-element xmlns:my-ns="uri">` as being called "my-ns:my-element" (leaving us to strip out the namespace prefix and resolve it to a URI). A SAX2 parser with this feature enabled will report "my-element" as the local name, provide the full URI reference of the namespace, and may also give us the prefix. Since we want to retain the namespace prefix (as this is more space-efficient than storing the full URI every time), we will enable these features with two Booleans, NAMESPACE_HANDLING and NS_PREFIX_HANDLING. The code for this class is shown in Listing 8.30.

Listing 8.30 xmlrepSAX Class

```
// Import core Java classes
import java.io.*;
import java.lang.*;
// Import SAX classes
import org.xml.sax.*;
import org.xml.sax.ext.*;
import org.xml.sax.helpers.*;
// The xmlrepSAX class
public class xmlrepSAX extends DefaultHandler {
   // Useful parameters
   protected static final String DEFAULT_PARSER_NAME =
"org.apache.xerces.parsers.SAXParser";
   protected static final String NAMESPACES_FEATURE_ID =
"http://xml.org/sax/features/namespaces";
   protected static final String NS_PREFIX_HANDLING_PROPERTY_ID =
"http://xml.org/sax/features/namespace-prefixes";
   protected static final String VALIDATION_FEATURE_ID =
"http://xml.org/sax/features/validation";
   protected static final String LEXICAL_EVENT_HANDLING_PROPERTY_ID =
"http://xml.org/sax/properties/lexical-handler";
   protected static final boolean NAMESPACE_HANDLING = true;
   protected static final boolean NS_PREFIX_HANDLING = true;
   // Variables
   String uri = null;
   FileReader r = null;
   XMLReader parser = null;
```

The parse() method instantiates a SAX parser, registers the various handlers, and invokes the parser, as shown in Listing 8.31.

Listing 8.31 parse Method

```
   public void parse(DefaultHandler xmlHandler, xmlrepSAX
errHandler, String uri) {
      // Create an XML reader
      try {parser =
            XMLReaderFactory.createXMLReader(DEFAULT_PARSER_NAME);
      } catch (Exception e) {
         genError("Error: Unable to instantiate parser ("
                  + DEFAULT_PARSER_NAME + ")");
      }
     // Register the SAX content handler
     try {parser.setContentHandler(xmlHandler);
     } catch (NullPointerException e) {
         genError("Could not set the ContentHandler.");}
     // Register the SAX error handler
     try {parser.setErrorHandler(errHandler);
     } catch (NullPointerException e) {
         genError("Could not set the ErrorHandler.");}
     // Set the namespace handling behavior
     try {parser.setFeature(NAMESPACES_FEATURE_ID,
NAMESPACE_HANDLING);
     } catch (SAXException e) {
         genError("Could not set namespace handling.");}
     // Set the namespace prefix handling behavior
     try {parser.setFeature(NS_PREFIX_HANDLING_PROPERTY_ID,
NS_PREFIX_HANDLING);
     } catch (SAXException e) {
         genError("Could not set namespace prefix handling.");}
     // Register the SAX lexical event handler
     try {parser.setProperty(LEXICAL_EVENT_HANDLING_PROPERTY_ID,
xmlHandler);
     } catch (SAXNotRecognizedException e) {
        System.out.println("Warning: lex property not
recognized.");
     } catch (SAXNotSupportedException e) {
        System.out.println("Warning: lex property not
supported.");}
     // Register the SAX DTD event handler
     try {parser.setDTDHandler(xmlHandler);
     } catch (NullPointerException e) {
```

```
        System.out.println("Warning: Could not set the DTD
handler.");}
      // Open the file and parse it
      try {r = new FileReader(uri);
      } catch (FileNotFoundException e) {
         System.out.println("File not found: " + uri);
         genError(e.toString());}
      try {parser.parse(new InputSource(r));
      } catch (Exception e) {
         System.out.println("Error encountered while parsing " +
uri);
         genError(e.toString());}
   }
```

Finally, we need exception-handling methods, as shown in Listing 8.32.

Listing 8.32 SAX Exception-Handling Methods

```
   // * A generic error handler (just outputs the message and
quits)
   public void genError(String msg) {
     System.out.println(msg);
     System.exit(1);
   }
   // -- SAX ErrorHandler methods
   // * Warnings
   public void warning(SAXParseException ex) {
     System.out.println("[Warning] " + ex.getMessage());
   }
   // * SAX errors
   public void saxError(SAXParseException ex) {
     System.out.println("[Error] " + ex.getMessage());
     System.exit(1);
   }
   // * Fatal errors
   public void fatalError(SAXParseException ex) throws SAXException
{
     System.out.println("[Fatal Error] " + ex.getMessage());
     System.exit(1);
   }
}
```

A SAX parser will report an error if the supplied XML file is not well formed, so we can avoid overburdening the database by scanning each file for well-formedness before we attempt to upload it. The `scanXML` class will do this for us (see Listing 8.33); it instantiates a SAX parser and provides dummy content-handling methods.

Listing 8.33 scanXML Class

```
// Import core Java classes
import java.io.*;
// Import SAX classes
import org.xml.sax.Attributes;
import org.xml.sax.DTDHandler;
import org.xml.sax.ext.LexicalHandler;
import org.xml.sax.helpers.DefaultHandler;
// Import our classes
import xmlrepSAX;
// The scanXML class
public class scanXML extends DefaultHandler
 implements LexicalHandler, DTDHandler {
   // Parse the document
   public void check(DefaultHandler handler, String uri) {
     // Variables
     xmlrepSAX saxParser = new xmlrepSAX();
     // Parse the file
     saxParser.parse(handler, saxParser, uri);
   }
   // -- ContentHandler methods
   public void startDocument() {/* Do nothing */}
   public void startElement(String namespaceURI, String localName,
      String rawName, Attributes attrs) {/* Do nothing */}
   public void endElement(String namespaceURI, String localName,
      String rawName) {/* Do nothing */}
   public void characters(char ch[], int start, int length)
      {/* Do nothing */}
   public void ignorableWhitespace(char ch[], int start, int
length)
      {/* Do nothing */}
   public void processingInstruction(String target, String data)
      {/* Do nothing */}
   public void endDocument() {/* Do nothing */}
   // -- LexicalEventListener methods
```

```
   public void startDTD(String name, String publicId, String
systemId)
      {/* Do nothing */}
   public void endDTD() {/* Do nothing */}
   public void comment(char ch[], int start, int length)
      {/* Do nothing */}
   public void startCDATA() {/* Do nothing */}
   public void endCDATA() {/* Do nothing */}
   public void startEntity(String name) {/* Do nothing */}
   public void endEntity(String name) {/* Do nothing */}
}
```

8.6.2 Stored Procedures for Data Entry

In order to load an XML document into the repository, our application will need to execute many `insert` and `update` statements. We can of course build these SQL statements on the fly, but for performance reasons, it would be better to create some stored procedures first. When *ad hoc* SQL is executed, the RDBMS will parse the SQL and create a "query plan" prior to execution; with a stored procedure, the query plan is determined upon first execution and then stored in the procedure cache, which means that subsequent execution will be considerably faster. The script create_xmlrep_db.sql contains numerous stored procedures that we will use later; the names are abbreviations referring to the activity and the table affected (e.g., `rep_i_an` involves an insert ("`i`") into the `attribute_name` ("an") table, and `rep` is just a prefix I have used for all the core stored procedures in the repository).

The procedure in Listing 8.34 creates an entry in the `doc` table and returns the unique `doc_id`.

Listing 8.34 Create rep_i_d Procedure

```
CREATE PROCEDURE dbo.rep_i_d
  @source         t_source,
  @contributor_id t_user_id AS
BEGIN
 INSERT doc (source, date_loaded, contributor_id)
 VALUES (@source, GETDATE(), @contributor_id)
 -- Result = doc_id
 SELECT @@identity AS value
END
GO
```

The procedure in Listing 8.35 creates an entry in the `node` table and returns the unique `node_id`. Note that at this stage, the document ID, type, and *x* index are known, but the *y* index is not (so it is not specified here).

Listing 8.35 Create rep_i_n Procedure

```
CREATE PROCEDURE dbo.rep_i_n
  @x_index      t_xy_index,
  @node_type_id t_node_type_id,
  @doc_id       t_doc_id AS
BEGIN
 INSERT node (doc_id, x, node_type_id)
 VALUES (@doc_id, @x_index, @node_type_id)
 -- Result = node_id
 SELECT @@identity AS value
END
GO
```

The procedure in Listing 8.36 inserts a row in the `element_name` table for an element node; the `node_id` refers back to the entry in the `node` table. The other parameters are the namespace prefix and the local name of the element.

Listing 8.36 Create rep_i_en Procedure

```
CREATE PROCEDURE dbo.rep_i_en
  @node_id    t_node_id,
  @ns_prefix  t_ns_prefix,
  @local_name t_element_name AS
INSERT element_name (node_id, ns_prefix, local_name)
VALUES (@node_id, @ns_prefix, @local_name)
GO
```

The procedure in Listing 8.37 inserts a row in the `attribute_name` table. Each entry has a reference back to the `element_name` entry (through `node_id`), a unique attribute ID (for this node), a namespace prefix, and a local name.

Listing 8.37 Create rep_i_an Procedure

```
CREATE PROCEDURE dbo.rep_i_an
  @node_id      t_node_id,
  @attribute_id t_seq_no,
```

```
  @ns_prefix    t_ns_prefix,
  @local_name   t_attribute_name AS
INSERT attribute_name (node_id, attribute_id, ns_prefix,
local_name)
VALUES (@node_id, @attribute_id, @ns_prefix, @local_name)
GO
```

The procedure in Listing 8.38 inserts a row in the attribute_value_leaf table; each entry has a reference back to the attribute_name table (through node_id and attribute_id). Long values will be split across leaves, each with a unique leaf_id (for the specified attribute).

Listing 8.38 Create rep_i_avl Procedure

```
CREATE PROCEDURE dbo.rep_i_avl
  @node_id      t_node_id,
  @attribute_id t_seq_no,
  @leaf_id      t_leaf_id,
  @leaf_text    t_leaf_text AS
INSERT attribute_value_leaf (node_id, attribute_id, leaf_id,
leaf_text)
VALUES (@node_id, @attribute_id, @leaf_id, @leaf_text)
GO
```

The procedure in Listing 8.39 inserts a row in the cdata_leaf table. Again, long values will be split across leaves.

Listing 8.39 Create rep_i_cdl Procedure

```
CREATE PROCEDURE dbo.rep_i_cdl
  @node_id   t_node_id,
  @leaf_id   t_leaf_id,
  @leaf_text t_leaf_text AS
INSERT cdata_leaf (node_id, leaf_id, leaf_text)
VALUES (@node_id, @leaf_id, @leaf_text)
GO
```

The procedure in Listing 8.40 inserts a row representing a leaf in the comment_leaf table.

Listing 8.40 Create rep_i_cl Procedure

```
CREATE PROCEDURE dbo.rep_i_cl
  @node_id   t_node_id,
  @leaf_id   t_leaf_id,
  @leaf_text t_leaf_text AS
INSERT comment_leaf (node_id, leaf_id, leaf_text)
VALUES (@node_id, @leaf_id, @leaf_text)
GO
```

The procedure in Listing 8.41 inserts a row in the `entity_reference` table.

Listing 8.41 Create rep_i_er Procedure

```
CREATE PROCEDURE dbo.rep_i_er
  @node_id     t_node_id,
  @entity_name t_entity_ref AS
INSERT entity_reference (node_id, entity_name)
VALUES (@node_id, @entity_name)
GO
```

The procedure in Listing 8.42 inserts a row in the `pi_data_leaf` table.

Listing 8.42 Create rep_i_pidl Procedure

```
CREATE PROCEDURE dbo.rep_i_pidl
  @node_id   t_node_id,
  @leaf_id   t_leaf_id,
  @leaf_text t_leaf_text AS
INSERT pi_data_leaf (node_id, leaf_id, leaf_text)
VALUES (@node_id, @leaf_id, @leaf_text)
GO
```

The procedure in Listing 8.43 inserts a row in the `pi_target_leaf` table.

Listing 8.43 Create rep_i_pitl Procedure

```
CREATE PROCEDURE dbo.rep_i_pitl
  @node_id   t_node_id,
  @leaf_id   t_leaf_id,
  @leaf_text t_leaf_text AS
```

```
INSERT pi_target_leaf (node_id, leaf_id, leaf_text)
VALUES (@node_id, @leaf_id, @leaf_text)
GO
```

The procedure in Listing 8.44 inserts a row in the `text_leaf` table.

Listing 8.44 Create rep_i_tl Procedure

```
CREATE PROCEDURE dbo.rep_i_tl
  @node_id    t_node_id,
  @ignorable BIT,
  @leaf_id    t_leaf_id,
  @leaf_text t_leaf_text AS
INSERT text_leaf (node_id, leaf_id, leaf_text, ignorable)
VALUES (@node_id, @leaf_id, @leaf_text, @ignorable)
GO
```

The procedure in Listing 8.45 returns the last value of `leaf_id` from the `cdata_leaf` table for the specified node.

Listing 8.45 Create rep_s_cdlid Procedure

```
CREATE PROCEDURE dbo.rep_s_cdlid
  @node_id t_node_id AS
SELECT ISNULL(MAX(leaf_id), 0) AS value
  FROM cdata_leaf
 WHERE node_id = @node_id
GO
```

The procedure in Listing 8.46 returns the last value of `leaf_id` from the `text_leaf` table for the specified node.

Listing 8.46 Create rep_s_tlid Procedure

```
CREATE PROCEDURE dbo.rep_s_tlid
  @node_id t_node_id AS
SELECT ISNULL(MAX(leaf_id), 0) AS value
  FROM text_leaf
 WHERE node_id = @node_id
GO
```

The procedure in Listing 8.47 returns the value of `node_id` for the last node in the specified document that has not yet had a *y* coordinate set.

Listing 8.47 Create rep_s_n_last Procedure

```
CREATE PROCEDURE dbo.rep_s_n_last
  @doc_id t_doc_id AS
SELECT node_id AS value
  FROM node
 WHERE doc_id = @doc_id
   AND x = (SELECT MAX(x)
              FROM node
             WHERE doc_id = @doc_id
               AND y IS NULL)
GO
```

The procedure in Listing 8.48 sets the value of *y* for the specified node.

Listing 8.48 Create rep_u_n_y Procedure

```
CREATE PROCEDURE dbo.rep_u_n_y
  @node_id t_node_id,
  @y_index t_xy_index AS
 UPDATE node
    SET y = @y_index
  WHERE node_id = @node_id
GO
```

The procedure in Listing 8.49 nulls the value of *y* for the specified node (we will discuss the reason for this requirement later).

Listing 8.49 Create rep_u_n_y_null Procedure

```
CREATE PROCEDURE dbo.rep_u_n_y_null
  @node_id t_node_id AS
UPDATE node
   SET y = NULL
 WHERE node_id = @node_id
GO
```

Finally, we need to set permissions for the stored procedures in Listing 8.50.

Listing 8.50 Set Permissions for Stored Procedures

```
GRANT EXECUTE ON dbo.rep_i_an TO xmlrep_user;
GRANT EXECUTE ON dbo.rep_i_avl TO xmlrep_user;
GRANT EXECUTE ON dbo.rep_i_cdl TO xmlrep_user;
GRANT EXECUTE ON dbo.rep_i_cl TO xmlrep_user;
GRANT EXECUTE ON dbo.rep_i_d TO xmlrep_user;
GRANT EXECUTE ON dbo.rep_i_en TO xmlrep_user;
GRANT EXECUTE ON dbo.rep_i_er TO xmlrep_user;
GRANT EXECUTE ON dbo.rep_i_n TO xmlrep_user;
GRANT EXECUTE ON dbo.rep_i_pidl TO xmlrep_user;
GRANT EXECUTE ON dbo.rep_i_pitl TO xmlrep_user;
GRANT EXECUTE ON dbo.rep_i_tl TO xmlrep_user;
GRANT EXECUTE ON dbo.rep_s_cdlid TO xmlrep_user;
GRANT EXECUTE ON dbo.rep_s_n_last TO xmlrep_user;
GRANT EXECUTE ON dbo.rep_s_tlid TO xmlrep_user;
GRANT EXECUTE ON dbo.rep_u_n_y TO xmlrep_user;
GRANT EXECUTE ON dbo.rep_u_n_y_null TO xmlrep_user;
GO
```

8.6.3 The uploadXML Class

Now we need a class (`uploadXML`) that will

1. Instantiate `scanXML` and parse the file with it to ensure well-formedness.
2. Start a database transaction.
3. Register itself as the content handler for the SAX parser and call its `parse()` method.
4. Commit the transaction—if the process completed satisfactorily—or roll back the transaction—if something went wrong—to ensure that the document-loading process succeeds or fails as a single unit.

The class will need all the same content-handling methods that `scanXML` provided, but this time we will do something with the content; we will call our stored procedures to insert the content into the database.

The class will also need to determine the Nested Sets coordinates of each node. The *x* coordinates are easy—we just start with `x = 1` and increment `x` every time we encounter a new node. When we encounter a leaf node, its *y* coordinate will be `x + 1` (we will need to increase `x` afterwards to `y + 1` before we continue, ready for the next node). The `y` coordinates of non-leaf nodes are a little trickier. When we create the document node or encounter element nodes, we do not yet know what the node's *y* coordinate will be, so we will have to leave it as a null value until it can be determined. Fortunately, because elements must nest correctly (i.e., `<a><b></b></a>` is well formed, but `<a><b></a></b>` is not), every time we encounter a closing tag (causing a SAX `endElement` event), we can be sure that this closing tag corresponds to the most recent opening tag that has not yet been closed; that is, we just need to query the node table for the last node with a null value of `y`, set it to `x + 1`, and then set `x = y + 1`, and so on, until all nodes have been closed (the document node will be the last). The code for the uploadXML class is shown in Listing 8.51.

Listing 8.51 uploadXML Class

```
// Import core Java classes
import java.io.*;
import java.lang.*;
import java.util.Date;
// Import SAX classes
import org.xml.sax.Attributes;
import org.xml.sax.DTDHandler;
import org.xml.sax.ext.LexicalHandler;
import org.xml.sax.helpers.DefaultHandler;
// Import our classes
import scanXML;
import xmlrepDB;
import xmlrepSAX;
// The uploadXML class
public class uploadXML extends DefaultHandler
   implements LexicalHandler, DTDHandler {
   // Parameter
   boolean keepIgnorableWS = true;
   // Variables
   boolean isCData = false;
   boolean isEntity = false;
   boolean verboseMode = false;
   int docID;
   int lastNodeID = -1;
   int lastNodeType = -1;
   int nodeID;
   int x = 0;
   String uri;
   xmlrepDB xmlrep = new xmlrepDB();
   xmlrepSAX saxParser = new xmlrepSAX();
```

The main() method instantiates the class, receives and checks the command-line arguments, and invokes the instance's uploadFile() method. This is shown in Listing 8.52.

Listing 8.52 Main Method for uploadXML

```
    public static void main(String args[]) {
      // Create an instance of this class
      uploadXML handler = new uploadXML();
      // Check we received a URI
      if (args.length == 0) {
        System.out.println("Usage:  java uploadXML uri (verbose)");
        System.out.println(" where");
        System.out.println("  uri     = URI of your XML document,");
        System.out.println("  verbose = 't' to switch on verbose
messaging.");
        System.exit(1);
      }
      // Verbose messaging?
      if (args.length >= 2) {
         if (args[1].equalsIgnoreCase("t")) {handler.verboseMode =
true;}}
      // Upload the XML file into the repository
      handler.uploadFile(handler, args[0]);
    }
```

The uploadFile() invokes a well-formedness check (scanXML) and (assuming all is well) connects to the repository, invokes the SAX parser (registering this object as the content handler), and—assuming successful completion—outputs a success message that includes the document ID that was assigned. The code for uploadFile is shown in Listing 8.53.

Listing 8.53 uploadFile Method

```
    public void uploadFile(DefaultHandler handler, String uri) {
      // Variables
      String successStr;
  this.uri = uri;
      // Parse the XML file to ensure it is well-formed
      scanXML sx = new scanXML();
      sx.check(sx, uri);
      // Start the upload process...
```

```
        try {
            // Connect to the repository
            xmlrep.connect();
            // Parse the file
            saxParser.parse(handler, saxParser, uri);
            // Close the connection
            xmlrep.disconnect();
            // Output the document ID
            successStr= "Document uploaded into the repository "
              + "with doc ID = " + docID + " (" + ((x + 1)/2) + "
nodes).";
            System.out.println(successStr);
        } catch (java.lang.Exception   ex) {xmlrep.javaEx(ex);}
    }
```

Next are the ContentHandler methods. The SAX parser invokes the startDocument() method (see Listing 8.54) when the document is opened; no arguments are passed (we know the URI of the document in any case), but it gives us the opportunity to insert a row into the doc table (using the rep_i_d procedure), grab the doc_id that is returned, and insert the document node into the node table (using the rep_i_n procedure).

Listing 8.54 startDocument Method

```
    // * Start document
    public void startDocument() {
        if (verboseMode) {System.out.println("* startDocument");}
        // Insert into doc table
        docID = xmlrep.intExecSQL("rep_i_d '" + uri + "',
'xmlrep_user';");
        // Increment counter and set node type = DOCUMENT [9]
        x++;
        int nodeType = 9;
        // Create a document node in the node table
        nodeID = xmlrep.intExecSQL("rep_i_n " + x + ", " + nodeType
            + ", "+ docID + ";");
        // Remember node type & ID
        lastNodeType = nodeType;
        lastNodeID = nodeID;
    }
```

The parser invokes the `startElement()` method shown in Listing 8.55 when an open tag—for example, `<myNS:message>`—is encountered. We ignore the `namespaceURI` and `localName` arguments; instead, we insert a node of type `ELEMENT` (using the `rep_i_n` procedure) and then slice the namespace URI (if any) from the element name, inserting the results into the `element_name` table (using `rep_i_n`). If there are any attributes, we will loop over them, inserting names and namespace prefixes into `attribute_name` (using `rep_i_an`) and values (spilt over leaves, if necessary) into `attribute_value` (using `rep_i_avl`). If element names, attribute names, or namespace prefixes exceed the maximum lengths, we will report an error and abort the process. In common with most of the other node-creation methods, we also need to keep a record of the last node type encountered; these are stored in `lastNodeType` and `lastNodeID` (respectively).

Listing 8.55 startElement Method

```
    // * Start element
    public void startElement(String namespaceURI, String localName,
String qName, Attributes attrs) {
        if (verboseMode) {System.out.println("* startElement ["
            + x + "]: qName = '" + qName + "'");}
        // Variables
        int lastColon;
        String name = qName;
        String namespace;
        // Increment counter and set node type = ELEMENT [1]
        x++;
        int nodeType = 1;
        // Insert to node table
        nodeID = xmlrep.intExecSQL("rep_i_n " + x + ", " + nodeType
            + ", "+ docID + ";");
        // Check that a valid nodeID was returned, if not report
error and exit
        if (nodeID < 1) {saxParser.genError(
            "[Error] Node was not successfully inserted: " + qName);}
        // Does the element's qualified name include a namespace?
        lastColon = name.lastIndexOf(":");
        if (lastColon > 0) {
            // Parse the qName to retrieve the namespace prefix and
            // the local element name
            namespace = "'" + name.substring(0, lastColon) + "'";
            name = name.substring(lastColon + 1, name.length());
            if (namespace.length() > xmlrep.nsPrefixLength) {
```

```
            saxParser.genError("[Error] : " + namespace
               + " exceeds the maximum length.");
         }
      } else {
          namespace = "null";
      }
      // Check element name does not exceed maximum length
      if (name.length() > xmlrep.elementNameLength) {
          saxParser.genError("[Error] : " + name
             + " exceeds the maximum length.");
      }
      // Insert to element_name table
      xmlrep.insertValue(false, "rep_i_en " + nodeID + ", "
         + namespace, name);
      // Loop over the element's attributes
      if (attrs != null) {
         int len = attrs.getLength();
         for (int i = 1; i <= len; i++) {
            // Attribute name (including namespace)
            name = attrs.getQName(i - 1);
            // Index of last colon
            lastColon = name.lastIndexOf(":");
            // Does the attribute name include a namespace?
            if (lastColon > 0) {
               namespace = "'" + name.substring(0, lastColon) +
"'";

               name = name.substring(lastColon + 1, name.length());
               if (namespace.length() > xmlrep.nsPrefixLength) {
                  saxParser.genError("[Error] : '" + namespace
                     + "' exceeds the maximum length.");
               }
            } else {
               namespace = "null";
            }
            // Insert to attribute_name table
            xmlrep.insertValue(false, "rep_i_an " + nodeID + ", "
               + i + ", " + namespace, name);
            // Insert to attribute_value_leaf table
            xmlrep.insertValue(true, "rep_i_avl " + nodeID + ", "
               + i, attrs.getValue(i - 1));
         }
      }
```

```
        // Remember node type & ID
        lastNodeType = nodeType;
        lastNodeID = nodeID;
    }
```

The processingInstruction() method shown in Listing 8.56 is called when a processing instruction—for example, <?target-application data-string?>—is encountered; string values for the target and data are supplied. Since we have allowed these to be of any length, we call the insertValue() method of the xmlrep object, which will split long strings into leaves and insert them to the appropriate tables.

Listing 8.56 processingInstructions Method

```
    // * Processing instruction
    public void processingInstruction(String target, String data) {
        if (verboseMode) {System.out.println("* processingInstruction
["
            + x + "] = '" + target + " " + data + "'");}
        // Increment counter and set node type =
PROCESSING_INSTRUCTION_NODE [7]
        x++;
        int nodeType = 7;
        // Insert to node table
        nodeID = xmlrep.intExecSQL("rep_i_n " + x + ", " + nodeType
            + ", " + docID + ";");
        // Insert to pi_target_leaf table
        xmlrep.insertValue(true, "rep_i_pitl " + nodeID, target);
        // Insert to pi_data_leaf table
        xmlrep.insertValue(true, "rep_i_pidl " + nodeID, data);
        // Update node table: set y value for this node
        // (since PI nodes do not have children)
        xmlrep.voidExecSQL("rep_u_n_y " + nodeID + ", " + (x + 1) +
";");
        x++;
        // Remember node type & ID
        lastNodeType = nodeType;
        lastNodeID = nodeID;
    }
```

The characters() method shown in Listing 8.57 is called in a number of situations—namely, when text, CDATA, or entity references are encountered. Unlike many applications that use a SAX parser, our application needs to differentiate between these types of content. Furthermore, in the case of entities, the SAX parser parses the entity reference for us. For example, suppose we have defined a `©right;` entity (to save us having to repeat a lengthy string every time we want to include standard copyright details in our documents). Every time the SAX parser encounters the entity reference `©right;` in our document, the `characters()` method will be called with the full copyright string. We need to override these behaviors; fortunately, help is at hand, thanks to SAX's LexicalEvent handler methods, which we will discuss shortly. For now, note that nothing happens if this method is called while the value of the Boolean `isEntity` is `true`. Otherwise, the character array is recast as a string and passed to the `handleText()` method.

Listing 8.57 characters Method

```
// * Characters
public void characters(char ch[], int start, int length) {
   // If the isEntity boolean is true, ignore this call (it is
   // a parsed entity)
   if (isEntity) {return;}
   // Treat as normal and flag as NOT ignorable
   handleText(new String(ch, start, length), 0);
}
```

The `ignorableWhitespace()` method shown in Listing 8.58 is called in place of `characters()` when the character data consists only of whitespace (spaces, tabs, and/or line feeds) and the SAX parser is able to determine that it is truly ignorable. This latter condition can be satisfied only if the supplied XML file has a reference to a schema (such as a DTD), which will dictate where text content may appear in the element hierarchy. If whitespace appears anywhere else (for example, if the file author used indentation and line feeds to make the XML document more human readable), then the SAX parser will call `ignorableWhitespace()` rather than `characters()`. Keeping `ignorable whitespace` is useful for readability and testing; however, if we prefer not to, we can change the value of `keepIgnorableWS` (in the variable definitions at the start of the class) to `false`.

Listing 8.58 ignorableWhitespace Method

```
   // * Ignorable whitespace
   public void ignorableWhitespace(char ch[], int start, int
length) {
       if (verboseMode) {System.out.println(
          "* ignorableWhitespace [" + x + "] = (" + start + ", "
          + length + ")");}
```

```
        // If user has specified that ignorable whitespace should be
        // kept, call the handling method (but flag as 'ignorable'
for
        // info). Otherwise, do nothing.
        if (keepIgnorableWS) {handleText(new String(ch, start,
length), 1);}
    }
```

The handleText() method in Listing 8.59 is one that was created to save having to write the same code twice in the characters() and ignorableWhitespace() methods (both of which invoke handleText()—and, in the latter case, only if we have specified that we want to keep ignorable whitespace). This method also handles a side effect of carriage return/newline characters on some operating systems; for XML files without schema definitions on certain combinations of operating system and parser, SAX will invoke the characters() method each time a carriage return/newline is encountered. This will have the side effect of splitting up text and CDATA sections into multiple nodes. To counter this situation, we make the assumption that—in the event that "this" node is of the same type (text or CDATA) as the "last" node—we will treat both as different leaves of the same node. We need to run rep_s_tlid (text) or rep_s_cdlid (CDATA) in order to determine the final leaf_id for the last node, before we execute rep_i_tl (text) or rep_i_cdl (CDATA) to add the new leaves.

Listing 8.59 handleText Method

```
    // * Handle character data
    public void handleText(String characterData, int isIgnorable) {
        if (verboseMode) {System.out.println(
            "* handleText [" + x + "] = '" + characterData + "'");}
        // A non-validating parser may split up CDATA and TEXT
sections...
        boolean isContinuation = false;
        int nodeType;
        int offset = 0;
        String abbrvTblNm;
        String extraArg = "";
        // Is the data CDATA or TEXT?
        if (isCData) {
            // Node type = CDATA_SECTION_NODE [4]
            if (lastNodeType == 4) {isContinuation = true;}
            nodeType = 4;
            abbrvTblNm = "cd";
```

```
        } else {
           // Node type = TEXT_NODE [3]
           if (lastNodeType == 3) {isContinuation = true;}
           nodeType = 3;
           abbrvTblNm = "t";
           extraArg = ", " + isIgnorable;
        }
        if (!isContinuation) {
           // Increment counter
           x++;
           // Insert to node table
           nodeID = xmlrep.intExecSQL("rep_i_n " + x + ", " +
nodeType
              + ", "+ docID + ";");
        } else {
           // Treat as a continuation: decrement counter
           x--;
           // Get the last leaf_id
           offset = xmlrep.intExecSQL("rep_s_" + abbrvTblNm + "lid "
              + lastNodeID + ";");
           // Null the y value of this node (since we are continuing
it)
           xmlrep.voidExecSQL("rep_u_n_y_null " + nodeID + ";");
        }
        // Insert to appropriate table
        xmlrep.insertValue(true, "rep_i_" + abbrvTblNm + "l " +
nodeID
           + extraArg, characterData, offset);
        // Update node table: set y value for this node
        xmlrep.voidExecSQL("rep_u_n_y " + nodeID + ", " + (x + 1) +
";");
        x++;
        // Remember node type & ID
        lastNodeType = nodeType;
        lastNodeID = nodeID;
    }
```

The `endElement()` method (see Listing 8.60) is invoked by the SAX parser when a closing tag is encountered (e.g., `</myNS:message>`). The element that this tag is closing will be the last node with a null value of y.

Listing 8.60 endElement Method

```
// * End element
public void endElement(String namespaceURI, String localName,
   String qName) {
   if (verboseMode) {System.out.println(
      "* endElement [" + x + "] = '" + qName + "'");}
   // Increment counter
   x++;
   // Find the node that this "end element" corresponds to
   nodeID = xmlrep.intExecSQL("rep_s_n_last " + docID + ";");
   // Check we found an element with null value for y
   if (nodeID < 1) {
      saxParser.genError("No element has null y.");
   }
   // Update node table: set y value for this node
   xmlrep.voidExecSQL("rep_u_n_y " + nodeID + ", " + x + ";");
   // Remember node type & ID
   lastNodeType = 1; // = ELEMENT [1]
   lastNodeID = nodeID;
}
```

The `startDTD()` and `endDTD()` methods shown in Listing 8.61 are invoked by the SAX parser at the beginning and end of a document type definition, respectively (and regardless of whether the DTD is stored inside the file or is external to it). In between, various methods will be invoked as the parser encounters notation declarations and entity definitions (and we can capture these if we register our class as the `DTDHandler` for the SAX parser). Aside from printing a message (if we are in "verbose" mode), we have chosen not to do anything with DTD events.

Listing 8.61 startDTD and endDTD Methods

```
// * Start DTD
public void startDTD(String name, String publicId, String
systemId) {
   if (verboseMode) {System.out.println("* startDTD (name = '"
      + name + "', publicId = '" + publicId + "', systemId = '"
      + systemId + "')");}
   // Do nothing
}
// * End DTD
public void endDTD() {
```

```
        if (verboseMode) {System.out.println("* endDTD");}
        // Do nothing
    }
```

The endDocument() method shown in Listing 8.62 is invoked by the SAX parser when the end of the file is reached; all we need to do when this stage is reached is to set the y value for the document node.

Listing 8.62 endDocument Method

```
    // * End document
    public void endDocument() {
        if (verboseMode) {System.out.println("* endDocument");}
        // Find the remaining node with null y (the document node)
        nodeID = xmlrep.intExecSQL("rep_s_n_last " + docID + ";");
        // Check we found a node with null value for y
        if (nodeID < 1) {
            saxParser.genError("Root node does not have null y.");
        }
        // Update node table: set y value for this node
        xmlrep.voidExecSQL("rep_u_n_y " + nodeID + ", " + (x + 1) +
";");
    }
```

The SAX parser invokes the methods shown in Listing 8.63 when lexical events are encountered. As with text and CDATA sections, the comment() method allowed comments to split across leaves. The startCDATA(), endCDATA(), startEntity(), and endEntity() methods toggle the values of the isCData and isEntity variables, so the character-handling methods (which will be called immediately afterwards by the SAX parser) know which type of character data they are dealing with.

Listing 8.63 LexicalHandler Methods

```
    // -- LexicalHandler methods
    public void comment(char[] ch, int start, int length) {
        if (verboseMode) {System.out.println("* comment [" + x +
"]");}
        // Increment counter and set node type = COMMENT_NODE [8]
        x++;
        int nodeType = 8;
        // Insert to node table
        nodeID = xmlrep.intExecSQL("rep_i_n " + x + ", " + nodeType
```

```
            + ", "+ docID + ";");
        // Insert to comment_leaf table
        xmlrep.insertValue(true, "rep_i_cl " + nodeID,
            new String(ch, start, length));
        // Update node table: set y value for this node
        xmlrep.voidExecSQL("rep_u_n_y " + nodeID + ", " + (x + 1) +
";");
        x++;
        // Remember node type & ID
        lastNodeType = nodeType;
        lastNodeID = nodeID;
    }
    public void startCDATA() {
        if (verboseMode) {System.out.println("* startCDATA [" + x +
"]");}
        // Next call to characters() will be treated as CDATA
        isCData = true;
    }
    public void endCDATA() {
        if (verboseMode) {System.out.println("* endCDATA [" + x +
"]");}
        // Next call to characters() will be treated as text
        isCData = false;
    }
    public void startEntity(String name) {
        if (verboseMode) {System.out.println("* startEntity [" + x +
"]");}
        // Set the isEntity boolean to true, so characters() calls
arising
        // due to entity parsing get ignored
        isEntity = true;
        // Increment counter and set node type =
ENTITY_REFERENCE_NODE [5]
        x++;
        int nodeType = 5;
        // Insert to node table
        nodeID = xmlrep.intExecSQL("rep_i_n " + x + ", " + nodeType
            + ", "+ docID + ";");
        // Check entity reference name does not exceed maximum length
        if (name.length() > xmlrep.entityRefLength) {
            saxParser.genError("[Error] : " + name
                + " exceeds the maximum length.");
```

```
        }
        // Insert to entity_reference table
        xmlrep.insertValue(false, "rep_i_er " + nodeID, name);
        // Update node table: set y value for this node
        xmlrep.voidExecSQL("rep_u_n_y " + nodeID + ", " + (x + 1) +
";");
        x++;
        // Remember node type & ID
        lastNodeType = nodeType;
        lastNodeID = nodeID;
    }
    public void endEntity(String name) {
        if (verboseMode) {System.out.println("* endEntity [" + x +
"]");}
        // Set the isEntity boolean to false
        isEntity = false;
    }
```

The SAX parser invokes the methods shown in Listing 8.64 when DTD events are encountered. Currently, we do not do anything in these situations, but we could add tables and procedures to deal with the information.

Listing 8.64 DTDHandler Methods

```
    // -- DTDHandler methods
    public void notationDecl(String name, String publicId,
        String systemId) {
        if (verboseMode) {System.out.println("* notationDecl");}
        // Do nothing
    }
    public void unparsedEntityDecl(String name, String publicId,
        String systemId, String notationName) {
        if (verboseMode) {System.out.println("*
unparsedEntityDecl");}
        // Do nothing
    }
}
```

Compile this class ("`javac uploadXML.java`"), and we're ready to test it with a sample XML file. On successful loading, the Java program returns a message indicating the document ID that was assigned (along with a count of the nodes that were created):

```
C:\xmlrep>java uploadXML wml-example.xml
Document uploaded into the repository with doc ID = 1 (25 nodes).
```

8.6.4 The extractXML Class

Running `rep_serialise_nodes` for a nontrivial document produces lots of output that is not particularly readable, so let's create a class (`extractXML.java`) that will call the procedure and knit the output back into recognizable XML. There is only one method, `main()`, which takes command-line parameters for the document ID (plus additional optional parameters) and executes `rep_serialise_nodes`. The code for extractXML is shown in Listing 8.65.

Listing 8.65 extractXML Class

```
// Import core Java classes
import java.lang.*;
import java.sql.ResultSet;
import java.sql.SQLException;
// Import our classes
import xmlrepDB;
// The extractXML class
class extractXML {
   public static void main(String[] args) {
      // Variables
      int docID;
      int startX = 1;
      int incMetadata = 0;
      Integer IntObj = new Integer(0);
      xmlrepDB xmlrep = new xmlrepDB();
      String xmlDoc = "";
      String xmlBit;
      String sqlCmd;
      // Check we received a docID
      if (args.length == 0) {
        System.out.println(
           "Usage:  java extractXML docID (startX) (incMetadata)");
        System.out.println(
           "   docID = ID of the document in the repository");
        System.out.println(
           "   startX = integer x index of the node with which to
start");
        System.out.println(
```

```
                "    incMetadata = 't' for attributes showing x & y
coordinates");
            System.exit(1);
        }
        // Document ID
        docID = IntObj.parseInt(args[0]);
        // Starting x_index specified?
        if (args.length >= 2) {startX = IntObj.parseInt(args[1]);}
        // Include metadata?
        if (args.length >= 3) {
           if (args[2].equalsIgnoreCase("t")) {incMetadata = 1;}}
        // Start the output
        System.out.println("<?xml version=\"1.0\"?>");
        // Handle errors
        try {
           // Connect to the repository
           xmlrep.connect();
           // Build the SQL command
           sqlCmd = "rep_serialise_nodes " + docID + ", " + startX
              + ", " + incMetadata + ";";
           try {
              // Execute the SQL
              ResultSet rs = xmlrep.stmt.executeQuery(sqlCmd);
              // Loop through the records
              while (rs.next()) {
                 // Read the fields & handle NULLs / empty strings
                 xmlBit = rs.getString("parsed_text");
                 if (!rs.wasNull()) {xmlDoc = xmlDoc + xmlBit;}
              }
           } catch (java.sql.SQLException ex) {xmlrep.sqlEx (ex,
sqlCmd);}
           // Output to screen
           System.out.println(xmlDoc);
           // Close the connection
           xmlrep.disconnect();
        } catch (java.lang.Exception ex) {
            // Print exception information as an XML comment
            System.out.println ("<!--");
            ex.printStackTrace ();
            System.out.println ("-->");
        }
```

```
    }
}
```

Compile this class ("`javac extractXML.java`"), and we can test it on the sample file we uploaded to the repository:

```
C:\xmlrep>java extractXML 1
```

If everything is working properly, the output should look exactly like the file that went in (you can pipe the output to a file, if you want to check). We can also run the process again for a fragment of the document, as shown in Listing 8.66.

Listing 8.66 Result for extractXML with Two Parameters

```
C:\xmlrep>java extractXML 1 37
<?xml version="1.0"?>
<card id="cSecond" title="Second card">
  <p align="center">
   Content of the second card.
  </p>
 </card>
```

In this case, we asked for the fragment of document 1 starting with the node with $x = 37$ (the second of the two `card` elements). If we were to repeat the process with the optional `inMetadata` parameter set to "`t`" (i.e., "`java extractXML 1 37 t`"), we would get a similar result but with additional attributes showing the values of `x`, `y`, and `node_id` for each element. Listing 8.67 shows the XML.

Listing 8.67 Result for extractXML with Three Parameters

```
C:\xmlrep>java extractXML 1 37 t
<?xml version="1.0"?>
<card xmlns:repository="http://www.rgedwards.com/"
repository:x="37"
      repository:y="46" repository:nodeID="52" id="cSecond"
      title="Second card">
  <p repository:x="40" repository:y="43" repository:nodeID="54"
     align="center">
   Content of the second card.
  </p>
 </card>
```

8.7 Querying the Repository

In this section, we will describe how to query the XML repository.

8.7.1 Ad Hoc SQL Queries

Once we have uploaded some documents into the database, we can start experimenting with queries. For example, the query in Listing 8.68 will return a list of the element names that appear, with their *x* and *y* coordinates and namespace prefixes (if any).

Listing 8.68 SQL Query

```
SELECT n.x, n.y, e.ns_prefix, e.local_name
  FROM element_name e, node n
 WHERE n.doc_id = 1 AND n.node_id = e.node_id;
```

The results for `wml-example.xml` (document ID = 1, if we loaded this document first) are shown in Listing 8.69.

Listing 8.69 Results for wml-example.xml

```
x    y    ns_prefix local_name
---- ---- --------- ----------
2    49   NULL      wml
5    34   NULL      card
8    19   NULL      p
11   12   NULL      img
15   16   NULL      br
22   31   NULL      p
25   28   NULL      a
37   46   NULL      card
40   43   NULL      p
(9 row(s) affected)
```

A variation on this theme is shown in Listing 8.70, where we return the element names (qualified with a namespace prefix, if any) with a count of their occurrences in the specified document (note the use of a `group by` expression).

Listing 8.70 Modified Query

```
SELECT ISNULL(e.ns_prefix + ':', '') + e.local_name AS qName,
       COUNT(1) AS occurrences
  FROM element_name e, node n
 WHERE n.doc_id = 1 AND n.node_id = e.node_id
 GROUP BY ISNULL(e.ns_prefix + ':', '') + e.local_name;
```

The results are shown in Listing 8.71.

Listing 8.71 Results for Modified Query

```
qName    occurrences
-------- -----------
a        1
br       1
card     2
img      1
p        3
wml      1
(6 row(s) affected)
```

For our simple example, the results are pretty obvious; there are two cards, one link, three paragraphs, and so on. However, for larger documents, the query can be very informative; for example, in an XHTML document, we can quickly determine how many paragraph elements there are, or how many images.

The query in Listing 8.72 will return a list of the attribute names that appear, with their *x* and *y* coordinates and namespace prefixes (if any).

Listing 8.72 More Informative Query

```
SELECT n.x, n.y, a.attribute_id, a.ns_prefix, a.local_name
  FROM attribute_name a, node n
 WHERE n.doc_id = 1 AND n.node_id = a.node_id;
```

The results for our example are shown in Listing 8.73.

Listing 8.73 Results for More Informative Query

```
x    y    attribute_id ns_prefix local_name
---- ---- ------------ --------- ----------
5    34   1            NULL      id
5    34   2            NULL      title
5    34   3            NULL      newcontext
8    19   1            NULL      align
11   12   1            NULL      src
11   12   2            NULL      alt
11   12   3            NULL      align
25   28   1            NULL      href
37   46   1            NULL      id
37   46   2            NULL      title
40   43   1            NULL      align
(11 row(s) affected)
```

To retrieve the text leaves for this document, run the query shown in Listing 8.74.

Listing 8.74 Text Leaves Query

```
SELECT n.x, t.leaf_id, t.leaf_text
  FROM text_leaf t, node n
 WHERE n.doc_id = 1 AND n.node_id = t.node_id
```

The results for our example are shown in Listing 8.75 (note that I've ignored whitespace nodes for brevity—there are 14 whitespace entries in addition to these three rows).

Listing 8.75 Results for Text Leaves Query

```
x    leaf_id leaf_text
---- ------- ---------------------------
17   1       Content of the first card.
26   1       Next card.
41   1       Content of the second card.
```

To return the text content of a specific element node (e.g., the second `card` element), see Listing 8.76.

Listing 8.76 Text Content Query

```
SELECT n.x, t.leaf_text
  FROM text_leaf t, node n
 WHERE n.doc_id = 1
   AND n.node_id = t.node_id
 AND n.x BETWEEN 37 AND 46;
```

where 37 and 46 are the *x* and *y* coordinates of the element node. The results are shown in Listing 8.77 (I've ignored whitespace again).

Listing 8.77 Results for Text Content Query

```
x    leaf_id leaf_text
---- ------- ---------------------------
41   1       Content of the second card.
```

We can generalize the last query to return, for a given document, all text nodes of elements with a specified name (in this case, all <a> elements), as shown in Listing 8.78.

Listing 8.78 Generalized Query

```
SELECT n2.x, n2.y, e.local_name, t.leaf_id, t.leaf_text
  FROM node n1, node n2, element_name e, text_leaf t
 WHERE n1.doc_id = 1
   AND n1.node_id = e.node_id
   AND e.local_name = 'a'
   AND n2.doc_id = 1
   AND n2.node_id = t.node_id
   AND n2.x BETWEEN n1.x AND n1.y;
```

In our example, there is only one <a> element, as shown in Listing 8.79.

Listing 8.79 Generalized Query Result

```
x   y   local_name leaf_id leaf_text
--- --- ---------- ------- ---------
26  27  a          1       Next card
(1 row(s) affected)
```

The queries in this section represent just a tiny sample of the queries we can dream up now that we have parsed XML into our relational database.

8.7.2 Searching for Text

The reader may have noticed a potential pitfall for applications that need to provide full text searching capabilities for document-centric XML. If we intend to run queries on large text nodes—for example, to find all text nodes that contain a certain word or words—we need to be mindful that the content may well be split over leaves. One solution would be to have the `leaf_text` column in our `text_leaf` table of type `text` rather than a `varchar` (this would also require some changes to the stored procedures that access this table, since the syntax for handling this type of content will differ). Another solution would be to build an indexing mechanism that creates a full text index at parse time, with references to the nodes that contain the text. Either approach will allow searches to weight hits according to information about the containing nodes (e.g., a word found in text content of a title element might be worth more than the same text found in a paragraph element).

8.7.3 Some More Stored Procedures

Time to introduce some more stored procedures that may prove useful in a number of applications. The first, `rep_s_parent`, selects the parent node of a specified node (identified by a document ID and *x* coordinate). This procedure makes use of the Nested Sets property that the parent of a given node *(x, y)* has the largest *x′* in the set defined by *x′*, *x* . *y′* (see Listing 8.80).

Listing 8.80 Create rep_s_parent Procedure

```
CREATE PROCEDURE dbo.rep_s_parent
  @doc_id  t_doc_id,
  @x_child t_xy_index AS
 SELECT n1.node_id,
        n1.x,
        n1.y,
        n1.node_type_id
   FROM node n1
  WHERE n1.doc_id = @doc_id
    AND n1.x = (SELECT MAX(n2.x)
                  FROM node n2
                 WHERE n2.doc_id = @doc_id
```

```
                    AND n2.x < @x_child
                    AND n2.y > @x_child)
GO
```

The next procedure, rep_s_children, shown in Listing 8.81 returns the child nodes of a specified node (again identified by a document ID and *x* coordinate). Descendants are easy (they are identified by *x*, *x'*, *y*; we have already exploited this property in rep_serialise_nodes), but immediate children are a bit harder to determine; the trick here is a correlated subquery that limits the results of the first section of the WHERE clause (the set of all descendants) to just those for which the specified node is the parent.

Listing 8.81 Create rep_s_children Procedure

```
CREATE PROCEDURE dbo.rep_s_children
  @doc_id    t_doc_id,
  @x_source t_xy_index AS
 SELECT n1.node_id,
        n1.x,
        n1.y,
        n1.node_type_id
   FROM node n1
  WHERE n1.doc_id = @doc_id
    AND n1.x > @x_source
    AND n1.y < (SELECT y
                  FROM node
                 WHERE doc_id = @doc_id
                   AND x = @x_source)
    AND @x_source  = (SELECT MAX(x)
                        FROM node n2
                       WHERE n2.doc_id = @doc_id
                         AND n2.x < n1.x
                         AND n2.y > n1.y)
  ORDER BY n1.x
GO
```

For our example document, we can (for example) ask for the parent node of the <p> element with $x = 40$, which produces the result shown in Listing 8.82.

Listing 8.82 Result for rep_s_parent with Two Parameters

```
rep_s_parent 2, 40
GO
node_id x   y   node_type_id
------- --- --- ------------
52      37  46  1
(1 row(s) affected)
```

As expected, this is the *x* coordinate of the second `<card>` element.

8.7.4 Generating XPath Expressions

The W3C's XPath recommendation provides a very useful syntax for querying XML documents. While a full implementation of XPath is beyond the scope of this chapter, we can at least make a start. We will create a stored procedure `rep_gen_xpath` (see Listing 8.83) that returns an XPath expression for the path between two nodes (identified by their *x* values: `x_source` and `x_target`) in a specified document. There is no error checking, and we need to specify valid *x* coordinates for two element nodes, or for the document node ($x = 1$) and an element node.

First we need to select (into a temporary table) the data needed to construct the path expression, and for each element in the path, we may also need a sequence number (if there is more than one element with the same name at the same level in the fragment).

Listing 8.83 Create rep_gen_xpath Procedure

```
CREATE PROCEDURE dbo.rep_gen_xpath
                 @doc_id   t_doc_id,
                 @x_source t_xy_index,
                 @x_target t_xy_index
AS
BEGIN
-- Returns an XPath expression for a given target element node
(starting at the source element node)
 -- Local variables
 DECLARE @seq_no          INTEGER
 DECLARE @this_element    t_leaf_text
 DECLARE @this_ns_prefix t_leaf_text
 DECLARE @xpath_expr      t_xpath_maxlen
 -- Build a temporary table
 SELECT n1.x,
```

```
        n1.y,
        (SELECT COUNT(1) + 1
           FROM node n3,
                element_name en2
          WHERE n3.doc_id = @doc_id
            AND n3.node_type_id = 1
            AND (SELECT MAX(n4.x)
                   FROM node n4
                  WHERE n4.doc_id = @doc_id
                    AND n4.node_type_id IN (1, 9)
                    AND n4.x < n3.x
                    AND n4.y > n3.x) = (SELECT MAX(n5.x)
                                          FROM node n5
                                         WHERE n5.doc_id = @doc_id
                                           AND n5.node_type_id IN
(1, 9)
                                           AND n5.x < n1.x
                                           AND n5.y > n1.x)
            AND n3.node_id = en2.node_id
            AND en2.local_name = en1.local_name
            AND n3.x < n1.x) AS seq_no,
        (SELECT COUNT(1)
           FROM node n6,
                element_name en3
          WHERE n6.doc_id = @doc_id
            AND n6.node_type_id = 1
            AND (SELECT MAX(n7.x)
                   FROM node n7
                  WHERE n7.doc_id = @doc_id
                    AND n7.node_type_id IN (1, 9)
                    AND n7.x < n6.x
                    AND n7.y > n6.x) = (SELECT MAX(n8.x)
                                          FROM node n8
                                         WHERE n8.doc_id = @doc_id
                                           AND n8.node_type_id IN
(1, 9)
                                           AND n8.x < n1.x
                                           AND n8.y > n1.x)
            AND n6.node_id = en3.node_id
            AND en3.local_name = en1.local_name) AS total_count,
        en1.ns_prefix,
        en1.local_name
```

```
    INTO #results
    FROM node n1,
         element_name en1
   WHERE n1.doc_id = @doc_id
     AND n1.x <= @x_target
     AND n1.y > @x_target
     AND n1.x >= @x_source
     AND n1.node_type_id = 1
     AND n1.node_id = en1.node_id
   ORDER BY n1.x
  -- Null sequence numbers if element is the only one of its type
  UPDATE #results
     SET seq_no = NULL
   WHERE seq_no = 1
     AND total_count = 1
```

Next we create a cursor to walk over the results set, building the XPath expression as we step through the rows, as shown in Listing 8.84.

Listing 8.84 Cursor to Walk the Results Set

```
  -- Initialize XPath expr (as a slash if we are starting from
  -- the root element or the document node)
  IF @x_source <= (SELECT MIN(x) FROM node
                   WHERE doc_id = @doc_id AND node_type_id = 1)
    SELECT @xpath_expr = '/'
  ELSE
    SELECT @xpath_expr = ''
 -- Create a cursor to walk through #results in depth order
  DECLARE xpath_generator CURSOR LOCAL FORWARD_ONLY STATIC READ_ONLY
 FOR
  SELECT seq_no, ns_prefix, local_name FROM #results ORDER BY x
  OPEN xpath_generator
  -- Loop over the entries
  FETCH NEXT FROM xpath_generator
   INTO @seq_no, @this_ns_prefix, @this_element
  WHILE @@FETCH_STATUS = 0
  BEGIN
   -- Append the element name, seq no (if required) and a slash
   SELECT @xpath_expr = @xpath_expr
      + ISNULL((@this_ns_prefix + ':'), '')
      + @this_element + ISNULL('[' + CONVERT(VARCHAR(10), @seq_no)
```

```
      + ']', '') + '/'
   -- Continue
   FETCH NEXT FROM xpath_generator
    INTO @seq_no, @this_ns_prefix, @this_element
  END
  -- Remove the final slash
  SELECT @xpath_expr = LEFT(@xpath_expr, DATALENGTH(@xpath_expr)
 - 1)
  -- Tidy up
  CLOSE xpath_generator
  DEALLOCATE xpath_generator
  DROP TABLE #results
  -- Return the XPath expression
  SELECT 'XPath(' + CONVERT(VARCHAR(4), @doc_id) + ', '
         + CONVERT(VARCHAR(4), @x_source) + ', '
         + CONVERT(VARCHAR(4), @x_target) + ')' AS parameter,
         RTRIM(@xpath_expr) AS value
END
GO
```

We can execute this procedure for our example document. For example, to obtain the path between the document node and the <p> element of the second <card> element would produce the result shown in Listing 8.85.

Listing 8.85 Result for rep_gen_xpath with Three Parameters

```
rep_gen_xpath 2, 1, 40
GO
parameter         value
---------------   --------------
XPath(2, 1, 40)   /wml/card[2]/p
(1 row(s) affected)
```

Note the sequence number 2 for the <card> element ("/wml/card/p" would match more than one node; the sequence number allows us to be specific).

8.8 Further Enhancements

This demonstration is really just a first step toward useful XML storage in relational databases. Keep an eye on http://www.rgedwards.com/ for news of future developments, such as a full DOM API for the repository. Aside from the benefits of being able to use DOM methods to manipulate large documents stored in the repository, this development will also allow us to support XSLT processing. A DOM API will allow us to render XML documents stored in the repository without first having to serialize them, and (since they are also XML) the XSLT stylesheets themselves can be stored alongside them. Clearly, this will be much slower than processing XML and XSLT files loaded into memory, but for large documents it will be a viable alternative.

8.9 Conclusion

We have investigated the practical implementation of a database model that can represent DOM node trees, and hence is able to store the content of any well-formed XML document. Since we are working at a higher level of abstraction than a schema-specific model, query building can prove more complex, but it does have the advantage of genericity. The merging of DOM with the Nested Sets Model allows us to navigate the document without recourse to walking the entire node tree. This feature allows for fast serialization and querying, but at the expense of slower updates (since insertions and deletions may require updates to the *(x, y)* coordinates of many nodes).

The major benefit of this exercise is that it provides the relational database programmer with the opportunity to experiment with XML data storage without recourse to implementing much (if any) new technology, and to do so in such a way that the XML can sit alongside traditional relational data without the need to build additional interfaces. The generic nature of the repository means that we are not constraining ourselves to any specific schema—a real advantage to those programmers that are not yet sure exactly what XML can do for them, or how it will fit with their future applications.

Chapter 9

An Object-Relational Approach to Building a High-Performance XML Repository

Paul G. Brown

9.1 Introduction

This chapter explores techniques for managing XML document data by exploiting the extensibility features of a modern Object-Relational Database Management System (ORDBMS). The motivation for this prototype system lies in the observation that new applications making use of XML are likely to coexist with preexisting information systems supported by SQL-centric (object-) relational databases. A further goal of the integrated data store described here is to investigate how to preserve all of the desirable quality-of-service features provided by an ORDBMS—read/write ACID transactions, scalability, standard client programming APIs (e.g., JDBC, ODBC), and a declarative data language interface—without compromising the potency of XML as a driver of inter-business communications.

We describe our prototype in cookbook fashion, explaining what its ingredients are and how they were assembled. Production-quality implementations of these ideas could make use of any number of freely available software libraries from the Internet. While this prototype was developed on one object-relational DBMS—namely IBM Informix IDS 9.x-the functionality needed to support its key features is implemented in a number of other DBMS products—notably the Java-based ORDBMS Cloudscape and the Open Source PostgreSQL DBMS—suggesting that the techniques described in this chapter should work equally well in these other systems. In other words, this prototype describes an approach to managing XML that has quite broad utility and does not require any engineering investment on the part of the DBMS vendors. Information systems developers need not wait for vendors to catch up or tolerate proprietary "extensions" to standards that characterize many vendor offerings.

We begin this chapter with an overview of the kind of use-case scenario addressed by our system. XML research is taking a number of divergent paths. Some researchers are focused on the unstructured and partially structured forms of XML, with applications in areas such as content management and information retrieval. This prototype system focuses instead on XML's likely use as an enabler for e-business communication. Pan-enterprise information systems—typified by supply chain management infrastructure—will tend towards much larger numbers of relatively small and more rigorously structured XML "documents" (with and without predefined schema). Participating business organizations will use XML as a *lingua franca* to exchange structured messages containing quantitative information: what, how much, how many, where, and when. It is thought that e-businesses will be motivated to retain these messages in a query-able repository in order to perform *post hoc* analysis involving components of the messages for which they had no operational use at the time the message was originally received.

Next, we describe the fairly conventional architecture of our prototype. Our description emphasizes logical architecture—the nature of the software modules making up the system and on the interfaces between them. Briefly, the prototype consists of a database schema that employs a number of SQL-3 user-defined types and functions and a small number of programs that convert XML and XPath into relational data and SQL-3 and back again. This logical architecture can be mapped to several physical architectures. In a modern DBMS, Java class libraries and even compiled binary libraries, which are conventionally integrated within some middleware or client program, can be dynamically linked into the DBMS runtime and treated as a kind of sophisticated stored procedure. Alternatively, the same class libraries may be loaded into middleware or even client programs. Deciding what physical model to adopt is contingent on the specifics of the system under construction.

We then move on to describe several of the more interesting features of the prototype in more detail. The areas of focus are

- The design of the object-relational database schema used by the prototype. Practical applications will need to build upon the simpleminded approach described here, and we suggest ways to employ other ORDBMS techniques to accommodate certain additional features of the XML data model.
- The functionality and design of the new types introduced into the ORDBMS in order to manage hierarchical structures efficiently. We emphasize how

the approach taken here meets the requirements of XML XPath processing, how it differs from other proposals, and what is required of the DBMS to support it.

- The algorithms used to convert XPath expressions into their equivalent SQL-3 given the schema design and user-defined types already introduced. XPath expressions constitute a sizeable portion of the XQuery specification. Because XML is conceived as a fundamentally hierarchical data model, getting XPath expressions to run efficiently presents a number of challenges to SQL query processors.

Finally we conclude this chapter with a review of the prototype and a summary of its key contributions.

9.2 Overview of XML Use-Case Scenario

The goal of this prototype is to implement an eXtensible Markup Language (XML) repository that coexists with a preexisting (object-)relational DBMS schema supporting an enterprise information system. In the context of business information systems, XML is typically described as a solution to the difficulties inherent in inter-systems (and inter-business) communications. As part of any negotiation, two business organizations must agree on a set of contractual obligations: quantities such as widget price, how many widgets, widget delivery schedule, and so on. When such negotiations are conducted face-to-face between representatives of the participating firms, the economic cost of coordinating such exchanges is relatively high. Higher transaction costs tend to push firms towards excess inventory and stocking levels and to financial management practices that require having plenty of cash on hand for "emergencies." One promise of the Internet is that electronic communications will lower the costs of business transactions and day-to-day business operations by reducing the need for face-to-face negotiations.

Consider, for example, a humble can of tomato soup. In the beginning, before there exists a single tomato, tin can, or label, farmers negotiate with representatives of agricultural supply companies for seed, fertilizer, and capital equipment. Having raised a crop of tomatoes, the farmer then negotiates with buyers from canneries on questions of volume, quality, and delivery dates, before the canners negotiate with their suppliers for tins and labels and with managers of retailer stores over wholesale prices, shelf space, and volume.

With perfect knowledge, all of these businesses could avoid excess and wastage but would not miss any business opportunities because a firm underestimated its cash or inventory requirements. Complicating the business communication problem is each firm's desire for independence: A business's problem domain overlaps the problem domains of the organizations adjacent to it in the supply chain, but it is in each firm's interests to retain its autonomy in terms of its management decision making. Business differentiation leads to diversity in the structure and functionality of the computer systems used to record the changing state of an organization and its assets. Consequently, no two businesses and no two business information systems are quite alike.

XML in e-business is therefore likely to be characterized by a very large number (due to lower transaction costs) of small, structured messages (due to the need for clarity in business communication). Even so, each business will need to concern itself with only a subset of the data in a message and will use the relevant subset as input to its own management systems. Also, the firm needs to convey information to other companies using XML. Consequently, the three principal requirements of any persistent storage system regarding XML are

1. The system must be capable of accepting high volumes of information formatted using XML. Further, the system should provide mechanisms for extracting the relevant information from these messages and storing it according to the (probably preexisting) data model that businesses design to support their own particular requirements.
2. An XML-enabled repository must also be capable of generating messages as XML from either the preexisting information systems or from the XML data it manages.
3. Because the original XML messages may contain information that has no place in the business's information systems and yet must be kept as a statement of record, many information systems will also be required to store XML messages for whatever duration the business requires, and to provide the business with the ability to manipulate (query) this message history.

Our prototype system's design priority, therefore, is managing a great many small XML messages: inquiries, quotes, orders, and invoices. These arrive, are stored within the repository, and the contents of these messages can be queried using SQL or XPath. Both XML schema (metadata) and XML document data are organized in a tightly integrated fashion. XPath-read queries span multiple messages (one can think of the repository as a single XML document that is constantly growing), and the system must be capable of executing XPath queries at the same time that new messages are being added to the repository.

9.3 High-Level System Architecture

The high-level logical architecture of the prototype—illustrated in Figure 9.1—is fairly orthodox. XML data and XPath expressions are passed into the repository at some pro-

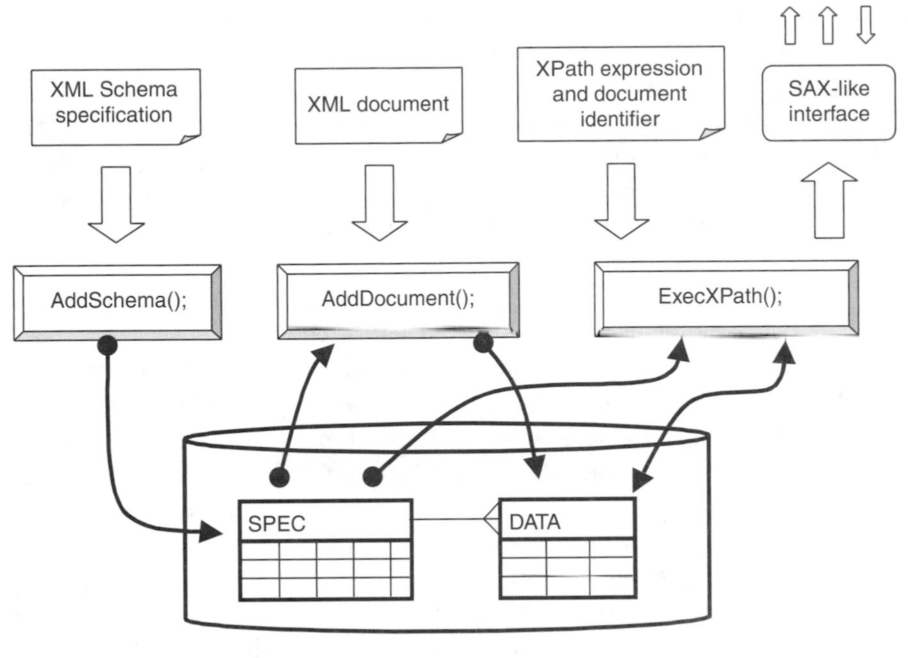

Figure 9.1 Logical Architecture of XML Repository Prototype

cedural mechanism: for example, a SOAP call or HTTP POST request. Three basic calls are provided by the prototype: `AddSchema()`, `AddDocument()`, and `ExecXPath()`.

The first two interfaces, `AddSchema()` and `AddDocument()`, add new schema specifications and document data to the repository, respectively. While the prototype relies upon the repository to manage both document data and the schema specification for each document, there is no requirement that each XML document must be preceded by its schema definition. As it parses a new XML document—shredding it into a sequence of document nodes—the prototype stores whatever schema structure it finds at the same time it stores the data. XML schema information is clearly very useful: Without knowledge of what data type a particular document node value belongs to, it is impossible to know precisely what is meant by the comparison operators in XPath. Metadata about the document's structure is used by the final function in the interface—`ExecXPath()`—to validate and interpret XPath expressions over documents.

The prototype stores XML schema and document data in relational tables. Each XML document node is stored in its own row. The first area where this prototype differs from others is in how the XML data are mapped to relational tables. Every XML document node is assigned a unique "value" that identifies it within the document independently of whatever data values the node contains. In fact, this node value identifies the new document node within the larger document consisting of the entire repository history. Further, the prototype's node identifier value can also be used to reason about the node's *position* in the hierarchy: its relationship to other nodes. (A more detailed description of the schema and the user-defined types used as node identifiers is discussed in Section 9.4.) The SQL-3 queries over the repository tables exploit the information contained within the node identifier to reason about the document's hierarchical structure.

In the `ExecXPath()` module, each incoming XPath expression is parsed and converted into an SQL-3 query expression that exploits the schema and user-defined types already mentioned. Given the repository design, the mapping from XPath expressions to SQL-3 queries is relatively straightforward, and these queries execute very efficiently. XPath is only a subset of the XQuery standard, which also includes a number of looping and set-manipulation aspects. In the prototype, we do not build a complete XQuery processor. Instead, we focus on the navigational XPath expressions because they constitute the most serious difficulties for an SQL database.

One interesting feature of our prototype concerns its handling of the results of an XPath expression from the `ExecXPath()` module. Most researchers have focused on XML as a document model. XML data in document form serves as the basic unit of input to the system, and most XML repositories output entire XML documents. This XML-as-document approach is clearly appropriate when XML is being used as a medium of communication: The whole point of the technology is to support self-contained and self-describing messages. But in the context of a centralized repository, the advantages of the XML-as-document approach are less clear. Our prototype takes a different approach.

Instead of handing an entire document back to the program that submitted the XPath query, the prototype instead hands back a *parser interface*, similar in its functionality to the SAX (Simple API for XML) interface. Not constructing the entire result document is made possible by the way the repository stores the XML data in a shredded format. Because of the way that the XML data are organized within the repository, the task of reconstructing a document to be returned incurs considerable computational overhead (whether or not the repository stores the document as a single contiguous byte stream). If the experience with SQL DBMS technology is any guide, applications requesting data from a repository are rarely interested in the entire result set for its own sake. A particularly common usage pattern is to iterate over some query results, discarding some results based on local (i.e., external to the DBMS) variable or end-user decision. Consequently, it seems likely that the first act of a program using an XML-as-document storage model repository will be to parse and shred any document returned. It seems wasteful to invest computational resources in putting a document together only to have it immediately pulled apart again.

In a similar vein, composing a document from its component parts is an example of what is known in query processing as a *blocking* operation. Before even the first byte of data can be returned to the external program, the repository is obliged to examine the entire result set. By streaming data out of the repository as soon as it is found to be part of the answer to the XPath expression, the prototype permits a degree of pipe-lining impossible in document-centric systems. An external program can be working on one part of the result document at the same time that the repository is producing the rest.

Replacing the XML-as-document model with an XML-as-data model yields one more advantage. In its current form, the XQuery language standard provides no mechanism for update operations over a persistent XML document. Even overwriting the value of a single `xsd:decimal` element requires replacing the entire document with a new version. Making matters worse, when a new XML document A is created by extracting a subdocument from some larger, persistently stored document B with some XPath expression, the new document's node identifiers are completely independent of the identifiers in the persistent store (node identifiers are scoped to the document). Thus it is not clear how an update operation over a data node identified in document A can be tied back to a node in document B. Only by providing an interface that maps back to the original, persistent data can an update be made reliably. We illustrate the problem in Figure 9.2.

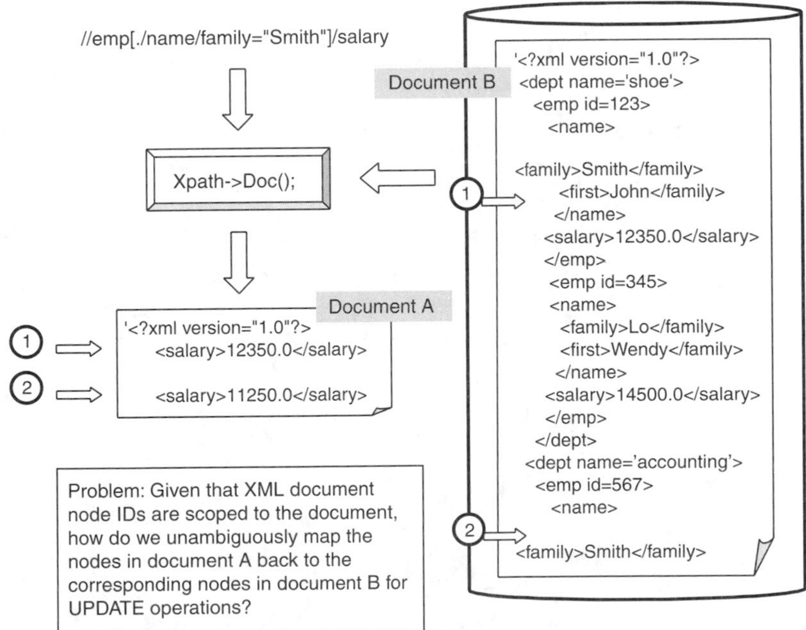

Figure 9.2 XML-as-Document Model and Repository Update Problem

To overcome this problem, our prototype abandons the XML-as-document model except when data are being added to the repository. Even the pair of functions—AddSchema() and AddDocument()—that do deal with documents are shims over identical internal logic that shreds each XML document and stores its contents in the prototype's internal structure. XML documents are not stored in BLOB (Binary Large Object) form (except for larger blocks of text in data nodes), and document data is never reparsed. Further, the prototype includes interface mechanisms allowing external programs to update document nodes stored in the repository in much the same way that SQL developers can use UPDATE WHERE CURRENT OF CURSOR.

In Listing 9.1 we present a sequence of operations to illustrate how the prototype is used. The schema and data introduced in Listing 9.1 are used as grist for examples later in this chapter. First, we show a call to AddSchema(), which adds a schema to the repository. This step is not strictly necessary, but the schema information, as we have mentioned already, is useful for discriminating among data types in an XML document. The second call adds a new document to the repository. In the prototype we adopt the practice of allowing a single schema to be used for multiple documents, and the AddDocument() call appends a new XML document to the end of an existing one (named in the second argument to AddDocument()). Alternative models of document management—multiple distinct documents or fewer instances of much larger documents—are not precluded by anything in the prototype's fundamental design.

Listing 9.1 Adding a New Schema and a Document to the Repository

```
$ AddSchema ('<xs:schema xmlns:xs=http://www.w3.org/2001/XMLSchema>
  <xs:element name="peach" type="part-type"/>
  <xs:complexType name="part-type">
    <xs:sequence>
      <xs:element name="variety" type="xs:string"/>
      <xs:element name="price" type="xs:decimal"/>
      <xs:attribute name="quantity" type="xs:integer"/>
    </xs:sequence>
    <xs:attribute name="quality" type="xs:string"/>
  </xs:complexType>
</xs:schema>', 'peaches');

$ AddDocument ('peaches','peach list # 1',
'<?xml version="1.0"?>
<peach quality="good">
    <variety>Belle of Georgia</variety>
    <price>1.25</price>
    <quantity>2500</quantity>
```

```
</peach>
<!<\#45><\#45>  This data is from two weeks ago <\#45><\#45>!>
<peach>
    <price>1.35</price>
    <quantity>1500</quantity>
</peach>
<peach quality="poor">
    <variety>Southland</variety>
    <price>0.95</price>
    <quantity>300</quantity>
</peach>');
```

In Listing 9.2, we present an example of an XML XPath expression together with the result produced by the expression evaluator. This XPath expression's plain language description would be: "List all of the peaches where the price is greater than $1.00." The results list shown in Listing 9.2 reflects only a fraction of the information the XPath evaluator returns. In fact, what the `ExecXPath()` function returns is a sequence of Parser Event Objects. Not shown in Listing 9.2 are the node identities of the schema node, and the document node, which are used within the repository to organize the XML data. The complete set of document node information is needed by both the UPDATE methods of the interface and whatever superstructure is required by a fully functional XQuery interpreter.

Listing 9.2 Evaluating an XPath Expression

```
$ Exec_XPath ('peaches list # 1','/peach[price>1.00]');

begin document
start element "peach"
start attribute "quality"
attribute data "good"
end attribute "quality"
start element "variety"
text data "Belle of Georgia"
end element "variety"
start element "price"
text data 1.25
end element "price"
start element "quantity"
text data 2500
end element "quantity"
```

```
end element "peach"
start element "peach"
start element "price"
text data 1.35
end element "price"
start element "quantity"
text data 1500
end element "quantity"
end element "peach"
end document
```

Because we have the luxury of working with an extensible DBMS the "objects" returned by the XPath interpreter are considerably more complex than the simple row sets or cursors with which SQL developers will be familiar. Instead, each result value is a self-contained "event" object. In our prototype, these are implemented as SQL-3 structured types, but other standards—such as the SQL-J standard for Java—provide a standard mechanism for returning Java objects directly from the DBMS. Since, in our prototype, this functionality is built into the framework provided by a commercial ORDBMS, product developers have a wide range of options for external APIs: ODBC (Open Database Connectivity), JDBC, or ESQL/C (Embedded SQL for C). All of the functional interfaces were developed in a mixture of C and the DBMS's own (proprietary) stored procedure language. In hindsight, this idea was a bad one as building a slow, buggy XML parser using a DBMS-stored procedure language added little to the sum of human knowledge. Fast, reliable, and free alternatives in the form of several C and Java parsers are available on the Internet.

Once indices have been added, experimental evidence suggests that the storage space requirement of our prototype is a little less than three times the storage space required to store the original documents uncompressed (although it is significantly more than the space required to store compressed XML). In compensation for the storage overhead, the schema and node identifier values together result in the useful situation where *every XPath expression over all of the document(s) in the repository is indexed.*

9.4 Detailed Design Descriptions

In this section we explore three aspects of the prototype in some detail: the object-relational DBMS schema used to hold the XML document schemas and data, the user-defined types needed to make hierarchical operations efficient, and the algorithms used to map XPath expressions to their corresponding SQL-3 queries.

Figure 9.3 presents the basic schema used in the prototype in an entity-relationship diagram, and Listing 9.3 shows the required SQL-3 DDL (Data Definition Language). What Figure 9.3 conveys can be thought of as a design pattern, rather than a complete schema. Because the prototype generates all of its SQL at runtime, it has considerable flexibility in terms of how it uses the table and schema management facilities of the underlying DBMS. For example, different subsets of an XML repository can be stored in separate pairs of tables. By extending the interface functions with a qualifying name, it becomes possible to discriminate among multiple pairs of tables.

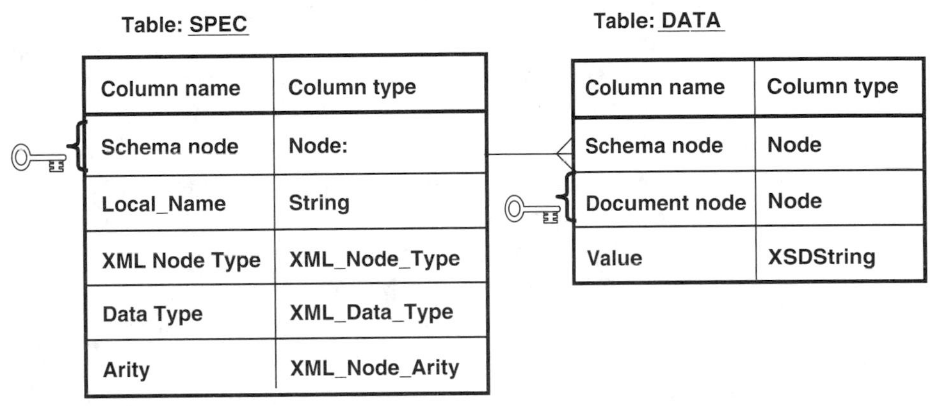

Figure 9.3 Entity-Relationship Diagram

Listing 9.3 SQL Definition of Repository Schema

```
CREATE TABLE Spec (
 Schema_Node      Node                PRIMARY KEY
                  CONSTRAINT Spec_Node_PK_Schema_Node,
 Local_Name       String              NOT NULL,
 XML_Node_Type    XML_Node_Type       DEFAULT 'ELEMENT'
 Data_Type        XML_Atomic_Type     DEFAULT 'xs:anyType',
 Arity            XML_Node_Arity      DEFAULT '[0..N]'
);
--
```

```
CREATE TABLE Data (
 Doc_Node          Node          PRIMARY KEY
                   CONSTRAINT Data_Doc_Node_PK,
 Schema_Node       Node          NOT NULL
                   REFERENCES Spec ( Schema_Node )
                   CONSTRAINT Data_Spec_FK_Schema_Node,
 Value             XSDSTRING     DEFAULT '<EMPTY>'
);
```

Each of the table data types in Listing 9.3 is an example of an *extended* data type managed by the ORDBMS. Many of these user-defined types are implemented to model aspects of the XML Schema and Data Model specification. For example, the specification provides for seven kinds of XML document nodes: Document, Element, Attribute, Namespace, Processing Instruction, Comment, and Text. Also, the XML Data Model includes a set of 19 primitive atomic types (in addition to a generic type known as `xsd:anyType`). Each atomic node value in the document must be of one of these types. XML Node Types and XML Atomic Data Type identifiers are modeled using the XML_Node_Type and XML_Data_Type SQL types.

Our prototype uses only a single pair of tables. In practice, an XML repository would need considerably more. XML's use of namespaces to assign semantic intent to tag names, for example, suggests that some additional columns are necessary. And although XML's "wire" format consists of ASCII strings, care must be taken to ensure that XPath expressions with range predicates (>, <, etc.) and the more complex set-membership operations evaluate correctly. Replacing the single `DATA` table from Figure 9.3 with a branching hierarchy of tables allows us to overload the data type used to define the `VALUE` column. The type system of the XML Schema and Data Model—which is considerably richer than the SQL-92 type system or the SQL-3 built-in types—can be modeled with user-defined types in an SQL-3 ORDBMS. We illustrate this approach with the E-ER diagram in Figure 9.4.

SQL-3 DBMS engines convert queries addressing the "table" `DATA` in Figure 9.4 into queries over the entire hierarchy of type-specific tables beneath it. A table per XML type approach is useful because it permits the DBMS to create a separate index per type/table ensuring that, for example, two `xsd:decimal` values 21 and 123 and two `xs:string` values "21" and "123" are handled in the manner appropriate to their type. Further, a distinct SQL-3 type/table per XML type simplifies the mapping from the typed operators specified in XQuery (>, >=, etc.) into SQL-3 equivalents. Although the XML Schema Specification includes about 40 types, the number of tables needed to manage them is fortunately much fewer. All 10 integer types, for example, can be stored in a single table. In all cases, typed data is converted back into an ASCII representation.

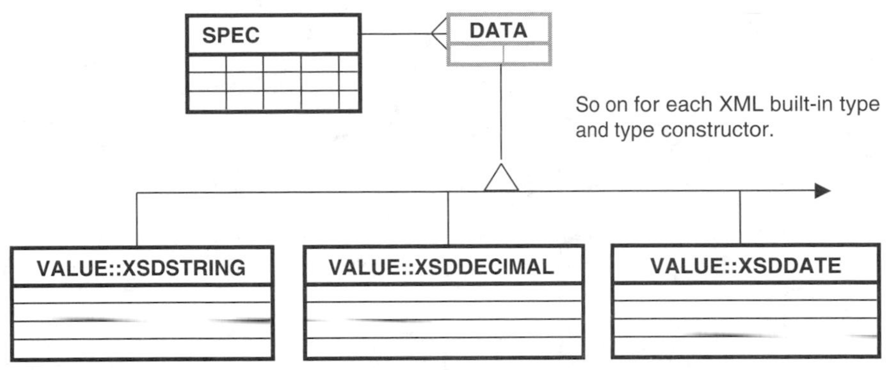

Figure 9.4 Extended-ER Diagram for OR Schema That Handles XML Built-in Data Type Information

Understanding how XML data are mapped to relational tables is central to understanding how the XPath expressions are mapped into fairly simple and efficient SQL-3 queries. We take a minute here to explain how this is done.

XML's data model is hierarchical (e.g., Figure 9.5). All XML documents combine *tags* that define the tree-like structure of the document with whatever data the document contains. Each item in an XML document is either a *node* (associated with the document's structure), or it is an *atomic value* (which makes up the data the document contains) bound to a node. XML nodes are organized into hierarchies; formally we can say that each node in a document has at most one other node that it can call its *parent* node, although it may have many *children* and an even larger number of *descendants*. Further, nodes have identity (every node is distinct from all other nodes within the document), and they are ordered within the document (XML documents have a well-defined node order).

Note that, without the schema specification, it is possible to determine the names and kinds (attributes, elements, etc.) of each node, although it is not clear how to extract data type information from a document. If the type of element or attribute data is unknown, then it is classified as being of `xsd:anyType`.

Among the various things standardized as part of XML is a set of operators for reasoning about the relative locations of nodes in a document tree. Collectively referred to as *path expressions*, these represent concepts such as "look for element node 'variety' *under* element node 'peach'", or "element node 'price' is a descendant of element node 'peach'", or "attribute node 'price' is a child of element node 'peach'". In the document data in Listing 9.1, for example, the <price></price> node associated with the "0.95" atomic value is a *descendant* of the <peach></peach> node that is the *parent of* the quality="poor" attribute node.

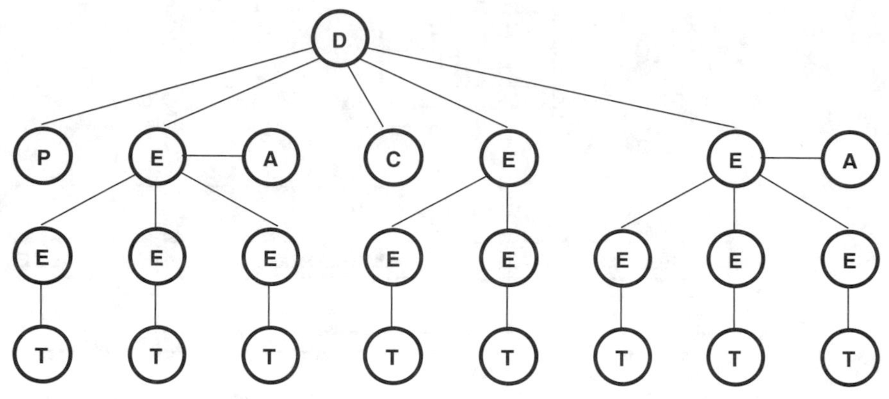

Figure 9.5 Hierarchical Structure of XML Document Data from Listing 9.1

Hierarchical operators are not part of the relational data model followed (more or less) by the implementers of SQL database management systems. An important challenge for our prototype, therefore, is to arrive at efficient ways to support hierarchical path operations in an object-relational DBMS.

We introduce hierarchical concepts into the DBMS through the mechanism of a new user-defined type (UDT) called "Node" (or "SQL Node" to distinguish it from "XML document node"), and a number of user-defined functions, which implement operators over the new type. You can see where the SQL Node type is used in Figure 9.3. SQL Node "values" consist of a variable length vector of positive integer values. Several internal representations suggest themselves, each with its own trade-off between complexity and performance. In the prototype we opted for the simplest possible representation: an array of 32-bit integers. The SQL Node type could easily be constructed to support *parent->child* branching or arbitrary width and of arbitrary depth by employing nonstandard integer representations.

In Tables 9.1 and 9.2 we present in tabular form what the SPEC and DATA tables would look like after the operations in Listing 9.1. SPEC stores nodes specified as part of an XML schema specification. DATA stores the actual data found in the XML documents stored in the repository with a reference back to the corresponding schema node.

SQL Node values are useful because they allow us to reason about hierarchies efficiently. Given two SQL Node values, it is possible to deduce what the relationship is between the corresponding XML document nodes. Other approaches to managing hierarchies (sometimes referred to in the literature as "containment" or "bill-of-materials" problems) require developers to reconstruct the relationship from data in several columns, or several rows, or both. Also, the query-processing techniques necessary to traverse the tree are very simple in the case of the SQL Node

Table 9.1 SPEC Table

Schema Node	XML_Node_ Type	Local_ Name	XML_Data_ Type	Arity	Fixed
6.1	ELEMENT	peach	part-type	1	
6.1.1	ELEMENT	variety	xsd:string	[0..N]	
6.1.2	ELEMENT	price	xsd:decimal	[0..N]	
6.1.3	ELEMENT	quantity	xsd:integer	[0..N]	
6.1.4	ATTRIBUTE	quality	xsd:string	[0..1]	

Table 9.2 DATA Table

Doc Node	Schema_ Node	Value	Doc_ Node	Schema_ Node	Value
4447.0	6.0	peaches	4447.2.1	6.1.2	1.35
4447.1	6.1	<EMPTY>	4447.2.2	6.1.3	1500
4447.1.1	6.1.4	good	4447.3	6.1	<EMPTY>
4447.1.2	6.1.1	Belle of Georgia	4447.3.1	6.1.4	poor
4447.1.3	6.1.2	1.25	4447.3.2	6.1.1	Southland
4447.1.4	6.1.3	2500	4447.3.3	6.1.2	0.95
4447.2	6.1	<EMPTY>	4447.3.4	6.1.3	300

approach—a B-tree index scan to extract a list of descendants, hash joins for equality—while they are considerably more complex in other approaches—iteratively constructing an intermediate result set in recursive query processing.

At the heart of the SQL Node UDT is a mechanism for ordering SQL Node values so that they can be indexed and compared in the manner required. This mechanism depends on a single user-defined function called `COMPARE()` that takes two SQL Node values and returns −1 if the first comes before the second, 1 if the first comes after the second, and 0 if they are the same value. In Listing 9.4 we present the pseudo code for this function.

Listing 9.4 Pseudo Code for Compare Function for SQL Node User-Defined Type

```
PROCEDURE COMPARE ( Node_A, Node_B )
RETURNS INTEGER
//  Node.GetElement ( INTEGER ) returns the element value at some
offset.
// If the INTEGER argument is larger than the number of elements in
the Node
// the method returns 0. The initial element of a Node must be a
positive
// integers.
  LOCAL:
     INTEGER  Result := NOT_FOUND,  // NOT_FOUND is out-of-band
placeholder.
              Offset := 1,
              FirstElement, SecondElement;

  WHILE ( Result == NOT_FOUND ) DO
     FirstElement  := Node_A.GetElement ( Offset );
     SecondElement := Node_B.GetElement ( Offset );
     IF ( FirstElement > SecondElement ) THEN
        Result := 1;
     ELSE IF ( FirstElement < SecondElement ) THEN
        Result := -1;
     ELSE IF ( FirstElement == 0 ) AND ( SecondElement == 0 ) THEN
        Result := 0;
     ELSE
        OffSet := OffSet + 1;
     END IF;
  END DO;
  RETURN Result;
 END COMPARE;
```

SQL-3 and XML developers never use the `COMPARE()` UDF. Rather, it is embedded within the ORDBMS, which makes use of it as part of SQL query processing. A number of other SQL operations can be built on `COMPARE()`. For example, all of the Boolean ordinal operators over two SQL Nodes—equals, greater than, less than, and so on—can be determined from the `COMPARE()` function's return result. And in a well-engineered ORDBMS, this same function can be used to overload the sorting, B-tree indexing facilities, as well as the `MIN()` and `MAX()` aggregate functions.

In Table 9.3 we present a list of hierarchical "axes" operations taken from the XPath version 2.0 and XQuery specification and show their corresponding representation as user-defined predicates over the SQL Node UDT. "Axes" operations are navigational "path" expressions involving an XML document's structure. Underlined operations are all user-defined functions. In SQL-3 queries, user-defined functions can be combined using the standard logical operators.

All of the expressions in the right column of Table 9.3 can be invoked as part of SQL-3 queries over the tables used to store the XML data. As part of its query-

Table 9.3 XML Hierarchical Operations and Node UDT Equivalent Expressions

XPath Axes Operations	Equivalent SQL Node User-Defined Type Expression, and Examples
is: Equivalent Document Node (or different Document Node)	EQUAL (Node_A, Node_B): '4447.1.4' = '4447.1.4', '6.1.3' <> '6.1.4'
descendant: Document Node A is descendant of Document Node B	GREATERTHAN (Node_A, Node_B) and LESSTHAN (Node_A, INCREMENT (Node_B)): '4447.1.4' > '4447.1' AND '4447.1.4' < (INCREMENT ('4447.1') == '4447.2') NOTE: The order-sensitive operations (GREATERTHAN() and LESSTHAN()) are determined by comparing each integer in each input node from left to right and returning when one integer is found to be different from the integer in the corresponding location in the other node. If no differences are found the result is an equality. If one node terminates before the other without there being any difference the terminating node is less than longer node. The INCREMENT (Node) function increments the least significant (last) integer value in the Node.
child: Document Node A is a child of Document Node B	GREATERTHAN (Node_A, Node_B) and LESSTHAN (Node_A, INCREMENT (Node_B)) AND LENGTH (Node_A) = LENGTH (Node_B) + 1; NOTE: The LENGTH (Node) function returns the number of integers or 'levels' in the Node. Thus LENGTH('4447.1') == 2.
ancestor: Document Node A is an Ancestor of Document Node B. (Note that this is simply the commutation of descendant).	GREATERTHAN (Node_B, Node_A) and LESSTHAN (Node_B, INCREMENT (Node_A)):

(continued)

Table 9.3 *continued*

XPath Axes Operations	Equivalent SQL Node User-Defined Type Expression, and Examples
parent: Document Node A is a parent of Document Node B. (Note that this is simply the commutation of child.)	EQUAL (Node_A, GETPARENT (Node_B)); NOTE: GETPARENT(Node) trims the least significant (last) integer from the input.
sibling: Document Node A is a sibling of Document Node B which occurs after it.	EQUAL (GETPARENT (Node_A), GETPARENT (Node_B)); NOTE: To compute the following or preceding sibling in a set it is necessary to find the MIN() or MAX() node value in the set matching the predicate above.

processing work, the ORDBMS engine calls the appropriate user-defined function in the appropriate places. As several of the examples in Table 9.3 imply, SQL Node values can be sorted into document order. For example, to reconstruct a list of all of the nodes in the documents, along with their tags, the kind of XML node and the XML node's data type all in document order, it is only necessary to use the query in Listing 9.5. Further, it is possible to use the relational concept of views in interesting ways. For example, the data in the `VIEW` in Listing 9.6 corresponds to a list of every possible subdocument in the repository (i.e., every possible target of an XPath expression over the repository). Clearly, for any reasonably large repository, selecting all of the data in this view is impossible. Even the 14 nodes in the single, small document added in Listing 9.1 by itself generates 37 "rows" in `XML_Doc_Trees`. In practice this view is used only to extract results from the repository, which means that other, very restrictive predicates are all applied over it.

Listing 9.5 SQL-3 Query to Reconstruct Entire XML Document from Repository Schema

```
SELECT S.XML_Node_Type AS Kind_of_Node,
       S.Local_Name    AS Tag_Name,
       S.XML_Data_Type AS Data_Type,
       D.Value         AS Value,
       D.Schema_Node   AS Schema_Node,
       D.Doc_Node      AS Doc_Node
  FROM Data D, Spec S
 WHERE D.Schema_Node = S.Schema_Node
 ORDER BY D.Doc_Node;
```

Listing 9.6 SQL-3 View Representing Every Possible Subtree in the Repository

```
CREATE VIEW XML_Doc_Trees AS
SELECT S1.Local_Name     AS Root_Tag_Name,
       S1.Schema_Node    AS Root_Schema_Node,
       D1.Doc_Node       AS Root_Doc_Node,
       S2.XML_Node_Type  AS Value_Data_Type,
       S2.Local_Name     AS Local_Tag_Name,
       S2.Data_Type      AS Data_Type,
       D2.Value          AS Value,
       D2.Doc_Node       AS Doc_Node,
       D2.Schema_Node    AS Schema_Node
  FROM Data D1, Spec S1, Data D2, Spec S2
 WHERE S1.Schema_Node = D1.Schema_Node  -- JOINS between Schema and
   AND S2.Schema_Node = D2.Schema_Node  -- DATA.
   AND D2.Doc_Node >= D1.Doc_Node       -- This pair of predicates
   AND D2.Doc_Node <                   -- specifies all of the Nodes
          Increment(D1.Doc_Node);       -- in D2 which are
descendants of
                                        -- each node in D2. See
Table 9.3.
```

How can such queries be made to scale to large documents or large numbers of documents? Database indexing is key to scalability, and providing the ability to support indexing operations over SQL Node user-defined type columns is critical to getting good performance out of the prototype. Not all modern DBMS products provide this functionality, and some that promote their user-defined indexing features implement the feature poorly. However, the Open Source PostgreSQL DBMS, IBM's Java-based Cloudscape, and Informix IDS products all implement such support quite well.

XML's document hierarchy is only one example of a data-modeling problem for which the Node UDT is suitable. Reporting hierarchies (employees, managers, and the manager's managers) and process hierarchies are other applications where the hierarchical structure of the information is a key challenge. In any data-modeling situation where there exists a parent/child relationship between objects of the same type can use the SQL Node UDT extension.

We now turn to a discussion of how the prototype converts XPath expressions into SQL-3 queries. In Listing 9.7 we provide a complex XML Schema definition, together with some example data. Figure 9.6 presents the same schema information as a graph.

Listing 9.7 XML Document for More Complex XPath Examples

```
$ AddDocument (
'INQUIRY','Inquiry List # 1',
'<?xml version="1.0"?>
  <inquiry reference-num="123" respond-by="2002-05-21">
     <inquiry-from>
        <name>Ajax Inc</name>
        <address country="US">
           <street>123 Ajax St</street>
           <city>Ajaxville</city>
           <state>CA</state>
           <zip>95123</zip>
        </address>
     </inquiry-from>
     <delivery-to country="US">
        <street>123 Ajax St</street>
        <city>Ajaxville</city>
        <state>CA</state>
        <zip>95123</zip>
     </delivery-to>
     <requested-order>
     <item partNum="ABC-123">
          <productName>Shoes</productName>
          <quantity>2</quantity>
       </item>
       <item partNum="CBA-321">
          <productName>Sox</productName>
          <quantity>2</quantity>
       </item>
    </requested-order>
 </inquiry>');
```

The primary purpose of XPath expressions is to identify interesting subsets of some XML data document. For example, a user may want address information of potential customers making inquiries or information about items that have a particular partNum. XPath expressions are deceptively simple. They derive their power from the flexibility of the underlying hierarchical data model. Each XPath expression describes a path within some target document. Names in the path expression correspond to element names (tags) in the document's structural schema, and each path expression will probably refer to a great many node locations in any particular document. Several examples of XPath path expressions and their interpretations are

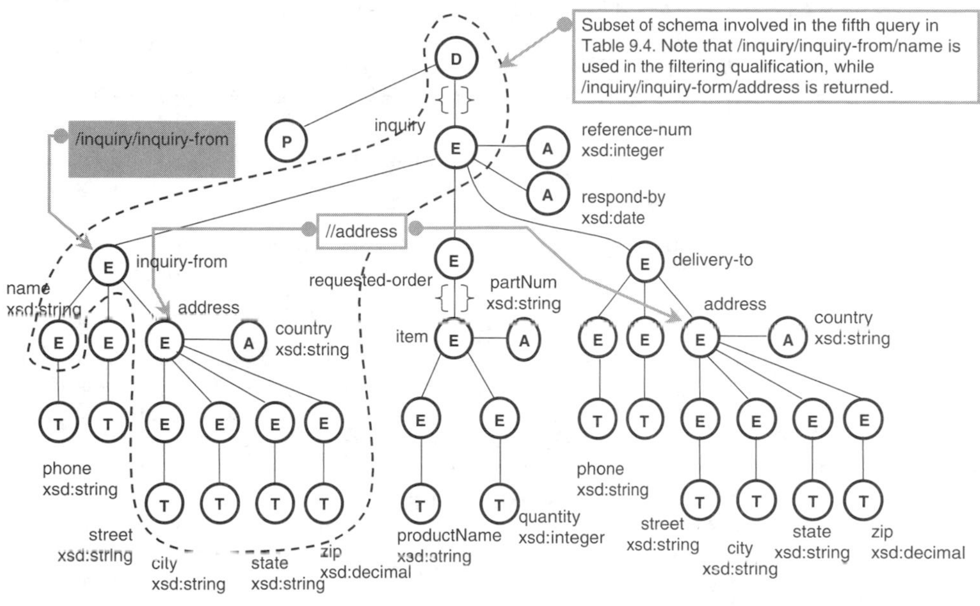

Figure 9.6 Tree Graph for XML Schema in Listing 9.7

to be found in Table 9.4. Note that the "//" or "descendant-of" path separator might produce as a result a situation where a single XPath expression addresses a number of nodes in the schema! And in an XML document subsets of a schema can be present multiple times.

At various points in the path, the XPath expression can add predicate expressions that filter (qualify) the set of possible document locations. Filter expressions are combinations of type-specific comparison operations. For example, the XPath standard includes a full set of comparison operators for numbers and strings as well as a set of mathematical and string-manipulation functions. In general, all of these are equivalent to a straightforward SQL-3 query statement.

Each path in an XPath expression is a sequence of node (element or attribute) names. Each has (at least) a hierarchical relationship (see Table 9.3) with the prior node in the list, with the initial node descending from some document root node or a current context node in the document. Consequently, an XPath expression in an XML document schema can be validated by joining the SPEC table from the prototype schema once with itself for each tag or label in the XPath expression. XPath expressions with a single node label require a single selection from the SPEC table: the root label of the result document. Each additional node label in the XPath expression adds another SPEC table join, with the join predicate depending on the

Table 9.4 XPath Expressions over Listing 9.7 Documents and Their Plain Language Interpretation

XPath Expression	Plain Language Interpretation
/inquiry	Return all of the document nodes descendant from the /inquiry path, together with the /inquiry node itself.
/inquiry/inquiry-from	Return all of the document nodes descendant from the '/inquiry/inquiry-from' path together the inquiry-from node itself.
//address	Return all of the document nodes which are descendants of an 'address' node together with the 'address' document node itself. Note that the '//' addressing says that the subsequent tag is either a descendant-or-self of the current node.
/inquiry//address [city eq "Ajaxville"]	Return all of the document nodes which are descendants of an 'address' node together with the 'address' document node itself, so long as the 'address' document node has a child node called 'city' whose value is equal to "Ajaxville".
/inquiry/inquiry-from [name eq "Ajax inc"]/address	Return all of the document nodes which are descendants of an 'address' node that is a child of an '/inquiry/inquiry-from' path together with the 'address' document node itself, so long as the 'inquiry-from' document node has a child node called 'name' whose value is equal to "Ajax Inc".
//address[zip intersect (94090, 95000 to 96000)]	Return all of the document nodes which are descendants of an 'address' node where a child node element called 'zip' has a value of 94090 or a value between 95000 and 96000.

axes relationship (descendant of, child of). If what separates the two nodes is a single "/", then the second element is a child of the first, and if the separator is a "//", or some relative path expression such as "..//", then a more complex hierarchical relationship is used in the join (*descendant*, or *descendant-of-parent*, respectively).

Having determined through a series of joins the schema node that is the root node of the XPath result, the SQL-3 query then needs to use the `XML_Doc_Trees` view from Listing 9.6 to retrieve the actual data. Listing 9.8 illustrates three SQL-3 queries that correspond to the first three XPath expressions in Table 9.4. Sorting the data—the last step in each of the queries in Listing 9.8—is necessary to meet the requirement that XML data always appear in document order. All of the predicates in the Table 9.4 queries are "indexable"—that is, the ORDBMS makes use of an index on the Data.Schema_Node column to compute the joins efficiently. Note that all of the navigational axes operations can be indexed if the schema size should be large enough to justify it. And a repository containing a very large number of schemas (where, for instance, each and every document produces its own schema as a side effect of parsing) presents no difficulty.

Listing 9.8 SQL-3 Equivalents for First Three XPath Expressions from Figure 9.6

```
SELECT X.*
  FROM XML_Doc_Trees X , Spec P1
 WHERE X.Root_Schema_Node = P1.Schema_Node
   AND P1.local_name = "inquiry
   AND Length (GetParent(P1.Schema_Node)) = 1
  ORDER BY X.Doc_Node;

SELECT X.*
  FROM XML_Doc_Trees X, Spec S1, Spec S2
 WHERE X.Root_Schema_Node = P2.Schema_Node
   AND P1.local_name = "inquiry"

   AND P2.local_name = "inquiry-from"
   AND P1.Schema_Node = GetParent(P2.Schema_Node)
   AND Length(GetParent(P1.Schema_Node)) = 1
   ORDER BY X.Doc_Node;

SELECT X.*
  FROM XML_Doc_Trees X ,Spec P1
 WHERE X.Root_Schema_Node = P1.Schema_Node

   AND P1.local_name = "address"

 ORDER BY X.Doc_Node;
```

Qualifiers in the XPath expression can also be checked in the SQL query. Nodes—attributes as well as elements—mentioned in qualification predicates can also be thought of as part of a path. In the fourth XPath example from Table 9.4, for instance, the "city" element (attributes are always preceded either by an "@" symbol or an "attribute::" expression) is a child of the "address" element, which is a descendant of the "inquiry" element, which makes up the root of the document path. The XPath qualifies only those addresses where the city element equals "Ajaxville". Another way of saying this is that the qualifier ensures that there exists a child element of address whose label name is "city" and whose value is "Ajaxville". It is this existential qualifier mechanism that the prototype exploits (see Listing 9.9).

Each qualifier identifies an element (or attribute) relative to one outer component of the XPath and provides an expression to evaluate over that element (or attribute). The prototype relegates the identification of the qualifier node and the qualifier check to a subquery. Multiple qualifiers in the XPath result in multiple subqueries.

Listing 9.9 SQL-3 Equivalent for Fourth XPath Expression in Table 9.4

```
SELECT X.*
  FROM XML_Tree X , Spec P1, Spec P2
 WHERE X.Root_Schema_Node = P2.Schema_Node
   AND P1.local_name = "inquiry"
   AND Length (GetParent(P1.Schema_Node)) = 1
   AND P2.Schema_Node > P1.Schema_Node
   AND P2.Schema_Node < Increment ( P1.Schema_Node )
   AND P2.local_name = "address"
   AND EXISTS ( SELECT 1
                 FROM Spec P3, Data D1
                WHERE D1.Schema_Node = P3.Schema_Node
                  AND P3.Local_Name  = "city"
         AND P2.Schema_Node = GetParent(D1.Schema_Node)
                  AND D1.Doc_Node     > X.Root_Doc_Node
                  AND D1.Doc_Node     < Increment ( X.Root_Doc_Node
)
                  AND D1.Value        = "Ajaxville")
 ORDER BY X.Doc_Node;
```

A qualifying filter expression may be the termination of an XPath expression. As you can see from the outlined subset of XML Schema Nodes in Figure 9.6, it is possible for a filtering qualifier to be applied over a path that branches from the path returned. In this case, the query needs to ensure that it is addressing only those data branches where an appropriate subnode exists. Our transformation algorithm achieves this by adding a join back to the DATA table in the outer query and adding another predicate to the subquery (see Listing 9.10).

Listing 9.10 SQL-3 Query Equivalent of the Fifth Query in Table 9.4

```
SELECT X1.*
  FROM Spec P1, Spec P2, Spec P3, Data D1,
       XML_Doc_Tree X1

 WHERE X1.Root_Schema_Node = P3.Schema_Node

   AND P1.local_name = "inquiry"
   AND Length (GetParent(P1.Schema_Node)) = 1

   AND P2.local_name = "inquiry-from"
   AND P1.Schema_Node = GetParent ( P2.Schema_Node )
   AND D1.Schema_Node = P2.Schema_Node
   AND GetParent(X1.Root_Doc_Node) = D1.Doc_Node

   AND P3.local_name = "address"
   AND P2.Schema_Node = GetParent ( P3.Schema_Node )

   AND EXISTS (
     SELECT 1
       FROM Spec P4, Data D2
      WHERE P4.local_name  = 'name'
        AND P2.Schema_Node = GetParent(P4.Schema_Node)
        AND D2.Schema_Node = P4.Schema_Node
        AND D2.Value       = 'Ajax Inc'
        AND D1.Doc_Node    = GetParent(D2.Doc_Node ))

 ORDER BY X1.Doc_Node;
```

Supporting update operations is another important objective of the repository. The `AddDocument()` interface call parses the input document and validates its contents against the schema. As it does so it stores the rows corresponding to input document nodes in a temporary table, inserting the entire set into the DATA table once it has validated the entire input document. In terms of the XML-as-document model what `AddDocument()` is doing is appending the new document to the end of the existing document data. Another kind of update operation modifies the data in a single document node: for example, changing a price in a catalog. And, of course, an entire subset of the document may be deleted. XPath and XQuery do not currently include support for update operations. Nevertheless they are likely to be important in any practical system of the kind the prototype addresses.

Storing XML documents as contiguous blocks of data presents a number of problems to concurrent read/write operations. If the locking granularity of the repository is at the document level—that is, if the system only supports document-level concurrency control—then different users may not be reading and writing different parts of the same document at the same time. Storing XML document data with one node-per-record offers the best possible granularity control: Modern DBMS products all support row-level locking. But any mechanism for supporting concurrent read/write access should do so with minimal cost overheads.

Support for INSERT and UPDATE operations over XML documents has proven to be a very hard problem because of the need to maintain document order. In Figure 9.7 we illustrate the problem. The tree graph on the left represents the before state of some subset of document nodes in an XML document. For completeness we include a sequence value representing node order. New nodes are added—an additional item might be in an inquiry document, for example—producing the tree on the right. All of the nodes to the left of the newly inserted nodes and all of the nodes to the left of the entire Figure 9.7 subtree have been modified. Consequently, adding new nodes to a document might have the side effect of modifying all of the node values coming after it in the document.

The Node UDT reduces but does not eliminate the problem. In Figure 9.8 we show the same subtree as in Figure 9.7, only this time using the SQL Node to enumerate the XML document nodes. As you can see, the addition of the new nodes has only modified the values of nodes descended from the after-siblings of the new root node. This is a significant improvement over the sequence value "worst case" of Figure 9.7.

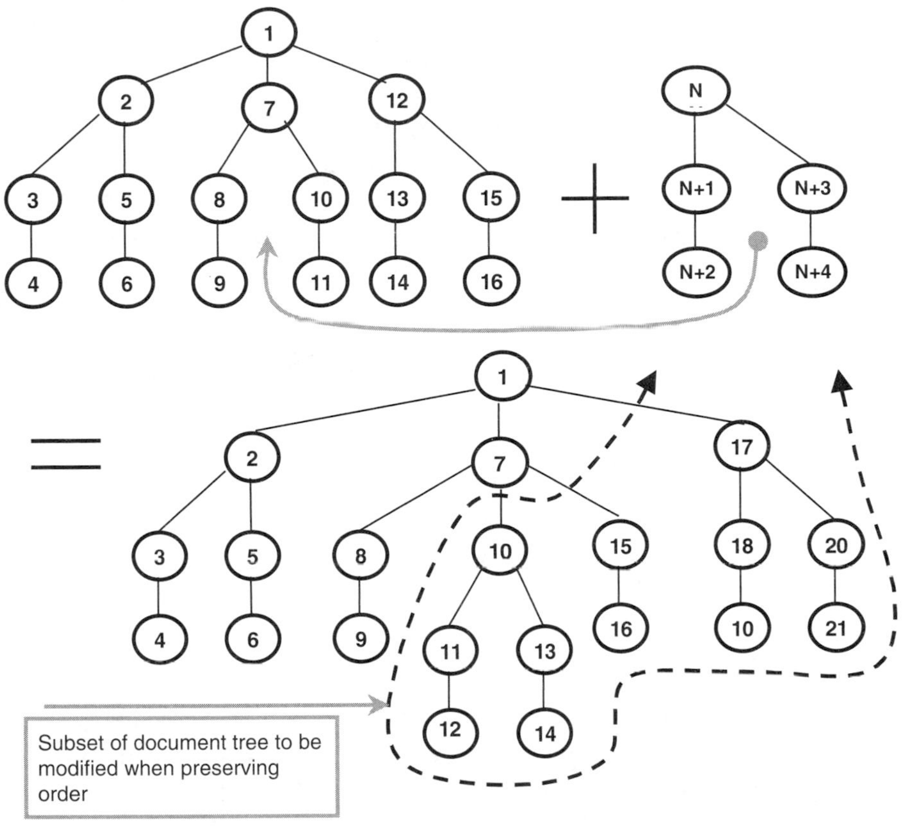

Figure 9.7 INSERTING Subtree into XML Document Preserving Document Order

Using the SQL Node type for XML document node identity reduces the amount of work required when adding (or deleting) values to (or from) an XML document stored in the repository. This represents more work than is required in other document management approaches—storing each "edge" in the document tree as a parent/child relationship between nodes allows for the absolute minimum of work—but it is less than certain other schemes. As a result, the XML repository prototype is fairly resilient to insert operations in the document tree.

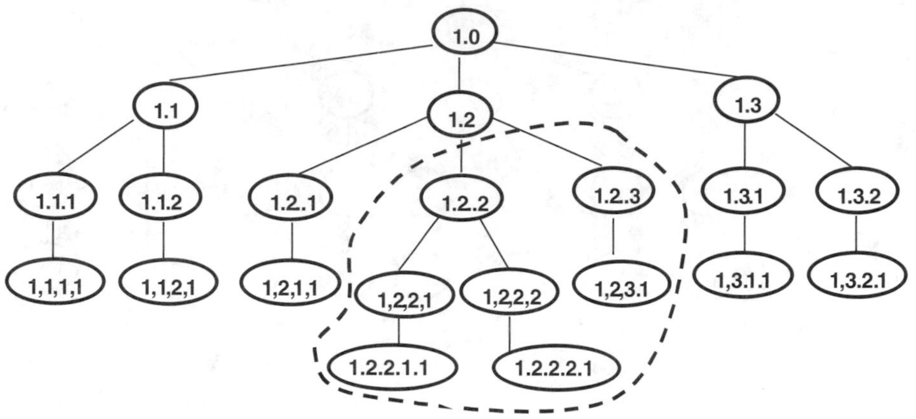

Figure 9.8 SQL Node Tree Hierarchy and Effect of INSERT Operation

9.5 Conclusion

In this chapter we have investigated a set of techniques for building an efficient XML repository using an extensible ORDBMS. The justifications for taking this approach—as opposed to building an XML-specific storage manager from scratch—were

1. Many applications using XML will be built around preexisting enterprise information systems that already use an (object-)relational DBMS.
2. We wanted to avoid having to build an (expensive) transactional, reliable, and scalable storage manager.

The key challenges to taking such an approach involve mapping the hierarchical XML data model into the SQL data model without losing any of the performance or flexibility of XML. The application focus of our prototype was XML in support of e-business: a scenario that envisions a multitude of smaller and fairly rigorously defined XML document messages.

Solving these two challenges involved developing some mechanism for representing hierarchies in a database schema, using this mechanism to devise a schema and storage model, and designing algorithms for rewriting XPath expressions into efficient SQL-3. In this chapter we have seen how to achieve all three.

The key functionality required of the DBMS core is an extensible indexing system: one where the comparison operator used for the built-in data types (such as

SQL INTEGER or VARCHAR) can be overloaded. At least three systems—IBM's Informix IDS 9.x and Cloudscape DBMS, along with the Open Source PostgreSQL DBMS, provide the desired functionality. In the prototype, we demonstrated how a new user-defined type (which we called the SQL Node type) can supply the necessary functionality for reasoning about node locations in a hierarchy. All of the XPath and XQuery "axes" operations for navigation in an XML document can be represented using operations over SQL Node type values.

The second contribution that the prototype makes is in the area of ORDBMS schema design for an XML repository. While other prototypes have adopted similar "shred and store" approaches, the range of XML types they support is fairly limited. By exercising the ORDBMS's extensible type system, it is feasible to introduce into the ORDBMS core equivalent types and operators to the ones standardized in XML. We also showed how a small modification to the schema and XPath query processor can support XML types in the repository.

Third, the prototype eschewed the traditional XML-as-document model in favor of an XML-as-data model approach. We showed how this provides a ready mechanism for implementing UPDATE operations in our prototype and argued that it presents a superior approach to XML-as-document in terms of computational efficiency and application flexibility.

Fourth, we showed how to map XPath expressions into SQL-3 queries over the schema. The algorithm and resulting SQL-3 queries depend upon the existence of the other parts of the prototype: the Node UDT and its operators, SQL-3 types corresponding to the XML data model's types, and a repository schema that tightly integrates XML Schema and XML Document information.

And finally, we explained how the design of this prototype allows for relatively low-cost inserts compared with other shredding approaches.

All of the techniques described in this chapter are suitable for use with a number of languages (e.g., C, Java) and a number of ORDBMS platforms (IBM's Cloudscape and Informix IDS, and the PostgreSQL Open Source ORDBMS). Overall, this prototype's most useful contribution is that it describes a way for developers to take advantage of XML without either abandoning their preexisting information management systems or waiting for vendors to catch up to the market.

Part IV

Applications of XML

This part presents several applications and case studies in XML data management ranging from bioinformatics and geographical and engineering data management, to customer services and cash flow improvement, through to large-scale distributed systems, data warehouses, and inductive database systems.

Chapter 10

Knowledge Management in Bioinformatics

Harry G. Direen, Jr.
Mark S. Jones

10.1 Introduction

With the publication of the seminal paper by Watson and Crick that proposed the DNA double helix in 1953, a course was set for the eventual explosion of scientific data related to DNA research. As we entered the twenty-first century, the Human Genome Project revolutionized the field of biology and created a need for efficient ways to manage enormous quantities of information stemming from gene research. New high-throughput sequencing technology now allows researchers to read genetic code at prodigious rates, generating vast amounts of new data. The requirement to manage the abundance of information from the Human Genome Project spawned the new field of bioinformatics. The following are a few of the key events in biology since the Watson and Crick discovery, up to the first drafts of the human genome:

- April 2, 1953: James Watson and Francis Crick publish in *Nature*: "A Structure for Deoxyribose Nucleic Acid."
- 1955: Frederick Sanger sequences the first protein; he later develops methods for sequencing DNA.
- 1966: Genetic code is cracked, showing how proteins are made from DNA instructions.
- 1980: A human protein project is proposed but not funded.

- 1990: The Human Genome Project (HGP) is launched by the public sector as an international effort to map all human genes. The U.S. HGP begins officially in 1990 as a $3 billion, 15-year program to find the estimated 80,000–100,000 human genes and determine the sequence of the 3 billion nucleotides that make up the human genome.
- 1998: A private-sector rival, Celera Genomics (headed by Craig Venter), joins the race.
- June 2000: Celera and the Human Genome Project (headed by Francis Collins) celebrate separate drafts of the human genome.
- February 2001: The draft human genome sequence is published in *Nature* and *Science*.

The information generated by the Human Genome Project is only the tip of the iceberg. This project is just the beginning of all the new information coming from the field of biology. Knowing the sequence of the over 3 billion base pairs that comprise the DNA in all 23 pairs of chromosomes in a human is comparable to having a byte dump of the Linux operating system without having any of the source code or code documentation, or for that matter, knowing the target for the machine code. The reverse-engineering problem from this starting point is astronomical!

On November 4, 1988, the late Senator Claude Pepper of Florida sponsored legislation that established the National Center for Biotechnology Information (NCBI at http://www.ncbi.nlm.nih.gov/). NCBI was established as a division of the National Library of Medicine (NLM) at the National Institutes of Health (NIH) to act as a national resource for molecular biology information. Other nations and regions have established their own centers and databases for biotechnology information, including Europe (http://www.ebi.ac.uk/), Japan (http://www.ddbj.nig.ac.jp), and Swiss-Prot (http://us.expasy.org/sprot/). Many other public and private databases have been established or are being established to capture the huge volumes of new information coming out of biological research today.

The intent of amassing information in these various public and private databases goes beyond creating repositories of data. A primary intent of these repositories is the building, management, and access of knowledge. A knowledge management system is a system that allows one to capture, store, query, and disseminate information that is gained through experience or study.

A key problem with many current data repositories is that the schema, which includes the data structure and the type of data stored, must be predefined. This implies that the creator of the repository (or the database) must have a priori knowledge of all information being stored in the database, which precludes handling "information gained through experience or study." XML provides a flexible, extensible information model that will grow with the discovery process. To support a growing knowledge base and the discovery process, the database technology must be as flexible, extensible, and schema independent as the XML information model.

10.2 A Brief Molecular Biology Background

One does not have to delve deeply to appreciate the intricacies, complexity, and interrelatedness of biological systems. A good place to start for those who do not have a background in genetics and molecular biology is the free publication "Primer on Molecular Genetics" published June 1992 by the U.S. Department of Energy. This publication is available online at http://www.ornl.gov/hgmis/publicat/primer/toc.html. Two other Internet sources are http://www.ornl.gov/hgmis/publicat/primer/intro.html and http://www.ornl.gov/hgmis/toc_expand.html#alpha. (Much of the overview in this section is drawn from the "Primer on Molecular Genetics.")

Life uses a quaternary, as opposed to binary, system to encode the entire blueprint of every living organism on earth. This quaternary system is our DNA (deoxyribonucleic acid). Inside almost every cell of the trillions of cells that make up a human being lies a nucleus that contains 23 pairs of chromosomes. The chromosomes are made up of long strands of DNA. Figure 10.1 depicts the chromosomes and the familiar double helix DNA structure.

The complete set of instructions for making up an organism is called its *genome*. DNA is constructed from a set of four base molecules: Adenine (A), Cytosine (C), Guanine (G), and Thymine (T). This is our quaternary code. These molecules are attached to a deoxyribose sugar-phosphate backbone. A backbone section with one base molecule, A, C, G, or T, is called a *nucleotide*. A key thing to note is that base molecules are attached to each other; these are called *base pairs*. The A and T bases have a double hydrogen bond, and the C and G bases have a triple hydrogen bond. Because of the molecular sizes and the bond structure only an A and a T will mate across from each other on a DNA strand, and only a C and a G will mate with each other. Viewing one half of a DNA strand, we may have any order of A, C, G, and Ts. Information is contained in the ordering of the A, C, G, and T bases. The opposite side of the DNA will always consist of the complement base structure. The complementary structure is very important in cell division (mitosis) when the DNA must make a copy of itself to go with the new cell. The complementary structure is also used when the DNA code is read or transcribed in order to make proteins.

The quaternary code of DNA defines the structure of all the proteins made and used in a given organism. The central dogma of molecular genetics defines how proteins are made from the information contained in the DNA. A section of DNA that codes for a protein is called a *gene*. Of the over 3 billion base pairs that make up the human genome, only approximately 10 percent of the nucleotides is code for

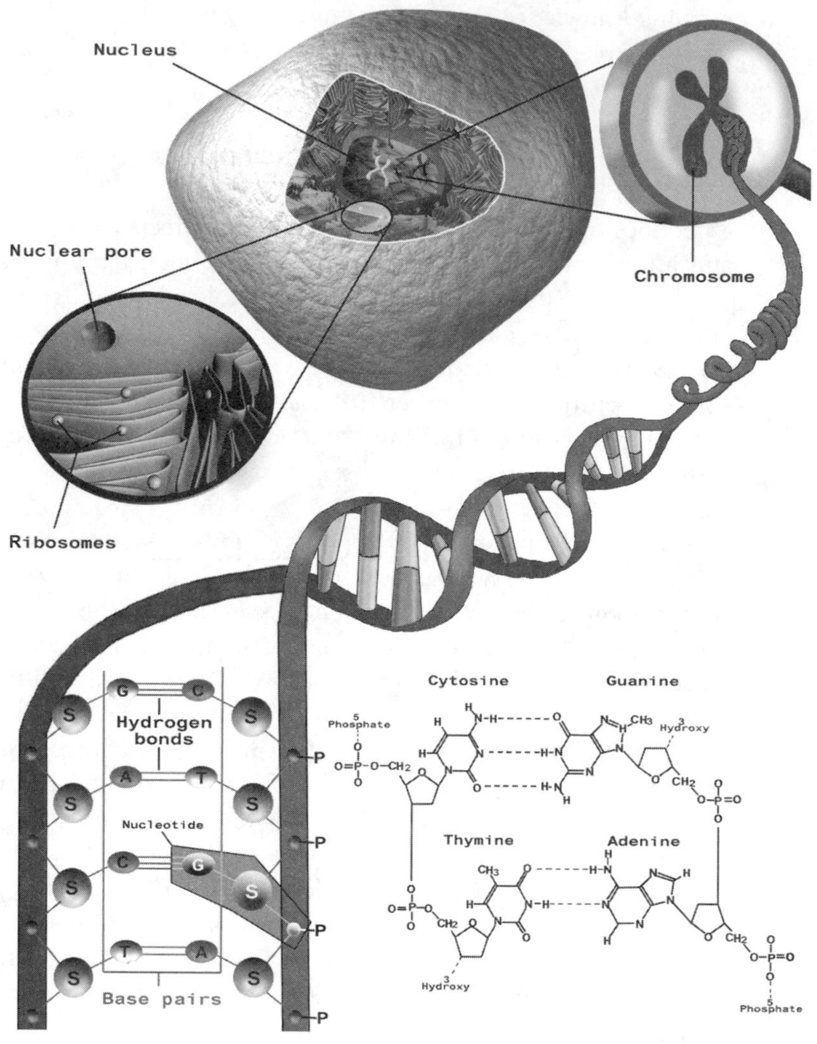

Figure 10.1 Chromosome and DNA Structure. Illustrated by James Direen.

proteins. The function of the other 90 percent of the DNA is in question at this time. The 10 percent of the DNA that codes for proteins is broken up into 30,000 to 40,000 genes. The exact number of genes, location of the genes, and function of the genes in the human genetic code are still hot areas of research.

Proteins are very large molecules or polypeptides made up of long chains of building blocks called *amino acids*. Twenty different amino acids are used in the construction of proteins. Proteins are used in almost every aspect of a living organism.

Life is a chemical process involving thousands of different reactions occurring in an organized manner. These reactions are called *metabolic reactions* and almost all of them are catalyzed by enzymes. Enzymes are proteins that are used to catalyze chemical reactions in our bodies. There are complex molecular machines made up of large protein complexes within cells. DNA polymerase, used to read or transcribe the DNA, is an example of a molecular machine. Ribosomes are another example of molecular machines; they are used in the process of making proteins. Proteins are also used in the chemical signaling processes in the body. Hormones such as insulin are utilized in chemical signaling. Insulin is a protein that controls the sugar or glucose usage in our bodies. Proteins are used as basic structural building blocks such as collagen fibres used in tendons or alpha-keratin in hair. The point is, wherever we look within a living organism, proteins are involved.

There are 20 amino acids from which to choose to make up the long chains that result in proteins. The DNA contains the code to define the sequence of amino acids that make up a given protein. It takes three nucleotides to code for one amino acid. Two nucleotides would only code for 4^2 or 16 possible things. Three nucleotides would code for 4^3 or 64 possible things, and since there are only 20 amino acids, there is redundancy in the coding. Each group of three nucleotides is called a *codon*.

Table 10.1 is the Genetic Code Table. It maps each codon to its corresponding amino acid. The amino acids are shown with both their three-letter abbreviation and their single-letter abbreviation. For instance, the codon ATG maps to the amino acid Methionine, Met or M.

To make proteins from DNA instructions, there is an intermediate messenger RNA (ribonucleic acid). The mRNA is created by a process called *transcription* when a particular gene is being expressed. DNA polymerase is involved in this transcription process. The mRNA then moves out of the nucleus of the cell into the cytoplasm. Ribosomes attach to the mRNA and are responsible for building proteins from the information contained in the mRNA. This process is called *translation*; the mRNA is translated into amino acid sequences. Transfer RNA (tRNA) in the cell are responsible for bringing the correct amino acid to the ribosome for building the proteins.

As can be seen from the diagram in Figure 10.2, the tRNA have a complementary anti-codon that matches a section of the mRNA. Start and stop codons help get the translation process started and terminated.

Hopefully the information in this section has given the reader enough basic molecular biology to make the rest of this chapter more intelligible. It is also hoped that this little snippet of biology entices one to delve deeper into this fascinating and rapidly growing field.

Table 10.1 Genetic Code Table

First Base	Second Base: T	Second Base: C	Second Base: A	Second Base: G	Third Base
T	TTT Phe (F)	TCT Ser (S)	TAT Tyr (Y)	TGT Cys (C)	T
	TTC Phe (F)	TCC Ser (S)	TAC Tyr (Y)	TGC Cys (C)	C
	TTA Leu (L)	TCA Ser (S)	TAA **STOP**	TGA **STOP**	A
	TTA Leu (L)	TCG Ser (S)	TAG **STOP**	TGG Trp(W)	G
C	CTT Leu (L)	CCT Pro (P)	CAT His (H)	CGT Arg (R)	T
	CTC Leu (L)	CCC Pro (P)	CAC His (H)	CGC Arg (R)	C
	CTA Leu (L)	CCA Pro (P)	CAA Gin (Q)	CGA Arg (R)	A
	CTG Leu (L)	CCG Pro (P)	CAG Gin (Q)	CGG Arg (R)	G
A	ATT Ile (I)	ACT Thr (T)	AAT Asn (N)	AGT Ser (S)	T
	ATC Ile (I)	ACC Thr (T)	AAC Asn (N)	AGC Ser (S)	C
	ATA Ile (I)	ACA Thr (T)	AAA Lys (K)	AGA Arg (R)	A
	ATG **Met (M)**	ACG Thr (T)	AAG Lys (K)	AGG Arg (R)	G
G	GTT Val (V)	GCT Ala (A)	GAT Asp (D)	GGT Gly (G)	T
	GTC Val (V)	GCC Ala (A)	GAC Asp (D)	GGC Gly (G)	C
	GTA Val (V)	GCA Ala (A)	GAA Glu (E)	GGA Gly (G)	A
	GTG Val (V)	GCG Ala (A)	GAG Glu (E)	GGG Gly (G)	G

Table obtained from http://molbio.mfo.nih.gov/molbio/gcode.html

10.3 Life Sciences Are Turning to XML to Model Their Information

It has been said that the difficulties in dealing with bioinformatics data come more from its idiosyncrasies than its quantity, and there certainly is no lack of quantity of information (Achard et al. 2001). Biological data are complex to model, and because of this complexity, our models must have the flexibility to grow. The complexity comes in part from the large variety of data types and their many interrelationships. In addition, new data types emerge regularly, and these new types modify our perception of the old types.

François Rechenmann confirms this synopsis by stating, "It is not so much the volume of data which characterizes biology, as it is the data's diversity and heterogeneity" (Rechenmann 2000). He wraps up his editorial with the statement, "The crucial role of computer science is now unanimously recognized for the management and the analysis of biological data; through knowledge modeling, it could be brought to play a role in life sciences similar to the role mathematics plays in physical sciences."

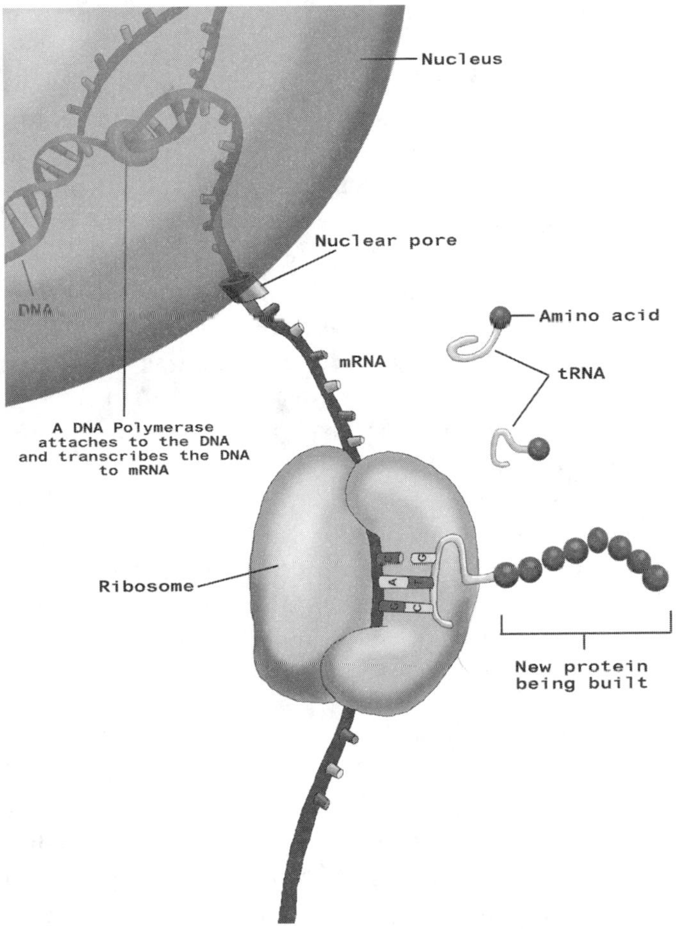

Figure 10.2 DNA to Proteins. Illustrated by James Direen.

Since the earliest origins of scientific thought, there have been efforts to collect, organize (i.e., categorize), and analyze data. A major alteration in scientific thought occurred with the publication in 1735 of *Systema Naturae* by Carolus Linnaeus. While the desire to organize data for eventual analysis predated this publication, the Linnaean classification system transformed the world of biology. The establishment of a common system for the identification of living organisms opened countless avenues to analyze the information gathered. This allowed vast increases in the overall knowledge base for biological science.

Interesting to note is that the Linnaean system, like XML, uses a hierarchical structure. The reason the Linnaean system was and XML is revolutionary is that they are flexible structures that support new information as it is discovered. Just as the Linnaean system of nomenclature allowed researchers to communicate in exact terms regarding specific organisms, XML, with its similar hierarchical nature, will allow researchers from widely diverse backgrounds to communicate information that leads to knowledge development.

Information is the combination of data and context. If someone gave you the sequence of letters "seat" without any context, you have no way of knowing to what he or she was referring. He or she could be referring to an uncomfortable seat or to a short amino acid sequence contained within the aspartokinase I protein in *E. coli*. The point is that data without context is incomplete. It is only when we combine data with its context that we have information. A system that locks context and only allows data to be modified, which is typical of many traditional data models, is unsuitable for a knowledge management system. Ideally, a knowledge management system will handle context (metadata) as freely and fluidly as it handles data (Direen et al. 2001).

XML is well suited for knowledge management systems in that it pairs data with its context via the hierarchical tag structure. XML is the first widely adopted standard for expressing information as opposed to just data. XML is also rapidly becoming an accepted information-modeling language for bioinformatics. A number of groups are developing standard XML markup languages in this area, including

- **BIOML (BIOpolymer Markup Language):** BIOML is used to describe experimental information about proteins, genes, and other biopolymers. A BIOML document will describe a physical object (e.g., a particular protein) in such a way that all known experimental information about that object can be associated with the object in a logical and meaningful way. The information is nested at different levels of complexity and fits with the tree-leaf structure inherent in XML. BIOML is a product of core working groups at Proteometrics, LLC and Proteometrics Canada, Ltd. More information is available at http://www.bioml.com/BIOML/.
- **BSML (Bioinformatic Sequence Markup Language):** The National Human Genome Research Institute (NHGRI) funded the development of BSML in 1997 as a public domain standard for the bioinformatics community. Among the early goals for BSML was to create a data representation model for sequences and their annotations. This model would enable linking the behavior of the display object to the sequences, annotations, and links it represents. The linking capability of BSML has paralleled the evolution of storage, analysis, and linking of biological data on computer networks. Sequence-related phenomena from the biomolecular level to the complete genome can be described using BSML. This flexibility provides a needed medium for genomics research. LabBook, Inc. (http://www.labbook.com/) is the author and owner of the copyrights for BSML.

- **PSDML:** The Protein Information Resource (PIR) database is a partnership between the National Biomedical Research Foundation at Georgetown University Medical Center, the Munich Information Center for Protein Sequences, and the Japan International Protein Information Database. The PIR is an annotated, public-domain sequence database that allows sequence similarity and text searching. The Protein Sequence Database Markup Language (PSDML) is used to store protein information in the PIR database. More information is available at http://pir.georgetown.edu/.
- **GAME:** Genome Annotation Markup Elements can be utilized to represent features or annotations about specific regions of a sequence. These annotations may be differentiated using GAME. Examples of this are features generated by a sequence analysis program and those generated by a professional lab worker. Facilitation of the exchange of genomic annotations between researchers, genome centers, and model organism databases will allow each to specify the conclusions they have drawn from their analysis and then share these descriptions in XML with each other. The first widely used version of GAME was created at the BDGP (Berkeley Drosophila Genome Project) by Suzanna Lewis and Erwin Frise. More information is available at http://www.bioxml.org/Projects/game/game0.1.html.
- **SBML (Systems Biology Markup Language):** The Systems Biology Workbench (SBW) project at the California Institute of Technology seeks to provide for the sharing of models and resources between simulation and analysis tools for systems biology. One of the two approaches that are being pursued to attain the goal has been the incremental development of the Systems Biology Markup Language (SBML). SBML is an XML-based representation of biochemical network models. More information is available at http://www.cds.caltech.edu/erato/index.html.
- **CellML:** CellML is an XML-based markup language whose purpose is to store and exchange computer-based biological models. CellML has primarily been developed by Physiome Sciences, Inc., in Princeton, New Jersey, and the Bioengineering Institute at the University of Auckland. CellML allows the sharing of models, even if they are using different model-building software and the reuse of components between models. This capability accelerates the model-building process. More information is available at http://www.cellml.org/.
- **MAGE-ML:** Microarray Gene Expression Markup Language has been automatically derived from Microarray Gene Expression Object Model (MAGE-OM). MAGE-ML is based on XML and is designed to describe and communicate information about microarray-based experiments. The information can describe microarray designs, manufacturing information, experiment setup and execution information, gene expression data, and data analysis

results. The Object Management Group (OMG) was primarily involved in the creation and distribution of MAGE-OM standards through the Gene Expression Request For Proposal (RFP). MAGE-ML replaced the MAML (Microarray Markup Language) as of February 2002. More information is available at http://www.mged.org/Workgroups/MAGE/introduction.html.

These are a few of the XML markup languages being defined for the bioinformatics arena. Hank Simon (Simon 2001) provides a more complete list, and Paul Gordon has a Web site devoted to XML for molecular biology (http://www.visualgenomics.ca/gordonp/xml/).

The unprecedented degree of flexibility and extensibility of XML in terms of its ability to capture information is what makes it ideal for knowledge management and for use in bioinformatics.

10.4 A Genetic Information Model

Let's envision a genetic-based information model. One method of basing our model is to start with a DNA sequence. This base is used by NCBI because GenBank is commissioned as a sequence database as opposed to a protein database such as Swiss-Prot. It is instructive to follow this starting point and see where it leads in terms of the variety of information that can be attached to a sequence that contains a gene. The information model and some of the data within the model will be somewhat contrived to bring out the key points. A detailed and accurate biological model is beyond the scope of this chapter.

Listing 10.1 is an XML document derived from an NCBI DNA sequence entry. For each sequence, a name or definition is provided along with a unique accession number to identify the sequence. This information is contained within the header element; also included in the header element are keywords. Notice how each keyword is contained within its own `<keyword>` tag. This makes database searching based on keywords much more efficient.

Listing 10.1 DNA Sequence Entry

```
<dna_sequence_entry>
 <header>
    <definition>
       Human Cu/Zn superoxide dismutase (SOD1) gene
    </definition>
```

```
    <accession_no>
       <base_no>L44135</base_no>
       <version>L44135.1</version>
       <GI>1237400</GI>
    </accession_no>
    <keyword>Cu/Zn superoxide dismutase</keyword>
    <keyword>Human SOD1 gene</keyword>
</header>
<source>
    <name>Human Cu/Zn superoxide dismutase (SOD1) gene, exon
    1.</name>
    <organism>Homo sapiens</organism>
    <taxonomy>
       <cell_type>Eukaryota</cell_type>
       <kingdom>Metazoa</kingdom>
       <phylum>Chordata</phylum>
       <subphylum>Vertebrata</subphylum
       <class>Mammalia</class>
       <infraclass>Eutheria</infraclass>
       <order>Primates</order>
       <family>Hominidae</family>
       <genus>Homo</genus>
       <species>sapiens</sapiens>
    </taxonomy>
</source>
<reference>
   <author> Levanon,D. </author>
   <author> Lieman-Hurwitz,J </author>
   <title>
      Architecture and anatomy of the chromosomal locus in human
chromosome 21 encoding the Cu/Zn superoxide dismutase
   </title>
   <journal> EMBO J. 4 (1), 77-84 (1985)</journal>
  </reference>
  <dna_sequence>
gtaccctgtttacatcattttgccattttcgcgtactgcaaccggcgggccacgccgtgaaaagaag
gttgttttctccacagtttcggggttctggacgtttcccggctgcggggcgggggggagtctccggcg
cacgcggccccttggcccgccccagtcattcccggccactcgcgacccgaggctgccgcaggggggcg
ggctgagcgcgtgcgaggccattggtttggggcc . . .
```

```
  </dna_sequence>
  <features>
     <protein>
        <type>CDS</type>
        <location>1..799</location>
        <gene>SOD1</gene>
        <codon_start>1</codon_start>
        <chromosome>21</chromosome>
        <map>21q22.1</map>
        <product>Cu/Zn-superoxide dismutase</product>
        <protein_id>AAB05661.1</protein_id>
        <db_xref>GI:1237407</db_xref>
        <amino_acid_sequence>
MATKAVCVLKGDGPVQGIINFEQKESNGPVKVWGSIKGLTEGLHGFHVHEFGDNTAGCTSAGPHFNP
LSRKHGGPKDEERHVGDL . . .
        </amino_acid_sequence>
     </protein>
  </features>
</dna_sequence_entry>
```

The next element in Listing 10.1 is source information. This information lets us know where and from what organism the sequence came. For most biologists the hierarchy in Listing 10.2 will be quite familiar.

Listing 10.2 Linnaean Classification of Humans

```
Kingdom:  Animalia
 Phylum:  Chordata
     Subphylum:  Vertebrata
        Class:  Mammalia
           Subclass:  Theria
              Infraclass:  Eutheria
                   Order:  Primates
                      Suborder:  Anthropoidea
                           Superfamily:  Hominoidea
                                  Family:  Hominidae
                                        Genus:  Homo
                                              Species:  sapiens
```

Listing 10.2 was taken from one of many Web sites that detail Linnaean classifications (http://anthro.palomar.edu/animal/humans.htm). While the degree of detail expressed in Listing 10.2 (outlining 12 classification categories from kingdom to species) may change depending on the source, it serves to illustrate the natural and efficient mechanism used to classify organisms. We have added acell type category to cover the Eukaryota/Prokaryota breakdown of a cell. Many databases put the primary taxonomic information within a single `<taxonomy>` tag (Eukaryota to Homo). The inclusion of most of the classification categories within one data item fails to respect the natural hierarchy of Linnaean classification and fails to unleash the strengths of XML. By mapping the natural hierarchical structure into XML, database searches for DNA sequences based on organism classification become more natural and efficient. It is surprising how often this point is missed.

The `<reference>` element in Listing 10.1 contains journal article information related to the DNA sequence. Often the researcher(s) who sequenced the section of DNA submits a journal article describing the sequence and information related to the sequence. The actual DNA sequence is contained within the `<dna_sequence>` element.

Finally, Listing 10.1 contains a features section, which contains information about features that are contained within the DNA sequence—in Listing 10.1, a section of the DNA (nucleotides 447 through 1934) code for a protein sequence. Some of the basic information on the protein is contained within the `<protein>` element.

If life were simple, we could stop here. We may want to add or remove some of the descriptive information about a sequence, but we might be able to lock down a data structure for capturing sequence information. Of course, life is not this simple, and we must consider how we might attach additional information to our base model and what forms this information might come in.

As noted previously, one of the sections in the XML in Listing 10.1 is a features section. In the brief biology introduction (Section 10.2), it was stated that DNA is composed of genes, and genes code for proteins. The feature shown in Listing 10.1 highlights a section of the DNA sequence, nucleotides 447–1934, which is a gene segment that codes for a protein. The protein ID is given along with the protein amino acid sequence. The more one understands and discovers about biology, the more information one would like to attach to the given DNA sequence. Here is a list of a few items that come to mind:

- DNA sequences are composed of genes. The actual gene section (or gene sections if there are multiple genes) of the sequence needs to be identified and noted in the information model (the XML). This would be noted by opening up a `<gene> . . . </gene>` element within the features section. The gene name, reference number, location, plus other information would be included within the element.

- Genes have promoter sections that control when the given gene is expressed. A gene is expressed if it is actively being transcribed into mRNA. Transcription factors (which are specialized proteins) bind to sections of the DNA in the promoter region to control gene expression and expression rates. The promoter sections need to be identified along with the specific transcription factors that control the gene at hand. Different genes use different transcription factors and different control mechanisms. This implies that, within a gene element, we would have a `<promoter> . . . </promoter>` element. Within the promoter element, we would have `<transcription_factor> . . . </transcription_factor>` elements. Within the transcription factor elements, there might be information as to where the promoter section binds with the transcription factor, and under what conditions.
- Genes have regions that code for proteins called *exons*, and interspersed within the gene may be regions that are not part of the coding for a protein; these regions are called *introns*. The information model must be able to handle the identification of these sections.
- The same gene may be used to code for multiple different proteins. It is somewhat of a mix and match use of the exon sections of the gene; this is called *alternative splicing of the mRNA*. Within each gene section, the various proteins that the gene codes for would be inserted. This would move the protein element in the example XML document in Listing 10.1 to be within a gene element. As we learn what control factors determine which proteins are made at which times, these control factors will be added to our model.
- Proteins control almost every biological process in a living organism and are used in the basic structure of organisms. In order to identify what a given gene is controlling or affects, one must know the function of the protein that the gene codes for. A protein function element could be added to the protein element to encode this information.
- A gene may be involved directly in a given organism trait such as eye color, hair color, baldness, number of fingers, and so on. The phenotype of a gene is this outward characteristic expression of the gene. For each gene we may want to have a `<phenotype> . . . </phenotype>` element. The subelements of the phenotype would depend heavily on the particular gene.
- A gene that goes awry can be the root cause of any number of diseases including sickle cell anemia, Huntington disease, cystic fibrosis, blindness, all kinds of cancers, and so on. A single nucleotide polymorphism (SNP)

is a single change in one base-pair on a DNA sequence. Sickle cell anemia is caused by an error in the gene that tells the body how to make hemoglobin. The defective gene tells the body to make the abnormal hemoglobin that results in deformed red blood cells. There is one amino acid substitution, a valine for glutamic acid in the beta sixth position that forms sickle beta chains, which is caused by a SNP on chromosome 11 where the beta chain of hemoglobin is coded. Sections for SNPs and related diseases may be added to capture this information.

Listing 10.3 shows the updated DNA sequence entry with some of this new information added.

Listing 10.3 Updated DNA Sequence Entry

```
<dna_sequence_entry>
 <header>
    <definition>
       Human Cu/Zn superoxide dismutase (SOD1) gene
    </definition>
    <accession_no>
       <base_no>L44135</base_no>
       <version>L44135.1</version>
       <GI>1237400</GI>
    </accession_no>
    <keyword>Cu/Zn superoxide dismutase</keyword>
    <keyword>Human SOD1 gene</keyword>
 </header>
 <source>
    <name> Human Cu/Zn superoxide dismutase (SOD1) gene, exon
    1.</name>
    <organism>Homo sapiens</organism>
    <taxonomy>
       <cell_type>Eukaryota</cell_type>
       <kingdom>Metazoa</kingdom>
       <phylum>Chordata</phylum>
       <subphylum>Vertebrata</subphylum
       <class>Mammalia</class>
       <infraclass>Eutheria</infraclass>
       <order>Primates</order>
       <family>Hominidae</family>
       <genus>Homo</genus>
       <species>sapiens</sapiens>
```

```
    </taxonomy>
 </source>
 <reference>
    <author> Levanon,D. </author>
    <author> Lieman-Hurwitz,J </author>
    <title>
Architecture and anatomy of the chromosomal locus in human
chromosome 21 encoding the Cu/Zn superoxide dismutase
    </title>
    <journal> EMBO J. 4 (1), 77-84 (1985)</journal>
 </reference>
 <dna_sequence>
gtaccctgtttacatcattttgccattttcgcgtactgcaaccggcgggccacgccgtgaaaagaag
gttgtttctccacagtttcggggttctggacgtttcccggctgcggggcgggggggagtctccggcg
cacgcggccccttggcccgccccagtcattcccggccactcgcgacccgaggctgccgcaggggggcg
ggctgagcgcgtgcgaggccattggtttggggcc . . .
 </dna_sequence>
 <features>
    <gene>
       <location>1..799</location>
       <phenotype>
          <eye_color>blue</eye_color>
       </phenotype>
       <promoter_section>
          <location>100..447</location>
          <transcription_factor>
             Various transcription factor info
          </transcription_factor>
          <transcription_factor>
             Various transcription factor info
          </transcription_factor>
       </promoter_section>
       <SNP>
mutation changing codon 102 from Asp->Gly and causing amyotrophic
lateral sclerosis
       </SNP>
       <exon>5</exon>
       <protein>
          <type>CDS</type>
          <location>1..799</location>
          <gene>SOD1</gene>
          <codon_start>1</codon_start>
```

```
            <chromosome>21</chromosome>
            <map>21q22.1</map>
            <product>Cu/Zn-superoxide dismutase</product>
            <protein_id>AAB05661.1</protein_id>
            <db_xref>GI:1237407</db_xref>
            <amino_acid_sequence>
MATKAVCVLKGDGPVQGIINFEQKESNGPVKVWGSIKGLTEGLHGFHVHEFGDNTAGCTSAGPHFNP
LSRKHGG . . .
            </amino_acid_sequence>
         </protein>
         <related_diseases>
Disease Information, AMYOTROPHIC LATERAL SCLEROSIS Lou GehrigFs
disease
         </related_diseases>
      </gene>
  </features>
</dna_sequence_entry>
```

It would be easy to imagine many more examples of all the possible information that can be associated with one DNA sequence. From this illustration, one quickly begins to realize why biological information is complex to model, and this example touched on only some of the issues at hand. Microbiology is still very much in the discovery phase. It is impossible to predict all of the information, context plus data, that researchers will want to capture against a given sequence. Therefore, it is imperative that the information model be flexible and easily scalable.

A few points about the DNA sequence model presented in Listing 10.3 are worth noting. First, all of the data items are contained within elements and not within attributes. Many of the XML schemas being developed for bioinformatics, and other fields as well, place a variety of their data items within attributes. While this is syntactically correct XML, it is poor information modeling. This practice blurs the distinction between an attribute and a data element. An attribute should tell us how to process or interpret data enclosed within the tag element and apply to all items within the tag element; it should not be data.

The tag structure in the DNA sequence model gives the entire context of related data items. We know based on tag structure, for instance, that "CDS" is a type of a protein coded by a gene that is a feature within a DNA sequence.

Hierarchy is used to show relationships within the model. For instance, a protein is contained within a gene. If the same gene codes for multiple proteins, multiple protein elements will be within the gene element. If the DNA sequence contains several genes, there will be several gene elements, each containing their own protein elements.

Finally, the model represents heterogeneous information, which is not obvious looking at one DNA sequence entry. If we looked across many DNA sequence entries, we would see that each DNA sequence contained different types of information. Some of the basic information types would remain the same; all would have a header element and a `<dna_sequence>` element, but not all would contain gene elements. This is due to the fact that much of the DNA in humans does not code for proteins and therefore does not contain genes. It is still a mystery what 90 percent of human DNA does! Based on this fact alone, the model must be flexible. Since genes that are in the DNA code for such a wide variety of proteins that are involved in a vast array of functions, it should be clear that the types of information captured for each gene will also vary widely. Therefore, our information model captures heterogeneous information.

10.5 NeoCore XMS*

Traditional databases were designed to manage data by creating a static framework to contain dynamic data—meaning data elements can be managed as long as all metadata (data's context) has been established in advance. This methodology falls short, by half, of true information or knowledge management. The solution to this dilemma is to manage metadata in exactly the same dynamic way as the data component. This offers two significant (if not profound) advantages. First, constraints on the use of dynamic data types are removed. New data types may simply be defined and added to the database. Second, the processes of database design and configuration (usually the most labor- and time-consuming aspect of system design) are reduced to practically nothing. NeoCore XMS (XML Management System) has been designed with precisely this feature: Metadata and data are handled in the same dynamic way. NeoCore XMS was designed to achieve the following goals:

- **Dynamic management of metadata.** All information is represented in an internal format called "information couplets"—pairings of data and complete metadata. Information couplets are treated as patterns, and those patterns can be arbitrary. Consequently, there are no rows or columns, and there is no need to predefine indices. Patterns can be as common or as unique as desired. A piece of information can be associated with a single fragment of information without having to be predefined, preallocated, or added to another information fragment. This means that an entirely new data type can be added to an application at any time without having to do anything to the database.

This section material is taken in part from (Direen et al. 2001). ©2001 IEEE Reprinted with permission, from Proceedings–23rd Annual Conference–IEEE/EMBS.

- **Immediate availability of information.** Information is "indexed" as soon as it is posted. In fact, there is no separate indexing process because there is no need to specify what should be indexed. NeoCore XMS automatically generates data patterns that allow information to be retrieved based on fully or partially qualified queries. Complex queries are accommodated through a hierarchical vector convergence algorithm, which quickly converges sets of individual pattern matches to locate information fragments based on multiple criteria. The vector convergence process operates on any information that has been posted, requiring no predefinition. The structure of the indices created within the XMS gives flat access time to all nodes within the system. There are no access time penalties based on the structure of the data stored in the XMS.
- **Schema independence.** NeoCore XMS was designed to be oblivious to schemas or DTDs, which is a more important feature than it may initially seem. Most XML data management systems require that all XML information be described by a schema or DTD for data-mapping reasons. The problem schema dependence imposes is that it destroys the ability to have heterogeneous data within similar document types. For example, suppose you want to add a new field to some, but not all, documents of the same type. How will the database know which schema applies unless a new schema is supplied? How will it know whether all the other documents of the same type need to be changed, or whether they should be treated as different document types? How will other applications know about this new document type? Ultimately, schema dependence makes it virtually impossible to use XML's most attractive feature—its extensibility. Schema independence implies that no database design needs to be done, and no penalty is imposed for change.
- **Scalability.** NeoCore XMS was designed to manage huge repositories of XML documents of all types. This was achieved by treating XML documents as aggregations of information. NeoCore XMS is aware of, but functionally oblivious to, the document-centric structure of XML information. XML data management systems are notorious for not scaling well—both as document size increases and as the number of documents increases. NeoCore XMS was designed to seamlessly scale to very large information management requirements, exhibiting remarkably flat performance as system size increases. Individual document size has no bearing on performance.
- **Efficient use of storage.** Information couplets represent a fundamental means of storing and managing information. Breaking the information into couplets, along with efficient indexing using NeoCore's patented Digital Pattern Processing (DPP) technology, creates a very efficient storage format. The upshot is the amount of storage used, for everything combined;

adds up to between one time and two times the size of the XML documents alone. This includes the documents, all indices, access control information—everything. This compares very favorably with all other methods of managing information, requiring less than half the storage of any database management system, and a tiny fraction of the space used by DOMs (Document Object Models).

By achieving these goals, NeoCore XMS is a perfect fit for managing complex biological information. Through NeoCore's membership and involvement with the Center for Computational Biology, NeoCore XMS is being tested in a research environment with biological information from a variety of sources. The Center for Computational Biology (CCB—http://www.cudenver.edu/ccb/) was created by Colorado University at Denver in association with the Colorado University Health Science Center for the purpose of bringing together computer science, mathematics/statistics, and biology (including relevant elements of chemistry and physics) in order to tackle many of the difficult problems coming out of the exploding field of bioinformatics. NeoCore XMS is being tested in the Computational Pharmacology Group located at the Health Science Center and directed by Dr. Lawrence Hunter.

Ron Taylor, a member of the Computational Pharmacology Group, has been running extensive tests on NeoCore XMS, using various biological information. Ron has also been developing specific interfaces to NeoCore XMS for their work. In one test, the entire Swiss-Prot protein database was loaded into NeoCore XMS. In addition, several bacterial genomes from NCBI were loaded into the database along with various ligand reaction, pathway, enzyme, and compound information, which is very diverse, heterogeneous information from disparate sources. Some of the findings of this test are:

- To load information into NeoCore XMS, a simple load command is issued with the file containing well-formed XML. NeoCore XMS determines the structure of the information based on the XML it receives, stores the information, and then fully indexes the information. A schema for the information is not required and there is no database design effort whatsoever to configure the database for the type of information being entered. The various types of information are simply loaded.
- The Swiss-Prot protein information consisted of 101,602 protein documents. The entire XML file was over 350MB, which loaded in approximately 30 minutes on a single processor, a Windows 2000 machine that had 512MB of RAM. This time includes storing all of the information and fully indexing it. The 350MB XML file consumed approximately 400MB of NeoCore XMS database resources, including all of the indexing. This means the footprint of the Swiss-Prot protein information was only 1.14 times the original XML. NeoCore XMS has the option of indexing data for

data-only queries. This allows, for instance, finding all occurrences of "blue" in the database regardless of the context. This option added another 85MB to the footprint. The 30 minutes of load time included this indexing also. The same database had an additional 73MB or 13,977 records of NCBI gene data, plus another 26MB of other ligand data.

- Query, retrieval, and access of the data stored was substantially faster in most cases than other database technologies the pharmacology group was using.
- Adding new structural information to a given protein record is as easy as targeting the location within the desired XML document using a simple XPath statement inside an insert command and providing the XML segment to be inserted. Only the targeted record is changed. The way NeoCore XMS is designed, adding new information structure to one document does not add unused fields to all similar documents in the database. This means that the space inside NeoCore XMS required to add unique information to a given record is limited to the specific information. There is no penalty for heterogeneous information. Information can be added as it is discovered.
- A Perl API was created by Ron Taylor to access NeoCore XMS. Specific storage and retrieval modules allow the laboratory easy access to the database for handling Affymetrix gene expression data.

The key point is that no database design is required in order to work with NeoCore XMS. Once information has been described in well-formed XML, the information may be stored, retrieved, modified, or deleted from the database via a simple HTTP interface. The information stored may be very heterogeneous, and structure can be added without changing the database in any way. These properties are essential for working with biological data. In addition, the storage footprint is efficient, and access is fast.

10.6 Integration of BLAST into NeoCore XMS

Sequence alignment tools are fundamental in the bioinformatics arena. A sequence alignment tool compares two or more sequences in order to determine how similar the sequences are or if subsections of the sequences are similar. A common use of the tool is for a researcher who sequences a section of DNA to then access a database and search for other DNA sequences that are similar to the one being studied. Finding other sequences in the database that are similar is a first step in trying to determine the functionality of the gene or to determine other organisms that may have a similar gene. Comparisons do not have to be comparing nucleotide sequence against nucleotide sequence or amino acid sequence against amino acid sequence. Since we know that nucleotide sequences code for amino acid sequences, we can convert nucleotide sequences to their equivalent amino acid sequence and compare sequences on those terms. This is often done because proteins are the functional element in life, and functional information is typically being sought.

Needleman-Wunsch are credited with coming up with the first global sequence alignment algorithm in 1970 (Needleman and Wunsch 1970). A global alignment compares the sequences over the entire length of both sequences. Gaps are added to force the two sequences to be the same length. Dynamic programming, a well-known optimization technique, is used to find the alignment(s) that produce the highest score. A more computationally efficient version was found by Gotoh in 1982.

Smith and Waterman generalized the Needleman-Wunsch algorithm in 1981 to find the highest-scoring subsequence matches between two sequences (Smith and Waterman 1981). Their method includes gap analysis and also uses a dynamic programming approach to find the best matches. The Smith-Waterman algorithm is still in popular use today.

The main problem with the Smith-Waterman sequence alignment algorithm is that it is computationally expensive and therefore very time consuming when comparing a given sequence against a large database of sequences. To improve search speed, a number of heuristic sequence alignment methods have been developed, such as those used in BLAST, FASTA, and SALSA. Of these heuristic methods, BLAST (Basic Local Alignment Search Tool) seems to be the most popular and well known (Altschul et al. 1990; Altschul et al. 1997). The heuristic algorithms are not guaranteed to find optimal alignment solutions, but they are far more practical for searching a large database of sequences, and they do a very good job of finding similar sequences.

It is beyond the scope of this chapter to go into the details of the various search algorithms. Numerous books are available that do cover these details, including (Durbin et al. 1998).

NeoCore developed its own sequence search plug-in module to go with NeoCore XMS. The NeoCore sequence search plug-in is similar to BLAST in operation but is based on NeoCore's patented digital pattern processing technology. The plug-in gives the power of a BLAST sequence search embedded (SSE) within a query of the XML database, which has the added advantage of being able to do targeted BLAST searches. In addition to looking for sequences that are similar to a query sequence, the query can restrict the search to DNA sequences from a particular organism or sequences involved in a particular metabolic pathway. Any set of sequences that can be targeted with an XPath query can have a BLAST search performed on it.

The NeoCore SSE plug-in is accessed via a function call within an XPath query. An example XPath query that calls the SSE is

```
/ND/dna_sequence_entry/dna_sequence{func("Blastn,-w11,-r1,-q3, -i
actgcggt . . . ")}/..
```

This query searches all DNA sequence entries within NeoCore XMS, targeted by `/ND/dna_sequence_entry/dna_sequence`. NeoCore XMS wraps all documents within the tags `<ND>`, hence the `/ND` at the beginning of the XPath query. The query returns all nucleotide sequences that are similar to the query sequence `actgcggt . . .`. Similarity is based on the BLAST scoring algorithm. The addition to the standard XPath query is the function call section starting and ending with curly brackets, `{ func("Blastn, . . . ")}`. Five separate function calls and a variety of parameters are supported by the NeoCore SSE. The five functions mimic those of BLAST and for convenience are named the same as BLAST calls.

10.6.1 Sequence Search Types

This section describes the various sequence search types supported by NeoCore SSE. The five functions supported are

- **Protein-Protein Search (Blastp)**
  This search compares an amino acid query sequence against amino acid sequences stored in the database.
- **Nucleotide-Nucleotide Search (Blastn)**
  This search compares a nucleotide query sequence against nucleotide sequences stored in the database.
- **Nucleotide-Protein Search (Blastx)**
  This search compares a nucleotide query sequence against amino acid sequences stored in the database. The nucleotide query sequence is first translated into a set of six possible amino acid sequences. The six amino acid sequences come from the six possible reading frames of the nucleotide sequence.
- **Protein-Nucleotide Search (tBlastn)**
  This search compares an amino acid query sequence against nucleotide sequences stored in the database. The nucleotide sequences in the database are dynamically translated in all six reading frames during the sequence search to their equivalent amino acid sequences and then compared to the protein sequence.
- **Translated Nucleotide-Nucleotide Search (tBlastx)**
  This search compares a nucleotide query sequence, translated into six possible amino acid sequences, against nucleotide sequences stored in the

database. The nucleotide sequences in the database are dynamically translated in all six reading frames during the sequence search and then compared to the six translated protein sequences.

Determining the set of nucleotides that make up a DNA sequence is but one step in the discovery process. The question arises as to how one goes about finding a gene, or a section of the DNA sequence that codes for a protein. It is not at all obvious from sequencing one side of a DNA strand where the genes lie. Similarity searches play a role in this process of discovering genes. If the sequence information that comes from one side of a DNA strand is translated into its various possible amino acid sequences via the genetic code table, a database of proteins can be searched looking for possible matches. If matches are found, then the corresponding section of the DNA may be a gene.

If the human genome may be thought of as the book of life that contains the blueprints for our construction, a mechanism must exist to indicate starting and stopping points. During protein construction within the cell, as genes are read, certain amino acids act as initiators and others act as terminators. The amino acid Methionine is the initiator or starting point for a gene and is coded for by the DNA sequence A-T-G in the genetic code table. As with any construction process, instructions for the ending or completion of the project must exist. Three stop codons serve this purpose. The DNA sequences T-A-A, T-G-A, or T-A-G do not code for an amino acid but act as signals to complete the protein under construction. The newly constructed protein begins with Methionine and ends just before one of the stop codons. Regions bounded by start and stop codons are known as Open Reading Frames (ORF). An ORF represents a possible gene-coding region in the nucleotide sequence. A DNA sequence may have six potential overlapping reading frames that must be evaluated.

As previously mentioned, DNA is a double-stranded molecule. Genes may be found on either the forward or reverse strand. The forward and reverse strands are related because of the pairing of the nucleotides across from one another. A Cytosine will pair only with a Guanine, and a Thymine will pair only with an Adenine.

Forward strand →
C A T G C A T G C A T C
G T A C G T A C G T A G
Reverse strand ←

In translating the forward sequence, the first three frames are found (remember that it takes three nucleotides to code for one amino acid, and we are not sure where the starting point is):

Frame 1:	CAT	GCA	TGC	ATC	DNA sequence (beginning with the first nucleotide)
	H	A	C	I	Translated amino acid sequence

Frame 2:	C	ATG	CAT	GCA	TC	Begin translating at the second nucleotide
		M	H	A	S	

Frame 3:	CA	TGC	ATG	CAT	C	Begin translating at the third nucleotide
		C	M	H		

To translate the reverse frames for evaluation the strand becomes:
G A T G C A T G C A T G

Frame 4:	GAT	GCA	TGC	ATG	Begin translation with the first nucleotide
	D	A	C	M	

Frame 5:	G	ATG	CAT	GCA	TG	Begin translation with the second nucleotide
		M	H	A		

Frame 6:	GA	TGC	ATG	CAT	G	Begin translation with the third nucleotide
		C	M	H		

Frames 2 and 5 begin with the Methionine initiator (M) or start signal. If one of these two strands ends with one of the stop codons, this would tend to indicate a gene-coding region that results in a manufactured protein. Another point that arises from this example is illustrated in Frame 2. Only two nucleotides are known at the end. No matter what the third nucleotide is, this codon will translate to amino acid S or serine. As previously mentioned, the genetic code contains redundancies in coding. Serine may be coded for by any of the following codons: TCA, TCG, TCT, TCC, AGT, and AGC. Methionine, the initiator of the protein chain, is coded for by the unique codon ATG. Except for BLASTp and BLASTn, examining the six reading frames is at the core of performing comprehensive BLAST searches. This search capability is an example of the ability to include powerful plug-ins within NeoCore XMS.

A couple of examples will demonstrate the use of the BLAST search engine with NeoCore XMS. NeoCore XMS was loaded with several bacterial genomes downloaded from NCBI. The XML format of the sequence entries can be assumed to be that shown in earlier sections of this chapter. The first example is a BLASTp. BLASTp compares an amino acid query sequence against amino acid sequences in the database. The XPath query is of the form shown in Listing 10.4.

Listing 10.4 XPath Query

```
/ND/dna_sequence_entry/features/gene/protein/amino_acid_sequence
{func("Blastn, -i  . . . KFGGTSVANAERFLRVADILESNARQGQVA . . .
")}/..
```

This query searches for all proteins similar to the query sequence ". . . KFGGTSVANA . . ." and targeted by XPath:

```
/ND/dna_sequence_entry/features/gene/protein/amino_acid_sequence
```

The trailing / . . . will cause the return XML to be at the <protein> element level. The return from this query will be of the form shown in Listing 10.5.

Listing 10.5 Result of the Query in Listing 10.4

```
<query_results>
      <protein>
            <gene>aspartokinase II</gene>
            <protein_id>AAC76922.1</protein_id>
            <db_xref>GI:1790376</db_xref>
            <amino_acid_sequence>
                  ...KFGGSSLADVKCYLRVAGIMAEYSQPDDMMVVSAA...
            <amino_acid_sequence>
      </protein>
</query_results>
```

NeoCore XMS always returns well-formed XML. To view details on the sequence matches, there is an option to output a file of search results. One of the results output from this search is shown in Listing 10.6.

Listing 10.6 File Containing Search Results for Listing 10.5

```
protein_id: AAC76922.1
DB Seq. Offset:   15
QuerySeq. Offset:  4
SA Length:        35
SA Score:         61
DB Sequence:      KFGGSSLADVKCYLRVAGIMAEYSQPDDMMVVSAA
Query Sequence:   KFGGTSVANAERFLRVADILESNARQGQVATVLSA
```

In this case a subsequence of 35 amino acids from query sequence starting at offset 4 from the beginning of the query sequence, matched a subsequence from the database, starting at offset 15, with a score of 61. The score is built by adding up alignment scores for each pair of amino acids over the subsequence at hand. Exact matches give the highest score. Over the set of 20 amino acids, there are amino acids that have similar properties to one another. Alignments with amino acids that have similar properties will still add to the score in a positive way. Alignments with amino acids that have dissimilar properties will cause a negative penalty to be added to the score. Sequence substitution matrices provide alignment scores for all possible combinations of two amino acids. It is beyond the scope of this chapter to go into how the sequence substitution matrix scoring is generated. The first couple of chapters in Durbin et al. 1998 provide a very readable development of sequence alignment methodologies and the generation of scoring matrices.

A more complex BLAST search can be performed using the tBLASTx option. The query format is shown in Listing 10.7.

Listing 10.7 A Complex Query Using the tBLASTx Option

```
/ND/dna_sequence_entry[source/taxonomy/cell_type="Eukaryota"]/dna_
sequence {func("tBlastx, -i
gtaccctgtttacatcattttgccattttcgcgtactgcaaccggcggg . . .
")}/../header/accession_no
```

This query performs a tBLASTx search against all DNA sequences in that database that come from a taxonomy cell type of Eukaryota. The query will return the accession number of all database sequences that meet the tBLASTx criteria. A typical result will look like Listing 10.8.

Listing 10.8 Result of the Query in Listing 10.7

```
<query_results>
      <accession_no>
            <base_no>AE000333</base_no>
            <version>AE000333.1</version>
            <GI>GI:1788805</GI>
      </accession_no>
</query_results>
```

A tBLASTx search first converts the query sequence into the six amino acid frames. The sequence search engine then compares the six query frames to each database sequence that is of the cell type Eukaryota. Before the comparison can be done, the database DNA sequences must first be dynamically converted to its six amino acid frames. The comparison is then performed at the amino acid sequence level. Using NeoCore's DPP technology, all six query sequences are compared to each database sequence in a single pass over the database sequences. The result is a very fast and accurate search. An example of one of the database matches is given in Listing 10.9.

Listing 10.9 Example Database Match for Amino Acid Sequence Comparison

```
Accession_no: AE000140.1
DB Seq Frame No:   2
Query Frame No:    6
DB Seq. Offset:    2728
QuerySeq. Offset:  592
SA Length:         32
SA Score:          53
DB Sequence:       FRVVAPSTHRRAGTGGVAGIQRNLLHSLHFRH
Query Sequence:    FRLVTQSEQGRAGAGDTARYRADFLRAMHHQQ
```

Notice how query sequence frame number 6 matched with a database sequence frame number 2. Since the query sequence match was on the reverse frame 6, the query sequence offset, 592, would be referenced from the tail end of the query nucleotide sequence. The database sequence matched on a forward frame 2, so the offset is from the beginning of the database nucleotide sequence. Nucleotide sequences tend to be much longer than amino acid sequences (at least by a factor of 3), hence the large offset numbers. The match subsequence is shown in the amino acid domain. The score is generated in the same fashion as a BLASTp type of search.

Sequence search and alignment tools are the heart and soul of data-mining in the high throughput genomics world. These are primary tools for the biologist today. The incorporation of a BLAST search engine into NeoCore XMS greatly enhances the database's ability to meet the information requirements of the exploding life sciences market.

Conclusion

The Human Genome Project has brought the field of biology over a high mountain pass and into a new, huge, unexplored, lush valley. We are standing at a precipice overlooking this valley and the wonders of what lies ahead are just beginning to sink in. It is like standing at a high vantage point in the early 1950s, overlooking what was ahead for the electronics industry. We are in a time of explosive growth in terms of knowledge and understanding of biological systems. The complexity of living organisms and the inherent information contained within is staggering. The tools we bring to bear to explore, discover, manipulate, and work with this new information will make an enormous difference in how fast and efficiently we are able to build this new information into knowledge and understanding.

XML is well suited and provides an excellent standard for capturing and expressing complex biological information. XML is a flexible, extensible information model that supports the heterogeneous characteristics of biological information and will grow with the discovery process. In order to support a growing knowledge base and the discovery process, the database technology must be as flexible, extensible, and schema independent as the XML information model. The database technology must work well with and support extremely heterogeneous information. NeoCore XMS uniquely meets these requirements. Through NeoCore's association with the UC Denver's Center for Computational Biology, NeoCore XMS is proving to meet the demands of the biological research community. The addition of a BLAST sequence search engine to NeoCore XMS further enhances the database's value in the exploding field of biology and life sciences. The ability to capture, manipulate, analyze, and grow the information discovered in the lush biological valley ahead will allow us to gain knowledge and understanding of the complex systems that make up living organisms. The gains here have the potential to revolutionize medicine.

Chapter 11

Case Studies of XML Used with IBM DB2 Universal Database

Lee Anne Kowalski

11.1 Introduction

The key question every company asks is: Why embrace a new technology? How will this new technology benefit our company goals? The case studies in this chapter illustrate how various companies might use XML and DB2 technology to solve business problems in those companies and industries. Each case study consists of:

- A company scenario and particular problem to solve
- What is currently stopping them
- How they used DB2 and XML to achieve that goal.

The reasons for choosing a particular technology combination and the lessons learned in each case are mentioned through each section.

The case studies covered in this chapter are

- Case Study 1: "Our most valued customers come first."
- Case Study 2: "Improve cash flow."

11.2 Case Study 1: "Our Most Valued Customers Come First"

In this section we describe the first case study.

11.2.1 Company Scenario

This company has a services unit where customers can report problems or file complaints by

- Calling in, speaking to a customer service representative who fills out and submits a Web form
- Filling out and submitting the form on the Web themselves

The type of information that is submitted is customer identification number, product ID, and severity of the problem (1=high to 4=low). Once the problem is submitted to the system, the customer relationship manager assigned to that customer ID is notified to respond to that customer.

Currently, the customer relationship managers respond to clients' problems on the basis of first come, first served. What the CEO of this services company wants is for the staff to act on the problems from their most important customers first.

What Does It Take to Solve This Problem?

What is stopping staff from responding to problems from their most important customers first? Each of the customer relationship managers covers a lot of individual clients. They need to be able to ask, "Is this customer with a high-severity problem one of my best customers?" so that they can respond to those clients first. To provide an answer to that question, the data on how valuable the customer is to the company has to be joined with the data about the problem, as shown in Table 11.1.

11.2.2 How This Business Problem Is Addressed

This section describes how the company solved this problem. The overall flow of the process is

Table 11.1 Problem Report Data and Customer History Data

Data source	Where managed
Problem reports submitted via Web form.	Files from the Web form
Customer history data: how much they've spent on the company's products, how good their past payment history is, etc.	DB2 relational database

1. The problem is submitted using the Web form.
2. The data are stored as an XML document.
3. The XML document is decomposed into relational data in the DB2 database where the customer history data is kept.
4. A trigger alerts the assigned customer relationship manager that a key client has submitted a high-severity problem.
5. The customer relationship manager responds to the client.

In this case, the DB2 XML Extender is used to decompose the problem report document into relational data.

Problem Reports: XML Documents

The client's problem is submitted as an XML document. This document contains this information:

- Customer information (name, e-mail, phone number)
- Product information (product name, version)
- Problem information (severity, symptoms)

Listing 11.1 presents an XML document.

Listing 11.1 XML Problem Submission Document

```
<?xml version="1.0"?>
<!DOCTYPE Problem SYSTEM "c:\dxx\dtd\newproblem.dtd">
  <Problem key="123">
    <Customer>
      <CustName>John Doe</CustName>
      <Email>parts@doe.com</Email>
```

```
      <Phone>4085552727</Phone>
    </Customer>
    <Product>
      <ProdName>GrandPlan</ProdName>
      <Version>3.5</Version>
    </Product>
    <SevCode>1</SevCode>
    <Symptoms>broken, cannot install
    </Symptoms>
  </Problem>
```

The XML document in Listing 11.1 is decomposed into the DB2 table in Table 11.2. With the combination of DB2 and the XML Extender, decomposition is done using the XML Extender's dxxShredXML stored procedure.

Notice that the symptoms, which are in the XML document, are not decomposed into the table. The company chooses to do this because the symptoms are not used to determine whether the customer relationship representative responds quickly to the client who submitted this report. Therefore, they do not have to be stored in the relational database table.

The symptoms will be useful when the customer relationship manager has already been alerted and is investigating the situation. For this reason, the company makes the decision to retain the XML problem documents intact for future use. For example, the customer relationship manager might use it later to display the symptoms that are reported.

Table 11.2 PROBLEMS Table

Column name	Data type	Length	Description
CUSTNAME	VARCHAR	10	Customer name
EMAIL	VARCHAR	20	Customer e-mail
PHONE	INTEGER		Customer phone number
PRODUCT	VARCHAR	8	Product name
VERSION	DECIMAL	3,1	Version of product with reported problem
SEVCODE	SMALLINT		Severity of reported problem

Order Data: Relational Data Stored in DB2

The importance of the client is judged by how much the client has spent on the company's products. In this company, customer order data has traditionally been stored in tables in the DB2 database. Some of the columns of their existing ORDERS table are listed in Table 11.3.

Table 11.3 ORDERS Table

Column name	Data type	Length	Description
INVCID	INTEGER		Invoice ID
CUSTID	INTEGER		Customer ID
CUSTNAME	VARCHAR	10	Customer name
PRODID	INTEGER		Product ID
PRODUCT	VARCHAR	8	Product name
TOTCOST	DECIMAL	6,2	Total cost for this order
REPID	INTEGER		ID for the customer relationship representative for this sale

Triggered Actions

When a row that has a SEVCODE = 1 is inserted into the PROBLEMS table, the SEV_PROBLEMS trigger is invoked and inserts a row into a table named SEVERE_PROBLEMS. Listing 11.2 shows how this can be done.

Listing 11.2 Create Trigger

```
CREATE TRIGGER SEV_PROBLEMS
  AFTER INSERT ON PROBLEMS
  REFERENCING NEW AS N
  FOR EACH ROW MODE DB2SQL
  WHEN (N.SEVCODE = 1)
  BEGIN ATOMIC
    INSERT INTO SEVERE_PROBLEMS
      VALUES (N.CUSTNAME, N.PRODUCT,(SELECT REPID FROM REPS
      WHERE (REPS.CUSTNAME = N.CUSTNAME)),
```

```
        (SELECT SUM(ORDERS.TOTCOST) FROM ORDERS
         WHERE (ORDERS.CUSTNAME = N.CUSTNAME)));
      END
```

The REPS table in the database stores data about the customer relationship representatives: their IDs, names, location, and so on. As shown in Table 11.4, the trigger uses that table to associate the customer that reported the problem with the ID of the representative who handles their relationship with the company.

When a row is inserted into SEVERE_PROBLEMS (Table 11.4), a trigger on it is invoked that sends a page to the customer relationship representative if the TOTPRICE exceeds a particular amount to alert the customer relationship representative. The customer representative can then immediately respond to the important customer.

Table 11.4 SEVERE_PROBLEMS Table

Column name	Data type	Length	Description
CUSTNAME	VARCHAR	10	Customer name
PRODUCT	VARCHAR	8	Product name
REPID	INTEGER		ID for the customer relationship representative for this sale
TOTSPENT	DECIMAL	7.2	Total amount of money that this customer has spent with the company. This is the sum of all TOTCOST for a particular CUSTID

11.2.3 Future Extensions

After solving the immediate problem and improving their response time to address the complaints from their most valued customers, the company has plans to expand this system into the following areas.

Immediate Response to the Customer

A trigger can be added to SEVERE_PROBLEMS so that when a row is inserted, an e-mail is sent to the customer that informs the customer that the assigned customer relationship manager has received their message and will be responding immediately. Using the XML composition functions, an XML document would be composed from the data in PROBLEMS for that customer, including the name of the customer relationship manager assigned to this case, and sent off to the customer's e-mail address.

More Accurate Marketing Strategies

From the data stored from the XML problem reports, the company's marketing department can easily see what customers have opened a number of problem reports about which products. If the marketing department is about to do a promotion about a product that a customer has complained about, the company can avoid further antagonizing this customer by automatically removing the customer's name from the list of people who would get that mailing.

Better Business Decisions for Future Product Lines

DB2 can be used to search XML documents stored intact external to DB2. If the XML problem report documents are stored intact outside the database, the `<SYMPTOMS>` element can be searched to find out if any patterns of symptoms are reported. That information can be used to influence plans for future models and product lines.

A product inventory table already exists in their DB2 database to track inventory. Data from the `INVENTORY` table can be joined with the `PROBLEMS` table to see which product is receiving the most reported problems.

11.3 Case Study 2: "Improve Cash Flow"

In this section we describe the second case study.

11.3.1 Company Scenario

A high school administrator wants to improve the school's cash flow by getting paid faster from the state's Department of Education for appropriate reimbursable expenses. "My teachers are complaining that they spend their own money buying supplies and then have to wait weeks to get reimbursed. The faster that I can get funds in the school's bank account, the faster I can reimburse the teachers, and they can focus their energies on what they love: teaching their students."

What Does It Take to Solve This Problem?

What is stopping the high school from submitting the claims quickly to the Department of Education and getting fast payment? Currently, the high school has to create paper documents to send to the Department of Education to request payment. The state's finance department won't pay claims for an individual school unless that school can show that it is maintaining a certain level of academic achievement. Along with the details about the expenses that it wants reimbursed, the school has to send data on current student grades and levels of attendance to show that the school is meeting the mandated levels. The finance department won't reimburse the school until someone at the Department of Education can go through that paperwork and verify that the school meets the educational criteria. If the high school could submit documents electronically with the necessary information directly to the Department of Education's data systems, the turn-around time would decrease dramatically.

11.3.2 How This Business Problem Is Addressed

The high school negotiates to do a pilot program with the Department of Education where the expense claims are submitted electronically. The benefits that they hope for are

- **High school:** They receive prompt payment from the state and can reimburse their teachers quickly.
- **Department of Education:** They reduce the amount of paperwork that they have to do. They also receive the school's performance data faster than they have before. They can then use this data for evaluating trends, for supporting evidence when requesting money from the federal government, or to report to the public to show how well the school is performing.

The high school stores their data in one type of system, and the Department of Education uses another system. Therefore, they decide to leverage XML as a common language to exchange the information and use XML-based Web Services.

The High School

The high school has a student and classroom record system based on a DB2 database that maintains information about each student, such as grades and attendance. When a teacher comes to the high school administrator with an out-of-pocket expense for reimbursement, the administrator uses a Web application to retrieve the teacher's classroom record and enter the information for the expense. A classroom reimbursement request document is created. Previously, that request document would have been submitted by fax or mail to the Department of Education. In the new process, the request document will be submitted to the Department of Education using a Web Service.

The Department of Education

The Department of Education has a reimbursement request system that maintains the criteria for reimbursing the various public schools in the state. When the Department of Education's Web Service receives the request document from the high school, it validates the request by accessing its reimbursement request system and returns a confirmation or rejection of approval back to the school. If the request is approved, the Department of Education also forwards the request to the state's finance department to initiate the process to transfer funds to the school.

The Department of Education's database does not have to be a DB2 database for this system to work. Because the information that is sent to the Department of Education is XML-based, they can access the data in the XML document as long as they are using a database that can extract the data from the document.

The High School Reimbursement Request Application

A teacher turns in a request for reimbursement to the school administrator. The reimbursement application is a Web application that first retrieves the classroom data, which is stored in DB2. The administrator opens the home page of the Web application and enters the classroom ID number for that teacher. The classroom ID number is then sent by a servlet that queries the database for the classroom record.

Table 11.5 shows a portion of the structure for the `CLASSROOM_RECORD` table that contains the classroom information.

Table 11.5 CLASSROOM_RECORD Table

Column name	Description
CLASS_ID	Classroom ID number (primary key)
TEACHER_ID	Teacher ID number
SUBJECT_ID	ID code for class subject
AVG_GRADE	Average grade for students in the class (aggregated from data stored for each student)
AVG_ATTDNCE	Average attendance (%) for students in the class

The application displays the query results and prompts the administrator for the following additional information:

- Category for the teacher's out-of-pocket expense (for example, purchasing paper)
- Amount requested for reimbursement

This additional information is submitted to a servlet that invokes the Web Service to go to the Department of Education's application for submitting reimbursement claims.

The Web Service returns the Department of Education's response to the claim. The high school administrator knows at once that the Department of Education has received the request and whether it has been approved.

The Department of Education Reimbursement Request Web Service

The high school submits the XML-based request document to this Web Service. The data that the high school must send as input to the Web Service is shown in Listing 11.3.

Listing 11.3 Input Data to Web Service

```
School identification number (SCHOOLID)
Class subject (SUBJECT_ID)
Average student grade for this class (AVG_GRADE)
Average student attendance (%) in this class (AVG_ATTDNCE)
Category of expense (EXPENSE_TYPE)
Amount requested (EXPENSE_AMT)
```

The output response data for the claim service is: School identification number (SCHOOLID) Approval flag (APPROVED = yes or no).

The response data is returned as an XML document (response.xml), which can be transformed to HTML and displayed in the high school's Web application immediately. The school administrator sees immediately whether the reimbursement is approved and can notify the teacher. This can be done as shown in Listing 11.4.

Listing 11.4 Response Data

```
<?xml version="1.0" ?>
<EXPENSE_APPROVAL>
  <SCHOOLID>3091578832</SCHOOLID>
```

```
  <APPROVED>yes</APPROVED>
</EXPENSE_APPROVAL>
```

The Department of Education has a relational database, possibly DB2 or another database system. This database stores information about the minimum criteria for class subjects, such as the average grades for each type of class and the attendance levels for those classes. It also stores the values reported by each state school.

The `SCHOOL_INFO` table (see Table 11.6) in that database stores the specifics about each school. The `SUBJECT_DATA` table (see Table 11.7) stores the information on standards that the state schools are mandated to meet in each subject. Table 11.6 contains the current average grade and attendance for that class in that specific school. Then Table 11.7 is used to look up the acceptable state standards for that class subject.

Table 11.6 SCHOOL_INFO Table

Column name	Description
SCHOOLID	State school identification number (primary key)
SUBJECTID	School subject (for example, math) ID code
AVGGRADE	Average grade for students in this class in this school
PCTATTDNCE	Average attendance percentage for students in this class in this school
APPROVED	A flag (yes or no) that shows whether this school is meeting the standards

Table 11.7 SUBJECT_DATA Table

Column name	Description
SUBJECT_ID	School subject ID code (primary key)
MIN_GRADE	Minimum acceptable average grade
MIN_ATTDNCE	Minimum acceptable average attendance

The flow of the process at the Department of Education's database once its Web Service has received the request from the school is

- Decompose the incoming XML document and update Table 11.6 with the values for the average student grade and attendance in that subject for that school. Set the APPROVED flag to no.
- Query the Table 11.7 for the values of acceptable average grades and attendance that correspond to the class subject ID that was submitted.
- Compare the data from Table 11.7 to the school's data in Table 11.6.
- If the comparison shows that the average grade and attendance level are higher than the minimum acceptable values, update Table 11.6 to set the APPROVED flag to yes.
- Query Table 11.6 for that SCHOOLID value and convert the result of the query to an XML document (Approval_Status.xml).
- Transform that XML document to the XML format of the desired response to send to the high school.
- Return the response document (response.xml) to the school.

In this case, the high school requires a particular XML format of the response they want (response.dtd). The benefit of using XML for data exchange is that to exchange data from the Department of Education's internal XML document (Approval_Status.xml) to another XML document, they need to know only the DTD of the required response and create an XSLT file to transform to it. This makes it easy to reuse their existing applications in the future. For example, suppose another school wants to use the Department of Education's Web Service and get a different response format back or the federal government might later define the format of response documents to be used by all schools in the country. The Department of Education would not have to change Approval_Status.xml. All they would have to do is have an XSLT to transform the Approval_Status.xml document to the desired response XML document.

The Approval_Status.xml document is shown in Listing 11.5.

Listing 11.5 Approval_Status XML Document

```
<?xml version="1.0" ?>
<SCHOOL_INFO>
  <SCHOOLID>3091578832</SCHOOLID>
  <SUBJECTID>1235</SUBJECTID>
  <AVGGRADE>2.9</AVGGRADE>
  <PCTATTNDCE>87</PCTATTNDCE>
```

```
  <APPROVED>yes</APPROVED>
</SCHOOL_INFO>
```

To transform this to the response.xml document to send back to the high school, the transform shown in Listing 11.6 is applied (response.xml).

Listing 11.6 Response XML Document

```
<?xml version="1.0" ?>
<xsl:transform xmlns:xsl="http://www.w3.org/1999/XSL/Transform"
version="1.0">
<xsl:output method="xml" indent="no" />
<xsl:strip-space elements="*" />
<xsl:template match="/">
<xsl:apply-templates select="//SCHOOL_INFO [1]" />
</xsl:template>
<xsl:template match="SCHOOL_INFO">
<EXPENSE_APPROVAL>
<SCHOOLID>
<xsl:value-of select="SCHOOLID[1]/text()" />
</SCHOOLID>
<APPROVED>
<xsl:value-of select="APPROVED[1]/text()" />
</APPROVED>
</EXPENSE_APPROVAL>
</xsl:template>
<xsl:template match="*|@*|comment()|processing-
instruction()|text()">
<xsl:copy>
<xsl:apply-templates select="*|@*|comment()|processing-
instruction()|text()" />
</xsl:copy>
</xsl:template>
</xsl:transform>
```

11.3.3 Future Extensions

After solving the immediate problem and improving cash flow, the high school has plans to expand this system. Now that they have a model for composing an XML document from their database of classroom and student records, the high school can expand in these areas:

- Create a Web site where parents can look up their children's records. Parents can monitor how their child is progressing week by week instead of waiting until the next report card.
- Enable teachers to determine the likelihood of getting approval for reimbursements before they make a purchase for the classroom. Because the Web Service exists at the Department of Education, the teacher can use a Web application to find out before making an out-of-pocket purchase whether it would be denied.

11.4 Conclusion

The case studies in this chapter have illustrated situations where a company or organization has embraced the technology combination of DB2 and XML to solve an immediate business problem. In one situation, the combination was used to make a company's internal business process more efficient for resolving issues for their customers. In the other situation, the combination made it easier for two separate organizations to work together and share the data they need to exchange more efficiently. Both case studies depict situations that are fairly commonplace and which can occur in any company. The combination of DB2 relational database technology and XML in these situations shows that it does not have to be reserved for complex business situations or high-technology industries. DB2 and XML technology can provide value in any part of a business's day-to-day operation, as well as be extended into unique uses, which then drive the development of new business processes for achieving the business's future goals.

Notices

IBM may have patents or pending patent applications covering subject matter described in this document. The furnishing of this document does not give you any license to these patents. You can send license inquiries, in writing, to:

IBM Director of Licensing
IBM Corporation
North Castle Drive
Armonk, NY 10504-1785
U.S.A.

The following paragraph does not apply to the United Kingdom or any other country where such provisions are inconsistent with local law:

INTERNATIONAL BUSINESS MACHINES CORPORATION PROVIDES THIS PUBLICATION "AS IS" WITHOUT WARRANTY OF ANY KIND, EITHER EXPRESS OR IMPLIED, INCLUDING, BUT NOT LIMITED TO, THE IMPLIED WARRANTIES OF NON-INFRINGEMENT, MERCHANTABILITY OR FITNESS FOR A PARTICULAR PURPOSE. Some states do not allow disclaimer of express or implied warranties in certain transactions, therefore, this statement may not apply to you. This information could include technical inaccuracies or typographical errors.

All statements regarding IBM's future direction or intent are subject to change or withdrawal without notice, and represent goals and objectives only.

This information contains examples of data and reports used in daily business operations. To illustrate them as completely as possible, the examples include the names of individuals, companies, brands, and products. All of these names are fictitious and any similarity to the names and addresses used by an actual business enterprise is entirely coincidental.

COPYRIGHT LICENSE

This information contains sample code. You may copy, modify, and distribute the sample code in any form without payment to IBM, for any purpose, but you do so at your own risk. The sample code is provided "AS IS" without warranty of any kind.

The following are trademarks or registered trademarks of IBM Corporation in the United States, other countries, or both: IBM, DB2, DB2 Universal Database.

Chapter 12

The Design and Implementation of an Engineering Data Management System Using XML and J2EE

Karen Eglin, Lily Hendra, and Odysseas Pentakalos

12.1 Introduction

JEDMICS is a large image management system that is accessed by a number of heterogeneous client applications, which require access to the same image repository. The Open Application Interface (OAI) is a new API for providing client application developers with a unified interface to the image repository, thereby introducing a layer of abstraction between the end user and the physical storage layer of the data and metadata that make up the image management system.

This chapter describes and discusses the design and implementation of the JEDMICS OAI system, an EJB-based API (Enterprise Java Bean–based API) that provides access to image data that is stored on a variety of storage media and metadata stored in a relational database system. The main focus of the chapter is the use of XML as the portable data exchange solution, and its integration with the object-oriented core of the system and the relational database that forms the persistent storage.

During the design and development of the OAI, we investigated the latest technologies and standards related to XML offered by different vendors, standards-governing, and user group communities (such as DOM, JDOM, JAXB, XSLT, Oracle XSU, etc.), to provide an effective solution for managing JEDMICS data. The chapter also presents our experiences with these technologies and standards, as well as the issues that we encountered while integrating them. We close this chapter by discussing the future directions of the OAI system.

12.2 Background and Requirements

JEDMICS (Joint Engineering Data Management Information and Control System) was conceived in the mid-1980s as the solution to the overwhelming problem of manually managing engineering data associated with weapon's system life cycle management. Originally, JEDMICS was developed as a client/server system for the U.S. Navy and the Defense Logistics Agency (DLA). During the last ten years, JEDMICS has been deployed to all branches of the service (JEDMICS started out in 1989 as EDMICS and was designated as a joint system in 1993). JEDMICS is specifically designed for controlling, managing, and distributing digitized engineering data.

JEDMICS is deployed at a total of 29 army, navy, marine, air force and DLA repository sites. It is used today by more than 38,000 Department of Defense (DoD) engineers, procurement specialists, repair technicians, and others worldwide to support the war-fighters by keeping their weapon systems at higher levels of readiness. JEDMICS is now in the process of being updated to an EJB-based, multitier client/server architecture (called the OAI) to carry it beyond its 2,005 life cycles in a Web-based environment. More than 77 million engineering documents are stored in JEDMICS repositories, including the engineering data for aircraft, ships, land vehicles, and helicopters. JEDMICS engineering documents consist of drawings that may have multiple revisions. Each revision contains multiple sheets and frames that uniquely identify images, stored on magnetic disk, contained in the drawing revision. Drawing revisions may also contain associated accompanying documents, which may also have multiple revisions containing multiple sheets and frames uniquely identifying images contained in the accompanying document revision. The engineering document and its component's metadata are stored in an Oracle database. Engineering data refers to the JEDMICS document's identifying metadata stored in an Oracle database and the associated images stored on magnetic disk.

OAI's primary requirement is to provide an Open Standards–based interface for external and internal clients to manage JEDMICS engineering data. This includes C, C++, Java, and Web clients. OAI intends to use a CORBA layer that interfaces the EJB server side to support clients written in languages other than Java.

Currently, JEDMICS includes a legacy API that supports C clients and several internally developed client/server GUI applications. Only a subset of the JEDMICS functionality provided by the GUI applications is available with the API. OAI's ultimate goal is to replace the legacy API and expose all of the current JEDMICS application functionality to external and internal clients written in Java or any language supported by CORBA. Until the legacy API can be replaced, OAI is constrained to the legacy database schema. No changes may be made to the database schema, which will break the current API or the internal GUI applications.

12.3 Overview

The OAI allows clients to access JEDMICS repository documents, document collections, and their associated metadata via its four external services. Clients connect through the Security Service, which authenticates and authorizes users and maintains the concept of a session between the client applications and the server tiers. Once connected, users can then obtain metadata through the Query Service that they can use to retrieve the physical data files corresponding to documents and images using the Image Query Service. Authorized clients may also print the files by using the Print Service.

Figure 12.1 illustrates the overall architecture of the OAI and the EJB components that it contains. The components are logically classified into three layers: external components, middle-layer services components, and persistence layer components. The current implementation of the OAI includes additional components that are not shown in the figure for the sake of conciseness. All external-layer components exchange data with the client using XML documents as the data transport. The reasons we chose this approach and the repercussions of this decision will be discussed in detail in Section 12.4, "Design Choices." The XML data coming into OAI is parsed and is either passed directly to the persistence layer services or passed to the middle layer services for further processing. Similarly, data coming from the persistence layer or the middle layer services is first converted into XML format before it is forwarded to the client. The following sections describe briefly each of the external layer components.

12.3.1 Security Service

The Security Service serves as the gateway to the OAI system, through which clients gain access to the system. A client application passes username and password information as part of the XML input to the Security Service interface method. The method returns a unique session identifier to indicate that the client is successfully connected. The client must pass this session identifier to the other OAI services in order to gain access to these services.

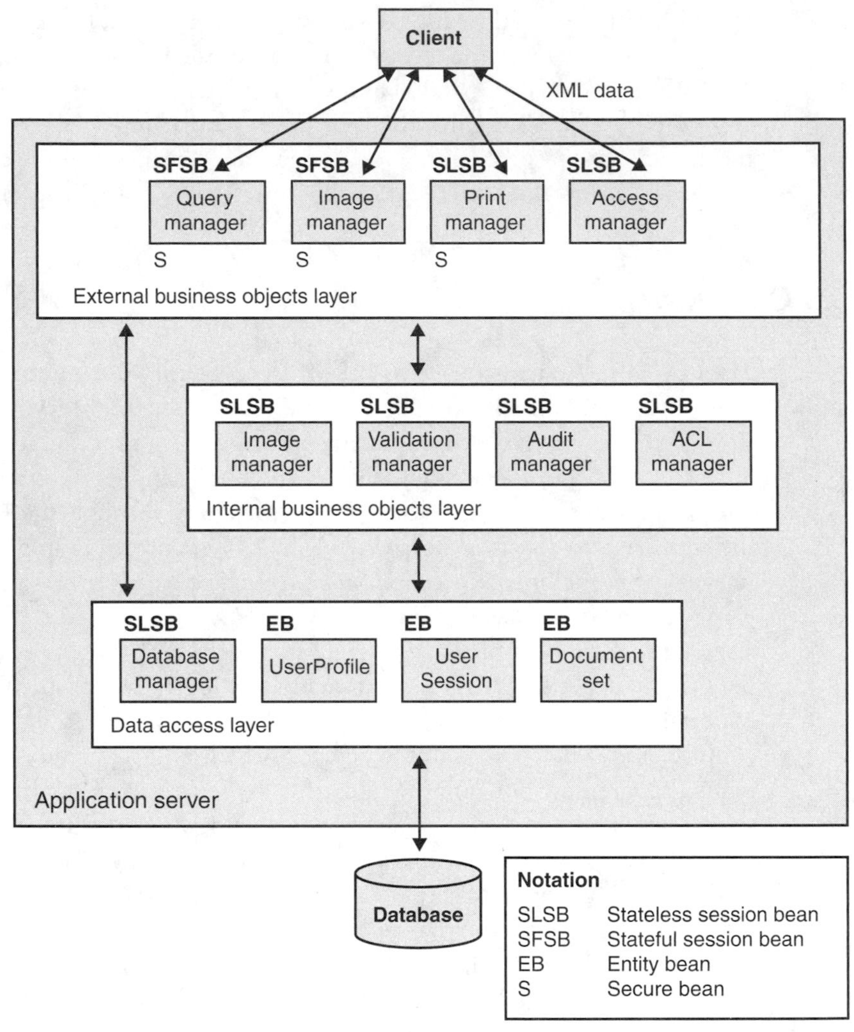

Figure 12.1 Component Architecture of the OAI

12.3.2 Query Service

The Query Service provides OAI clients with methods to query for document (drawings or accompanying documents), document components, and document collection metadata. Clients can also make specific queries for summary and detail-level document-related metadata as well as metadata specific to certain types of document collections. The component architecture of the OAI is illustrated in Figure 12.1.

12.3.3 Image Query Service

The Image Query Service provides OAI clients with methods to retrieve physical images based upon their identifying key fields. Through this service, clients obtain the actual representation of a drawing or accompanying document from the JEDMICS repository. However, only authorized clients are allowed to view certain images, and the enforcement of this access control is based on the client's user profile with respect to the image's access level attributes.

12.3.4 Print Service

The Print Service provides OAI clients with methods to print drawings, accompanying documents, images, and document collections. Just like the Image Query Service, the Print Service applies restrictions on the images and document collections that a client can print. Clients can make a request to create a print job, and subsequently attach items to be printed to the job. All items in the print job will be queued and remain on "hold" status until a request to submit it is made by the client. Clients may also cancel or abort print jobs.

12.4 Design Choices

While designing OAI, we made a number of decisions that impacted the overall architecture of the system. To comply with the requirement of having to support multiple heterogeneous clients, we chose to use XML as the data transport for exchanging data between the client and the OAI system. This design choice introduced a number of issues on how to deal with the data requests to OAI that arrive in the form of XML documents and how to return data also in the form of XML documents in an efficient way. In this section, we discuss in detail each of the choices we made including the available options in each case, the advantages and disadvantages of each option, and the reason for our final selection.

12.4.1 Using XML in OAI

One of the limitations presented by the JEDMICS legacy system is its inability to select and return different types of data to the client in a single call without returning complex/heavy client objects or the proprietary internal scheme. For example, if the client needs all the information about an engineering drawing, the system requires several client calls: one call to retrieve the drawing metadata, another call to retrieve the images for the drawing, another call to retrieve the part number associations, and another call to retrieve the Weapon System Code associations. A proprietary scheme was developed internally for retrieving this information, but it is not easily read or parsed. In addition, external clients do not know how to process the proprietary scheme. OAI uses XML documents for input and output to external client interfaces, which resolves the problem. It allows for a nonproprietary method for clients to specify what data to retrieve and to return, in an easily understandable format that is platform independent. Currently, there is no XML industry standard for defining engineering documents. Therefore, OAI developed its own DTDs for defining engineering documents and their components. External clients can parse this data with any XML parser. OAI also has a requirement to support CORBA clients. Since XML documents are returned as a String element, any CORBA client can easily access the data. The following are several advantages offered by XML, which make it an excellent choice for OAI's external interfaces:

- **Portability:** XML is a good match for Java. It pairs Java's code portability feature with its data portability, as well as strengthening Java's ease-of-use feature. XML's portability is made possible by its text format and the need for no formatting instructions. Since the OAI system will have multiple clients connecting to it, portability is the key design issue. Data needs to be readable and usable by all clients, regardless of their platforms and applications. Text data are both portable and easy to use, readable by both humans and text-editing software.
- **Extensibility:** XML tags are extensible, allowing us to define and use our own XML tags to describe data content. The OAI system needs to be able to use the same data format for different functionality. That is why XML becomes useful: We can extend and customize the tags to fit the different needs of each function. We can also easily combine results of several queries into one XML document.
- **Control over presentation:** Separation between the management of content and its presentation allows developers to reuse and/or reformat data in different ways. The internal OAI processes do not have to worry about the different presentation requirements; they only need to know how to manage the data content. When the process is done, then presentation can be customized according to the needs of the requesting client.
- **Interoperability:** XML allows access to single data by heterogeneous applications. The OAI system is the core JEDMICS application interface that processes and returns single data to heterogeneous clients/applications. And since XML describes the structure of the data (and not its format), the single data can be used by different applications, and therefore interoperability is preserved.

12.4.2 Conversion of XML Input into Objects

While XML is an ideal choice for external client interfaces, it is not efficient for internal application processing. During the design and implementation of the OAI, we evaluated many methods for processing the XML documents passed in from the client. We prototyped the use of Simple API for XML (SAX) and Document Object Model (DOM) parsers, JDOM, generic hash table, and tree java objects to convert the XML document, and JAXB (Java Architecture for XML Binding) to generate Java classes based on the XML document's DTD.

SAX processes XML data like a text stream, which is fairly fast. However, the structure is not stored in memory; hence it is hard to retrieve specific elements of a collection without processing the whole document. In addition, SAX does not allow adding, removing, or changing elements in the document (since it provides a read-only model to the XML document), it does not provide a method to output XML, and it only provides structural validation (field validation must be done programmatically). For the aforementioned reasons, SAX does not provide the processing power that OAI needs, and parsing using SAX proves to be slower than parsing XML documents into JAXB-generated Java classes.

The DOM translates an XML document into an in-memory tree structure. DOM provides powerful document-processing capabilities including support for adding, deleting, and changing elements and outputting XML documents. However, DOM requires additional overhead to support these capabilities, and it provides only structural validation (field validation must be done programmatically), and the document is interpreted, which is slower than dealing with compiled code. OAI only uses a limited subset of the DOM capability, but incurs the overhead to support all the unused capability, and it proves to be slower than parsing XML documents into JAXB-generated Java classes.

JDOM is a Java API for manipulating XML documents. JDOM provides capabilities similar to the DOM API but without as much overhead. Our experience shows that JDOM is still slower than parsing XML documents into JAXB-generated Java classes.

JAXB (which we will describe in more detail later in this chapter) takes an XML DTD and generates Java classes representing the XML document structure. The generated classes include code to validate the data as well as the structure. The code has to be compiled, and therefore, it is much faster than SAX, DOM, or JDOM. The generated classes also make it obvious what is expected in the document, whereas with SAX, DOM, or JDOM, developers must refer to the DTD or XML schema to determine what the XML document contains. JAXB-generated classes are much easier to work with for development and maintenance. Whenever the DTD changes, re-running JAXB will generate the Java classes based on the changed DTD. The JAXB classes that are generated, in addition to methods for marshaling and unmarshaling XML, include accessors and mutators for each of the elements of the class.

To add support for additional application-specific validation, we would need to extend the classes that are generated by JAXB using derived classes that provide the validation code.

12.4.3 Conversion of Database Data into XML

One of the major functions of the OAI is to provide support for retrieving image data stored in the JEDMICS repository as well as image metadata, stored in a relational database. Therefore, the ability to extract the data and output it in XML format is crucial. It is important that the whole conversion process is done efficiently. For these reasons, and the fact that the database system used to store the image metadata is Oracle, it was decided that the Oracle XSU (XML SQL Utility) be utilized. The utility automatically transforms relational data into XML (and vice versa) without any need for extra coding on the OAI server. It allows for the extraction of data from an object-relational or pure relational format into XML, as well as insertion, update, or deletion of column/attribute values within a table or a view using XML input extracted from an XML document. In addition to the features mentioned earlier, Oracle XSU also enables the OAI system to generate output DTD and XML Schema, which will become critical when the system moves towards the future. The main advantage of XML Schema over DTD is its support for a broad set of predefined data types as well as support for user-defined data types. The disadvantage of XML Schema at this point is that it does not have sufficient tool support, but this will change over time as more and more systems incorporate its use in their architecture.

12.4.4 Conversion of Image Data into XML

The Image Query Service receives requests that specify the attributes that uniquely identify one or more images within the OAI system and returns these images after retrieving them from the appropriate image server and enforcing access control. Due to the definition of what represents a valid character within an XML document and due to the encoding and decoding processes at the sending and receiving side, we cannot directly embed the image's binary data within the XML document that forms the response to the caller. To resolve this issue, we evaluated three different encoding schemes before making our selection. The first choice was to encode each byte in the image with its two-character hexadecimal representation. This scheme is easy to implement but results in an XML document that is twice the size of the original binary image. The next choice was to use base64 encoding, which represents each 3-byte sequence as four 6-bit blocks that are each encoded as a single character from a 64-character set. This scheme is fairly easy to implement, and various versions exist in the public domain. At the same time, the base64 encoding scheme results in a document that is 1.34 times the size of the original image. The last scheme we evaluated was the use of Huffman codes. Huffman coding uses the statistical properties of the document to encode a document using variable-length codes. In this case the size of the resulting document is dependent on the statistical properties of the original binary document that is being encoded. For the particular implementation that we evaluated, the size of the resulting document would range between 1.0 and 1.75 times the size of the original document depending on the distribution of the byte values within the image. We finally decided to use the base64 encoding scheme due to the ease of implementation and its lack of dependence on the nature of the data encoded. Another reason we did not select the Huffman codes approach is that most of the images that are stored in our system use a proprietary compression scheme that would result in encoded document sizes towards the higher end of the range specified earlier.

12.4.5 Database Access

OAI supports several different user communities. A large portion of the user community retrieves document data and document collection data but does not update the data. A smaller subset of the users manipulates potentially large collections of documents for procurement and bid-set purposes. Another subset of the users is responsible for quality assurance of the engineering data, which requires updates to a limited set of data. We chose to use JDBC statements for constructing ad hoc queries against the Oracle database for retrieving metadata, Oracle stored procedures for manipulating OAI collections, and entity beans for limited updates to the Oracle database.

OAI uses JDBC statements for retrieving metadata for several reasons. Oracle provides the capability to return query results as XML documents, which eliminated the need for OAI to programmatically convert the Oracle query result sets into XML documents. The use of stored procedures or entity beans would have required additional custom code to convert the data into an XML document. The clients of OAI use XML documents to customize, in a user-friendly manner, the queries that are used for retrieving metadata from the system. JDBC-executed statements provide a flexible means to dynamically generate *ad hoc* queries based on the client-supplied search criteria.

OAI uses stored procedures for manipulating collections of data. OAI provides many capabilities that require accessing large collections of data such as adding the contents of one collection to another collection or moving full or partial engineering drawings and all their cross-reference associations to another drawing. The user is interested in only whether the action completed successfully and does not need to see every item that was affected. Stored procedures allow us to manipulate these collections within Oracle, which are much more efficient than pulling all the data from the database to the server, processing each row individually, and inserting each row individually back into the database. In many cases, the collections could be manipulated with one SQL statement inside the stored procedure. The additional advantage of using the stored procedures is that they are compiled, and therefore we save the parsing time required in processing JDBC queries. Using either JDBC statements or entity beans would have been very costly because we would have to process each row in the collection individually.

OAI uses entity beans for updating engineering drawings and collection metadata. The main advantage of container-managed entity beans over the use of JDBC statements or stored procedures is the reduced development time. Developing an entity bean involves defining the bean interface and then mapping the bean's member fields to database fields in a table. The container is then responsible for generating the code that implements the queries for retrieving, storing, updating, and deleting data from the database. In theory, container-managed beans are easy to develop and are database independent. This convenience does come as a trade-off against performance and fine control over the execution of the queries against the database. The EJB specification defines the life cycle of an entity bean so as to guarantee that the data mapped into object is always synchronized with the corresponding data in the database. The enforcement of the life cycle of each entity bean by the container introduces considerable performance overhead in using entity beans. As a result, we chose to use entity beans for cases where we needed the convenience and development efficiency of entity beans, and for those parts of the system where requests against them will be a small fraction of the overall workload. At a later stage, if we determine that those entity beans are forming a bottleneck, we will need to replace them with either stored procedures or JDBC statements.

When we decided to use XML as the data transport for external data, we considered the option of storing XML directly in the database, as opposed to parsing the XML documents first and storing the data only. In making this decision we investigated the option of using a native XML database. Using a native XML database is the natural choice for storing XML data since there is a direct mapping between the original XML document and its physical representation within the database. Another feature of native XML databases, referred to as "round-tripping," is important to us since we often need to return responses to a caller in the form of XML documents, which were previously submitted to our system in the form of an XML document. Finally, the use of XPath or XQL for generating queries against a native XML database would be a direct fit with our requirement of having to allow clients to generate queries against the image management system using XML documents to specify the queries.

Despite those positive features of storing XML directly in the database, we chose not to consider a native XML database for a number of reasons. The primary reason is that at least for the early releases of the OAI system, we need to support the relational database that is currently used by the legacy applications. Therefore, using another data store at this point would require every operation that modified data to apply the changes in a transactional manner to two different databases. The second reason is the negative publicity regarding the performance of native XML databases specifically for our needs. We need to query the database using various different attributes and at different levels of the image metadata hierarchy. XML databases tend to perform very well against queries that fit the document hierarchy that was used to store the documents. However, they do not do well for more *ad hoc* queries, unless indexes are used extensively (which hinders the performance of update requests). We believe that using Oracle XSU to XML-enable our native Oracle databases is currently a good solution for JEDMICS. With future developments of Oracle and other XML technologies, more options may be available.

12.4.6 Validation

Querying the JEDMICS repository is a major function of OAI. Despite its many advantages, free-format XML makes it hard to guarantee that clients will always provide valid input required for processing. The OAI system, therefore, has to make sure that the client input is validated before it is processed to prevent unnecessary access to the database. This input validation is done in two steps:

1. Structure validation

   The OAI system needs to know that the client provided required fields needed for processing. This is done automatically by specifying the XML input's schema (in this case we use DTDs). When the data are parsed against the appropriate DTD, unmatched input (missing or unexpected fields, fields appearing in incorrect order) will create exceptions, which will be thrown to indicate to the client that the input is invalid. The fields needed for processing are based on the query called by the client, and therefore different queries have different requirements.

2. Content validation

   The OAI system also validates field content. Certain fields can only have certain values (and this is sometimes based on the query called by a client). Due to the limitations presented by the current DTD specification, this validation has to be done in the code. Once the input passes the structure validation, the system calls the validation bean, which does the content-based validation. Invalid input will also be thrown to the client before database processing is undertaken.

This two-step validation helps the system prevent unnecessary overload to the system. The Query Service is the most heavily accessed service provided by OAI. Therefore, it is crucial to reject invalid data before executing queries to reduce the load on the database. It is not possible, however, for the validation to fully protect the system from bad data, simply due to the extensiveness of the image data stored in the system.

The OAI system integrates an early implementation of JAXB, provided by Sun Microsystems, to validate input fields using the appropriate DTD and for representing the XML data within the system using an object format. Based on the DTD provided, the JAXB compiler generates Java classes that provide a two-way conversion mechanism between the XML document and the Java objects. We decided to incorporate JAXB because of its tight integration between Java technology and XML, as well as its guarantee for valid data. With JAXB, we define input syntax in the DTD for field validation and then extend the classes to include some or all content-based validation rules. Representing data with Java objects also has the advantage of easier access to data from within the objects.

XML schema and DTD are the different forms of schema used to model a whole class of XML documents. DTD has been around as long as XML has, whereas XML Schema has only lately gained popularity. XML Schema's popularity is due to a number of limitations that DTD presents. Some of the limitations of DTD are the non-XML syntax it is written in, its limited datatyping, and its complex and fragile extension mechanism based on string substitution. XML Schema tries to overcome this limitation by being more expressive than DTD. The intrinsic expressiveness value lets developers exchange XML data in a more robust way without having to rely heavily on validation tools and/or processes.

Many tools do not yet support XML Schema since it is fairly new. One such application, regrettably, is the JAXB implementation, which is currently still based on the use of DTD to create Java classes. When the support for XML Schema in JAXB becomes a reality, the system will be equipped with a pattern-matching validation scheme and content-based validation rules, and thus a more robust validation capability. The other advantages of using XML Schema in the system is to define occurrence constraints as well as simple and complex types. The JAXB compiler is then used to generate Java objects, which will make sure that fields defined in the XML Schema appear in the input as expected. Despite their advantages, however, XML Schema and JAXB alone may not do all the validations we need. In some cases, we still need to do manual content-based validation in the code. We can do that easily by extending the Java classes created by the JAXB compiler to validate content on user input based on the field and other criteria.

12.5 Future Directions

In this section we look at the future directions of relevant technologies.

12.5.1 XSLT

One of the technologies related to XML that has become a powerful complementary tool to use along with XML is the eXtensible Stylesheet Language (XSL). XSL is a language for transforming XML documents and consists of three parts: the XSL language specification itself, XSL Transformations (XSLT), and XML Path (XPath). The combination of XSLT and XPath provides a powerful tree-oriented language for transforming XML documents into other forms including HTML, XML, and PDF. Future versions of the OAI need to provide the client the ability to dynamically select a subset of the fields returned through a query, instead of the full set, which is what is currently returned. The Query Service currently returns query results in the form of an XML document. By processing the user's request to obtain the subset of the selected fields, we can generate the style sheet that can then be used to transform the XML document that includes the full set of fields from the query into an XML document that only includes the client-specified subset. XSLT simplifies the task of transforming the returned document without having to first parse it and regenerate it. This approach is not the most efficient solution for the dynamic field selection problem. It would be more efficient to submit a subset of the original query to obtain the required fields. Our short-term goal is to be able to cache these fixed queries, so that we can at least gain some performance advantage. XSLT in the short run fits our needs best, although we are exploring approaches to efficiently generate dynamically generated queries based on the client-specified fields.

12.5.2 Web Services

Another technology that we plan to explore and possibly utilize in the future is the umbrella of technologies referred to as Web Services. Web Services provide the capability of exporting services to the Web that can be located and accessed by any type of client regardless of their programming language or platform. A Web Service can be as simple as a single method call (such as get the stock price for a given symbol) or a complicated business process. The current set of technologies that form Web Services consists of SOAP, XML Schema, WSDL, and UDDI. The Simple Object Access Protocol (SOAP) is an XML-based protocol for making Remote Procedure Calls (RPCs). The Web Services Description Language (WSDL) is used to describe the service and how to invoke it, and serves a similar purpose as the IDL for a CORBA service. Universal Discovery Description Integration (UDDI) is a standard-based service for exporting Web Services by the service provider and for locating them for the clients.

Using Web Services fits very nicely with some of the requirements of OAI. The platform and language-independence features of Web Services will resolve our requirement of having to support multiple heterogeneous clients. The ability to export services across the Internet will help us meet the requirement of having to support the exchange of image data across repositories in a secure way.

12.5.3 Mass Transfer Capability

A future enhancement of OAI will require for the mass transfer of JEDMICS data between sites and/or external applications. Importing/exporting complete engineering drawings and collections, including all cross-reference associations and the image data itself from remote OAI sites is of major importance to the JEDMICS community. JEMDICS sites need to be able to easily share their data.

Currently, JEDMICS provides several tools to allow the bulk transfer of information (both index data and image files) between JEDMICS sites. However, the current tools are intended for use by the JEDMICS system administrative staff and require the user to run several different applications to define, assemble, export, and finally import the data from the remote JEDMICS site into the local JEDMICS site. It is because of these limitations that a new, consolidated approach is needed for the end users and system administrators. Defining the JEDMICS data as XML documents provides for a platform- and language-independent means of transferring this data. The XML document is easily read and understood and is parsable by any client application. Without the use of XML, OAI would need to develop a proprietary data interchange format, which would not be easily manipulated by external clients.

12.5.4 Messaging

Messaging is a method of communication between software components or applications. Messaging enables distributed communication that is loosely coupled, which means that the sender and receiver do not need to know about each other. A messaging system makes the best effort to deliver messages asynchronously and reliably. Reliability means that messages are delivered to the client once and only once. Asynchronous means that the provider can deliver messages to the client as they arrive, and the client does not have to request messages in order to receive them. It also means that both clients and providers do not need to wait until messages are received, processed, or sent. Clients can continue with other tasks while the message request is processed in the background. This is very useful, especially when the client needs only to make sure that the request will be processed and not necessarily when the request has been processed.

It would be useful for the future release of OAI to incorporate messaging capability into the system. One such use may be applied to the printing bean, where sometimes a print job is associated with many images (and therefore involves many data files), and where delays might be associated with the print queue. Therefore, it makes sense for the clients to be able to submit print jobs once and be assured that they will get printed, without having to wait. The current JEDMICS system already has the capability to query and produce reports on print jobs submitted, and this capability will still be in use when the messaging is utilized.

There are two ways by which messaging can be done in the context of the OAI system:

1. Using JMS.

   JMS stands for Java Messaging System, which is an API that J2EE 1.3 platforms were required to implement to allow components (i.e., EJBs) to send or synchronously receive messages. The J2EE 1.3 platform also provides a new message-drive bean, which enables the asynchronous consumption of messages. In addition to that, message sends and receives can be coupled with the Java Transaction API. Since OAI already does use J2EE as its middleware technology, the use of the JMS API should be directly applicable to the printing bean (rewriting it as a message-driven bean) and be used by the three different OAI clients (Java, Web, and CORBA).

2. JAXM.

   JAXM (Java API for XML Messaging) is an XML-based lightweight messaging Java API for the development of XML-based applications. JAXM message exchange may be synchronous or asynchronous, but it has to be document centric. JAXM providers must support the HTTP protocol, although they may also choose to implement other standard networking protocols, such as FTP and SMTP. In all cases, JAXM assumes SOAP messages are being transported. JAXM presents a more flexible way of sending messages for the reasons stated previously. However, since JAXM only supports SOAP messages, this option cannot be realized until OAI exports its current services in the form of Web Services. JAXM would be a good candidate to facilitate the mass data transfer capability between JEDMICS sites that was mentioned in an earlier section.

12.6 Conclusion

In this chapter we discussed the design and implementation of the OAI, specifically focusing on the central role of XML on the structure of the system. After describing each of the components that make up the OAI and its relationship to the JEDMICS system, we described the use of XML as the means to submit requests and receive responses from the OAI and the consequences of making that decision. We covered in detail the design decisions we made in processing the XML input on its flow through the OAI, including structural validation through the use of DTDs, conversion into Java objects through the use of JAXB, and field validation by extending the JAXB-generated classes. We also discussed the conversion of the database data into XML, through the use of database-specific utilities, to generate the responses from the OAI and the development of an encoding mechanism for conversion of binary image data into XML. We closed the chapter by briefly reviewing some of the future directions we plan to take with the OAI. This includes the use of XSLT for filtering the XML documents returned to the clients, the use of Web Services for exporting the OAI functionality across JEDMICS sites, the need for a mass transfer capability for exchanging data across sites, and the use of messaging to move some of the processing that is currently synchronous into an asynchronous mode of operation.

Chapter 13

Geographical Data Interchange Using XML-Enabled Technology within the GIDB System

Ruth Wilson, Maria Cobb, Frank McCreedy, Roy Ladner, David Olivier, Todd Lovitt, Kevin Shaw, Fred Petry, Mahdi Abdelguerfi

13.1 Introduction

The Geospatial Information Data Base (GIDB) System is an object-oriented (OO) digital-mapping database system designed by the Digital Mapping, Charting and Geodesy Analysis Program (DMAP) of the Naval Research Laboratory. Development of the GIDB System began in 1994 to demonstrate that representation of spatial data is less cumbersome and more optimal in object format versus relational format. Smalltalk was chosen as the programming language for the database, since at that time it was the most robust pure OO language available. Initially, all management of spatial objects was done in memory. As development grew to the point where memory management was no longer feasible, first ObjectStore and later GemStone was chosen as the OO database management system in which the GIDB database spatial data was stored.

When Java made its debut in 1995, the DMAP team began monitoring its usefulness in Internet-based capabilities. The DMAP team began work on Internet-based digital-mapping capabilities in 1997. This work has resulted in the GIDB Java mapping application and applet, which gives users access to mapping data via the Internet. Given the success of the GIDB mapping application and the growth and stability of the Java programming language, the DMAP team migrated all GIDB database and system code from Smalltalk to Java in 2001. The database component of the GIDB database is now implemented in an Open Source, all-Java, OO database management system called Ozone. Information on Ozone, including documentation and downloads, is available at http://www.ozone-db.org/.

The GIDB database, implemented in Ozone, is able to store spatial data from a variety of sources. Most of the mapping data in the GIDB database is obtained from the National Imagery and Mapping Agency (NIMA). Other data sources include the Naval Oceanographic Office, the U.S. Geological Survey, the National Ocean Survey, the U.S. Census Bureau, and the U.S. Army Corps of Engineers. The most common format of GIS data that can be read by the GIDB System and stored in the database is vector data such as NIMA's Vector Product Format (VPF) (NIMA 1996) and ESRI's Shapefile format (ESRI 1998). The GIDB System can also read in images, audio clips, video clips, and specialized text or binary files. Each data type is ingested into a common object model for uniform retrieval. This common object model was designed primarily to facilitate data retrieval in a mapping environment and so it organizes data in terms of scale, thematic layers, and feature classification types. The structure generally follows the organization of VPF data, the most complex and common data type in the GIDB database. The combination of data structure and spatial indexing facilitates storage of data with worldwide coverage and efficient retrieval for a given area of interest.

Since its inception, the GIDB System has been gradually moving from a monolithic to a truly distributed database system. The latest step in this migration has been the development of the GIDB portal, which allows for connection to and retrieval from many disparate databases, in addition to the GIDB Ozone database. With the widespread use of the Internet, many new sources of geospatial data are available for access. Since storage of the plethora of new data available within a single database system would be impractical, the DMAP team has instead focused on accessing these data sources directly through a GIDB portal. The GIDB portal establishes a common data request format and a common data transfer format. The GIDB mapping application, as well as any other application that interfaces with this common data transfer format, is able to make use of the data that the portal accesses. Use of the GIDB portal allows retrieval of data from many existing data repositories, regardless of whether they are relational, hybrid, or pure OO database management systems. It is important to note that no changes are required by the data source providers in order for the GIDB portal to access the data. All translation of the data from native format to the common transfer format occurs within the portal. For each new type of data source, a driver is written to perform this translation, and this new driver becomes a part of the overall GIDB portal. Each driver provides a common interface between the data source and the GIDB System, hiding the underlying details of how the data source is accessed. Figure 13.1 shows the overall GIDB System architecture.

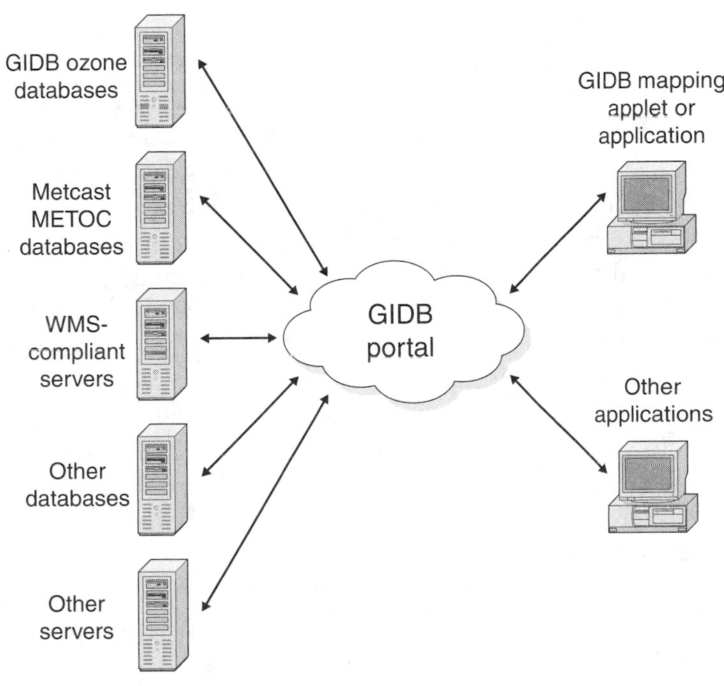

Figure 13.1 Basic GIDB System Architecture

The overwhelming success of the GIDB System has been due in part to its ability to take advantage of new technologies and standards as they become available. The focus of the rest of this chapter is on how the GIDB System has utilized XML (Walmsley 2002) and XML-based standards to expand its mapping portal capabilities. Initially, a driver was written for the portal to access meteorological and oceanographic data, using an XML catalog to determine the available data and how to retrieve it. Additionally, the DMAP team developed a driver to allow for a portal connection to OpenGIS Consortium (OGC) Web Map Service (WMS) compliant data providers on the Internet. Finally, the DMAP team has implemented the capability to read and write vector data in the OGC's Geographic Markup Language (GML) format (Cox et al. 2001), an XML-based specification for standard data interchange with other Geographic Information System (GIS) applications.

13.2 GIDB METOC Data Integration

In this section we describe the integration of Meteorological and Oceanographic (METOC) data into the GIDB System.

13.2.1 Background

METOC data is remotely retrieved via Metcast (DII 2001), which is a system for the distribution of METOC data to the navy developed by the Fleet Numerical Meteorology and Oceanography Center (FNMOC). Metcast is a client/server architecture in which the Metcast server application serves data from a METOC database containing a variety of products, including satellite imagery and model outputs of weather and ocean conditions describing the current and future state of the environment around the globe. The server publishes a catalog of currently available products. This catalog is in XML format and describes the database's hierarchy of products and an appropriate set of metadata parameters for each product. A Metcast client may request a catalog from any known Metcast server and then, using the catalog to identify desired products, request those products. Products are requested using a Metcast-specific request language, the Metcast Broker Language (MBL), which, although not XML itself, closely mirrors the structure of the XML catalog. The server returns the requested products to the client in their native formats.

The products available from the Metcast server are arranged according to the Metcast data model—that is, they're arranged hierarchically, grouping products into sets and subsets as shown in Figure 13.2. A real catalog would typically be populated with a much larger selection of products.

The products are grouped first according to type, whether they are satellite images or grids. Gridded products are outputs from meteorological and oceanographic models, which describe current and future conditions of the atmosphere or oceans by describing their state at gridded intervals over some area. Images are grouped according to area and then, within that, are described by the specific product type such as an infrared or a visible image. Grids are first grouped by the production center (the agency that generated it), then by the model that produced it, and then by the particular parameter it describes such as winds or temperature. Finally, grids are fully specified by the specific level and tau. Level represents the specific altitude within the atmosphere, and tau represents the number of hours into the future relative to the time of the model run that the grid describes.

The Metcast catalog is hierarchically structured according to this scheme. It describes elements corresponding to the nodes of this hierarchy with their appropriate attributes as specified in the Metcast Catalog Document Type Definition (DTD). For example, the model element has associated attributes describing its

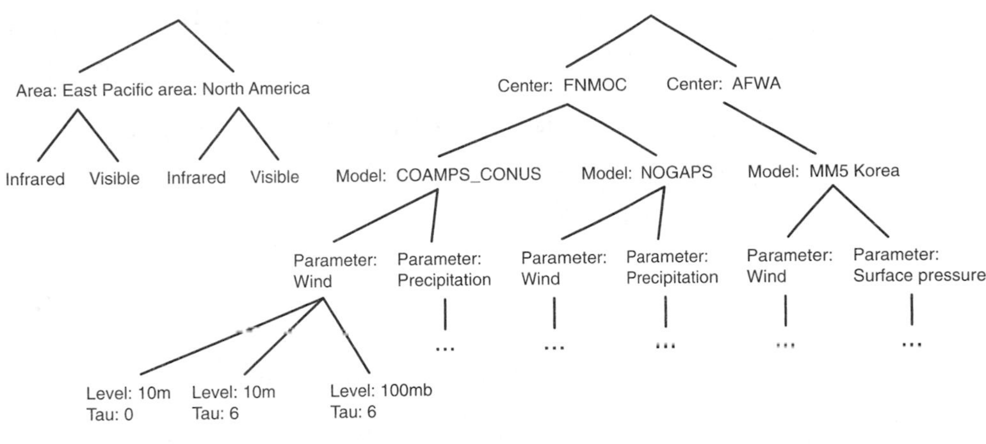

Figure 13.2 Products Arranged According to the Metcast Data Model

resolution in the x and y directions, and the parameter element has an attribute specifying the units.

When a user selects a product or set of products, the Metcast client software must generate an MBL request specifying the product or products. MBL is a relatively simple text-based request language in which each request is in the form of an S-expression (DII 2001). Each request specifies the product or products by designating an area of interest for which a data product is desired and a set of attributes fully describing the desired product for that area.

13.2.2 Implementation

In the existing Metcast system, a standalone Metcast client application uses Metcast's protocols for acquiring data products from the remote server. Our goal was to add Metcast connectivity to the GIDB System, extending its functionality so that it behaved as a Metcast client, allowing for the seamless integration of METOC data. The user would be able to browse up-to-date information on atmospheric and oceanic conditions side by side with data extracted from other local and remote geospatial data sources. To accomplish this we developed a GIDB Metcast driver, essentially a software bridge between the two systems. The GIDB System requires a standard interface to access any one of its data stores. The driver provides this common interface, hiding the underlying details of how the data source is accessed.

The general process of acquiring products from Metcast (or any other data source) is illustrated in Figure 13.3 and involves the following:

- Available products are discovered (a catalog is acquired from Metcast).
- Desired products are requested.
- Requested products are delivered.

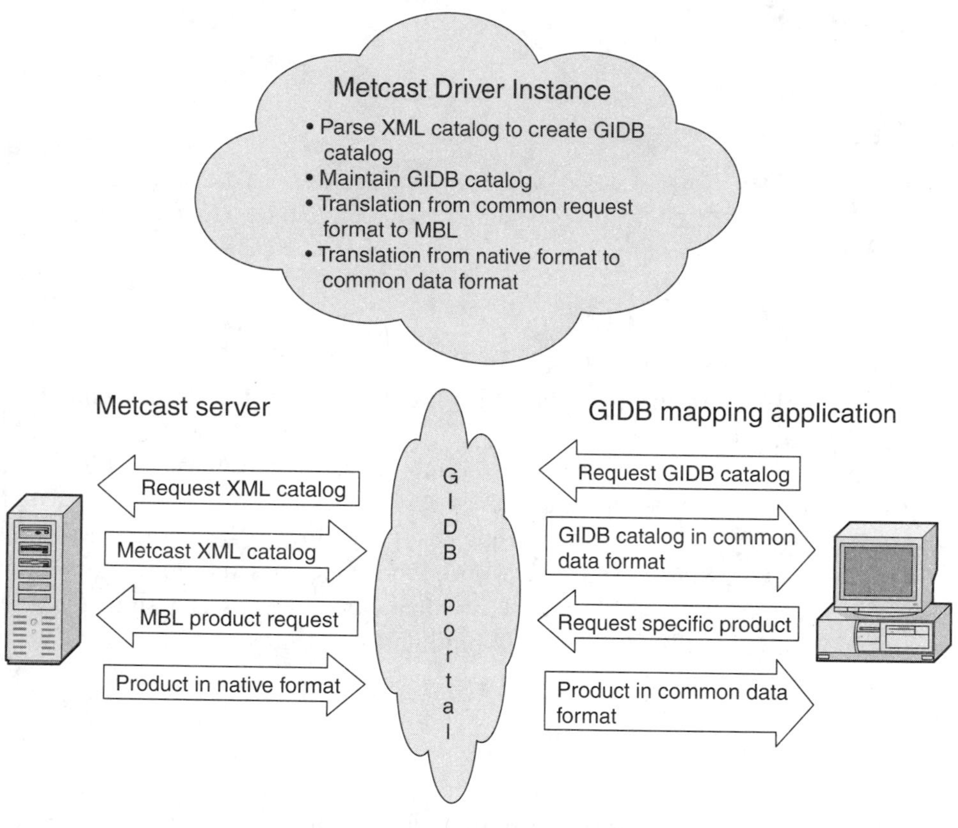

Figure 13.3 Complete Set of Steps to Acquire a Data Product from Metcast

During this process, the Metcast driver has three principal translations to perform:

1. To translate the organization of products in the Metcast catalog into the organizational form in which they are delivered through the GIDB portal
2. To translate GIDB mapping application requests for products to Metcast's MBL requests for products

3. To translate the resulting products from the native formats in which they are delivered to the GIDB portal's common data transfer format

Since the Metcast catalog is an XML document, we will consider the first translation in detail. We will also touch upon the second. As Metcast data products are returned in a non-XML format, we will not discuss the third translation here.

First, let us consider the translation from the Metcast catalog to the GIDB portal's catalog. This portal's catalog structures data products into the following hierarchy: Database—Library (or scale)—Coverage (or thematic layer)—Feature Class—Feature. An example of this structure is shown in Figure 13.4.

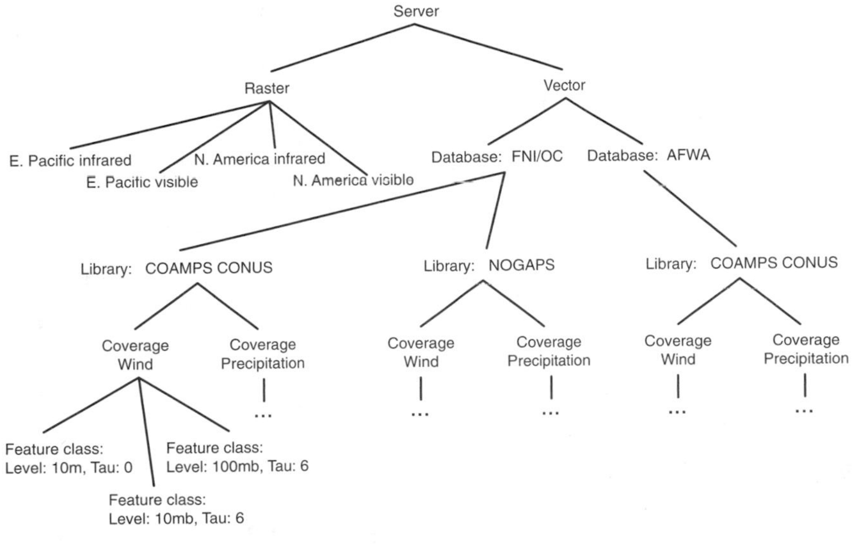

Figure 13.4 Metcast Data Products Organized According to the GIDB Data Model

The GIDB mapping application allows the user to select products of interest by navigating through the hierarchy, selecting a database, then selecting a library, and so on, down to individual products. For databases that the GIDB System maintains locally within Ozone, the data can actually be structured in this hierarchy. For Metcast, however, we have no control over how the data are structured. A catalog is received and organized according to the Metcast structure. Therefore, the GIDB Metcast driver must transform this hierarchy into the GIDB hierarchy. The user navigates the new GIDB hierarchy until a product is selected.

Translating the Metcast catalog is a two-step process. Since good third-party XML parsers already exist, we do not wish to directly parse the XML catalog ourselves. Instead we use the Apache Xerces XML parser to generate a Document Object Model (DOM) tree. The DOM tree is a generic object-oriented Java tree embodying the same structure and information as the original XML document. This DOM tree forms the input to our mapping. The driver applies a series of transformations to the tree that navigate down through its hierarchy. As the navigation proceeds, a new GIDB catalog tree is constructed, embodying the same information but in a new structure. The new tree could also be a DOM tree. In fact, for convenience's sake, we developed our own tree node objects with convenient helper methods, including methods useful for navigating geospatial data (such as queries for the minimum-bounding-rectangle circumscribing the data under a node). Figure 13.5 shows an example of the DOM-to-GIDB mapping process. The XML sample is slightly simplified from the original. The actual catalog contains some additional information that is not relevant to our purposes.

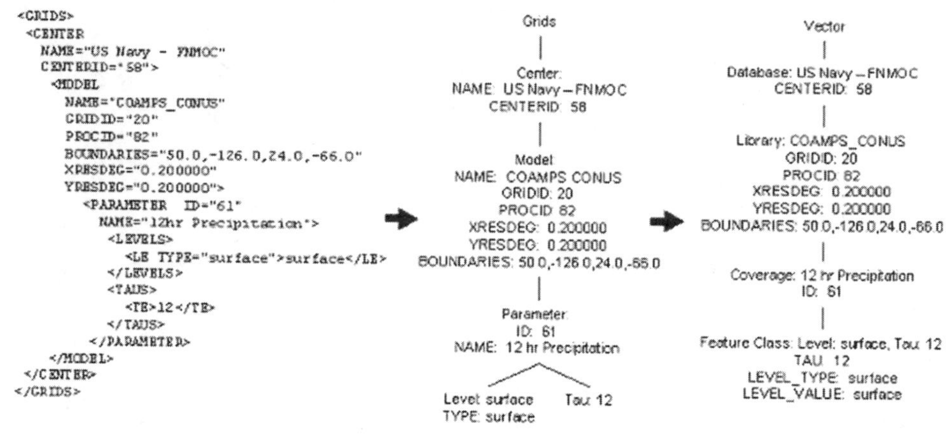

Figure 13.5 Mapping from a Catalog Entry to a DOM Tree Branch to a GIDB Tree Branch

For example, the *Center* element of the Metcast DOM tree is mapped to a *Database* node in the GIDB tree. The database node is given the center ID and Name attributes from the *Center*. When the driver navigates down to a DOM tree *Model* node, a new GIDB *Library* node is built. The Grid ID, Process ID, and resolution attributes from the original *Model* are added to the new *Database*. This process continues down each level of the tree and continues until each branch of the DOM tree has been navigated down to each leaf and a completely new GIDB tree has been constructed representing the equivalent information. This new tree is the GIDB catalog that the Metcast driver will use to inform the GIDB mapping application user of the products that are available.

Once the user has navigated through the GIDB catalog tree and identified a particular product of interest, another translation must occur. This translation entails taking the user's selection from the GIDB catalog tree and constructing an MBL request that is meaningful to the Metcast system. The selection of a product in the GIDB catalog tree is the request, and the complete branch that leads to this product is the full specification of the product and forms the basis of the translation from the GIDB request to the Metcast MBL request (see Figure 13.6). The "bounding-box" in the MBL request is the area for which data is requested. It must be a subset of the boundaries of the requested product.

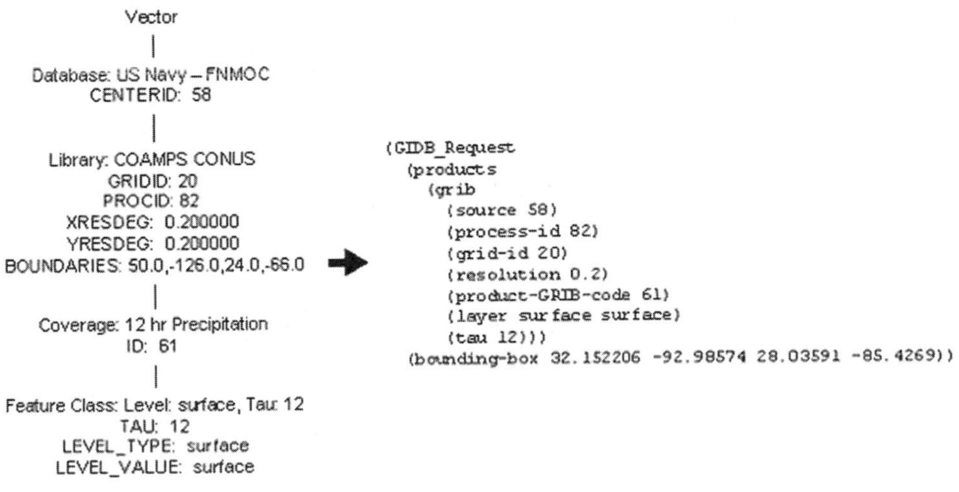

Figure 13.6 Mapping from a GIDB Tree Branch to an MBL Request

When generating the MBL request, the driver traverses the given branch from its leaf node (the product) to the root, extracting relevant attributes about the product and using them to construct a request. We will not go into the details of the S-expression syntax of the MBL statement, but a quick visual inspection (see Listing 13.1) shows that it embodies information in the original XML document describing the product (see Listing 13.2).

Listing 13.1 MBL Request

```
(GIDB_Request
  (products
    (grib
      (source 58)
      (process-id 82)
      (grid-id 20)
      (resolution 0.2)
      (product-GRIB-code 61)
```

```
      (layer surface surface)
      (tau 12)))
    (bounding-box 32.152206 -92.98574 28.03591 -85.4269))
```

Listing 13.2 Original Catalog Entry

```
<GRIDS Timestamp="1003338720">
 <CENTER
   NAME="US Navy - FNMOC"
   CENTERID="58">
    <MODEL
      NAME="COAMPS_CONUS"
      GRIDID="20"
      PROCID="82"
      BOUNDARIES="50.0,-126.0,24.0,-66.0"
      XRESDEG="0.200000"
      YRESDEG="0.200000">
        <PARAMETER  ID="61"
          NAME="12hr Precipitation">
           <LEVELS>
             <LE TYPE="surface">surface</LE>
           </LEVELS>
           <TAUS>
             <TE>12</TE>
           </TAUS>
        </PARAMETER>
    </MODEL>
 </CENTER>
</GRIDS>
```

The request is sent to the server, which in turn delivers the appropriate product back to the client. This last step completes the process for retrieving a product. Figure 13.7 shows a display screen of data retrieved through this process. The data in the figure was retrieved via Metcast and displayed in the GIDB application.

The Metcast catalog in XML provides fundamental information about the available products and their organization, forming the basis of the product retrieval process. The GIDB Metcast driver uses this information, transforming it into another scheme. Products are selected and mapped back to Metcast's scheme. These translations all occur behind the scenes, allowing a user of the GIDB System to access Metcast data without any knowledge of the disparate data models and protocols.

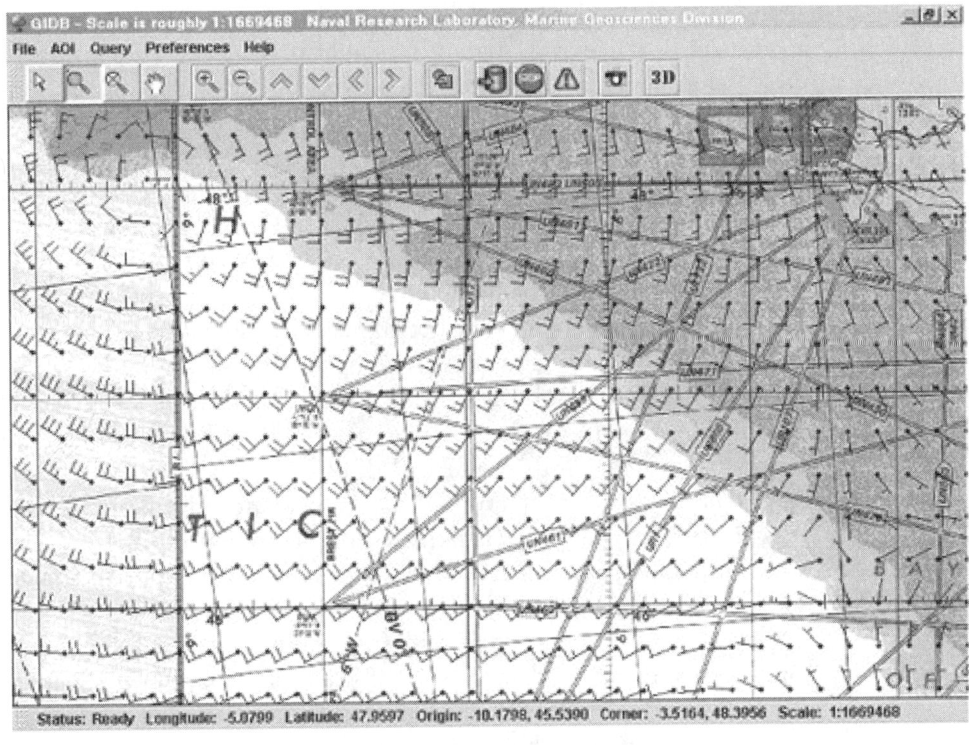

Figure 13.7 A View of the Winds off the West Coast of France

13.3 GIDB Web Map Service Implementation

In this section, we will look at the OpenGIS Consortium's (OGC) Web Map Service (WMS) Interface Specification and how it is utilized within the GIDB System. This specification is a set of open protocols that allow Web map servers to provide uniform services to HTML clients. By definition of the specification, a Web map server has three basic responsibilities:

1. Publish a list of maps it can provide, together with the query abilities of each.
2. Reply to queries concerning map content.
3. Generate a map.

Actual map data can be provided in a number of formats, including pictures or images, basic graphical elements (vector), or sets of geographic feature data. The standardization of map requests can allow users, via HTML clients, to create custom layered maps with information from possibly different Web map servers.

Requests are submitted through Web browsers in the form of uniform resource locators (URLs). The URL parameters indicate relevant request information, such as the portion of the earth to be mapped, coordinate system, output format, map and location to be queried, or the holdings of a particular server. A map server provides three interfaces: Capabilities, Map, and FeatureInfo. The Capabilities and Map interfaces are required for conformance to the WMS specification, while the implementation of a FeatureInfo interface is optional. The Capabilities interface provides clients with machine-parseable lists of supported interfaces, map layers, and formats. Capabilities must be provided in an XML format to be considered conformant. The Map interface provides the actual maps to clients. To do this, the interface may possibly access multiple map servers. If the request cannot be satisfied, the server must throw an exception according to instructions received in the request. The FeatureInfo interface provides clients with additional information about points in maps that were previously returned as a result of a Map request. The map server developer is free to determine the information to be returned in response to a FeatureInfo request (detailed information for developers can be found in the *OpenGIS Web Map Server Interface Implementation Specification* at http://www.opengis.org/).

A GIDB portal driver was written to allow the GIDB mapping application to connect to and retrieve data from WMS-compliant map servers. Currently, the GIDB portal driver for WMS servers only implements the required request interfaces: Capabilities and Map. The FeatureInfo request interface is not implemented since it is optional, and at the time of initial development, no WMS servers could be found that provided this interface.

It is possible to connect to many WMS-compliant servers at the same time. To accomplish this, a driver instance is registered with the GIDB portal by submitting a URL request for the Capabilities interface. The WMS server should respond with a Capabilities XML document that complies with the WMS Capabilities DTD (http://www.digitalearth.gov/wmt/xml/capabilities_1_1_1.dtd). The driver software then parses the Capabilities XML document using the Apache Xerces XML parser. The Capabilities XML document contains information about the layers of mapping data available, the coordinate reference systems used, the geographic bounds the data covers, and how the data can be retrieved. As the GIDB portal driver parses the document, it translates the information into a structure that facilitates rapid understanding of available data and quick retrieval by the GIDB mapping application.

The driver instance maintains an array of geographical layer objects as a result of parsing the Capabilities XML document. A geographical layer object is defined to have a unique name, descriptive title, output map format, data location URL, and minimum geographic bounding rectangle. Listing 13.3 is an example of a layer in a Capabilities XML document.

Listing 13.3 Example of a Geographical Layer

```
<Layer>
  <Title>The GLOBE Program Visualization Server</Title>
  <SRS>EPSG:4326 AUTO:42003 AUTO:42005</SRS>
  <LatLonBoundingBox minx="-180" miny="-90" maxx="180" maxy="90" />
  <Layer>
    <Title>Physiography</Title>
    <Layer queryable="0">
      <Name>RTOPO</Name>
      <Title>Topography and Bathymetry</Title>
      <Abstract>Topography and Bathymetry. Availability:
special,19941231.  Units: m.</Abstract>
    </Layer>
  </Layer>
</Layer>
```

In Listing 13.3, the *Topography and Bathymetry* layer inherits its bounding box from its parent layer. The resulting geographical layer object that is created and maintained in the driver instance is defined in Listing 13.4.

Listing 13.4 Resulting Geographical Layer in the Driver Instance

```
Name: RTOPO
Title: Topography and Bathymetry
Map Format: PNG: Topography and Bathymetry
Data URL: http://viz.globe.gov/viz-bin/wmt.cgi?
Bounding Box: -180, -90, 180, 90
```

The GIDB portal uses the array of geographical layers to determine which map data, if any, exists in the user's area of interest. Since the GIDB WMS implementation does not include FeatureInfo requests, the only types of maps returned by WMS-compliant servers will be image or raster maps such as JPEG, GIF, TIFF, and PNG image formats. These map images can then be displayed in the GIDB mapping application and overlaid with data from other sources.

To utilize the GIDB WMS portal driver, the GIDB mapping application will first ask the WMS driver instance for a list of its available map formats. This list is obtained from the output map formats in the geographical layer object array. Examples of map formats include topographic map layer, elevation data layer, aerial photography layer, and water bodies layer. When a user of the GIDB mapping application selects a particular map format for display, the request is sent to the WMS driver instance. The driver instance will then structure the WMS URL request based on the selected geographical layer object and the user's area of interest. A sample URL request is shown in Listing 13.5.

Listing 13.5 Example URL Request

```
http://viz.globe.gov/viz-
bin/wmt.cgi?&request=map&wmtver=1.0&SRS=EPSG:4326&LAYERS=RTOPO&BBOX
=-
134.08163,15.81284,-
57.857143,54.901443&WIDTH=1024&HEIGHT=641&STYLES=default&FORMAT=-
PNG&TRANSPARENT=TRUE
```

Given this request, the WMS-compliant server will return a PNG image, which can then be displayed in the GIDB mapping application, as shown in Figure 13.8.

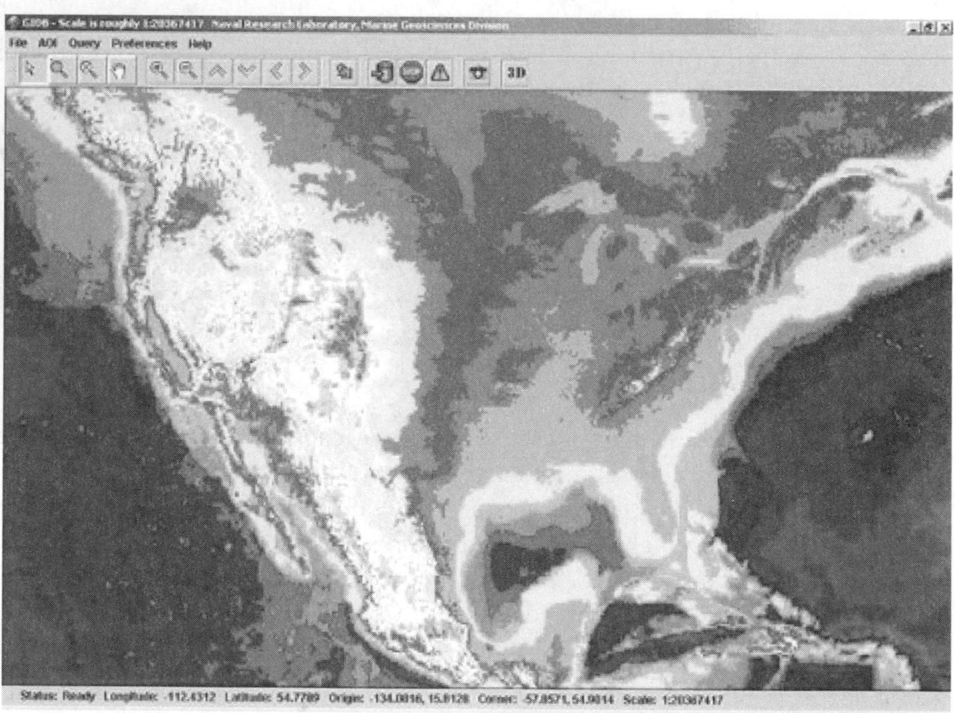

Figure 13.8 The Display within the GIDB Mapping Application of a PNG Image that Was Returned from a WMS-Compliant ServerRequest

A summary of the GIDB WMS architecture is shown in Figure 13.9. Note its similarity to the Metcast architecture shown earlier in Figure 13.3.

The WMS specification provides a standard mechanism for map data interchange over the Internet. This technology uses XML, coupled with URL requests, to provide georeferenced map images. The implementation of a WMS driver for the GIDB portal has demonstrated that this XML-enabled technology can be used to successfully integrate mapping data from many distinct and disparate databases over the Internet into a single application for display and analysis.

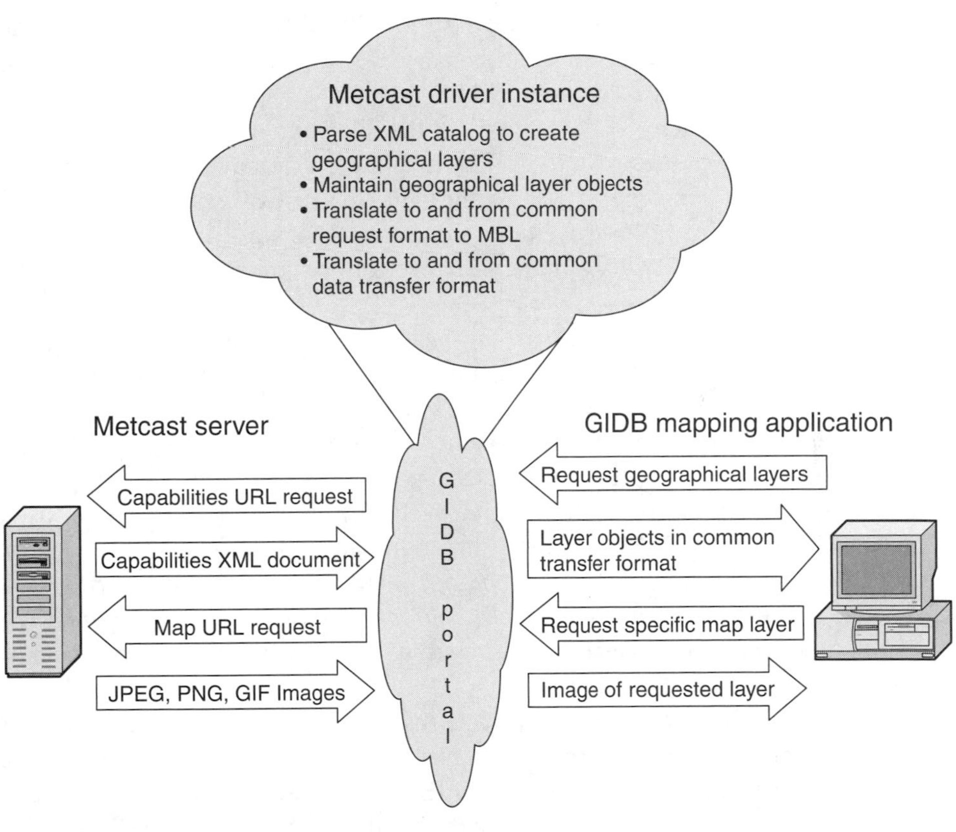

Figure 13.9 GIDB WMS Architecture

13.4 GIDB GML Import and Export

GML represents a continuation of the OpenGIS Consortium's work in interoperable geoprocessing through interface specifications. GML is an XML extension that allows developers to encode geographic information for both transfer and storage. The XML base provides a means to separate the actual geographic data from the representation or visualization of the data, and ensures that the data is accessible by a large variety of software systems. GML is comprised of three base XML schema documents: general feature-property model (feature.xsd), detailed geometry components (geometry.xsd), and XLink attributes (xlinks.xsd). An application schema is needed to declare the application-specific feature types that are derived from types in the standard GML schemas.

The GIDB System now has the ability to export any of the available vector data to GML in the form of an instance document (.XML) with a corresponding application schema document (.XSD). The GML application schema developed for the GIDB System was written to be flexible enough to include any point, line, or area vector features with the ability to add more complex vector types in the future. The application schema will be the same for all GML exports, but clearly the instance document will be specific to the data set that was exported. The GIDB System's ability to import GML data is still a work in progress and will be completed in the near future.

We will now describe the design behind the application schema document with target namespace, "*gidb.*" Namespaces are case sensitive and used to provide a container for names used in XML. For example, "*gml:AbstractFeatureType*" is the syntax used to represent the element "*AbstractFeatureType*" that is defined in the GML namespace, "`gml.`" Our GML application schema vector features were designed to be a good fit with the existing vector feature objects in the database interface module of the GIDB System as shown in Table 13.1.

The root element in the *gidb* namespace is *FeatureCollection,* which is derived from *gml:AbstractFeatureCollectionType. gidb:FeatureCollection* contains *gml* namespace elements *description, name, boundedBy*, and zero or more *featureMembers* as shown in Figure 13.10.

The feature type *gidb:VectorFeatureType*, derived from *gml:AbstractFeatureType*, is the base for the concrete feature types *PointFeatureType, LineFeatureType*, and *AreaFeatureType* (all in the `gidb` namespace). The *gidb:VectorFeatureType* contains zero or more abstract *gidb:_featureAttribute* elements as well as the *gml:AbstractFeatureType* elements it inherits (see Figure 13.11). The *gidb:_featureAttribute* elements are used to describe the feature attribute name and value pairs for a feature as in the fragment of GML instance code from the `gidb` namespace shown in Listing 13.6.

Table 13.1 Comparison of GIDB SystemVector Feature Objects to GML Application Schema Vector Features

GIDB System VectorFeature (Java)	GIDB-GML VectorFeature (XML)
FeatureAttribute[n] (array of n attributes)	gidb:_featureAttribute (n attribute elements)
name	gidb:featureAttributeName
value	gidb:featureAttributeValue
BoundingBox	gml:boundedBy
minX, minY	gml:box
maxX, maxY	gml:coordinates (pair of coordinate tuples)
POINT as Point2DFloat[1][1]	pointFeature as gidb:PointFeatureType
(single coordinate tuple)	gml:PointType
x, y	gml:coordinates (single coordinate tuple)
LINE as Point2DFloat[m][n] (m line segments, n points in each segment) x, y	lineFeature as gidb:LineFeatureType gml:MultiLineStringType gml:lineStringMember (1 or more) gml:coordinates (2 or more coordinate tuples)
AREA as Point2DFloat[m][n] (m rings, n points in each ring) x, y	areaFeature as gidb:AreaFeatureType gml:MultiPolygonType gml:polygonMember (1 or more) gml:coordinates (2 or more coordinate tuples)

Listing 13.6 Fragment of GML Instance Code

```
<featureAttributeInteger>
  <featureAttributeName>Population</featureAttributeName>
  <featureAttributeValue>45000</featureAttributeValue>
</featureAttributeInteger>
```

The use of substitution groups with feature attributes simplifies content models and allows us to substitute the abstract *gidb:_featureAttribute* with concrete subtypes. The head of the substitution group is *gidb:_featureAttribute,* and *featureAttributeString, featureAttribute-Integer, featureAttributeDecimal*, and

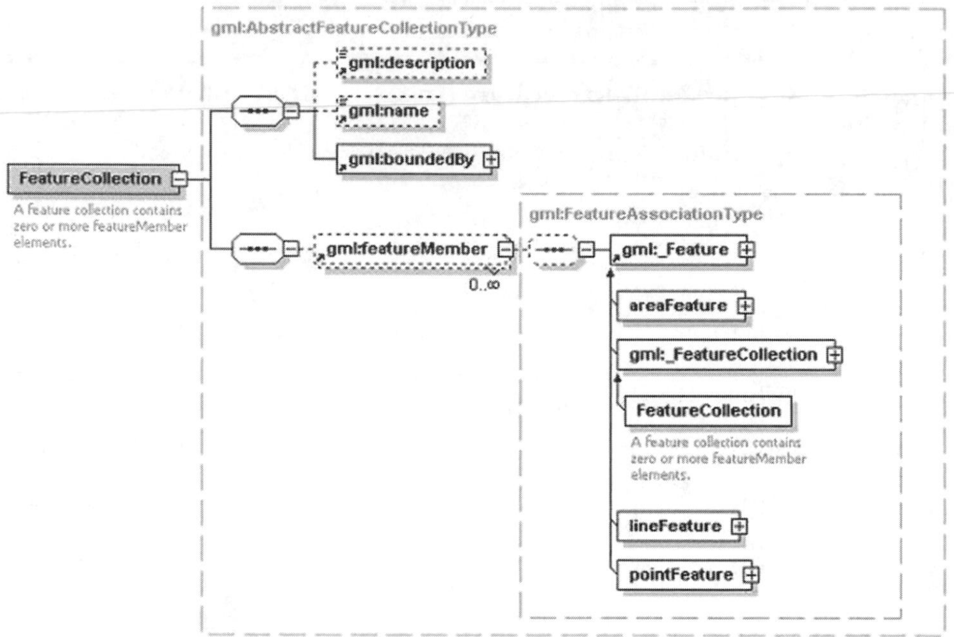

Figure 13.10 FeatureCollection Content Model

featureAttributeDate are the members (all in the `gidb` namespace). This means that any of the members of the substitution group can be substituted in place of the head.

The XML code shown in Listing 13.7, taken from our `gidb` namespace application schema `gidb.xsd`, shows how the feature attributes with string or integer values are defined and included in the base feature type `gidb:VectorFeatureType`. The feature attribute types for decimal and date, omitted in Listing 13.7, are defined in the same manner as strings and integers.

Listing 13.7 XML Code from gidb Namespace

```
<element name="_featureAttribute"
type="gidb:AbstractFeatureAttributeType" abstract="true"/>

<element name="featureAttributeString" type=
"gidb:FeatureAttributeStringType"
```

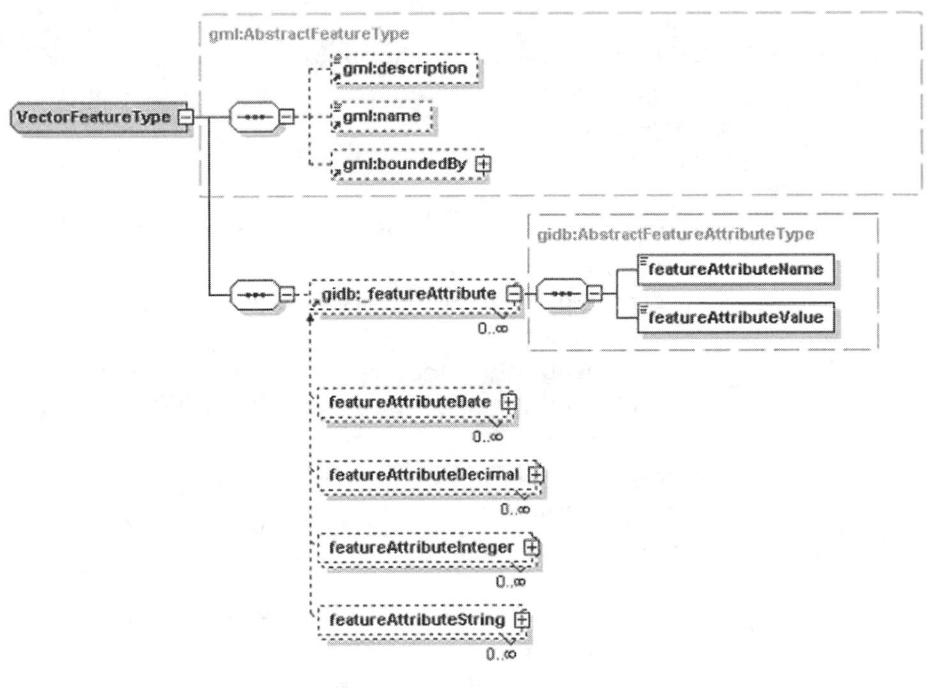

Figure 13.11 VectorFeatureType Content Model

```
substitutionGroup="gidb:_featureAttribute"/>

<complexType name="VectorFeatureType">
  <complexContent>
    <extension base="gml:AbstractFeatureType">
      <sequence>
        <element ref="gidb:_featureAttribute" minOccurs="0"
maxOccurs="unbounded"/>
      </sequence>
    </extension>
  </complexContent>
</complexType>
```

```
<complexType name="AbstractFeatureAttributeType" abstract="true">
  <sequence>
    <element name="featureAttributeName" type="string"/>
    <element name="featureAttributeValue" type="anySimpleType"/>
  </sequence>
</complexType>

<complexType name="FeatureAttributeStringType">
  <complexContent>
    <restriction base="gidb:AbstractFeatureAttributeType">
      <sequence>
        <element name="featureAttributeName" type="string"/>
        <element name="featureAttributeValue" type="string"/>
      </sequence>
    </restriction>
  </complexContent>
</complexType>

<complexType name="FeatureAttributeIntegerType">
  <complexContent>
    <restriction base="gidb:AbstractFeatureAttributeType">
      <sequence>
        <element name="featureAttributeName" type="string"/>
        <element name="featureAttributeValue" type="integer"/>
      </sequence>
    </restriction>
  </complexContent>
</complexType>
```

Types defined in the `gidb` namespace *PointFeatureType, LineFeatureType*, and *AreaFeatureType extend VectorFeatureType* by appending GML-specific geometry properties. *PointFeatureType* adds the element *gml:pointProperty; LineFeatureType* adds the elements *gml:lineStringProperty* and *gml:multiLineStringProperty*; and *AreaFeatureType* adds the elements *gml:polygonProperty* and *gml:multiPolygonProperty* to describe the geometry of the associated point, line, or area feature. The geometry elements of *PointFeatureType* are shown in Figure 13.12.

The GIDB System's GML export capability adds yet another way that we can interchange data with other standard GIS applications. Also, this use of industry-

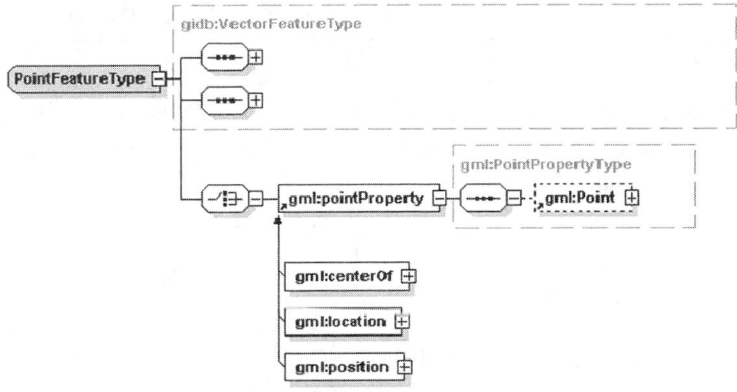

Figure 13.12 PointFeatureType Content Model (geometry only)

standard XML encoding in GML to transport and store geographic features opens up large stores of diverse data types to customers locally and throughout the world.

13.5 Conclusion

The decision to expand the GIDB capabilities to the realm of XML was first motivated by customer requirements. For the GIDB to retrieve Metcast data, the XML catalog must be utilized. Of course, the decision to publish the catalog in XML has had wide-ranging benefits, including the ability to express the information in a widely understood format and the ability to utilize standardized tools to interpret the information. Additionally, XML's hierarchical format is well suited for expressing a data model catalog such as that for Metcast. The Metcast Document Type Definition also allowed us to understand specific data structures, which provided a powerful tool for application development. The benefits of an XML-based approach to interoperability were readily apparent to team members by the end of the development process.

In this chapter, we have shown how XML-enabled technology has been used by the GIDB System to enhance the ability to exchange geographical data over the Internet. The GIDB System has demonstrated successful retrieval of meteorological and oceanographic data using a METOC community XML catalog and retrieval system. Implementation of the OpenGIS WMS specification has allowed the display of georeferenced map layers from numerous WMS-compliant servers on the Internet. In addition, the ability to import and export vector data in standard GML format will make it possible for any GML-enabled application to utilize data from the GIDB Ozone database repository.

The need for interoperability and geographical data exchange is very important in the GIS domain. The Internet provides a wealth of geographic data sources, and the DMAP team has worked to provide access to this data through the GIDB System. Use of XML-enabled technology has been a contributing factor to the pursuit and continuing achievement of this goal.

Chapter 14

Space Wide Web by Adapters in Distributed Systems Configuration from Reusable Components

David C. Rine

14.1 Introduction

Human exploration and development of space will involve opening the space frontier by exploring, using, and enabling the development of space through information technology, while expanding the human experience into the far reaches of space. At that point in time we assert that the current primitive World Wide Web (Web) will be replaced and dramatically expanded into an interstellar Space Wide Web (SWW). The current state-of-the-art low-orbit communications satellites constellations will be dramatically expanded to higher orbits and to orbits supporting work on remote human colonies. This will be necessary in order to furnish in a human-friendly way the necessary software and information that will be needed in support of interstellar spacewide information technologies. Many of the problems encountered in conceiving of, modeling, designing, and deploying such a facility will be different from those problems encountered in today's Web. Future research and development work will be to identify some of these problems and to conceptually model a few of their solutions. In this work we describe research into the development of scalable tools and techniques that reduce the effort associated with component integration, both with respect to network environments and with respect to other components within the application. Our approach is also targeted at increasing the reusability of software components and software architectures. Our research is to investigate current problems in leveraging adapters as a means to configure large-scale next-generation distributed systems software from reusable architectures and components. Our approach to solving this problem is through the development of a novel configuration model and network-aware runtime environment called SWWACXML, an abbreviation for Space Wide Web Adapter Configuration eXtensible Markup Language. SWWACXML provides support for cross-layer architectural configuration at both the application level and the level of individual network connections. The language associated with this environment captures component interaction properties and network-level QoS constraints. Adapters will be generated automatically from SWWACXML specifications. These adapters are part of the SWWACXML runtime system. The runtime system includes facilities for automatic configuration and runtime reconfiguration, as well as efficient management of network connections and QoS options. This facilitates reuse because components are not tied to interactions or environments. Another aspect of this work will focus on development and experimentation with a novel Web-based interaction paradigm that allows client adapters to tailor themselves to servers at runtime. One of the strengths of our approach is that clients do not have to be tied to specific servers at implementation time. Rather, a client's adapter loads an SWWACXML configuration page from the server. The SWWACXML configuration page defines the appropriate interaction, including management of heterogeneous network QoS options. We believe our approach is amenable to facilitate a style of dynamic reconfiguration, where clients can at runtime change server, communication, or interaction protocol. Future researchers and developers will design and implement the SWWACXML system in a distributed test bed. They will develop performance analysis techniques to judge the success and efficiency of our approach.

14.2 Advanced Concept Description: The Research Problem

Twenty-first century Space Wide Web (SWW) distributed component-based software applications will dwarf today's increasingly complex World Wide Web (WWW) environments, supported by earth-bound low-orbit satellite constellations, and will represent a far more significant investment in terms of development costs, deployment, and maintenance. As we now move into the twenty-first century, part of the cost will come in the effort required to develop, deploy, and maintain the individual software components. Many of these components will be on numerous remote satellites. As now, part of this effort will include implementing the required functionality of components, implementing the required interactions for components, and preparing components to operate in some remote runtime environment. One way to reduce the cost of component development will continue to be the reuse of existing commercial software components that meet the functional requirements. However, in either approach (SWW or Web), the task of integrating these components into vast twenty-first century spacewide distributed systems will be even more substantial because reasoning about and implementing the interactions in such distributed software systems is even now a complex process, even if the underlying communication mechanisms are homogeneous (Bonsard et al. 1997; Garlan et al. 1995).

Once a space application has been fielded, the cost of maintaining and extending this application can be substantial. One common maintenance change made to existing applications is porting to a new environment. However, because new space community environments potentially involve many differences in communication mechanisms and in underlying spacewide networks, making such a change is not trivial. Replacement of existing components is also a common maintenance upgrade, but this can be difficult, particularly if the signature of some service either used or provided is different from signatures of clients.

For these reasons, developing ways to increase the reusability both of the software components and of the applications' architectures is vital. The current benefits of reusing components are many; the development cost is amortized over multiple applications, and if we make no changes to the component, the testing obligations for this component are generally minimal (Rine and Sonnemann 1996, 1998).

There is also a great deal of interest in the idea of reusing the architecture of the applications themselves. The development of new products from the product-line reusable architecture (Rine and Sonnemann 1998) assumes that the following scenario or one similar to it has taken place. Suppose a company has a product that is doing well in the market. Because of an identified possible expansion of the current customer base, a conservative expansion of the current product is formulated by identifying a few variation points based on a variety of new services or functions (Jaber, Rine 1998; Jaber, Nada 1998; Nada and Rine 1998; Nada et al. 1998). Thereafter, the company develops an experience-based software architecture as the centerpiece of this expanding market's new products. Taking advantage of the variation points then leverages the reuse of this architecture.

The product-line reusable architecture is, therefore, initially comprised of abstract components and connectors representing the topology of the architecture and applications (products) to be derived from it (Abowd et al. 1995; Allen and Garlan 1997; Garlan et al. 1995; Shaw and Garlan 1996). At the endpoints of certain connectors, there are specifications of variation points where adapters will be introduced (Jaber, Rine 1998; Jaber, Nada 1998). The variation points were determined as part of the requirements of the software architecture and were selected in cooperation between market and development departments as variations between new product releases. An adapter in the design represents the specification of each variation point in the requirements. The representation of each adapter is incomplete, since at this point adapters that are supposed to communicate and interact with each other on behalf of corresponding components' services have not been introduced. And none of the numerous syntactical mismatches between client and server signatures has yet been resolved.

Unfortunately, neither of these two types of reuse is adequately supported with current technologies. The software architecture and its details are usually not explicitly defined; rather they are implicit in the software components' implementations, making it difficult to reuse. Components are difficult to reuse as well because they are tied to runtime environments and to interactions and must often be modified before reuse. The issue of reuse is even more difficult for components where only the interface of the component is available (e.g., COTs products) (Brown and Wallnau 1996; Clements 1995; Dellarocas 1997a, 1997b).

In this early stage there will be research into the development of scalable tools and techniques that increase the reusability of software components and software architectures. The approach should be based on the idea of developing adapters outside (i.e., external to) components to interconnect and isolate their interactions in message-based systems supporting the utilization of many components. These adapters also need to be quality of service aware in order to allow interoperation over entirely different network types. The requirements of the component interfaces and of the interactions are expressed separately from the component, meaning that we can generate adapters automatically. Because interconnection and interaction issues are addressed separately and implemented automatically, this method decreases the components' perceived complexity, increases their reusability, and simplifies their integration.

Before describing the adapter-based approach to software configuration, a more detailed description is made of the issues that make integration in a component-based system difficult and provide a simple telecommunications-based example. This example is used to illustrate some of the integration problems and how adapters can be used to solve these problems.

14.2.1 Future Supporting Communications Satellites Constellations

In this section we will discuss issues and requirements for a Space Wide Web.

A Scenario Using Future SWW

Considering a future scenario involving planetary and deep space satellites motivates the need for an adaptive Web-based configuration language. Assume that several teams of researchers are scattered across Mars, and that communication between these researchers is supported by a constellation of low-orbit communication satellites, like the present LEOS. Further, suppose that there is a deep space probe exploring the asteroid zone between Mars and Jupiter. Scientists on both Mars and earth would like to be able to dynamically access data from this probe, via a relay between their low-orbit constellations and a ground- or space-based relay station. This access can include running different sets of measurements, changing sensor configuration, and so on. Further, when appropriate, earth scientists would like to share results with their Mars colleagues using push technology, and vice versa. Finally, scientists will want to run their experiments on the deep space probe by writing and then loading the equivalent of a Java-like applet onto the probe.

This scenario raises a number of technological challenges. First, the earth-based and Mars-based scientists may have quite different capabilities in terms of the type and amount of data they can receive from the probe. It may even be desirable to first send the data to earth, have it processed, and then send it back up to Mars. Second, all space-based communication is costly in terms of power consumption, available bandwidth, and round-trip propagation delay. Finally, the dynamics of this situation change due to factors such as changing orbits and relative positions. For instance, it may be better for the probe at times to send to Mars, or to earth, or both. These routing decisions are based upon both the needs of the application and the physical configuration of the communication satellites. In order to make appropriate use of minimal bandwidth and limited power, it is desirable that these semantics are directly reflected from the application down to the network layer. The challenge is to do this in a way that both does not unduly burden the application writer (i.e., the scientist writing the satellite applet) and also makes appropriate usage of network resources. This is possible by developing the SWW-XML and by placing communication control in the appropriate adapters.

Current Low-Orbit Communications Satellite Constellations

The present state-of-the-art low-orbit communications satellite constellations around earth are an integrated combination of ground stations, gateways, uplinks, downlinks, planes, sequences of links between satellites (online and backup), commercial and government satellites, L-bands, K-bands, and so forth. The physics of reliable telephone-like or network-like communications currently depends on low-orbit satellites (e.g., 350–450 miles, L4, etc.) and power utilization based upon current technology. These satellites are often circling above the earth in one of several polar orbit planes, and a number of satellites (online and backup) are in each plane. Communications from users (cellular phones, network computers, Web users, client components, etc.) are routed through a gateway to an initial satellite. From this satellite a nearest neighbor satellite in the constellation is selected, and the "call" route is expanded through additional nearest neighbors until a final satellite is found to send the call down to the receiver (server component, etc.) of the call. Software in orbit-installed satellites are maintained by (1) frequently sending (uplinking) "patches" or modifications to on-board software and (2) continually testing the on-board software either through line-of-sight testing while the satellite is in "view" or by extensive use of on-board testing software when the satellite is not in line-of-sight (i.e., not in "view"). Unfortunately, on-board testing and quality assurance software in the satellite's computer memory take up a significant amount of memory space. Also, the functionality of satellites needs to be modified and adapted as new "environmental" requirements are imposed on the satellites, which is an additional set of quality assurance requirements of the on-board satellite software. If in the future, space, power, and maintenance requirements of satellites significantly increase, how will these requirements be met?

Adaptive Spacecraft Software

To support a space web (e.g., SWW), a futuristic spacecraft (satellite) orbiting a distant planet or moon needs to robustly self-adapt to its target environment. Sometimes this self-adaptation will be needed in order to respond to SWW user commands from earth or from another space colony, and sometimes this self-adaptation will be needed as a satellite reconfigures itself to allow it to perform more effectively or efficiently in a new physical environment. Let us imagine a satellite orbiting a different planet or a different orbit around the same planet for a period of time (e.g., a month). Environmental factors can be different versions of sunlight, temperature, magnetic field, gravity, and solar wind. Suppose a satellite supporting SWW in this research supports imaging. Let us use a client/server model. Suppose the client is the ground station on earth and the server is this satellite. Suppose three software subsystems are embedded in this satellite: command and data handling (CD), flight control, and payload control. Each of these software subsystems runs on a different processor. The CD is basically for receiving uplink commands and routing them through constellations to a given satellite and to a given processor. The flight control software is mainly for the attitude determination and attitude control system (ACS). The payload interface processor (PIP) is for controlling the imaging camera and sending images back to the client. We illustrate an idea of an adaptive ACS. In the future, this idea can be applied to adaptive PIP software.

The ACS follows the control model with three kinds of components: sensor, decision (control) logic, and actuator (Wertz 1997). Generally the set of sensors includes star tracker, sun sensor, magnetometer, gyroscope, and reaction wheel (see Figure 14.1).

The decision logic includes attitude determination and attitude control. The actuator can be a reaction wheel and a torque coil. In fact, the sensor and actuator hardware has some built-in logic to make it flexible. Any of these components can be made adaptive. Let the input sensors be sun sensors, magnetometers, and accelerometers. Let the actuator be torque coils. Assume all these hardware components' performances are acceptable in a new environment. Only the control logic is subjected to modification. For simplicity, let the ACS control logic be only for controlling precession and spinning. In precession (imaging) mode, the goal is to keep

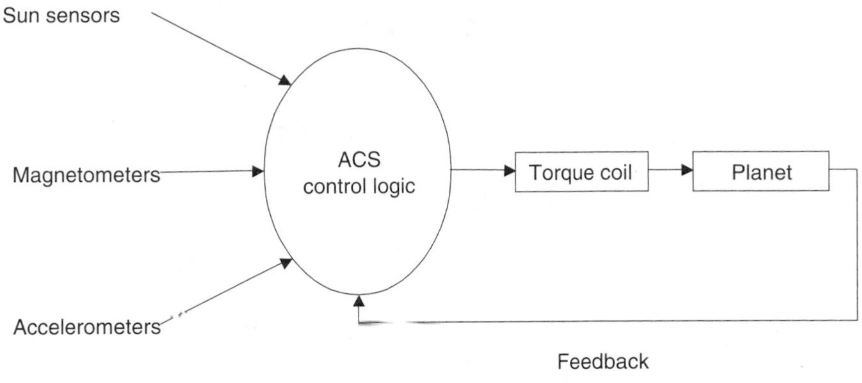

Figure 14.1 Adaptive Spacecraft Software: Control Model

the satellite pointing to the sun within a threshold (e.g., 0.2 degree), so that the solar array can observe to maximum solar energy and the finest image can be taken (see Figure 14.2).

In spinning (at night) mode, the goal is to maintain the satellite spinning at a desired period about Z-axis (see Figure 14.3).

Software component adaptation approaches have been developed (Chen 1998; White 1995). One of the tasks in the research is to explore this approach further in the spacecraft software domain. The adaptation procedure can be abstractly suggested by means of the steps shown in Listing 14.1.

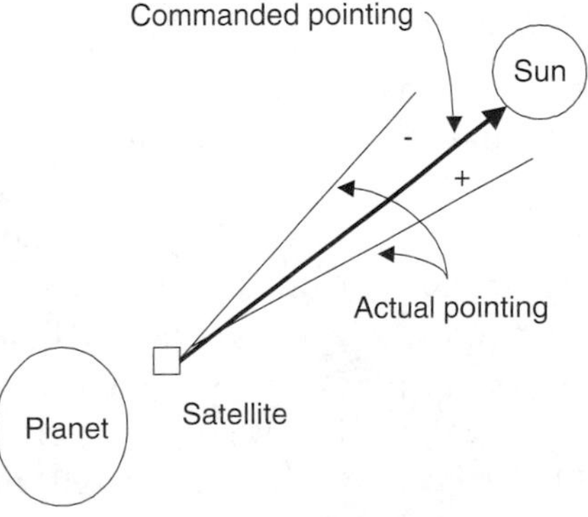

Figure 14.2 Adaptive Spacecraft Software: Precession Model

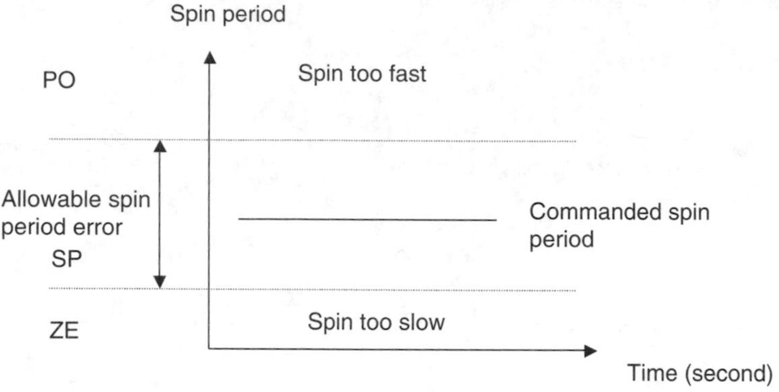

Figure 14.3 Adaptive Spacecraft Software: Spinning Model

Listing 14.1 Algorithm for Adaptation

```
WHILE (Server's Performance is Unsatisfactory) DO
BEGIN
The client (ground) receives telemetry (environmental data, state
of health) from the server (satellite).
The client adapts the ACS software component by using dynamic
compilation algorithms.
The client initializes the adapted ACS software component in the
server.
END.
```

In practice, on-board memory of the spacecraft is limited. Hence, we robustly adapt the software in the client (step 2). After adaptation, the satellite should well support improved imaging for the space web. A space web client on earth issues service commands to a space satellite to adjust orbit and attitude parameters in order that the satellite payload (e.g., a camera) can take photographs of a planetary body of interest. The client-service commands must be preprocessed by the client's adapter software component so that the commands can be sent in the correct form to the adapter software of the service satellite's software component. Therefore, the service satellite's adapter must have knowledge of the environmental parameters in which the service satellite currently exists. Initially three complementary models must exist for the correct adjustments to be made to the satellite so that it can be in a correct state to begin taking the required images. These three models are depicted in Figures 14.1 (Control Model for the ACS), 14.2 (Precession Model for the ACS), and 14.3 (Spinning Model for the ACS).

14.3 Integration of Components with Architecture

Many current technologies, including CORBA, DCOM (Distributed Component Object Model), and Java RMI (Remote Method Invocation), can provide a *de facto* standard for local and distributed object communication (Baker 1998; Mowbray and Ruh 1997; OMG 1999; Rine and Retnadhas 1980; Rine and Ahmed 1997; Trevor et al. 1994). For these tools to be useful, the component implementations must be prepared to conform to the *de facto* standard imposed by the environment. These technologies provide client/server communications. However, each of these uses different incompatible styles. This simple requirement may make functionally useful commercial products impossible to use in some chosen environment.

Because interaction code for a given environment is part of the component's implementation, moving it to a different environment involves making changes to source code; changing the source code for a commercial product is generally not an option. In addition, as software components move to new environments, the underlying network often changes. Different networks offer different types of reliability and quality of service (QoS), and are managed and controlled in different ways. This heterogeneity is a source of complexity for software architects and designers of distributed applications, especially as the variety of network types and QoS options increases.

Integration can be difficult when even considering a single runtime environment and a *de facto* standard interaction style such as client/server (Beach 1992; Meyer 1992; White and Purtilo 1992; White 1995), particularly in the context of reuse and maintenance (Rine and Chen 1996, 1998; Rine 1997, 1998). Many problems can arise: differences in parameter ordering, differences in data types, differences in the expected interaction mechanism, and differences in the meaning or semantics of the interfaces themselves. These differences can sometimes be fixed by adapting the component source code; however, this usually leads to multiple different versions of the same component and means that the new version of the component should be retested, negating one of the benefits of reuse.

In general solving the interface problems of software components involves the study of three dimensions:

1. Varying interface syntax
2. Varying interface semantics
3. Varying interface pragmatics

The problems addressed in this research include the varying mismatches between the interfaces of different software components.

Network performance is characterized by various QoS parameters, such as bandwidth, reliability, and end-to-end delivery delay. Different networks offer different QoS service levels, such as best effort, controlled, and guaranteed (Zhang 1996).

Best-effort service networks do not provide applications assurance that a particular QoS request will be satisfied, but rather are engineered to deliver the best possible performance. An example of a best-effort network is the current Internet, which at times experiences significant levels of congestion and poor performance. Controlled and guaranteed service networks provide assured performance levels through combinations of admission control tests, traffic-policing mechanisms and packet-scheduling policies. Examples of these types of networks include the future-generation Internet proposals (Bradshaw 1997) and some types of ATM networks (ATM 1996).

Distributed applications must use different service networks in different ways. In a best-effort network, an application simply sends data using network send primitives. In controlled and guaranteed architectures, the application must specify a variety of desired QoS parameters before data are sent (Bradshaw 1997; Zhang 1996). Further, because of admission control and QoS restrictions, the network itself may reject or seek to modify the request. In order for applications to take advantage of these options, the networks' semantic differences must be reflected back through to the distributed application (Ahlgren et al. 1998; Clark and Tennenhouse 1990). By moving this management complexity into interface adapters, components can take advantage of entirely different network architectures without needing to have their code modified.

An example of the need for this type of control arises from a distributed educational software and course presentation system (Pullen 1998). An instructor uses distributed instructional software for slide presentations and real-time annotations. A possible scenario is to connect to a remote classroom by a high-bandwidth guaranteed service network capable of transporting two-way audio and video. At the same time, a student may be participating from home over a slow modem connection and a student may have a wireless mobile laptop. These two students have sufficient network connectivity for audio and slide only presentations. Further, the underlying network architectures supporting the remote classroom, the at-home student, and the student with the wireless unit are completely different from each other. It is desirable to support all three types of network connectivity without having to change the instructional software. This is possible by placing communication control in the appropriate adapters. This technical approach is being used at George Mason University, using the NEW distance education tools kit invented by Pullen, to teach distributed/distance education information technology and engineering courses.

■ 14.4 Example

To illustrate potential integration problems and the utility of adapters, we use a small client/server application from the telephone-based telecommunications domain that uses a signaling protocol called Signaling System 7 (SS7). We use the telecommunications domain because advances in this domain will be key elements in supporting the interstellar SW Web. The illustrative system contains two components, a monitor (MT) responsible for monitoring the signaling links of the space system and a manager (MG) component responsible for handling requests (from the monitor) to bring space links into service, inhibit links, and take links out of service.

Consider the services provided by the monitor component (see Listing 14.2).

Listing 14.2 Monitor Services

```
MT interface {
  Monitor-links();                  // To monitor a link
  Inservice-result(result: int);    // Result of inservice request
  Inhibit-result(result: int);      // Result of inhibit request
  Outservice-result(result: int);   // Result of outservice request
}
```

The monitor expects the services shown in Listing 14.3 to be defined in another component.

Listing 14.3 External Services

```
In-service(link-id: short int, time: long int);
Inh-service(link-id: short int, time: long int);
Out-service(link-id: short int, time: long int);
```

The manager component provides the services shown in Listing 14.4.

Listing 14.4 Manager Services

```
MG interface {
  Inservice(time-in: float, link-num: long int);
  Inhibit(time-inh: float, link-num: long int);
  Outservice(time-out: float, link-num: long int);
}
```

The manager also expects to send an integer result that indicates success or failure of the service request to the component that invoked the service. The underlying communication mechanism is asynchronous message passing. For this application we need two queues, one that holds messages traveling from MT to MG and another that holds messages traveling from MG to MT. The communication mechanism has an interface that looks like that in Listing 14.5.

Listing 14.5 Communication Interface

```
Message-Object interface {
Result create-queue(queue-id: int);
Result attach-queue(queue-id: int);
Result put-Msg(Msg);
Result get-Msg(Msg);
}
```

Integrating these components involves providing ways for these components to interact. Consider the "inservice" interaction. The service name and the signatures for MG and MT do not match: Component MT expects to send a short int to represent the link and a long int to represent the time, while component MG expects to receive a float to represent the time followed by a long int for the link number. The standard solution to this type of problem is to manually modify one of the component implementations to fix the mismatch.

Consider the same application with adapters. The component signatures are as shown previously, but we have one adapter associated with each component. In an adapter-based system, interaction between the client and the server is handled as follows. The client generates a request that is received by its adapter. The adapter takes the request and forwards it to the server's adapter. Finally, the server adapter sends the request to the actual server. One purpose of these adapters is to handle potential mismatches in the communication. In the previous example we have a simple mismatch in the data types and ordering of the parameters. If code to handle the mismatch could be made part of the client's adapter, then neither the client nor the server would have to be modified to correct the mismatch; the adapters would handle it. The mismatch can be described using a notation like Nimble (Purtilo 1991). Nimble provides a way to describe both the formal (server) and actual (client) interfaces, as well as a map between them. If the map is well formed, Nimble produces code that performs the mapping.

In Nimble, we describe the formal parameters, the actual parameters, and then the map between them (see Listing 14.6).

Listing 14.6 Nimble Example

```
SERVICE In-service
ACTUAL PATTERN: link-id: short int, time: long int
FORMAL PATTERN: float, long int
NIMBLE MAP: FLOAT(time), LONG(link-id)
```

This is a relatively simple map that swaps the actual parameters and coerces their types to match the formal parameters. In addition to providing built-in coercions, Nimble also provides ways to describe masking out of parameters, introduction of new parameters (with default values), and adding user-defined coercion routines. In an adapter-based system, this specification defines a map between what this adapter receives and what is sent to the manager component's adapter.

Nimble provides a nice way to describe data heterogeneity (parameter mismatches) but cannot describe mappings between interaction mismatches. Consider the situation where we introduce a different server that meets the same functional requirements (adding, removing, and inhibiting links) but does not return a result value to the client. If the client waits for this value to return, as is done in many client/server interactions, no further progress will be made in the client. Obviously, one solution is to modify the client so that this expectation is removed; a solution that requires no change to the client is one in which the adapter generates a return value after the request is sent to the server. Describing both the mismatch and the solution requires a richer language. Contributing such an improved language is one of the research tasks.

14.5 Future Generation NASA Institute for Advanced Concepts, Space Wide Web Research, and Boundaries

An integrated research approach in the multiple disciplines of software reuse and distributed computer systems is needed to carry out this future research (Rine and Sonnemann 1998; Simon and Znati 2000; White 1995). In support of future human exploration and development of space, the research investigates future-generation software problems in complex application design and support systems through a new programming model. The research investigates current problems in leveraging adapters as a means to configure large-scale future distributed systems software from reusable architectures and components. Therefore, this research directly attacks current problems in the design and support of complex applications using a novel future development and runtime support environment, which we coin SWWACXML. This new environment will reduce complexity through a system's architectural layers from specified requirements of distributed components interactions and interconnections to the design and deployment of the supporting system architecture.

14.6 Advanced Concept Development

In this section we will discuss advanced concept development.

14.6.1 The Research Approach

As components move to new environments, the underlying network on which they had previously been used often changes. Different networks offer different types of reliability and quality of service (QoS), and they are managed and controlled in different ways. This heterogeneity is a source of complexity for software architects and designers of distributed applications, especially as the variety of network types and QoS options increases.

Part of the challenge in developing adapter interface technology is reducing the complexity of communication control and providing access to QoS support for distributed applications. Research is conducted into developing adapter communication auto-configuration techniques and "drill-down" methods. Auto-configuration allows adapters to run over different types of networks without having to rewrite communication management code (Huitema 1996). Drill-down methods expose to the adapter different network and transport layer QoS options (NSF 1997). Research in auto-configuration and QoS drill-down is conducted within the framework of a new type of adapter configuration language design.

In addition to the ability to easily move applications across environments, it is also important to be able to construct these applications out of reused components and to be able to easily change the application components. This means that an adapter configuration language must also be powerful enough to describe the properties of the software components and the interactions between software components in a way to make it possible to find and reason about potential mismatches in these interactions (Astley and Agha 1998; Braden et al. 1998; Yellin and Strom 1997). These mismatches include not only parameter or data mismatches, but control-oriented mismatches as well.

The requirements of any configuration language are that it should be easy to use and should be interoperable with existing and evolving standards for information representational languages. There should be a way to associate properties with the components and the connectors of the application, as well as describe how these basic elements will fit together. For communication control, it should be able to express the full range of QoS requirements on connectors for different types of real-time applications and networks. Finally, it is desirable that a full range of GUI tools exist to edit the representational language, and that these tools run on multiple platforms.

The eXtensible Markup Language (XML) is currently a language that meets many of these requirements. It is used for structured document interchange on the Web, as a way of providing application metadata, and as a syntactical basis for a variety of application languages. Examples of these languages include MATHML for mathematical expressions, SMIL for synchronized multimedia, and a schema representation language. As part of our approach, we investigate the development of an XML-compliant representational language in order to fulfill the requirements of our adapter configuration language.

The next section of this paper provides the technical details of our approach. An example of an XML-compliant representational language for adapter autoconfiguration called SWWACXML is presented. Because it provides a way to describe component interactions and connector properties, the XML-compliant language we describe primarily facilitates component reuse. It will be necessary to see how higher-level architecture description languages can be used to describe systems and can be mapped down to this type of language (Allen and Garlan 1997; Luckham et al. 1995). This part of the research addresses the issue of providing ways to reuse software architectures.

14.6.2 The Research Tasks

The major focus of the research efforts is toward the development of a language that can be used to describe both the QoS aspects of integration as well as the interaction requirements of the components. We are currently designing an XML-compliant language, SWWACXML, which meets these requirements. Extending a runtime QoS communication control system for use with SWWACXML is investigated in this paper.

Interaction Support for Adapter Communication

Our approach to adding interaction support for adapter-based applications has several primary parts. The first part, described in the sections "Research Approach: Configuration Language" and "Architecture Description Languages (ADLs)," addresses languages that can be used to drive the integration process. The task of using this information to generate adapters is discussed in the section "Building the Adapters with Generated Mapping Code." Finally, we are interested in exploring the utility of a new interaction style based on the way Web-based servers have been interacting with clients. This part of the interaction support research is described in the section "QoS-aware Configuration Language."

Research Approach: Configuration Language

In this section, we focus on the aspects of SWWACXML that allow us to address the task of generating adapters to support component interactions, even in the face of mismatches. The language we describe can be considered a rudimentary architecture description language (ADL). Just as with emerging high-level ADLs (Allen and Garlan 1997; Luckham et al. 1995), we define the base elements of a software system to be components and connectors. Components are the self-contained computational units of the application, consisting of code and state. Connectors capture the interaction (and communication) aspects of the application. The components and connectors have some relationships that define the application as a whole.

Since the goal is to be XML compliant, SWWACXML is composed of `<tag attribute> . . . <\tag>` pairs, as can be seen in the listings in this section. In SWWACXML, connectors and components of an application are listed explicitly in the `<SWWACXML-elements> . . . </SWWACXML-elements>` section of the specification. The properties of components that we are interested in are the services provided by a component (exported interfaces) and the services that the component expects to use (imported interfaces). Exposing both the services provided and services needed allows us not only to more easily determine what adapters are needed, but also provides us with information for performing a static check on the intended connections in the application. For example, it is possible to determine from an SWWACXML specification whether any services are missing.

The connectors in the application are explicitly defined and may have properties as well; these are used along with general application communication properties in establishing efficient network connections. These aspects of the language are described in the section "QoS-aware Configuration Language," and a network runtime communication control system is described in the section "Runtime Network Control System." In the SWWACXML specification of this section, we assume connectors are one-way, from a source to a destination. Extending this to a static set of connector types is straightforward and is part of the initial planned language development.

In Listing 14.7, we focus on the MT and MG interactions associated with putting a link into service.

Listing 14.7 MT and MG Interactions

```
<SWWACXML-elements>
  <Component name=MT>
      <export-interface name="Inservice-result">
        <param name="result" type=INT>
      </export-interface>
      <import-interface name="Inservice">
        <param name="link" type=SHORT>
        <param name="time" type=LONG>
      </import-interface>
      . . .
  </component>
  <Component name=MG>
      <export-interface name="In-service">
        <param name="time" type=FLOAT>
```

```
        <param name="link" type=LONG>
      </export-interface>
      <import-interface name="In-service-result">
        <param name="result" type=INT>
      </import-interface>
      . . .
  </component>
  <Connector name=C1>
      . . .
  </connector>
  <Connector name=C2>
      . . .
  </connector>
</SWWACXML-elements>
```

One thing to notice is that the automatically generated adapters need to occur at the boundary between components and connectors. The components and connectors described in the first part are composed in the <SWWACXML-build> . . . </SWWACXML-build> part of the specification (see Listing 14.8). Given the types of connectors we are initially considering, setting up a connection means providing a source and destination for each connector, and then describing what adapters are needed at sources and destinations. Multiple interactions between the given source and destination components may occur across a single connection. The adapter is where the binding between the names of the imported and exported interfaces is done, as well as the mapping (if needed) between the parameters. In this preliminary version of SWWACXML, the mapping notation is similar to the Nimble notation described in the introduction. The formal and actual parameters are included in the individual component interfaces; in the adapter, parameter maps can be defined. In these specifications, multiple adapters are described. These descriptions are merged into a single runtime adapter for the component.

Listing 14.8 SWWACXML-build

```
<SWWACXML-build>
  <client-server connector=C1 source=MT dest=MG>
    <adapter source-name="Inservice" dest-name="In-service">
      <param-map="MG.time = FLOAT(MT.time)">
      <param-map="MG.link = LONG(MT.link)">
      . . .
    </adapter>
      . . .
  <client-server connector=C2 source=MG dest=MT>
    <adapter source-name="In-service-result" dest-name="Inservice-
```

```
result">
        . . .
    </adapter>
        . . .
</SWWACXML-build>
```

One important problem to be addressed during the development of SWWACXML is how to formalize the notation used to describe the adapters. Obviously this language needs to be straightforward both to write and to place in the adapters. In addition, it is important that the mapping language have a well-defined definition of what it means to be well formed. The Nimble notation could be the basis of such a language; however, it does not provide a way to express some of the types of mismatch we are interested in handling. For example, in the introduction, we describe a simple control mismatch that could be handled by the adapters. A way to provide for this mismatch and its solution to be specified as part of the adapter specification is necessary.

Generating adapters requires the ability to extract the relevant information from a given specification; for this reason, an obvious first step is to build a tool that can parse SWWACXML specifications. This tool will be the front end of the adapter generator, as well as other tools in the overall system. SWWACXML as described previously is relatively simple, and generating adapters to do the appropriate mapping for the interactions is a straightforward task. We expect this task to become more interesting as the language evolves.

One question that arises is whether or not adapters need to be generated, compiled, and then turned into executables, or whether it would be better for an adapter to interpret these specifications. There are obvious design trade-offs between these choices. In particular, generating and compiling an adapter may be more efficient in terms of runtime performance. However, if we are addressing applications that might move between architectures, either statically (at configuration time) or dynamically (at runtime), interpreting the specification may prove to be the more flexible approach to adapter generation. Part of this research is to study the trade-offs between these approaches in different situations.

The configuration language, as described previously, focuses on techniques to make components more reusable and does little to address reuse of the architectures themselves. One problem is that the language is by necessity low level in order to drive the integration process. We believe that higher-level architecture description languages, discussed in the section "Architecture Description Languages (ADLs)," later in this chapter, must also be part of any advances toward software architecture reusability.

Building the Adapters with Generated Mapping Code

Once the components have been identified, this information is input into our application (product) compiler (assembler). The compiler develops all of the necessary generated mapping codes for each of the previously incompletely represented adapters. The compiled result produces completely represented adapters that can now communicate with each other on behalf of corresponding components' services having now been introduced. And the numerous syntactical mismatches between client and server signatures have been resolved, while maintaining the semantic requirements of each client.

Now a component sending a request for a service provided by another component uses generated adapter-level code to map its request's parameters to the service signature performing the request. The adapter-level generated code maps the request and solves the syntactic interface mismatch (service name, and its parameters order, names, and types) between the request and the syntax of the signature performing the request, while maintaining the semantics required of a client. The generated mapping code is included in the requesting component's associated adapter at compile or interpretation time.

Architecture Description Languages (ADLs)

Applications are often described using a high-level specification of the application (e.g., a MIL- [Prieto-diaz and Neighbors 1986] or an ADL-like approach), which describes components and connectors abstractly. This allows us to deal separately with issues of programming in the large versus the small. Architecture description languages (ADLs) such as Wright (Allen and Garlan 1997) and Rapide (Luckham et al. 1995) provide ways to describe interactions themselves and could potentially be used to describe dependencies between interactions, which are capabilities not provided by SWWACXML. These higher-level ADLs also often provide modeling- or theorem-proving capabilities to allow a designer to reason about the architecture of an application. Despite their strengths, they are generally too abstract to be used for integration purposes.

The SWWACXML notation is a lower-level approach to describing the structure and properties of the components and connectors of an application. Part of this is driven by the need to be able to describe some basic network information. In this notation, connectors may have network-level properties, but the interactions are limited to a static set of low-level primitives. This allows us to reason about how to generate adapters and how to integrate the components of the application into its architecture.

We are interested in developing ADLs that can be used to drive the integration process. This builds on previous work in using high-level specifications to generate and integrate interface software (White 1995; White and Purtilo 1992). However, rather than generating interface code directly as we have done in the past, we intend to extract the relevant interaction information and use it to generate the interaction part of SWWACXML specifications automatically. One of the difficulties in this part of the research is to determine how to decompose connector interactions into adapters. By their very nature, ADLs capture interactions as a single entity; however, at runtime the code implementing an interaction is by necessity spread across more than one runtime element. A general solution to this problem may be unsolvable; however, we hope to be able to find solutions for some classes of interactions.

Web-Based Interconnection

Using XML-like notations also introduces some interesting possibilities for potential interactions. Consider the way SMIL, an XML-compliant language, is used to allow real-time interactions. When it connects to a server, a client receives an SMIL specification. Based on the client's properties, the SMIL specification is translated at the client to HTTP calls that implement one of the protocols expected by the server. In this framework, the client does not have to be tailored in advance to the server; this tailoring is done at connection time.

During this research, we explored the use of a similar approach for client/server interaction for non-Web-based applications. Interactions in general software applications would work as follows. The server has an XML-compliant specification for its protocol or protocols. When a client's adapter first connects, the server's adapter reacts by sending this specification to the new client adapter. When the client receives this specification, it is used to direct the client's interaction with the server. This "use" could either be an interpretation of the specification, or the specification could be compiled into an executable. How the specification is instantiated (i.e., what the adapter looks like) is based both on the client's needs and on the underlying environment (network).

This approach has several advantages that we are interested in exploring. First, the client and server do not have to be tailored to each other, although they still can be if desired. Instead, the client needs only the ability to use this high-level description. Another advantage of this approach is that the protocols do not have to be defined in advance, and new protocols can be added at runtime, which is a style of dynamic reconfiguration that has not been studied. If at runtime a client needs to be changed to interact with a different server that uses a different protocol, the client's adapter could change at runtime based on the protocol exported by the new server. Part of the initial efforts involves both assessing the utility of this novel approach to interconnection and building an integration system capable of allowing this interaction.

It may also be the case that other dynamic reconfiguration (Chowdhary et al. 1997; Hofmeister et al. 1993) styles could be described and facilitated with an approach like this. Recent work in building applications that can dynamically reconfigure themselves has focused on putting as much of the work into the connectors (i.e., the interaction) as possible (Oreizy and Taylor 1998). Making the adapters aware of how to react to situations that potentially require a dynamic change to the application would be a useful step in this direction.

Quality of Service Support for Adapter Communication

It is necessary to develop a platform-neutral QoS-aware language introduced in the previous section for adapter configuration and communication control, along with runtime control mechanisms for network management and QoS control. We will illustrate the generality of our configuration and drill-down approach by demonstrating its use through Web-based applications running over multiple network types.

The major benefit of making adapters QoS aware is the ability to take advantage of different QoS options, to increase the maintainability and portability of adapter communication code, and to allow client/server code to operate over entirely different network architectures without having to rewrite or recompile component code. Our approach is to develop, within the framework of the SWWACXML language described earlier, QoS-aware techniques for adapter configuration. The adapter configuration methods will interact with local environment communication runtime systems for network control. As adapters move to different environments, the adapter communication language specifies the range of options suitable for component communication. The local communication runtime system interacts with the adapter to establish connections.

Our goal is to allow client and server component code to migrate to different platforms and to be properly configured through system architectural levels by simply loading SWWACXML configuration pages. We will focus on three basic issues. First, we will develop QoS-aware configuration languages, which are accessible through and compatible with World Wide Web technology. Second, we will develop runtime communication control systems based on multimedia call modeling. We focus on multimedia connection control systems because they have already been shown to be capable of managing a wide range of QoS options and data types. Finally, conducting performance studies via empirical measurements and the development of analytical models are required.

QoS-Aware Configuration Language

Each SWWACXML specification consists of several sections for network auto-configuration and QoS drill down. One of the sections is a <meta-head> section, providing meta-level information such as application name, security, and so on. Another section is <`SWWACXML-info`>, containing information pertaining to general, application-level QoS options, and information for QoS drill down. Examples include compiler option information and network QoS information such as desired network service type and end-to-end message delivery delay. This information can be used by the local compiler and by the local communication management system. An additional section of SWWACXML is <`SWWACXML-connector`>. This section describes how connectors communicate and includes auto-configuration information and different QoS options in the case of multistream connectors (e.g., audio and video).

An example of the QoS portions of SWWACXML is shown in Listing 14.9. This example extends the SS7 tool. It shows how the tool can be automatically configured to run on a single machine or across a network with different QoS options.

The <meta-head> section contains the application name and description. The <SWWACXML-info> section contains information about targeted message delivery delay and a priority ordering of the network service desired, if the application is distributed. In our example, the desired component-to-component message delivery delay is 150ms. The <SWWACXML-connector> section describes either a shared memory location or a network connection. These identifiers may be resolvable at runtime, if required. Listing 14.9 includes network QoS information, including requested bandwidth and a network policing interval. The policing interval is an application-specified traffic characterization used in establishing QoS over ATM or future-generation Internet networks.

Listing 14.9 SWWACXML QoS Example

```
<SWWACXML>
  <meta-head>
    <meta app="SS7-monitoring"/>
    <meta name="Configuration" content="Adapter Config"/>
  </meta-head>
  <SWWACXML-info>
    <target-message-delay delay=150ms>
    <ordered-switch>
      <target-network-service service="guaranteed">
      <target-network-service service="best-effort">
    </ordered-switch>
  </SWWACXML-info>
  <SWWACXML-connector>
    <client-server-com source=MT dest=MG>
    <switch>
      <local connection-id="100">
      <networked connection-id="channel" bandwidth=10kbps policing-
interval=50ms>
    </switch>
    <client-server-com source=MG dest=MT>
    <switch>
      <local connection-id="200">
      <networked connection-id="channel" bandwidth=10kbps policing-
interval=50ms>
    </switch>
  </SWWACXML-connector>    *
```

*
*
*
*

</SWWACXML>

Runtime Network Control System

Part of our research focus is to design SWWACXML to enable it to run on different types of platforms and across different networks. We will design runtime communication control systems capable of this level of heterogeneous control. To accomplish this goal, we will extend an integrated multimedia communication tool we have designed and implemented, called the Distributed Interprocess Communication System (DIPCS) (Simon, Znati 1995; Simon 1996). DIPCS is a distributed multimedia call management tool targeted towards running over both best-effort and real-time networks. It consists of a high-level call model for managing heterogeneous multimedia devices and a set of integrated best-effort and ISN-based network-level algorithms. It is specifically designed to provide a lightweight communication control mechanism for applications using heterogeneous platforms and networks.

Real-time applications use DIPCS by interacting with a connection manager. The connection manager provides primitives for specifying communication endpoints, QoS requirements, and communication control. The connection manager interacts with local network control modules and QoS options. Within DIPCS, actual communication management and control is specified by using network- and platform-independent objects, called DEVICEs and STREAMs. The advantage of DIPCS over other distributed call models such as CORBA 2.x and Java RMI is that DIPCS explicitly supports a wide range of QoS connection options, which are described in (Simon 1997) and (Simon and Sood 1997). CORBA and Java RMI have limited QoS support (Schmidt et al. 1999).

DEVICEs are defined as objects that represent communication endpoints. DEVICEs can be used to represent, from the point of view of the network, all objects that produce and consume data. DEVICEs manage system heterogeneity; each DEVICE may be a buffer in computer memory, an instrumentation device directly connected to the network, a local area network as represented by a bridge or router, and so on. Communication occurs directly between DEVICEs after an appropriate channel is established in the network.

STREAMs represent instances of a DEVICE's communication requirements. A STREAM inherits the type of media (e.g., video) and the direction of media (e.g., source or sink) from the DEVICE it represents. The STREAM encapsulates the QoS requirements of a connection between DEVICEs and is used to derive the characteristics of a supporting network communication channel. Matching a source STREAM and a sink STREAM of the same type forms a network connection.

Multiple source STREAMs may be connected to a single sink STREAM, if the DEVICE associated with the sink STREAM permits mixing. One example is an audio output device, such as a speaker, which can receive data from multiple audio input devices, such as microphones.

Separating STREAMs from DEVICEs allows a single-source DEVICE to be shared simultaneously by several sink DEVICEs, each with different QoS requirements. For instance, one STREAM may be a TCP connection, while another STREAM may represent RTP data. This separation of STREAMs from DEVICEs permits better utilization of network resources, since each network connection is supported only at its required QoS level.

We have successfully implemented DIPCS in a working distributed multimedia system, called Multi-Media MedNet (Simon, Krieger 1995). The primary mission of MedNet is to provide real-time monitoring and multiparty consultation and collaboration during brain surgery. MedNet functions as a real-time medical command, control, and communication system, running in a general-purpose hospital computing environment. MedNet allows continuous surveillance of the patient's condition during surgery and provides a full range of neurophysiological monitoring and diagnostic functions. It is used on a daily basis at seven hospitals and multiple diagnostic and research laboratories at the University of Pittsburgh. As of 1998, MedNet has been used to monitor approximately 1,300 cases per year.

Extending the DEVICE and STREAM model for use with SWWACXML, DEVICEs can represent components and variation points, while STREAMs can represent different types of network QoS. Local connection managers provide the ability to do QoS drill down. We will investigate ways of integrating the DIPCS approach with the adapter technology described earlier. Notice, for instance, that STREAMs can be specified in the `<SWWACXML-connector>` section. Connection managers can utilize information from the `<SWWACXML-info>` section. Further, DEVICEs appear to be one potential way to model adapters for network control. Since DIPCS already works with multiple network types, we believe that our approach towards demonstrating runtime support is quite general.

Experiments in Future Distance Education Technologies

Constructing a test bed for our runtime SWWACXML system is another interesting issue. A planned investigation of several application domains is required, and one of our primary areas of interest is distance education technology. We have extensive experience using distance learning applications, including several years of teaching network classes using both synchronous and asynchronous technology (Pullen 1998). The synchronous application uses real-time multimedia technology, including audio, video, and shared whiteboard connections. The asynchronous application uses prerecorded lectures that provided synchronized audio, mouse, and slide presentations over the Internet. Using these experiences in the development of the initial applications within our test bed will be important.

Performance Evaluation

Performance validation and evaluation are critical to the success of future-generation software systems. Developing instrumentation methods for performance monitoring and evaluation of our test bed is required. Three elements affect the end-to-end performance of the system we have described. The first is the overhead caused by our adapter and configuration methods. The second is the amount and type of data generated by the application. The third is how the underlying end-systems and networks behave under different traffic loads. For two different reasons, we are interested in evaluating the first element. First, application data generation and network/system performance are outside the control of the adapter configuration technology. Second, our adapter configuration technology will be successful if it simplifies the problem of reuse and configuration and if it does not become a software bottleneck.

Our approach to evaluating adapter configuration technology is to conduct software-timing measurements via code instrumentation. It will then be necessary to compare different configurations on an end-to-end application sender to application receiver basis. One comparison point will be application and system overhead measurements without the use of adapter configuration methods. This will be achieved by hand configuration of a test case. We will also develop an analytical model for performance prediction and analysis. This model will be based on a queuing model we have developed for performance prediction of rate- and deadline-based network service disciplines (Simon and Znati 2000). We will extend this model to include adapter configuration software delays. We can compare this analytical model against actual performance data obtained from the test bed.

Application-Level Network QoS Control

There has been extensive related research in QoS control at the distributed application layer. Here we cite some relevant related work. Schmidt, Levin, and Cleeland have developed a CORBA extension to deal with QoS issues (Schmidt et al. 1999). Examples of XML-compliant languages incorporating QoS include SMIL, a language for synchronized multimedia presentation. There has also been work in developing application-layer communication architectures incorporating network-level QoS control. The OMEGA endpoint architecture provides end-to-end QoS guarantees through the use of a QoS broker (Nahrstedt and Smith 1996). QoS parameters are translated between the application and the underlying system. Admission control is via end-to-end tests. The Lancaster QoS-A (Quality of Service Architecture) is a layered architecture of services and mechanisms for QoS management and control of continuous media flows (Hutchison et al. 1994). The COMET group at Columbia University is developing XRM (eXtended integrated Reference Model), a framework for controlling multimedia telecommunications networks (Lazar 1997). Our approach differs from these efforts because of our emphasis on cross-layer auto-configuration, in addition to communication specification. Our work will extend the DIPCS control model (Simon, Znati 1995; Simon 1996).

Several research groups have developed performance and analytical models for end-to-end network performance modeling and analysis of client/server and distributed objects. These models include Layered Queuing Networks (Rolia and Sevcik 1995), the DAMSON system, and an analysis of DoD's object-oriented HLA architecture (Srinivasan and Reynolds 1998). Our approach differs from this work because we will develop models targeting QoS-enabled networks, some of which are presented in (Simon and Znati 2000).

14.7 Conclusion

The eXtensible Markup Language (XML) is evolving as a standard digital systems language for representing, exchanging, sharing, and publishing information. XML-based formats for data and metadata are evolving to support many different kinds of knowledge organization and agents' communication on the Internet/Web, driving the need for new techniques capable of extracting and organizing knowledge from various heterogeneous data. However, both the vision of XML and Internet/Web are also evolving in ways that are only imagined in the future. Also humankind pushes exploration onto a much broader playing field (namely "space")—new challenges to performance, integration, and very large-scale systems adaptation will have to be overcome.

Later twenty-first century Space Wide Web (SWW) distributed component-based software applications will dwarf today's increasingly complex World Wide Web (WWW) environments, supported by mere earth-bound low-orbit satellite constellations, and will represent a far more significant investment in terms of development costs, deployment, and maintenance. As we now move into the twenty-first century, part of the cost will come in the effort required to develop, deploy, and maintain the individual software components, including vast, shared knowledge bases. Many of these components will be on remote, numerous satellites, attracting information through the next generation of XML-like technologies. As of now, part of this effort will include implementing the required functionality of components, implementing the required interactions for components, and preparing components to operate, using information technologies of the future, in some remote runtime environment. One way to reduce the cost of component development will continue to be the reuse of existing commercial software components that meet the functional requirements.

Chapter 15

XML as a Unifying Framework for Inductive Databases

Rosa Meo and
Giuseppe Psaila

15.1 Introduction

Information technology applications present new challenging requests to the database research field. These requests are motivated by the widespread use of database applications and by the complex and new needs that these applications present. Furthermore, the volume of data is growing everyday and is reaching dimensions of terabytes, while the response must be fast and precise.

Instances of these applications are the data warehouse analysis procedures that perform several scans of huge databases in order to provide an answer to a single request. These queries ask the system to perform huge computations based on the aggregation of data. They define a new typology of database applications: the OLAP (On-Line Analytical Processing) applications.

Other instances of these new applications that, like data warehouse applications, work on huge volumes of data and require fast response times are data-mining applications. These are called to extract descriptive patterns from the data in order to represent information on the data itself that is useful for decision making. Examples of these applications are classifiers. They assign the analyzed data to a set of classes, having previously learned the rules that allow the system to assign a data example to a class. Data examples are taken from a subset of the data, the training set, already classified by an expert. Clustering applications perform a similar task but with no supervision of the expert and with a number of classes that is not given in advance.

Other examples are *basket analysis* applications, which extract patterns such as association rules and sequential patterns. These patterns give a representation of the laws that govern the distribution of the data in the database. They are designed in order to give, to the user/analyst, an intuitive explanation of the underlying laws that guide the customer in his or her purchases.

All these different techniques share the goal to extract data patterns from the database, in order to obtain a description that can be used as a prediction tool for future data. Therefore, all of them constitute a potentially useful tool for the analyst, in order to give an explanation of the patterns themselves and help the analyst in the hard interpretation task of the extracted patterns. In this way extracted patterns are themselves considered data to be analyzed (and not necessarily with the same analysis tool that was used to obtain them).

These are the motivations that inspired Imielinski and Mannila to launch the idea of an inductive database, a general-purpose database in which both the data and the patterns can be represented, retrieved, and manipulated together or separately (Imielinski and Mannila 1996). Inductive databases should help the analyst in the hard task of extracting knowledge from the database and successively in interpreting it with the same suite of analysis tools. This process is known as the Knowledge Discovery process (KDD process for short). It consists of a sequence of data preprocessing steps, data-mining steps (extracting patterns), and post-processing steps (providing the interpretation of the extracted patterns). According to Imielinski and Mannila, inside the inductive database framework, the knowledge discovery process becomes a simple querying sequence, where each query is an instance of a specialized query language, provided with a highly expressive power. With inductive databases, all the analysis techniques previously described should be integrated inside the same framework, the inductive database management system, in order to be used and intermixed in the analysis process when needed.

However, the underlying analysis models are rather different and require data to be represented, retrieved, and manipulated in different ways. Classifiers and clustering procedures usually adopt a data model that is a classification tree, while the basket analysis problem is solved representing data with the use of a set enumeration model. On the other side, source raw data are very often represented in the relational data model (because they reside inside relational databases), whose simplicity does not provide an easy way to manage data represented in different models.

In this chapter, we explore the feasibility of using XML as the language for the representation and integration of the different models previously cited. XML is particularly suitable for this task, because it can represent at the same time, and in a flexible way, both the data schema and the data values. This allows more generality in the definition of patterns and in the representation of the adopted models. In particular, we propose here a new model called XDM (XML for Data Mining) specifically designed to be adopted inside the unifying framework of inductive databases. We show the features that make it suitable for inductive database applications. The first one is that it allows source raw data and patterns to be represented at the same time in the model. The second one is that it represents, together with patterns, also the pattern definition that results from the pattern derivation process. This is determinant for the phase of pattern interpretation and allows pattern reuse by the inductive database management system. As we explain later in this chapter, this fact may speed up future pattern extractions because it allows an incremental computation of patterns. Furthermore, we show that the use of XML allows the description of complex formats, such as trees, enabling the effective integration of several heterogeneous data-mining techniques and models in the same framework. Finally, we show that the framework can be easily extended with new data-mining operators. In this way inductive databases really become open systems that are easily customizable according to the kinds of patterns in which the user/analyst is interested.

This chapter is organized as follows. In Section 15.2 "Past Work," we discuss the work that motivates the proposed model: We discuss the problem of the extraction and evaluation of association rules, and the problem of data classification. Then, we present the concept of inductive databases, and finally we present a previous proposal concerning both XML and data mining—that is, the Predictive Model Mark-up Language (PMML).

The running example introduced in Section 15.2, "Past Work," will be the basis for Section 15.3, "The Proposed Data Model: XDM": XDM, our proposal for inductive databases, is presented in that section. In particular, we first introduce the basic XDM concepts and notions, and then we show the application of XDM to concrete problems, by exploiting the running examples.

Section 15.4, "Benefits of XDM," presents the benefits of the new model. Section 15.5, "Toward Flexible and Open Systems," presents the inductive database system as an open and flexible framework. Section 15.6, "Related Work," discusses related work, and finally we draw our conclusions.

15.2 Past Work

The ideas illustrated in this chapter originate from past work on the integration of database technology and data-mining tools, and from the notion of an inductive database. In order to make clear our proposal, it is necessary to report this past work, showing the background that inspired our present work. In particular, we will consider two main data-mining problems: the association rule extraction problem and the classification problem.

15.2.1 Extracting and Evaluating Association Rules

We describe here a classical market basket analysis problem that will serve as a running example throughout the chapter to illustrate association rule mining problems.

We are looking for associations between two sets of items bought by customers in the same purchase transaction, with the purpose of discovering the behavior of customer purchases.

The source database from which association rules might be extracted is shown in Table 15.1.

Table 15.1 The Purchase Transactions Table

transaction_ID	customer	item	price
1	c1	A	25
1	c1	B	12
1	c1	C	30
1	c1	D	20
2	c2	C	30
2	c2	D	20
2	c2	B	12
3	c1	A	25
3	c1	B	12
4	c3	A	25
4	c3	C	30
4	c3	B	12
5	c4	A	25
5	c4	B	12
5	c4	C	30
5	c4	F	16
6	c5	A	25
6	c5	F	16

Association Rules

An association rule is a pair of two sets of items extracted from within purchase transactions. An example of an association rule extracted from the Transactions Table is *{A}⇒{B}*. *A* is the antecedent (or body), and *B* the consequent (or head) of the rule. In Table 15.1, *{A}⇒{B}* is satisfied by the customer c1, c3, and c4, because both items *A* and *B* are bought by those customers in the transactions 1, 3, 4, and 5, respectively. The intuitive meaning of *{A}⇒{B}* is that the customers that buy *A* in a transaction also tend to buy *B* in the same transaction. Association rules are extracted from the database having computed the value of two statistical measures, whose purpose is to give the association rules frequency and statistical relevance.

Support is the statistical frequency with which the association rule is present in the table. It is given by the number of transactions in the source table in which both the sets of items (the antecedent and the consequent) are present, divided by the total number of transactions in the table (in the example of Table 15.1, *{A}⇒{B}* has support 4/6).

Confidence is the conditional probability with which customers buy, in a transaction, the consequent of the association rule (in the example *B*), given that the transaction contains the antecedent (*A*). Confidence may be obtained by the ratio between the number of transactions containing both the antecedent and the consequent and the number of transactions containing the antecedent. Therefore, in the example of Table 15.1, *{A}⇒{B}* has confidence 4/5.

The analyst usually specifies minimum values for support and confidence, so that only the most frequent and significant association rules are extracted.

MINE RULE Operator

The purpose of this paragraph is to introduce a running example that will be used to discuss the problem of mining association rules. Therefore this paragraph is not to be considered as a complete overview of the `MINE RULE` operator. For full details, the reader is directed to (Meo et al. 1998a).

The `MINE RULE` operator has been introduced with the purpose to request the extraction of association rules from within a relational database, by means of a declarative, SQL-like, query. The problem of extracting the simplest association rules, as described in the preceding paragraph, is specified by the `MINE RULE` statement in Listing 15.1.

Listing 15.1 MINE RULE Statement

```
MINE RULE Rule_Set1 AS
SELECT DISTINCT 1..n item AS BODY, 1..1 item AS HEAD
FROM Transactions
GROUP BY transaction_ID
EXTRACTING RULES WITH SUPPORT: 0.5, CONFIDENCE: 0.8
```

The GROUP BY clause logically partitions the source Transactions table (FROM clause) in groups, such that each group is made by items bought in the same transaction. The SELECT clause selects association rules made by a set of one or more items in the body (1..n item AS BODY), and one single item in the head (1..1 item AS HEAD), coming from the same transaction (group). From all the possible association rules, only those ones that have a support that is at least 0.5 and a confidence at least 0.8 (EXTRACTING clause) are extracted. Finally the extracted association rules, output of the MINE RULE operator, are inserted into a new table, named Rule_Set1. The output of the MINE RULE statement in Listing 15.1 is shown in Table 15.2.

Table 15.2 The Output Table Rule_Set1

Body	**Head**	**Support**	**Confidence**
{A}	{B}	0.667	0.8
{B}	{A}	0.667	0.8
{B}	{C}	0.667	0.8
{C}	{B}	0.667	1
{A,C}	{B}	0.5	1

EVALUATE RULE Operator

If we want to *cross over* between extracted rules and the original relation, for instance, in order to select the tuples of the source table that satisfy the rules in a given rule set, we need an operator that does the reverse task of the extraction of association rules: It selects the original tuples from the source table for which certain rules hold. A possible operator that does this task is named EVALUATE RULE and has been introduced in Psaila (2001). With this operator, it is also possible to perform aggregations on the rules and other sophisticated operations. Although in this chapter, we consider only a very simple rule evaluation problem, this is still an exemplary instance of the problems that belong to the class of post-processing operations. These are operations, executed after the proper mining operations, that have the purpose of analyzing, with certain detail, the result set of the mining step.

Suppose we want to find those customers for which at least one association rule in the result set Rule_Set1 holds. This problem is expressed by means of the EVALUATE RULE operator in Listing 15.2.

Listing 15.2 EVALUATE RULE Operator

```
EVALUATE RULE InterestingCustomers AS
SELECT DISTINCT customer, BODY, HEAD
USING RULES Rule_Set1
ASSOCIATING item AS BODY, item AS HEAD
FROM Transactions
GROUP BY customer
DIVIDE BY transaction
```

From table `Transactions` (`FROM` clause), the `EVALUATE` statement retrieves those customers for which at least an association rule holds in the result set `Rule_Set1` (clause `USING RULES`). Furthermore, for those customers, it also reports the body and the head of the association rules that hold (clause `SELECT DISTINCT customer, BODY, HEAD`). Clause `ASSOCIATING` and clause `DIVIDE BY` specify, respectively, how association rules have been defined and how they have been extracted from table `Transactions`; finally, clause `GROUP BY` specifies that rules are evaluated considering transactions of each single customer. In other words, tuples are grouped by customer, because we want to know for which customer rules hold; then, groups are subdivided by transaction, so that rules are evaluated on these subgroups, a customer separately by other customers. The result set is a table, named `InterestingCustomers`, which is shown in Table 15.3.

Table 15.3 Table InterestingCustomers, Result of the Operator EVALUATE RULE

Customer	Body	Head
c1	{A}	{B}
c1	{B}	{A}
c1	{B}	{C}
c1	{C}	{B}
c1	{A, C}	{B}
c2	{B}	{C}
c2	{C}	{B}
c3	{A}	{B}

(continued)

Table 15.3 *continued*

Customer	**Body**	**Head**
c3	{B}	{A}
c3	{B}	{C}
c3	{C}	{B}
c3	{A, C}	{B}
c4	{A}	{B}
c4	{B}	{A}
c4	{B}	{C}
c4	{C}	{B}
c4	{A, C}	{B}

The reader will notice that in the `EVALUATE RULE` operator, it is necessary to include some of the clauses of the `MINE RULE` statement that were used when the association rule set was extracted and stored in the referenced table (`Rule_Set1`). This is necessary in order to indicate the meaning of the association rules and to ensure consistency between the association rules and the analysis performed on the source data through those rules. Unfortunately, this information is not present in the relational database, since tables are stored without keeping track of the actual statement that generated the table. This means that tables generated by the `MINE RULE` or the `EVALUATE RULE` operators are meaningless for a user who has no knowledge of the actual statements that generated those tables. Indeed, the user/analyst is expected to remember the `MINE RULE` statement that generated the rule set.

This intrinsic limitation of the relational model provides an important observation that constitutes one of the main motivations for the new model based on XML presented in this chapter.

15.2.2 Classifying Data

Another typical data-mining problem is the classification problem. A generic classification problem consists of two distinct phases: the *training phase* and the *test phase*. In the training phase, a set of classified data, called *training set*, is analyzed in order to build a classification model—that is, a model that, based on features appearing in the training set, determines in which cases a given class should be used. For example, the training set might describe data about car insurance applicants. Usually, the risk class of insurance applicants has been established by an expert or is based on historical observations: The classification model says which class to apply, depending on the characteristics of applicants (e.g., age, car type, etc.).

The training phase is then followed by the *test phase*. In this phase, the classification model built in the previous phase is used to classify new unclassified data. For instance, when new car insurance applicants submit their application form, an automatic system may refer to the classification model and assign the proper risk class to each applicant, depending, for example, on the age and/or the car type.

From the algorithmic point of view, the classification problem has been widely studied in the past, so that several algorithms are available. However, we do not want to focus on algorithms, but on the issue of specifying a classification problem. A possible solution, based on the same idea that inspired the `MINE RULE` operator, has been introduced by P. L. Lanzi and G. Psaila (Lanzi and Psaila 1999). In this work, an operator able to specify classification problems is proposed. This operator, named `MINE CLASSIFICATION`, is based on the relational model: It operates on relational tables and is based on an SQL-like syntax. We now give a brief description of this operator.

Training Phase

Suppose we want to obtain a classification model from a sample training set for the car insurance application domain. The training set might be the one contained in the table `Training_Set`, reported in Table 15.4.

This is a very simple training set, in which attributes AGE and CAR-TYPE are the features that characterize applicants, while attribute RISK is the class label. This attribute can assume only two values, "Low" and "High," meaning that we consider only two risk classes.

The classification model that can be produced analyzing this training set is basically represented in two distinct, yet equivalent formats: a *classification tree* or a *classification rule set*. The classification tree for our case is depicted in Figure 15.1. Nonleaf nodes are labeled with a condition: If the condition is evaluated to true, the branch labeled with "True" is followed; otherwise, the branch labeled with "False" is followed. When a leaf node is reached, it assigns a value to the class. For example, if an applicant owns a truck and is 18 years old, the condition evaluated in the root node is false, and therefore the false branch is followed. Then the condition in the following node (`AGE<=23`) is evaluated. Being true, it leads to a leaf node with the High value assigned to the `Risk` class.

Table 15.4 The Table Training_Set, Containing the Training Set for the Classification Process

Age	Car-type	Risk
17	Sports	High
43	Family	Low
68	Family	Low
32	Truck	Low
23	Family	High
18	Family	High
20	Family	High
45	Sports	High
50	Truck	Low
64	Truck	High
46	Family	Low
40	Family	Low

The same classification model might be described by means of classification rules. A possible rule set corresponding to the classification tree depicted in Figure 15.1 follows:

1. IF AGE $\leq$ 23 THEN RISK IS "High"
2. IF CAR-TYPE = "Sports" THEN RISK IS "High"
3. IF CAR-TYPE IS {"Family", "Truck"} AND AGE > 23 THEN RISK IS "Low"
4. DEFAULT RISK IS "Low"

The numbers preceding each rule denote the order in which the rules are evaluated (from the first rule to the following ones) until a rule is satisfied. If no rule is satisfied, the DEFAULT rule is applied. Observe that the condition part of a rule can contain complex conditions, composed using the logical operators.

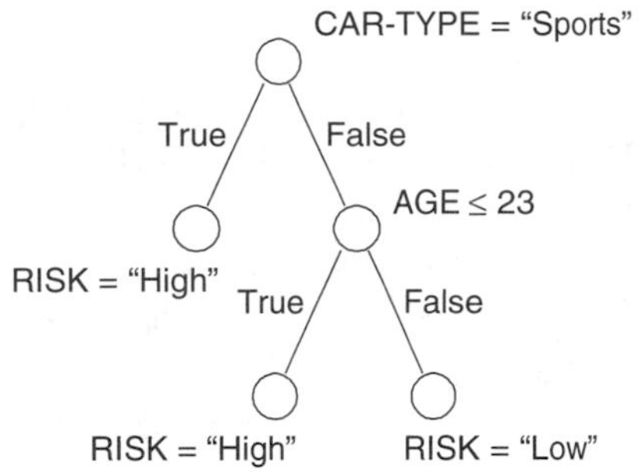

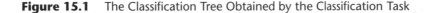

Figure 15.1 The Classification Tree Obtained by the Classification Task

The data-mining task that leads to the generation of the classification models can be specified, by means of the `MINE CLASSIFICATION` operator, as shown in Listing 15.3.

Listing 15.3 MINE CLASSIFICATION Operator

```
MINE CLASSIFICATION Classification_Model AS
SELECT DISTINCT RULES ID, AGE, CAR-TYPE, CLASS
FROM Training_Set
CLASSIFY BY RISK
```

The statement in Listing 15.3 can be read as follows. The `FROM` clause specifies the table containing the training set, in this case named `Training_Set`. Then the `CLASSIFY BY` clause indicates that the `RISK` attribute is used as class label. Finally, the `SELECT` clause specifies the structure of the output table, named `Classification_Model`: The first attribute of this table is named ID and is the rule identifier; the second and third attributes (`AGE` and `CAR-TYPE`) are the attributes on which the conditions of the classification model (expressed in the nodes of the classification tree) are represented. The fourth and last attribute is the class label.

Although it is possible to represent a classification tree in a table, this representation would be unreadable; the `MINE CLASSIFICATION` operator generates a tabular representation of a classification rule set, where each row corresponds to a rule. We omit the description of this table since it does not add any particular and useful information for the purposes of the present discussion.

Test Phase

Once the classification model has been generated, it should be used to classify new (unclassified) data. Suppose we have a table named `New_Applicants`, describing data about a set of new applicants for car insurance (see Table 15.5).

Suppose we want to assign each applicant the proper risk class, based on the previously generated model. In practice, we want to obtain table `Classified_Applicants` (Table 15.6). This table has been obtained by extending rows in Table 15.5 and adding the risk class, obtained by evaluating the classification model on each single row.

Table 15.5 The Table New_Applicants, Containing Unclassified Data

Name	**Age**	**Car-type**
John Smyth	22	Family
Marc Green	60	Family
Laura Fox	35	Sports

Table 15.6 The Table Classified_Applicants, Obtained by Extending Table New_Applicants with Class Labels

Name	**Age**	**Car-type**	**Risk**
John Smyth	22	Family	High
Marc Green	60	Family	Low
Laura Fox	35	Sports	High

By means of the `MINE CLASSIFICATION` operator, it is possible to specify the test phase as well. Table 15.6 might be obtained by Listing 15.4.

Listing 15.4 Test Phase

```
MINE CLASSIFICATION TEST Classified_Applicants AS
SELECT DISTINCT *, CLASS
FROM New_Applicants
USING CLASSIFICATION FROM Classification_Model AS RULES
```

The FROM clause denotes the table containing the data to classify; the SELECT clause denotes that the output table will be obtained by taking all the attributes in the source table (denoted by the star) and adding the class attribute; finally, the last clause (USING CLASSIFICATION FROM) specifies that the classification model is stored in table Classification_Model. This is the simplest form of the MINE CLASSIFICATION TEST operator: In fact, it provides constructs to map attributes in the table containing the data to be classified into attribute names appearing in the classification model. Since they are outside the scope of this chapter, they are not reported here.

To conclude, we want to observe that the classification problem seen from a global point of view is intrinsically a two step process: Although the hard task of this process is the training phase, a system whose aim is to provide a global support to data-mining and knowledge discovery activities must necessarily provide adequate support for the other activities. Indeed, it is necessary to keep track of the analysis process and provide the user complete semantics about the data and model stored in the system.

Consequently, as argued in Lanzi and Psaila 1999 and later in Psaila 2001, the MINE RULE, MINE CLASSIFICATION, and EVALUATE RULE operators constitute a *relational database-mining framework*, which is a precursor of the notion of an inductive database.

15.2.3 Inductive Databases

The notion of an inductive database has been introduced by T. Imielinski and H. Mannila (Imielinski and Mannila 1996) as a first attempt to address the previously mentioned drawbacks arising with data-mining operators built on top of relational databases: The relational database does not maintain information about the statement and/or the process that generated a table, storing patterns extracted by data-mining operators.

Let us briefly introduce them, by taking the definition and examples from J.-F. Boulicaut et al. (Boulicaut et al. 1998, 1999).

The *schema of an inductive database* is a pair $R = (\mathbf{R}, (Q_R, e, V))$, where $\mathbf{R}$ is a database schema, Q_R is a collection of patterns, e is the *evaluation function* that defines how patterns occur in the data, and V is a set of *result values* resulting from the application of the evaluation function. More formally, this function maps each pair $(\mathbf{r}, \theta_i)$ to an element of V, where $\mathbf{r}$ is a database of $\mathbf{R}$ and θ_i is a pattern from Q_R, (i.e., $Q_R = \{\theta_i\}$).

An *Instance* $(\mathbf{r}, s)$ of an inductive database over the schema R consists of a database $\mathbf{r}$ over the schema $\mathbf{R}$ and a subset $s \subseteq Q_R$.

Let us explain the preceding formal concepts by means of a practical example. A simple and compact way to define association rules (see Agrawal and Srikant

1994), also called *binary association rules*, is the following. Given a schema **R** = $\{A1, \ldots, An\}$ of attributes with domain $\{0, 1\}$, and a relation **r** over **R**, an *association rule* over **r** is an expression of the form $X \Rightarrow B$, where $X \subseteq \mathbf{R}$ and $B \in \mathbf{R} - X$.

The binary model for association rules is an alternative model to the one adopted in section 15.2.1, "Extracting and Evaluating Association Rules." In the binary model, we need a binary attribute for each value of the `item` attribute in the source table. A binary attribute takes the true value in a transaction that contains the corresponding item; false otherwise. For instance, the association rule $\{A\} \Rightarrow \{B\}$ can be represented with the two binary attributes A and B and is satisfied for those transactions in which the condition A *and* B is true.

We choose to adopt this alternative model in the context of this description of inductive databases because the following presentation becomes simpler.

Suppose now we want to define an inductive database for binary association rules. At first, we have to define the set of patterns Q_R, then the evaluation function e, which induces a set of result values V.

The set of patterns is defined as $Q_R = \{X \in B \mid X \subseteq \mathbf{R}, B \in R - X\}$—that is, it contains all possible binary association rules. For each association rule, we wish to evaluate the support and confidence. In some references, the support evaluation function is called *frequency*, while support of a set W of binary attributes is defined as the total number of rows that have a *1* for each binary attribute of W. Indeed we can obtain support by means of a frequency function: given a set of items $W \subseteq \mathbf{R}$, $freq(W, \mathbf{r})$ is the fraction of rows of **r** that have a *1* in each column of W. Consequently, the support of the rule $X \Rightarrow B$ in **r** is defined as $freq(X \cup \{B\}, \mathbf{r})$, while the *confidence* of the rule is defined as $freq(X \cup \{B\}, \mathbf{r}) / freq(X, r)$. As a result, the evaluation function e is defined as $e(\mathbf{r}, \theta) = (f(\mathbf{r}, \theta), c(\mathbf{r}, \theta))$, where $f(\mathbf{r}, \theta)$ and $c(\mathbf{r}, \theta)$ are the support and the confidence of the rule θ in the database **r**.

Finally, the set V of result values induced by the evaluation function e, is defined on the domain $[0, 1]^2$, which contains pairs of real values in the range $[0, 1]$, where the first value is the support and the second value is the confidence.

Table 15.7 shows an instance of an inductive database. On the left side, we find the source table containing data from which association rules are extracted; on the right side, we find the inductive part of the inductive database. Each row describes a pattern (an association rule) and the values of support and confidence.

The definition provided by J.-F. Boulicaut et al. (Boulicaut et al. 1998, 1999) for inductive databases also considers the notion of queries. In particular, queries can be performed both on the instance of a relational database and on the set of patterns.

A typical example is the selection of association rules having support and confidence greater than a minimum; if this threshold is set to 0.5 for support and 0.7 for confidence, we obtain the new inductive database instance illustrated in Table 15.8.

Although the notion of an inductive database is interesting, we think that its definition is not mature enough to be exploited in real systems. In particular, we find two major problems.

Table 15.7 Basic Instance of an Inductive Database

A	B	C	QR	f(r, θ)	c(r, θ)
1	0	0	θ_1: A ⇒ B	0.25	0.33
1	1	1	θ_2: A ⇒ C	0.50	0.66
1	0	1	θ_3: B ⇒ A	0.25	0.50
0	1	1	θ_4: B ⇒ C	0.50	1.00
			θ_5: B ⇒ A	0.50	0.66
			θ_6: C ⇒ B	0.50	0.66
			θ_7: A B ⇒ C	0.25	1.00
			θ_8: A C ⇒ B	0.25	0.50
			θ_9: B C ⇒ A	0.25	0.50

Table 15.8 Derived Instance of an Inductive Database

A	B	C	QR	f(r, θ)	c(r, θ)
1	0	0	θ_4: B⇒ C	0.50	1.00
1	1	1			
1	0	1			
0	1	1			

The first problem is that it is not clear which kinds of patterns can be represented. For example, it seems that trees and other semi-structured formats cannot fit into the formal definition of an inductive database.

The second problem with inductive databases is that an instance of an inductive database is tailored to deal with a specific type of pattern, which is due to the fact that when the inductive database schema is defined, it is necessary to specify in advance the patterns that will be extracted and stored in the inductive database instance. As a result, it seems hard to integrate in the same database instance different patterns, in order to exploit them in the more general and complex knowledge discovery processes. Consequently, a system based on the definition of an inductive database would not be flexible enough to support these processes.

15.2.4 PMML

The idea of using XML to effectively describe complex data models is not completely new in the research area of data mining. The Data Mining Group (DMG) is working on a proposal called Predictive Model Mark-up Language (PMML). PMML (http://www.dmg.org/pmml-v2-0.htm) is an XML-based language that provides a way for applications to define statistical and data-mining models and to share models between PMML-compliant applications. In other words, PMML plays the role of standard format to share, among different software applications, complex data models concerning data-mining and knowledge discovery tasks.

Due to these premises, PMML is based on a precise DTD that defines the XML structure for a given set of data models; the current version provides XML structure definitions for models based on trees, regression models, cluster models, association rules, sequences, neural networks, and Bayesian nets. In this section, we briefly introduce the main characteristics of a PMML document by means of an example based on association rules.

Suppose we want to describe, by means of a PMML document, the same extraction of association rules discussed in section 15.2.1, "Extracting and Evaluating Association Rules," in order to present the `MINE RULE` operator. Recall that the goal of the discussed `MINE RULE` statement was to extract association rules associating product items, found in the same purchased transactions having support greater than or equal to 0.5 and confidence greater than or equal to 0.8. A PMML-aware system might generate the PMML document shown in Listing 15.5.

Listing 15.5 PMML Document

```
<PMML version="2.0" >
   <Header copyright="www.dmg.org"
           description="example model for association rules"/>
   <DataDictionary numberOfFields="2" >
     <DataField name="Transaction_ID" optype="categorical" />
     <DataField name="Item" optype="categorical" />
   </DataDictionary>
   <AssociationModel
       functionName="associationRules"
       numberOfTransactions="6" numberOfItems="5"
       minimumSupport="0.5"     minimumConfidence="0.8"
       numberOfItemsets="7"     numberOfRules="5">
```

```
    <MiningSchema>
           <MiningField name="Transaction_ID"/>
           <MiningField name="Item"/>
    </MiningSchema>

<!-- We have five items in our input data -->
  <Item id="1" value="A" />
  <Item id="2" value="B" />
  <Item id="3" value="C" />
  <Item id="4" value="D" />
  <Item id="5" value="F" />

<!-- three frequent itemsets with a single item -->
  <Itemset id="1" support="0.833" numberOfItems="1">
    <ItemRef itemRef="1" />
  </Itemset>
     <Itemset id="2" support="0.833" numberOfItems="1">
    <ItemRef itemRef="2" />
  </Itemset>
  <Itemset id="3" support="0.667" numberOfItems="1">
    <ItemRef itemRef="3" />
  </Itemset>

<!-- three frequent itemsets with two items. -->
<Itemset id="4" support="0.667" numberOfItems="2">
   <ItemRef itemRef="1" />
   <ItemRef itemRef="2" />
</Itemset>
<Itemset id="5" support="0.5" numberOfItems="2">
   <ItemRef itemRef="1" />
   <ItemRef itemRef="3" />
</Itemset>
<Itemset id="6" support="0.667" numberOfItems="2">
   <ItemRef itemRef="2" />
   <ItemRef itemRef="3" />
</Itemset>

<!-- one frequent itemset with three items. -->
<Itemset id="7" support="0.5" numberOfItems="2">
   <ItemRef itemRef="1" />
   <ItemRef itemRef="2" />
   <ItemRef itemRef="3" />
```

```
    </Itemset>


    <!-- Three rules satisfy the requirements -->
    <AssociationRule support="0.667" confidence="0.8"
                     antecedent="1" consequent="2" />
    <AssociationRule support="0.667" confidence="0.8"
                     antecedent="2" consequent="1" />
    <AssociationRule support="0.667" confidence="0.8"
                     antecedent="2" consequent="3" />
    <AssociationRule support="0.667" confidence="1.0"
                     antecedent="3" consequent="2" />
    <AssociationRule support="0.5" confidence="1.0"
                     antecedent="5" consequent="2" />
  </AssociationModel>
</PMML>
```

We now give a brief description of this document. The first meaningful element is the `DataDictionary` element: It specifies that association rules have been extracted from a data set whose relevant attributes are `Transaction_ID` and `Item`; both of these attributes are categorical.

Then element `AssociationModel` specifies both the parameters that characterize the association rule extraction process and the set of extracted association rules. As far as the parameters are concerned, notice that a set of XML attributes (whose name is self-explanatory) specifies the total number of transactions in the source data set, the total number of items, the minimum thresholds for support and confidence, the total number of item sets, and the total number of rules that can be found with the previously described parameters. Then, a `MiningSchema` element (with `MiningField` children) specifies the attributes in the source data set that are considered for mining.

The PMML model for association rules summarizes most of the overall association rule extraction process. In fact, elements `Item` describe all the items found in the source data set; elements named `Itemset` report all item sets having sufficient support, where it is possible to observe that the content refers to single items by means of a unique item identifier. Finally, elements `AssociationRules` describe association rules with both sufficient support and confidence; observe that these elements refer to item set identifiers, by means of attributes `antecedent` and `consequent`; furthermore, for each association rule, attributes `support` and `confidence` report its support and confidence, respectively.

To conclude this short description of PMML, we can notice that it is tailored on a set of predefined data models, since it is meant to be a standard communication format. In contrast, PMML does not consider at all the problem of integrating data and models in a unifying framework, based on the notion of a database for data-mining operations.

15.3 The Proposed Data Model: XDM

In this section, we introduce the proposed data model, XDM (XML for Data Mining). We first show the basic idea that is behind a knowledge discovery process conducted through XDM; then we illustrate, by means of several examples, how XDM can be effectively used.

15.3.1 Basic Concepts

Past experience shows that data-mining tasks should be supported by a database system for several reasons. The first one is that data come from large databases and are often stored in data warehouses. The second reason is that if data-mining tasks are supported by a database, it helps to keep track of the intermediate and final results of the knowledge discovery process.

Nevertheless, the database support need not be necessarily provided by a relational (or an object-relational) database. In this chapter, we want to show that better support can be provided by an XML database—that is, a database that stores semi-structured data. The result is a more flexible way to represent heterogeneous data patterns and data transformation models.

XDM Database State

An XDM database is a set of *XDM data items*. An XDM data item is a fragment of a semi-structured tree, represented as an XML fragment rooted in an `XDM-DATA-ITEM` node (element). The root node has three mandatory attributes. The first one, named `Name`, defines the name given to the data item; the second one, named `Derived`, indicates if the data item is (value "`YES`") or is not (value "`NO`") derived; the third attribute, named `Date`, indicates the creation date for the data item.

A *nonderived data item* is a data item that is not the result of the application of a data-mining operator; in this case, the `XDM-DATA-ITEM` element has only one child element—that is, the root of the actual data fragment.

A *derived data item* is the result of the application of a data-mining operator. In this case, the `XDM-DATA_ITEM` element has two children: The first one is an `XDM-DERIVATION` node (element) and describes the application of the data-mining operator that generated the data described by the data item; the second child node (element) is the root of the actual derived data.

For example, a generic nonderived XDM data item has the aspect shown in Listing 15.6.

Listing 15.6 A Nonderived XDM Data Item

```
<XDM Database="host.xdm/AssociationRulesData">
<XDM-DATA-ITEM Name="Purchases" Derived="NO"
               Date="23/3/2002">
      <TRANSACTIONS>
       <PRODUCT TID="1" CUSTOMER="c1" ITEM="A"  PRICE="25"/>
       <PRODUCT TID="1" CUSTOMER="c1" ITEM="B"  PRICE="12"/>
       <PRODUCT TID="1" CUSTOMER="c1" ITEM="C"  PRICE="30"/>
       <PRODUCT TID="1" CUSTOMER="c1" ITEM="D"  PRICE="20"/>
       <PRODUCT TID="2" CUSTOMER="c2" ITEM="C"  PRICE="30"/>
       <PRODUCT TID="2" CUSTOMER="c2" ITEM="D"  PRICE="20"/>
       <PRODUCT TID="2" CUSTOMER="c2" ITEM="B"  PRICE="12"/>
        . . .  . . .  . . .  . . .  . . .  . . .  . . .  . . .
      </TRANSACTIONS>
</XDM-DATA-ITEM>
</XDM>
```

The example in Listing 15.6 shows a fragment of the content of table `Transactions` on purchase transactions data previously discussed in Section 15.2.1, "Extracting and Evaluating Association Rules." However Listing 15.6 and Listing 15.7 will be described in full detail in Section 15.3.3, "Association Rules with XDM," later in this chapter.

The root element is named `XDM`, whose attribute `Database` denotes the database instance named `AssociationRulesData` hosted by a hypothetical XDM Database Management System residing on a computer named `host.xdm`. The `XDM-DATA-ITEM` has a name and a date, and its attribute `Derived` is false. Observe that the actual data are described by elements inside the `TRANSACTIONS` element.

In contrast, a derived XDM data item describing extracted patterns (association rules) from the `XDM-DATA-ITEM` in Listing 15.6 is shown in Listing 15.7.

Listing 15.7 A Derived XDM Data Item Containing Association Rules

```
<XDM Database="host.xdm/AssociationRulesData">
<XDM-DATA-ITEM Name="rules" Derived="YES" Date="28/3/2002">
  <XDM-DERIVATION>
    <MINE-RULE>
      <SOURCE select="//XDM-DATA-ITEM[ @Name='Purchases']"/>
```

```
specification section of a mining operator (e.g., MINE RULE)

      <OUTPUT Type="RULE-SET"/>
    </MINE-RULE>
  </XDM-DERIVATION>
  <ASSOCIATION-RULE-SET>

specification section of the set of extracted association rules

  </ASSOCIATION-RULE SET>
</XDM-DATA-ITEM>
</XDM>
```

In Listing 15.7, we omitted the parameters that characterize the data-mining task; they depend on the particular data-mining operator and will be discussed in Section 15.3.3, "Association Rules with XDM," later in this chapter. It is important to note here that the first child element of the XDM-DATA-ITEM element is an XDM-DERIVATION element. This one describes the source data item (in the SOURCE element) and the type of the output (the OUTPUT element). Then the second child of the XDM-DATA-ITEM element is the ASSOCIATION-RULE-SET element, which contains the derived set of association rules.

XDM Database State Transitions

An XDM database instance evolves thorough *state transitions*. A state transition consists of the application of a data-mining operator to a set of XDM data items and extends the database state with a set of new derived XDM data items.

The state transition is described by an XML document whose root node is named XDM-TRANSITION. It includes the name of the database instance on which the state transition is performed, the mining statement that performs the state transition, the set of source XDM data items, the data-mining operator, the relevant parameters for the data-mining task, and the name and possibly the format of the new derived XDM data items.

The documents specifying state transitions are not stored in the XDM database instance as they are; in contrast, these documents are submitted to the system, similarly to classical SQL statements. When the system generates and stores new derived XDM data items, the XDM-DERIVATION tags report about the statement that generated the data item.

Let us consider a sample state transition submitted to the system (see Listing 15.8).

Listing 15.8 A State Transition Applied to the XDM Data Item of Listing 15.6

```
<XDM-TRANSITION Database="host.xdm/AssociationRulesData">
<XDM-STATEMENT>
  <MINE-RULE>
    <SOURCE select="//XDM-DATA-ITEM [@Name='Purchases']"/>

fragment describing the parameters of the state transition

    <OUTPUT Type="RULE-SET" Name="rules"/>
  </MINE-RULE>
</XDM-STATEMENT>
</XDM-TRANSITION>
```

This document is submitted to the system in order to perform a data-mining operation, namely the extraction of association rules using the `MINE-RULE` operator (the XDM version of the `MINE RULE` operator previously discussed). For the moment, we still omit the parameters that characterize the data-mining task; they will be discussed later.

Here it is important to note that the XDM state transition is described by an `XDM-TRANSITION` element applied to the XDM data item of the same database instance shown in Listing 15.6. The `XDM-TRANSITION` contains an `XDM-STATEMENT` element describing the actual XDM statement. This latter, in turn, contains a child element corresponding to a data-mining operator—in this case, the `MINE-RULE` element. Elements corresponding to a data-mining operator must contain one or more `SOURCE` elements that refer to the source XDM data item through an XPath expression (see the `select` attribute). The `OUTPUT` element, instead, defines the output format and the name of the XDM data item being generated.

Figure 15.2 shows a typical XDM state transition that occurs when an XDM operator is applied to an initial database state.

XDM Database Views

A view of an XDM database is a subset of XDM data items, involved in a complex knowledge discovery process. A view can be *complete* or *partial*: Specified a given target XDM data item, a *complete view* contains all the XDM data items derived by the process and the source data items; a *partial view* is similar to a complete view, but it contains only a user-defined set of XDM data items.

In an orthogonal way, a view can be a *detailed* view or an *abstract* view: In the former, all the included XDM data items are fully described; in the latter, only references to the actual XDM data item are reported, and, in the case of a derived data item, the derivation process description.

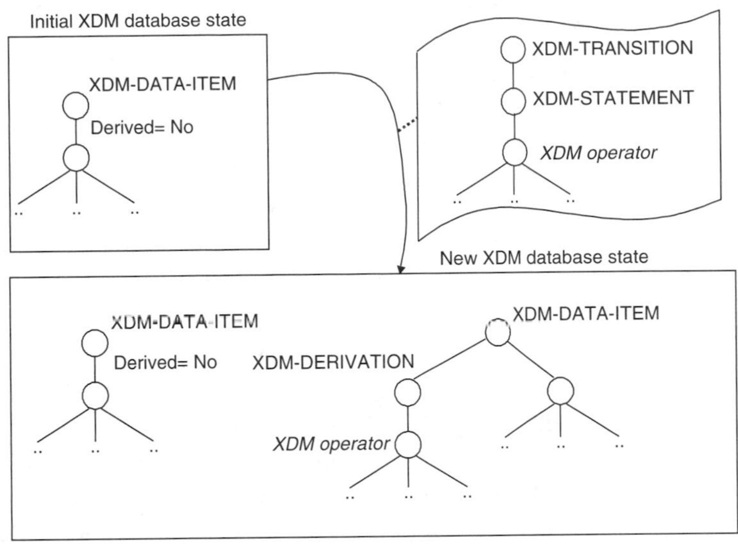

Figure 15.2 A Typical XDM State Transition

In the following sections, we will explain the previously introduced concepts by means of two typical application cases: classification and association rule extraction.

15.3.2 Classification with XDM

Let us now consider a typical data-mining problem—that is, the classification problem. Recall that the classification problem is divided into two steps: the training phase and the test phase. During the training phase, a classification model is built analyzing the so-called training set—that is, a set of classified data. During the test phase, the classification model is applied to new and unclassified data. Hence, the knowledge discovery process based on the classification task necessarily requires the sequential application of two operators.

Initial XDM Database State

Suppose we are creating an XDM database instance, named `ClassificationData`, hosted by a hypothetical XDM Database Management System identified as `host.xdm`; the complete URI for the XDM database instance might be `host.xdm/ClassificationData`.

The initial XDM database state is constituted by one data item—the training set. If we take as an example the training set described in Table 15.4, this state can be described by the XML document shown in Listing 15.9.

Listing 15.9 The XDM Data Item Containing the Training Set of a Classification Problem

```
<XDM Database="host.xdm/ClassificationData">
<XDM-DATA-ITEM Name="Training Set" Derived="NO" Date="22/3/2002">
  <CAR-INSURANCE>
    <PROFILE AGE="17" CAR-TYPE="Sports" RISK="High" />
    <PROFILE AGE="43" CAR-TYPE="Family" RISK="Low" />
    <PROFILE AGE="68" CAR-TYPE="Family" RISK="Low" />
    <PROFILE AGE="32" CAR-TYPE="Truck"  RISK="Low" />
    <PROFILE AGE="23" CAR-TYPE="Family" RISK="High" />
    <PROFILE AGE="18" CAR-TYPE="Family" RISK="High" />
    <PROFILE AGE="20" CAR-TYPE="Family" RISK="High" />
    <PROFILE AGE="45" CAR-TYPE="Sports" RISK="High" />
    <PROFILE AGE="50" CAR-TYPE="Truck"  RISK="Low" />
    <PROFILE AGE="64" CAR-TYPE="Truck"  RISK="High" />
    <PROFILE AGE="46" CAR-TYPE="Family" RISK="Low" />
    <PROFILE AGE="40" CAR-TYPE="Family" RISK="Low" />
  </CAR-INSURANCE>
</XDM-DATA-ITEM>
</XDM>
```

The root element has an attribute, named `Database`, which denotes the URI of the database instance.

The data item is described by element `XDM-DATA-ITEM`, is named `"Training Set"`, is not derived, and its creation date is `22/3/2002`.

Notice that the actual data are contained in the `CAR-INSURANCE` element. The data are described by a set of empty elements named `PROFILE`, and their attributes describe properties (e.g., `AGE` and `CAR-TYPE`) that characterize each classified profile and the class that they have been assigned to (`Risk` Attribute).

Observe that this is one possible representation of the training set. A possible alternative representation, allowed by the semi-structured nature of XML, might be the one shown in Listing 15.10.

Listing 15.10 An Alternative Representation of Listing 15.9

```
<XDM Database="host.xdm/ClassificationData">
<XDM-DATA-ITEM Name="Training Set 2" Derived="NO" Date="22/3/2002">
  <CAR-INSURANCE>
    <PROFILE> <AGE>17</AGE> <CAR-TYPE>Sports</CAR-TYPE>
              <RISK>High</RISK> </PROFILE>
    <PROFILE> <AGE>43</AGE> <CAR-TYPE>Family</CAR-TYPE>
```

```
              <RISK>Low</RISK> </PROFILE>
    <PROFILE> <AGE>68</AGE> <CAR-TYPE>Family</CAR-TYPE>
              <RISK>Low</RISK> </PROFILE>
    <PROFILE> <AGE>32</AGE> <CAR-TYPE>Truck</CAR-TYPE>
              <RISK>Low</RISK> </PROFILE>
    <PROFILE> <AGE>23</AGE> <CAR-TYPE>Family</CAR-TYPE>
              <RISK>High</RISK> </PROFILE>
    <PROFILE> <AGE>18</AGE> <CAR-TYPE>Family</CAR-TYPE>
              <RISK>High</RISK> </PROFILE>
    <PROFILE> <AGE>20</AGE> <CAR-TYPE>Family</CAR-TYPE>
              <RISK>High</RISK> </PROFILE>
    <PROFILE> <AGE>45</AGE> <CAR-TYPE>Sports</CAR-TYPE>
              <RISK>High</RISK> </PROFILE>
    <PROFILE> <AGE>50</AGE> <CAR-TYPE>Truck</CAR-TYPE>
              <RISK>Low</RISK> </PROFILE>
    <PROFILE> <AGE>64</AGE> <CAR-TYPE>Truck</CAR-TYPE>
              <RISK>High</RISK> </PROFILE>
    <PROFILE> <AGE>46</AGE> <CAR-TYPE>Family</CAR-TYPE>
              <RISK>Low</RISK> </PROFILE>
    <PROFILE> <AGE>40</AGE> <CAR-TYPE>Family</CAR-TYPE>
              <RISK>Low</RISK> </PROFILE>
  </CAR-INSURANCE>
</XDM-DATA-ITEM>
</XDM>
```

Notice that this representation pushes single pieces of data into the content of elements named AGE, CAR-TYPE, and RISK. Although less synthetic, it is equivalent to the former representation.

Building the Classification Model

The first step for solving a classification problem is to build the classification model based on the training set. Suppose that a suitable operator is available in our framework; to obtain the classification model, it is necessary to apply such an operator to the training set, which constitutes the initial state of the XDM database. In other words, we have to perform a *state transition* that produces a new database state, augmenting the initial state with a new data item describing the classification model.

Let us see how the state transition might be described, by means of an XML document rooted in the XDM-TRANSITION element (see Listing 15.11).

Listing 15.11 The Transition Performed by the Generation of the Classification Model

```
<XDM-TRANSITION Database="host.xdm/ClassificationData">
  <XDM-STATEMENT>
    <MINE-CLASSIFICATION>
      <SOURCE select="//XDM-DATA-ITEM[ @Name='Training Set']/CAR-
INSURANCE"/>
      <CLASSIFICATION-UNIT select="PROFILE">
        <PARAM name="AGE" select="@AGE" Type="Integer"/>
        <PARAM name="CAR-TYPE" select="@CAR-TYPE" Type="String"/>
        <CLASS-PARAM select="@RISK"/>
      </CLASSIFICATION-UNIT>
      <OUTPUT Type="CLASSIFICATION-TREE" Name="Risk Classes"/>
    </MINE-CLASSIFICATION>
  </XDM-STATEMENT>
</XDM-TRANSITION>
```

The first thing to note in Listing 15.11 is the root element of the XML document: It is the XDM-TRANSITION node. Indeed Listing 15.11 specifies a mining task or a state transition. The attribute named Database specifies the XDM database instance on which the specified state transition must be performed.

The applied operator is named MINE-CLASSIFICATION and is described by the homonymous element. Elements in their content define parameters necessary to drive the classification process.

The SOURCE element selects the data item that constitutes the training set; in particular, the selection is performed through the XPath query specified in the select attribute. The reported XPath expression:

```
//XDM-DATA-ITEM[ @Name='Training Set']/CAR-INSURANCE
```

denotes that the training set is within the CAR-INSURANCE element contained in the XDM data item whose name is Training Set (see Listing 15.9).

The next element appearing in the state transition specification, named CLASSIFICATION-UNIT, denotes which elements inside the selected CAR-INSURANCE element must be considered for building the classification model. In particular, the select attribute denotes (through an XPath expression that implicitly operates in the context defined by the SOURCE element) the set of elements in the training set whose properties must be used to build the classification model. Inside the CLASSIFICATION-UNIT element, a nonempty set of PARAM elements denotes the properties that will be used to build the classification model (always through XPath expressions). The Type attribute specifies the data type (e.g., integers, real numbers, strings, etc.) that will be used for the evaluation of the property. Notice that this is necessary to overcome the absence of data types in XML. Finally, the CLASS-PARAM element specifies the property inside the classification unit that defines the class (always by means of an XPath expression denoted by the select attribute).

In our sample case, the elements named PROFILE are the classification units, as specified by the select attribute (select="PROFILE") in the CLASSIFICATION-UNIT node. The PARAM nodes denote that the properties that will be used for the classification model are the attributes AGE and CAR-TYPE, through the XPath expressions @AGE and @CAR-TYPE in the PROFILE nodes. The class label is included in attributes RISK, as specified by the XPath expression @RISK in the CLASS-PARAM node.

To conclude the specification, it is necessary to specify the output, by means of the OUTPUT element. Its attribute named Name specifies the name of the newly generated XDM data item. Attribute Type allows the specification of the format chosen for the classification model: In this case, a classification tree is specified, but we can suppose that implementations of this operator generate both classification trees and classification rules.

Observations

At first, notice the fact that elements that constitute the MINE-CLASSIFICATION operator are not prefixed as XDM elements. This is motivated by the fact that XDM is an open framework, which is not based on any predefined data-mining operator. In contrast, XDM is devised in order to be extended with any operator, provided that its application can be specified by means of an XML specification.

A second thing to notice is the following. The use of XPath provides several advantages. At first, XPath expressions are simple to write and easy to understand. Furthermore, they make transparent the information sources to the operator. To explain this concept, suppose we had to build the same classification model moving from the alternative representation of the training set described by the XDM data item named Training Set 2; we can specify the application of the MINE-CLASSIFICATION operator by using a state transition identical to the previously discussed one, apart from the content of the CLASSIFICATION-UNIT element, which becomes as follows:

```
<CLASSIFICATION-UNIT select="PROFILE">
  <PARAM name="AGE" select="AGE/." Type="Integer"/>
  <PARAM name="CAR-TYPE" select="CAR-TYPE/." Type="String"/>
  <CLASS-PARAM select="RISK/."/>
</CLASSIFICATION-UNIT>
```

Observe that only the value of the select attributes has changed with respect to the example of Listing 15.11. In particular, we now consider the content of elements named AGE, CAR-TYPE, and RISK (through the XPath expressions "AGE/.", "CAR_TYPE/.", and "RISK/.", respectively).

The Classification Model

The state transition discussed so far produces a new XDM data item containing a classification tree. Consequently, the state of the XDM database now contains two data items. The first is the original one, and the second is the new generated one. For the sake of saving space, we do not report the complete database state, but the *partial view* that reports only the data item describing the classification tree.

In the following examples of XDM code, when necessary, we will show in normal font the portion of code that has already been described in previous examples and has been inserted in the current example for the sake of the derivation process. The new portion of the XDM code is shown in bold font. However, the code in normal font need not to be reexamined by the reader since it is the same as the code already explained. For example, in Listing 15.12, the code already shown in Listing 15.11 is in normal font.

Listing 15.12 The XDM Data Item with the Classification Tree Obtained after the Transition of Listing 15.11

```
<XDM Database="host.xdm/ClassificationData">
  <XDM-DATA-ITEM Name="Risk Classes" Derived="YES" Date="5/4/2002">
    <XDM-DERIVATION>
      <MINE-CLASSIFICATION>
      <SOURCE select="//XDM-DATA-ITEM[@Name='Training Set']/CAR-
INSURANCE "/>
      <CLASSIFICATION-UNIT select="PROFILE">
        <PARAM name="AGE" select="@AGE"/>
        <PARAM name="CAR-TYPE" select="@CAR-TYPE"/>
        <CLASS-PARAM select="@RISK"/>
      </CLASSIFICATION-UNIT>
      <OUTPUT Type="CLASSIFICATION-TREE" Name="Risk Classes"/>
      </MINE-CLASSIFICATION>
    </XDM-DERIVATION>
    <CLASSIFICATION-TREE>
      <CLASS-PARAM Name="RISK"/>
      <CONDITION>
        <EQ> <PARAM Name="CAR-TYPE"/> <VALUE String5"Sports"/>
</EQ>
      </CONDITION>
```

```
        <TRUE-BRANCH>
          <CLASS Value="High"/>
        </TRUE-BRANCH>
        <FALSE-BRANCH>
          <CONDITION>
            <LEQ> <PARAM Name="AGE"/> <VALUE Integer="23"/> </LEQ>
          </CONDITION>
          <TRUE-BRANCH>
            <CLASS Value="High"/>
          </TRUE-BRANCH>
          <FALSE-BRANCH>
            <CLASS Value="Low"/>
          </FALSE-BRANCH>
        </FALSE-BRANCH>
      </CLASSIFICATION-TREE>
    </XDM-DATA-ITEM>
  </XDM>
```

Since the classification tree is a derived data item, the first element in the content of the XDM-DATA-ITEM element is an XDM-DERIVATION element. This element reports the state transition that generated the data item.

Consider now the element CLASSIFICATION-TREE that describes the classification tree generated by the application of the data-mining operator. Notice that while it is hard to effectively represent a classification tree in a table, XML is really suitable for this purpose, due to the a priori unlimited nesting levels. In fact, consider the sample classification tree depicted in Figure 15.1. The first child element in the content of element CLASSIFICATION-TREE, named CLASS-PARAM, specifies which parameter constitutes the class (the risk property). Then, a sequence of three elements, named CONDITION, TRUE-BRANCH, and FALSE-BRANCH, describes the condition to be applied in the root node, the branch to follow if the condition is evaluated to true, and the branch to follow when it is false, respectively.

Inside a branch, it is possible to find either a class assignment (denoted by element CLASS, which is also a leaf of the tree) or another triple, CONDITION, TRUE-BRANCH, and FALSE-BRANCH, and so forth.

As far as conditions are concerned, they are usually based on comparisons between properties and numerical ranges or categorical values; the syntax chosen in our sample classification tree is just an example to show that it is possible to represent conditional expressions in XML. The reader can anyway notice that the XML representation corresponds to the classification tree of Figure 15.1.

The Test Phase

Typically, the classification model is used to classify unclassified data. For example, we can think that a new data item is loaded into the XDM database, consisting of unclassified applicants' profiles. Then a suitable state transition is performed: It takes the unclassified data set and the classification tree and generates the classified data set.

Let us describe such a process by means of our sample XDM database. Suppose that a new set of applicants is loaded into the database. This might be described by the following XDM data item, named `New Applicants` (see Listing 15.13).

Listing 15.13 The XDM Data Item Containing the Test Set

```
<XDM Database="host.xdm/ClassificationData">
<XDM-DATA-ITEM Name="New Applicants" Derived="NO" Date="10/4/2002">
  <NEW-APPLICANTS>
    <APPLICANT Name="John Smyth" AGE="22" CAR-TYPE="Family"/>
    <APPLICANT Name="Marc Green" AGE="60" CAR-TYPE="Family"/>
    <APPLICANT Name="Laura Fox" AGE="35" CAR-TYPE="Sports"/>
  </NEW-APPLICANTS>
</XDM-DATA-ITEM>
</XDM>
```

Observe that the root element (`NEW-APPLICANTS`) and the elements in its content (`APPLICANT` elements), which describe single profiles of new applicants, are different with respect to the corresponding elements of the training set—for example, `CAR-INSURANCE` and `PROFILE` (see Listing 15.9); in particular, data about applicants also describe applicants' names. With XDM, this is not a problem because the XPath expressions used in state transition specifications make the applied data-mining operator unaware of the root element.

At this point, we have to define an XDM state transition, whose goal is to generate a new data item: This new data item is obtained by adding an attribute, which denotes the risk class, to each `APPLICANT` element in the data item named `New Applicants` (see Listing 15.13); the class value is determined by applying the classification tree generated by the previous state transition (see Listing 15.12). Suppose the XDM system provides such an operator, named, for example, `TEST-CLASSIFICATION`. The desired state transition might be as shown in Listing 15.14.

Listing 15.14 The XDM State Transition Leading to the Classified Test Set

```
<XDM-TRANSITION Database="host.xdm/ClassificationData">
<XDM-STATEMENT>
  <TEST-CLASSIFICATION>
```

```
  <SOURCE select="//XDM-DATA-ITEM[@Name='New Applicants']/NEW-
APPLICANTS"/>
  <CLASSIFICATION-MODEL Type="CLASSIFICATION-TREE"
        select="//XDM-DATA-ITEM [@Name='Risk Classes']
            [ @Date='5/4/2002']/CLASSIFICATION-TREE"/>
  <CLASSIFICATION-UNIT select="APPLICANT">
    <PARAM name="AGE" select="@AGE"/>
    <PARAM name="CAR-TYPE" select="@CAR-TYPE"/>
  </CLASSIFICATION-UNIT>
  <EXTEND-WITH-CLASS Name="Risk" Type="Attribute"/>
  <OUTPUT Name="Classified Applicants"/>
  </TEST-CLASSIFICATION>
</XDM-STATEMENT>
</XDM-TRANSITION>
```

This state transition specification can be read as follows. The element `SOURCE` specifies the XDM data items to classify, through the XPath expression in the `select` attribute. This is:

```
Select="//XDM-DATA-ITEM [ @Name='New Applicants']/NEW-APPLICANTS"
```

and states that the data set to classify is contained in the XDM data item whose name is `New Applicants`, rooted in the node `NEW-APPLICANTS` (see Listing 15.13).

Then the `CLASSIFICATION-MODEL` element specifies the XDM data item that contains the classification model to apply on the data to classify. In fact, the XPath expression that constitutes the value of the `select` attribute:

```
select="//XDM-DATA-ITEM[ @Name='Risk Classes']
 [ @Date='5/4/2002']/CLASSIFICATION-TREE"
```

says that the classification tree is contained in the XDM data item whose name is `Risk Classes` and the generation date is `5/4/2002` (see Listing 15.12).

Similarly to the `MINE-CLASSIFICATION` operator, the `CLASSIFICATION-UNIT` element specifies the nodes in the data item that contain the data to classify. In this case, the select attribute says that nodes named `APPLICANT` contain data to classify (`select="APPLICANT"`). Inside this element, a set of `PARAM` elements denotes the nodes in the data item that describe the classification model parameters. In this case:

```
<PARAM name="AGE" select="@AGE"/>
<PARAM name="CAR-TYPE" select="@CAR-TYPE"/>
```

Attributes AGE and CAR-TYPE (see the XPath expressions in the select attributes) in the APPLICANT nodes are mapped to the homonymous parameters in the classification tree.

The next element, named EXTEND-WITH-CLASS, specifies how the data to classify are extended with the class label, when the new data item containing classified data is generated. In particular, in our case:

```
<EXTEND-WITH-CLASS Name="RISK" Type="Attribute"/>
```

The element says that a new object is added to the APPLICANT node; this object is called RISK and is an attribute (alternatively, it is possible to add a node/element).

Finally the OUTPUT element denotes the name of the new data item (the TEST-CLASSIFICATION operator is polymorph with respect to the structure of classified data, so no output type must be specified). In our case:

```
<OUTPUT Name="Classified Applicants"/>
```

says that the new generated data item is called Classified Applicants. This data item is shown in the next section.

The Derivation of the Classified Test Data

In this section we describe the derivation of the classified test data, starting with the derived XDM data item in Listing 15.15.

Listing 15.15 The Derived XDM Data Item Containing the Classified Test Data

```
<XDM Database="host.xdm/ClassificationData">
  <XDM-DATA-ITEM Name="Classified Applicants" Derived="YES"
                 Date="10/4/2002">
  <XDM-DERIVATION>
  <TEST-CLASSIFICATION>
    <SOURCE
       select="//XDM-DATA-ITEM[ @Name='New Applicants']/NEW-
APPLICANTS"/>
    <CLASSIFICATION-MODEL Type="CLASSIFICATION-TREE"
       select="//XDM-DATA-ITEM[ @Name='Risk Classes']
             [ @Date='5/4/2002']/CLASSIFICATION-TREE"/>
    <CLASSIFICATION-UNIT select="APPLICANT">
      <PARAM name="AGE" select="@AGE"/>
      <PARAM name="CAR-TYPE" select="@CAR-TYPE"/>
    </CLASSIFICATION-UNIT>
```

```
    <EXTEND-WITH-CLASS Name="RISK" Type="Attribute"/>
  </TEST-CLASSIFICATION>
  </XDM-DERIVATION>

  <CLASSIFIED-NEW-APPLICANTS>
    <APPLICANT Name="John Smyth" AGE="22" CAR-TYPE="Family"
RISK="High"/>
    <APPLICANT Name="Marc Green" AGE="60" CAR-TYPE="Family"
RISK="Low" />
    <APPLICANT Name="Laura Fox" AGE="35" CAR-TYPE="Sports"
RISK="High"/>
  </CLASSIFIED-NEW-APPLICANTS>
</XDM-DATA-ITEM>
</XDM>
```

Notice the XDM-DERIVATION element, which reports the state transition (described with Listing 15.14) and the CLASSIFIED-NEW-APPLICANTS element, which contains the classified data. Observe that each APPLICANT element has now a new attribute, named RISK, which describes the class; its value has been determined based on the classification tree. The reader can easily check these values—for example, by using the graphical representation of the classification tree reported in Figure 15.1.

To conclude our discussion about the test phase, we report a view that describes the test phase previously described (see Listing 15.16).

Listing 15.16 The XDM Database View Showing the Test Phase

```
<XDM Database="host.xdm/ClassificationData">
<XDM-DATA-ITEM Name="New Applicants" Derived="NO" Date="10/4/2002">
  <NEW-APPLICANTS>
    <APPLICANT Name="John Smyth" AGE="22" CAR-TYPE="Family"/>
    <APPLICANT Name="Marc Green" AGE="60" CAR-TYPE="Family"/>
    <APPLICANT Name="Laura Fox" AGE="35" CAR-TYPE="Sports"/>
  </NEW-APPLICANTS>
</XDM-DATA-ITEM>

<XDM-DATA-ITEM Name="Classified Applicants" Derived="YES"
               Date="10/4/2002">
  <XDM-DERIVATION>
    <TEST-CLASSIFICATION>
    <SOURCE
       select="//XDM-DATA-ITEM[ @Name='New Applicants']/NEW-
```

```
APPLICANTS"/>
    <CLASSIFICATION-MODEL Type="CLASSIFICATION-TREE"
       select="//XDM-DATA-ITEM[@Name='Risk Classes']
              [ @Date='5/4/2002']/CLASSIFICATION-TREE"/>
    <CLASSIFICATION-UNIT select="APPLICANT">
      <PARAM name="AGE" select="@AGE"/>
      <PARAM name="CAR-TYPE" select="@CAR-TYPE"/>
    </CLASSIFICATION-UNIT>
    <EXTEND-WITH-CLASS Name="RISK" Type="Attribute"/>
    </TEST-CLASSIFICATION>
  </XDM-DERIVATION>
  <CLASSIFIED-NEW-APPLICANTS>
    <APPLICANT Name="John Smyth" AGE="22" CAR-TYPE="Family"
RISK="High"/>
    <APPLICANT Name="Marc Green" AGE="60" CAR-TYPE="Family"
RISK="Low" />
    <APPLICANT Name="Laura Fox" AGE="35" CAR-TYPE="Sports"
RISK="High"/>
  </CLASSIFIED-NEW-APPLICANTS>
</XDM-DATA-ITEM>
</XDM>
```

The Overall Classification Process

At this point, it is important to summarize the overall classification process, by means of Figure 15.3.

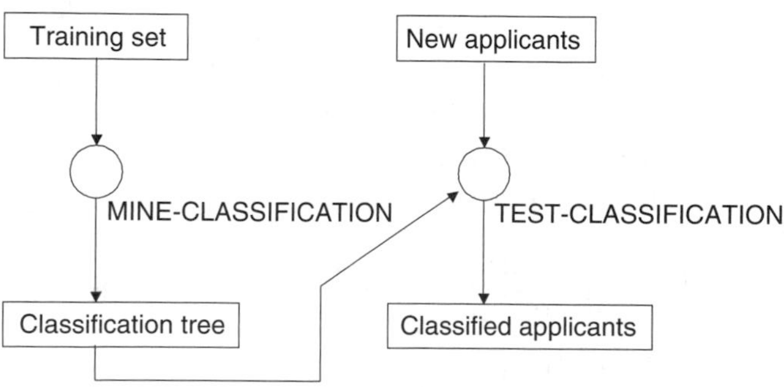

Figure 15.3 The Overall Classification Process

In the figure, we represent XDM data items as labeled rectangles, where the label denotes the data item name; with labeled circles, we denote the application of XDM data-mining operators, where the label denotes the applied operator.

The first step is constituted by the extraction of the classification model, represented as a classification tree, by means of the `MINE-CLASSIFICATION` operator applied to the XDM data item named `Training Set`; this operator generates the XDM data item named `Classification Tree`.

Then the application of the `TEST-CLASSIFICATION` operator allows us to classify data in the XDM data item named `New Applicants` based on the classification model in the XDM data item named `Classification Tree`; the operator generates the new XDM data item named `Classified Applicants`, which contains the same data of the data item named `New Applicants` extended with the class label.

From now on, any other data-mining or analysis task might be performed. The advantage of XDM is that the overall process, even complex, is traced by the system.

15.3.3 Association Rules with XDM

In this section, the example of the extraction of association rules presented in Section 15.2.1, "Extracting and Evaluating Association Rules," is discussed with the use of XDM.

We want to create here another XDM database instance, named `Association-RulesData`, hosted by the hypothetical XDM Database Management System `host.xdm`; the complete URI for the XDM database instance is therefore `host.xdm/AssociationRulesData`.

The initial XDM database state is constituted by one data item, `Purchases`, the source data that we want to analyze by means of association rules. The initial state is described by the following XML document in Listing 15.17. Notice that the attribute `Derived` is false.

Listing 15.17 The XDM Data Item Containing the Purchase Transaction Data

```
<XDM Database="host.xdm/AssociationRulesData">
<XDM-DATA-ITEM Name="Purchases" Derived="NO"
             Date="23/3/2002">
     <TRANSACTIONS>
       <PRODUCT TID="1" CUSTOMER="c1" ITEM="A"  PRICE="25"/>
       <PRODUCT TID="1" CUSTOMER="c1" ITEM="B"  PRICE="12"/>
       <PRODUCT TID="1" CUSTOMER="c1" ITEM="C"  PRICE="30"/>
       <PRODUCT TID="1" CUSTOMER="c1" ITEM="D"  PRICE="20"/>
       <PRODUCT TID="2" CUSTOMER="c2" ITEM="C"  PRICE="30"/>
       <PRODUCT TID="2" CUSTOMER="c2" ITEM="D"  PRICE="20"/>
```

```
            <PRODUCT TID="2" CUSTOMER="c2" ITEM="B"  PRICE="12"/>
            . . .  . . . . . . . . . . . . . . . . . .  . . . .  . . .
        </TRANSACTIONS>
    </XDM-DATA-ITEM>
    </XDM>
```

The actual data are contained in the TRANSACTIONS element and are described by a set of empty elements named PRODUCT, where the attributes describe the properties that characterize each purchased product (TID is the transaction identifier, customer; item and price are the homonymous attributes already seen in Transactions shown in Table 15.1). Observe that, analogously as already said with the representation of classification data, this is only a possible representation of the source data set. An alternative representation might include the content of the attributes of the transactions in the children elements of PRODUCT.

The Extraction of Association Rules

We suppose at this point that an implementation of the MINE-RULE operator is available in this framework. This MINE-RULE implementation extracts association rules from an XDM data item, according to MINE-RULE semantics described in Section 15.2.1, "Extracting and Evaluating Association Rules." In other words, it performs a *state transition* that produces a new database state augmenting the initial state with a new data item. In Listing 15.18 we provide the description of the state transition by means of an XML document rooted in the XDM-TRANSITION element.

Listing 15.18 The XDM State Transition Produced by the MINE RULE Operator

```
<XDM-TRANSITION Database="host.xdm/AssociationRulesData">
<XDM-STATEMENT>
  <MINE-RULE>
    <SOURCE select="//XDM-DATA-
ITEM[@Name='Purchases']/TRANSACTIONS"/>
    <GROUPING select="PRODUCT" common-value="@TID"/>
    <RULE-SCHEMA>
      <BODY-SCHEMA>
        <RULE-ELEMENT name="ITEM" select="@ITEM"/>
        <CARD min="1" max="N"/>
      </BODY-SCHEMA>
      <HEAD-SCHEMA>
        <RULE-ELEMENT name="ITEM" select="@ITEM"/>
```

```
        <CARD min="1" max="N"/>
      </HEAD-SCHEMA>
    </RULE-SCHEMA>
    <MEASURES>
      <SUPPORT threshold="0.5"/>
      <CONFIDENCE threshold="0.8"/>
    </MEASURES>
      <OUTPUT Type="RULE-SET" Name="rules"/>
  </MINE-RULE>
</XDM-STATEMENT>
</XDM-TRANSITION>
```

Notice that the root node, named XDM-TRANSITION, recalls that the document considered here specifies a mining task, or a state transition to the database instance AssociationRulesData.

The XDM-STATEMENT, as already said, provides a description of the syntactic elements of the MINE RULE operator described by the MINE-RULE element. Again analogously to the MINE-CLASSIFICATION operator, SOURCE identifies the source of the data from which association rules will be extracted, through an XPath expression described by attribute select.

The GROUPING element specifies how source data is grouped (that is, by keeping together data having a common property). Grouping constitutes one of the most important operations in association rule mining because the association rules will be extracted, taking elements from within groups. Therefore, select defines the elements that are grouped together, and common-value defines the common property to the elements of the group.

```
<GROUPING select="PRODUCT" common-value="@TID"/>
```

This GROUPING element specifies that groups will be composed of PRODUCT elements found in the XDM data item (select attribute) such that given a group all PRODUCT nodes share the same value for attribute TID (common-value attribute).

RULE-SCHEMA defines the schema of the association rules by separately defining the body and head of rules through elements named BODY-SCHEMA and HEAD-SCHEMA. Both of them allow the children nodes RULE-ELEMENT and CARD.

The node RULE-ELEMENT defines elements that constitute the body of the rule; the XPath expression specified by select denotes either attributes or #PCDATA nodes, whose values are associated by rules; attribute name specifies the name given to the body element. The body schema definition is completed by the CARD element, whose attributes min and max denote the minimum and maximum number of elements appearing in the body; the value "N" for attribute max specifies that the maximum cardinality is unlimited.

In our sample state transition, the body schema is defined as follows:

```
<BODY-SCHEMA>
  <RULE-ELEMENT name="ITEM" select="@ITEM"/>
  <CARD min="1" max="N"/>
</BODY-SCHEMA>
```

The MEASURES element in the MINE-RULE operator introduces, by means of *ad hoc* subelements, minimum support and confidence threshold values.

Notice that here it is possible to extend the semantics of the operator and allow other evaluation measures (such as *conviction* or *lift*) known in the literature on association rules.

Finally, element OUTPUT tells us the type of the derived XDM data item (RULE-SET) and its name (rules).

The Derivation of the Association Rules

The XML document in Listing 15.19 describes the XDM data item produced by the state transition and named rules. Notice that attribute derived is set to "YES". The child node ASSOCIATION-RULE-SET contains the set of association rules extracted by the MINE-RULE operator. The XDM-DERIVATION child element explains how this data item has been derived, resuming the state transition that generated the data item; in particular, it contains the definition of the extracted association rules.

Listing 15.19 The XDM Data Item with Association Rules Obtained by the State Transition

```
<XDM Database="host.xdm/AssociationRulesData">
<XDM-DATA-ITEM Name="rules" Derived="YES" Date="28/3/2002">
  <XDM-DERIVATION>
    <MINE-RULE>
      <SOURCE select="//XDM-DATA-ITEM[ @Name='Purchases']
/TRANSACTIONS"/>
      <GROUPING select="PRODUCT" common-value="@TID"/>
      <RULE-SCHEMA>
        <BODY-SCHEMA>
          <RULE-ELEMENT name="ITEM" select="@ITEM"/>
          <CARD min="1" max="N"/>
        <BODY-SCHEMA/>
        <HEAD-SCHEMA>
```

```
        <RULE-ELEMENT name="ITEM" select="@ITEM"/>
        <CARD min="1" max="N"/>
      <HEAD-SCHEMA/>
    <RULE-SCHEMA/>
    <MEASURES>
      <SUPPORT threshold="0.5"/>
      <CONFIDENCE threshold="0.8"/>
    <MEASURES/>
    <OUTPUT Type="RULE-SET" Name="rules"/>
  </MINE-RULE>
</XDM-DERIVATION>
<ASSOCIATION-RULE-SET>
  <RULE>
    <BODY>
      <ELEMENT Name="ITEM"> A </ELEMENT>
    </BODY>
    <HEAD>
      <ELEMENT Name="ITEM"> B </ELEMENT>
    </HEAD>
    <SUPPORT value="0.667">
    <CONFIDENCE value="0.8">
  </RULE>
  <RULE>
    <BODY>
      <ELEMENT Name="ITEM"> B </ELEMENT>
    </BODY>
    <HEAD>
      <ELEMENT Name="ITEM"> A </ELEMENT>
    </HEAD>
    <SUPPORT value="0.667">
    <CONFIDENCE value="0.8">
  </RULE>
  <RULE>
    <BODY>
      <ELEMENT Name="ITEM"> B </ELEMENT>
    </BODY>
    <HEAD>
      <ELEMENT Name="ITEM"> C </ELEMENT>
    </HEAD>
    <SUPPORT value="0.667">
    <CONFIDENCE value="0.8">
  </RULE>
```

```
      <RULE>
        <BODY>
          <ELEMENT Name="ITEM"> C </ELEMENT>
        </BODY>
        <HEAD>
          <ELEMENT Name="ITEM"> B </ELEMENT>
        </HEAD>
        <SUPPORT value="0.667">
        <CONFIDENCE value="1">
      </RULE>
      <RULE>
        <BODY>
          <ELEMENT Name="ITEM"> A </ELEMENT>
          <ELEMENT Name="ITEM"> C </ELEMENT>
        </BODY>
        <HEAD>
          <ELEMENT Name="ITEM"> B </ELEMENT>
        </HEAD>
        <SUPPORT value="0.5">
        <CONFIDENCE value="1">
      </RULE>
    </ASSOCIATION-RULE-SET>
  </XDM-DATA-ITEM>
  </XDM>
```

In the ASSOCIATION-RULE-SET node, BODY and HEAD children nodes contain a set of ELEMENT nodes that are the elements that have been associated with each other in an association rule. Each ELEMENT node has an attribute Name, which indicates the name given to the rule element (as specified by the RULE-ELEMENT tag in the state transition); the content of the ELEMENT node is the value associated by the rule.

Finally, the SUPPORT element gives the value of support of an association rule, and analogously of the CONFIDENCE element.

For example, rule $\{A,C\} \Rightarrow \{B\}$, which associates itemset $\{A, C\}$ to itemset $\{B\}$ with support 0.5 and confidence 1, is represented as shown in Listing 15.20.

Listing 15.20 Rule Example

```
<RULE>
  <BODY>
    <ELEMENT Name="ITEM"> A </ELEMENT>
    <ELEMENT Name="ITEM"> C </ELEMENT>
  </BODY>
```

```
    <HEAD>
      <ELEMENT Name="ITEM"> B </ELEMENT>
    </HEAD>
    <SUPPORT value="0.5">
    <CONFIDENCE value="1">
  </RULE>
```

Observe that the presented data item is the XDM representation of the rule set depicted in Table 15.2; hence, the state transition described is the XDM counterpart of the MINE-RULE statement described in Section 15.2.1, "Extracting and Evaluating Association Rules."

As a final comment, notice that the elements that constitute the MINE-RULE operator and its result set (RULE-SET) are not prefixed as XDM elements, as happened with MINE-CLASSIFICATION. This is motivated again by the fact that XDM is an open framework and might be extended with any operator, provided that its application is specified with an XML specification.

Evaluation of Association Rules with XDM

We present in this paragraph the evaluation of association rules with XDM. The association rules that must be evaluated have been already extracted during the mining step with the XDM MINE-RULE operator whose state transition is detailed in Listing 15.8.

We suppose that an implementation of the EVALUATE-RULE operator, described by the element EVALUATE-RULE in XDM, is available. This operator extracts its results from two XDM data items, the transaction data and the association rule set—and performs a *state transition* whose result is a new data item and a new database state, with the set of evaluated association rules. The state transition that applies the EVALUATE-RULE operator to the sample database instance obtained by the previous application of the MINE-RULE operator is described in Listing 15.21), rooted in the XDM-TRANSITION element.

Listing 15.21 The XDM State Transition Performed by the EVALUATE Operator

```
<XDM-TRANSITION Database="host.xdm/AssociationRulesData">
  <XDM-STATEMENT>
    <EVALUATE-RULE>
      <DATA-SECTION>
        <SOURCE select="//XDM-DATA-ITEM[ @Name='Purchases']/
TRANSACTIONS"/>
        <EVALUATION-FEATURE name="CUSTOMER" select="@CUSTOMER"/>
        <GROUPING select="PRODUCT" common-value="@TID"/>
```

```
      </DATA-SECTION>
      <RULE-SECTION>
        <SOURCE
        select="//XDM-DATA-ITEM[ @Name='rules']/ASSOCIATION-RULE-
SET"/>
      </RULE-SECTION>
      <RULE-SCHEMA>
        <BODY-SCHEMA>
          <RULE-ELEMENT name="ITEM" select="@ITEM"/>
        </BODY-SCHEMA>
        <HEAD-SCHEMA>
          <RULE-ELEMENT name="ITEM" select="@ITEM"/>
        </HEAD-SCHEMA>
      </RULE-SCHEMA>
      <OUTPUT Type="DATA-WITH-RULES" Name="Rules with Customers"/>
    </EVALUATE-RULE>
  </XDM-STATEMENT>
</XDM-TRANSITION>
```

The XDM-STATEMENT provides a description of the syntactic elements of the EVALUATE-RULE operator. Recall from Section 15.2.1, "Extracting and Evaluating Association Rules," that the operator evaluates an association rule set over the source data set; in the example case, the goal is to evaluate the association rule set over the transaction data, in order to obtain, for each rule, the set of customers for which the rule holds.

For this reason, the EVALUATE-RULE tag contains four elements: the DATA-SECTION element specifies the data item on which the association rule set must be evaluated; the RULE-SECTION specifies the data item containing the association rule set; the RULE-SCHEMA element specifies the structure of association rules; finally, the OUTPUT element specifies the output data item.

In more detail, the DATA-SECTION element specifies the data item on which the rules must be evaluated and how the evaluation must be performed. Hence, in its content we find a SOURCE element whose select attribute specifies an XPath expression that selects the data item. Then, an element named EVALUATION-FEATURE specifies the feature for which the rules must be evaluated: In particular, the attribute name specifies the feature name, while the attribute select defines the XPath expression that locates the evaluation feature. Finally, the GROUPING element specifies how data in the source data item are grouped (analogously to the MINE-RULE operator). To clarify, the fragment in Listing 15.22 says that the data item named Purchases (see Listing 15.6) will be selected in order to evaluate association rules.

Listing 15.22 Purchases Example

```
<DATA-SECTION>
  <SOURCE select="//XDM-DATA-ITEM[ @Name='Purchases']/
TRANSACTIONS"/>
  <EVALUATION-FEATURE name="CUSTOMER" select="@CUSTOMER"/>
  <GROUPING select="PRODUCT" common-value="@TID"/>
</DATA-SECTION>
```

The evaluation will be performed with respect to customers. To do so, data are partitioned based on the CUSTOMER attribute, in order to have in a partition all transaction data concerning the same customer. Then, all transaction data concerning a single customer (a partition) are further grouped by transaction IDs (attribute TID). Consequently, an association rule holds for a customer if it is present in at least one group (which contains all transaction data referring to the same transaction ID). That group appears in the partition corresponding to the transaction data of that customer.

The RULE-SCHEMA element contains only a SOURCE element, which specifies, through an XPath expression, the XDM data item containing the rule set that must be evaluated. In our example, the XDM data item named rules is selected (see Listing 15.19). The element named RULE-SCHEMA simply contains body schema and head schema definitions, rooted in the BODY-SCHEMA and in the HEAD-SCHEMA elements, respectively. They are the same elements appearing also in the MINE-RULE operator. Body schema and head schema definitions in MINE-RULE and EVALUATE-RULE are the same, apart from the fact that in EVALUATE-RULE they do not contain the CARD element. Indeed, since rules have already been extracted, it is not necessary to specify a constraint on the cardinality of body and head.

For example, our state transition contains the RULE-SCHEMA definition shown in Listing 15.23.

Listing 15.23 RULE-SCHEMA Definition

```
<RULE-SCHEMA>
  <BODY-SCHEMA>
    <RULE-ELEMENT name="ITEM" select="@ITEM"/>
  </BODY-SCHEMA>
  <HEAD-SCHEMA>
    <RULE-ELEMENT name="ITEM" select="@ITEM"/>
  </HEAD-SCHEMA>
</RULE-SCHEMA>
```

The RULE-SCHEMA definition shows how to associate values of the ITEM attribute to the transaction data.

The Derivation of the Evaluated Association Rules

The state transition produces a new, derived XDM-DATA-ITEM, named Rules with Customers, containing the association rules in rules and, for each rule, the set of customers for which the rule is satisfied. The XDM-DERIVATION element contained in the XML document in Listing 15.24 explains how this data item has been derived. In particular, it contains the specification of the EVALUATE-RULE statement used to verify the validity of each reported rule (see Listing 15.19).

Listing 15.24 The Derivation of the XDM Data Item with the Evaluated Association Rules

```
<XDM Database="host.xdm/AssociationRulesData">
<XDM-DATA-ITEM Name="Rules with Customers" Derived="YES"
               Date="30/3/2002">
  <XDM-DERIVATION>
    <EVALUATE-RULE>
    <DATA-SECTION>
      <SOURCE select="//XDM-DATA-
ITEM[@Name='Purchases']/TRANSACTIONS"/>
      <EVALUATION-ELEMENT name="CUSTOMER" select="@CUSTOMER"/>
      <GROUPING select="PRODUCT" common-value="@TID"/>
    </DATA-SECTION>
    <RULE-SECTION>
      <SOURCET select="//XDM-DATA-ITEM[@Name='rules']/ASSOCIATION-
RULE-SET"/>
    </RULE-SECTION>
    <RULE-SCHEMA>
      <BODY-SCHEMA>
        <RULE-ELEMENT name="ITEM" select="@ITEM"/>
      </BODY-SCHEMA>
      <HEAD-SCHEMA>
        <RULE-ELEMENT name="ITEM" select="@ITEM"/>
      </HEAD-SCHEMA>
    </RULE-SCHEMA>
    <OUTPUT Type="DATA-WITH-RULES"/>
    </EVALUATE-RULE>
  </XDM-DERIVATION>
  <DATA-AND-RULE-SET>
    <RULE>
```

```
  <BODY>
    <ELEMENT Name="ITEM"> A </ELEMENT>
  </BODY>
  <HEAD>
    <ELEMENT Name="ITEM"> B </ELEMENT>
  </HEAD>
  <EVALUATED-FOR>
    <ELEMENT Name="CUSTOMER"> c1 </ELEMENT>
    <ELEMENT Name="CUSTOMER"> c3 </ELEMENT>
    <ELEMENT Name="CUSTOMER"> c4 </ELEMENT>
  </EVALUATED-FOR>
</RULE>
<RULE>
  <BODY>
    <ELEMENT Name="ITEM"> B </ELEMENT>
  </BODY>
  <HEAD>
    <ELEMENT Name="ITEM"> A </ELEMENT>
  </HEAD>
  <EVALUATED-FOR>
    <ELEMENT Name="CUSTOMER"> c1 </ELEMENT>
    <ELEMENT Name="CUSTOMER"> c3 </ELEMENT>
    <ELEMENT Name="CUSTOMER"> c4 </ELEMENT>
  </EVALUATED-FOR>
</RULE>
<RULE>
  <BODY>
    <ELEMENT Name="ITEM"> B </ELEMENT>
  </BODY>
  <HEAD>
    <ELEMENT Name="ITEM"> C </ELEMENT>
  </HEAD>
  <EVALUATED-FOR>
    <ELEMENT Name="CUSTOMER"> c1 </ELEMENT>
    <ELEMENT Name="CUSTOMER"> c2 </ELEMENT>
    <ELEMENT Name="CUSTOMER"> c3 </ELEMENT>
    <ELEMENT Name="CUSTOMER"> c4 </ELEMENT>
  </EVALUATED-FOR>
</RULE>
<RULE>
  <BODY>
    <ELEMENT Name="ITEM"> C </ELEMENT>
```

```
      </BODY>
      <HEAD>
        <ELEMENT Name="ITEM"> B </ELEMENT>
      </HEAD>
      <EVALUATED-FOR>
        <ELEMENT Name="CUSTOMER"> c1 </ELEMENT>
        <ELEMENT Name="CUSTOMER"> c2 </ELEMENT>
        <ELEMENT Name="CUSTOMER"> c3 </ELEMENT>
        <ELEMENT Name="CUSTOMER"> c4 </ELEMENT>
      </EVALUATED-FOR>
    </RULE>
    <RULE>
      <BODY>
        <ELEMENT Name="ITEM"> A </ELEMENT>
        <ELEMENT Name="ITEM"> C </ELEMENT>
      </BODY>
      <HEAD>
        <ELEMENT Name="ITEM"> B </ELEMENT>
      </HEAD>
      <EVALUATED-FOR>
        <ELEMENT Name="CUSTOMER"> c1 </ELEMENT>
        <ELEMENT Name="CUSTOMER"> c3 </ELEMENT>
        <ELEMENT Name="CUSTOMER"> c4 </ELEMENT>
      </EVALUATED-FOR>
    </RULE>
  </DATA-AND-RULE-SET>
</XDM-DATA-ITEM>
</XDM>
```

Notice that the DATA-AND-RULE-SET element contains a set of association rules, described by the element RULE. The content of RULE elements is similar to the content of RULE elements in the data item named `rules` (see Listing 15.19). However, it differs for two reasons:

1. Elements named SUPPORT and CONFIDENCE are missing, since this information is useless at this level.
2. The EVALUATED-FOR element is added to each rule, and it reports the entity for which the rule holds.

Consider the fragment in Listing 15.20, taken from the data item in Listing 15.19.

Listing 15.20 XML Fragment

```
<RULE>
  <BODY>
    <ELEMENT Name="ITEM"> A </ELEMENT>
    <ELEMENT Name="ITEM"> C </ELEMENT>
  </BODY>
  <HEAD>
    <ELEMENT Name="ITEM"> B </ELEMENT>
  </HEAD>
  <EVALUATED-FOR>
    <ELEMENT Name="CUSTOMER"> c1 </ELEMENT>
    <ELEMENT Name="CUSTOMER"> c3 </ELEMENT>
    <ELEMENT Name="CUSTOMER"> c4 </ELEMENT>
  </EVALUATED-FOR>
</RULE>
```

The fragment in Listing 15.20 says that rule $\{A,C\} \Rightarrow \{B\}$ holds for customer *c1*, *c3,* and *c4*.

The overall data item is the XDM representation of Table 15.3 obtained by the `EVALUATE RULE` statement reported in Section 15.2.1, "Extracting and Evaluating Association Rules."

15.4 Benefits of XDM

In this section, we summarize the benefits achieved by XDM.

- **Flexibility:** A major critique of the data-mining research field is that each technique has been developed with data models that strongly differ from the models of other techniques. This causes difficulties in integrating different data-mining techniques in the same system. Furthermore, the need for database support has been widely recognized, but relational databases are not suitable for managing with ease data represented in other models (such as trees). With XDM, we exploit the flexible structure of XML to integrate any kind of data representation in the XDM database, including trees.
- **Derivation dependencies:** The derivation process is maintained inside the XDM database, which is important for two reasons. The first one is that in this way the database maintains the meaning of each derived data item. This fact plays an important role when data are successively interpreted.

This may be one of the most important limitations of the relational database-mining framework, because relational databases do not maintain this kind of information and tables lose their meaning. The second benefit of maintaining the derivation process of each data item arises when a source data item changes: all derived data items are no longer valid and must be recomputed. If the derivation process is not maintained inside the database state, it is impossible to know which data items are still valid and which are not. Furthermore, this information may allow the exploitation of incremental computation techniques for derived data items considering only the changes in the source data items.

- **Open description:** XDM is an open representation of data and derivation processes. This may be exploited by the user, since she/he can clearly read the data and the process descriptions. However, we think that advanced data-mining operators may better exploit this fact. Indeed, process descriptions can be considered as *background knowledge* about data mining, and new operators can use it to better perform new sophisticated derivations.

The major drawback of choosing XML as the basis for our unifying framework is the amount of space required by XML representations, if compared with flat text or binary representations. For instance, source data sets might significantly increase their size, when they are described in XML format, due to the introduction of markups and attributes. Consequently, we can expect that for huge data sets, it is necessary to take into account this problem.

Comparison with PMML

Earlier, we briefly introduced the Predictive Model Mark-up Language (PMML). We said that this language, developed by the DMG group, is the first attempt to define an XML language for interchange of data-mining and knowledge discovery models among heterogeneous applications over the Internet. Here we want to compare PMML features with XDM, in order to highlight differences and benefits provided by XDM with respect to PMML-based solutions.

- PMML is devised to be a standard communication format. For this reason, it is not suitable to be the basis for an integrated database environment that unifies several complex data-mining and knowledge discovery tasks under the same framework. In fact, PMML is not aware of the concept of database state and is unable to represent both source data and patterns.
- PMML is devised to describe patterns. However, it does not consider at all that patterns might be extracted by a variety of different data-mining tools

with different semantics. Even if these tools produce the same kinds of patterns, their meaning can change significantly.

- PMML does not describe processes or multistep derivations. In fact, nothing is said about how to reuse the patterns generated by a mining step; this task is left to the specific tools that receive the PMML documents.

For these reasons, PMML is not a good data model for advanced data-mining systems, like inductive databases. In the next section, we will present a new generation of data-mining systems that can be developed on the basis of XDM. In fact, the main advantage of XDM is that it copes with notions such as database state, derivation of data items, description of complex patterns, and complex mining statements.

15.5 Toward Flexible and Open Systems

The features of XDM open the way toward a new generation of *flexible and open systems* for data mining and knowledge discovery. In this section, we give a brief discussion of the set of functionalities that a system based on XDM should provide.

- **Flexibility:** XDM is defined on top of XML, the eXtensible Markup Language. The aim of XDM is to exploit the extensibility characteristics provided by XML. Hence, an XDM-based system should be able to deal with any kind of data and pattern representation, provided that it is described as an XML fragment. Furthermore, the fact that XML provides a representation for semi-structured data means that an XDM-based system can easily deal with complex formats and not flat formats such as trees.
- **Extensibility:** An XDM-based system should not be tailored on any data-mining algorithm or problem. In contrast, it should be open, in order to be extended with any data-mining operator and allowing its implementation, provided that the operator and its implementation comply with the API interface provided by the system. In particular, we think that an XML Schema definition for the operator and for the data items generated by the operator should be provided. In fact this can be useful in order to extend the system with a new operator and its implementation.
- **Incremental computations:** An XDM-based system should provide support for incremental computations. In fact, since XDM data items represent both data and the statement that generated them, it is possible to trace the knowledge discovery process performed by the user. This fact may allow us to set up an incremental computation mechanism that recomputes derived data items when source data items are updated. This might be done in an efficient way if an incremental implementation of the operators is provided,

or in a naive way simply recomputing from scratch each derived data item (in this case, a background task might be activated in order to perform recomputations when the system is not loaded with heavy computations).

- **User interaction:** The user should be provided with a user interface that exploits XDM peculiarities. This means that the interface should provide clever support for navigating inside the set of XDM data items, by showing the computation trace, or by giving the possibility of showing, in different windows, several XDM data items. But a feature that the user interface of an XDM-based system should certainly provide is the automatic suggestion of new statements. This idea can be easily clarified if we consider the `EVALUATE-RULE` operator: A statement based on this operator makes sense only if the evaluation of association rules is coherent with the `MINE-RULE` statement that generated the association rule set, in terms of the rule schema and grouping features. Once the user selected the XDM data item containing the rule set to evaluate, the user interface might automatically complete the statement taking, for example, the rule schema specification from the `MINE-RULE` statement.

15.6 Related Work

The topic addressed by this chapter embraces two wide research areas: the research area of data mining and knowledge discovery, and the research area of XML data management. In both the areas, a large amount of work has been done, although the work in both areas has been rather recent (no more than ten years for data mining and no more than five years for XML data management). Therefore, when writing about this topic, it is difficult to be exhaustive.

The research community considers R. Agrawal's paper (Agrawal et al. 1993a) the work that originated the field of data mining: In that work the authors demonstrated that it is possible to extract patterns from large raw data with acceptable performance. The papers that followed that work provided a large variety of algorithms for efficiently mining association rules (Agrawal et al. 1993b; Agrawal and Srikant 1994; Bayardo 1998; Han et al. 2000—to cite only the most widely known in the field of association rule mining) and other kinds of knowledge, such as classification models, sequential patterns, and so on (see, for example, Kamber et al. 1997; Li et al. 2001; Mehta et al. 1996; Srikant and Agrawal 1996; Quinlan 1993).

Then the problem of integrating data-mining algorithms and databases emerged. Several works addressed the topic. First of all, the problem has been addressed from the language perspective in works by R. Meo et al. (Meo et al. 1996, 1998a), T. Imielinski et al. (Imielinski et al. 1996; Imielinski and Virmani 1998), and J. Han et al. (Han et al. 1996). Different query languages for data mining based on the SQL syntax are proposed: The common idea is to extend SQL with specific constructs in order to enable the user to specify in a declarative form data-mining statements over relational databases. The main advantage of this proposal is the fact that data, patterns, and mining statements belong to the same framework—that is, the relational framework, where data are usually stored. P. L. Lanzi and G. Psaila (Lanzi and Psaila 1999; Psaila 2001) tried to stress this idea, showing that the relational database framework could be effectively used to host several SQL-like data-mining operators, thus transforming the relational database framework in a relational database-mining framework.

The alternative way to address the problem of integrating data-mining technologies and databases considered the integration of data-mining algorithms and databases. On this topic, we cite the works of R. Agrawal and K. Shim (Agrawal and Shim 1996) and R. Meo et al. (Meo et al. 1998b): The former gives an overview of different solutions and problems arising when data-mining algorithms are integrated with relational databases; the latter shows that a specific design for algorithms can take advantage of the presence of the underlying relational database.

Finally, as far as the data-mining area is concerned, we recall that the idea of developing a unifying framework and system for data mining led to the definition of inductive databases. While the idea of an inductive database was introduced for the first time by T. Imielinski and H. Mannila (Imielinski and Mannila 1996), J.-F. Boulicaut et al. (Boulicaut et al. 1998) formally defined this notion for the first time, taking the `MINE-RULE` operator introduced by R. Meo et al. (Meo et al. 1996) as the first example of an inductive database query language; consequently, it is possible to see that the work of P. L. Lanzi and G. Psaila (Lanzi and Psaila 1999; Psaila 2001) confirms the idea that inductive databases and the relational database-mining framework are two sides of the same coin. Then the work of J.-F. Boulicaut et al. (Boulicaut et al. 1999) gave a better formalization of the concept of inductive databases, although we think that the definition provided in that paper (and reported in this chapter) is still inadequate to give a full support for flexible data-mining systems.

As far as the research area related to XML is concerned, the situation is still more difficult. XML has been introduced by a W3C recommendation. The language was immediately an object of interest because it easily describes semi-structured and/or complex data, is an open format, and is suitable for data exchange over the Internet.

The research work on XML moved in several directions. At first, query languages for XML were proposed, with the aim of querying XML documents to extract information. XPath is a simple and powerful query language: Its simplicity makes it suitable to be incorporated inside other languages, such as XSLT. At the moment, the work on query languages for XML is converging around XQuery, the official W3C language for querying XML documents and generating other XML documents; however, it is not stable yet, since it is ongoing work.

As far as the connection between database systems and XML is concerned, some work has been done to explore the problem of storing and managing XML documents inside relational, object-relational, and object-oriented databases (see, for example, Klettke and Meyer 2000, Schmidt et al. 2000, Kappel et al. 2000). The common idea behind these works is to map XML documents into the relational or object-oriented structure; then retrieval is performed by translating queries over XML documents to the corresponding database schema.

From a commercial point of view, the most famous database system to store collections of XML documents is Tamino by Software AG: It provides support for XML document storage in their native format, in order to freely manage collections of XML documents without knowing their structure in advance.

Finally, we recall that at the moment the gap between XML and data mining has been filled only by two proposals. The first one is the Predictive Model Mark-up Language (PMML—http://www.dmg.org/pmml-v2-0.htm). This proposal is devised to create a standard format, in order to enable different systems to exchange patterns extracted from within data sets by data-mining tools. Unfortunately, because of the goal for which PMML has been designed, PMML cannot be exploited for improving the notion of an inductive database. Instead, this is exactly the main goal of XDM. Certainly, the open nature of XDM may allow the use of PMML in order to represent patterns and models inside XDM.

The second proposal is introduced in a recent work by D. Braga et al. (Braga et al. 2002): This paper follows the way traced for the `MINE-RULE` operator (Meo et al. 1996, 1998a) to define an operator for mining association rules from within XML documents based on the XQuery syntax. The clauses on which the operator is based, the `MINE-RULE` XDM statement, were illustrated in this chapter in Section 15.3.3, "Association Rules with XDM."

■ 15.7 Conclusion

In this chapter we presented a new data model, named XDM, based on XML and designed to be adopted inside the framework of inductive databases. We have presented a set of data-mining operations on data (classification, association rules extraction, and evaluation) and shown how these operations can be described and obtained using XDM to represent data and patterns.

The new model presents several positive features. It allows the contemporaneous representation of raw data and pattern data inside the inductive databases. It allows also the representation of several heterogeneous typologies of patterns, such as trees and association rules. Thanks to the semi-structured nature of the data that can be represented by XML, XDM also allows the management of semi-structured and complex patterns. Furthermore, XDM explicitly represents the pattern definition—that is, the pattern derivation process, in order to keep track of the knowledge discovery process from which the patterns are generated. In XDM pattern definition is represented together with data. This allows the reuse of patterns by the inductive database management system and the efficient incremental computation of new patterns. The latter is an important feature of XDM that helps to overcome one of the limits of inductive databases based on the relational model—that is, they do not keep track of the pattern derivation process in the pattern definition.

The new model also allows more flexibility and generality in the representation of the conceptual tools that are used during the knowledge discovery process (classification trees, enumeration sets, etc.). Finally, the flexibility of the XDM representation allows extensibility to new pattern models and new mining operators, provided that the models are represented in XML and the implementation of the operators are compliant to an API interface provided by the XDM database management system. This gives to the framework the characteristic to be an open system, easily customized by the analyst.

One drawback of the use of XML in data mining, however, could be the large volumes reached by the source data represented in XML (due to the addition of markup tags and attributes).

The future work with XDM consists of studying the formal properties that may be obtained considering the database state and the transitions performed by the derivation processes. This theory should provide the foundation to deal with the problem of the incremental computation of the database state. Moreover, it will be certainly necessary to deliver an implementation of an XDM-based system and of the operators that we have mentioned in this chapter (classification, `MINE-RULE`, and `EVALUATE-RULE` operator). This would allow us to obtain actual figures of performance evaluation of a KDD process in the inductive database framework based on the XDM data model.

Chapter 16

Designing and Managing an XML Warehouse

Xavier Baril and Zohra Bellahsène

16.1 Introduction

Data present on the Web is unstructured, or has incomplete, irregular, or frequently changed structure. XML is becoming the universal data exchange model on the Web. It has been shown that XML is well suited for representing semi-structured data. Compared to HTML, XML provides explicit data structuring, and data presentation is separated from data content. The aim of this chapter is to present a method for designing and managing an XML warehouse. We have designed and implemented a browser to graphically define XML views in order to simplify and improve the specification of XML views. Furthermore, we also have proposed a strategy for storing XML data in a relational DBMS.

16.1.1 Why a View Mechanism for XML?

The need for information personalization or adaptation for various types of users is crucial in many Web applications, since the gathered information is huge. Moreover, the data are heterogeneous and unstructured, or have incomplete, irregular, or frequently changed structure. XML is taking an important and increasing share of the data published on the Web. The W3C has proposed XSL (eXtensible Stylesheet Language), a language that provides a means for XML document restructuring. This language is designed to define style sheets over XML documents. However, XSL cannot be considered as a view definition language, as its expressive power is insufficient. This is why we have defined a view mechanism for XML data. We propose a view mechanism for XML data in order to customize and adapt the gathered information according to user requirements. Indeed, different users sharing XML data may want to see the same data differently.

Besides, views in a semi-structured (e.g., XML) environment can be used to provide: (1) a unified view of heterogeneous data sources and (2) the means to add a structured interface on top of semi-structured data. This last feature makes query optimization easier on semi-structured data and easier to use classical programming languages for application development. We have defined and implemented a view model for XML data. A view in the relational data model is a virtual relation that combines information from several base relations. While in our approach, a view is a "virtual" document that combines parts of different real documents. The resulting XML documents are stored in a repository, which provides a unified view of heterogeneous information sources and allows us to quickly answer user queries independently of the availability if the data sources. We call this repository an *XML warehouse*, which is built as a set of materialized views over multiple information sources.

Our system supports filtering documents and storing them in a DBMS. In this chapter, we will focus on that part of the system that allows the XML view specification and its mapping to relational tables in a MySQL database system.

16.1.2 Contributions

The main contributions of this chapter are

- A general architecture for a data warehouse integrating XML data
- A formalism for a data warehouse specification
- A mapping to store the warehouse in a relational DBMS
- A graphic tool implementing our approach: DAWAX

16.1.3 Outline

This chapter is organized as follows. Section 16.2, "Architecture," presents the general architecture of our system. Section 16.3, "Data Warehouse Specification," follows this. The next section, 16.4, "Managing the Metadata," presents the metadata defining the warehouse. Section 16.5, "Storage and Management of the Data Warehouse," contains the storage techniques for the warehouse in a relational database. Our system for designing and managing the data warehouse, DAWAX, is presented in section 16.6 where we also discuss implementation details. This is followed by section 16.7, "Related Work," and finally our conclusions.

16.2 Architecture

This section presents the architecture of our system for defining and implementing an XML data warehouse. Our system has been designed to integrate XML sources, using a data-warehousing approach. The data warehouse is defined as a set of XML materialized views.

The architecture depicted in Figure 16.1 is based on three main components:

1. The data warehouse specification module, which allows us to design the data warehouse
2. The data warehouse implementation module, which allows us to store XML data in a relational DBMS and manages data extraction and maintenance
3. The query manager module for querying the data warehouse

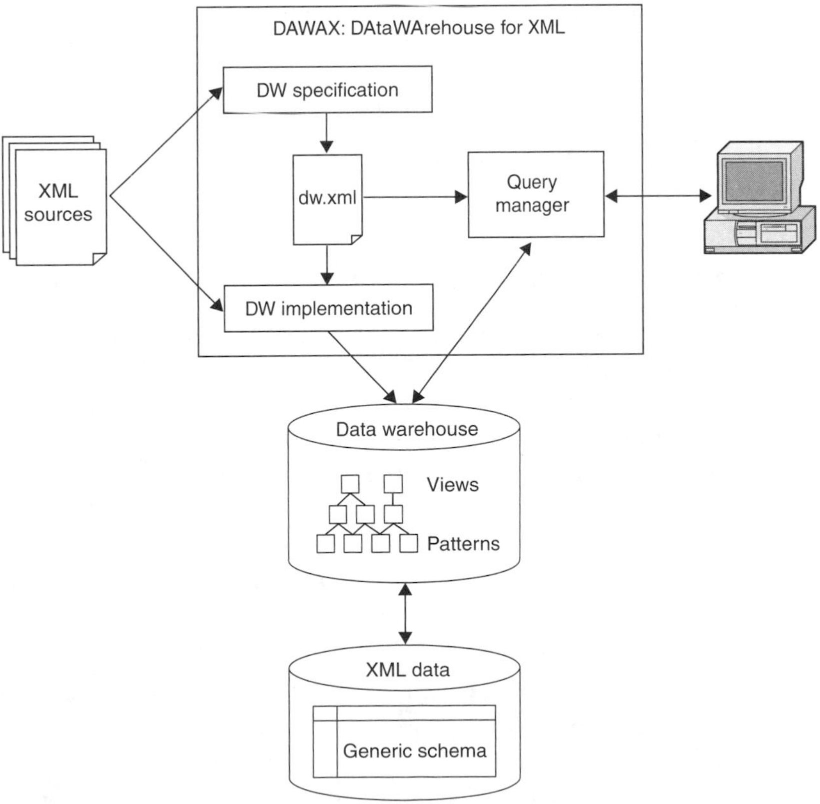

Figure 16.1 System Architecture

The *Datawarehouse specification* component allows us to design data warehouse content. It provides a graphic editor that produces an XML document containing the data warehouse specification. This specification is composed of information on XML sources and view specifications.

The Datawarehouse implementation component is responsible for creating the relational database of the data warehouse. The XML data are stored in a relational DBMS, to take advantage of the performance of this type of system. We distinguished two levels of data storage: (1) the *Datawarehouse* component stores the metadata (i.e., patterns and views organization data) and (2) the *XML data* component stores the content of XML elements or attributes.

The *query manager* is responsible for reconstructing XML documents from the relational data. In the future, we plan to use query-rewriting techniques (Manolescu et al. 2001) to translate an XML query on the data warehouse interface to an SQL query.

16.3 Data Warehouse Specification

This section deals with the data warehouse specification. An XML data warehouse is defined as a set of materialized views. In the first subsection we present our view model for XML documents. Next, we present the graphic tool that enables the data warehouse designer to specify the XML views.

16.3.1 View Model for XML Documents

Since the data warehouse is defined as a set of views, the main issue of data warehouse definition is the view model. We present briefly in this section the main characteristics of our view model. This model has been presented in detail in work by X. Baril and Z. Bellahsène (Baril and Bellahsène 2000).

Our view model fulfills the following requirements:

- **Closure property:** A view defined on XML document(s) should yield an XML document as output. This allows us to transparently use a view or a document. From the data warehouse point of view, this property implies that the unified view of sources is an XML document.
- **Restructuring possibilities:** The view mechanism enables restructuring elements of the source(s) document(s). We can distinguish two classes of views: (1) *select views* that extract existing documents from sources, and (2) *composite views* that create new elements or attributes. For this latter class, new elements of the result may be created from several source

elements. Furthermore, aggregation functions (i.e., sum, avg, min, max, count, etc.) can be used to define new values. Moreover, sorting and grouping elements is also provided.

- **DTD inference:** The view result should be associated to a DTD. This DTD is inferred from the view definition and possibly from source DTDs if they exist. The inferred DTD can be used to optimize the view storage or to query the view. From the data warehouse point of view, the inferred DTD is used to give a global integrated schema on which user queries can be formulated.

Each view is composed of a *result* pattern that specifies the structure of the result. This result pattern uses *variables* that are defined in *fragments*. A fragment is a collection of *patterns*: Each pattern uses variables to define data to match in a source. A fragment is composed of several patterns defining the same variables on different sources and provides the union of their data.

For example, let us consider a source "`senior.xml`" containing information about senior researchers and a source "`senior.xml`" containing information about Ph.D. students. To define a fragment "f1" containing the names and birthdays of senior researchers and Ph.D. students, we would define two patterns: one pattern matching names and birthdays of the senior researchers on source "senior.xml" and another one matching names and birthdays of the Ph.D. students on source "student.xml".

To define composite views, the result pattern can be based on several fragments. For this purpose, fragments are linked using *join* conditions. A join condition involves two variables defined in two different fragments.

Listing 16.1 shows a complete example of a view specification involving two fragments. Let us consider a view retrieving for each author their name, surname, and a list of the titles of their publications. The view is composed of a result pattern, two fragments, and a join condition. The fragment "f3" contains a pattern that matches the "author" elements, while "f4" contains a pattern that matches the "inproceedings" elements, with their "title" attribute and "authorlink" subelements. These subelements contain a "ref" attribute that references the author of the publication. The join element gives the join condition between the two fragments "f3" and "f4". The result element contains the result pattern. Each item of the view result is an "author" element, containing a "name" attribute (having the value of the "name" variable) and a "title" subelement (having the value of the "title" variable). The group-by element indicates that the result is grouped by "name" values (i.e., for an author there are possibly several "title" subelements). The part of the DTD validating this specification is presented in section 16.4.2, "View Definition," later in this chapter.

Listing 16.1 Example of View Definition

```
<view id="authorspublications">
<result>
 <result.node name="author" type="element">
  <result.node name="name" type="attribute">
   <result.node name="name" type="variable"></result.node>
  </result.node>
  <result.node name="title" type="element">
   <result.node name="title" type="variable"></result.node>
  </result.node>
 </result.node>
 <groupby name="name"></groupby>
</result>
<fragment id="f3">
 <pattern id="p3" source="1">
  <pattern.node name="author" type="element">
   <pattern.node name="id" type="attribute"
                 bind="id"></pattern.node>
   <pattern.node name="name" type="attribute"
                 bind="name"></pattern.node>
   <pattern.node name="surname" type="attribute"
                 bind="surname"></pattern.node>
  </pattern.node>
 </pattern>
</fragment>
<fragment id="f4">
 <pattern id="p4" source="1">
  <pattern.node name="inproceedings" type="element">
   <pattern.node name="title" type="attribute"
bind="title"></pattern.node>
   <pattern.node name="authorlink" type="element">
    <pattern.node name="ref" type="attribute"
bind="ref"></pattern.node>
   </pattern.node>
  </pattern.node>
 </pattern>
</fragment>
<join leftfragment="f3" leftvariable="id"
      rightfragment="f4" rightvariable="ref">
</join>
</view>
```

16.3.2 Graphic Tool for Data Warehouse Specification

We propose a graphic tool to help the user in the specification of the data warehouse. The editor allows us to create this specification without knowledge of the exact structure of the warehouse definition. We have proposed (in Baril and Bellahsène 2001) helpers for view definitions that we plan to integrate with DAWAX. These helpers allow us to define patterns without knowledge of the source structure. They use the DTD (if available) and the dataguide to propose choices for the pattern specification.

Figure 16.2 shows the graphic editor for the data warehouse specification. The XML document defining the data warehouse is represented as a tree. New elements

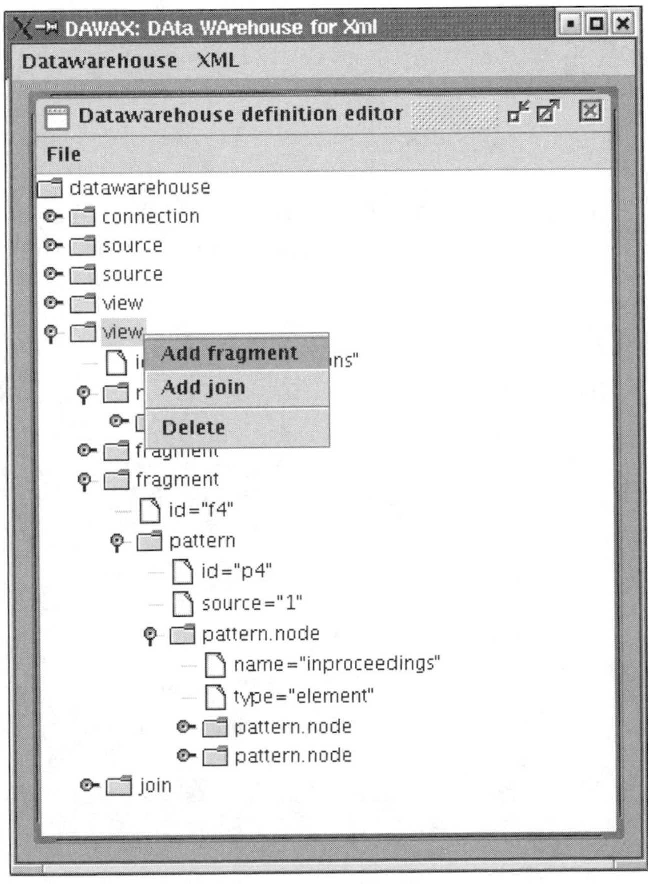

Figure 16.2 Data Warehouse Definition Editor

(sources, views, fragments, etc.) can be added by way of a contextual popup menu. The popup menu suggests possible choices for adding or updating the current element. In the example, the popup menu for a view element suggests the addition of a fragment or a join, and the deletion of a view.

The fragment "f4" of the view given as an example is displayed in Figure 16.2. It contains a pattern ("p4") with an identifier and a source attribute. The root pattern node of the pattern is displayed, and due to space limitations, its child nodes are not expanded in the tree.

16.4 Managing the Metadata

The specification of the data warehouse is stored in an XML document. This document contains the metadata of the warehouse, including:

1. Information about the JDBC connection for XML data storage
2. Data source URLs
3. View specifications

We chose an XML format for metadata storage because of portability and easy parsing. We present now the DTD validating the warehouse metadata.

16.4.1 Data Warehouse

The root element of the data warehouse specification is declared as follows:

```
<!-- datawarehouse element -->
<!ELEMENT datawarehouse (connection, source*, view*) >
```

- "connection" element contains data about the JDBC connection. This data is used to connect the data warehouse manager with the DBMS (MySQL) used to store data of the warehouse.
- "source" element contains data about the XML sources.
- "view" element contains a view definition.

The element describing a source is shown in Listing 16.2.

Listing 16.2 Element Describing an XML Source

```
<!-- source element -->
<!ELEMENT source EMPTY >
<!ATTLIST source
          id  ID    #REQUIRED
          url CDATA #REQUIRED
>
```

A "source" element contains two attributes: "id" identifies the source, and "url" gives the XML source URL. Elements describing sources are not encapsulated in pattern elements to easily recognize sources that are used in several patterns.

16.4.2 View Definition

This section describes the part of the DTD that defines a view. The "view" element is described as shown in Listing 16.3.

Listing 16.3 Element Describing a View

```
<!-- view element -->
<!ELEMENT view (fragment+, join*, result) >
<!ATTLIST view
          id ID #REQUIRED
>
```

A "view" element is composed of several fragments (one at least), several join conditions, and a result pattern.

Fragment Definition

A "fragment" element describes data to match in one or more XML sources. The part of the DTD shown in Listing 16.4 describes a fragment definition.

Listing 16.4 Element Describing a Fragment

```
<!-- fragment element -->
<!ELEMENT fragment (pattern+) >
<!ATTLIST fragment
          id ID #REQUIRED
>
```

A fragment is composed of several pattern subelements (one at least).

The "pattern" element describes data to match in an XML source. A pattern is linked to a source with the "source" attribute, which references a previously defined source. A "pattern" element is composed of a "pattern.node" element indicating the pattern root and one or more "condition" elements. A condition adds a restriction on values of a variable to be matched by the pattern. Listing 16.5 is the part of the DTD describing a pattern definition.

Listing 16.5 Elements Describing a Pattern

```
<!-- pattern element -->
<!ELEMENT pattern (pattern.node, condition*) >
<!ATTLIST pattern
          id     ID    #REQUIRED
          source IDREF #REQUIRED
>
<!-- pattern node -->
<!ELEMENT pattern.node (pattern.node*) >
<!ATTLIST pattern.node
          name CDATA #REQUIRED
          type CDATA #REQUIRED
          bind CDATA #IMPLIED
>
```

A pattern is described with "pattern.node" elements that describe the pattern to match in the XML source. For this purpose, a "pattern.node" element contains two attributes: The "type" attribute indicates if the node matches an element or an attribute in the XML source and the "name" attribute indicates the name of the element or attribute to match. The "bind" attribute, if it exists, indicates the variable name that binds the matched element or attribute in the XML source.

The "condition" element allows us to add a condition on the variables defined in the pattern. The part of the DTD shown in Listing 16.6 describes the condition element definition.

Listing 16.6 Element Describing a Condition

```
<!-- condition node -->
<!ELEMENT condition EMPTY >
<!ATTLIST condition
          left     CDATA #REQUIRED
          operator CDATA #REQUIRED
          right    CDATA #REQUIRED
>
```

Join Definition

A "join" element contains the join condition between the fragments defined in the view. The part of the DTD shown in Listing 16.7 describes the join element definition.

Listing 16.7 Element Describing a Join

```
<!-- join node -->
<!ELEMENT join EMPTY >
<!ATTLIST join
          leftfragment  IDREF #REQUIRED
          leftvariable  CDATA #REQUIRED
          rightfragment IDREF #REQUIRED
          rightvariable CDATA #REQUIRED
>
```

The "join" element contains four attributes indicating fragments and variables defining the join condition. The "leftfragment" and "rightfragment" attributes are IDREF attributes referencing the left and right fragments to join. The "leftvariable" and "rightvariable" contain the names of the variables of the left and right fragments used in the join condition.

Result Definition

Finally, the "result" element contains the definition of the view result pattern (see Listing 16.8).

Listing 16.8 Elements Describing a Result and Grouping Constraints

```
<!-- result -->
<!ELEMENT result (result.node, groupby*) >
<!-- result node -->
<!ELEMENT result.node (result.node*) >
<!ATTLIST result.node
          name CDATA #REQUIRED
          type CDATA #REQUIRED
>
<!-- group by -->
<!ELEMENT groupby EMPTY >
<!ATTLIST groupby
          variable CDATA #REQUIRED
>
```

The "result" element contains the description of the view result structure. It is composed of a "result.node" element containing the result pattern and zero or more "groupby" elements indicating how result data will be organized.

16.4.3 Mediated Schema Definition

The main role of a data warehouse is to provide integrated and uniform access to heterogeneous and distributed data. For this purpose, a mediated schema is provided to users on which they can formulate their queries. Metadata are used to create this schema. In the following, we will present how this schema is generated.

To provide an integrated view of heterogeneous sources, the data warehouse is considered as an entire XML document, containing the result of all the views. The fragment of DTD describing the data warehouse (with "N" views) is as follows:

```
<!ELEMENT datawarehouse (view1, view2,  . . . , viewN) >
```

The view model allows us to generate a DTD on a view specification. This DTD is defined with the result pattern and could possibly be completed with the source definition. The generated DTD for the view that is specified in Listing 16.1 is shown in Listing 16.9.

Listing 16.9 DTD Generated for the View in Listing 16.1

```
<!ELEMENT authorspublications (author*) >
<!ELEMENT author (title+) >
<!ATTLIST author name CDATA #REQUIRED >
<!ELEMENT title (#PCDATA) >
```

The root of the view result is an element, of which the type is the view name "authorspublications". The "author" element is composed of one or more "title" elements, because of the group-by clause, and has one attribute containing the author's name.

The mediated schema is aimed at querying the XML data in the warehouse. Currently, the query manager evaluates the XML views from the database system. In the future, the query manager capabilities will be extended to enable the processing of XPath queries with a DTD-driven tool.

■ 16.5 Storage and Management of the Data Warehouse

This section presents the data warehouse implementation. First, we enumerate different solutions to store XML data. Next, we present the mapping we propose for storing XML data using a relational DBMS. Finally, we present the solution we have implemented to store the mapping rules concerning views in the data warehouse.

16.5.1 The Different Approaches to Storing XML Data

We briefly present here the different approaches to storing XML data. We can distinguish at least three categories:

1. **Flat Streams:** In this approach XML data are stored in their textual form, by means of files or BLOB attributes in a DBMS. This method is very fast and easy for storing or retrieving whole documents. On the other hand, querying the data on structure (i.e., metadata) is not efficient because parsing all the data is mandatory for each query.
2. **Metamodeling:** In this approach, XML data are shredded and stored in a DBMS using its data model. The main issue of this approach is to define a schema mapping from XML data to the target DBMS data model. This mapping may be generic (i.e., valid for all XML documents), or schema driven (i.e., valid for documents that are instances of a DTD or XML Schema). These mappings improve query response time on XML data, but storage is more difficult because a parsing phase is necessary. In the database literature, many mapping schemes have been studied for relational DBMSs (e.g., Florescu and Kossmann 1999a; Manolescu et al. 2000; Yoshikawa et al. 2001; Sha et al. 1999).
3. **Mixed:** Finally, the two previous approaches could be merged to use the best of each one. A hybrid approach consists of defining a certain level of data granularity. Structures coarser than this granularity are stored using the metamodeling approach and structures finer are stored using the flat streams approach. A special-purpose XML DBMS has been proposed by C.-C. Kanne and G. Moerkotte (Kanne and Moerkotte 1999), using this technique. Another approach is to store data in two redundant repositories, one flat and one metamodeled.

16.5.2 Mapping XML to Relational

We chose a relational DBMS to store XML data of the warehouse. The mapping schema that we used is presented in Listing 16.10. Primary keys are in bold characters and foreign keys are in italic characters.

Listing 16.10 Mapping Schema for XML Data

```
Document (d_docID, d_url)
Element (e_elemID, e_type)
Attribute (a_attID, a_name)
XmlNode (xn_nodeID, xn_type, xn_elemID, xn_attID, xn_value,
xn_docID)
Children (c_father, c_child, c_rank)
AllChildren (ac_father, ac_child)
```

The "`Document`" table contains source URLs. The "`Element`" and "`Attribute`" tables are dictionaries containing all element types or attributes names of XML data in the data warehouse. These dictionaries will accelerate queries. The "`XmlNode`" table contains XML nodes. The "`xn_type`" attribute indicates the node type: element, attribute, or text. The foreign keys "`xn_elemID`" or "`xn_attID`" indicate the element type or the attribute name. The "`xn_value`" attribute gives the value of an attribute node or a text node. Finally, the "`xn_docID`" foreign key indicates the source from where the node came. This information is useful for warehouse maintenance. The "`Children`" table indicates parent-child relationships between nodes, and the "`AllChildren`" table indicates all parent-child relationships between nodes. This last table introduces redundancies in XML data but is useful for the query manager.

16.5.3 View Storage

As depicted in Figure 16.1, data warehouse storage is performed with two main components: (1) the *XML data* component (used to store XML data), and (2) the *Datawarehouse* component (used to store mapping rules).

The XML data component is organized according to the relational schema presented in Listing 16.10. Each XML node is identified by a "nodeID" attribute. This identifier is used to reference XML data in the Datawarehouse component.

We will now describe the organization of the Datawarehouse component. As for XML data, we use a relational DBMS to store mapping rules between the variables and XML data. The base relations are a result of patterns, and the other nodes of the graph are defined with relational operations to create fragments and views.

- **Patterns:** A table is created for each pattern. The name of this table is P-pid with "pid" being the identifier of the pattern. For each variable of the pattern, a column is created in the pattern table. This column is named by the variable name and contains the identifier of the XML node in the XML data component.

- **Fragments:** Tables are created for fragments. The name of this table is F-fid with "fid" being the identifier of the fragment. This table uses relational operators to compute the fragment result with the appropriate pattern tables.
- **Views:** Tables are created for views. The name of this table is V-vid with "vid" being the identifier of the view. This table uses relational operators to perform joins between the different fragment tables used by the view.

16.5.4 Extraction of Data

This section explains how data are extracted from source. For storage space optimization, we store the XML data component once in the XML nodes that match several pattern variables.

For data extraction, we consider all patterns that have the same data source. The challenge is to avoid introducing redundancies in the XML data component. For this purpose, we process as follows:

1. All patterns are grouped by sources, so that patterns having the same source are evaluated together.
2. For a group of patterns, the source is parsed, and an object document model is generated. Each XML node has an object identifier assigned by the system.
3. Each pattern of the group is evaluated, and nodes matching the pattern specification are stored by the way of an Xml2Sql component.

The Xml2Sql component ensures that each XML element will be stored only once in the datawarehouse. For this purpose, we use a hash table associating the identifier of the parsed node and the value of the "nodeID" attribute in the XML data component. Before adding the XML data, the Xml2Sql component checks if the node has already been stored. If the node is already stored, the Xml2Sql component retrieves the "nodeID" attribute value in the hash table. In the case where the node is not already stored, the node is added in the XML data component and in the hash table. During the extraction phase, the fragment tables are populated, and the "nodeID" attribute is necessary to reference XML data.

At this time, we propose only a basic maintenance strategy for data. When a source is updated, we maintain the warehouse by recomputing patterns that use this source. Views using modified patterns are also recomputed. This strategy is possible thanks to our storage technique that separates storage of each pattern in a table. We plan to investigate a more sophisticated strategy: incremental maintenance.

16.6 DAWAX: A Graphic Tool for the Specification and Management of a Data Warehouse

This section presents the implementation of the system that we have developed for the specification and the management of an XML warehouse. DAWAX (DAta WArehouse for XML) is composed of three main tools:

1. The graphic editor for data warehouse specification, which was presented in section 16.3, "Data Warehouse Specification."
2. The data warehouse manager, which is responsible for the creation and management of the warehouse in a relational DBMS (MySQL). It is presented in the next section.
3. The data warehouse query manager, which is not presented here.

16.6.1 Data Warehouse Manager

In this section, we present the part of the application dedicated to the data warehouse implementation. As we have seen in Section 16.5, "Storage and Management of the Data Warehouse," the XML data are stored in a MySQL Database System. DAWAX automatically creates the warehouse and extracts metadata from a specification file.

Figure 16.3 shows the graphic interface for the management of XML data. When opening the implementation manager, the user chooses a specification file (previously defined with the graphic editor). Then the implementation manager loads the data warehouse specification, connects to the SQL database and displays its graphic interface. The frame is composed of two panels: one for data warehouse creation and another one for data maintenance. The creation panel contains a create button and is in charge of creating the SQL database and extracting data from sources. The second panel, which is shown in Figure 16.3, is dedicated to data maintenance. It displays the source list and is responsible for refreshing data extracted from the selected source. Then, the system refreshes the XML data, the patterns using this source, and views using the updated patterns.

16.6.2 The Different DAWAX Packages

The application has been written in the Java language because of its portability and universality. We used a MySQL server for storing XML data, essentially because it's a free DBMS running under Linux.

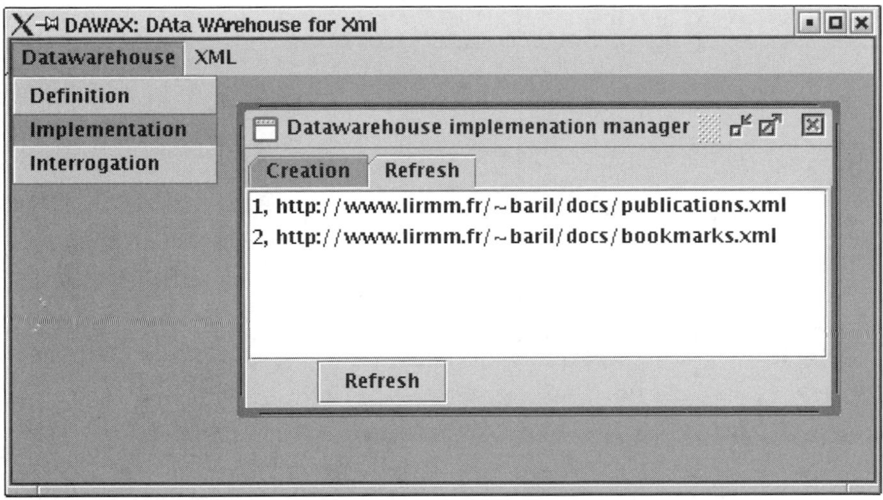

Figure 16.3 Data Warehouse Implementation Manager

The different functionalities are implemented by the following Java packages:

- "dawax": Contains the main functionality of the application, allowing us to start one of the three components (i.e., specification, management, interrogation).
- "dawax.specification": Contains the graphic editor for the data warehouse specification.
- "dawax.management": Contains the JDBC interface with the MySQL server and the `Xml2Sql` class that stores XML data in MySQL.
- "dawax.interrogation": Contains the query manager (not presented in this chapter) that is responsible for recomposing XML documents representing views, with the `Sql2Xml` class.
- "dawax.xml.documentmodel": Contains the implementation of the document model for XML.
- "dawax.xml.parser": Contains the parser for the document model (based on a SAX parser).

16.7 Related Work

In this section, we first present related work on XML query languages, which is useful for view definition. Then, we present an overview of XML data integration projects.

16.7.1 Query Languages for XML

Today, there is not yet a W3C standard for an XML query language. However, the W3C has proposed recently a working draft for a future query language standard: XQuery (Boag et al. 2002). XQuery is derived from a query language named Quilt (Chamberlin et al. 2000), which borrowed features from existing query languages. XPath (Clark and DeRose 1999) and XQL (Robie et al. 1998) were used for addressing parts of an XML document. XML-QL (Deutsch, Fernandez, Florescu et al. 1999) was used for its restructuring capabilities. XML-QL is based on pattern matching and uses variables to define a result pattern. We also use the concept of pattern matching for our view specification.

16.7.2 Storing XML Data

Many approaches have been proposed for storing XML data in databases. We presented the main techniques to store XML data in section 16.5.1, "The Different Approaches to Storing XML." Different mapping schemas for relational databases have also been proposed (e.g., Manolescu et al. 2000; Yoshikawa et al. 2001; Sha et al. 1999). In D. Florescu and D. Kossmann, several mappings are compared using performance evaluations (Florescu and Kossmann 1999a). Mappings based on DTDs have also been proposed by J. Shanmugasundaram et al. (Shanmugasundaram et al. 1999). The STORED system has explored a mapping technique using an object-oriented database system (Deutsch, Fernandez, and Suciu 1999). Recently, the LegoDB system (Bohannon et al. 2002) has proposed a mapping technique using adaptive shredding.

16.7.3 Systems for XML Data Integration

Many research projects have focused on XML data integration, given the importance of this topic.

The MIX (Mediation of Information using XML—http://www.npaci.edu/DICE/MIX) system was designed for mediation of heterogeneous data sources. The system is based on wrappers to export heterogeneous sources. The work by C. Baru (Baru 1999) deals with relational-to-XML mapping. Views are defined with XMAS (Ludäscher et al. 1999), which was inspired by XML-QL. The language proposes a graphic interface (BBQ) but only considers XML documents that are validated by a DTD. Other documents are not considered. As the approach is virtual, XML data storage has not been considered.

Xyleme is an XML data warehouse system designed to store all data on the Web as data. This ambitious aim underlines interesting issues. XML data acquisition and maintenance is studied in L. Mignet et al. and A. Marian et al. (Mignet et al. 2000; Marian et al. 2000). XML data are stored in a special-purpose DBMS named NATIX (Kanne and Moerkotte 1999), which uses the hybrid approach we described earlier. To provide a unified view of data stored in the warehouse, Xyleme provides an *abstract DTD* that can be seen as the ontology of a domain. Then a mapping is defined between the DTD of the stored documents (*concrete DTD*) and the DTD of the domain modeled by the document (*abstract DTD*) (Reynaud et al. 2001). Compared to our system, Xyleme is aimed at storing all XML documents dealing with a domain, without storage space consideration, while our approach allows us to filter XML data to be stored by a view specification mechanism.

Recently, an original system for optimizing XML data storage has been proposed. The LegoDB (Bohannon et al. 2002) is a cost-based XML storage-mapping engine that explores a *space* of XML-to-relational mappings and selects the best mapping for a given application. Parameters to find the best mapping are: (1) an extension of the XML Schema containing data statistics on sources and (2) an XQuery workload. LegoDB cannot be considered a complete integration system because it considers only storage and proposes an efficient solution to storing XML data according to an XQuery workload.

16.8 Conclusion

Many research projects have focused on providing efficient storage for XML repositories. Our focus in this chapter has been on filtering and adapting XML documents according to user requirements before storing them.

In this chapter, we have presented a global approach for designing and managing an XML data warehouse. We have proposed a view model and a graphical tool for the data warehouse specification. Views defined in the warehouse allow filtering and restructuring of XML sources. The warehouse is defined as a set of materialized views and provides a mediated schema that constitutes a uniform interface to querying the XML data warehouse. We have also proposed mapping techniques using a relational DBMS. This mapping allows us to store XML data without redundancies and then optimizes storage space. Finally, our approach has been implemented in a complete system named DAWAX.

We are planning to investigate two main research issues. First, we plan to improve the maintenance strategy. In the context of monitored XML sources, we plan to develop an incremental maintenance technique. Second, we plan to investigate query-rewriting techniques to enhance the capabilities of the query manager. This technique will benefit from the mapping schema that we have presented here.

Part V

Performance and Benchmarks

XML database management systems face the same stringent efficiency and performance requirements as any other database technology. Therefore, the final part of this book is devoted to a discussion of benchmarks and performance analyses of such systems.

Chapter 17

XML Management System Benchmarks

Stéphane Bressan, Mong Li Lee, Ying Guang Li, Zoé Lacroix, and Ullas B. Nambiar

17.1 Introduction

Introduced as a schema-less, self-describing data representation language, XML (Bray et al. 2000) has rapidly emerged as the standard for information interchange on the World Wide Web. Database researchers have actively participated in developing standards centered on XML, in particular data models and query languages for XML. Many XML query languages have been proposed, and some XML Management Systems (XMS) with those query languages implemented are available for use.

Current XMS can be divided into two categories: XML-enabled databases and native XML databases. XML-enabled databases, typically relational databases, such as DB2 XML Extender from IBM, Informix, Microsoft SQL Server 2000, and Oracle-8i and -9i (Bourret 2001a; Chang et al. 2000), provide XML interfaces that allow the storage of XML data in their proprietary relational format, and querying and publishing through an XML representation. Such systems are generally designed to store and retrieve data-centric XML documents. On the other hand, native XML databases such as Kweelt (Sahuguet 2001), IPEDO, Tamino, 4SuiteServer, DBDOM, dbXML (Bourret 2001a), and so on either store the entire XML document in text form with limited retrieval capabilities or store a binary model (e.g., Document Object Model) of the document in an existing or custom data store. With so many XMS being developed and proposed, it is necessary to start designing and adopting benchmarks that allow comparative performance analysis of the tools and systems.

The rest of this chapter is organized as follows. The next section gives benchmark specifications. This is followed by a section that describes three existing XMS benchmarks—the XOO7 benchmark, the XMach-1 benchmark, and the XMark benchmark. Finally, the chapter concludes with a brief comparison of the three benchmarks.

17.2 Benchmark Specification

Various domain-specific benchmarks have been developed because no single metric can measure the performance of computer systems for all applications. *The Benchmark Handbook* by Jim Gray (Gray 1993) has laid down the following four key criteria for a domain-specific benchmark:

- **Relevance:** The benchmark must capture the characteristics of the system to be measured.
- **Portability:** The benchmark should be able to be implemented in different systems.
- **Scalability:** The benchmark should be able to test various databases in different computer systems.
- **Simplicity:** The benchmark must be understandable; otherwise it will not be credible.

Basically, a benchmark is used to test the peak performance of a system. Different aspects of a system have varying importance in different domains. For example, the transaction cost is crucial in a network system, while the processing time and storage space are critical in a database system. Hence, it is important that a benchmark captures the characteristics of the system to be measured. In addition, systems vary in hardware and software support. Some run on Windows, while others run on Linux. As a consequence, it is important that a benchmark be portable and scalable. Finally, it is obvious that a benchmark should be easy to understand, and the results analyzable.

There are many domain-specific benchmarks. For example, the Wisconsin benchmark (Bitton et al. 1983) is widely used to test the performance of relational query systems on simple relational operators; the AS^{3}AP benchmark (Turbyfill et al. 1989) provides a more complete evaluation of relational database systems by incorporating features such as testing utility functions, mix batch and interactive queries, and multiuser tests; the Set Query benchmark (O'Neil 1997) evaluates the ability of systems to process complex queries that are typical in decision-support and data-mining applications; TPC-D is used for online transaction processing (OLTP); TPC-H, TPC-R, and APB-1 (OLAP 1998) are used for decision support and information retrieval; Sequoia (Stonebraker et al. 1993) is used for spatial data management, OO7 (Carey et al. 1993) for object-oriented databases, BUCKY (Carey et al. 1997) for object-relational databases, and the most recent TPC-W benchmark (see http://www.tpc.org/) for e-commerce. These benchmarks mainly evaluate query-processing performance. Each of these benchmarks meets the important criteria of being relevant to its domain, portable, simple, and scalable.

The design of a benchmark to evaluate XML management systems is a nontrivial task. The XML is a self-describing data representation language that has emerged as the standard for electronic information interchange. Thus its potential use covers a variety of complex usage scenarios. The objective of the benchmarks presented in this chapter is not to capture all possible uses of XML but rather to focus on the query-processing aspect of XML. In fact, for the sake of fairness and simplicity, the XML query-processing tools are evaluated in the simplest possible setup—that is, with locally stored data (without data transaction over a network) and in a single machine/single user environment.

In the following sections, we will discuss the various issues that arise when developing a benchmark for XML management systems. This involves designing a benchmark data set and the corresponding set of benchmark queries that adhere to the four criteria for benchmark design. We note that these criteria are interrelated, often to the extent of being conflicting. This may affect the ability of a benchmark to adequately capture the performance of the systems under evaluation. For example, if the test data of an XML management system benchmark is too simple (*simplicity*), it will not be able to capture the ability of XML to represent complex structures (*relevance*). On the other hand, if the schema of the XML data is very complex (*relevance*), then some XML systems may not have the capability to store the data properly (*portability*), and it may be difficult to change the size of the data (*scalability*).

17.3 Benchmark Data Set

The structure of a relevant benchmark data set must be complex enough to capture all characteristics of XML data representation. XML and relational data models are radically different. In particular, XML provides an implicit ordering of its elements since it is designed as a subset of SGML to represent documents. XML also provides references, deep nesting, as well as hyperlinks. These features, which we elaborate upon in the next section, are similar to those found in object-oriented models. In addition to the traditional object-oriented complex object-modeling features, the benchmark database should also capture the document (i.e., the implicit order of elements) and navigation (references) features while providing an understandable semantics and structure. The scalability of a system can be measured by using data sets of varying sizes. Since XML data can be represented as a tree, the depth and width of the tree should be adjustable. This can be achieved as follows:

- The depth of a tree can be controlled by varying the number of repetitions of recursive elements.
- The width of the tree can be adjusted by varying the cardinality of some elements.

Since XML itself is platform and application independent, portability is not a major issue here. We observe that unlike XML elements, the ordering of attributes in XML is optional. Hence, an XML management system can return the results of a query without preserving the attribute order.

17.3.1 Benchmark Queries

The performance of the implementations of query languages for XML depends greatly on their expressive power—that is, the functionalities they provide. Bonifati and Ceri address the functionalities of XML query languages by carrying out a comparative analysis of the major XML query languages (Bonifati and Ceri 2000). The W3C XML Query Language Working Group has also published a list of "must have" requirements for XML query languages (Chamberlin et al. 2001). Table 17.1 presents these requirements. Note that the requirement R21 represents the functionality based upon element ordering, an important feature of XML representation assumed by the document community that has dramatic impact on the expressive power of query languages (Fernandez et al. 2000).

The requirements enumerated by the W3C specify an XML query language that provides data-centric, document-centric, and navigational capabilities. XML can represent structured and unordered data, and an XML query language must be as expressive as a structured query language such as SQL is for relational databases. Such data-centric capabilities or *relational queries* include various types of join operations (R9), aggregation (R10), sorting (R11), and so on. Queries that use the implicit and explicit order of elements or use textual operators are classified as *document queries*. Such document-centric capabilities are required when order and document structure need to be preserved in some form (R17, R21). Queries that require traversal of XML document structure using references/links as supported by XLink/XPointer specification (DeRose, Maler, Daniel 2001; DeRose, Maler, Orchard 2001) are called navigational queries (R13, R20).

Some XMS may have limited query-processing capabilities and it is possible that many benchmark queries cannot be executed on such systems. For example, XPath (Clark and DeRose 1999) supports only the `count` function but not the `avg` (average) function. A benchmark query that tests the performance of both `count` and `avg`

Table 17.1 Desired Functionalities of XML Query Languages

Id	Description
R1	Query all data types and collections of possibly multiple XML documents.
R2	Allow data-oriented, document-oriented, and mixed queries.
R3	Accept streaming data.
R4	Support operations on various data models.
R5	Allow conditions/constraints on text elements.
R6	Support hierarchical and sequence queries.
R7	Manipulate NULL values.
R8	Support quantifiers ($\exists$, $\forall$, and $\sim$) in queries.
R9	Allow queries that combine different parts of document(s).
R10	Support for aggregation.
R11	Able to generate sorted results.
R12	Support composition of operations.
R13	Allow navigation (reference traversals).
R14	Able to use environment information as part of queries (e.g., current date, time etc.)
R15	Able to support XML updates if data model allows.
R16	Support type coercion.
R17	Preserve the structure of the documents.
R18	Transform and create XML structures.
R19	Support ID creation.
R20	Structural recursion.
R21	Element ordering.

functions cannot be evaluated on systems that implement XPath. This problem can be resolved by having separate benchmark queries, each testing a different type of aggregation. Furthermore, depending on the application, users may want to test only a subset of the functionalities covered by some queries. For example, some applications may never need to update the database while others do not need to restructure the retrieved results. Hence, it is important to distribute the various functionalities into different queries so that users can always choose the queries according to the functionalities they need. Separating the functionalities also facilitates the analysis of the experiment results since it will be very clear which feature is being tested. Finally, the benchmark queries should allow the range of values of selected attributes to be varied in order to control the percentage of data retrieved by queries—that is, the selectivity of queries.

17.4 Existing Benchmarks for XML

In this section we discuss and compare three benchmarks currently available that test XML systems for their query-processing abilities: XOO7 (Bressan, Dobbie 2001; Bressan, Lee 2001), XMach-1 (Böhme and Rahm 2001), and XMark (Schmidt, Waas, Kersten, Florescu, Manolescu et al. 2001). We will first describe the three benchmarks before comparing them.

17.4.1 The XOO7 Benchmark

The XOO7 benchmark was developed using the well-established OO7 benchmark as the starting point. The XOO7 benchmark is an XML version of the OO7 benchmark with new elements and queries added to test the features that are unique in XML.

The XOO7 Database

The basic data structure in the XOO7 benchmark comes from the OO7 benchmark. Figure 17.1 shows the conceptual schema of the database modeled using the ER diagram. We have translated this schema into the corresponding DTD as shown in Listing 17.1.

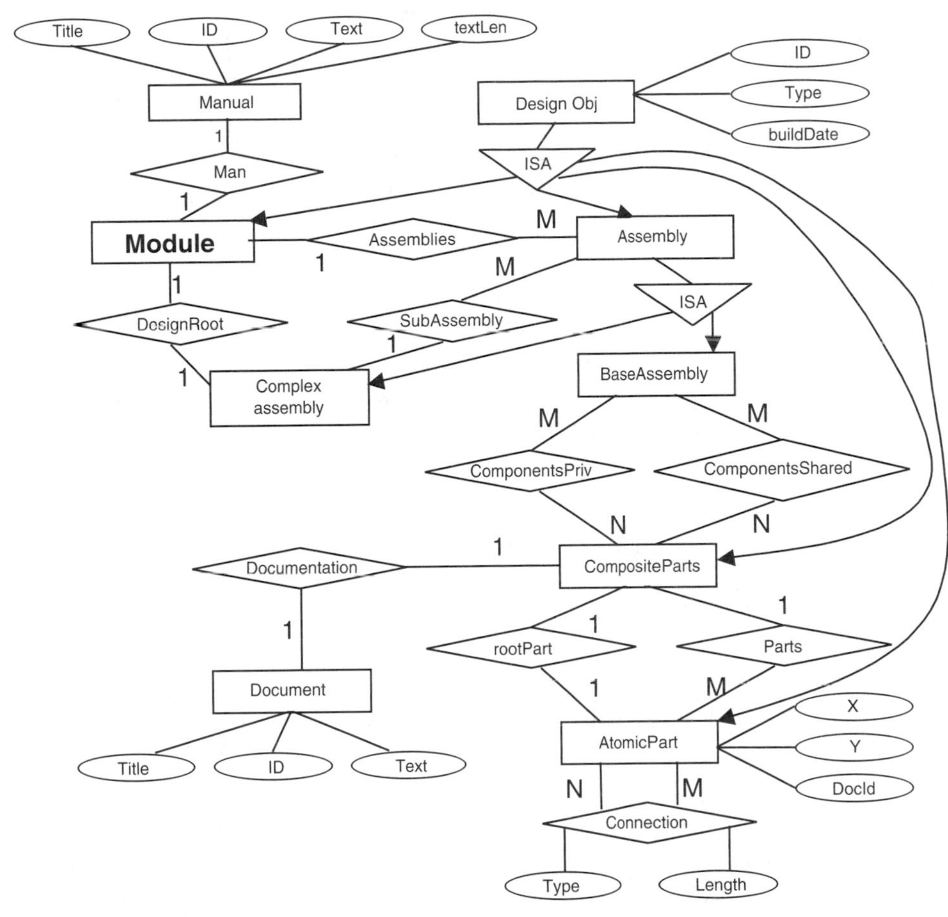

Figure 17.1 Entity Relationship Diagram for the OO7 Benchmark

Listing 17.1 DTD of XOO7 Database

```
<!ELEMENT Module        (Manual, ComplexAssembly)>
<!ATTLIST Module        MyID       NMTOKEN   #REQUIRED
                        type       CDATA     #REQUIRED
                        buildDate  NMTOKEN   #REQUIRED>

<!ELEMENT Manual        (#PCDATA)>
<!ATTLIST Manual        MyID       NMTOKEN   #REQUIRED
                        title      CDATA     #REQUIRED
                        textLen    NMTOKEN   #REQUIRED>
```

```
<!ELEMENT ComplexAssembly (ComplexAssembly+ | BaseAssembly+)>
<!ATTLIST ComplexAssembly MyID      NMTOKEN   #REQUIRED
                          type      CDATA     #REQUIRED
                          buildDate NMTOKEN   #REQUIRED>
<!ELEMENT BaseAssembly    (CompositePart+)>
<!ATTLIST BaseAssembly    MyID      NMTOKEN   #REQUIRED
                          type      CDATA     #REQUIRED
                          buildDate NMTOKEN   #REQUIRED>
<!ELEMENT CompositePart   (Document, Connection+)>
<!ATTLIST CompositePart   MyID      NMTOKEN   #REQUIRED
                          type      CDATA     #REQUIRED
                          buildDate NMTOKEN   #REQUIRED>
<!ELEMENT Document        (#PCDATA | para)+>
<!ATTLIST Document        MyID      NMTOKEN   #REQUIRED
                          title     CDATA     #REQUIRED>
<!ELEMENT para            (#PCDATA)>
<!ELEMENT Connection      (AtomicPart, AtomicPart)>
<!ATTLIST Connection      type      CDATA     #REQUIRED
                          length    NMTOKEN   #REQUIRED>
<!ELEMENT AtomicPart      EMPTY>
<!ATTLIST AtomicPart      MyID      NMTOKEN   #REQUIRED
                          type      CDATA     #REQUIRED
                          buildDate NMTOKEN   #REQUIRED
                          x         NMTOKEN   #REQUIRED
                          y         NMTOKEN   #REQUIRED
                          docId     NMTOKEN   #REQUIRED>
```

Since XML does not support ISA relationships, we have to preprocess the inheritance of attributes and relationships. We choose <Modulei> as the root element of the XML document. Although XML is supposed to be portable and independent of any platform, some systems designate special functions to certain attributes. For example, Lorel (Abiteboul et al. 1997) uses the name of the root element to identify an XML document, while the majority of the XMS uses the filename as the identifier. XOO7 assigns a unique root name to each XML file so that the XML data can be stored and queried in most systems.

Two <para> elements are created in <Document> to cater to the document-centric aspect of XML. In fact, the <Document> element provides for a liberal use of free-form text that is "marked up" with elements. <Document> contains two attributes, MyID (integer) and title (string). Since two attributes are in the `connection` relation, we choose to convert `connection` to a subelement of `CompositePart` with attributes `type` and `length`. Then `AtomicPart` becomes a subelement of `connection` instead of `CompositePart`.

Table 17.2 The XOO7 Database Parameters

Parameters	Small	Medium	Large
NumAtomicPerComposite	20	200	200
NumConnectionPerAtomic	3, 6, 9	3, 6, 9	3, 6, 9
DocumentSize (bytes)	500	1000	1000
ManualSize (bytes)	2000	4000	4000
NumCompositePerModule	50	50	500
NumAssemblyPerAssembly	3	3	3
NumAssemblyLevels	5	5	7
NumCompositePerAssembly	3	3	3
NumModules	1	1	1

Similar to OO7, the XOO7 benchmark allows data sets of varying size to be generated: small, medium, and large. Table 17.2 summarizes the parameters and their corresponding values that are used to control the size of the XML data.

Note that there are some important differences in the XOO7 benchmark database parameters compared to those in the OO7 benchmark:

- While seven levels of assemblies are in the OO7 benchmark, only five levels are used in the small and medium databases because existing XML tools have limitations in the amount of data they can manipulate.
- There are ten modules in the large database in the OO7 benchmark. In XOO7, the number of modules is fixed at one because the module element is chosen as the root of the XML document.
- Since the XML data set can be represented as a tree, the data size can be changed in two directions: depthwise and breadthwise. The depth of the tree can be varied by changing the value of NumAssemblyLevels, while the breadth of the tree can be controlled by the value of NumAtomicPerComposite or NumCompositePer Module. Furthermore, users can include different amounts of text data according to their application by changing the size of Document and Manual.

The XOO7 Queries

The queries generated from the OO7 benchmark do not cover a substantial number of the XML query functionalities we identified earlier (compare Table 17.1 and the OO7 queries in S. Bressan et al. [Bressan, Lee 2001]). In fact, the majority of the OO7 queries focus on the data-centric query capabilities of object-oriented database systems. It is therefore imperative that the benchmark be extended to include queries to test document-processing capabilities. Table 17.3 lists the complete set of

Table 17.3 Queries in the XOO7 Benchmark

Group	ID	Description	Comments	Coverage
I	Q1	Randomly generate 5 numbers in the range of AtomicParts MyID. Then return the AtomicPart according to the 5 numbers	Simple selection. Number comparison is required.	R1, R2
	Q2	Randomly generate 5 titles for Documents. Then return the first paragraph of the document by lookup on these titles.	String comparison and element ordering are required in this query.	R1, R2
	Q3	Select 5% of AtomicParts via buildDate (in a certain period).	Range query. Users can change the selectivity.	R4
	Q4	Join AtomicParts and Documents on AtomicParts docId and Documents MyID.	Test join operation. It is commonly tested in many benchmarks.	R9
	Q5	Randomly generate 2 phrases among all phrases in Documents. Select those documents containing the 2 phrases.	Text data handling. Contains-like functions are required (Contains is a function defined in the XQuery specification. It checks if a string occurs in another string).	R5
	Q6	Repeat query 1 but replace duplicated elements using their IDREF.	This is to test the ability to reconstruct a new structure.	R1, R18
	Q7	For each BaseAssembly count the number of documents.	Test count aggregate function.	R9, R10
	Q8	Sort CompositePart in descending order where buildDate is within a year from current date.	Test sorting and use of environment information.	R11, R14

(continued)

Table 17.3 *continued*

Group	ID	Description	Comments	Coverage
	Q9	Return all BaseAssembly of type "type008" without any child nodes.	Users only require a single level of the XML document without child nodes included.	R18
II	Q10	Find the CompositePart if it is later than BaseAssembly it is using (comparing the buildDate attribute).	Compare attributes in parent nodes and child nodes. It tests the basic relation in XML data.	R13
	Q11	Select all BaseAssemblies from one XML database where it has the same "type" attributes as the BaseAssemblies in another database but with later buildDate.	Selection from multiple XML documents. It performs string and number comparison as well.	R9
	Q12	Select all AtomicParts with corresponding CompositeParts as their subelements.	Users may have various choices to store the same data, so they always require switching the parent nodes with the child nodes.	R18
	Q13	Select all ComplexAssemblies with type "type008".	Note ComplexAssembly is a recursive element, so it tests on regular path expression. An XMS should not browse every node.	R20
	Q14	Find BaseAssembly of not type "type008".	Robustness in presence of negation.	R8
	Q15	Return all Connection elements with length greater than Avg(length) within the same composite part without child nodes.	Avg function and group-by-like functions are required in this query.	R9, R10
	Q16	For CompositePart of type "type008", give 'Result' containing ID of CompositePart and Document.	Part of information of an element is required in this query. Test data transformation.	R17, R18
III	Q17	Among the first 5 Connections of each CompositePart, select those with length greater than "len".	Test element order preservation. It is a document query.	R9, R21
	Q18	For each CompositePart, select the first 5 Connections with length greater than "len".	Similar to above. It is to check if some optimization is done.	R9, R21

queries in the XOO7 benchmark together with comments and coverage. The XOO7 queries are divided into three main groups. Group I consists of traditional database queries. Most of these functionalities are already tested in many existing database benchmarks. Group II consists of navigational queries. They were designed because of the similarities between XML data and semi-structured data (Abiteboul et al. 2000; Buneman 1997). These queries test how traversals are carried out in the XML tree. Group III consists of document queries. These queries test the level of document-centric support given by systems and test the ability of data to maintain order.

These three groups of queries are relevant to the characteristics of XML data and cover most of the functionalities. All of the queries are simple, and each query covers only a few functionalities. The majority of the queries is supported in many XMS, which makes them very portable. Users can always choose a subset of queries to test the features required in their applications.

17.4.2 The XMach-1 Benchmark

The XMach-1 benchmark (Böhme and Rahm 2001) is a multiuser benchmark designed for B2B applications. In this chapter, we did not analyze the multiuser part of the benchmark but we consider only the special case of the XMach-1 benchmark, a single-user issuing queries from a local machine. The benchmark models a Web application using XML as follows: XML manipulations are performed through an XML-based directory system sitting on top of XML files.

The XMach-1 Database

The XMach-1 benchmark limits the XML data to be simple in data structure and small in size. It supports both schema-based and schema-less XMS and allows implementing some functionality at the application level. Figure 17.2 shows the ER diagram of XMach-1 database and the corresponding DTD is given in Listing 17.2. Attributes have been omitted to simplify the diagram. Each of the XML files simulates an article with elements like title, chapter, section, paragraph, and so on. The element section is a recursive element. Text data are taken from the natural language text. Users can vary an XML file size by modifying the number of the article elements. Varying the number of XML files controls the size of the database. Note that XMach-1 assumes that the size of the data files exchanged in Web applications will be small (1–14KB).

Listing 17.2 DTD of XMach-1 Database

```
<!ELEMENT document   (title, chapter+)>
<!ATTLIST document   author     CDATA         #IMPLIED
                     doc_id     ID            #IMPLIED>
```

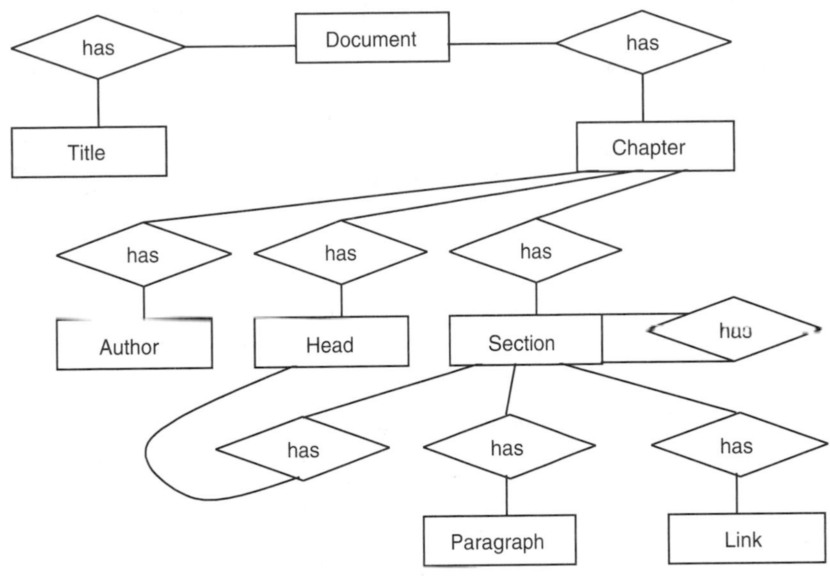

Figure 17.2 ERD of XMach-1 Database

```
<!ELEMENT author      (#PCDATA)>
<!ELEMENT title       (#PCDATA)>
<!ELEMENT chapter     (author?, head, section+)>
<!ATTLIST chapter     id          ID              #REQUIRED>
<!ELEMENT section     (head, paragraph+, subsection*)>
<!ATTLIST section     id          ID              #REQUIRED>
<!ELEMENT subsection  (head, paragraph+, subsection*)>
<!ATTLIST subsection  id          ID              #REQUIRED>
<!ELEMENT head        (#PCDATA)>
<!ELEMENT paragraph   (#PCDATA | link)*>
<!ELEMENT link        EMPTY>
<!ATTLIST link        xlink:type (simple)         #FIXED "simple"
                      xlink:href CDATA            #REQUIRED>
```

The XMach-1 Queries

XMach-1 evaluates standard and nonstandard linguistic features such as insertion, deletion, querying URL, and aggregate operations. The benchmark consists of eight queries and two update operations as shown in Table 17.4. For the sake of a consistent comparison, we divide the queries into four groups according to the common characteristics they capture. Group I consists of simple selection and projection queries with comparisons on element or attribute values. Group II queries

Table 17.4 Queries Specified in the XMach-1 Benchmark

Group	ID	Description	Comment
I	Q1	Get document with given URL.	Return a complete document (complex hierarchy with original ordering preserved).
	Q2	Get doc_id from documents containing a given phrase.	Text retrieval query. The phrase is chosen from the phrase list.
	Q5	Get doc_id and id of parent element of author element with given content.	Find chapters of a given author. Query across all DTDs/text documents.
II	Q3	Return leaf in tree structure of a document given by `doc_id` following first child in each node starting with document root.	Simulates exploring a document with unknown structure (path traversal).
	Q4	Get document name (last path element in directory structure) from all documents that are below a given URL fragment.	Browse directory structure. Operation on structured unordered data.
	Q6	Get doc_id and insert date from documents having a given author (document attribute).	Join operation.
III	Q7	Get doc_id from documents that are referenced by at least four other documents.	Get important documents. Needs some kind of group by and count operation.
	Q8	Get doc_id from the last 100 inserted documents having an author attribute.	Needs count, sort, and join operations and accesses metadata.
IV	M1	Insert document with given URL.	The loader generates a document and URL and sends them to the HTTP server.
M2		Delete a document with given doc_id.	A robot requests deletion, e.g., because the corresponding original document no longer exists in the Web.

require the systems to use the element order to extract results. Group III queries test aggregation functions and the use of metadata information. Group IV are update operations. We observe that while the proposed workload and queries are interesting, the benchmark has not been applied, and no performance results are available.

17.4.3 The XMark Benchmark

The XML benchmark project at CWI (Schmidt, Waas, Kersten, Florescu, Manolescu et al. 2001) recently proposed the XMark benchmark. This benchmark consists of an application scenario that models an Internet auction site and 20 XQuery (Boag et al. 2002) challenges designed to cover the essentials of XML query processing.

The XMark Database

Figure 17.3 shows the ER diagram of the XMark database. The corresponding DTD can be seen in Listing 17.3. We have again omitted the attributes to simplify the diagram. The main entities in the database are item, person, open auction, close auction, and category. Items are the objects that are for sale or are sold already; person entities contain subelements such as name, e-mail address, phone number; open auctions are auctions in progress; close auctions are the finished auctions; categories feature a name and a description. The XMark benchmark enriches the references in the data, like the item IDREF in an auction element and the item's ID in an item element. The text data used are the 17,000 most frequently occurring words of Shakespeare's plays. The standard data size is 100MB with a scaling factor of 1.0, and users can change the data size by 10 times from the standard data (the initial data) each time.

Listing 17.3 DTD of XMark Database

```
<!ELEMENT site             (regions, categories, catgraph, people,
open_auctions, closed_auctions)>

<!ELEMENT categories       (category+)>
<!ELEMENT category         (name, description)>
<!ATTLIST category         id ID #REQUIRED>
<!ELEMENT name             (#PCDATA)>
<!ELEMENT description      (text | parlist)>
<!ELEMENT text             (#PCDATA | bold | keyword | emph)*>
<!ELEMENT bold             (#PCDATA | bold | keyword | emph)*>
<!ELEMENT keyword          (#PCDATA | bold | keyword | emph)*>
<!ELEMENT emph             (#PCDATA | bold | keyword | emph)*>
<!ELEMENT parlist          (listitem)*>
<!ELEMENT listitem         (text | parlist)*>

<!ELEMENT catgraph         (edge*)>
<!ELEMENT edge             EMPTY>
<!ATTLIST edge             from IDREF #REQUIRED to IDREF #REQUIRED>
```

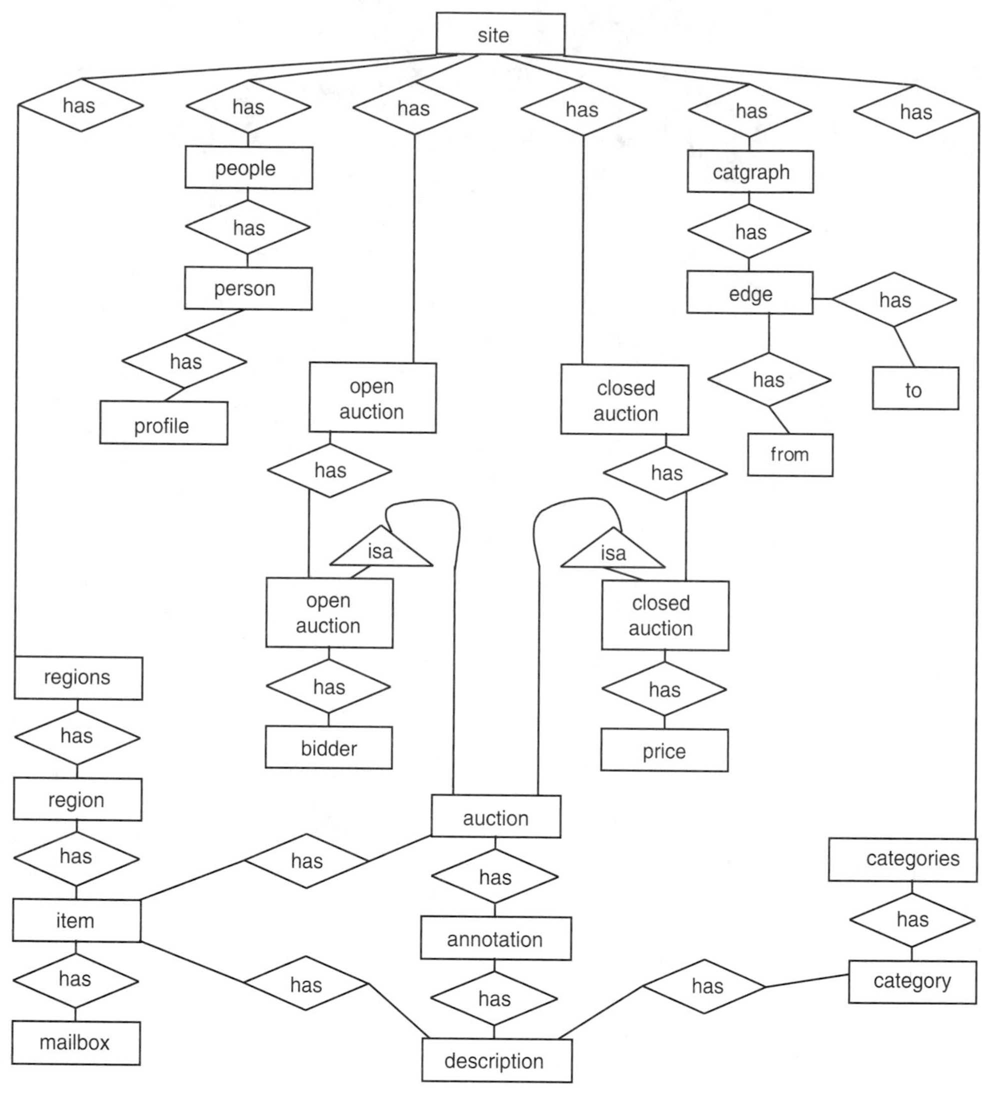

Figure 17.3 Queries Specified in the XMark Benchmark

```
<!ELEMENT regions        (africa, asia, australia, europe,
namerica, samerica)>
<!ELEMENT africa         (item*)>
<!ELEMENT asia           (item*)>
<!ELEMENT australia      (item*)>
```

```
<!ELEMENT namerica        (item*)>
<!ELEMENT samerica        (item*)>
<!ELEMENT europe          (item*)>
<!ELEMENT item            (location, quantity, name, payment,
description, shipping, incategory+, mailbox)>
<!ATTLIST item            id ID #REQUIRED
                          featured CDATA #IMPLIED>
<!ELEMENT location        (#PCDATA)>
<!ELEMENT quantity        (#PCDATA)>
<!ELEMENT payment         (#PCDATA)>
<!ELEMENT shipping        (#PCDATA)>
<!ELEMENT reserve         (#PCDATA)>
<!ELEMENT incategory      EMPTY>
<!ATTLIST incategory      category IDREF #REQUIRED>
<!ELEMENT mailbox         (mail*)>
<!ELEMENT mail            (from, to, date, text)>
<!ELEMENT from            (#PCDATA)>
<!ELEMENT to              (#PCDATA)>
<!ELEMENT date            (#PCDATA)>
<!ELEMENT itemref         EMPTY>
<!ATTLIST itemref         item IDREF #REQUIRED>
<!ELEMENT personref       EMPTY>
<!ATTLIST personref       person IDREF #REQUIRED>

<!ELEMENT people          (person*)>
<!ELEMENT person          (name, emailaddress, phone?, address?,
homepage?, creditcard?, profile?, watches?)>
<!ATTLIST person          id ID #REQUIRED>
<!ELEMENT emailaddress    (#PCDATA)>
<!ELEMENT phone           (#PCDATA)>
<!ELEMENT address         (street, city, country, province?,
zipcode)>
<!ELEMENT street          (#PCDATA)>
<!ELEMENT city            (#PCDATA)>
<!ELEMENT province        (#PCDATA)>
<!ELEMENT zipcode         (#PCDATA)>
<!ELEMENT country         (#PCDATA)>
<!ELEMENT homepage        (#PCDATA)>
<!ELEMENT creditcard      (#PCDATA)>
<!ELEMENT profile         (interest*, education?, gender?,
business, age?)>
<!ATTLIST profile         income CDATA #IMPLIED>
```

```
<!ELEMENT interest        EMPTY>
<!ATTLIST interest        category IDREF #REQUIRED>
<!ELEMENT education       (#PCDATA)>
<!ELEMENT income          (#PCDATA)>
<!ELEMENT gender          (#PCDATA)>
<!ELEMENT business        (#PCDATA)>
<!ELEMENT age             (#PCDATA)>
<!ELEMENT watches         (watch*)>
<!ELEMENT watch           EMPTY>
<!ATTLIST watch           open_auction IDREF #REQUIRED>

<!ELEMENT open_auctions   (open_auction*)>
<!ELEMENT open_auction    (initial, reserve?, bidder*, current,
privacy?, itemref, seller, annotation, quantity, type, interval)>
<!ATTLIST open_auction    id ID #REQUIRED>
<!ELEMENT privacy         (#PCDATA)>
<!ELEMENT initial         (#PCDATA)>
<!ELEMENT bidder          (date, time, personref, increase)>
<!ELEMENT seller          EMPTY>
<!ATTLIST seller          person IDREF #REQUIRED>
<!ELEMENT current         (#PCDATA)>
<!ELEMENT increase        (#PCDATA)>
<!ELEMENT type            (#PCDATA)>
<!ELEMENT interval        (start, end)>
<!ELEMENT start           (#PCDATA)>
<!ELEMENT end             (#PCDATA)>
<!ELEMENT time            (#PCDATA)>
<!ELEMENT status          (#PCDATA)>
<!ELEMENT amount          (#PCDATA)>

<!ELEMENT closed_auctions (closed_auction*)>
<!ELEMENT closed_auction  (seller, buyer, itemref, price, date,
quantity, type, annotation?)>
<!ELEMENT buyer           EMPTY>
<!ATTLIST buyer           person IDREF #REQUIRED>
<!ELEMENT price           (#PCDATA)>
<!ELEMENT annotation      (author, description?, happiness)>

<!ELEMENT author          EMPTY>
<!ATTLIST author          person IDREF #REQUIRED>
<!ELEMENT happiness       (#PCDATA)>
```

The XMark Queries

XMark provides 20 queries that have been evaluated on an internal research prototype, Monet XML, to give a first baseline. Table 17.5 shows the XMark queries and our comments. For the sake of a consistent comparison, we divide the queries into four groups based on the query functionality. Group I contains simple relational queries with comparisons on various types of data values. Queries in Group II are

Table 17.5 Queries Specified in the XMark Benchmark

Group	ID	Description	Comment
I	Q1	Return the name of the person with ID 'person0' registered in North America.	Check ability to handle strings with a fully specified path.
	Q5	How many sold items cost more than 40.	Check how well a DBMS performs since XML model is document oriented. Checks for typing in XML.
	Q14	Return the names of all items whose description contains the word 'gold'.	Text search but narrowed by combining the query on content and structure.
II	Q2	Return the initial increases of all open auctions.	Evaluate cost of array lookups. Authors cite that a relational backend may have problems determining the first element. Essentially query is about order of data which relational systems lack.
	Q3	Return IDs of all open auctions whose current increase is at least twice as high as initial.	More complex evaluation of array lookup.
	Q4	List reserves of those open auctions where a certain person issued bid before another person.	Querying tag values capturing document orientation of XML.
	Q11	For each person, list the number of items currently on sale whose price does not exceed 0.02% of person's income.	Value-based joins. Authors feel this query is a candidate for optimizations.
	Q12	For each richer-than-average person list the number of items currently on sale whose price does not exceed 0.02% of the person's income.	As above.

(continued)

Table 17.5 *continued*

Group	ID	Description	Comment
	Q17	Which persons don't have a homepage?	Determine processing quality in presence of optional parameters.
III	Q6	How many items are listed on all continents?	Test efficiency in handling path expressions.
	Q7	How many pieces of prose are in our database?	Query is answerable using cardinality of relations. Testing implementation.
	Q8	List the names of persons and the number of items they bought.	Check efficiency in processing IDREFs. Note a pure relational system would handle this situation using foreign keys.
	Q9	List the names of persons and the names of items they bought in Europe (joins person, closed auction, item).	As above.
	Q10	List all persons according to their interest. Use French markup in the result.	Grouping, restructuring, and rewriting. Storage efficiency checked.
	Q13	List names of items registered in Australia along with their descriptions.	Test ability of database to reconstruct portions of XML document.
	Q15	Print the keywords in emphasis in annotations of closed auctions.	Attempt to quantify completely specified paths. Query checks for existence of path.
	Q16	Return the IDs of those auctions that have one or more keywords in emphasis.	As above.
IV	Q18	Convert the currency of the reserve of all open auctions to another currency.	User defined functions checked.
	Q19	Give an alphabetically ordered list of all items along with their location.	Query uses SORT BY, which might lead to an SQL-like ORDER BY and GROUP BY because of lack of schema.
	Q20	Group customers by their income and output the cardinality of each group.	The processor will have to identify that all the subparts differ only in values given to attribute and predicates used. A profile should be visited only once.

document queries that preserve the element order. Group III contains navigational queries. For example, Q8 and Q9 check the navigational performance in the presence of ID and IDREF, while Q15 and Q16 test long path traversals. Queries in Group IV require aggregate handling and sort operations.

17.5 Conclusion

The XOO7, XMach-1, and XMark benchmarks have been designed to investigate the performance of different XMS. All three benchmarks provide complex data sets to capture the essential characteristics of XML data such as recursive elements and various data types. In terms of simplicity, XMach-1 has the most straightforward database description. It models a document, which is easy for users to understand. XOO7 adapts and extends the OO7 database on modules, which can be understood quite easily. XMark simulates an auction scenario, which is a very specialized interest area, containing many elements and attributes that may be difficult for users to understand.

Table 17.6 shows the coverage of the queries in the three benchmarks. Clearly, XMark and XOO7 cover most of the functionalities. It makes sense that XMach-1

Table 17.6 Benchmark Coverage of the XML Query Language Functionalities

Coverage	XMach-1	XMark	XOO7
R1	✓	✓	✓
R2	✓	✓	✓
R3			
R4	✓	✓	✓
R5	✓	✓	✓
R6			
R7		✓	
R8		✓	✓
R9	✓	✓	✓
R10	✓	✓	✓

(continued)

Table 17.6 *continued*

Coverage	XMach-1	XMark	XOO7
R11		✓	✓
R12			
R13		✓	✓
R14			✓
R15	✓		
R16			
R17		✓	✓
R18		✓	✓
R19			
R20			✓
R21		✓	✓

covers the least number of functionalities since it has relatively fewer queries. We observe that both XOO7 and XMach-1 give simple queries that test one or two functionalities, while the majority of the queries in XMark are complex and cover many features. The latter may lead to difficulty in analyzing the results of a query since it may not be clear which feature contributes most to the response time. Furthermore, it is possible that some queries in XMark may not be executable or applicable because the system under test supports only a subset of the complex features.

Varying the number of elements in the XML files can scale the data sets of the three benchmarks. XOO7 allows users to change the file size both depthwise and breadthwise. XMark changes the database size by a certain factor (e.g., 10 times). Since XMach-1 assumes that the XML files are small, changing the number of XML files varies the database size.

As we have shown, the quality of an XMS benchmark can be analyzed with respect to four criteria: simplicity, relevance, portability, and scalability. Our study of the extent to which these criteria are met by each of the three major existing XMS benchmarks, XOO7, XMach-1, and XMark, shows that the definition of a complete XMS benchmark is a challenging ongoing task.

Chapter 18

The Michigan Benchmark: A Micro-Benchmark for XML Query Performance Diagnostics

Jignesh M. Patel and H. V. Jagadish

18.1 Introduction

With the increasing popularity of the XML as a representation format for a wide variety of data, it is clear that large repositories of XML data sets will soon emerge. The effective management of XML in a database thus becomes a pressing issue. Several methods for managing XML databases have emerged, ranging from retrofitting commercial RDBMSs to building native XML database systems. There has naturally been an interest in benchmarking the performance of these systems, and a number of benchmarks have been proposed (Böhme and Rahm 2001; Bressan, Dobbie 2001; Schmidt, Waas, Kersten, Florescu, Manolescu et al. 2001). The focus of currently proposed benchmarks is to assess the performance of a given XML database in performing a variety of representative tasks. Such benchmarks are valuable to potential users of a database system in providing an indication of the performance that users can expect on their specific application. The challenge is to devise benchmarks that are sufficiently representative of the requirements of *most* users. The TPC series of benchmarks accomplished this, with reasonable success, for relational database systems. However, no benchmark has been successful in the realm of ORDBMS and OODBMS, which have extensibility and user-defined functions that lead to great heterogeneity in the nature of their use. It is too soon to say whether any of the current XML benchmarks will be successful in this respect—we certainly hope that they will.

One aspect that current XML benchmarks do not focus on is the performance of the basic query evaluation operations, such as selections, joins, and aggregations. A *micro-benchmark* that highlights the performance of these basic operations can be very helpful to a database developer in understanding and evaluating alternatives for implementing these basic operations. A number of questions related to performance may need to be answered: What are the strengths and weaknesses of specific access methods? Which areas should the developer focus attention on? What is the basis for choosing between two alternative implementations? Questions of this nature are central to well-engineered systems. Application-level benchmarks, by their nature, are unable to deal with these important issues in detail. For relational systems, the Wisconsin benchmark (DeWitt 1993) provided the database community with an invaluable engineering tool to assess the performance of individual operators and access methods. Inspired by the simplicity and the effectiveness of the Wisconsin benchmark for measuring and understanding the performance of relational DBMSs, we develop a comparable benchmarking tool for XML data management systems. The benchmark that we propose is called the Michigan benchmark.

A challenging issue in designing any benchmark is the choice of the data set that is used by the benchmark. If the data are specified to represent a particular "real application," they are likely to be quite uncharacteristic for other applications with different data distributions. Thus, holistic benchmarks can succeed only if they are able to find a real application with data characteristics that are reasonably representative for a large class of different applications.

For a micro-benchmark, the benchmark data set must be *complex* enough to incorporate data characteristics that are likely to have an impact on the performance of query operations. However, at the same time the benchmark data set must be *simple* so that it is not only easy to pose and understand queries against the data set, but the queries must also guide the benchmark user to the precise component of the system that is performing poorly. We attempt to achieve this balance by using a data set that has a simple schema. In addition, random number generators are used sparingly in generating the benchmark's data set. The Michigan benchmark uses random generators for only two attribute values and derives all other data parameters from these two generated values. In addition, as in the Wisconsin benchmark, we use appropriate attribute names to reflect the domain and distribution of the attribute values.

When designing benchmark data sets for relational systems, the primary data characteristics that are of interest are the distribution and domain of the attribute values and the cardinality of the relations. In addition, there may be a few additional secondary characteristics, such as clustering and tuple/attribute size. In XML databases, besides the distribution and domain of attribute values and cardinality, several other characteristics, such as tree fanout and tree depth, are related to the structure of XML documents and contribute to the rich structure of XML data. An XML benchmark must incorporate these additional features into the benchmark data and query set design. The Michigan benchmark achieves this by using a data set that incorporates these characteristics without introducing unnecessary complexity into the data set generation, and by carefully designing the benchmark queries that test the impact of these characteristics on individual query operations.

The remainder of this chapter is organized as follows. The next section presents related work. Following this, we discuss the rationale of the benchmark data set design. We then describe the queries of the benchmark data set. Then, we present our recommendation on how to analyze and present the results of the benchmark. Finally, we summarize the contribution of this benchmark.

18.2 Related Work

Several proposals for generating synthetic XML data have been proposed (Aboulnaga et al. 2001; Barbosa et al. 2002). Aboulnaga et al. proposed a data generator that accepts as many as twenty parameters to allow a user to control the properties of the generated data. Such a large number of parameters adds a level of complexity that may interfere with the ease of use of a data generator. Furthermore, this data generator does not make available the schema of the data that some systems could exploit. Most recently, Barbosa et al. proposed a template-based data generator for XML, which can generate multiple tunable data sets. In contrast to these previous data generators, the data generator in the Michigan benchmark produces an XML data set designed to test different XML data characteristics that may affect the performance of XML engines. In addition, the data generator requires only a few parameters to vary the scalability of the data set. The schema of the data set is also available to exploit.

Three benchmarks have been proposed for evaluating the performance of XML data management systems (Böhme and Rahm 2001; Bressan, Dobbie 2001; Schmidt, Waas, Kersten, Florescu, Manolescu et al. 2001). XMach-1 (Böhme and Rahm 2001) and XMark (Schmidt, Waas, Kersten, Florescu, Manolescu et al. 2001) generate XML data that models data from particular Internet applications. In XMach-1, the data are based on a Web application that consists of text documents, schemaless data, and structured data. In XMark, the data are based on an Internet auction application that consists of relatively structured and data-oriented parts. XOO7 (Bressan, Dobbie 2001) is an XML version of the OO7 Benchmark (Carey et al. 1993) that provides a comprehensive evaluation of OODBMS performance. The OO7 schema and instances are mapped into a Document Type Definition (DTD) and the corresponding XML data sets. The eight OO7 queries are translated into three respective languages of the query-processing engines: Lore (Goldman et al. 1999; McHugh et al. 1997), Kweelt (Sahuguet et al. 2000), and an ORDBMS. While each of these benchmarks provides an excellent measure of how a test system would perform against data and queries in their targeted XML application, it is difficult to extrapolate the results to data sets and queries that are different from ones in the targeted domain. Although the queries in these benchmarks are designed to test different performance aspects of XML engines, they cannot be used to perceive the system performance change as the XML data characteristics change. On the other hand, we have different queries to analyze the system performance with respect to different XML data characteristics, such as tree fanout and tree depth, and different query characteristics, such as predicate selectivity.

A desiderata document (Schmidt, Waas, Kersten, Florescu, Carey et al. 2001) for a benchmark for XML databases identifies components and operations, and ten challenges that the XML benchmark should address. Although the proposed benchmark is not a general-purpose benchmark, it meets the challenges that test performance-critical aspects of XML processing.

18.3 Benchmark Data Set

In this section, we first discuss characteristics of XML data sets that can have a significant impact on the performance of query operations. Then we present the schema and the generation algorithms for the benchmark data.

18.3.1 A Discussion of the Data Characteristics

In the relational paradigm, the primary data characteristics are the selectivity of attributes (important for simple selection operations) and the join selectivity (important for join operations). In the XML paradigm, several complicating characteristics must be considered as discussed in the sections that follow.

Depth and Fanout

Depth and fanout are two structural parameters important to tree-structured data. The depth of the data tree can have a significant performance impact when we are computing containment relationships that include an indirect containment between ancestor and descendant and a direct containment between parent and child. It is possible to have multiple nodes at different levels satisfying the ancestor and the descendant predicates. Similarly, the fanout of the node tree can affect the way in which the DBMS stores the data and answers queries that are based on selecting children in a specific order (for example, selecting the last child).

One potential way of testing fanout and depth is to generate a number of distinct data sets with different values for each of these parameters and then run queries against each data set. The drawback of this approach is that the large number of data sets makes the benchmark harder to run and understand. In this chapter, our approach is to create a base benchmark data set of a depth of 16. Then, using a "level" attribute of an element, we can restrict the scope of the query to data sets of certain depth, thereby quantifying the impact of the depth of the data tree.

To study the impact of fanout, we generate the data set in the following way There are 16 levels in the tree, and each level has a fanout of 2, except levels 5, 6, 7, and 8. Levels 5, 6, and 7 have a fanout of 13, whereas level 8 has a fanout of 1/13 (at level 8 every thirteenth node has a single child). This variation in fanout is designed to permit queries that measure the effect of the fanout factor. For instance, the number of nodes is 2,704 for nodes at levels 7 and 9. Nodes at level 7 have a fanout of 13, whereas nodes at level 9 have a fanout of 2. Queries against these two levels can be used to measure the impact of fanout. The distribution of nodes is shown in Table 18.1.

Table 18.1 Distribution of the Nodes in the Base Data Set

Level	Fanout	Nodes	% of Nodes
1	2	1	0.0
2	2	2	0.0
3	2	4	0.0
4	2	8	0.0
5	13	16	0.0
6	13	208	0.0
7	13	2,704	0.4
8	1/13	35,152	4.8
9	2	2,704	0.4

(continued)

Table 18.1 *continued*

Level	Fanout	Nodes	% of Nodes
10	2	5,408	0.7
11	2	10,816	1.5
12	2	21,632	3.0
13	2	43,264	6.0
14	2	86,528	11.9
15	2	173,056	23.8
16	-	346,112	47.6

Data Set Granularity

To keep the benchmark simple, we chose a single large document tree as the default data set. If it is important to understand the effect of document granularity, one can modify the benchmark data set to treat each node at a given level as the root of a distinct document. One can compare the performance of queries on this modified data set against queries on the original data set.

Scaling

A good benchmark needs to be able to scale in order to measure the performance of databases on a variety of platforms. In the relational model, scaling a benchmark data set is easy—we simply increase the number of tuples. However, with XML, there are many scaling options, such as increasing the number of nodes, depth, or fanout. We would like to isolate the effect of the number of nodes from the effects due to other structural changes, such as depth and fanout. We achieve this by keeping the tree depth constant for all scaled versions of the data set and changing the number of fanouts of nodes at only a few levels.

The default data set, which was described earlier, is called **DSx1**. This data set has about 728K nodes, arranged in a tree of a depth of 16 and a fanout of 2 for all levels except levels 5, 6, 7, and 8, which have fanouts of 13, 13, 13, 1/13, respectively. From this data set we generate two additional "scaled-up" data sets, called **DSx10** and **DSx100** such that the numbers of nodes in these data sets are approximated 10 and 100 times the number of nodes in the base data set, respectively. We achieve this scaling factor by varying the fanout of the nodes at levels 5–8. For the data set **DSx10** levels 5–7 have a fanout of 39, whereas level 8 has a fanout of 1/39. For the data set **DSx100** levels 5–7 have a fanout of 111, whereas level 8 has a fanout of 1/111. The total number of nodes in the data sets **DSx10** and **DSx100** is 7,180K and 72,350K, respectively (which translates into a scale factor of 9.9x and 99.4x, respectively).

In the design of the benchmark data set, we deliberately keep the fanout of the bottom few levels of the tree constant. This design implies that the percentage of nodes in the lower levels of the tree (levels 9–16) is nearly constant across all the data sets. This allows us to easily express queries that focus on a specified percentage of the total number of nodes in the database. For example, to select approximately 1/16 of all the nodes, irrespective of the scale factor, we use the predicate `aLevel = 13`.

18.3.2 Schema of Benchmark Data

The construction of the benchmark data is centered on the element type `BaseType`. Each `BaseType` element has the following attributes:

- **`aUnique1`**: A unique integer generated by traversing the entire data tree in a breadth-first manner. This attribute also serves as the element identifier.
- **`aUnique2`**: A unique integer generated randomly.
- **`aLevel`**: An integer set to store the level of the node.
- **`aFour`**: An integer set to `aUnique2` mod 4.
- **`aSixteen`**: An integer set to `aUnique1 + aUnique2` mod 16. Note that this attribute is set to `aUnique1 + aUnique2` mod 16 instead of `aUnique2` mod 16 to avoid a correlation between the predicate on this attribute and one on either `aFour` or `aSixtyFour`.
- **`aSixtyFour`**: An integer set to `aUnique2` mod 64.
- **`aString`**: A string approximately 32 bytes in length.

The content of each `BaseType` element is a long string that is approximately 512 bytes in length. The generation of the element content and the string attribute `aString` is described further below.

In addition to the attributes listed above, each `BaseType` element has two sets of subelements. The first is of type `BaseType`. The number of repetitions of this subelement is determined by the fanout of the parent element, as described in Table 18.1. The second subelement is an `OccasionalType` and can occur either 0 or 1 time. The presence of the `OccasionalType` element is determined by the value of the attribute `aSixtyFour` of the parent element. A `BaseType` element has a nested (leaf) element of type OccasionalType if the aSixtyFour attribute has the value 0. An OccasionalType element has content that is identical to the content of the parent but has only one attribute, aRef. The OccasionalType element refers to the BaseType node with aUnique1 value equal to the parent's aUnique1-11 (the reference is achieved by assigning this value to aRef attribute). In the case where no BaseType element has the parent's aUnique1-11 value (e.g., top few nodes in the tree), the OccasionalType element refers to the root node of the tree.

The XML Schema specification of the benchmark data is shown in Listing 18.1.

Listing 18.1 Benchmark Specification in XML Schema

```
<?xml version="1.0"?>
<xsd:schema xmlns:xsd="http://www.w3.org/2001/XMLSchema"
  targetNamespace="http://www.eecs.umich.edu/db/mbench/bm.xsd"
  xmlns="http://www.eecs.umich.edu/db/mbench/bm.xsd"
  elementFormDefault="qualified">
 <xsd:complexType name="BaseType" mixed="true">
  <xsd:sequence>
   <xsd:element name="eNest" type="BaseType" minOccurs="0">
    <xsd:key name="aU1PK">
     <xsd:selector xpath=".//eNest"/>
     <xsd:field xpath="@ aUnique1"/>
    </xsd:key>
    <xsd:unique name="aU2">
     <xsd:selector xpath=".//eNest"/>
     <xsd:field xpath="@aUnique2"/>
    </xsd:unique>
   </xsd:element>
   <xsd:element name="eOccasional" type="OccasionalType"
        minOccurs="0" maxOccurs="1">
    <xsd:keyref name="aU1FK" refer="aU1PK">
    <xsd:selector xpath="../eOccasional"/>
    <xsd:field xpath="@aRef"/>
    </xsd:keyref>
   </xsd:element>
  </xsd:sequence>
  <xsd:attributeGroup ref="BaseTypeAttrs"/>
 </xsd:complexType>
 <xsd:complexType name="OccassionalType">
  <xsd:simpleContent>
   <xsd:extension base="xsd:string">
    <xsd:attribute name="aRef" type="xsd:integer" use="required"/>
```

```
    </xsd:extension>
   </xsd:simpleContent>
  </xsd:complexType>
  <xsd:attributeGroup name="BaseTypeAttrs">
   <xsd:attribute name="aUnique1" type="xsd:integer"
use="required"/>
   <xsd:attribute name="aUnique2" type="xsd:integer"
use="required"/>
   <xsd:attribute name="aLevel" type="xsd:integer" use="required"/>
   <xsd:attribute name="aFour" type="xsd:integer" use="required"/>
   <xsd:attribute name="aSixteen" type="xsd:integer"
use="required"/>
   <xsd:attribute name="aSixtyFour" type="xsd:integer"
use="required"/>
   <xsd:attribute name="aString" type="xsd:string" use="required"/ >
  </xsd:attributeGroup>
</xsd:schema>
```

18.3.3 Generating the String Attributes and Element Content

The element content of each BaseType element is a long string. Since this string is meant to simulate a piece of text in a natural language, it is not appropriate to generate this string from a uniform distribution. Selecting pieces of text from real sources, however, involves many difficulties, such as how to maintain roughly constant size for each string, how to avoid idiosyncrasies associated with the specific source, and how to generate more strings as required for a scaled benchmark. Moreover, we would like to have benchmark results applicable to a wide variety of languages and domain vocabularies.

To obtain the string value that has a distribution similar to the distribution of a natural language text, we generate these long strings synthetically, in a carefully stylized manner. We begin by creating a pool of 2^{16} -1 (over sixty thousands) synthetic words. This is roughly twice the number of entries in the second edition of the *Oxford English Dictionary*. However, half the words that are used in the benchmark are "derived" words, produced by appending "ing" to the end of the word. The words are divided into 16 buckets, with exponentially growing bucket occupancy. Bucket i has 2^{i-1} words. For example, the first bucket has only one word, the second has two words, the third has four words, and so on. The words are not meaningful in any language but simply contain information about the bucket from which they are drawn, and the word number in the bucket. For example, "15twentynineB14" indicates that this is the 1,529th word from the fourteenth bucket. To keep the size of the vocabulary in the last bucket at roughly 30,000 words, words in the last bucket are derived from words in the other buckets by adding the suffix "ing" (to get exactly 2^{15} words in the sixteenth bucket, we add the dummy word "oneB0ing").

The value of the long string is generated from the template shown in Listing 18.2, where "PickWord" is actually a placeholder for a word picked from the word pool described above. To pick a word for "PickWord", a bucket is chosen, with each bucket equally likely, and then a word is picked from the chosen bucket, with each word equally likely. Thus, we obtain a discrete Zipf distribution of parameter roughly 1. We use the Zipf distribution since it seems to reflect word occurrence probabilities accurately in a wide variety of situations. The value of `aString` attribute is simply the first line of the long string that is stored as the element content. Through the above procedures, we now have the data set that has the structure that facilitates the study of the impact of data characteristics on system performance and the element/attribute content that simulates a piece of text in a natural language.

Listing 18.2 Generation of the String Element Content

```
Sing a song of PickWord,
A pocket full of PickWord
Four and twenty PickWord
All baked in a PickWord.
When the PickWord was opened,
The PickWord began to sing;
Wasn't that a dainty PickWord
To set before the PickWord?
The King was in his PickWord,
Counting out his PickWord;
The Queen was in the PickWord
Eating bread and PickWord.
The maid was in the PickWord
Hanging out the PickWord;
When down came a PickWord,
And snipped off her PickWord!
```

18.4 Benchmark Queries

In creating the data set above, we make it possible to tease apart data with different characteristics and to issue queries with well-controlled yet vastly differing data access patterns. We are more interested in evaluating the cost of individual pieces of core query functionality than in evaluating the composite performance of application-level queries. Knowing the costs of individual basic operations, we can estimate the cost of any complex query by just adding up relevant piecewise costs (keeping in mind the pipelined nature of evaluation, and the changes in sizes of intermediate results when operators are pipelined).

One clean way to decompose complex queries is by means of algebra. While the benchmark is not tied to any particular algebra, we find it useful to refer to queries as "selection queries," "join queries," and the like, to clearly indicate the functionality of each query. A complex query that involves many of these simple operations can take time that varies monotonically with the time required for these simple components.

In the following sections, we describe each of these different types of queries in detail. In these queries, the types of the nodes are assumed to be `BaseType` (`eNest` nodes) unless specified otherwise.

18.4.1 Selection

Relational selection identifies the tuples that satisfy a given predicate over its attributes. XML selection is both more complex and more important because of the tree structure. Consider a query, against a popular bibliographic database, that seeks `books`, published in the `year 2002`, by an `author` with `name` including the string `"Bernstein"`. This apparently straightforward selection query involves matches in the database to a four-node "query pattern," with predicates associated with each of these four (namely `book`, `year`, `author`, and `name`). Once a match has been found for this pattern, we may be interested in returning only the `book` element, all the nodes that participated in the match, or various other possibilities. We attempt to organize the various sources of complexity in the following sections.

Returned Structure

In a relation, once a tuple is selected, the tuple is returned. In XML, as we saw in the example above, once an element is selected, one may return the element, as well as some structure related to the element, such as the subtree rooted at the element. Query performance can be significantly affected by how the data are stored and when the returned result is materialized.

To understand the role of returned structure in query performance, we use the query, selecting all elements with `aSixtyFour = 2`. The selectivity of this query is 1/64 (1.6%).

This query is run in the following cases:

- **QR1:** Return only the elements in question, not including any subelements
- **QR2:** Return the elements and all their immediate children
- **QR3:** Return the entire subtree rooted at the elements
- **QR4:** Return the elements and their selected descendants with `aFour = 1`

The remaining queries in the benchmark simply return the unique identifier attributes of the selected nodes (`aUnique1` for `eNest` and `aRef` for `eOccasional`), except when explicitly specified otherwise. This design choice ensures that the cost of producing the final result is a small portion of the query execution cost.

Simple Selection

Even XML queries involving only one element and a single predicate can show considerable diversity. We examine the effect of this single selection predicate in this set of queries.

Exact Match Attribute Value Selection

Selection based on the value of a string attribute.

QS1. Low selectivity: Select nodes with `aString = "Sing a song of oneB4"`. Selectivity is 0.8%.

QS2. High selectivity: Select nodes with `aString = "Sing a song of oneB1"`. Selectivity is 6.3%.

Selection based on the value of an integer attribute.

We reproduce the same selectivities as in the string attribute case.

QS3. Low selectivity: Select nodes with `aLevel = 10`. Selectivity is 0.7%.

QS4. High selectivity: Select nodes with `aLevel = 13`. Selectivity is 6.0%.

Selection on range values.

QS5: Select nodes with `aSixtyFour between 5 and 8`. Selectivity is 6.3%.

Selection with sorting.

QS6: Select nodes with `aLevel = 13` and have the returned nodes sorted by `aSixtyFour` attribute. Selectivity is 6.0%.

Multiple-attribute selection.

QS7: Select nodes with attributes `aSixteen = 1` and `aFour = 1`. Selectivity is 1.6%.

Element Name Selection

QS8: Select nodes with the element name `eOccasional`. Selectivity is 1.6%.

Order-Based Selection

QS9: Select the second child of every node with `aLevel = 7`. Selectivity is 0.4%.

QS10: Select the second child of every node with `aLevel = 9`. Selectivity is 0.4%.

Since the fraction of nodes in these two queries is the same, the performance difference between queries QS9 and QS10 is likely to be on account of fanout.

Element Content Selection

QS11: Select `OccasionalType` nodes that have `"oneB4"` in the element content. Selectivity is 0.2%.

QS12: Select nodes that have `"oneB4"` as a substring of element content. Selectivity is 12.5%.

String Distance Selection

QS13. Low selectivity: Select all nodes with element content that the distance between keyword `"oneB5"` and keyword `"twenty"` is not more than four. Selectivity is 0.8%.

QS14. High selectivity: Select all nodes with element content that the distance between keyword `"oneB2"` and keyword `"twenty"` is not more than four. Selectivity is 6.3%.

Structural Selection

Selection in XML is often based on patterns. Queries should be constructed to consider multinode patterns of various sorts and selectivities. These patterns often have "conditional selectivity." Consider a simple two-node selection pattern. Given that one of the nodes has been identified, the selectivity of the second node in the pattern can differ from its selectivity in the database as a whole. Similar dependencies between different attributes in a relation could exist, thereby affecting the selectivity of a multiattribute predicate. Conditional selectivity is complicated in XML because different attributes may not be in the same element, but rather in different elements that are structurally related.

In this section, all queries return only the root of the selection pattern, unless otherwise specified.

Parent-Child Selection

QS15. Medium selectivity of both parent and child: Select nodes with `aLevel = 13` that have a child with `aSixteen = 3`. Selectivity is approximately 0.7%.

QS16. High selectivity of parent and low selectivity of child: Select nodes with `aLevel = 15` that have a child with `aSixtyFour = 3`. Selectivity is approximately 0.7%.

QS17. Low selectivity of parent and high selectivity of child: Select nodes with `aLevel = 11` that have a child with `aFour = 3`. Selectivity is approximately 0.7%.

Order-Sensitive Parent-Child Selection

QS18. Local ordering: Select the second element below *each* element with `aFour = 1` if that second element also has `aFour = 1`. Selectivity is 3.1%.

QS19. Global ordering: Select the second element with `aFour = 1` below *any* element with `aSixtyFour = 1`. This query returns at most one element, whereas the previous query returns one for each parent.

QS20. Reverse ordering: Among the children with `aSixteen = 1` of the parent element with `aLevel = 13`, select the last child. Selectivity is 0.7%.

Ancestor-Descendant Selection

QS21. Medium selectivity of both ancestor and descendant: Select nodes with `aLevel = 13` that have a descendant with `aSixteen = 3`. Selectivity is 3.5%.

QS22. High selectivity of ancestor and low selectivity of descendant: Select nodes with `aLevel = 15` that have a descendant with `aSixtyFour = 3`.Selectivity is 0.7%.

QS23. Low selectivity of ancestor and high selectivity of descendant: Select nodes with `aLevel = 11` that have a descendant with `aFour = 3`. Selectivity is 1.5%.

Ancestor Nesting in Ancestor-Descendant Selection

In the ancestor-descendant queries above (QS21–QS23), ancestors are never nested below other ancestors. To test the performance of queries when ancestors are recursively nested below other ancestors, we have three other ancestor-descendant queries. These queries are variants of QS21–QS23.

QS24. Medium selectivity of both ancestor and descendant: Select nodes with `aSixteen = 3` that have a descendant with `aSixteen = 5`.

QS25. High selectivity of ancestor and low selectivity of descendant: Select nodes with `aFour = 3` that have a descendant with `aSixtyFour = 3`.

QS26. Low selectivity of ancestor and high selectivity of descendant: Select nodes with `aSixtyFour = 9` that have a descendant with `aFour = 3`.

The overall selectivities of these queries (QS24–QS26) cannot be the same as that of the "equivalent" unnested queries (QS21–QS23) for two situations. First, the same descendants can now have multiple ancestors they match, and second, the number of candidate descendants is different (fewer) since the ancestor predicate can be satisfied by nodes at any level. These two situations may not necessarily cancel each other out. We focus on the local predicate selectivities and keep these the same for all of these queries (as well as for the parent-child queries considered before).

QS27: Similar to query QS26, but return both the root node and the descendant node of the selection pattern. Thus, the returned structure is a pair of nodes with an inclusion relationship between them.

Complex Pattern Selection

Complex pattern matches are common in XML databases, and in this section, we introduce a number of *chain* and *twig* queries that we use in this benchmark. Figure 18.1 shows an example of each of these types of queries.

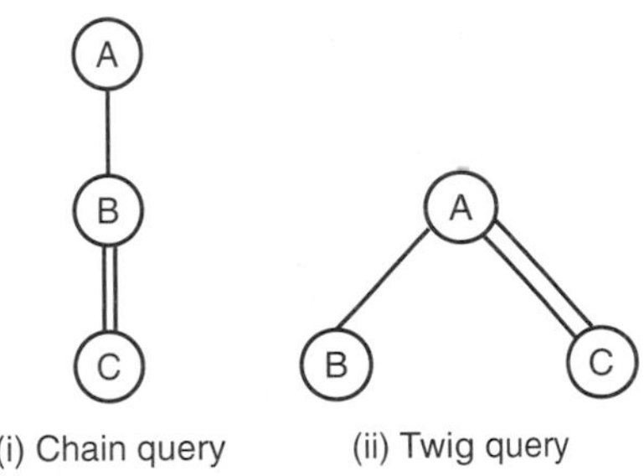

Figure 18.1 Samples of Chain and Twig Queries

In the figure, each node represents a predicate such as an element tag name predicate, an attribute value predicate, or an element content match predicate. A structural parent-child relationship in the query is shown by a single line, and an ancestor-descendant relationship is represented by a double-edged line. The chain query shown in (i) finds all nodes that match the condition A, such that there is a child node that matches the condition B, such that some descendant of the child node matches the condition C. The twig query shown in (ii) matches all nodes that satisfy the condition A, and have a child node that satisfies the condition B, and also has a descendant node that satisfies the condition C.

We use the following complex queries in our benchmark.

Parent-Child Complex Pattern Selection

QS28. One chain query with three parent-child joins with the selectivity pattern: high-low-low-high: The query is to test the choice of join order in evaluating a complex query. To achieve the desired selectivities, we use the following predicates: `aFour = 3`, `aSixteen = 3`, `aSixteen = 5`, and `aLevel = 16`.

QS29. One twig query with two parent-child selection (low-high, low-low): Select parent nodes with `aLevel = 11` (low selectivity) that have a child with `aFour = 3` (high selectivity) and another child with `aSixtyFour = 3` (low selectivity).

QS30. One twig query with two parent-child selection (high-low, high-low): Select parent nodes with `aFour = 1` (high selectivity) that have a child with `aLevel = 11` (low selectivity) and another child with `aSixtyFour = 3` (low selectivity).

Ancestor-Descendant Complex Pattern Selection

QS31–QS33: Repeat queries QS28–QS30 but using ancestor-descendant in place of parent-child.

QS34. One twig query with one parent-child selection and one ancestor-descendant selection: Select nodes with `aFour = 1` that have a child of nodes with `aLevel = 11` and a descendant with `aSixtyFour = 3`.

Negated Selection

QS35: Find all `BaseType` elements below which do not contain an `OccasionalType` element.

18.4.2 Value-Based Join

A value-based join involves comparing values at two different nodes that need not be related structurally. In computing the value-based joins, one would naturally expect *both* nodes participating in the join to be returned. As such, the return structure is a tree per join-pair. Each tree has a join-node as the root, and two children, one corresponding to each element participating in the join.

QJ1. Low selectivity: Select nodes with `aSixtyFour = 2` and join with themselves based on the equality of `aUnique1` attribute. The selectivity of this query is approximately 1.6%.

QJ2. High selectivity: Select nodes based on `aSixteen = 2` and join with themselves based on the equality of `aUnique1` attribute. The selectivity of this query is approximately 6.3%.

18.4.3 Pointer-Based Join

The difference between these following queries and the join queries based on values QJ1–QJ2 is that references that can be specified in the DTD or XML Schema may be optimized with logical OIDs in some XML databases.

QJ3. Low selectivity: Select all `OccasionalType` nodes that point to a node with `aSixtyFour = 3`. Selectivity is 0.02%.

QJ4. High selectivity: Select all `OccasionalType` nodes that point to a node with `aFour = 3`. Selectivity is 0.4%.

Both of these pointer-based joins are semi-join queries. The returned elements are only the `eOccasional` nodes, not the nodes pointed to.

18.4.4 Aggregation

Aggregate queries are very important for data-warehousing applications. In XML, aggregation also has richer possibilities due to the structure. These are explored in the next set of queries.

QA1. Value aggregation: Compute the average value for the `aSixtyFour` attribute of all nodes at level 15. Note that about 1/4 of all nodes are at level 15. The number of returned nodes is 1.

QA2. Value aggregation with group by: Group nodes by level. Compute the average value of the `aSixtyFour` attribute of all nodes at each level. The return structure is a tree, with a dummy root and a child for each group. Each leaf (child) node has one attribute for the level and one attribute for the average value. The number of returned trees is 16.

QA3. Value aggregate selection: Select elements that have at least two occurrences of keyword `"oneB1"` in their content. Selectivity is 0.3%.

QA4. Structural aggregation. Among the nodes at level 11, find the node(s) with the largest fanout. 1/64 of the nodes are at level 11. Selectivity is 0.02%.

QA5. Structural aggregate selection: Select elements that have at least two children that satisfy `aFour = 1`. Selectivity is 3.1%.

QA6. Structural exploration: For each node at level 7 (have `aLevel` = 7, determine the height of the subtree rooted at this node. Selectivity is 0.4%. Other functionalities, such as casting, also can be significant performance factors for engines that need to convert data types. However, in this benchmark, we focus on testing the core functionality of the XML engines.

18.4.5 Updates

QU1. Point Insert: Insert a new node `BaseType` node below the node with `aUnique1 = 10102`. The new node has attributes identical to its parent, except for `aUnique1`, which is set to some new large, unique value.

QU2. Point Delete: Delete the node with `aUnique1 = 10102` and transfer all its children to its parent.

QU3. Bulk Insert: Insert a new `BaseType` node below each node with `aSixtyFour = 1`. Each new node has attributes identical to its parent, except for `aUnique1`, which is set to some new large, unique value.

QU4. Bulk Delete: Delete all leaf nodes with `aSixteen = 3`.

QU5. Bulk Load: Load the original data set from a (set of) document(s).

QU6. Bulk Reconstruction: Return a set of documents, one for each subtree rooted at level 11 (have `aLevel = 11`) and with a child of type `eOccasional`.

QU7. Restructuring: For a node `u` of type `eOccasional`, let `v` be the parent of `u`, and `w` be the parent of `v` in the database. For each such node `u`, make `u` a direct child of `w` in the same position as `v`, and place `v` (along with the subtree rooted at `v`) under `u`.

18.5 Using the Benchmark

Since the goal of this benchmark is to test individual XML query operations, we do not propose a single benchmark number that can be computed from the individual query execution times. While having a single benchmark number can be very effective in summarizing the performance of an application benchmark, for a non-application-specific benchmark, such as this benchmark, it may be meaningless.

Similarly, it may be useful to run the benchmark queries in both *hot* and *cold* modes, corresponding to running the queries using a buffer pool that is warmed up by a previous invocation of the same query and running the query with no previously cached data in the buffer pool, respectively.

In our own use of the benchmark, we have found it useful to produce two tables: a *summary* table that presents a single number for a group of related queries and a *detail* table that shows the query execution time for each individual query. For the summary table, we use the groups that are shown in Table 18.2. For each group,

Table 18.2 Benchmark Groups

Group	Group Description	Queries
A	Returned Structure	QR1–QR4
B	Exact Match Attribute Value Selection	QS1–QS7
C	Element Name Selection	QS8
D	Order-Based Selection	QS9–QS10
E	Element Content Selection	QS11–QS12
F	String Distance Selection	QS13–QS14
G	Parent-Child Selection	QS15–QS17

(continued)

Table 18.2 *continued*

Group	Group Description	Queries
H	Order-Sensitive Parent-Child Selection	QS18–QS20
I	Ancestor-Descendant Selection	QS21–QS23
J	Ancestor Nesting in Ancestor-Descendant Selection	QS24–QS26
K	Parent-Child Complex Pattern Selection	QS27–QS30
L	Ancestor-Descendant Complex Pattern Selection	QS31–QS34
M	Negated Selection	QS35
N	Value-Based Join	QJ1–QJ2
O	Pointer-Based Join	QJ3–QJ4
P	Value-Based Aggregation	QA1–QA3
Q	Structural Aggregation	QA4–QA6
R	Point Updates	QU1–QU2
S	Bulk Updates	QU3–QU7

we compute the geometric mean of the execution times of the queries in that group. When comparing different systems, or when evaluating the scalability of a system using the benchmark, the summary table quickly identifies the key strengths and weaknesses of the system(s) being evaluated. The detailed table then provides more precise information on the performance of the individual query operations. We expect that this approach of using two tables to summarize the benchmark results will also be useful to other users of this benchmark.

18.6 Conclusion

The Michigan benchmark that is described in this chapter is a micro-benchmark that can be used to tune the performance of XML query-processing systems. In formulating this benchmark, we paid careful attention to the techniques that we use in generating the data and the query specification, so as to make it very easy for a benchmark user to identify any performance problems. The data generation process uses random numbers sparingly and still captures key characteristics of XML data sets, such as varying fanout and depth of the data tree. The queries are carefully chosen to focus on individual query operations and to demonstrate any performance problems related to the implementation of the algorithms used to evaluate the query operation. With careful analysis of the benchmark results, engineers can diagnose the strengths and weaknesses of their XML databases and quantitatively examine the impact of different implementation techniques, such as data storage structures, indexing methods, and query evaluation algorithms. The benchmark can also be used to examine the effect of scaling up the database size on the performance of the individual queries. In addition, the benchmark can also be used to compare the performance of various primitive query operations across different systems. Thus, this benchmark is a simple and effective tool to help engineers improve the performance of XML query-processing engines.

In designing the benchmark, we paid careful attention to the key criteria for a successful domain-specific benchmark that have been proposed by J. Gray (Gray 1993). These key criteria are relevant, portable, scalable, and simple. The proposed Michigan benchmark is *relevant* to testing the performance of XML engines because proposed queries are the core basic components of typical application-level operations of XML application. The Michigan benchmark is *portable* because it is easy to implement the benchmark on many different systems. In fact, the data generator for this benchmark data set is freely available for download from the Michigan benchmark's Web site (http://www.eecs.umich.edu/db/mbench). It is *scalable* through the use of a scaling parameter. It is *simple* since it contains only one data set and a set of simple queries, each with a distinct functionality test purpose.

We are continuing to use the benchmark to evaluate a number of native XML data management systems and traditional (object) relational database systems. We plan to publish the most up-to-date benchmark results at the Web site for this benchmark.

Chapter 19

A Comparison of Database Approaches for Storing XML Documents

Cosima Schmauch and Torsten Fellhauer

19.1 Introduction

The number of XML documents will grow rapidly in the future due to the increasing importance of XML as a data exchange format and as a language describing structured text. Serious thought is required on how to store XML documents while preserving their structure and allowing efficient access to parts of the structured documents. The latter calls for database techniques that primarily view XML documents as semi-structured data.

There are many standard database systems—relational, object-oriented, object-relational, as well as directory servers—and more recently the so-called native XML database systems. We would like to determine the suitability of these alternatives for storing XML documents. In this chapter we show the results of an intensive comparison of the time and space consumed by the different database systems when storing and extracting XML documents. In a suite of benchmark tests, we stored different-sized XML documents using different kinds of database management systems, extracted complete documents, selected fragments of documents, and measured the performance and disk space used. Our data-respective object models for the standard database approaches also used the Document Object Model, which maps XML documents into trees and thus reduces the problem to storing and extracting trees (i.e., hierarchical structures). We used the pure standard database techniques without any extensions in order to demonstrate their true capabilities in solving this task.

19.2 Data Models for XML Documents

A small example will illustrate the application of the different approaches. In Listing 19.1, we introduce the Document Type Definition (DTD) (W3C 1998b) for XML documents that contain `personnel`, a set of `professor[s]` with their `name[s]` and their `course[s]`. The name consists of a `firstname` and a `lastname`, and the courses have a `title` and a `description`. Both, `professor` and `course`, have an attribute—`employeeNo` and `courseNo`, respectively.

Listing 19.1 DTD for University Personnel

```
<!ELEMENT personnel (professor+)>
<!ELEMENT professor (name, course+)>
<!ATTLIST professor employeeNo ID #REQUIRED>
<!ELEMENT name (firstname, lastname)>
<!ELEMENT course (title, description)
<!ATTLIST course courseNo ID #REQUIRED>
<!ENTITY % textdata "(     firstname, lastname, title,
description)">
<!ELEMENT % textdata; (#PCDATA)>
```

The XML document in Listing 19.2 applies this DTD and will be used during this chapter. It contains a `professor` with `employeeNo`, `firstname`, and `lastname`. The `professor` gives a `course` with `title` and `description`.

Listing 19.2 Sample XML Document

```
<?xml version=(1.0(?>
<personnel>
 <professor employeeNo=(0802(>
  <name>
   <firstname>Sissi</firstname>
   <lastname>Closs</lastname>
  </name>
  <course courseNo=(TR1234(>
    <title>Document Structuring with SGML
    </title>
    <description>In this course  . . .
```

```
        </description>
      </course>
    </professor>
  </personnel>
```

The Document Object Model (DOM) of the WWW Consortium (W3C 1998a) is based on an object-oriented viewpoint of documents and their parts. It organizes them hierarchically in a document tree. The elements of a document become the inner nodes of the DOM tree. Attributes, comments, processing instructions, texts, entities, and notations form the leaves of the tree.

19.2.1 The Nontyped DOM Implementation

In a nontyped DOM implementation, one class is defined for every interface of the DOM. Figure 19.1 shows an excerpt of the DOM in the notation of the Unified Modeling Language (UML) (OMG 1999). The class `NodeImpl` that implements the interface `Node` contains attributes called `nodeName`, `nodeValue`, and `nodeType` to store the content of a node, and attributes called `parentNode` and `childNodes` to implement the tree and to allow navigation from a tree node to its children and from a node to its parent. It also implements the predefined methods, like `firstChild`, `lastChild`, `nextSibling`, and so on. By means of these methods, the tree can be built and traversed. Subclasses like `ElementImpl` and `AttrImpl` implement the subinterfaces like `Element` and `Attribute` and provide, if necessary, additional attributes and the required method definitions.

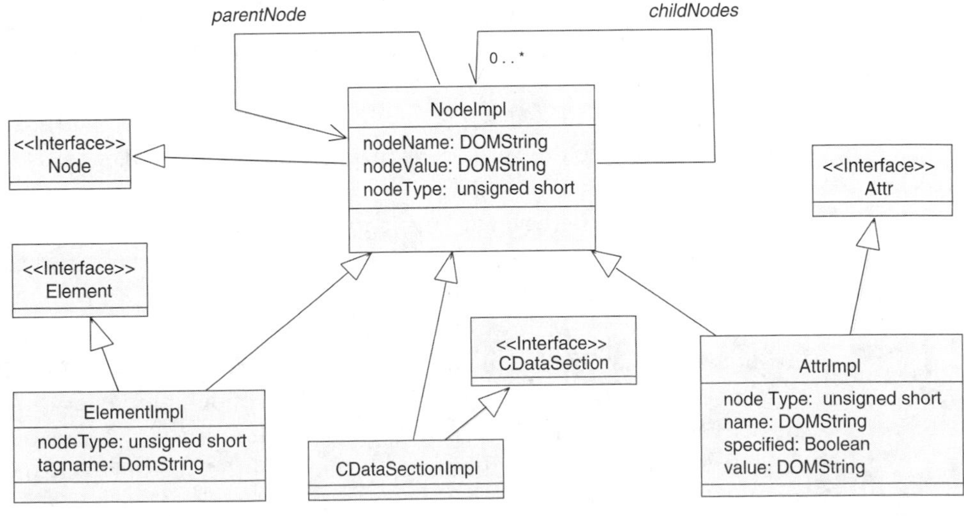

Figure 19.1 Excerpt of the DOM

The nontyped implementation of the DOM is document neutral—it does not reflect the structure of the documents. M. Yoshikawa et al. call this the "model-mapping approach" (Yoshikawa et al. 2001). For the interface `Element` there exists a unique class `ElementImpl`, even though many different element types can occur in an XML document. They also do not explicitly reproduce the nesting: It cannot be seen from the classes that certain elements are subelements of others.

To summarize, using the DOM the whole XML document is kept in a set of instances belonging to classes that implement the interfaces. The instances and not the classes contain the document-specific information.

19.2.2 The Typed DOM Implementation

As an extension to the nontyped implementation of the DOM, a subclass of the class `ElementImpl` can now be defined for every element type of an XML document. These classes have relationships to their subelements, attributes, and text nodes represented by compositions. The association `childNodes` proposed by the DOM is then superfluous.

When applying the typed DOM implementation to our example, the classes `Personnel`, `Professor`, `Name`, `Firstname`, and `Lastname` are defined as subclasses to the class `ElementImpl`, which implements the interface `Element`. The class `EmployeeNo` is defined as subclass to the class `AttrImpl`. Figure 19.2 shows these classes and their attributes and the relationships between them in UML. The class `Personnel` has a multivalued and ordered composition to the class `Professor`. This relationship is derived from the definition of the element `personnel` included in the DTD—a `personnel` element contains one or several `professor` elements:

```
<!ELEMENT personnel (professor+)>
```

Compositions are also created between the classes `Professor`, `Name`, and `EmployeeNo`; between the classes `Name`, `Firstname`, and `Lastname`; as well as between the latter and `CDATASectionImpl`.

The difference between the two approaches is that in the first approach the document structure is reproduced only in the states of the instances. By contrast, in the second approach, the structure of the document is shown in the composition hierarchy of the classes. M. Yoshikawa et al. call this the "structure-mapping approach" (Yoshikawa et al. 2001). In the nontyped implementation of the DOM, the subelement `name` of the element `professor` is one node among several child nodes of the `professor` node. In the typed implementation, it is by contrast an instance of a class `Name` that is referenced from an instance of the class `Professor`.

Assigning the nodes a type forces the application that is processing the XML document to recognize the document structure. When running through the DOM

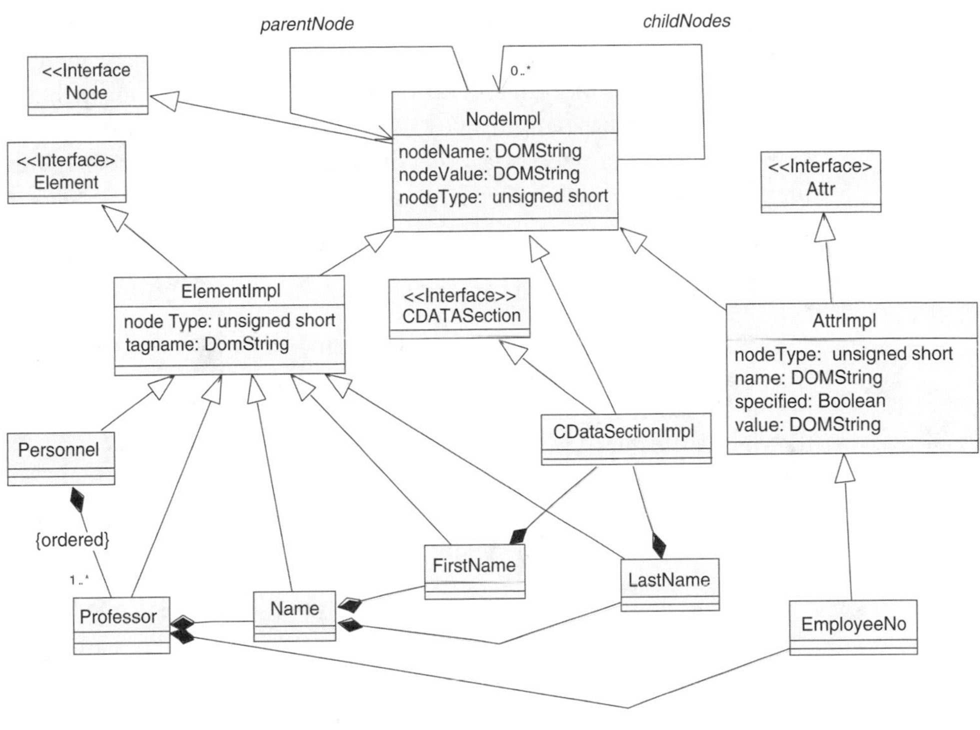

Figure 19.2 A Typed DOM Implementation

tree, the application must follow the typed composition paths. A `Name` instance can only be reached from a `Professor` instance via a composition of the type `Name`. This is a very strong restriction since the application that processes the document tree has to know the names and types of the composition—that is, the subelements. If it uses the interface `Node` instead of the typed classes, which is allowed because of the subtyping, it actually deals with the nontyped implementation of the DOM.

19.3 Databases for Storing XML Documents

Although XML documents are text only and thus can easily be stored in files, they are so-called semi-structured data, which need to be accessed via the structure. (Semi-structured data have been intensively studied by Abiteboul et al. (Abiteboul et al. 2000)). It is therefore worthwhile to draw upon database technologies for their storage and retrieval. In doing so, the XML document structure has to be mapped to the database schema, which is required by every database management system. The structure of XML documents does not correspond to any schema model of the widely used database approaches and therefore has led, on the one hand, to extensive studies of the necessary transformation and, on the other hand, to the implementation of so-called native XML databases.

19.3.1 Relational Databases

The storing of XML documents in relational databases means describing hierarchical, tree-type structures with relations. In the object-oriented world, the DOM builds the basis for these structures. But it is just the relational database approach that poses the question whether we should build on an object model. We will therefore point to two alternative data models for XML documents, the so-called edge approach applied by D. Florescu and D. Kossman (Florescu and Kossmann 1999b) and XRel developed by M. Yoshikawa et al. (Yoshikawa et al. 2001).

A Simple Nontyped DOM Implementation

By using the DOM, these tree-type structures have already been transformed into trees by the implementation classes of the DOM interfaces. Two associations form the tree: the `childNodes` and the `parentNode` association. The `childNodes` association is multivalued, which leads to a one-to-many relationship between nodes. We have to reverse this relationship to meet the relational database constraint that does not allow composed attribute values. But the `parentNode` association already defines the reverse relationship.

The value of the `parentNode` field of a table entry identifies the superordinate element that is defined by its own table entry. The elements are, however, no longer unique as soon as they are removed from the context of the XML document. Therefore, every element receives a unique identification number that is also used as the key of its table entry. The identification numbers also allow us to store the sequence of the subordinate elements. For example, the identification number of `firstname` is smaller than the identification number of `lastname`. Table 19.1 shows the unique element table for the XML document of our example in Listing 19.2. `Personnel` is the topmost element with ID 1; it has no parent. `Professor` has ID 2 and is contained in `personnel`, which is its parent with ID 1. `Name` is contained in `professor`, `firstname` and `lastname` are contained in `name`, `course` is contained in `professor`, and `title` and `description` are contained in `course` with ID 6.

The actual contents of an XML document refer from the `CDATASection` table to entries in the element table. In this way a link is established between the `CDATASection` table and the `element` table that we can create using a foreign key in the field `parentNode`. Moreover, each row in the `CDATASection` table possesses an

Table 19.1 Unique Element Table

ID	tagname	parentNode
1	personnel	null
2	professor	1
3	name	2
4	firstname	3
5	lastname	3
6	course	2
7	title	6
8	description	6

identification number as a key and a value stored in the field `data`. Table 19.2 shows the text contents of the XML document in Listing 19.2. For example, Sissi, the first name of a professor, points to entry `firstname` with ID 4 in the `element` table.

The attribute table contains the specific fields of the `Attr` node—`value` and `specified`, an identification number for the sequence and, in the field `parentNode`, the identification number of the element to which it is defined as the foreign key. Table 19.3 shows the entries for the example in Listing 19.2. `PersonnelNo` with value 0802 belongs to the entry `professor` with ID 2 in the `element` table.

In addition to the attribute values, the actual contents of the XML document are stored in the data fields of the records in the `CDATASection` table. The values of this field can, however, vary randomly in size, from short strings to page-long texts. A

Table 19.2 CDATASection Table for the Example Document

ID	data	parentNode
1	Sissi	4
2	Closs	5
3	Document structuring with SGML	7
4	In this course . . .	8

Table 19.3 Attribute Table for the Example Document

ID	Name	value	specified	parentNode
1	personnelNo	0802	null	2
2	courseNo	TR1234	null	6

differentiation can take place by means of different tables: Short strings are stored in a string table; long texts in a text table. Both tables then replace the `CDATASection` table. Tables 19.4 and 19.5 show this once again for the example in Listing 19.2.

If we want to extract a text from the database, either we need the special support of the database manufacturer who, as in the case of Oracle, has complemented its database with the SQL construct `Connect-By` for the extraction of hierarchical structures. Or, starting at the root, we can use an SQL instruction for every element, similar to a recursive descent into the DOM tree. A construct like `Connect-By` is not offered by all manufacturers of relational databases. The second solution requires database access for every subelement. The typed implementation of the DOM could be an improvement.

Table 19.4 String Table for the Example Document

ID	data	parentNode
1	Sissi	4
2	Closs	5
3	Document Structuring with SGML	7

Table 19.5 Text Table for the Example Document

ID	data	parentNode
1	In this course . . .	8

The Typed DOM Implementation

The typed implementation of the DOM defines a class for every element and stores the class instances in a table of the same name. The nesting of elements, which is realized by composition, also has to take place by means of an identification number. These form the key for the entries. They must, however, be unique throughout all special element tables. The values of the `parentNode` fields are no longer foreign keys, as they would have to refer to the same table. However, two entries of a specific element table, as elements in an XML document, can be included in two different superordinate elements.

The elements of the example document in Listing 19.2 require the definition of eight tables, as shown in Table 19.6. The `attribute` and `CDATASection` tables and the `string` and `text` tables remain the same as with the nontyped DOM approach.

It is obvious that for a highly structured XML document many tables with few entries result. Extracting an XML document takes place by joining all element tables to a single table. This must be expressed by an SQL query. Beginning with the table of the root element, it selects the value for `tagname` in two tables at a time when the value of the `ID` field of the first table is identical to the value of the `parentNode` field of the second table.

The creation of this `Select` statement requires knowledge of the document structure. The structure is, however, reflected only in the names of the tables. As the tables are not linked to each other via the foreign key, the nesting of the elements is also not expressed in the database schema. The advantages of the typing—the validation of the document using the database and the metadata for the structure of the document—are not present with relational databases. But the advantage remains that parts of the documents can be accessed via element names.

Table 19.6 Tables Corresponding to Elements

Personnel		Professor		Name		Firstname		Lastname	
ID	parent Node	ID	parent Node	ID	parent Node	ID	parent Node	ID	parent Node
1	null	2	1	3	2	4	3	5	3
Course		**Title**		**Description**					
ID	**parent Node**	**ID**	**parent Node**	**ID**	**parent Node**				
6	2	7	6	8	6				

19.3.2 Object-Oriented Databases

Object-oriented databases are the natural storage technology for the DOM. They store DOM trees without having to map the objects and their relations to other data concepts. Because they are based on a schema, as relational database systems are, the implementation variants of the DOM are reflected in the schema and have to be weighed against each other.

With the typed implementation, the specialized element classes complement the schema, and the names of the elements and their nested data are stored as metadata in the database. This can be advantageous when an application wants to validate a document using the database schema or wants to obtain information about the structure of the documents. Accessing subelements of an element also takes place via named references directly from the element and is therefore fast. With the nontyped implementation, subelements are instances in the `childNodes` set and have to be searched for. The class extents in object-oriented databases also bring an advantage in speed. They collect all references to the instances of a class and thus offer direct access to them. Using these, all `course` elements, for example, can be extracted from an XML document.

The typed compositions between the classes can, however, also be a great hindrance. If we want to extract the complete XML document again, which corresponds to running through the complete DOM tree, we do not take the typed access path but have to visit the nontyped nodes of the `childNodes` sets.

Modifications of the DTD also have a disadvantageous effect. Object-oriented database systems do indeed allow a dynamic customization of the schema. However, as this represents the document structure, a modification can lead to invalid documents that follow the original DTD.

These disadvantages speak in favor of the nontyped implementation of the DOM that optimally supports the running through of a DOM tree to the complete output of an XML document. Quick access to the child nodes of an element node can however be achieved by an indexing of the node set. Object-oriented database systems provide a means of indexing. In this way, indices to the attribute `nodeName` and to the ordering number of the child nodes can compensate for the speed differences of the different implementations.

To summarize, there is the attempt to represent hierarchical data by mapping XML documents on the schema of the various database models. This fact suggests the examination of a further type of database whose data can be organized hierarchically: the directory server.

19.3.3 Directory Servers

Although hardly discussed, directory servers could be another interesting database approach for storing XML documents. Usually, they store huge quantities of simply structured data like personnel or inventory data of a company and allow very fast read access but significantly worse write access of the data. Another important feature is the existence of a tree—the so-called directory information tree—as a means of organizing the data.

Directory servers are widespread as address databases that are accessed by using the Lightweight Directory Access Protocol (LDAP), a simple variant of the X.500 ISO standard (Howes et al. 1995). Entries in an LDAP directory contain information about objects such as companies, departments, resources, and people in a company. They are ordered hierarchically, as people normally work in departments of companies. Entries consist of attributes and their values or value sets.

Although directory servers were originally developed for providing central address books, which is reflected in the attribute names—"o" for "organization", "ou" for "organizational unit", "sn" for "surname"—they can include entries of any object classes (i.e., with self-defined attribute types).

An entry for a professor of a department is presented in LDIF (Lightweight Directory Interchange Format), a text format for the exchange of directory data, in Listing 19.3.

Listing 19.3 A Directory Entry

```
dn: personnelNo=1012, ou=FBWI, o=fh-karlsruhe.de
objectclass: professor
objectclass: employee
objectclass: person
objectclass: top
cn: Cosima Schmauch
givenname: Cosima
sn: Schmauch
personnelNo: 1012
uid: scco0001
telephone: 2960
roomNo: K111
courses: courseNo=wi2034, ou=FBWI, o=fh-karlsruhe.de
courses: courseNo=wi2042, ou=FBWI, o=fh-karlsruhe.de
```

Every entry in the directory server is given a so-called distinguished name (dn) that uniquely identifies it. The distinguished name is derived from a defined relative distinguished name (rdn) consisting of attribute value pairs and extensions of namespaces. The namespaces are ordered hierarchically and are normally represented as trees—directory information trees. Figure 19.3 shows a section of the directory information tree at the Karlsruhe University of Applied Sciences.

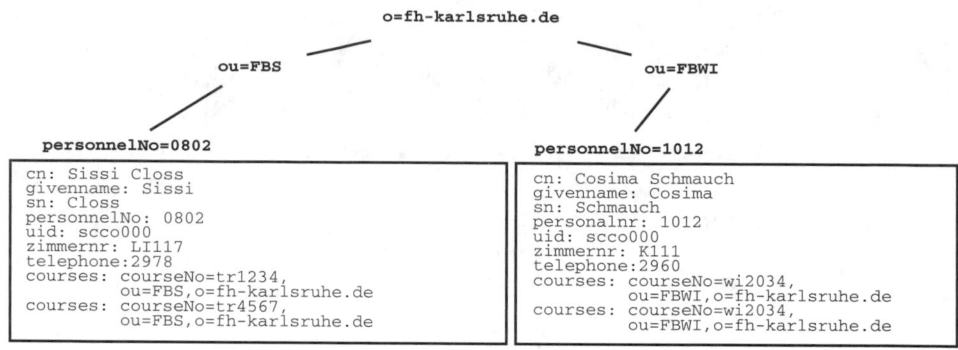

Figure 19.3 A Section of the Directory Information Tree of the Karlsruhe University of Applied Sciences

Just as with object-oriented databases, we define the directory server schema using classes. Relationships between directory server classes are, however, established using distinguished names. An example of this is the `professor` entry, which is linked to several `course` entries. A link between directory server entries is not typed—it is a string or a set of strings, which are marked as distinguished names.

The typed DOM implementation can therefore affect only the names of the directory server classes but not the relationship between the classes. The directory server schema, similar to an implementation using relational databases, cannot reflect the document structure. We have selected therefore the nontyped DOM implementation as the basis for the directory server schema.

For the interfaces of the DOM, 13 classes are defined for their implementation—there was no implementation of the abstract class for the interface `CharacterData`. Figure 19.4 shows these classes. The class `xmlnode` implements the interface `Node` and is the base class for all remaining classes. It makes the attributes `XMLname`, `XMLtype`, and `XMLvalue` for storing the document-specific information available to them. The remaining classes add attributes, if required.

We are left to decide how the parent-child relationships of the DOM tree are implemented. We could use distinguished names. The `childNodes` relationship between elements can be realized through a corresponding multivalued attribute at the class `xmlnode`. Because we already have the LDAP directory information tree, we can also map the DOM tree to it. We do not have to implement the tree using relations, as it is necessary with object-oriented databases via the `childnodes` association. We can rely on the directory information tree that is built by the form of the distinguished names. Therefore the base class `xmlnode` is given an additional attri-

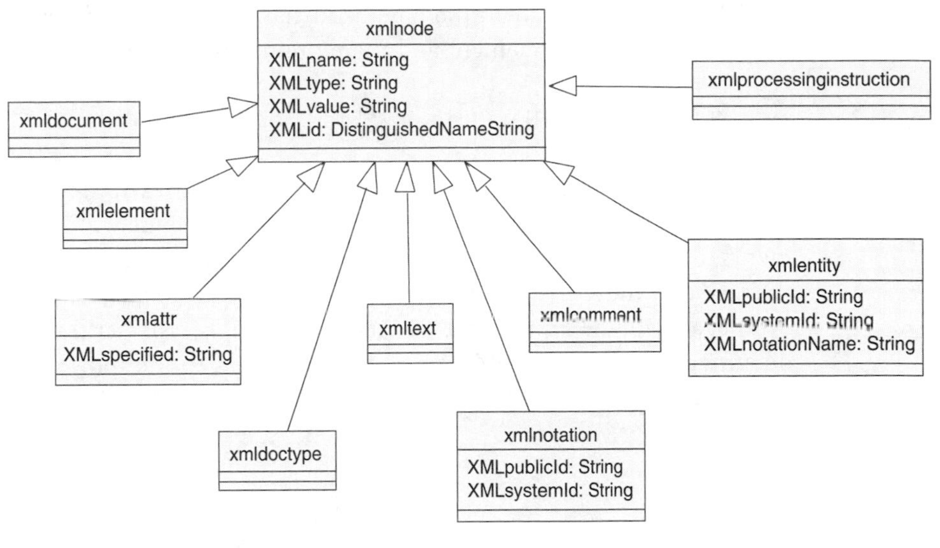

Figure 19.4 The Classes of the Directory Server Schema

bute `XMLid` that contains a number and thus retains the order of the subelements. This id at the same time will form the relative distinguished name of the entry.

An XML document is now mapped to the directory information tree so that—modeled on the DOM tree—the element entries form the inner nodes, while all others become leaves. Figure 19.5 shows the directory information tree for the XML document from the example document of Listing 19.2. Every entry in the directory server is positioned in the directory information tree. It consists of the attribute values that are defined by its class. The `personnel` element is entered in the tree under the nodes with the distinguished name `ou=xml`. It has the following attribute values:

```
XMLname = personnel,
XMLvalue = null,
XMLtype = Element,
XMLid = 1
```

Thus the entry is given the distinguished name `XMLid=1, ou=xml`.

The `course` element, which is subsumed under the `professor` element as the third element after `name` and `telephone`, is given the value 3 as its `XMLid` and therefore the distinguished name

```
XMLid=3,XMLid=1,XMLid=1,ou=xml.
```

The attribute `personnelNo` obtains its name as a value of `XMLid`. It is subsumed under the `professor` element and therefore has the distinguished name

```
XMLid=personnelNo,XMLid=1,XMLid=1,ou=xml.
```

The ordering number given to every entry by the attribute `XMLid` contributes to its distinguished name. This allows it to retain the sequence of the elements, comments, and text parts. The value for the `XMLid` is assigned, and from its position in the tree and the `XMLid`, a new distinguished name is formed.

Because of the nontyped DOM implementation, a parser must validate the XML document, create the DOM tree, and allow access to the root of the DOM tree that represents the document. Starting at the root, the tree is then traversed completely.

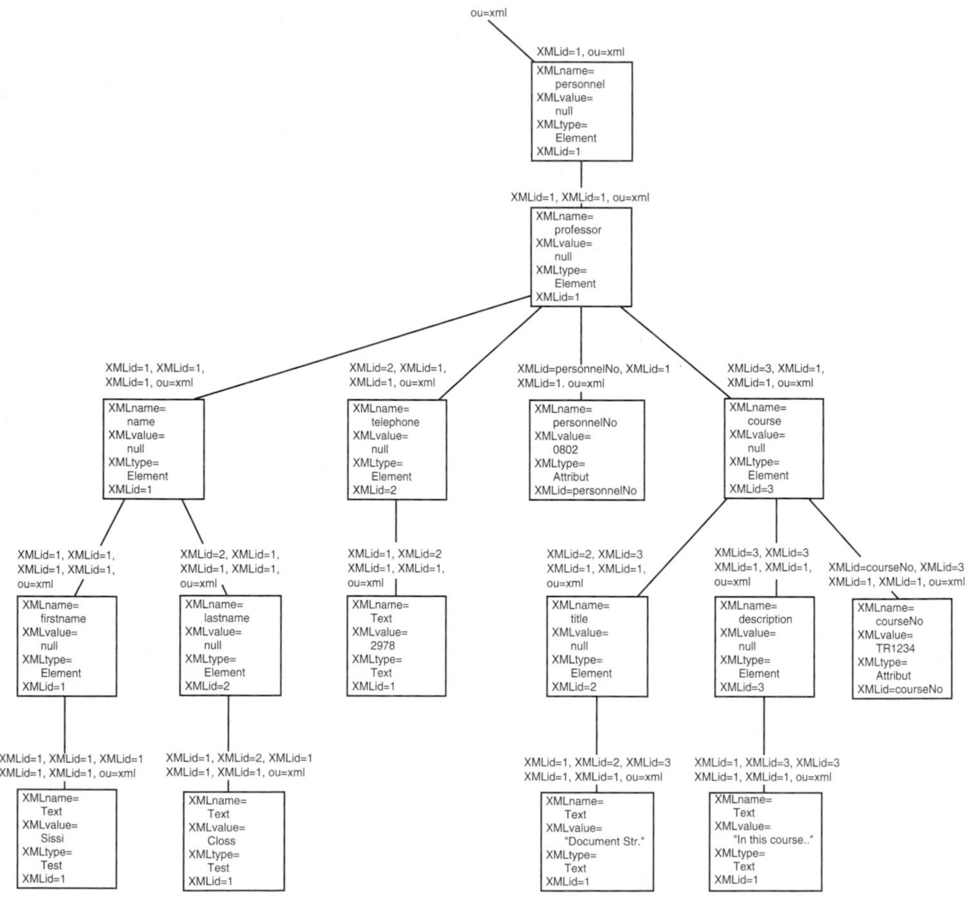

Figure 19.5 The Directory Information Tree for the Example Document

While doing so, the type is determined for every node, the corresponding LDAP entry is created with a distinguished name, the rest of the attribute values of the entry are set, and the entry is stored into the directory server. Then its child nodes are processed.

19.3.4 Native XML Databases

Finally, we should have a look at native XML databases, which are specialized to store and process XML documents. The database system we use has to know the DTD. From the DTD, it creates a database schema. Using a Java API, the XML document has to be parsed with the integrated DOM parser, which returns a reference to the root object. This root object will then be inserted into the database.

19.4 Benchmarking Specification

This work focuses on the use of directory servers as XML data management systems and a comparison with relational, object-oriented, and native XML database systems approaches. Besides the native XML database system that includes a proprietary query language to access the database, we have to implement the access to each of the other databases. The standardization of an XML query language has just been completed, and because of the missing implementations of the final version, we rely on general requirements that the storage of XML documents has to meet. These requirements were published by the WWW Consortium (in Maier 1998) and can serve as the provisional basis for storage procedures until the officially adopted query language is implemented.

XML documents should be stored in a database and be able to be modified in part. In addition, XML query languages have to fulfill the following requirements:

- A document or parts of a document can be searched for, using the structure, the content, or attribute values.
- A complete XML document or parts of an XML document can be extracted.
- A document can be reduced to parts by omitting subelements.
- Parts can be restructured to create a new document.
- Elements can be combined to create a document.

Although these statements refer to XML query languages, they make clear the kind of performance that is required of storage technologies.

19.4.1 Benchmarking a Relational Database

In the case of relational databases, we implemented the typed and the nontyped approach, indexing the `parentNode` in both cases. To insert and extract the XML documents into and from the database, we used pure SQL. However, some database management system providers offer additional statements to extract hierarchical structures from relations.

XML documents are stored by traversing the DOM tree and inserting every node represented by its identification number and the reference to its parent node into the appropriate table. In the typed approach, each element is inserted in its own element table. In the nontyped approach, the tag name also has to be stored in the unique element table common to all elements.

The extracting procedure iteratively collects all parts of an XML document starting with the `personnel` entry. In the typed approach, it has to find all element entries in the element table with their parent node identical to its own identification number. When an element is selected from the element table, it is also put on a stack that then contains all open tags in the right order. If the procedure does not find a subelement, it writes the end tag and removes the corresponding open tag from the top of the stack. The typed approach has to search for the subelements of an element in all element tables. Because this is very expensive, we consult the DTD to decide on the tables. If the procedure has to find the subelements of `professor`, it searches only the tables `name` and `course` to find its subelements. This is the only difference between the typed and the nontyped approach.

Deleting complete XML documents is similar to extracting them—starting with the root element, all subelements are iteratively identified and deleted.

The statements for extracting and replacing parts of XML documents have to be transformed into SQL statements that select database entries and replace them or even insert new entries. The latter could affect the identification number of the following entries. Therefore, the replacing procedure has to adjust the identification numbers of all entries that are sibling nodes of the replaced node.

19.4.2 Benchmarking an Object-Oriented Database

The object-oriented database environment we used provides special classes to make a DOM tree persistent. This is done by traversing the DOM tree that is built by the DOM parser. Every node of the tree has to be converted into a persistent node that is automatically written into the object-oriented database. The persistent DOM implementation uses the nontyped DOM implementation.

To extract a complete document from the database, the DOM tree is restored beginning at the root node, is transformed into text, and is output by using an XML serializer class.

Deleting a complete XML document by deleting the root node seems to be very fast but not effective—the objects were not removed from the disk. Also deletion of the tree by deleting node by node was not successful.

Selecting parts of documents could not be implemented by using the search function but had to be done by reconstructing the DOM tree and searching the document parts in the tree. The search functions on the persistent tree showed very poor performance.

Replacing document parts was done on the persistent DOM tree although it includes a search of the part that has to be replaced. But replacing the part on a reconstruction of the DOM tree has to make the new tree persistent and therefore has to delete the old tree.

19.4.3 Benchmarking a Directory Server

To store an XML document in a directory server, we traverse the DOM tree, create entries, and insert them in the directory information tree.

A complete XML document is extracted by selecting the entries in the directory information tree. The selection method of LDAP allows the return of the whole tree in a result set that is unfortunately not ordered. After storing an XML document in the directory server, the sequence of entries in the result set will be identical to the sequence of elements. But the first update of an entry will no longer preserve that sequence. Ordering the result set containing the whole tree would be very expensive. We decided to select just the set of child nodes of an entry, order this small set, and process it by printing the element name as well as attribute value pairs, and then recursively select the set of child nodes.

LDAP also provides a rich set of methods to search for entries based on their distinguished names and on the specification of filters.

Parts of documents have to be replaced by deleting the entries representing the document part and inserting the new entries. This will cause an update of entries that follow in the sequence of the replaced part if the set of replacing entries is larger. The updating is restricted to entries in the subtree of the node that represents the replaced part.

19.4.4 Benchmarking a Native XML Database

The XML database provides methods for inserting an XML document into the database and extracting the complete document from the database. It also implements an XML query and updating language that allows us to express the statements of our benchmarking specification.

19.5 Test Results

The benchmarking tests were run on an Intel Pentium III server with 450MHz, 256MB RAM, and two mirrored UW-SCSI hard disks. The clients included an Intel Pentium III processor with 350MHz and 128MB RAM. They were connected to the server by a 10-Mbit local area network. The storing strategies used a well-known relational DBMS, object-oriented DBMS, directory server, and native XML DBMS (for legal reasons the products cannot be named).

The documents used were automatically generated based on a DTD that defines the structure of project descriptions. The DTD contains 26 elements with a maximum nesting size of 8 and 4 attributes. XML documents based on this DTD contain information on the project members, such as names and addresses, as well as information on the publications, such as articles. This allows us to easily produce different-sized documents.

To compare the different database types, we run a set of tests that do the following:

- Store XML documents
- Extract complete XML documents
- Delete complete XML documents
- Extract parts of documents identified by the position of elements in the document
- Replace parts of documents

The benchmarks were specified and run by Fellhauer (see Fellhauer 2001 for the complete list of test results).

19.5.1 Evaluation of Performance

We ran the benchmarks five times with every document of every size, dropped the best and the worst results, and took the average of the remaining three values as the result value. Table 19.7 shows the results of storing XML documents.

All figures in Table 19.7 measure the times for inserting the XML document into the database including the time consumed by the DOM parser. The object-oriented database is the best. The native XML database shows a relatively high growth rate, which we could not confirm for larger documents because of the limited space of our test installation—an 11MB document took 35MB disk space of the 50MB space of the test version. Almost surprising is the bad result of storing the 25MB document into the typed relational database: It took more than 12 hours. We would like to investigate this further to determine if the number of tables involved is the reason. We were not able to store the 64MB document in the databases due to the

Table 19.7 Test Results for Storing XML Documents

Size of XML Documents	Directory Server	Non-Typed Relational Database	Typed Relational Database	Object-Oriented Database	Native XML Database
125 KB	18.1 s	19.8 s	28.3 s	4.3 s	10.5 s
500 KB	55.7 s	42.2 s	61.5 s	9.5 s	38.1 s
2,000 KB	90.0 s	74.4 s	123.6 s	20.7 s	166.3 s
8,000 KB	361.0 s	251.4 s	983.6 s	107.6 s	906.8 s
16,000 KB	386.8 s	713.4 s	2,774.7 s	213.9 s	*
32,000 KB	1,512.7 s	> 12 hours	> 12 hours	1,167.3 s	*
64,000 KB	> 12 hours	> 12 hours	> 12 hours	> 12 hours	*

*Failed because of license restrictions.

256MB main memory. The DOM tree could be built, but the traversal of the tree resulted in permanent swapping. Table 19.8 shows the results of extracting complete XML documents.

The native XML database shows the best results, better than the directory server, which is known for its fast read access. It is not surprising that the relational databases consume a lot of time for reconstructing the documents. We do not know whether the size of the unique element table in the nontyped relational database will produce a result worse than the typed relational database result. The number of tables could influence the results for the 8MB document, especially when we apply proprietary statements for selecting hierarchically connected entries.

To extract parts of the XML documents, we ran queries that determine elements in the XML document and return these elements or parts of their content. All databases show similar results independent of the size of the document; there is no sequential search. The relational databases are the fastest, where the difference between the nontyped and the typed approaches is due to the runtime of consulting the DTD. Table 19.9 shows the test results for the query "Select the first heading of the third publication of a project determined by a project number."

The nontyped relational database shows surprisingly good results especially for the selection of small document parts. It leaves the directory servers, which are known for fast read accesses, far behind. The poor results of the object database are caused by the reconstruction and searching of the DOM tree.

Table 19.8 Test Results for Extracting Complete XML Documents

Size of XML Documents	Directory Server	Non-Typed Relational Database	Typed Relational Database	Object-Oriented Database	Native XML Database
125 KB	11.8 s	26.9 s	31.0 s	12.9 s	8.7 s
500 KB	22.2 s	81.1 s	75.9 s	26.5 s	9.5 s
2,000 KB	39.1 s	307.4 s	275.6 s	49.9 s	12.7 s
8,000 KB	153.4 s	2,369.7 s	1,620.3 s	175.2 s	28.7 s
16,000 KB	206.7 s	-	-	232.2 s	-
32,000 KB	413.4 s	-	-	904.2 s	-

Table 19.9 Test Results for Extracting Parts of XML Documents

Size of XML Documents	Directory Server	Non-Typed Relational Database	Typed Relational Database	Object-Oriented Database	Native XML Database
125 KB	3.7 s	0.2 s	3.4 s	12.9 s	8.9 s
500 KB	3.6 s	0.2 s	3.6 s	24.9 s	9.5 s
2,000 KB	3.7 s	0.2 s	3.5 s	45.4 s	12.4 s
8,000 KB	3.8 s	0.2 s	3.6 s	154.4 s	235.1 s
16,000 KB	3.6 s	0.2 s	3.5 s	199.7 s	-
32,000 KB	3.6 s	-	-	396.7 s	-

Finally, Table 19.10 shows the results of updating parts of an XML document—for example, the whole `person` element determined by the last name and the project number should be replaced by a new `person` element given as are XML document.

The native XML database shows dramatically decreasing performance. The poor results of the object database are due to the bad performance of the search functions applied to the persistent DOM tree.

Table 19.10 Test Results for Replacing Parts of an XML Document

Size of XML Documents	Directory Server	Non-Typed Relational Database	Typed Relational Database	Object-Oriented Database	Native XML Database
125 KB	17.8 s	7.3 s	5.9 s	809.0 s	19.6 s
500 KB	17.3 s	7.2 s	5.8 s	798.9 s	52.0 s
2,000 KB	17.2 s	7.3 s	5.8 s	798.7 s	195.9 s
8,000 KB	17.2 s	7.2 s	5.8 s	794.4 s	198.9 s
16,000 KB	17.1 s	7.4 s	5.6 s	796.7 s	692.3 s
32,000 KB	16.9 s	-	-	795.8 s	-

19.5.2 Evaluation of Space

Table 19.11 shows the disk space each database management system uses to store the schema and the XML documents of different sizes. The typed relational database approach defines a table for each element type, which increases space for the schema. However, disk space to store the XML documents is very efficient.

The directory server and the native XML database produce a lot of overhead, when compared to the original XML document.

19.5.3 Conclusion

The benchmarks have shown that the nontyped relational database approach has advantages over all other solutions. The weak point is the reconstruction of complete XML documents, which should be improved. As long as a standardized XML query language does not support inserting and updating functionality, the reconstruction of XML documents will be an important operation.

We do not know whether the bad results of the searching function of the object-oriented database system are representative for this database type. But it supports our belief that searching large object trees will cause large loading times due to the techniques the systems apply. To avoid this, special indexing techniques like B-trees have to be applied. Although content management systems based on object-oriented databases implement this improvement, we used the bare object-oriented database approach to show its capabilities.

Table 19.11 Disk Space Usage in Kilobytes

Size of XML Documents	Directory Server	Non-Typed Relational Database	Typed Relational Database	Object-Oriented Database	Native XML Database
Schema/0 KB	440	672	3,484	512	5,178
125 KB	2,064	117	118	615	760
500 KB	4,952	820	546	1,536	2,088
2,000 KB	11,240	3,164	2,182	3,738	7,060
8,000 KB	40,848	15,157	10,547	13,722	28,780
16,000 KB	53,280	26,562	18,476	22,630	> 50,000*
32,000 KB	120,024	-	-	43,991	-
64,000 KB	-	-	-	-	-

*Space restriction of 50 MB.

The directory server shows disappointing results compared to the relational database. The expected very fast reading times could not be achieved. There might be some improvements in the mapping of the DOM tree into the directory information tree, too. Also the space consumed by the directory server is critical. Additional experiments will be necessary to determine the reasons.

19.6 Related Work

At the time we were conducting these evaluations, the public discussion of comparing XML data management approaches was poor. Most work was done in the field of semi-structured data, where database management systems and query languages were developed. The first publications that explored the role of relational database systems in storing and retrieving XML documents were presented by researchers from INRIA (Florescu and Kossmann 1999b) and from the University of Wisconsin (Shanmugasundaram et al. 1999).

In the meantime, several research teams have studied this subject and published their results. Their work can be divided into three categories. The first category contains studies in additional improvements of the mapping of XML document structures into data and object models. Researchers in the second category are developing benchmarks for XML data management systems based on existing benchmarks for the common database management systems like relational and object-oriented. The work in the third category focuses on guidelines for benchmarking XML databases to support the decisions of users and of developers of XML data management systems.

19.6.1 Studies in Storing and Retrieving XML Documents

Most of the published work deals with the mapping between XML document structures and relations. Due to the extreme difference between the highly nested, hierarchical structure of XML documents and the flat table structure of relational databases, several substantially different approaches have been developed. The object-oriented view of XML documents provided by the Document Object Model suggests storing XML documents in object-oriented databases but also bringing object-relational databases into play.

19.6.2 XML and Relational Databases

The so-called edge approach was intensively studied at INRIA by D. Florescu and D. Kossmann (Florescu and Kossmann 1999b) and AT&T Labs by A. Deutsch, M. Fernandez, and D. Suciu (Deutsch, Fernandez, Suciu 1999). It is derived from the graphical representation of semi-structured data (Abiteboul 1997; Buneman 1997), which maps the labels of the data—corresponding to XML tags—to labels of the graph. To do this, the elements in a document get identification numbers and are mapped to the nodes of the tree. The element names appear as labels of the edges between these nodes. The sequence of the elements of one level can be determined by ordering the edges. The attributes that belong to an element and which possess a name and a value are represented by an edge bearing their names from the element node to the value node. The mapping of this tree to relations is represented quite easily now. The edges have a source, a target, and a name, and they are ordered. This information can be stored in a table. The key is composed of the values of the source and the number.

As with our typed DOM implementation, the single large element table can be split into many small tables using the edge approach. The tables receive the name of the element. Here, too, the key is formed from the value of the source and the number. The target of a table entry is either a value or the identification number of a node that occurs in one of the tables as the source. As the identification number is only a part of the key and the table is not uniquely defined, the target field cannot contain a foreign key. For the extraction of a complete document, all tables must be unified into one table, as with the typed DOM approach. The `Select` statement must determine the equality of target and source values of the edges with the names of nested elements.

A different approach was published by J. Shanmugasundaram et al. (Shanmugasundaram et al. 1999), who first established the relationship between XML elements—defined by the Document Type Definition and applied as XML tags—and relations. The database schema is created from the DTD, which is done by building a so-called DTD graph and constructing an element graph from it. When the schema is created, several inlining techniques that flatten nested elements can be applied to avoid the fragmentation of the XML document over several tables. The authors developed benchmarks to compare the different inlining techniques but were not able to relate to other approaches at this early stage of research.

The idea of J. Shanmugasundaram et al. was adopted and developed by a number of other researchers. We only mention a few of them (Bourret 2002; Kappel et al. 2001; Lee and Chu 2000; Mani et al. 2001; Williams et al. 2001). They all use the typed approach while improving and extending the original.

One publication that does not follow the typed approach is XRel—a path-based approach to storing XML documents in relational databases. This work was done by researchers from the Nara Institute of Science and Technology in Japan together with IBM Japan (see Yoshikawa et al. 2001). The idea is to store the textual content of an XML document in a table together with a link to the position of the text in the document tree. The position is expressed by the path from the root to the element in the tree together with the information where the text starts and ends within the document. Four tables are necessary: the path table that contains all paths of the document tree; the element table that contains a relationship to the path table, the start and end position of the element in the XML document, and a number for ordering issues; the text table that contains a relationship to the path table, the start and end position of the element in the XML document, and the value (i.e., the text itself); the attribute table that contains a relationship to the path table, the start and end position of the element in the XML document, and the value of the attribute. All tables have a `docID` attribute referring to the XML document. Although this interesting technique is compared to the edge approach of D. Florescu and D. Kossmann, and is very successful in querying the database, no figures were published for storing and reconstructing the complete XML document.

19.6.3 XML and Object-Relational Databases

Object-relational databases allow database developers to define their own data types and to use them as scopes for relations. Looking at a relation as a data type, relations can then be defined via relations—that is, tables can be stored in tables. This seems to be the ideal way for storing XML documents, which can then nest elements by embedding tables in tables or defining object types and assigning them to attributes of tables. The problem of mapping element types to tables, attributes, or even object types has encouraged several research teams to study the subject.

A simple method maps element types with complex content to object types and element types with PCDATA content to attributes of the parent element. This may cause a strong reduction of the relational portion of the object-relational database system and raises the question whether an object-oriented database system might be more appropriate. Additionally, the document structure is reflected in the database schema—the nesting of the elements determines the nesting of the tables of linked object types. A modification of the document structure also forces a modification of the database schema and makes previously stored, valid documents invalid.

More complex methods use the relational portion of object-relational database systems more intensively (see Runapongsa and Patel 2002). They apply the mapping described by J. Shanmugasundaram et al. (Shanmugasundaram et al. 1999) and define a new type, the XADT (XML Abstract Data Type). Attributes of type XADT can store a fragment of an XML document. The operations of the XADT provide the programmer with data contained in the attribute value of type XADT.

It seems that additional research is required to prove the contribution of object-relational database techniques to the storage and retrieval of XML documents.

19.6.4 XML and Object-Oriented Databases

Although several content management systems—especially commercial systems—are based on object-oriented databases, only minor discussions and publications are known. There might be several reasons for this. First, applying object-oriented database techniques is less difficult compared to relational and object-relational techniques. Second, publications on this subject would have to disclose technical details not suited for publication. Finally, the absence of a query language has hindered the development of tests to compare these implementations.

Nevertheless, several technical papers indicate that XML documents are mapped to persistent object trees. Thereby, the nontyped approach is applied. Sometimes, DTD and XML schemas are implemented additionally to support validation of documents. Implementing the nontyped approach, the database schema does not depend on the DTD or the XML schema and allows importation of different DTDs and changes to the imported DTDs. Special indexing techniques like B-trees are used to guarantee fast access to parts of the object tree.

19.6.5 XML and Directory Servers

The combination of XML and directory servers is rarely discussed. Only a few projects use directory servers to organize huge quantities of XML documents. As described by K. Polatschek (Polatschek 2000), Tagesspiegel Online stores articles as

XML documents in files and organizes these within a directory server. The organization of the documents is stored, not their content. Yet, the latter is done by P. Marrón et al. (Marrón and Lausen 2001) who propose a mapping between a DOM tree and a directory information tree. It corresponds to our approach described earlier.

19.6.6 Benchmarks for XML Databases

Even today, performance evaluations of applications processing XML documents in databases are rare. F. Tian et al. (Tian et al. 2000) published performance evaluations of four storage approaches including relational databases, object-oriented databases, and a file system. They implement the edge approach of Florescu and Kossmann, use an object-oriented database with support by a B-tree implementation and files parsed by an XML parser. The data are created from the DBLP (Database systems and Logic Programming) database of bibliographical entries and have a size of 65MB. The benchmark contains the reconstruction of the original document, selection queries, join queries, and updates. A comparison to other performance tests is difficult due to the nonstandardized benchmark.

Today, interest in performance evaluations of XML data management systems is growing, and the first benchmarks have been published. The XOO7 benchmark (Bressan, Dobbie 2001) is derived from the OO7 benchmark for measuring the performance of object-oriented database management systems. The benchmark contains a DTD and parameters to control the production of XML documents. There are eight queries taken from OO7 and an additional five queries covering special XML aspects. The benchmark has been used to compare a public domain database management system for semi-structured data, a file system, and a commercial object-relational database system.

XMach-1 is a multiuser benchmark developed by T. Böhme and E. Rahm (Böhme and Rahm 2001). Documents and queries are derived from Web applications. The documents contain structured data and structured text. They are produced by assigning values to a number of parameters and by randomly generating text. Thus, the sizes of the documents vary. Four different-sized databases with 10,000 to 10,000,000 documents can be created. Böhme and Rahm propose eight query operations covering reconstruction of a complete document, text search, path traversal, test of efficient index implementation, and application of group-by, join, sort, as well as three manipulation operations including insertion of a document, deletion of a document, and update of an element in a document.

The Michigan benchmark (Runapongsa et al. 2002), which is discussed in Chapter 18 of this book, was developed to support engineers in designing improved XML-processing engines. It is inspired by the Wisconsin benchmark for measuring the performance of relational database management systems. Among the 49 queries are several that hit the core of an XML database implementation. The benchmark contains parameters to generate XML documents of different sizes that are characterized by the number and fanout of the nodes and the depth of the document trees. The benchmark was applied to compare a native XML database management system developed at the University of Michigan and a commercial object-relational database management system.

19.6.7 Guidelines for Benchmarking XML Databases

The XMark project is designed to provide a benchmark suite that allows users and developers to gain insights into the characteristics of their XML repositories. It is described by A. Schmidt et al. (Schmidt, Waas, Kersten, Florescu, Manolescu et al. 2001). The project has produced guidelines for developing XML database benchmarks that comprise ten general challenges for performance analysis (as described in Schmidt, Waas, Kersen, Florescu, Carey et al. 2001). These challenges cover

1. Bulk loading of XML documents into the database
2. Reconstruction of the original documents
3. Path traversal to retrieve parts of the document
4. Casting of text to data types
5. Handling of missing elements
6. Ordering of elements
7. References between elements
8. Join operations on values
9. Construction of large results
10. Containment and full text search

With this list, Schmidt et al. make an important contribution but do not emphasize the data-centric view of XML documents. Challenge 10 focuses on the aspect that documents can contain large quantities of text that have to be searched for words. Challenges 1 and 2 also contribute to the document-centric view so far as documents are created, stored, and either completely reconstructed or exist in parts. We also have to consider that the standardized query language XQuery is no more than a query language and not a manipulation language. It does not contain operations like insert and update. Therefore, manipulation of XML documents could probably do without this functionality. Updating the document could be done by means of an XML-authoring tool. Thus, reconstruction and repeated storage of XML documents gain special importance that should be supported by efficient storage techniques.

19.7 Summary

Storage and retrieval of XML documents is an interesting and important subject. The techniques and research results discussed in this chapter prove this to be a very big challenge. Several reasons may cause the technological clash that has been produced by the rise of XML and the necessity of storing XML documents. First, file-based storage techniques are too weak; second, research on semi-structured data is not so well known. Furthermore, the widespread database management techniques barely fit, and finally, the requirements of the XML data management systems have not been fully explored. Therefore, we should not miss the opportunity to develop either new storage techniques for the known database systems or even new database management systems, like the native XML data management systems. They could lead to a totally new awareness of the definition and usage of data and documents.

Chapter 20

Performance Analysis between an XML-Enabled Database and a Native XML Database

Joseph Fong, H. K. Wong, and Anthony Fong

20.1 Introduction

HTML dominates the Internet as a standard to present data and information in the twenty-first century. XML is replacing HTML in many domains as the next-generation standard for data representation and exchange. As e-commerce development grows rapidly, XML documents are also growing in ever increasing numbers. Hence, many XML-related applications and software are available to satisfy market demands. In this chapter, we concentrate on an XML-enabled database and a native XML database by comparing their performance (for legal reasons the products cannot be named). The XML-enabled database is a relational database that transfers data between XML documents and relational tables. It retrieves data for maintaining the relational properties between tables and fields, rather than to model XML documents. The native XML database stores XML data directly. It maps the structure of XML documents to the database without any conversion.

The XML-enabled database, with a relational database engine, stores XML data in relations. The XML document schema must be translated into the relational schema before accessing the corresponding tables. Similarly, the XML query language must be translated into SQL to access the relations. Figure 20.1 shows the

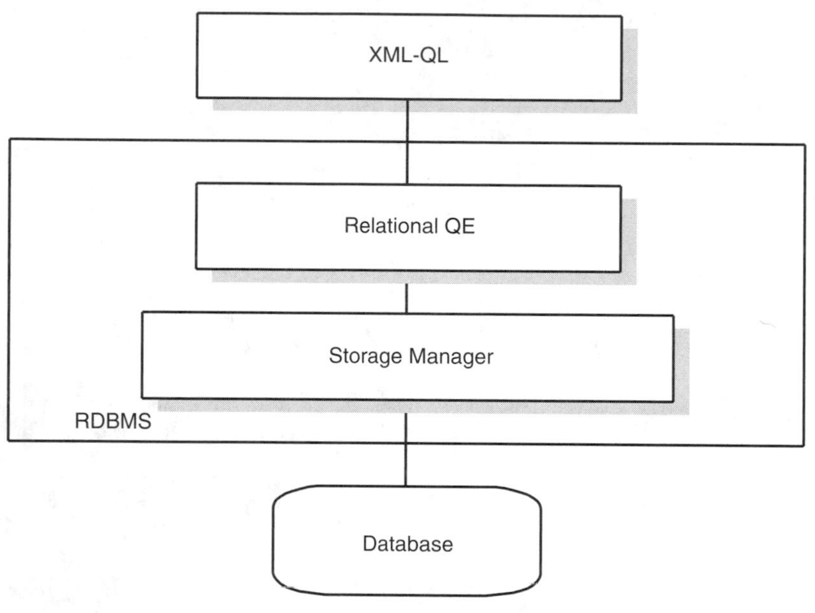

Figure 20.1 Architecture of the XML-Enabled Database

architecture of the XML-enabled database. The XML-QL (XML Query Language) is implemented as an add-on function to the RDBMS. The relational QE (query engine) parses the XML-QL and translates it into SQL. The SQL is executed inside the RDBMS to perform operations with the storage manager. The XML-QL must be implemented separately. Since XML data instances are stored in relational tables, translated SQL may involve retrieval and join operations, which may consume considerable CPU power and cause performance degradation.

The native XML database stores XML data directly. The database engine accesses the XML data without performing any conversion. This is the main difference between an XML-enabled database and a native XML database. This direct access in a native XML database can reduce processing time and provide better performance. The XML engine stores XML documents in and retrieves them from their respective data sources. The storage and retrieval are based on schemas defined by the administrator. The native XML database implements performance-enhancing technologies, such as compression and buffer pool management, and reduces the workload related to database administration. The diagram in Figure 20.2 shows the storing and retrieving of XML data through the XML engine. The XML parser checks the syntactical correctness of the schema and ensures the incoming XML data objects are well formed. The object processor is used to store objects in the native XML store. The query language is XML Query Language (XQL). The query interpreter

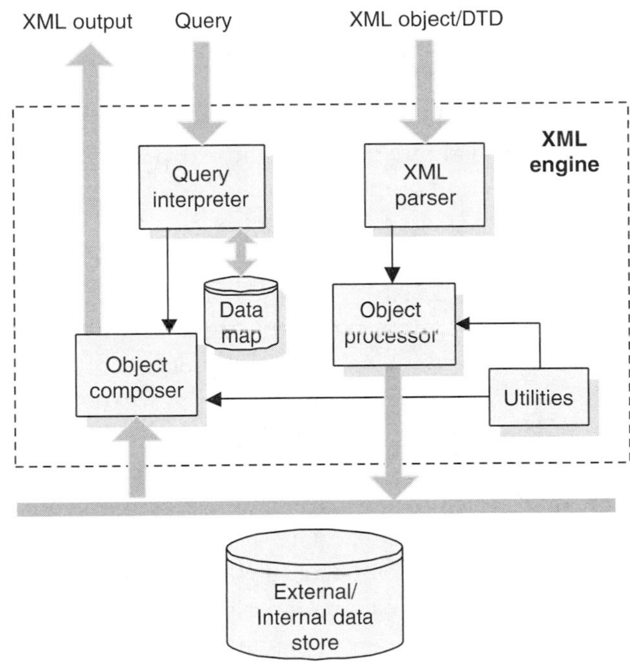

Figure 20.2 Architecture of Native XML Database XML Engine

resolves incoming requests and interacts with the object composer to retrieve XML objects according to the schemas defined by the administrator. Using the storage and retrieval schemas, the object composer constructs the information objects and returns them as XML documents.

The arrival of native XML databases has been fairly rapid. However, the maturity of the technology may be questionable. How well do such products perform? Can they really replace traditional (relational) database products? The goal of this chapter is to try to answer these questions. We will implement some performance tests to compare a modern XML-enabled database with a native XML database. Through various procedures and operations, we will measure and record the outcome. The data will then be analyzed, and we will then draw our conclusions.

20.2 Related Work

One of the first attempts to develop a benchmark for XML databases was XMach-1 (Böhme and Rahm 2001). It is a multiuser benchmark for the performance evaluation of XML data management systems. The benchmark application is Web based.

The XML data types are text documents, schema-less data, and structured data. In their paper, the authors specify the benchmark database first. Then they determine the performance of an application by defining a set of SQL queries. Their most important performance metric is defined as Xqps (XML queries per second) for measuring throughput. By identifying the performance factors for XML data storage and query processing, they claim that XMach-1 can be used to evaluate both native and XML-enabled database products.

Another benchmark, the "XML Benchmark Project," was recently completed (Schmidt, Waas, Kersten, Florescu, Manolescu et al. 2001). According to the authors, their set of queries captures the essential factors of managing XML data: path expression, NULL values query processing, full-text search, hierarchical data processing, reconstruction, ordering, aggregation, join, indexing, and coercion between data types. In their results, they conclude that there is no single best generic mapping from text documents to database.

Other research papers have mainly concentrated on mapping schemes for storing XML data in relational databases and studying the performance of relational databases to process XML data (e.g., Florescu and Kossmann 1999a). F. Tian et al. (Tian et al. 2000) compare both design and performance of storing XML data using different strategies. Their evaluation includes loading databases and reconstructing XML documents, selection query processing, indexing, scan selection, join query processing, and containment query processing. Their conclusion is that the use of a DTD is necessary for achieving good performance and complex-structured data presentation. C. Zhang et al. (Zhang et al. 2000) compare the performance of two relational database products using XML for an information retrieval system.

20.3 Methodology

Our methodology is based on XMach-1 (Böhme and Rahm 2001). That benchmark requires a Web-based application to model a general XML data management system. Based on the Web application, a number of performance measurements are taken: database population and scaling, document generation by queries, data manipulation operations, and operation mix. The methodology has two phases. The first phase is to explore the functionality of an XML-enabled database in handling XML documents. The second phase is to evaluate the performance of the XML-related libraries or gateway supported by the XML-enabled database.

Our methodology for measuring the performance of the two databases being tested (the XML-enabled database and the native XML database) is similar. The main difference is in the database design. We apply the method developed by K. Williams et al. (Williams et al. 2001) to convert a relational schema into a DTD. Then we use this DTD to generate an XML schema and store it in a database. A fixed number of records in text format are assigned to be imported into a database. The measurements are repeated from 100, 1,000, 10,000 and 50,000 sales records. Each measurement is repeated three times, and the average value is taken.

First, the database size is measured for both schema mappings. The objective is to investigate how efficient the database server stores XML documents. The size for building indexes is measured in megabytes.

We then examine the efficiency of the mapping schemes for the two database products. The time for XML document reconstruction from the database is measured in seconds. This tests the performance of the database engine. The time required to import from external XML sources into the databases is also recorded in seconds.

In our experiments, a sales order application was implemented for evaluating performance. The implementation involves using an XML gateway or XML libraries for mapping or data conversion. To cope with the performance measurements, the application has the following functions:

- GUI interfaces to perform insert, update, delete, and search functions for single records
- GUI interfaces to perform transactions (insert and delete) for bulk size records
- A number of reports and queries to evaluate query optimizations

In developing the application, Java DOM APIs were used to directly access the native XML database server. The entire application was written using Java servlets. X-Query was used instead of SQL for reporting because X-Query was required to access the server using the HTTP protocol.

Since two versions of the application were implemented in this project, a number of APIs from the two database products were used. Our focus will also be on API usability comparisons, ease of programming, program size, program readability, compatibility, supported features, debugging tools, and functions related to their development environments.

After collecting data from the above-mentioned experiments, we were able to perform a detailed analysis. From the study of XML-related features of both databases, we were able to draw some conclusions that we present below.

20.4 Database Design

The first step was to design a database to use XML features as much as possible. We implemented a system to model book sales and reports. Listing 20.1 contains the core relational schema we used.

Listing 20.1 Relational Schema for the Book Sales and Reports System

```
Relation Customer (Customer_no, Customer_name, Sex, Postal_code,
Telephone, Email)
Relation Customer_address (Customer_no, Address_type, Address,
City, Sate, Country, Is_default)
Relation Invoice (Invoice_no, Customer_no, Quantity,
Invoice_amount, Invoice_date, Shipment_type, Shipment_date)
Relation Invoice_item (Invoice_no, Item_no, quantity, Unit_price,
Invoice_price, Discount)
Relation Item (Item_no, Item_name, Catalog_type, Author, Publisher,
Item_price)
Relation Category (Catalog_type, Catelog_description)
Relation Shipment (Shipment_type, Shipment_description)
Relation Monthly_sales (Year, Month, Quantity, Total)
Relation Customer_sales (Year, Month, Customer_no, Quantity, Total)
Relation Item_sales (Year, Month, Item_no, Quantity, Total)
```

Figure 20.3 shows the EER diagram of the relational schema.

The next step was to translate the relational schema into an XML schema. We adopted the methodology used by K. Williams et al. (Williams et al. 2001). Listing 20.2 contains the final DTD produced from this process.

Listing 20.2 DTD Corresponding to the Relational Schema in Listing 20.1

```
<!ELEMENT           Sales (Invoice*, Customer*, Item*,
Monthly_sales*)>
<!ATTLIST           Sales
  Status            (New|Updated|History) #required>
<!ELEMENT           Invoice (Invoice_item*)>
<!ATTLIST           Invoice
  Quantity          CDATA     #REQUIRED
  Invoice_amount    CDATA     #REQUIRED
  Invoice_date      CDATA     #REQUIRED
  Shipment_type     (Post|DHL|UPS|FedEx|Ship) #IMPLIED
  Shipment_date     CDATA     #IMPLIED
  Customer_idref    IDREF     #REQUIRED>
<!ELEMENT           Customer (Customer_address*)>
<!ATTLIST           Customer
  Customer_id       ID        #REQUIRED
  Customer_name     CDATA     #REQUIRED
  Sex               CDATA     #IMPLIED
```

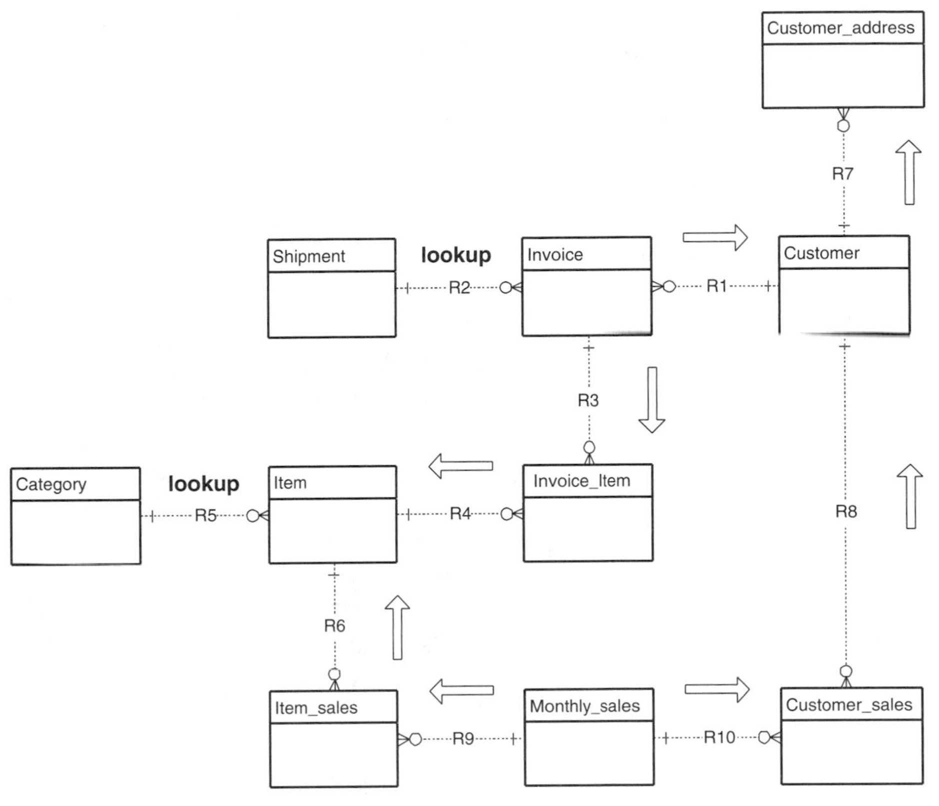

Figure 20.3 EER Diagram

```
  Postal_code       CDATA    #IMPLIED
  Telephone         CDATA    #IMPLIED
  Email             CDATA    #IMPLIED>
<!ELEMENT           Customer_address EMPTY>
<!ATTLIST           Customer_address
  Address_type      (Home|Office) #REQUIRED
  Address           NMTOKENS #REQUIRED
  City              CDATA    #IMPLIED
  State             CDATA    #IMPLIED
  Country           CDATA    #IMPLIED
  Is_default        (Y|N) "Y">
<!ELEMENT           Invoice_Item EMPTY>
<!ATTLIST           Invoice_Item
  Quantity          CDATA    #REQUIRED
```

```
  Unit_price        CDATA    #REQUIRED
  Invoice_price     CDATA    #REQUIRED
  Discount          CDATA    #REQUIRED
  Item_idref        IDREF    #REQUIRED>
<!ELEMENT           Item EMPTY>
<!ATTLIST           Item
  Item_id           ID       #REQUIRED
  Item_name         CDATA    #REQUIRED
  Category_type     (Art|Comp|Fict|Food|Sci|Sport|Trav) #REQUIRED
  Author            CDATA    #IMPLIED
  Publisher         CDATA    #IMPLIED
  Item_price        CDATA    #REQUIRED>

<!ELEMENT           Monthly_sales (Item_sales*, Customer_sales*)>
<!ATTLIST           Monthly_sales
  Year              CDATA    #REQUIRED
  Month             CDATA    #REQUIRED
  Quantity          CDATA    #REQUIRED
  Total             CDATA    #REQUIRED>
<!ELEMENT           Item_sales EMPTY>
<!ATTLIST           Item_sales
  Quantity          CDATA    #REQUIRED
  Total             CDATA    #REQUIRED
  Item_idref        IDREF    #REQUIRED>
<!ELEMENT           Customer_sales EMPTY>
<!ATTLIST           Customer_sales
  Quantity          CDATA    #REQUIRED
  Total             CDATA    #REQUIRED
  Customer_idref    IDREF    #REQUIRED>
```

The root element, <Sales>, is related to the meaning of the document. The corresponding content elements that follow are <Invoice>, <Customer>, <Item>, and <Monthly_sales>. Every element has its attributes, which can be seen from the DTD in Listing 20.2.

20.5 Discussion

Two approaches to modeling the columns in an RDBMS as an XML DTD structure are

- **Element approach:** Define the table name as the root element. It is nested by its columns, which are also defined as elements. An example is

```
<! ELEMENT Person (Name, Sex, Age)>
<! ELEMENT Name (#PCDATA)>
<! ELEMENT Sex (#PCDATA)>
<! ELEMENT Age (#PCDATA)>
```

- **Attribute approach:** The columns are defined as attributes of the root element. The previous example becomes

```
<! ELEMENT Person>
<! ATTLIST Person
Name CDATA #REQUIRED
Sex CDATA #REQUIRED
Age CDATA #REQUIRED>
```

In a relational database, data and structures are defined. Columns represent data. Tables and relationships form structure. This can be managed well in searching for data and for database navigation. XML attributes refer to the data. XML elements and subelements build the structure. In addition, attributes do not have the concept of ordering. This is similar to columns in a table. No matter how one changes the position of a column in a table, the data content inside a table does not change. For the first approach, tables and columns are both defined as element types. It may be ambiguous to a parser to decide the role of an element. The flexibility of searching for child elements is less than the attribute approach. This is because an element does have ordering meaning. Hence, it cannot fully represent the location-independence of data from an RDBMS concept.

Performance is another critical issue. There are two technologies in parsing XML documents: DOM and SAX. Our application can only use the native XML database Java DOM API. The principle of DOM is to pull the document into memory first and then present it as a tree. The process of converting the document to a tree structure involves traversal through the document. For example, the steps for retrieving the invoice price of the second item from an invoice are: (1) Go to parent element Invoice; (2) go to second Invoice_item child of Invoice; (3) get the price value from this Invoice_item.

If the element approach is used for the sample database, more steps are involved: (1) Go to parent element Invoice; (2) go to second Invoice_item child; (3) go to invoice price child of the second Invoice_item; (4) get the text value portion of invoice price.

Coding may be simpler if the attribute approach is used. Also when using attributes, there is the option of using enumerated types such that the value of a column can be constrained by a defined value.

Document size is another issue. For the element approach, a starting tag must be defined first, followed by the content, and then followed by an end tag. This is not necessary for the attribute approach. The syntax is "attribute_name = attribute_value". As the database size increases, the difference could be significant. The element approach costs time in parsing documents. Hence, the performance will be affected, since a mass of records must be processed. In addition, more disk space is required to store tags.

In defining the relationships between elements, containment is used for one-to-one and one-to-many cases. The ID/IDREF pointer approach is not recommended because XML is designed with the concept of containment. Using pointers costs more processing time, because DOM and SAX do not provide efficient methods to handle ID/IDREF relationships. Furthermore, navigating from an ID field to an IDREF field may not be easy. This becomes more difficult for IDREFS, since all IDREFS fields need to be tokenized. Each token is examined for all possible ID fields. Hence, containment is introduced to build relationships at the start. The pointer approach is used for those relationships that can go either way.

20.6 Experiment Result

Table 20.1 provides a summary of the tests we used in our performance evaluation. We discuss our results following the table.

20.6.1 Database Size

Database size is the disk space required for storing data after the conversion procedures in the database server. Index size is also investigated. The unit of measurement is megabytes (MBs).

As shown in Figure 20.4, the native XML database needs more disk space to store both data and indexes than the XML-enabled database. The growth is almost exponential. The result is more serious as the number of records increases. For 50,000 records, the native XML database has an indexing size over 150 times that of the XML-enabled database. The XML-enabled database controls the sizing much better than the native XML database. From 100 to 10,000 records, the indexing size is approximately 0.11 MB. The larger indexing in the native XML database can be

Table 20.1 Summary of Performance Tests

Test	Description
Q1, Q2	evaluate insert operation performance
Q3, Q4	evaluate update operation performance
Q5, Q6	evaluate delete operation performance
Q7, Q8, Q9	measure the running time in searching for record by using index key
Q10, Q11	measure the running time for bulk load
Q12, Q13	measure the running time for bulk mass delete
Q14, Q15	measure the running time for bulk mass update
Q16, 17	evaluate the efficiency in executing a complicated query using regular expression
Q18	evaluate the efficiency in executing a complicated query using join (one-to-many relationship)
Q19	investigate the performance of more complicated queries that combine selection and sorting

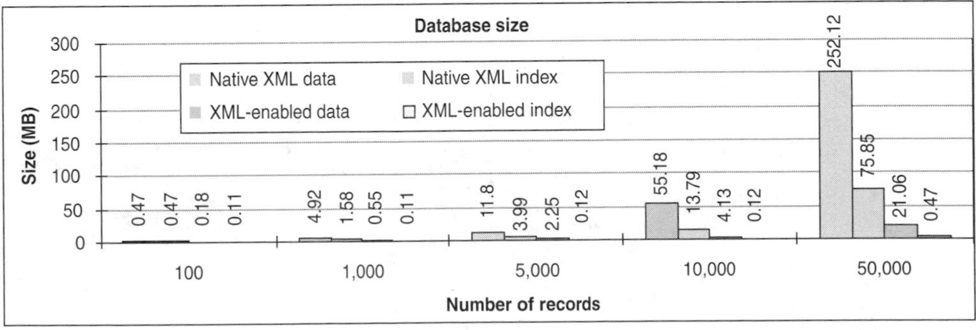

Figure 20.4 Results of Database Size

explained by the fact that more comprehensive indexing support is provided, such as full-text searching. Storing XML in the native XML database is not any less space-efficient than decomposing the same data and storing it in a relational database. The only reason for this large size is that the native XML database must store tag names, both elements and attributes, in order to retain the native XML features of the document source.

20.6.2 SQL Operations (Single Record)

The objective of Q1 and Q2 is to measure insert performance (see Figure 20.5). Q1 is a single insert statement with only one table (item) involved. Q2 consists of a master-details relationship (`customer` and `customer_address`). As the results indicate, the XML-enabled database has better performance than the native XML database in all cases. However, both products have steady figures no matter how large the database is. We conclude that insert operation performance is not affected by the database size. Furthermore, Q2 costs more time than Q1 as Q2 needs to handle more than one table.

The objective of Q3 and Q4 is to measure update performance (see Figure 20.6). We obtained results similar to the insert operation (shown in Figure 20.5). The XML-enabled database has better performance than the native XML database. The update timing is less than the cost of insert. This is reasonable as the insert operation needs to check data integrity and unique indexing before execution. Before an update/delete operation, the record has already been retrieved from the database. Hence, time is saved. Both products have steady figures no matter how large the database is. We conclude that update performance is not affected by the database size.

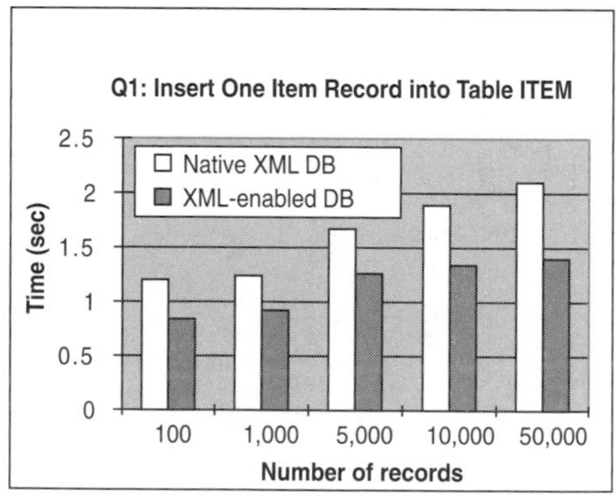

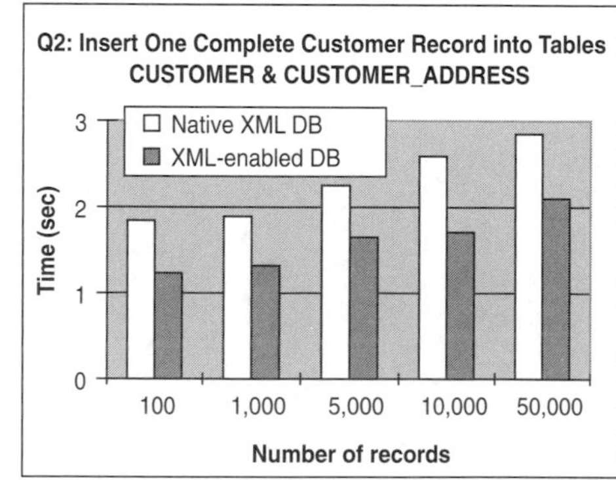

Figure 20.5 Results of Q1 and Q2—Insert

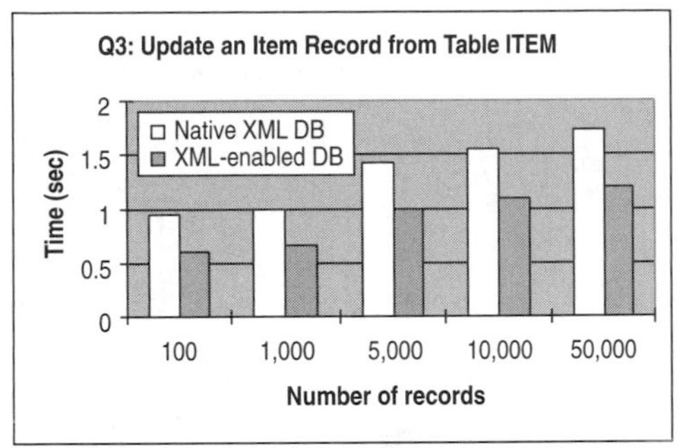

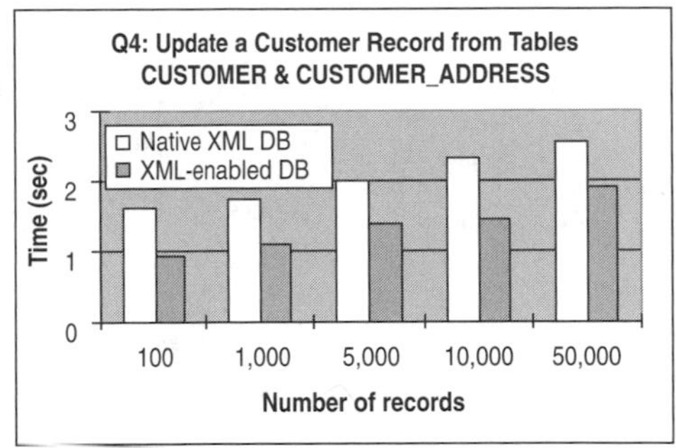

Figure 20.6 Results of Q3 and Q4—Update

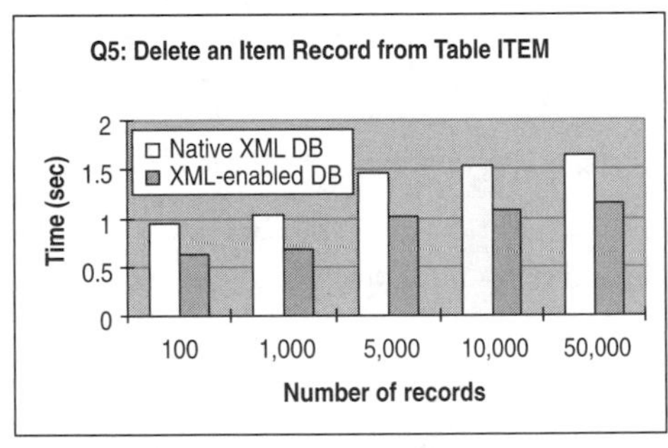

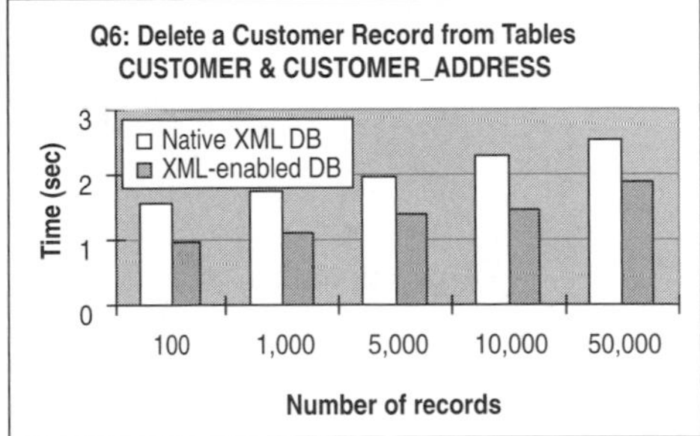

Figure 20.7 Results of Q5 and Q6—Delete

The objective of Q5 and Q6 is to measure delete performance (see Figure 20.7). We obtain results similar to Q1–Q4. The XML-enabled database has better performance than the native XML database. Since the update and the delete functionalities are of the same logic, there is not much performance difference between `update` and `delete`. Both products have steady figures no matter how large the database is. We conclude that delete performance is not affected by the database size.

Q7, Q8, and Q9 measure the time to search for a record using an index key (see Figure 20.8). For 100 or 1,000 records, the results for both products are very similar. From 5,000 records onward, the native XML database outperforms the XML-enabled database. The native XML database provides steady performance in all cases. We conclude that the native storage strategy and indexing approach is efficient enough for searching in a database.

For this section, we conclude that the XML-enabled database outperforms the native XML database in single SQL operations, but the native XML database

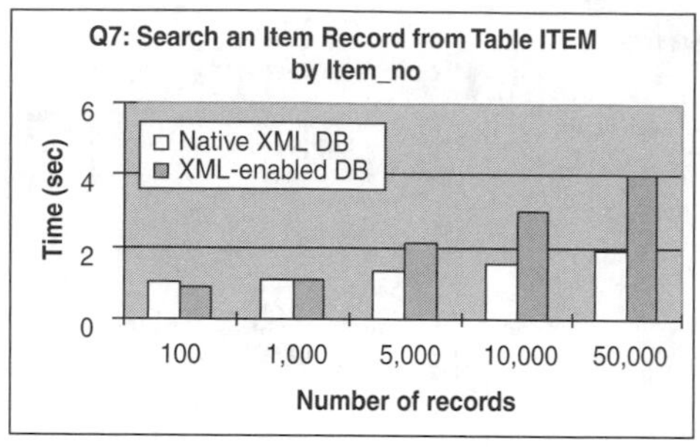

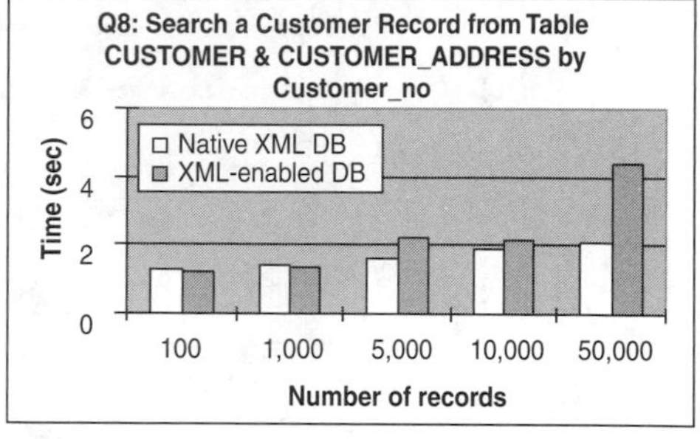

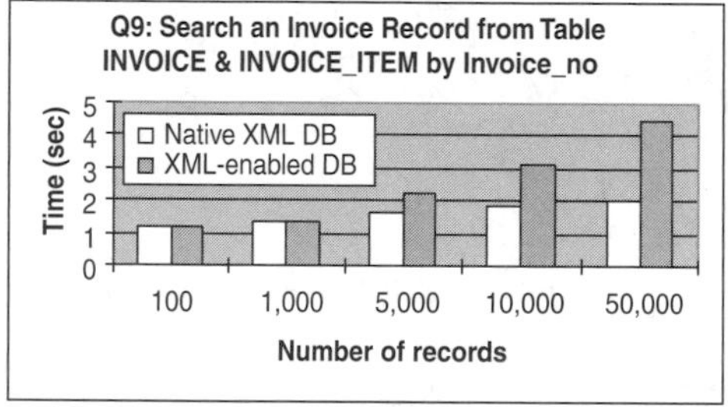

Figure 20.8 Results for Q7, Q8, and Q9—Searching

outperforms the XML-enabled database in index searching. It seems that the XML parser in either database has no impact on our performance results.

20.6.3 SQL Operations (Mass Records)

Q10 and Q11 are the bulk load operations for `Item` and `Customer` records (see Figure 20.9). As the figures indicate, the native XML database has better performance than the XML-enabled database as data size becomes larger. The XML-enabled database runs faster than the native XML database for 100 and 1,000 records. For larger record numbers, the native XML database costs at most half of the running time as the XML-enabled database. This may be due to the native XML database's storage strategy. The API gateways of the XML-enabled database could be the bottleneck for larger data sizes. Furthermore, the running time for `Customer` records is more than the running time for `Item` records as size becomes larger.

Q12 and Q13 are the mass delete operations for `Item` and `Customer` records (see Figure 20.10). As the figures indicate, the XML-enabled database has better performance than the native XML database except for 50,000 records. For the XML-enabled database, a simple structural and powerful SQL query can perform a mass delete. In contrast, the servlet program for the native XML database needs to exe-

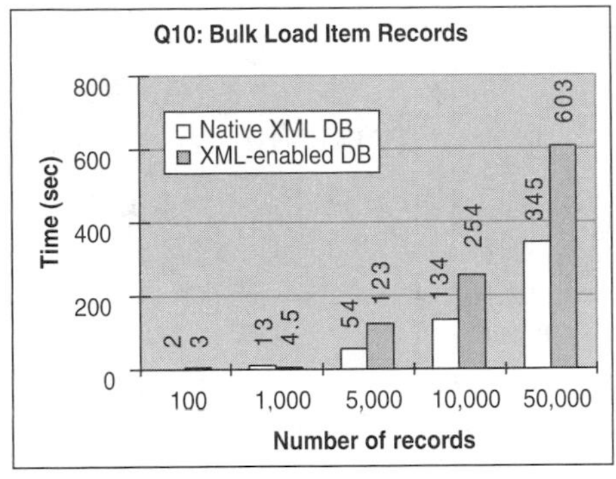

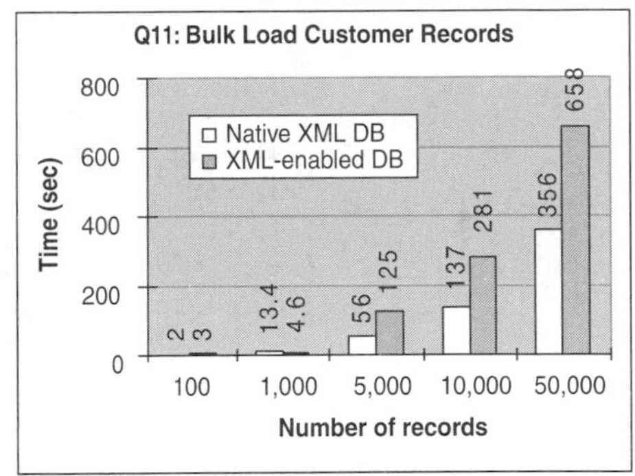

Figure 20.9 Results for Q10 and Q11—Bulk Load

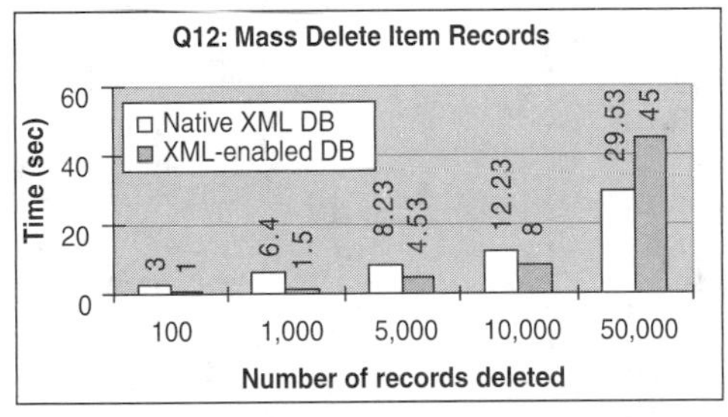

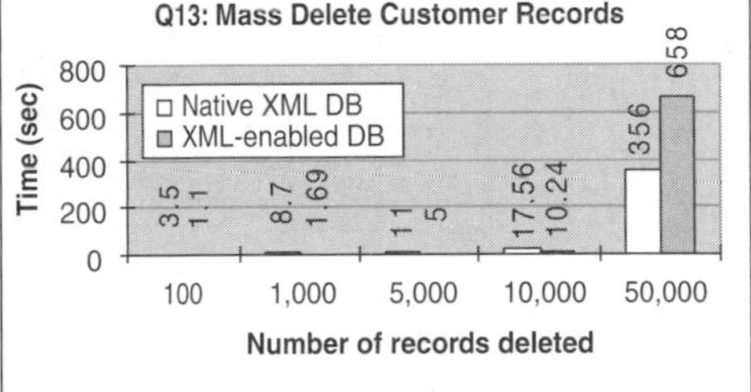

Figure 20.10 Results for Q12 and Q13—Mass Delete

cute an additional query prior to retrieving all possible `Customers/Items`. Then the program uses the temporary list to remove records.

Q14 and Q15 are the mass update process for `Item` and `Customer` records (see Figure 20.11). As the figures indicate, the XML-enabled database has better performance than the native XML database except in the case of 50,000 records. We conclude that this is due to the same reasons outlined above for Figure 20.10.

20.6.4 Reporting

The following are the results from the reporting section of the sample application. Similar results are measured for Q16 and Q17 (see Figure 20.12). The native XML database has steady performance in implementing regular expressions. The XML-enabled database results are more variable.

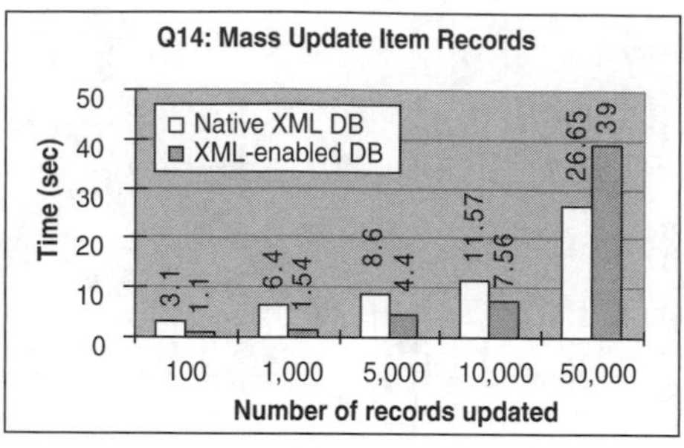

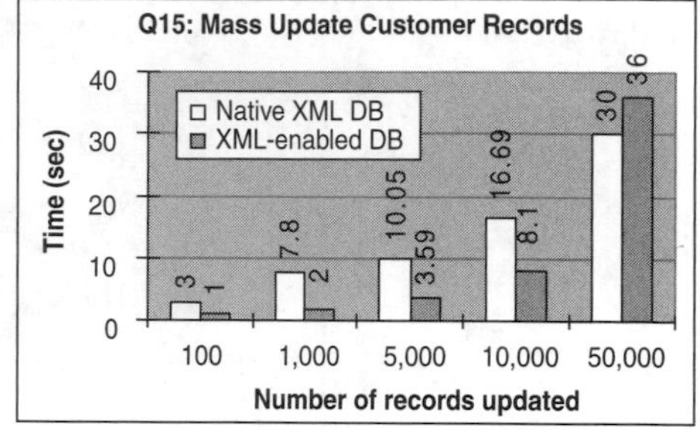

Figure 20.11 Results for Q14 and Q15—Mass Update

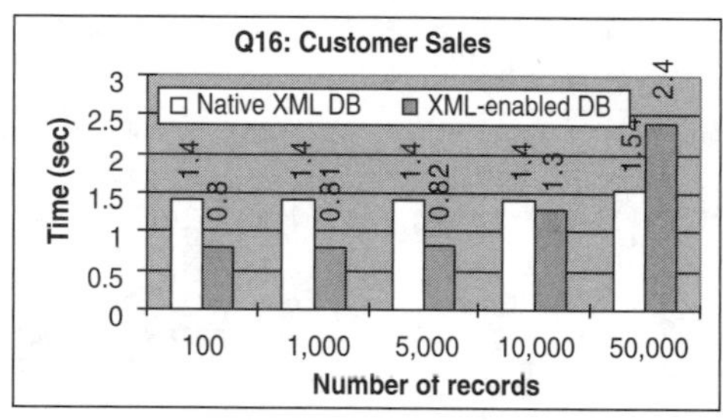

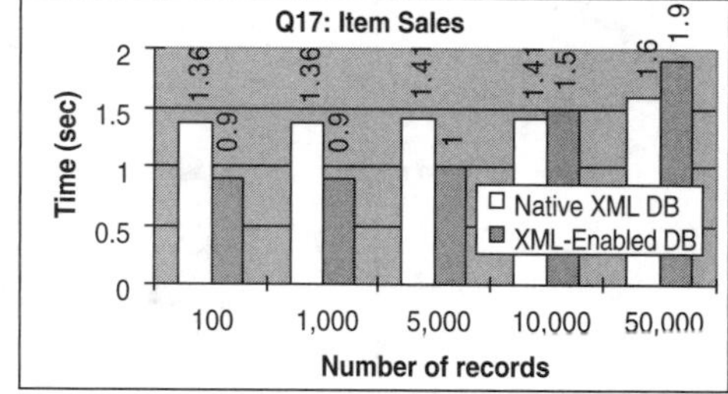

Figure 20.12 Results for Q16 and Q17—Reporting

Q18 aims to measure the join property (one-to-many relationship) of records/documents inside `invoice` and `invoice_item`. The results in Figure 20.13 are similar to Q5. For rich-content documents or records, the native XML database outperforms the XML-enabled database. This result is clear from 10,000 records. In this case, the native XML database cannot give a steady result. The running time goes up as data size increases. But it is not as serious as the XML-enabled database. Q19 combines selection criteria and sorting. The result is similar to Q4. This time the XML-enabled database provides steady performance within the testing range. It outperforms the native XML database until at 10,000 records, and even at 50,000 records, the two products are quite similar.

We conclude that the native XML database has better query optimization than the XML-enabled database for large data sizes. However, the XML-enabled database does dominate for small data sizes.

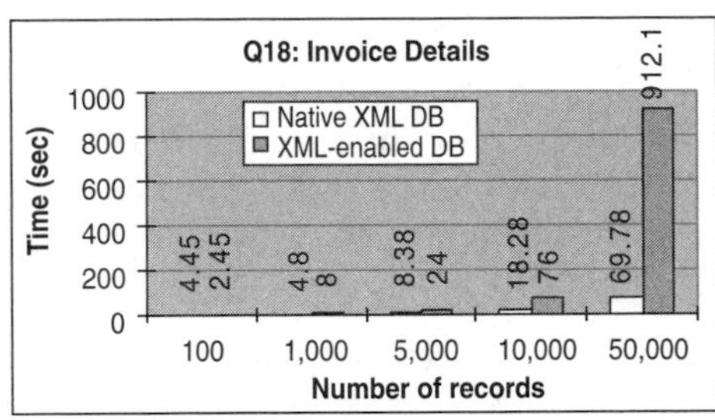

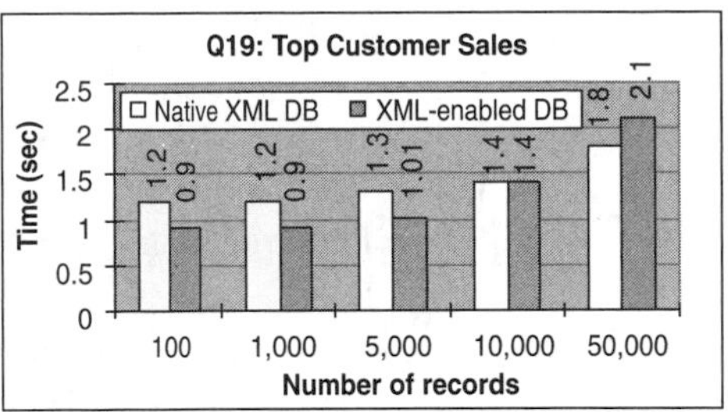

Figure 20.13 Results for Q18 and Q19

20.7 Conclusion

After analyzing the above results, we conclude that the native XML database has better performance than the XML-enabled database for handling XML documents with larger data sizes. Although the XML-enabled database has better performance for small document sizes (number of records <= 1,000), it cannot handle large-sized documents as efficiently due to conversion overhead. In contrast, the native XML database engine directly accesses XML data without conversion.

Although the native XML database provides high performance in handling XML documents, it does have some disadvantages. From calibrating the database size, both data and index size consumed by the native XML database is much larger than in the XML-enabled database.

Both databases have steady performance in single data operations: insert, delete, and update. From 100 records to 50,000 records, the result is more or less the same. The native XML database has better performance in searching by index.

For mass record operations, the native XML database shows advantages in handling large quantities of XML data. Both the results of bulk loading and delete operations are very similar to the results in reconstruction. The XML-enabled database has better performance in small database sizes. The native XML database provides better scalability as the database grows. For mass updates, the native XML database still has advantages, but the difference is not so obvious as in the previous case. As the XML-enabled database needs one SQL statement to perform mass updates, the native XML database achieves this indirectly. We have tried to discover any API of the native XML database that provides mass update functionality but without success. It seems that update functionality is a weakness for this native XML database. Instead, we have to retrieve a single document, change it by another API, and then return the results to the database or display them through XSL. This consumes quite a lot of running time.

The native XML database produced better results in the reporting section, which implies that the native XML database X-Query has performance gains from query optimization. Most of the figures show that the XML-enabled database starts better but becomes worse as data size grows. The difference becomes obvious as the query becomes more complicated. Q17 and Q18 in Figures 20.12 and 20.13 demonstrate this.

Both products have advantages and disadvantages in developing applications. In using the native XML database APIs, the compatibility is high for applications written in Java. Since the XML-enabled database is a proprietary product, the application can run only in certain operating system environments. When compared to the XML-enabled database, Java is a relatively low-level language. More coding is required, and hence the debugging time and also the maintenance cost are increased if the application becomes complicated. Since the native XML database is a new product, the technology related to this product is not well known to most developers. It takes time for most IT developers to get accustomed to this new product.

Both the XML-enabled database and the native XML database provide good graphical user interfaces. The native XML database uses a Web-based application, which acts as the centralized database administration software, while the XML-enabled database is a Windows-based application. In order to communicate with the database, both the XML-enabled database and the native XML database use the same approach by sending HTTP requests that use a URL syntax. The XML-enabled database needs the annotated schema as a middle tier to map the XML objects into the corresponding database object. The XML-enabled database is developed so that programmers do not have to learn from scratch. However, since the native XML database is a new product, programmers need time to learn new concepts and functions before using it.

Since the native XML database is developed using Java and is Web based, its portability and accessibility outperform the XML-enabled database. This accommodates the Internet trend as information should be accessed anywhere. Portable database features are welcome if the performance is acceptable. The native nature and technology of a native XML database handle XML efficiently as scalability increases. The APIs (e.g., JavaScript, ActiveX, VBScript, etc.) increase its compatibility as well. Despite its poor performance in handling large XML documents, the XML-enabled database does have an advantage in being relatively fast to develop, which is welcome to business requests. Hence, we do not have a preference in choosing between the two products. But if one wants to develop a system that has very complex structure, nesting, and so on, we recommend the native XML database. Our results are summarized in Table 20.2.

Table 20.2 Summary

	Native XML database	**XML-enabled database**
Schema	DTD	XDR
Commands	XQL	XPath
Performance (single record)	Low	High
Performance (mass records)	High	Low
User Interface:		
User Friendliness	Good	Good
Implementation	Good	Fair
Maintenance	Fair	Good

Chapter 21

Conclusion

XML is definitely a hot technology today. The question is for how long? In a series of articles for executives in "OT Land" (http://www.otland.com), Paul Harmon explains nicely the typical cycle in the introduction of new technologies:

> *First, new technologies are proclaimed and leading theorists explain how they are going to solve many different problems. Then, after companies begin to experiment with them, it is realized that a lot of infrastructure is going to be needed to make the new technology really useful. Thus, a lull sets in, while the infrastructure is developed. Later, with the infrastructure in place, companies begin again, more modestly, with a much better idea of what the new technology is really good for (Harmon 2002).*

Let us briefly review what has happened since the introduction of XML by the W3C in 1998. The Internet Engineering Task Force (IETF) has also accepted XML as a standard. This is very important, since IETF is a powerful organization that governs the Internet. So from the beginning, XML received an official endorsement. This was not necessarily the only reason that XML was accepted as a standard by the market, but it definitely was a prerequisite.

Although XML might not be the most efficient protocol for passing data over the Internet, it has two key advantages:

1. It is an open, international standard designed for the Internet by the W3C.
2. It allows users to define the data types of information and include the data type information in the same file as the data itself.

The second point is an important technical improvement with respect to older data protocols. XML allows various applications to communicate data, including the semantics of the data itself. At the time, this sounded like the silver bullet needed to build a network of cooperative Web sites for the Internet, a vision often referred to as the "Semantic Web." Soon expectations ran very high. The business press started to become interested in XML and praised it as the new "lingua franca of the Internet." However, as always with the introduction of new technologies, after high expectations, reality sets in.

The real test for a new technology is when a company starts using it for real business applications. By using XML, companies explored its limits and at the same time looked for new ways to use it for their businesses. The result was the need to introduce a solid infrastructure to support XML for business (mainly for the Internet, though not exclusively).

At the time of writing this book, the W3C has made over 20 extensions to the original definition of XML and has defined a new XML Schema Language, and a variety of XML languages made by numerous companies and consortia has also been defined. So, more than the "lingua franca of the Internet," at first sight XML looks like the Tower of Babel of different languages of the Internet. Of course reality is, as always, in the middle. XML isn't a silver bullet, but it's a technology that's here to stay, one that will play a significant role for the Internet.

Why all of these XML extensions? To understand, it is useful to look more closely at the way XML is used or is proposed to be used. XML was originally designed to be an Internet protocol that allowed companies to pass data over the Internet. However, if several companies want to communicate with each other about some specific information related to their businesses, they need to agree first and standardize the use of a set of XML tags (or data types). Unless the companies agree on the meaning of the tags, they will not understand the data being passed. This basically means that XML can be used to create other XML languages. A set of tags (a DTD set) defines a language. The W3C has introduced an XML Schema for help defining new XML languages. We are tempted to call such languages "XML dialects." So you will find XML dialects for all kinds of vertical domains, such as banking, insurance, and retail. They are all XML, but only if you can speak the "dialect" can you understand the real meaning of the data exchanged.

It is clear that, once you can agree on the information you want to exchange with a partner company, then the next thing you can do with the data is to use it. This is when things really get complicated. Once you start linking different applications together (for example, to implement a set of Web Services), then immediately the need for an XML infrastructure for integration arises. But XML was not originally designed for this. XML was not supposed to be a middleware technology. XML was simply a file format. No security mechanisms were provided; no distributed features were provided. Notwithstanding this, XML has been used as a base to develop new middleware technologies. Notable examples are the earlier proposal called SOAP (Simple Object Access Protocol), UDDI, and WSDL (Web Service Description Language), which have all been created to allow an XML message to automatically locate target applications on the Web and to return messages to the sender.

A significant effort in defining an XML middleware architecture is the work of the OASIS (Organization for the Advancement of Structured Information Standards) consortium. It works jointly with the UN/CEFACT standards body. The initiative is called ebXML, for electronic business XML. The ebXML initiative is basically creating a complete middleware architecture based on XML. In this respect, it is an alternative to earlier proposals such as SOAP. Part of the work of ebXML has been influenced by the work of the OMG (Object Management Group), a consortium defining standards for middleware. One of the contributions of the OMG in the XML area is the definition of a DTD language, called XMI, to allow information to be passed on UML diagrams and documents. UML (the Unified Modeling Language) is an OMG standard widely adopted to model complex information systems. But there is more. XML has found another area of applicability: XML for storing information. This aspect of XML has been extensively dealt with in this book.

To better understand this aspect of XML, let us use an example. With XML, a company owning information can create a report with text, figures, tables, and photographs and decide to store each individual element as an XML file in a content management system. Later, the company may decide to make the entire report available on its Web site, or the company may decide to send only selected paragraphs of the report to targeted people via devices, such as cell phones and/or Palm Pilots.

All this is possible because the basic content is stored as XML files. Figures and photos can be reused and modified while in the content management system, and it is possible because the information has not been stored as a text document or a photograph created in some special program, but as XML files.

Assuming that a predefined set of XML data types (tags) have been agreed upon among a group of cooperating companies, then since each XML file describes all the data contained in that file, a company has the ability to manipulate the data in the files. Therefore, XML can be used as a technology to implement so-called "Web Services." Web Services are designed to help business people creating virtual business applications combining the strengths of several companies. Since Web Services are a kind of set of cooperating Web sites on the Net, all working together to achieve a common business goal, it is clear that XML is a key technology for their implementation.

Many companies are working to incorporate XML in their products. For example, Microsoft is rearchitecting its operating system using an XML-based architecture called .NET. Sun is incorporating XML capabilities into Java and J2EE. Tool vendors are modifying their products to support and generate XML files. Most package software vendors are moving to the use of XML as their primary data-passing or middleware technology.

Database and application server vendors are extending their products to store and manipulate XML files, which is exactly why we (the editors) put this book together, to help you (the reader) understand and exploit the database technology created to support XML files. In addition, major industry consortia are working on specialized XML languages for specific business areas.

The Gartner Group predicts that by the end of 2003, 80 percent of Web-based B2B traffic will be passed as XML documents. However, XML is not the ultimate silver bullet. XML was designed for the Internet and not for the problems one faces when integrating legacy applications with new applications. However, XML promises to be an important technology in the overall distributed computing architecture. Something you cannot miss.

References

(Abiteboul 1997) Abiteboul, S. 1997. "Querying Semi-Structured Data," *Proceedings of the International Conference on Database Theory*. Delphi, Greece, pp. 1–18.

(Abiteboul et al. 1997) Abiteboul, S., Quass, D., McHugh, J., Widom J., and J. L. Wiener. 1997. "The LOREL Query Language for Semistructured Data," *International Journal on Digital Libraries* 1(1):68–88.

(Abiteboul et al. 2000) Abiteboul, S., Buneman, P., and D. Suciu. 2000. "Data on the Web: From Relations to Semistructured Data and XML." (Morgan Kaufmann Publishers).

(Aboulnaga et al. 2001) Aboulnaga, A., Naughton, J., and C. Zhang. 2001. "Generating Synthetic Complex-Structured XML Data," *Informal Proceedings of the International Workshop on the Web and Databases*. Santa Barbara, California.

(Abowd et al. 1995) Abowd, G. D., Allen, R. B., and D. Garlan. 1995. "Formalizing Style to Understand Descriptions of Software Architecture," *ACM Transactions on Software Engineering and Methodology* 4(4):319–64.

(Achard et al. 2001) Achard, F., Vaysseix, G., and E. Barillot. 2001. "XML, Bioinformatics and Data Integration," *Bioinformatics Review* 17(2):115–125.

(Aggarwal et al. 1998) Aggarwal, S., Hung, F., and W. Meng. 1998. "WIRE—A WWW-Based Information Retrieval and Extraction System," *Proceedings of the International Workshop on Database and Expert System Applications*. Vienna, Austria, pp. 887–92.

(Agrawal and Shim 1996) Agrawal, R., and K. Shim. 1996. "Developing Tightly-Coupled Data Mining Applications on a Relational Database System," *Proceedings of the International Conference on Knowledge Discovery and Data Mining*. Portland, Oregon, pp. 287–90.

(Agrawal and Srikant 1994) Agrawal, R., and R. Srikant. 1994. "Fast Algorithms for Mining Association Rules in Large Databases," *Proceedings of the International Conference on Very Large Data Bases*. Santiago de Chile, Chile, pp. 487–99.

(Agrawal et al. 1993a) Agrawal, R., Imielinski, T., and A. N. Swami. 1993. "Database Mining: A Performance Perspective," *IEEE Transactions on Knowledge and Data Engineering* 5(6):914–25.

(Agrawal et al. 1993b) Agrawal, R. Imielinski, T., and A. N. Swami. 1993. "Mining Association Rules between Sets of Items in Large Databases," *Proceedings of the ACM SIGMOD International Conference on Management of Data*. Washington D.C., pp. 207–16.

(Ahlgren et al. 1998) Ahlgren, B., Björkman, M., and P. G. Gunningberg. 1998. "The Applicability of Integrated Layer Processing," *IEEE Journal on Selected Areas in Communications* 16(3):317–31, 1998.

(Allen and Garlan 1997) Allen, R., and D. Garlan. 1997. "A Formal Basis for Architectural Connection," *ACM Transactions on Software Engineering and Methodology* 6(3):213–49.

(Altschul et al. 1990) Altschul, S. F., Gish, W., Miller, W., Myers. E. W., and D. J. Lipman. 1990. "Basic Local Alignment Search Tool," *Journal of Molecular Biology* 215:403–10.

(Altschul et al. 1997) Altschul, S. F., Madden, T. L., Schaffer, A. A., Zhang, J., Zhang, Z., Miller, W., and D. J. Lipman. 1997. "Gapped BLAST and PSI-BLAST: A New Generation of Protein Database Search Programs," *Nucleic Acids Research* 25:3389–402.

(Astley and Agha 1998) Astley, M., and G. Agha. 1998. "Customization and Composition of Distributed Objects: Middleware Abstractions for Policy Management," *Proceedings of the ACM SIGSOFT International Symposium on the Foundations of Software Engineering*. Lake Buena Vista, Florida, pp. 1–9.

(ATM 1996) ATM (Asynchronous Transfer Mode). 1996. "ATM Forum Traffic Management Draft Standard," aftm-0056.000, ftp://ftp.atmforum.com/pub/approved-specs/af-tm-0056.000.pdf.

(Baker 1998) Baker, S. 1998. *CORBA Distributed Objects: Using Orbix* (Reading, Massachusetts: Addison-Wesley; New York: ACM Press).

(Banerjee et al. 2000) Banerjee, S., Krishnamurthy, V., Krishnaprasad, M., and R. Murthy. 2000. "Oracle8i—The XML Enabled Data Management System," *Proceedings of the International Conference on Data Engineering*. San Diego, California. pp. 561–68.

(Barbosa et al. 2002) Barbosa, D., Mendelzon, A., Keenleyside, J., and K. Lyons. 2002. "ToXgene: An Extensible Template-based Data Generator for XML" *Informal Proceedings of the International Workshop on the Web and Databases*. Madison, Wisconsin, pp. 49–54.

(Baril and Bellahsène 2000) Baril, X., and Z. Bellahsène. 2000. "A View Model for XML Documents," *Proceedings of the International Conference on Object-Oriented Information Systems*. London, U.K., pp. 429–41.

(Baril and Bellahsène 2001) Baril, X., and Z. Bellahsène. 2001. "A Browser for Specifying XML Views," *Proceedings of the International Conference on Object-Oriented Information Systems*. Calgary, Canada, pp. 164–74.

(Baru 1999) Baru, C. 1999. "XVviews : XML Views of Relational Schemas," *Proceedings of the International Workshop on Database and Expert System Applications*. Florence, Italy, pp. 700–05.

(Bayardo 1998) Bayardo, R. 1998. "Efficiently Mining Long Patterns from Databases," *Proceedings of the ACM SIGMOD International Conference on Management of Data*. Seattle, Washington, pp. 85–93.

(Beach 1992) Beach, B. 1992. "Connecting Software Components with Declarative Glue," *Proceedings of the International Conference on Software Engineering*. Melbourne, Australia, pp. 120–37.

(Bitton et al. 1983) Bitton, D. J. DeWitt, and C. Turbyfill. 1983. "Benchmarking Database Systems: A Systematic Approach," *Proceedings of the International Conference on Very Large Data Bases*. Florence, Italy, pp. 8–19.

(Boag et al. 2002) Boag, S., Chamberlin, D., Fernandez, M. F., Florescu, D., Robie, J., Siméon, J., and M. Stefanescu, eds. 2002. "XQuery 1.0: An XML Query Language," W3C Working Draft, http://www.w3.org/TR/2002/WD-xquery-20020430/.

(Bohannon et al. 2002) Bohannon, P., Freire, J., Roy, P., and J. Siméon. "From XML Schema to Relations: A Cost-Based Approach to XML Storage," *Proceedings of the International Conference on Data Engineering*. San Jose, California.

(Böhme and Rahm 2001) Böhme, T., and E. Rahm. 2001. "XMach-1: A Benchmark for XML Data Management," *Proceedings of the German Database Conference (BTW2001)*. Oldenburg, Germany, pp. 264–73.

(Bonifati and Ceri 2000) Bonifati, A., and S. Ceri. 2000. "Comparative Analysis of Five XML Query Languages," *SIGMOD Record*, 29(1):68–79.

(Boulicaut et al. 1998) Boulicaut, J.-F., Klemettinen, M., and H. Mannila. "Querying Inductive Databases: A Case Study on the MINE RULE Operator," *Proceedings of the International Conference on Principles of Data Mining and Knowledge Discovery*. Nantes, France, pp. 194–202.

(Boulicaut et al. 1999) Boulicaut, J.-F., Klemettinen, M., and H. Mannila. 1999. "Modeling KDD Processes within the Inductive Database Framework,"

Proceedings of the International Conference on Data Warehousing and Knowledge Discovery. Florence, Italy, pp. 293–302.

(Bourret 2001a) Bourret, R. P. 2001. "XML Database Products," http://www.rpbourret.com/xml/XMLDatabaseProds.htm.

(Bourret 2001b) Bourret, R. P. 2001. "Middleware for Transferring Data between XML Documents and Relational Databases," http://www.rpbourret.com/xmldbms/index.htm.

(Bourret 2002) Bourret, R. P. 2002. "XML and Databases", http://www.rpbourret.com/xml/XMLAndDatabases.htm.

(Braden et al. 1998) Braden, B., Clark, D., Crowcroft, J., Davie, B., Deering, S., Estrin, D., Floyd, S., Jacobson, V., Minshall, G., Partridge, C., Peterson, L., Ramakrishnan, K., Shenker, S., Wroclawski, J., and L. Zhang. 1998. "Recommendations on Queue Management and Congestion Avoidance in the Internet," RFC 2309, http://xml.resource.org/public/rfc/html/rfc2309.html.

(Bradshaw 1997) Bradshaw, J. 1997. "Software Agents," *American Association for Artificial Intelligence* (Menlo Park, California: AAAI Press).

(Braga et al. 2002) Braga, D., Campi, A., Klemettinen, M., and P. L. Lanzi. "Mining Association Rules from XML Data," *Proceedings of the International Conference on Data Warehousing and Knowledge Discovery.* Aix en Provence, France.

(Bray et al. 2000) Bray, T., Paoli, J., Sperberg-McQueen, C. M., and E. Maler. 2000. "Extensible Markup Language (XML) 1.0," 2nd ed., http://www.w3.org/TR/REC-xml.

(Bressan, Dobbie et al. 2001) Bressan, S., Dobbie, G., Lacroix, Z., Lee, M. L., Li, Y. G., Nambiar, U., and B. Wadhwa. 2001. "XOO7: Applying OO7 Benchmark to XML Query Processing Tools," *Proceedings of the ACM International Conference on Information and Knowledge Management*. Atlanta, Georgia, pp. 167–74.

(Bressan, Lee et al. 2001) Bressan, S., Lee, M. L., Li, Y. G., Lacroix, Z., and U. Nambiar. 2001. "The XOO7 XML Management System Benchmark," Technical Report TR21/00, Computer Science Department, National University of Singapore.

(Bronsard et al. 1997) Bronsard, F., Bryan, D., Kozaczynski, W., Liongosari, E. S., Ning, J. Q., Ólafsson, Á., and J. W. Wetterstrand. 1997. "Toward Software Plug and Play," *Proceedings of the Symposium on Software Reusability*. Boston, Massachusetts, pp. 19–29.

(Brown and Wallnau 1996) Brown, A., and K. Wallnau. 1996. "Engineering of Component-Based Systems," *Proceedings of the IEEE International Conference on Engineering of Complex Systems*. Montreal, Canada.

(Buneman 1997) Buneman, P. 1997. "Semistructured Data," *Proceedings of the Symposium on Principles of Database Systems*. Tucson, Arizona, pp. 117–121.

(Carey et al. 1993) Carey, M. J., DeWitt, D. J., and J. F. Naughton. 1993. "The OO7 Benchmark," *Proceedings of the ACM SIGMOD International Conference on Management of Data*. Washington D.C., pp. 12–21.

(Carey et al. 1997) Carey, M. J., DeWitt, D. J., Naughton, J. F., Asgarian, M., Brown, P., Gehrke, J. E., and D. N. Shah. 1997. "The BUCKY Object-Relational Benchmark," *Proceedings of the ACM SIGMOD International Conference on Management of Data*. Tucson, Arizona, pp. 135–46.

(Carey et al. 2000) Carey, M. J., Florescu, D., Ives, Z. G., Lu, Y., Shanmugasundaram, J., Shekita, E. J., and S. N. Subramanian. 2000. "XPERANTO: Publishing Object-Relational as XML," *Informal Proceedings of the International Workshop on the Web and Databases*. Dallas, Texas. pp. 105–10.

(Celko 2000) Celko, J. 2000. *SQL for Smarties: Advanced SQL Programming* 2nd ed. (San Francisco: Morgan Kaufmann Publishers).

(Chamberlin et al. 2000) Chamberlin, D., Robie, J., and D. Florescu. 2000. "Quilt: An XML Query Language for Heterogeneous Data Sources," *Informal Proceedings of the International Workshop on the Web and Databases*. Dallas, Texas, pp. 53–62.

(Chamberlin et al. 2001) Chamberlin, D., Clark, J., Florescu, D., Robie, J., Siméon, J., and M. Stefanescu. 2001. "XQuery 1.0: An XML Query Language," W3C Working Draft, http://www.w3.org/TR/2001/WD-xquery-20010607/.

(Chang et al. 2000) Chang, B., Scardina, M., Karun, K., Kiritzov, S., Macky, I., Novoselsky, A., and N. Ramakrishnan. *ORACLE XML Handbook* (Oracle Press).

(Chen 1998) Chen, J. 1998. "A Training Approach to Develop Reusable Software Components by Combining Adaptation Algorithms," Ph.D. diss., George Mason University.

(Cheng and Xu 2000a) Cheng, J., and J. Xu. 2000. "IBM DB2 XML Extender—An End to End Solution for Storing and Retrieving XML Documents," IBM Corporation white paper, http://www-3.ibm.com/software/data/db2/extenders/xmlext/xmlextbroch.pdf.

(Cheng and Xu 2000b) ——. 2000. "XML and DB2," *Proceedings of the International Conference on Data Engineering*. San Diego, California, pp. 569–73.

(Chowdhary et al. 1997) Chowdhary, A., Nicklas, L., Setia, S., and E. White. 1997. "Supporting Dynamic Space-Sharing on Clusters of Non-dedicated Workstations," *Proceedings of Seventeenth International Conference on Distributed Computing Systems*. Baltimore, Maryland.

(Chung, Wilson, Ladner et al. 2001) Chung, M., Wilson, R., Ladner, R., Lovitt, T., Cobb, M., Abdelguerfi, M., and K. Shaw. 2001. "The Geospatial Information Distribution System (GIDS),"*Succeeding with Object Databases* (New York: John Wiley & Sons).

(Chung, Wilson, Shaw et al. 2001) Chung, M., Wilson, R., Shaw, K., Petry, F., and M. Cobb. 2001. "Querying Multiple Data Sources via an Object-Oriented Spatial Query Interface and Framework," *Journal of Visual Languages and Computing* 12(1):37–60.

(Clark and DeRose 1999) Clark, J., and S. DeRose, eds. 1999. "XML Path Language (XPath) Version 1.0," W3C Recommendation, http://www.w3.org/TR/1999/REC-xpath-19991116.

(Clark and Tennenhouse 1990) Clark, D. D., and D. L. Tennenhouse. 1990. "Architectural Considerations for a New Generation of Protocols," *Proceedings of the ACM Symposium on Communications Architectures & Protocols*. Philadelphia, Pennsylvania, pp. 200–08.

(Clements 1995) Clements, P. 1995. "From Subroutines to Subsystems: Component-Based Software Development," *American Programmer* 8(11).

(Cox et al. 2001) Cox, S., Cuthbert, A., Lake, R., and R. Martell, eds. 2001. "Geography Markup Language (GML) Implementation Specification 2.0," OGC Document #01-029, http://opengis.net/gml/01-029/GML2.html.

(Dellarocas 1997a) Dellarocas, C. 1997. "The Synthesis Environment for Component-Based Software Development," *Proceedings of the International Workshop on Software Technology and Engineering Practice*. London, U.K, pp. 434–43.

(Dellarocas 1997b) —— 1997. "Towards a Design Handbook for Integrating Software Components," *Proceedings of International Symposium on Assessment of Software Tools*. Pittsburgh, Pennsylvania, pp. 3–13.

(DeRose, Maler, Daniel 2001) DeRose, S., Maler, E., and R. Daniel. 2001. "XML Pointer Language (XPointer)", W3C Candidate Recommendation, http://www.w3.org/TR/2001/WD-xptr-20010108/.

(DeRose, Maler, Orchard 2001) DeRose, S., Maler, E., and D. Orchard. "XML Linking Language (XLink)," W3C Recommendation, http://www.w3.org/TR/2000/REC-xlink-20010627/.

(Deutsch, Fernandez, Florescu et al. 1999) Deutsch, A., Fernandez, M. F., Florescu, D., Levy, A. Y., Maier, D., and D. Suciu. 1999. "Querying XML Data," *IEEE Data Engineering Bulletin* 22(3):10–18.

(Deutsch, Fernandez, Suciu 1999) Deutsch, A., Fernandez, M., and D. Suciu. 1999. "Storing Semistructured Data with STORED," *Proceedings of the ACM SIGMOD International Conference on Management of Data*. Philadelphia, Pennsylvania, pp. 431–42.

(DeWitt 1993) DeWitt, D. J., 1993. "The Wisconsin Benchmark: Past, Present, and Future," *The Benchmark Handbook for Database and Transaction Processing Systems* 2nd ed. (San Francisco: Morgan Kaufmann Publishers).

(DII 2001) DII (Defense Information Infrastructure). 2001. "Common Operating Environment (COE) Programmer's Guide for Data Retrieval via METCAST," draft version 1.5, Space and Naval Warfare Systems Command METOC Systems Program Office. SPAWAR PMW-185. San Diego, California.

(Direen et al. 2001) Direen, H., Brandin, C., Jones, M., Hedgepeth, C., and D. Shin. 2001. "Knowledge Management through a Fully Extensible, Schema Independent, XML Database," *Proceedings of the IEEE/EMBS Annual Conference*. Istanbul, Turkey.

(DMG) DMG Group. "The Data Mining Group," http://www.dmg.org/.

(Durbin et al. 1998) Durbin, R., Eddy, S., Krogh, A., and G. Mitchison. *Biological Sequence Analysis, Probabilistic Models of Proteins and Nucleic Acids* (Cambridge: Cambridge University Press).

(Eisenberg and Melton 2001) Eisenberg, A., and J. Melton. 2001. "SQL/XML and the SQLX Informal Group of Companies," *SIGMOD Record* 30(3):105–108.

(ESRI 1998) ESRI (Environmental Systems Research Institute). 1998. "ESRI Shapefile Technical Description." ESRI white paper, http://www.esri.com/library/whitepapers/pdfs/shapefile.pdf.

(Fellhauer 2001) Fellhauer, T. 2001. "Managing XML Documents with Directory Servers and Other Database Management Systems." Diploma thesis, Karlsruhe University of Applied Sciences.

(Fernandez et al. 2000) Fernandez, M., Siméon, J., and P. Wadler. 2000. "XML Query Languages: Experiences and Exemplars," http://www-db.research.bell-labs.com/user/simeon/xquery.html.

(Fiebig and Moerkotte 2000) Fiebig, T., and G. Moerkotte. 2000. "Evaluating Queries on Structure with eXtended Access Support Relations," *Informal Proceedings of the International Workshop on the Web and Databases*. Dallas, Texas, pp. 41–46.

(Florescu and Kossmann 1999a) Florescu, D., and D. Kossmann. 1999. "Storing and Querying XML Data Using an RDBMS," *IEEE Data Engineering Bulletin* 22(3):27–34.

(Florescu and Kossmann 1999b) ——. 1999. "A Performance Evaluation of Alternative Mapping Schemes for Storing XML Data in a Relational Database," Technical Report no. 3680, INRIA, Le Chesnay Cedex, France.

(Garlan et al. 1995) Garlan, D., Allen, R., and J. Ockerbloom. 1995. "Architectural Mismatch or Why It's Hard to Build Systems Out of Parts," *Proceedings of the International Conference on Software Engineering*. Seattle, Washington, pp. 179–85.

(Goland et al. 1999) Goland, Y., Whitehead, E., Faizi, A., Carter, S., and D. Jensen. 1999. "HTTP Extensions for Distributed Authoring—WebDAV," Network Working Group RFC no. 2518, http://asg.Web.cmu.edu/rfc/rfc2518.html.

(Goldman et al. 1999) Goldman, R., McHugh, J., and J. Widom. 1999. "From Semistructured Data to XML: Migrating to the Lore Data Model and Query Language," *Informal Proceedings of the International Workshop on the Web and Databases*. Philadelphia, Pennsylvania, pp. 25–30.

(Gray 1993) Gray, J., ed., "The Benchmark Handbook for Database and Transaction Processing Systems," 2nd ed. (San Francisco: Morgan Kaufmann Publishers).

(Han et al. 1996) Han, J., Fu, Y., Kopersky, K., Wang, W., and O. Zaïane. 1996. "DMQL: A Data Mining Query Language for Relational Databases," *Proceedings of the ACM SIGMOD International Workshop on Data Mining and Knowledge Discovery*. Montreal, Canada.

(Han et al. 2000) Han, J., Pei, J., and Y. Yin. 2000. "Mining Frequent Patterns without Candidate Generation," *Proceedings of the ACM SIGMOD International Conference on Management of Data*. Dallas, Texas, pp. 1–12.

(Harmon 2002) Harmon, P. 2002. " An OMG Update for Managers: XML and MDA (May '02), OT Land, available at http://www.otland.com.

(Hofmeister et al. 1993) Hofmeister, C., White, E., and J. Purtilo. 1993. "SURGEON: A Packager for Dynamically Reconfigurable Distributed Applications," *IEE Software Engineering Journal* 8(2):95–101.

(Howes et al. 1995) Howes, T., Yeong, W., and S. Kille. "Lightweight Directory Access Protocol," The Internet Society, RFC 1770.

(Huitema 1996) Huitema, C. 1996. *IPv6: The New Internet Protocol.* (Upper Saddle River, New Jersey: Prentice Hall).

(Hutchison et al. 1994) Hutchison, D., Coulson, G., Campbell, A., and G. S. Blair. 1994. "Quality of Service Management in Distributed Systems," *Network and Distributed Systems Management* (Reading, Massachusetts: Addison-Wesley).

(Imielinski and Mannila 1996) Imielinski, T., and H. Mannila. 1996. "A Database Perspective on Knowledge Discovery," *Communications of the ACM* 39(11):58–64.

(Imielinski and Virmani 1998) Imielinski, T., and A. Virmani. 1998. "Association Rules . . . and What's Next? Towards Second Generation Data Mining Systems," *Proceedings of the International Conference on Advances in Databases and Information Systems*. Poznan, Poland, pp. 6–15.

(Imielinski et al. 1996) Imielinski, T., Virmani, A., and A. Abdulghani. 1996. "DataMine: Application Programming Interface and Query Language for Database Mining," *Proceedings of the International Conference on Knowledge Discovery and Data Mining*. Portland, Oregon, pp. 256–62.

(Jaber, Nada et al. 1998) Jaber, K., Nada, N., and D. Rine. 1998. "Towards the Design and Integration of Multi-Use Components," *Proceedings of the International Conference on Information Systems Analysis and Synthesis*. Orlando, Florida.

(Jaber, Rine et al. 1998) Jaber, K., Rine, D., and N. Nada. 1998. "Using Adapters at Variation Points in Component-Based Software Development: A Case Study," *Proceedings of the European Reuse Workshop*. Madrid, Spain.

(Kamber et al. 1997) Kamber, M., Winstone, L., Gon, W., and J. Han. 1997. "Generalization and Decision Tree Induction: Efficient Classification in Data Mining," *Proceedings of the International Conference on Research Issues in Data Engineering*. Birmingham, U.K., pp. 111–21.

(Kanne and Moerkotte 1999) Kanne, C.-C., and G. Moerkotte. 1999. "Efficient Storage of XML Data," Technical Report no. 8, Faculty of Mathematics and Informatics, University of Mannheim, Germany.

(Kanne and Moerkotte 2000) ——. 2000. "Efficient Storage of XML Data," *Proceedings of the International Conference on Data Engineering*. San Diego, California. p. 198.

(Kappel et al. 2000) Kappel, G., Kapsammer, E., Rausch-Schott, S., and W. Retschitzegger. 2000. "X-Ray—Towards Integrating XML and Relational Database Systems," *Proceedings of the International Conference on Conceptual Modeling*. Salt Lake City, Utah, pp. 339–53.

(Kappel et al. 2001) Kappel, G., Kapsammer, E., and W. Retschitzegger. "XML and Relational Database Systems—A Comparison of Concepts," *International Conference on Internet Computing*. Las Vegas, Nevada.

(Klettke and Meyer 2000) Klettke, M., and H. Meyer. 2000. "XML and Object-Relational Database Systems—Enhancing Structural Mappings Based on Statistics," *Informal Proceedings of the International Workshop on the Web and Databases*. Dallas, Texas. pp. 63–68.

(Lanzi and Psaila 1999) Lanzi, P. L., and G. Psaila. 1999. "A Relational Database Mining Framework with Classification and Discretization," *Proceedings of SEBD 1999*. Como, Italy, pp. 101–15.

(Lazar 1997) Lazar, A. A., "Programming Telecommunication Networks," Keynote address at the International Workshop on Quality of Service, Columbia University, New York.

(Lee and Chu 2000) Lee, D., and W. Chu. "Constraints—Preserving Transformation from XML Document Type Definition to Relational Schema," *Proceedings of the International Conference on Conceptual Modeling*. Salt Lake City, Utah.

(Lee et al. 1996) Lee, Y. K., Yoo, S. J., Yoon, K., and P. B. Berra. 1996. "Index Structures for Structured Documents," *Proceedings of the ACM International Conference on Digital Libraries*. Bethesda, Maryland. pp. 91–99.

(Li and Moon 2001) Li, Q., and B. Moon. 2001. "Indexing and Querying XML Data for Regular Path Expressions," *Proceedings of the International Conference on Very Large Data Bases*. Rome, Italy, pp. 361–70.

(Li et al. 2001) Li, W., Han, J., and J. Pei. 2001. "CMAR: Accurate and Efficient Classification Based on Multiple Class-Association Rules," *Proceedings of the IEEE International Conference on Data Mining*. San Jose, California, pp. 369–76.

(Luckham et al. 1995) Luckham, D., Kenney, J., Augustin, L., Vera, J., Bryan, D., and W. Mann. 1995. "Specification and Analysis of System Architecture Using Rapide," *IEEE Transactions on Software Engineering* 21(4):336–55.

(Ludäscher et al. 1999) Ludäscher, B., Papakonstantinou, Y., Velikhov, P., and V. Vianu. 1999. "View Definition and DTD Inference for XML," *Proceedings of the Post ICDT Workshop on Query Processing for Semistructured Data and Non-Standard Data Formats*. Jerusalem.

(Maier 1998) Maier, D. 1998. "Database Desiderata for an XML Query Language," http://www.w3.org/ TandS/QL/QL98/pp/maier.html.

(Mani et al. 2001) Mani, M., Lee, D., and R. Muntz. 2001. "Semantic Data Modeling using XML Schema," *Proceedings of the International Conference on Conceptual Modeling*. Yokohama, Japan.

(Manolescu et al. 2000) Manolescu, I., Florescu, D., Kossmann, D., Xhumari, F., and D. Olteanu. 2000. "Agora: Living with XML and Relational," *Proceedings of the International Conference on Very Large Data Bases*. Cairo, Egypt, pp. 623–26.

(Manolescu et al. 2001) Manolescu, I., Florescu, D., and D. Kossmann. 2001. "Pushing XML Queries inside Relational Databases," Technical Report no. 4112, INRIA, Le Chesnay Cedex, France.

(Marian et al. 2000) Marian, A., Abiteboul, S., and L. Mignet. 2000. "Change-Centric Management of Versions in an XML Warehouse," *Journées Bases de Données Avancées*. Blois, France, pp. 281–303.

(Marrón and Lausen 2001) Marrón, P., and G. Lausen. "On Processing XML in LDAP," *Proceedings of the International Conference on Very Large Data Bases*. Rome, Italy, pp. 601–10.

(McHugh and Widom 1999) McHugh, J., and J. Widom. 1999. "Query Optimization for XML," *Proceedings of the International Conference on Very Large Data Bases*. Edinburgh, Scotland, pp. 315–26.

(McHugh et al. 1997) McHugh, J., Abiteboul, S., Goldman, R., Quass, D., and J. Widom. 1997. "Lore: A Database Management System for Semistructured Data," *SIGMOD Record* 26(3):54–66.

(Mehta et al. 1996) Mehta, M., Agrawal, R., and J. Rissanen. 1996. "SLIQ: A Fast Scalable Classifier for Data Mining," *Proceedings of the International Conference on Extending Database Technology*. Avignon, France, pp. 18–32.

(Melton 2002) Melton, J., ed. 2002. "Database Languages—SQL—Part 14: XML-Related Specifications (SQL/XML)—Final Committee Draft, H2-2002-063, WG3:ICN-011," ISO/IEC JTC 1/SC 32/WG 3, ftp://sqlstandards.org/SC32/ WG3/Progression_Documents/FCD/4FCD1-14–XML-2002-03.pdf.

(Meo et al. 1996) Meo, R., Psaila, G., and S. Ceri. 1996. "A New SQL-like Operator for Mining Association Rules," *Proceedings of the International Conference on Very Large Data Bases*. Mumbai, India, pp. 122–33.

(Meo et al. 1998a) Meo, R., Psaila, G., and S. Ceri. 1998. "An Extension to SQL for Mining Association Rules," *Journal of Data Mining and Knowledge Discovery* 2(2):195–224.

(Meo et al. 1998b) ——. 1998. "A Tightly-Coupled Architecture for Data Mining," *Proceedings of the International Conference on Data Engineering*. Orlando, Florida, pp. 316–23.

(Meyer 1992) Meyer, B. 1992. "Applying 'Design by Contract,'" *IEEE Computer* 25(10):40–51.

(Michigan Benchmark) The Michigan Benchmark Team. "The Michigan Benchmark Homepage," http://www.eecs.umich.edu/db/mbench.

(Mignet et al. 2000) Mignet, L, Abiteboul, S. Ailleret, S., Amann, B., Marian, A., and M. Preda. 2000. "Acquiring XML Pages for a WebHouse," *Journées Bases de Données Avancées*. Blois, France, pp. 241–63.

(Mowbray and Ruh 1997) Mowbray, T., and W. Ruh. 1997. *Inside CORBA: Distributed Object Standards and Application* (Reading, Massachusetts: Addison-Wesley).

(Nada and Rine 1998) Nada, N., and D. Rine. 1998. "Component Management Infrastructure: A Component-Based Software Reuse Reference Model M," *Proceedings of the ICSE98 International Workshop on Component-Based Software Engineering*. Kyoto, Japan.

(Nada et al. 1998) Nada, N., Rine, D., and K. Jaber. 1998. "Towards Components-Based Software Development," *Proceedings of the European Reuse Workshop*. Madrid, Spain.

(Nahrstedt and Smith 1996) Nahrstedt, K., and J. Smith. 1996. "Design, Implementation and Experiences of the OMEGA End-Point Architecture," *IEEE Journal on Selected Areas in Communications* 14(7):1263–79.

(Needleman and Wunsch 1970) Needleman, S. B., and C. D. Wunsch. 1970. "A General Method Applicable to the Search for Similarities in the Amino Acid Sequence of Two Proteins," *Journal of Molecular Biology* 48:443–53.

(NIMA 1996) NIMA (National Imagery and Mapping Agency). 1996. "Department of Defense Interface Standard for Vector Product Format." MIL-STD-2407, http://www.nima.mil/publications/specs/ .

(NSF 1997) NSF (National Science Foundation). 1997. Workshop on Priorities in Wireless and Mobile Communications and Networking. Airlie House, Virginia.

(O'Neil 1997) O'Neil, P. E. 1997. "Database Performance Measurement," *Computer Science and Engineering Handbook* (Boca Raton, Florida: CRC Press).

(OLAP 1998) OLAP Council. 1998. "APB-1 OLAP Benchmark," release II, http://www.olapcouncil.org/research/bmarkly.htm.

(OMG 1999) OMG (Object Management Group). 1999. CORBA 3.0 specification, http://www.omg.org.

(Oreizy and Taylor 1998) Oreizy, P., and R. Taylor. 1998. "On the Role of Software Architectures in Runtime System Reconfiguration," *Proceedings of the International Conference on Configurable Distributed Systems (ICCDS 4)*. Annapolis, Maryland.

(Polatschek 2000) Polatschek, K. 2000. "XML and LDAP for Online Publications," Presentation at the Opening of the XML Competence Centre at GMD-IPSI, Darmstadt.

(Prieto-diaz and Neighbors 1986) Prieto-diaz, R., and J. Neighbors. 1986. "Module Interconnection Languages," *The Journal of Systems and Software* 6:307–34.

(Psaila 2001) Psaila, G. 2001. "Enhancing the KDD Process in the Relational Database Mining Framework by Quantitative Evaluation of Association Rules," *Knowledge Discovery for Business Information Systems* (Norwell, Massachusetts: Kluwer Publishers).

(Pullen 1998) Pullen, J. M. 1998. "Synchronous Distance Education and the Internet," *Internet Society Annual Conference*. Geneva, Switzerland.

(Purtilo 1991) Purtilo, J. 1991. "The Polylith Software Bus," Technical Report no. TR-2469. University of Maryland.

(Quinlan 1993) Quinlan, J. R. 1993. *C4.5: Programs for Machine Learning* (San Francisco: Morgan Kaufmann Publishers).

(Rechenmann 2000) Rechenmann, F. 2000. "From Data to Knowledge," *Bioinformatics* 16 (5):411–16.

(Reynaud et al. 2001) Reynaud, C., Sirot, J. P., and D. Vodislav. 2001. "Semantic Integration of XML Heterogeneous Data Sources," *Proceedings of the International Database Engineering and Applications Symposium*. Grenoble, France, pp. 199–208.

(Rine 1997) Rine, D. 1997. "Supporting Reuse with Object Technology," *IEEE Computer* 30(10):43–45.

(Rine 1998) ——. 1998. "Development of Soft Computing Application: Using the Software Reuse Function Framework," *Journal of Soft Computing*.

(Rine and Ahmed 1997) Rine, D., and M. Ahmed. 1997. "A Reusable Intelligent Autopilot: A Framework," *International Journal of Applied Software Technology*.

(Rine and Chen 1996) Rine, D., and J. Chen. 1996. "Testing Trainable Software Components by Combining Genetic Algorithms and Backpropagation Algorithms," *Proceedings of the Conference on Artificial Neural Networks in Engineering*. St. Louis, Missouri.

(Rine and Chen 1998) Rine, D., and J. Chen. 1998. "Training Reusable Software Components by Combining Adaptation Algorithms," *International Journal of Applied Software Technology*.

(Rine and Retnadhas 1980) Rine, D., and C. Retnadhas. 1980. "Design of a Ring-Based Local Area Network for Microcomputers: Improved Architecture using Interface Node Adapters," *Proceedings of the Conference on Local Computer Networks*. Minneapolis, Minnesota.

(Rine and Sonnemann 1996) Rine, D. and R. Sonnemann. 1996. "Investments in Reusable Software: A Study of Software Reuse Investment Success Factors," *Measuring Information Technology Investment Payoff: Contemporary Approaches* (Hershey, Pennsylvania: Idea Group).

(Rine and Sonnemann 1998) ——. 1998. "Investments in Reusable Software. A Study of Software Reuse Investment Success Factors," *The Journal of Systems and Software* 41:17–32.

(Robie et al. 1998) Robie, J., Lapp, J., and D. Schach. 1998. "XML Query Language (XQL)", QL'98, The Query Languages Workshop, Boston, Massachusetts, http://www.w3.org/TandS/QL/QL98/.

(Rolia and Sevcik 1995) Rolia, J. A., and K. C. Sevcik. 1995. "The Method of Layers," *IEEE Transactions on Software Engineering* 21(8):689–99.

(Runapongsa and Patel 2002) Runapongsa, K., and J. Patel. "Storing and Querying XML Data in Object-Relational DBMSs," *EDBT 2002 Workshop on XML-Based Data Management*, Prague, Czech Republic.

(Runapongsa et al. 2002) Runapongsa, K., Patel, J., Jagadish, H. V., and S. Al-Khalifa. 2002. "The Michigan Benchmark: Towards XML Query Performance Diagnostics," http://www.eecs.umich.edu/db/mbench/.

(Rys 2001) Rys, M. 2001. "Bringing the Internet to Your Database: Using SQL Server 2000 and XML to Build Loosely-Coupled Systems," *Proceedings of the International Conference on Data Engineering*. Heidelberg, Germany, pp. 465–72.

(Sahuguet 2001) Sahuguet, A. 2001. "Kweelt: More than just 'yet another framework to query XML!'" SIGMOD Demonstration Session, Santa Barbara, California.

(Sahuguet et al. 2000) Sahuguet, A., Dupont, L., and T. L. Nguyen. 2000. "Querying XML in the New Millennium," http://cheops.cis.upenn.edu/Kweelt/.

(Salton and McGill 1983) Salton, G., and M. J. McGill. 1983. *Introduction to Modern Information Retrieval* (Berkeley, California: McGraw-Hill).

(Schmidt et al. 1999) Schmidt, D., Levin, D., and C. Cleeland. 1999. "Architectures and Patterns for Developing High-Performance, Real-time ORB Endsystems," *Advances in Computers* (San Diego, California: Academic Press).

(Schmidt et al. 2000) Schmidt, A., Kersten, M. L., Windhouwer, M., and F. Waas. 2000. "Efficient Relational Storage and Retrieval of XML Documents," *Informal*

Proceedings of the International Workshop on the Web and Databases. Dallas, Texas, pp. 47–52.

(Schmidt, Waas, Kersten, Florescu, Carey et al. 2001) Schmidt, A., Waas, F., Kersten, M., Florescu, D., Carey, M., Manolescu, I., and R. Busse. 2001. "Why and How to Benchmark XML Databases," *SIGMOD Record* 30(3).

(Schmidt, Waas, Kersten, Florescu, Manolescu et al. 2001) Schmidt, A. R., Waas, F., Kersten, M. L., Florescu, D., Manolescu, I., Carey, M. J., and R. Busse. 2001."The XML Benchmark Project", Technical Report INS-R0103, CWI, Amsterdam, The Netherlands.

(Schöning and Wäsch 2000) Schöning, H., and J. Wäsch. 2000. "Tamino—An Internet Database System," *Proceedings of the International Conference on Extending Database Technology*. Konstanz, Germany, pp. 383–87.

(Sha et al. 1999) Sha, F., Gardarin, G., and L. Nemirovski. 1999. "Managing Semistructured Data in Object-Relational DBMS," *Journées Bases de Données Avancées*. Bordeaux, France, pp. 101–15.

(Shanmugasundaram et al. 1999) Shanmugasundaram, J., Tufte, K., Zhang, C., He, G., DeWitt, D. J., and J. F. Naughton. 1999. "Relational Databases for Querying XML Documents: Limitations and Opportunities," *Proceedings of the International Conference on Very Large Data Bases*. Edinburgh, Scotland. pp. 302–14.

(Shanmugasundaram et al. 2000) Shanmugasundaram, J., Shekita, E., Barr, R., Carey, M., Lindsay, B., Pirahesh, H., and B. Reinwald. 2000. "Efficiently Publishing Relational Data as XML Documents," *Proceedings of the International Conference on Very Large Data Bases*. Cairo, Egypt, pp. 65–76.

(Shanmugasundaram et al. 2001) Shanmugasundaram, J., Kiernan, J., Shekita, E., Fan C., and J. Funderburk. 2001. "Querying XML Views of Relational Data," *Proceedings of the International Conference on Very Large Data Bases*. Rome, Italy, pp. 261–70.

(Shaw and Garlan 1996) Shaw, M., and D. Garlan. 1996. *Software Architecture*. (Upper Saddle River, New Jersey: Prentice-Hall).

(Shin et al. 1998) Shin, D., Jang, H., and H. Jin. 1998. "BUS: An Effective Indexing and Retrieval Scheme in Structured Documents," *Proceedings of the ACM International Conference on Digital Libraries*. Pittsburgh, Pennsylvania, pp. 235–43.

(Shinagawa et al. 2000) Shinagawa, N., Kitagawa, H., and Y. Ishikawa. 2000. "X2QL: An eXtensible XML Query Language Supporting User-Defined Foreign Functions," *Proceedings of Current Issues in Databases and Information Systems—East European Conference on Advances in Databases and Information Systems*. Prague, Czech Republic, pp. 251–64.

(Simon 1996) Simon, R. 1996. "An Integrated Communication Architecture for Distributed Multimedia Applications," Ph.D. diss., University of Pittsburgh.

(Simon 1997) Simon, R. 1997. "Peer-to-Peer Communication Protocols for Interactive Multimedia Applications," *Proceedings of the Pacific Conference on Distributed Multimedia Systems*. Vancouver, Canada, pp. 110–17.

(Simon 2001) Simon, H. 2001. "XML: Data about Data," *Journal on Modern Drug Discovery*. 4(3):69–70.

(Simon and Sood 1997) Simon, R., and A. Sood. 1997. "Load-Balanced Routing for Collaborative Multimedia Communication," *Proceedings of IEEE High Performance Distributed Systems*. Portland, Oregon, pp. 81–91.

(Simon and Znati 2000) Simon, R., and T. Znati. 2000. "Performance Analysis of Routing and Channel Establishment Procedures for Multimedia Communication," *International Journal of Parallel and Distributed Systems and Networks* 3(2):82–94.

(Simon, Krieger et al. 1995) Simon, R., Krieger, D., Znati, T., Lofink, R., and R. Sclabassi. 1995. "MultiMedia MedNet: A Medical Diagnosis and Consultation System," *IEEE Computer* 28(5):65–73.

(Simon, Znati et al. 1995) Simon, R., Znati, T., and R. Sclabassi. 1995. "DIPCS: An Interprocess Communication Architecture for Distributed Multimedia Systems," *Journal of Multimedia Tools and Applications* 1(3):263–93.

(Smith and Waterman 1981) Smith, T. F., and M. S. Waterman. 1981. "Identification of Common Molecular Subsequences," *Journal of Molecular Biology* 147:195–97.

(Srikant and Agrawal 1996) Srikant, R., and R. Agrawal. 1996. "Mining Sequential Patterns: Generalizations and Performance Improvements," *Proceedings of the International Conference on Extending Database Technology*. Avignon, France, pp. 3–17.

(Srinivasan and Reynolds 1998) Srinivasan, S., and P. Reynolds. 1998. "Communications, Data Distribution and Other Goodies in the HLA Peformance Model," *Proceedings of HLA Workshop*. Atlanta, Georgia.

(Srivastava et al. 2002) Srivastava, D., Al-Khalifa, S., Jagadish, H. V., Koudas, N., Patel, J. M., and Y. Wu. 2002. "Structural Joins: A Primitive for Efficient XML Query Pattern Matching," *Proceedings of the International Conference on Data Engineering*. San Jose, California.

(Stonebraker et al. 1993) Stonebraker, M., Frew, J., Gardels, K., and J. Meredith. 1993. "The SEQUOIA 2000 Storage Benchmark," *Proceedings of the ACM SIGMOD International Conference on Management of Data*. Washington, D.C., pp. 2–11.

(Tian et al. 2000) Tian, F., DeWitt, D. J., Chen, J., and C. Zhang. 2000. "The Design and Performance Evaluation of Alternative XML Storage Strategies," Report, Computer Sciences Department, University of Wisconsin.

(Trevor et al. 1994) Trevor, J., Rodden, T., and J. Mariani. 1994. "The Use of Adapters to Support Cooperative Sharing," *Proceedings of the Conference on Computer Supported Cooperative Work*. Chapel Hill, North Carolina, pp. 219–30.

(Turbyfill et al. 1989) Turbyfill, C., Orji, C., and D. Bitton. 1989. "AS3AP: A Comparative Relational Database Benchmark," *Proceedings of IEEE COMPCON*.

(Unicode Consortium 2000) The Unicode Consortium. 2000. *The Unicode Standard, Version 3.0* (Boston: Addison-Wesley).

(W3C 1998a) WWW Consortium. 1998. "Document Object Model 1.0," http://www.w3.org/REC-DOM-Level-1-19981001.

(W3C 1998b) WWW Consortium. 1998. "XML 1.0 Recommendation," http://www.w3.org/TR/1998/ REC-xml-19980210.

(Walmsley 2002) Walmsley, P. 2002. *Definitive XML Schema* (Upper Saddle River, New Jersey: Prentice-Hall PTR).

(Wertz 1997) Wertz, J. R., ed. 1997. *Spacecraft Attitude Determination and Control* (Dordrecht, The Netherlands: Kluwer Publishers).

(White 1995) White, E. 1995. "Control Integration in Heterogeneous Distributed Systems," Ph.D. diss., University of Maryland.

(White and Purtilo 1992) White, E., and J. Purtilo. 1992. "Integrating the Heterogeneous Control Properties of Software Modules," *Proceedings of the ACM SIGSOFT Symposium on Software Development Environments*. pp. 99–108.

(Williams et al. 2001) Williams, K. ed., Brundage, M., Dengler, P., Gabriel, J., Hoskinson, A., Kay, M., Maxwell, T., Ochoa, M., Papa, J., and M. Vanmane. 2001. *Professional XML Databases* (Chicago: Wrox Press).

(Yellin and Strom 1997) Yellin, D., and R. Strom. 1997. "Protocol Specifications and Component Adapters," *ACM Transactions on Programming Languages and Systems* 19(2):292–333.

(Yoshikawa et al. 2001) Yoshikawa, M., Amagasa, T., Shimura, T., and S. Uemura. 2001. "XRel: A Path-Based Approach to Storage and Retrieval of XML Documents Using Relational Databases," *ACM Transactions on Internet Technology* 1(1):110–41.

(Zhang 1996) Zhang, H. 1996. "Service Disciplines for Guaranteed Performance Service in Packet-Switching Networks," *Proceedings of the IEEE* 83(10).

(Zhang et al. 2000) Zhang, C., Luo, Q., DeWitt, D., Naughton, J., and F. Tian. 2000. "On the Use of a Relational Database Management System for XML," Report, Department of Computer Sciences, University of Wisconsin.

(Zhang et al. 2001) Zhang, C., Naughton, J. F., DeWitt, D. J., Luo, Q., and G. M. Lohman. 2001. "On Supporting Containment Queries in Relational Database Management Systems," *Proceedings of the ACM SIGMOD International Conference on Management of Data*. Santa Barbara, California, pp. 425–36.

Contributors

Editors

Akmal B. Chaudhri has been working with objects and databases for over ten years. He has been a regular presenter on Java, XML, and databases at a number of international conferences. He has edited the books *Object Databases in Practice* (Prentice-Hall, 1998), *Succeeding with Object Databases* (John Wiley & Sons, 2000), and *Java and Databases* (Hermes Penton Science, 2002). At present, he works for IBM developerWorks where he is editor for the Special Projects Zone. He has previously worked for Reuters, Logica, Computer Associates, and Informix Software. He holds a B.S. in computing and information systems, M.S. in business systems analysis and design, and a Ph.D. in computer science.

Awais Rashid has worked in the area of objects and databases for six years. His principal research interests are in improving the customizability, extensibility, and evolvability of such systems and their use to support new software technologies such as XML and aspect-oriented development. He has published actively on these topics and has regularly served on the program and organizing committees of a number of relevant international events. Recently he edited *IEE Proceedings—Software* special issue on *Aspect-Oriented and Component-Based Software Engineering* and is currently coediting the British Computer Society's *Computer Journal* special section on *Aspect-Oriented Programming and Separation of Crosscutting Concerns.*

Presently he is a faculty member at Lancaster University, U.K., where he teaches courses on database technologies. Previously he has worked as a postgraduate researcher at Lancaster and at Xerox Research Centre Europe, Cambridge. He holds a B.S. in electronics engineering, an M.S. in software engineering methods, and a Ph.D. in computer science.

Roberto Zicari, born 1955 in Milano, is full professor of computer science at the Johann Wolfgang Goethe University in Frankfurt, Germany. Previously he was associate professor at Politecnico di Milano, Italy; visiting scientist at IBM Almaden Research Center, U.S. and University of California at Berkeley, U.S.; visiting professor at EPFL in Lausanne, Switzerland and the National University of Mexico City, Mexico. Roberto Zicari is an internationally recognized expert in the field of object technology, in particular in object databases and in middleware. He has consulted and lectured in Europe, the U.S., and Japan. He is a coeditor of the books *Succeeding with Object Databases* (John Wiley & Sons, 2000), *Advanced Database Systems* (Morgan Kaufmann, 1997), and *Conceptual Modeling, Databases and Case* (John Wiley & Sons, 1992). Roberto Zicari holds a doctor of engineering degree from Politecnico di Milano.

Chapter 1: Information Modeling with XML

Chris Brandin is chief technology officer of NeoCore, Inc. Brandin is the inventor and chief architect of NeoCore's technology and products and a pioneer in parallel processing computing. Before NeoCore, he was the CEO of Business Operating Systems, Inc., where he developed computer systems used by the New York Stock Exchange and other exchanges. He also designed control integrated circuits for PC I/O bus management, music synthesizer hardware and software, and other products marketed by Symantec, NEC, Alcatel, and others. Brandin has consulted on patent issues for Motorola, AT&T, Bell Labs, Belcore, Wang, IBM, Intel, and others.

Chapter 2: Tamino—Software AG's Native XML Server

Harald Schöning has been active in database research and development for 15 years. At present, he works as a Tamino architect for Software AG, a German company that has produced database systems for more than 30 years. In addition, he regularly presents seminars on XML and databases. He also serves on the board of the database systems group of the German Informatics Society (GI) and on numerous conference and workshop program committees. He holds a diploma and a doctorate in computer science.

Chapter 3: eXist Native XML Database

Wolfgang M. Meier founded eXist as an Open Source project in January 2001. He has been working with SGML/XML and databases for several years. After graduating from Frankfurt University in 1999 with a degree in sociology, he became a member of the TELOS working group at Darmstadt University of Technology, where he is involved with various projects in the field of digital libraries and XML-based information systems.

Chapter 4: Embedded XML Databases

John Merrells is an expert in the fields of object-oriented software and application-specific database systems. He currently leads the Berkeley DB XML project at Sleepycat Software. Prior to Sleepycat, he was principal architect of a business service, helping companies to optimize their order-to-cash cycle time. He was responsible for defining the architectural platform for the business services and led a team building an XML database for financial document reconciliation. Previously John worked on three major releases of the LDAP Directory Server at Netscape and held a lead architectural role. He led the IETF LDUP Working Group defining the architecture for interoperable directory replication and has filed a number of patent applications in the area of directory architecture. He continues his work editing the Association of C and C++ Users, C++ Special Interest Group magazine, *Overload*. John received his formal education at Hertfordshire University and earned a B.S. in computer science with honors.

Michael Olson has been working in database technology for 17 years. He was a key contributor to the POSTGRES research project at the University of California at Berkeley and joined Illustra Information Technologies, the company formed to commercialize that research, in 1993. Illustra was the first company to offer a commercial object-relational database, based on the academic POSTGRES system. After the acquisition of Illustra by Informix, Michael managed the company's DataBlade development efforts to produce extensions to the core Informix database engine for commercial use. Michael was an early contributor to the Berkeley DB project. He is currently president and CEO of Sleepycat Software.

Chapter 5: IBM XML-Enabled Data Management Product Architecture and Technology

Shawn Benham has been part of IBM database, middleware, and business intelligence software development in the Silicon Valley Lab for 8 years. Previously, he worked at IBM's CAD/CAM enterprise software development lab in Santa Monica. Currently he is the pervasive and integrated user technology department manager. Shawn holds a B.A. degree in English from UCLA.

Chapter 6: Supporting XML in Oracle9i

Dr. Uwe Hohenstein is principal research scientist at Siemens Corporate Technology in Munich, Germany. His responsibility is to coach the efficient and effective use of database technologies in modern software architectures. He has gained experience with relational, object-oriented, object-relational, and XML database systems over the past 15 years. Based on this knowledge, he has published nearly 50 papers in the field of formal semantics of query languages, benchmarking databases, data migration, and federated database systems at international conferences. He has also coauthored three books on database semantics, evaluating object-oriented database systems, and the object-relational features of Oracle9i.

Chapter 7: XML Support in Microsoft SQL Server 2000

After finishing his Ph.D. at the Swiss Federal Institute of Technology in Zurich (ETHZ) in the area of database systems, Michael Rys went to Stanford University for a postdoc, where he worked on semi-structured databases and distributed heterogeneous information integration. In late 1998, he joined Microsoft Corporation in Redmond where he is now a program manager for SQL Server's XML technologies. He has been a regular presenter and panelist on XML and databases. Michael has previously worked for I. P. Sharp, ETHZ, and Reuters and is also a member of the W3C XML Query Language Working Group and a member of ACM and IEEE.

Chapter 8: A Generic Architecture for Storing XML Documents in a Relational Database

Richard Edwards graduated with a Ph.D. from Leeds University in 1995 and spent 4 years in industry as a software developer, specializing in relational databases, GUI development, OLAP, and data warehousing. In 1999 he returned to academia, taking a post in the School of Education at the University of Wales, Bangor (UWB), where he codeveloped the Electronic Village—a DfES-funded groupware system for U.K. and French schools—which showcased at the BBC's Tomorrow's World Live event in 2000. He now works as a research officer in the Software Engineering & Systems Integration (SESI) research group of the School of Informatics at UWB. His principal research interests include XML databases (on which subject he has presented to the British Computer Society, the British Library, and at a number of conferences), XML transformation using XSLT and the semantic mapping metalanguage SML, and supporting online communities with next-generation groupware. He is cofounder and a director of Semantise Ltd., an ICT consultancy business based in North Wales.

Chapter 9: An Object-Relational Approach to Building a High-Performance XML Repository

Paul G. Brown works for IBM Research in Almaden, California. Before that he worked for Informix Software. He has worked on databases and DBMS-related technologies for about 10 years. He is responsible for eliminating bugs in three (trying for four) DBMS engines. He is the author of *Object-Relational Database Development: A Plumber's Guide* (Prentice-Hall, 2001), the coauthor of *Object-Relational DBMS: Tracking the Next Great Wave* (Morgan Kaufmann Publishers, 1999), and has been a contributor to several other books on database topics. He remains puzzled by XML.

Chapter 10: Knowledge Management in Bioinformatics

Dr. Direen is a senior consulting engineer with NeoCore, Inc., where he is involved in finite field and statistical analysis of the company's patented Digital Pattern Processing (DPP) algorithms and has several patents pending from this work. He is responsible for the design and coding of DPP algorithms used in the database and for the development of a BLAST plug-in module to aid in the search for DNA and protein sequences stored in NeoCore XMS. Dr. Direen has over 20 years of diverse design and development experience including control systems design, embedded hardware and software design, high-power RF and microwave amplifier design, analog signal-processing design and mixed signal semi-custom IC design for use in MRI systems, semiconductor processing equipment, and other systems. Dr. Direen holds a B.S. in electrical engineering from the University of California at Irvine and a Ph.D. in electrical engineering from the University of Colorado for his work in neural network and wavelet-based adaptive control systems.

Mark S. Jones has worked for NeoCore, Inc., since February 2001. During this time Mr. Jones has assisted with NeoCore's positioning in the life sciences sector. He came to NeoCore with a background in teaching biological sciences and has extensive academic experience with graduate work in finance and environmental studies. Mr. Jones obtained his B.A. in biology and chemistry from the University of

Colorado at Colorado Springs. He has wide-ranging experience in curriculum and standards development in education.

Chapter 11: Case Studies of XML Used with IBM DB2 Universal Database

Lee Anne Kowalski is a user assistance architect in the data management organization at IBM Silicon Valley Lab. Her activities include designing and implementing pervasive user assistance and information delivery mechanisms for IBM's DB2 Universal Database and related products. She has presented on user experience and user assistance methodologies at a number of national conferences. Lee Anne joined IBM in 1992. Over the past 10 years, she has developed online information systems in both application development and database products. Lee Anne holds a Ph.D. in physics from Stanford University.

Chapter 12: The Design and Implementation of an Engineering Data Management System Using XML and J2EE

Karen Eglin is a technical engineering lead with Northrop Grumman Information Technology. She is tasked with designing and developing an Enterprise Java Bean–based Open Application Interface (OAI) for the Joint Engineering Data Management Information and Control System (JEDMICS) repository, made up of engineering drawings stored on magnetic disks and drawing metadata stored in an Oracle database. Ms. Eglin has experience in all phases of system life cycle development including designing and developing client- and server-side applications using Java, Enterprise Java Beans, C++, and CORBA.

Lily Hendra is an engineer with Northrop Grumman Information Technology working on the JEDMICS program. She focuses on developing enterprise applications using J2EE and XML to interface with backend databases. Prior to JEDMICS, she has worked in the area of distributed objects and database technology, focusing on Java, C++, CORBA, and object-relational database systems. She has coauthored papers published in conferences and journals sponsored by the ACM and IEEE, as well as contributed to technical reports published by Cutter Consortium and CSIRO Australia.

Odysseas Pentakalos is vice-president of SYSNET International, Inc., where he focuses on architecture, design, and development of large distributed systems that utilize Java and J2EE technologies. His clients have included major government agencies and corporations such as NASA Goddard Space Flight Center, the U.S. Army Research Lab, Sun Microsystems, Concert Communications, KPMG, and

Northrop Grumman. He holds a Ph.D. in computer science with a specialization in performance management of computer systems. He is the author of the book *Windows 2000 Performance Guide* (O'Reilly & Associates, 2002), has published over two dozen papers in conference proceedings and journals, and is a frequent speaker at industry conferences.

Chapter 13: Geographical Data Interchange Using XML-Enabled Technology within the GIDB System

Ruth Wilson is a mathematician for the Naval Research Laboratory (NRL). She has been a lead developer of the Geospatial Information Database System and Portal for over 8 years. Her research interests include object-oriented programming, mathematical techniques to improve digital mapping, and distributed communication of mapping data between servers and users in real time. Wilson received a B.S. in mathematics from the University of Southern Mississippi in 1993 and an M.S. in mathematics from McNeese State University in 1997. She can be reached at ruth.wilson@nrlssc.navy.mil.

Maria A. Cobb is an associate professor in the Department of Computer Science & Statistics at the University of Southern Mississippi. Dr. Cobb received a Ph.D. in computer science from Tulane University in 1995. She was previously employed by the Naval Research Laboratory as a computer scientist. Her primary research interests are spatial data modeling, including techniques for modeling and reasoning about spatial data under uncertainty, and distributed object-oriented systems.

Frank McCreedy has been a software developer for 4 years. Primarily working with Java, his work has included such topics as servlets, applets, client/server architectures, interaction with various database systems, and geographic mapping. Currently he works at the Naval Research Laboratory at Stennis Space Center as a computer scientist. He gained a B.S. in computer science from University of Southern Mississippi in 1998.

Roy Ladner received an M.S. in computer science and a Ph.D. in engineering and applied science from the University of New Orleans. He works as a research scientist at the Naval Research Laboratory at Stennis Space Center. His work emphasizes the investigation of spatio-temporal database issues and advanced methods to improve delivery of spatio-temporal data over the Internet. His research has been published in national and international conference proceedings and journals.

David Olivier is a member of the Digital Mapping, Charting, & Geodesy Analysis Program, Marine Geosciences Division at the Naval Research Laboratory, Stennis Space Center. He received a B.A. in philosophy and the history of math and science from St. John's College in 1994 and an M.S. in computer science from the

University of New Orleans in 2001. His research interests include geographic information systems and distributed applications.

Todd Lovitt is a computer scientist and mathematician with Planning Systems, Inc. He has been working with the Naval Research Laboratory on the design and development of object-oriented databases of digital mapping data. His research interests include visualization of 2D/3D GIS data and distributed techniques for integration and display of disparate geospatial data types across the Internet. He received a B.S. in mathematics with a computer science minor from Mississippi State University in 1989. He can be reached at todd.lovitt@psislidell.com.

Kevin B. Shaw leads a Naval Research Laboratory R&D team that focuses on advanced geospatial modeling, object-oriented database design, and portal implementation for improved naval, DoD, and government agencies' usage. Mr. Shaw received a B.S. in electrical engineering from Mississippi State University in 1984, an M.S. in computer science from the University of Southern Mississippi in 1987, and an M.E.E. in electrical engineering from Mississippi State University in 1988. Mr. Shaw can be reached at shaw@nrlssc.navy.mil.

Fred Petry received B.S. and M.S. degrees in physics and a Ph.D. in computer and information science from Ohio State University in 1975. He has been on the faculty of the University of Alabama in Huntsville and Ohio State University and is currently a full professor in the Department of Electrical Engineering & Computer Science at Tulane University. His recent research interests include representation of imprecision via fuzzy sets and rough sets in databases, GIS and other information systems, and artificial intelligence including genetic algorithms. His research has been funded by NSF, NASA, DOE, NIH, various DoD agencies, and industry. He has directed 20 Ph.D. students in these areas in the past 10 years. Dr. Petry has over 250 scientific publications including over 85 journal articles/book chapters and 5 books written or edited. His monograph on fuzzy databases has been widely recognized as the definitive volume on this topic. He is currently an associate editor of IEEE Transactions on Fuzzy Systems, *Neural Processing Letters*, and an area editor of information systems for *Fuzzy Sets and Systems* and was general chairperson of FUZZ-IEEE '96. He was selected as an IEEE Fellow in 1997 for his research on the use of fuzzy sets for modeling imprecision in databases and was chosen as a recipient of the 2002 Tulane School of Engineering Outstanding Researcher Award.

Dr. Mahdi Abdelguerfi is currently professor and chair of the computer science department at the University of New Orleans. His research interests include terrain databases, 3D synthetic environments, and spatio-temporal information systems.

Chapter 14: Space Wide Web by Adapters in Distributed Systems Configuration from Reusable Components

David Rine has been practicing software development, computational sciences, and software systems engineering for 37 years. He joined George Mason University in June 1985 and was the founding chair of the Department of Computer Science, as well as co-developer of the School of Information Technology and Engineering. He is presently Professor of computer science, Professor of Information Systems and Software Systems Engineering, and Professor on the Faculty of the Institute for Computational Sciences and Informatics. He has been researching, teaching, consulting, working with the software industry and directing research projects in the areas of software systems engineering, computational science, information systems, computer science, and science and engineering education. Within the span of his career in computing, he has published over 200 papers and books in the general areas of computer science, engineering, information systems, computer applications, computational science, science and engineering education, systems engineering, and software engineering. Dr. Rine is internationally known for his work in science and engineering education, having accumulated many years of experience in directing curriculum, large-scale software, computational science, and systems projects.

Chapter 15: XML as a Unifying Framework for Inductive Databases

Rosa Meo was born in Torino, Italy, in 1966. She obtained her "Laurea" degree in *ingegneria elettronica* (electronic engineering) in July 1993 and her Ph.D. in *ingegneria informatica e dei sistemi* (computer science and systems engineering) in September 1997, both at the Politecnico di Torino, Italy. Since November 1999 she has been a researcher in the Department of Computer Science, Università degli Studi di Torino, where she works in the database and data mining research fields.

Giuseppe Psaila is researcher at the Faculty of Engineering, University of Bergamo, Italy. He received the Degree of Electronic Engineer from Politecnico di Milano in 1993 with a thesis on Semantic Evaluation Techniques for Artificial Languages. He received his Ph.D. from Politecnico di Torino in 1998 with a thesis on the Integration of Data Mining Techniques and Relational Databases. His research interests cover databases, data mining, XML, and artificial languages.

Chapter 16: Designing and Managing an XML Warehouse

Xavier Baril studied computer science at the University of Toulouse III, France, and the University of Pau, France. He received his M.S. (DEA) from the University of Toulouse III in 1999 and is now working as a Ph.D. student in the database group of the LIRMM, Montpellier, France. His research area covers XML data warehousing, semistructured data, XML views, and XML querying.

Zohra Bellahsène is a senior lecturer, HDR, in computer science at the University of Montpellier II, France. She received her "Habilitation à Diriger des Recherches" (HDR) from the University of Montpellier II in 2000. She has devoted her recent research and publications on various aspects of view mechanisms, organizing database summer schools, and serving on the committees of French and international conferences. She has organized or chaired several workshops, invited sessions, and conferences. She was PC cochair of the international conference on Object-Oriented Information Systems (OOIS'02) and chair of the workshop on Data Integration over the Web (DIWeb'01 and DIWeb'02). She has published on the following topics: query optimization, object-oriented database views, meta-modeling, human genome databases, schema evolution, distributed database systems, view adaptation in data-warehousing systems, data warehouse design, data integration, and XML views management.

Chapter 17: XML Management System Benchmarks

Stéphane Bressan received his Ph.D. in computer science in 1992 from the Laboratoire D'informatique Fondamentale of the University of Lille. He is a senior fellow in the computer science department of the School of Computing (SoC) of the National University of Singapore. Dr. Bressan's main areas of research are information and knowledge management, Web applications and services, the integration of distributed and heterogeneous information systems, and the design and implementation of database management systems.

Mong Li Lee received her Ph.D. in computer science from the National University of Singapore in 1999. She is an assistant professor in the School of Computing, National University of Singapore. Her research interests include database performance issues, cleaning, integrating, and querying heterogeneous and semi-structured data.

Li Ying Guang received his B.S. from the School of Computing in the National University of Singapore in 2000 and is now an M.S. student at the School of Computing in the National University of Singapore. His research topic is XML query processing and storage.

Zoé Lacroix received her Ph.D. in Computer Science in 1996 from the University of Paris XI (France). She has been a researcher at the French Institut National de la Recherche en Informatique et Automatique (INRIA), and at the Institute for Research in Cognitive Science (IRCS) at the University of Pennsylvania (USA). Since then she has been working at Gene Logic and at SurroMed, two biotech companies, where her research focused on bioinformatics. In addition, she was involved in the XML working groups XML Query Language and XML Forms at the World Wide Web Consortium (W3C). Recently she joined Arizona State University where she started new projects on electronic business hubs, integration of biological databases, optimization, semantics of Web queries, and Semantic Web.

Ullas Nambiar received his B.S. and engineering degree from M.S University, India in 1997 and is pursuing his Ph.D. in computer science with a focus on data integration. His research interests are data integration, extracting source statistics for Web sources, adaptive query plan execution, and distributed mediation services.

Chapter 18: The Michigan Benchmark: A Micro-Benchmark for XML Query Performance Diagnostics

Jignesh M. Patel is an assistant professor at the University of Michigan. He graduated with a Ph.D. from the University of Wisconsin in 1998. As a graduate student, he led the efforts to develop the Paradise database system, a parallel object-relational database system, which was purchased by NCR Corporation in 1998. After graduating from the University of Wisconsin, he joined NCR where he helped with the efforts to commercialize the Paradise system. Since 1999, he has been a faculty member at the University of Michigan, where his research has focused on XML data management systems, bioinformatics, and spatial data management systems. He has served on a number of program committees including ACM SIGMOD, VLDB, and IEEE TKDE, and is currently the associate editor for the Systems and Prototype section of *ACM SIGMOD Record*.

H. V. Jagadish is a professor of computer science and engineering at the University of Michigan. After earning his Ph.D. from Stanford in 1985, he spent over a decade at AT&T Bell Laboratories, eventually becoming head of AT&T Labs database research department at the Shannon Laboratory. He has also served as a professor at the University of Illinois in Urbana-Champaign. Professor Jagadish is well known for his broad-ranging research on databases and has over 80 major papers and 20 patents. He is the founding editor of the *ACM SIGMOD Digital Review*. Among the many professional positions he has held, he has previously been an associate editor for the *ACM Transactions on Database Systems* (1992–1995) and program chair of the ACM SIGMOD annual conference (1996).

Chapter 19: A Comparison of Database Approaches for Storing XML Documents

Cosima Schmauch is a full professor at the University of Applied Sciences in Karlsruhe, Germany. She has been teaching software engineering, distributed systems, and knowledge-based systems since she joined the university in 1991. Her research interests lie in developing distributed systems with CORBA and Web Services, storing XML in different kinds of databases, and applying game theory to negotiating software agents. She has previously worked for several companies as a consultant for knowledge-based systems. She holds a diploma in computer science from the Universität des Saarlandes in Saarbrücken and a Ph.D. in computer science from the Universität Kaiserslautern.

Torsten Fellhauer is a system administrator for UNIX at iXpoint Informationssysteme. He holds a diploma in business information systems from the University of Applied Sciences in Karlsruhe.

Chapter 20: Performance Analysis between an XML-Enabled Database and a Native XML Database

Joseph Fong is an associate professor in the computer science department at the City University of Hong Kong. He graduated with a B.S. in computer engineering from the State University of New York at Buffalo in 1975, an M.S. in computer engineering from the State University of New York at Stony Brook in 1976, an M.B.A. from Golden Gate University in San Francisco in 1985, and a Ph.D. in computing at the University of Sunderland in the U.K. in 1993. He gained 12 years' data-processing experience in the United States before returning to Hong Kong in 1987 to be an academic. His main research area is database technology, and he has obtained two Hong Kong patents in database reengineering and interoperability. He is the founder-chairman of the Hong Kong Web Society and the Sybase Hong Kong User Group and was also the chairman of the Hong Kong Computer Society Database Special Interest Group.

Hing Kwok Wong is a full-time Ph.D. student in the computer science department at the City University of Hong Kong. He received a B.S. in information technology, with first class honors, from the electronic engineering department, and an M.S. in computer science at the City University of Hong Kong in 1999 and 2001, respectively. He has published several research journal and conference papers in data mining. His current research interests are online analytical mining, Web usage mining, and XML-enabled databases.

Anthony Fong received his B.S. degree from Villanova University, Pennsylvania in 1969. He worked at Philco-Ford Corporation as a programmer before he returned to the university in 1971. He received his M.S. degree in computer science from the State University of New York at Buffalo in 1973. He then joined Digital Equipment Corporation in Massachusetts as a design engineer, responsible for the design and development of DEC Systems 10 and 20, and the VAX11/780 Systems. In 1977, he moved to the Data General Corporation as a senior design engineer, working on the FHP Project in Research Triangle Park in North Carolina. He was later project leader working on MV/20000 designs and development. He joined Wang Laboratories in 1984 as a hardware section manager, responsible for the design and development of the VS-300 FPU and the VS-10000. He was elected to the Chairman's Club in 1989. He was also a part-time instructor at Northeastern University, Boston, from 1981 to 1983. In 1991 he joined the City University of Hong Kong as a senior lecturer in the Department of Electronic Engineering. At present he is an associate professor and the director of the EDA Centre. He is also a visiting professor at the Institute of Electronics, Chinese Academy of Science. Anthony Fong has been awarded six U.S. patents, all on computer architecture and design. He has published more than 40 papers on computer architecture and design and databases.

Index

B

D

E

F

G

H

I

K

L

M

O

P

Q

R

S

T

U

V

W

X

Z

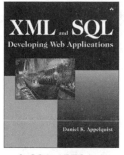

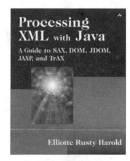

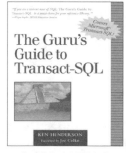